THE HISTORY OF
EXERCISE
AND
SPORT SCIENCE

THE HISTORY OF
EXERCISE
AND
SPORT SCIENCE

John D. Massengale, EdD
University of Nevada, Las Vegas

Richard A. Swanson, PhD
University of North Carolina, Greensboro

Editors

Human Kinetics

Library of Congress Cataloging-in-Publication Data

The history of exercise and sport science / John D. Massengale
(editor), Richard A. Swanson (editor).
    p. cm.
   Includes bibliographical references and index.
   ISBN 0-87322-524-4
   1. Physical education and training--Study and teaching (Higher)-
-United States--History. 2. Sports--Study and teaching (Higher)-
-United States--History. 3. Exercise--Study and teaching (Higher)-
-United States--History. 4. Physiology--Study and teaching
(Higher)--United States--History. I. Massengale, John D.
II. Swanson, Richard A. (Richard Albin), 1939-   .
GV223.H57   1997   96-10555
613.7'1'071173--dc20   CIP

ISBN: 0-87322-524-4

Developmental Editors: Anne Mishakoff Heiles and Nanette Smith; **Assistant Editors**: Erin Cler and Henry Woolsey; **Editorial Assistant**: Coree Schutter; **Copyeditor**: Tom Taylor; **Proofreader**: Sue Fetters; **Indexer**: Tom Taylor; **Graphic Artist**: Yvonne Winsor; **Graphic Designer**: Judy Henderson; **Photo Editor**: Boyd LaFoon; **Cover Designer**: Jack Davis; **Printer**: Braun-Brumfield

Printed in the United States of America   10 9 8 7 6 5 4 3 2 1

Human Kinetics
Web site:
http: //www.humankinetics.com/

United States: Human Kinetics
P.O. Box 5076
Champaign, IL 61825-5076
1-800-747-4457
e-mail: humank@hkusa.com

Canada: Human Kinetics
Box 24040
Windsor, ON N8Y 4Y9
1-800-465-7301 (in Canada only)
e-mail: humank@hkcanada.com

Europe: Human Kinetics
P.O. Box IW14
Leeds LS16 6TR, United Kingdom
(44) 1132 781708
e-mail: humank@hkeurope.com

Australia: Human Kinetics
57A Price Avenue
Lower Mitcham, South Australia 5062
(08) 277 1555
e-mail: humank@hkaustralia.com

New Zealand: Human Kinetics
P.O. Box 105-231, Auckland 1
(09) 523 3462
e-mail: humank@hknewz.com

Contents

Contributors

Linda L. Bain, PhD

Linda L. Bain is a professor in the Department of Human Performance, and the Provost/Academic Vice-President at San José State University. She has published 5 books, 13 chapters in books, and more than 40 articles in various professional periodicals. She is the past president of the Research Consortium of the American Alliance for Health, Physical Education, Recreation and Dance (AAHPERD), and holds Fellow status in both AAHPERD's Research Consortium and the American Academy of Kinesiology and Physical Education.

Elsworth R. Buskirk, PhD

Elsworth R. Buskirk is the Marie Underhill Noll Professor of Human Performance, and director of the Noll Laboratory for Human Performance Research at The Pennsylvania State University. He has authored or coauthored over 225 publications in the scientific literature, served as the editor of *Medicine and Science in Sports and Exercise*, and served on the editorial boards of 12 other professional journals in his chosen field of study. He is a past president of the American College of Sports Medicine (ACSM), and is a recipient of ACSM's highest recognition, the Honor Award.

Karen P. DePauw, PhD

Karen P. DePauw is a professor in the Department of Physical Education, Sport and Leisure Studies, and the associate dean of the Graduate School at Washington State University. She has more than 90 articles in the professional literature, and has published 7 books and 20 chapters in books. She is past president of the National Association for Physical Education in Higher Education (NAPEHE) and past president of the Western Society of Physical Education for College Women (WSPECW). She is a Fellow in the Research Consortium of the American Alliance for

Health, Physical Education, Recreation and Dance (AAHPERD), and has been recognized with several prestigious awards from the aforementioned organizations.

Diane L. Gill is a professor in the Department of Exercise and Sport Science, and associate dean of the School of Health and Human Performance at the University of North Carolina at Greensboro. She has published over 50 research articles, several book chapters, and the book *Psychological Dynamics of Sport*. She is a former editor of the *Journal of Sport & Exercise Psychology*, past president of the North American Society for the Psychology of Sport and Physical Activity (NASPSPA), and a Fellow in the Association for the Advancement of Applied Sport Psychology (AAASP), as well as the American Academy of Kinesiology and Physical Education.

Diane L. Gill, PhD

R. Scott Kretchmar is a professor and former head of the Department of Exercise and Sport Science at The Pennsylvania State University. He has published over 30 articles in professional periodicals, several chapters in books, and the book *A Practical Philosophy of Sport and Physical Education*. He is a Fellow in the American Academy of Kinesiology and Physical Education, and the past president of both the Philosophy Academy of the American Alliance for Health, Physical Education, Recreation and Dance (AAHPERD) and the Philosophic Society for the Study of Sport.

R. Scott Kretchmar, PhD

John D. Massengale is a professor in the Department of Kinesiology, and the former dean of the College of Human Performance and Development at the University of Nevada, Las Vegas. He has published more than 40 articles in professional periodicals, 11 chapters in books, and 5 books in the areas of physical education and coaching. He is a former editor of *Quest*; past president of the National Association for Physical Education in Higher Education (NAPEHE); a Fellow in the Research Consortium of the American Alliance for Health, Physical Education, Recreation and Dance (AAHPERD); and a past recipient of AAHPERD's Research Writing Award.

John Massengale, EdD

George H. Sage, EdD

George H. Sage is professor emeritus in the Department of Kinesiology and the Department of Sociology at The University of Northern Colorado. He has published more than 50 articles in the professional literature, 7 books, and several chapters in books. He is past president of the National Association for Physical Education in Higher Education (NAPEHE) and past president of the North American Society for the Sociology of Sport (NASSS); he holds Fellow status in the American Academy of Kinesiology and Physical Education, as well as the Research Consortium of the American Alliance for Health, Physical Education, Recreation and Dance (AAHPERD), and has been designated as an Alliance Scholar by AAHPERD.

Claudine Sherrill, EdD

Claudine Sherrill is a professor in the Department of Kinesiology at Texas Woman's University. She has published 10 books, 29 chapters in books, and more than 80 articles in various professional periodicals. She is past president of the National Consortium on Physical Education and Recreation for the Handicapped, a Fellow in the American Academy of Kinesiology and Physical Education, and a recipient of the National Honor Award from the American Alliance for Health, Physical Education, Recreation and Dance (AAHPERD).

Nancy L. Struna, PhD

Nancy L. Struna is associate professor in the Department of Kinesiology and affiliate associate professor in the Department of History at the University of Maryland. She has more than 30 articles in the professional literature and 7 chapters in books, and has published the book *Sport and Changing Relations of Work and Leisure in Early American Society*. She is past president of the North American Society for Sport History (NASSH), a former editor of *Quest*, and a recipient of the Distinguished Scholar Award from the National Association for Physical Education in Higher Education (NAPEHE); she holds Fellow status in the American Academy of Kinesiology and Physical Education, as well as the Research Consortium of the American Alliance for Health, Physical Education, Recreation and Dance (AAHPERD).

Richard A. Swanson is a professor in the Department of Exercise and Sport Science, and the former dean of the School of Health and Human Performance at the University of North Carolina at Greensboro. He has numerous publications in the professional literature, and coauthored the book *History of Sport and Physical Education in the United States*. He is past chair of the History of Sport and Physical Education Academy and a recipient of the Honor Award from the College and University Administrators' Council (CUAC) of the American Alliance for Health, Physical

Richard Swanson, PhD

Education, Recreation and Dance (AAHPERD); he serves as an archivist/historian for the National Association for Physical Education in Higher Education (NAPEHE).

Jerry R. Thomas is a professor in the Department of Exercise Science and Physical Education at Arizona State University. He has published 9 books, 19 chapters in books, and more than 100 articles in professional periodicals. He is a former editor of the *Research Quarterly for Exercise and Sport*, past president of the North American Society for the Psychology of Sport and Physical Activity (NASPSPA), and past president of the American Academy of Kinesiology and Physical Education; he has been designated as the Alliance Scholar by the American Alliance for Health, Physical

Jerry R. Thomas, EdD

Education, Recreation and Dance (AAHPERD).

Charles M. Tipton is a professor in the Department of Exercise and Sport Sciences and a professor in the Department of Surgery at the University of Arizona. He has authored or coauthored over 300 publications in the scientific literature, served as the editor of *Medicine and Science in Sports and Exercise*, and served on the editorial boards of many of the most prestigious journals in his chosen field of study. He is a Fellow in the American Academy of Kinesiology and Physical Education and a past president of the American College of Sports Medicine (ACSM).

Charles M. Tipton, PhD

Jerry D. Wilkerson, PhD

Jerry D. Wilkerson is a professor in the Department of Kinesiology at Texas Woman's University. She is the coauthor of *The Teaching of Team Sports: A Coeducational Approach*, and has over 50 other publications in the professional literature. She is a former chair of the Kinesiology Academy of the American Alliance for Health, Physical Education, Recreation and Dance (AAHPERD), a Fellow in AAHPERD's Research Consortium, and an editorial board member and reviewer for nine professional periodicals in her chosen field of study.

Preface

The main purpose of this book is to record, examine, and analyze, for the first time in depth, the historical development of subdisciplines within the field of Exercise and Sport Science. The book is a special publishing project of the National Association for Physical Education in Higher Education (NAPEHE). The publisher, the editors, and the officers of the NAPEHE immediately agreed upon the critical importance of moving forward on this project while many primary records and people were still available.

Nine subdisciplines were identified, and contributing authors were selected. The selection of contributors involved many considerations, such as their professional stature in their respective subdisciplines, their long association with their subdisciplines, their appreciation of history, their involvement and commitment to NAPEHE, and (perhaps of most importance) their dedication to the task of accurately recording, detailing, and explaining the history of their subdiscipline.

In every instance, the authors were carefully selected for their potential to work with, or actually serve as, primary sources. The importance of primary sources cannot be overstated in the preparation of this book. In some cases, the contributor was an original active participant in the early development and/or organization of the subdiscipline. Contributing authors were also selected for their knowledge of, and ability to access, key sources, including significant persons, photographic and printed materials, official records, and personal records and correspondence.

During the twentieth century the field of Physical Education evolved, from an almost exclusive focus on the delivery of instructional services to children and youth, into a field that is often conceptualized as a group of loosely organized and affiliated endeavors capable of providing multiple services to an almost limitless population. As the general field of study evolved, so did the concept of exercise and sport science, with all of its attendant specializations and eventual subdisciplines. Although the antecedents of some subdisciplines extend back to the early years of the twentieth century, the phenomenon took root and became central to the field during the 1960s and 1970s. In a relatively brief period of time it became the primary framework for graduate education and research in physical education.

Subdiscipline development has influenced the entire profession/discipline of physical education in many different ways. The name, label, or term "physical education" has evolved to the point that many different descriptors are used—kinesiology, exercise and sport science, exercise science, human performance, and so on. For this particular book the editors have elected to use the term "exercise and sport science" to describe the general field with its many subdisciplines.

This book takes the position that the acceptance of subdisciplines has evolved to the point that graduate programs with high degrees of specialization are generally regarded as being of a higher quality. At the same time, it appears that those same programs are producing a sizable majority of the earned doctorates in the field. A concomitant concern has developed as the profession/discipline has attempted to distinguish between specialization and fragmentation: Many have taken the position that the profession is in danger of specializing itself right out of existence.

It is the assumption of the editors that fragmentation is not an automatic outcome of specialization, and that the latter is a normal or natural result of the evolution of any profession or field of study. The editors also assume that specialization and subdiscipline development are positive occurrences that have resulted from research and thought by outstanding scholars in the field. It is also our position that the same scholarly effort can be applied to the strengthening of the central core of exercise and sport science.

The editors realize that this book is the first attempt at recording the history of all of the subdisciplines that comprise exercise and sport science. Editorial commentary throughout the book attempts to provide ties across the subdisciplines, thus illustrating common bases as well as unique contributions and problem areas. The editors trust that this book will be a highly important project for the field. By identifying, acknowledging, and embracing the history of the subdisciplines, it is anticipated that we will better understand the entire profession/discipline. Finally, rather than supporting the potential fragmentation that concerns many colleagues, we trust that an historical understanding will stimulate creative thinking that will lead to a strengthened field of study and service.

The contributing authors were invited to research, record, describe, and analyze the history of their respective subdiscipline, following a similar organizational format and addressing a number of common questions. In addition, the editorial boards of subdiscipline journals were invited to review the chapters in their respective fields as a further attempt to assure the highest level of accuracy, thoroughness, and quality.

Finally, the editors would like to thank NAPEHE, Human Kinetics Publishers, the contributing authors, and the many professionals whose cooperation and helpful suggestions enabled the publication of this work. Being the first of its kind, this book chronicles the events and people who have truly developed the highly specialized profession/discipline of exercise and sport science.

John D. Massengale
Richard A. Swanson

Exercise and Sport Science in 20th-Century America

Richard A. Swanson
University of North Carolina at Greensboro
John D. Massengale
University of Nevada, Las Vegas

It was early in the second half of the century that two scholars, one from within and one from outside physical education, published words that sent shock waves through, and a challenge to, the field. In 1963 James Bryant Conant, former president of Harvard University, published *The Education of American Teachers*, the third in a series of works based on a study of American public education. In this book Conant singled out physical education for special criticism. He was particularly harsh in his condemnation of graduate programs that were nothing more than a continuation of the "methods"-based curricula for undergraduate teacher preparation. He wrote,

> I am far from impressed by what I have heard and read about graduate work in the field of physical education. If I wished to portray the education of teachers in the worst terms, I should quote from the descriptions of some graduate courses in physical education. To my mind, a university should cancel graduate programs in this area. If the physical education teacher wishes to enter into a research career in the field of physiology of exercise and related subjects, he should use the graduate years to build on his natural science background a knowledge of the physiological sciences that will enable him to stand on an equal footing with the undergraduate major in these sciences. (Conant, 1963, p. 201)

Several months later, Franklin Henry, professor of physical education at the University of California at Berkeley, without citing the Conant criticism, wrote, "It would perhaps not be overly presumptuous to suggest that there is an increasing need for the organization and study of the academic discipline herein called physical education" (Henry, 1964, p. 9). Certainly echoing Conant, he stated,

> Learning the rules and strategy of sports may well be intellectual, but it is highly doubtful if a course on rules and strategy can be justified as a major component of an academic field of knowledge at the upper division college or university level. There simply is not enough time for such specifics within the undergraduate years. (Henry, 1964, p. 8)

Henry, himself a product of rigorous academic training in the biological sciences outside of physical education, was calling his colleagues to the task of identifying and organizing a body of knowledge that would serve as the foundation of an academic discipline. Regardless of career goals, undergraduate and graduate students in physical education would be steeped in the physical education discipline. Additional professional course work would then prepare them for specific career objectives.

These two events, coming close together as they did, were catalysts for monumental changes in the way physical education scholars perceived the field and its future. While there was much hand-wringing following Conant's pronouncement, there was even more positive interest in the challenge Henry presented. After all, as you will read in the coming chapters, isolated research work in a variety of areas related to, and sometimes within, physical education had been proceeding for several decades, especially following World War II. In addition, an increasing number of younger scholars were pursuing doctoral studies, many under the tutelage of serious researchers. Over the next two decades the drive to identify and organize the body of knowledge led to the ascendency of research, the administrative and curricular reorganization of departments in colleges and universities, and the creation of subdisciplines and specialties.

Even at this early stage of analysis, it was clear that the movement to identify the field's body of knowledge was perhaps the single most significant step in its evolution. The movement began the transformation of the discipline from a field devoted almost exclusively to the *teaching* of exercise and sport activities and the preparation of physical education teachers into an academic discipline concerned with the *study* of the art and science of exercise and sport.

1885-1920

To comprehend the enormity of the changes that took place in the 1960s and 1970s, one must know and appreciate the evolution of physical education during the first 65 years of the century. In many colleges and universities physical education, unlike most other academic subjects, had developed a two-fold purpose by the early 1920s. First, there was an aim to provide activity-based and health-content courses to the general student population. The purpose here was to engage the students in learning situations that would contribute to their immediate physical and emotional well-being, as well as stimulate them to a lifelong commitment to live active healthy lives. Second, the preparation of physical education teachers and athletic coaches became a primary focus in those institutions that counted teacher education as a major part of their academic mission. These schools at first included the public normal (or teachers') colleges and later, the large state universities and such private institutions as Columbia and New York University.

As the 19th century gave way to the 20th, it was no longer the exception to find physical education courses included in the curricula of liberal arts colleges and universities. Taught by either a non-faculty "gymnasium director" or a competent member of the faculty, the courses in most schools emphasized the formal "gymnastics" or "training" promoted by Edward Hitchcock at Amherst, Dudley Sargent at Harvard, Delphine Hanna at Oberlin, or one of several practitioners of the German or Swedish gymnastic systems. While sports and games, popularized through intercollegiate and interscholastic programs, were increasingly included in physical training classes at many colleges and high schools, the more formal approaches dominated through the credibility of these and other early leaders, most of whom had their academic training in medicine, and were proponents of scientifically based, systematic programs of exercise.

For these very reasons, Edward Mussey Hartwell, PhD, MD, was a strong advocate of the German and Swedish systems. In November 1889, while director of the gymnasium at Johns Hopkins University, Hartwell was asked to give the keynote address at the now famous Boston Conference in the Interest of Physical Training. While lauding the recreational benefits of play, he clearly identified formal gymnastics as educationally superior:

> In the athletic sports of young men we see the highest and fullest expression of the play instinct. The essential difference between athletics and gymnastics is one of aim. The aim of athletics, unless of the illegitimate professional sort, is pleasurable activity for the sake of recreation; that of gymnastics is discipline or training for pleasure, health, and skill. We have but to compare the aims, methods, and results of each, and to call to mind the characteristics of the nations which have affected athletics on the one hand and gymnastics on the other, to perceive that gymnastics are more highly developed and present more features of educational value. Gymnastics, as compared with athletics, are more comprehensive in their aims, more formal, elaborate, and systematic in their methods, and are productive of more solid and considerable results. (Hartwell, 1889, p. 19)

In spite of such strong support, however, the encroachment of games and sport continued slowly but steadily throughout the 1890s and into the next decade. A classic illustration of student preference (and power) for sport occurred at the International YMCA Training School in December 1891. Faced with increasing student rebelliousness against a formal gymnastics emphasis during the indoor season of the winter months, young James Naismith was charged by his department head, Dr. Luther Gulick, to create an indoor game that would provide vigorous exercise while satisfying the demand of the students for sport. His invention of basketball, of course, became the premier indoor game for both men and women during the 20th century. By 1920, sport activities had become the bedrock of the required and elective programs of physical education in U.S. colleges, universities, and secondary schools.

By the end of the first decade of the new century, literally all colleges and universities in the United States offered some kind of course work in physical education for the general student. Some, however, began to offer study leading to preparation for teaching careers in this new field. In the 1880s and 1890s it was primarily the private normal schools, most situated in the northeast, that offered programs of study leading to a certificate in physical education, varying in length from several months to two years. Some, like Sargent's Harvard Summer School, offered teachers the opportunity to receive this specialized training during their summer vacation over a two- or three-year period. The Sargent Normal School of Physical Training (Cambridge, Massachusetts), The Brooklyn Normal School, The Boston Normal School of Gymnastics, the North American Gymnastics Union (German Turners, Milwaukee, Wisconsin), and the YMCA Training School (Springfield, Massachusetts) were examples of these private institutions that offered nondegree programs.

Given the scientific and medical bias of their founders and directors in these normal schools, it is not surprising that the curricula were heavily weighted toward physical education. While each exhibited some differences consistent with their respective educational philosophy, they all offered anatomy and physiology; most taught anthropometry and physics. Other courses offered physiological psychology, the relation of body and mind, mechanics of the body, and sphygmography. With the exception of the YMCA Training School, all offered a very modest sports program. The Springfield school boasted an extensive sports offering while the others included sport on a limited basis.

Since the objective of the schools was limited—the preparation of teachers in a relatively singular system of physical training that emphasized physical fitness—the curriculum and the limited research conducted by these physical educators centered primarily around anthropometric measurement and some applied work by Sargent that contributed to the development of new exercise apparatus. The anthropometric work was influenced by Hitchcock and Sargent and was carried out at a number of institutions including Harvard, Amherst, Yale, Oberlin, the University of Nebraska, Beloit College, and Wellesley, between 1885 and 1900 (Swanson and Spears, 1995). Students were measured and individual statistics recorded on size, growth, and strength development. Comparisons were made over the years in an effort to find the "typical" college man and woman. From these studies, prescriptions for specific exercises and activities were made for individual students.

Five colleges and universities were offering four-year degree programs at the turn of the century: Harvard University, Oberlin College, Stanford University, the University of California, and the University of Nebraska. By the time the United States entered World War I in 1917, the public and private four-year colleges and universities exceeded the private normal schools in the graduation of teachers (Bowen, 1922). Teachers' College of Columbia University awarded the nation's first master's degree in physical education in 1910; within seven years, graduate work was offered by the Normal College of the American Gymnastic Union, Wellesley College, the University of Southern California, and the University of Oregon (Swanson and Spears, 1995).

1920-1945

By 1920 the focus of the physical education major was clearly established: the preparation of teachers and coaches for the grammar and secondary schools as well as the colleges and universities of the nation. Public-school enrollment was increasing at a rapid rate, creating an unprecedented demand for teachers. Between 1920 and 1940 the number of boys and girls graduating from high school increased from 311,266 to 1,221,475. Adding to the pressures, during World War I high military draft rejection rates due to physical deficiencies encouraged many states to join those that had already passed legislation requiring physical education in the public schools.

Another factor creating a demand for physical education teachers, and contributing greatly to the curricular emphasis on sport, was the tremendous growth in the popularity of interscholastic and intercollegiate athletics. According to Lewis (1969) the practical need for coaches dictated much of the shift from gymnastics to sport-based professional programs:

Well-intentioned administrators, assisted by a tremendous increase in the number and size of physical education programs, forced physical educators to adopt the sports program. From this point formulation of a philosophy was merely a practice in justifying the existence of programs already sanctioned by higher authority. Accommodation, then, of varsity athletics was the key factor in the transformation of the profession. The status of competitive athletics established the location of physical education in high schools and colleges; facilities, equipment, and staff secured for varsity sports determined the content of the curricula and the nature of the programs. (p. 42)

Responding to the demand for new teachers provided even more incentive for college and university departments of physical education to focus entirely on teacher preparation with the curriculum clearly centered around sport. Furthermore, the new generation of college faculty were coming from graduate programs steeped in education theory rather than the natural and biological sciences of the earlier medical doctors. The progressive education movement, inspired by John Dewey, legitimized play as a learning medium, thus broadening the purposes of physical education from training the body to educating the "whole" person. The play experience was now seen to provide the laboratory for character building, sociobehavioral learning, and skill development, as well as fitness training. Perhaps the major proponent of this philosophy was Jesse Feiring Williams of Columbia University Teachers' College, who saw physical education as "education through the physical" rather than "education of the physical."

While sport continued to be the dominant feature of American physical education, there was not total unanimity regarding its purposes. Besides Williams there were two other prominent voices in the profession during the 1930s and 1940s: Jay Bryan Nash of New York University and Charles H. McCloy of the University of Iowa. Nash, also a major figure in the recreation movement, believed that children should be educated for lifelong leisure-time pursuits as well as for a vocation. Therefore, skill development and appreciation for the activity were the focal points of his philosophy. McCloy, on the other hand, established an enviable reputation as a researcher specializing in exercise physiology. He proposed that physical education should focus on the development of the body. He "believed in organic power, physical development, strenuous exercise, and the mastery of physical skills" (Swanson & Spears, 1995, p. 228).

Each of these leaders had his own group of followers. As a result, variations in the physical education curriculum from one institution to another were common. Seward Staley of the University of Illinois proposed in 1931 that, since sport was the major component of physical education, the name should be changed to "sport education." He argued that within the context of modern psychological and educational thought, the old mind-body dualism (translated to classroom education for the mind and physical education for the body), on which the nineteenth century American concept of physical education had been based, was no longer plausible. Regarding the purposes of the program he noted that "sports" education would "undoubtedly produce interested, intelligent spectators at sport contests, but . . . the vital objective and outcome should be the production of participants" (Staley, 1931, p. 82). While the idea did not spread, it reinforced the concept of sport as central to American physical education.

While the curricular focus of professional programs of physical education remained on the preparation of teachers and coaches, most college and university faculty thought of themselves as broad generalists and taught a variety of courses. The emphasis was on teaching and advising students; most faculty did not carry on active programs of research in any area of specialization. Two areas did, however, attract a good deal of research attention, albeit by a small number of scholars, especially after 1920: exercise physiology with a focus on cardiovascular fitness assessment; and tests and measurements with emphasis on physical fitness, general motor ability, specific skill development, and physical efficiency. The two areas were closely related and found great acceptance, both in teacher preparation and in the K-through-12 physical education programs of the period. According to Van Dalen and Bennett (1971), "Tests and measurements as used in physical education at this time had two basic functions:

1. To provide accurate data regarding the health, abilities, and capacities of pupils in order to ascertain individual needs.
2. To measure progress or achievement of pupils according to the objectives of the physical education program. The results could be used both as a basis for grading and for evaluating teaching efficiency." (pp. 468-469)

This type of work dominated the research program of physical education for the next three to four decades until the 1960s, when growing interest in other aspects of exercise and sport science led to the creation of several subdisciplines, most of which are focused on in the coming chapters. In recognition and support of the increasing interest in research evidenced during the 1920s, the American Physical Education Association in 1930 established the *Research Quarterly* as a publishing outlet for researchers in its membership. Over the ensuing 65 years, the scope, sophistication, and quality of the work published in the *Quarterly* have steadily increased.

During this era, gender-separate departments of physical education existed in literally all colleges and universities, as well as in all secondary schools. While sport was at the center of both the women's and men's programs, the women's programs also included modern dance and an emphasis on body mechanics and movement analysis. One of the leading institutions that featured gender-separate departments, typical of this era, was the University of Wisconsin, where Margaret H'Doubler and Ruth Glassow were on the faculty. Whereas her male counterparts across the country concentrated more heavily on measuring such factors as motor ability and skill achievement, Glassow concentrated on the analysis of movement, and was particularly interested in demonstrating the importance of kinesiology to the teacher of physical education. Like McCloy, she promoted research in her area but always with the objective of strengthening the pedagogical foundations of physical education. The reasons for this gender difference in research emphasis has yet to be thoroughly analyzed.

1945-1994

The focus on teacher education continued throughout the first 20 years of the post-World War II era. Nevertheless, a small but steady change was taking place in terms of the knowledge base of the field. Public interest in the results of the 1953 Kraus-Weber tests, which compared muscular strength and flexibility levels of youth in Europe and the United States, sparked a new surge of activity in fitness assessment and promotion. The poor showing of the American subjects (56.6% failure rate compared to 8% for European subjects, ages 6-19) brought new cries for stronger physical education programs in the schools. A few years later the heart attack of President Dwight D. Eisenhower and the exercise-based rehabilitative work of his physician, Dr. Paul Dudley White, focused additional attention on the benefits of lifelong exercise. Within physical education, exercise physiology received another boost of support, as both faculty and new graduate students were attracted to the area. The creation of the American College of Sports Medicine in the early 1950s brought physical education-based researchers together with their counterparts in medicine in a concerted effort to organize the specialty and to encourage further research.

Physical education theoreticians, such as Delbert Oberteuffer of The Ohio State University, and Eleanor Metheny of the University of Southern California, wrote and spoke extensively on the philosophical bases of physical education and sport, albeit usually within the context of teacher education. In addition, a few people were becoming interested in the sociocultural issues in physical education, although it would not be until the late 1960s that the first sports studies courses began to appear on college campuses.

This then was the setting of physical education in the early 1960s when Conant and Henry challenged physical educators. Teacher education was the professional focus. Sport was the primary medium through which physical educators worked. Men and women, for the most part, dwelled in separate departments. Curricula, especially within the men's departments, varied from one institution to another. Even at major research universities, faculty in physical education were often not expected to engage in systematic programs of research.

In retrospect, it should come as no surprise that the conversion of physical education into exercise and sport science would begin in the 1960s. It was a period of social, political, and intellectual foment. Conant's criticism came in the same year that Betty Friedan published *The Feminine Mystique* (1963), heralding the beginning of the women's movement. It was also the height of the drive for civil rights for the African-American minority. At the same time, the nation was engaged in a race with the Soviet Union to explore outer space, and committed itself to land a spaceship on the moon by the end of the decade. In support of this cause, a premium was placed on mathematics and science in the schools. New colleges and universities were established, and existing campuses expanded, to meet the demand presented by the first wave of "baby boomers." Henry's challenge, emanating from the University of California at Berkeley, coincided with that campus's "Free Speech Movement," which was the first of a decade-long series of nationwide campus disruptions over that issue and others, including the Vietnam War, civil rights, and even the relevancy of the curriculum.

It was, therefore, more than coincidence that physical education should find itself engaged in self-reflection and change. Broad societal forces have acted throughout history to effect changes in educational institutions. The rekindling of interest in classical civilization created Renaissance Europe, with its experimentation with the structure of knowledge, and the dissemination of that knowledge through schools and universities. Succeeding centuries brought the Reformation, the age of science, the Enlightenment, and the nineteenth-century idealists. Because movement caused major change in the content and method of education—the challenge of the "space race" with the Soviet Union, a new emphasis on math and science, a close examination of the entire school curriculum and its educational purpose—physical education was forced to scrutinize itself and join the other disciplines in the academy in the quest for new knowledge through research.

As the decade progressed and more and more people began questioning what they saw as a growing gap between the ideal and the reality of the American experience, scholars within physical education and related fields began calling for a closer examination of sport as a major social institution. Thus began an examination that went beyond the physiological disciplines and beyond the traditional confines of teacher education curricula. In 1965 two members of the physical education faculty at the University of Wisconsin, Gerald Kenyon and John Loy, urged American scholars to work with them in developing a sociology of sport. By the end of the decade, many curriculums, either in departments of sociology or physical education, boasted courses in this area. Textbooks serving the new curriculums were beginning to appear.

Scholars interested in the psychological dimensions of sport also began to organize during the 1960s. Suddenly, many faculty in the doctoral-granting research universities found themselves admitting students with very definite academic specialties in mind. No longer interested in pursuing a rather generalized program of studies, these students sought competency in specific areas of interest. The growing recognition of sport as an important institution, combined with a society increasingly critical of many of its structures, provided a fruitful environment for these two areas of social and behavioral science to flourish.

Throughout the late 1960s and early 1970s, many scholars were engaged in the effort to identify and organize the "body of knowledge" of what was still being called physical education. This effort was certainly in direct response to Henry's call of 1964 and to the early efforts in sport sociology and sport psychology to join the more traditional interests in exercise physiology and pedagogy. The Big Ten universities initiated an ongoing "Body of Knowledge" project consisting of several conferences in various specialties during the 1970s and 1980s. Sessions at annual conventions of the professional associations were devoted to the subject. In 1967 one of the leading scholarly journals in the field, *Quest*, focused one entire issue on identifying the nature of a discipline; several other issues over the ensuing years contained individual papers.

By the middle of the 1970s some graduate and even undergraduate physical education programs were beginning to resemble those found in other established disciplines in the arts and sciences. Increasingly, men's and women's departments of physical education were merging, sometimes of their own volition, as it became clear that the study of exercise and sport science was not necessarily gender-specific and sometimes, for fiscal reasons, at the insistence of the central administration of the campus. In 1970 the State University of New York, College at Brockport, announced an undergraduate major in sport science. Students in the new program pursued the "study of man as he develops and participates in the social institutions that supply his varied needs and wants for competitive physio-cognitive behavior" (Whited, 1970, p. 227). In 1973 the University of Massachusetts at Amherst also unveiled a new program in sport studies. By 1980, literally all of the leading graduate programs in the nation offered specializations such as exercise physiology, biomechanics, sport history, motor development, sport sociology, sport psychology, sport management, sport philosophy, and adapted physical activity and education, in addition to teacher education.

The creation of undergraduate non-teacher education-based programs in colleges and universities increased as the demand for elementary and secondary school teachers dramatically abated throughout the 1970s. College and university faculties began to explore other career options for the graduates of their programs. The growing popularity of health and fitness clubs, and the recognition of the value of rehabilitation centers in hospitals and nursing homes, provided more and more employment possibilities for those specializing in the sport sciences. The success of early programs in sport management at Ohio University and the University of Massachusetts at Amherst encouraged others to develop similar options. The area of sport psychology experienced a boom in interest during the 1980s as more and more elite athletes began seeking individual counseling in the quest for a competitive edge. At the same time, the level of research scholarship in sport psychology was raised as its first significant generation of scholars achieved maturity. As a result of these two circumstances and the accompanying media attention, more and more graduate students began to seek advanced degrees in the field, and competition for places in the leading programs became increasingly intense.

The evolution from physical education to exercise and sport science did not come without controversy and concern. For many of those in midcareer who saw themselves as generalists, the era of specialization contained a frightening edge; others saw it as an opportunity to retrain in an area of long-held interest in which they were not expert. The drive to develop an academic discipline out of what had been considered a profession brought with it the need to create and organize a body of knowledge, and in turn an intense commitment to research that would intensify the creation of subdisciplines and further specialization. For the vast majority of college and university faculty whose only research may have begun and ended with their own doctoral dissertation, this development was a new threat. Would they be relegated to the sidelines when new and younger faculty, thoroughly steeped in research, gained prestige and position within their departments? Did departments in *all* institutions have to be engaged in this quest for new knowledge? Would it lead to elitism within departments as research and the funds generated by grants assumed greater importance?

By the late 1970s another question was being raised by no less a light than Franklin Henry, who had first called attention to the need to identify the body of knowledge in physical education 14 years earlier. In 1964 he had urged a cross-disciplinary approach to graduate education from which students would emerge, not as sport sociologists or exercise physiologists, but as scholars of sport, exercise, and movement. In 1978 he was concerned

> that when a physical education department demonstrates that many of its courses and the research of its students and faculty are, in fact, possible within the various traditional disciplines, it also signals the university administration that it can be phased out, that the students will not suffer since an interdisciplinary group major set up from courses in the traditional disciplines will presumably take care of their needs, and faculty research will continue since it is within those disciplines anyway. (Henry, 1978, p. 2)

While in no way repudiating his earlier call for cross-disciplinary work and the identification of a unique body of knowledge, Henry was sounding a major warning to his younger colleagues about the seeming headlong rush to create discrete subdisciplines within the overall discipline of exercise and sport science. Had the move to a discipline, with its consequent specialization, led to fragmentation rather than the strengthening of the field? In a debate carried on in the pages of the *Journal of Physical Education, Recreation and Dance*, S.J. Hoffman and J.R. Thomas grappled with this disturbing possibility. Echoing Henry's concern, Hoffman wrote, "I . . . worry about the academic character of some of the Ph.D.'s we are graduating, exceptionally narrow people—technicians almost—who lack a scholar's understanding of how their discipline relates to the broader framework of physical education and academic life, and who studiously avoid anything that looks or sounds too philosophical" (1985a, p. 20). He later concluded, "The critical question is not whether or not graduate programs in physical education deserve to be absorbed and/or eliminated, but whether we have so fragmented the body of knowledge and, in the wake of it, our professional identities, that extermination of graduate education in physical education is the most appealing managerial alternative" (1985b, p. 22).

In response to Hoffman's essay, Thomas acknowledged the need for doctoral students in physical education to have a broad base "of understanding in both the professional aspects and the subdisciplines of our field" (1985, p. 22). He was, however, concerned that insuring a broad base would come at the expense of interdisciplinary work. It was the latter, he claimed, that had strengthened physical education's move to disciplinary status over the preceding 20 years.

In 1995 the debate continues over the exact nature of the body of knowledge, as well as over the resulting ramifications of the ensuing specialization within the discipline. It is abundantly clear, however, that the field of exercise and sport science is far different from when Conant insulted, and Henry first challenged, physical educators some three decades ago. The effort to define the body of knowledge resulted in the creation of areas of specialization so discrete as to be designated subdisciplines, but was this the sole direction that could have been taken? Clearly, based upon his later statements, it was not what Henry had in mind in 1964. Quite possibly some scholars, initially prepared as physical educators, saw the subdisciplinary route as a means to escape association with the negative stereotype of traditional physical education while building ties to more basic and higher-status academic disciplines. Perhaps others felt it would be the only way to break with the traditional generalist approach, suitable for the preparation of K-through-12 teachers but not necessarily for the advancement of new knowledge. While each of these factors might have contributed, the primary cause of specialization may well have been the recognition that other more traditional and established disciplines in the physical, behavioral, and social sciences, as well as the humanities, had largely ignored the subjects of exercise science and sport. Therefore, the void of research-based data was so great that nothing less than highly focused efforts in all related areas would suffice if a significant body of knowledge was to be created. Finally, the lack of a single universally accepted plan for identifying and creating a unified body of knowledge may have also contributed to the era of specialization in which we find ourselves today.

In the nine chapters to follow, the story will be told of the development of each of the primary subdisciplines or areas of specialization that comprise contemporary exercise and sport science. Outstanding scholars from each of these areas were commissioned to document and relate this remarkable history. The concluding chapter will attempt to summarize the whole, and peer into the immediate future as the field prepares for the twenty-first century.

References

Bowen, W.P. (1922). Seven years of progress in preparing teachers of physical education. *American Physical Education Review*, **27**, 64-65.

Conant, J.B. (1963). *The Education of American Teachers*. New York: McGraw-Hill.

Friedan, B. (1963). *The Feminine Mystique*. New York: Morton.

Hartwell, E.M. (1890). The nature of physical training and the best means of securing its ends. In I.C. Barrows (Ed.), *Physical Training: A Full Report of the Papers and Discussions of the Conference Held in Boston in November, 1889* (pp. 5-22). Boston: George H. Ellis Press.

Henry, F.M. (1964). Physical education—An academic discipline. *Proceedings: Annual Meeting of the National College Physical Education Association for Men*, **67**, 6-9.

Henry, F.M. (1978). The academic discipline of physical education. *Quest*, **29**(Winter), 13-29.

Hoffman, S.J. (1985a). Specialization + fragmentation = Extermination: A formula for the demise of graduate education. *Journal of Physical Education, Recreation and Dance*, **56**(6), 19-22.

Hoffman, S.J. (1985b). Hoffman replies. . . . *Journal of Physical Education, Recreation and Dance*, **56**(9), 23.

Lewis, G.M. (1969). Adoption of the sports program, 1906-39: The role of accommodation in the transformation of physical education. *Quest*, **12**(Spring), 34-46.

Staley, S.C. (1931). The four year curriculum in physical (sports) education. *Research Quarterly*, **2**(1), 82, 90.

Swanson, R.A., & Spears, B. (1995). *History of Sport and Physical Education in the United States*. Dubuque, IA: Brown.

Thomas, J.R. (1985). Physical education and paranoia—synonyms. *Journal of Physical Education, Recreation and Dance*, **56**(9), 20-22.

Van Dalen, D.B., & Bennett, B.L. (1971). *A World History of Physical Education*. Englewood Cliffs, NJ: Prentice Hall.

Whited, C.V. (1970). Sport science, the modern disciplinary concept of physical education. *Proceedings: Annual Meeting of the National College Physical Education Association for Men*, **74**, 223-230.

2

Sport Pedagogy

Linda L. Bain
San José State University

Pedagogy's recognition and identity as a distinct area of scholarly inquiry have coincided with the development of exercise and sport science during the last 20 years. Pedagogists, like their colleagues in other subdisciplines, have developed a research tradition and a body of knowledge. Many of them have resisted the term *subdiscipline*, however, because the debate about the relationship between the discipline of kinesiology (or exercise and sport science) and the profession of teaching physical education has generated tensions that remain unresolved. (See *Quest 42* [3] and *Quest 43* [2].)

Pedagogy research focuses on four general areas:

- Teaching and coaching
- Teacher education
- Teachers' lives and careers
- Curriculum

North Americans tend to simply use the term *pedagogy*, although the phrase *sport pedagogy* is more common in Europe. Americans and Europeans, however, in general agree in defining pedagogy as "disciplined inquiry from different perspectives into teaching and coaching in a variety of contexts in order to inform and improve practice" (Pieron, Cheffers, & Barrette, 1990, p. 24). Most researchers in sport pedagogy study teachers and students in their natural settings. Furthermore, they are committed characteristically not only to understanding but also to improving the practice of teaching. Pedagogists have learned how complex and challenging it is to conduct field research intended to improve practice.

Early Foundations

Concern for the quality of instructional programs was shared by physical educators throughout the late 19th century and first half of the 20th

▼

A Chronology of Sport Pedagogy

Early Foundations

Year   Event

1963   Brown & Cassidy, *Theory in Physical Education*

1963   Gage (Ed.), *Handbook of Research on Teaching*

1965   AAHPER Design Conference on Physical Education as an Area of Scholarly Study and Research

1968   Metheny, *Movement and Meaning*

1969   AAHPER Physical Education Theoretical Structure Project

Organization

Year   Event

1975   Formation of NASPE Curriculum & Instruction Academy

1979   First Curriculum Theory Conference at the University of Georgia

1981   First issue of *Journal of Teaching in Physical Education*

1982   CIC Big Ten Symposium on Research on Teaching in Physical Education

1984   Inclusion of pedagogy research in Olympic Scientific Congress

1986   Establishment of American Educational Research Association (AERA) Special Interest Group for Research on Learning and Instruction in Physical Education

Development

Year   Event

1971   *Quest 15* Educational Change in the Teaching of Physical Education

1972   *Quest 18* Teaching Teachers

1973   Nixon & Locke, Research on Teaching Physical Education in *Second Handbook of Research on Teaching*

1978   Publication of monograph, *What's Going on in Gym?*, describing Teachers College Data Bank Project (Anderson & Barrette, Eds.)

1982   Hal Lawson's presentation at Big Ten Symposium marks transition to multiple paradigm field (Lawson, 1983a)

1986   *Journal of Teaching in Physical Education* monograph on qualitative research

Don Hellison

John Nixon

Mike Metzler

Eleanor Metheny

Larry Locke

Daryl Siedentop

Ann Jewett

Teachers College Databank Project. Standing from left to right: Mitch Levison, Silvia Fishman, Gary Barrette, Bill Anderson, Chuck Tobey, Rachelle Goldsmith, Linda Catelli, and Ed Kennedy. Kneeling (friends from Teachers College): Ree Arnold and Ruth Skinner. Missing from the picture: John Costello, Dick Hurwitz, Susan Laubach, Bruce Morgenegg, Sue Kelly, and Leroy Weissberg.

century. Until the 1960s, physical education was defined as a teaching field, not as an academic discipline. Leaders in the field gave considerable attention to the quality of physical education programs. However, there were no systematic programs of research on curriculum or instruction in physical education, and no doctoral programs to train experts in pedagogical research. Most of the professors who taught "methods" classes to undergraduate students were chosen not because they had formal training but because they had extensive experience teaching or coaching. Most of the content of the methods courses was based on a view of teaching as a craft learned primarily through apprenticeship (Zeichner, 1983).

Before the 1960s, the research on teaching primarily consisted of master's theses and doctoral dissertations. Graduate students, especially teachers earning master's degrees for career advancement, often conducted small research projects designed to evaluate and improve instructional practice. This work was largely atheoretical, and generally employed psychometric measurement or the comparison of method A with method B. The psychometric studies often utilized paper-and-pencil tests, sometimes designed by the researcher, to measure attitudes about

physical education. Because of the use of small and/or nonrandom samples and primitive statistical analyses, little generalizable knowledge
was produced.

The method-A-versus-method-B studies produced a body of inconsis-
tent and often insignificant results. When a study did find a significant
difference between methods, the results were difficult to explain or to
generalize because of the absence of theory and lack of a detailed description of the teaching practices used. For these reasons, the research did
not produce a cumulative body of knowledge about teaching physical
education; however, the psychometric studies and the methods research
demonstrated an early recognition of the importance of studying teaching.

Although the publication of a classic article by Franklin Henry (1964),
"Physical Education as an Academic Discipline," is usually cited as a
turning point within the field, a series of conferences and publications
during the 1960s had a more direct impact on the area of pedagogy, in
particular on the area of curriculum. Two pivotal sets of events occurred
for the development of pedagogy as an area of scholarly inquiry.

First, in response to the launching of Sputnik in 1957 and the subsequent
criticism of American schools, professionals in many fields began projects
to identify the theoretical structure of their disciplines as a basis for
curricular improvement. The American Association for Health, Physical
Education, and Recreation (AAHPER, after 1979 AAHPERD) initiated
such a project in 1961, holding a series of meetings that culminated in
1965 in the Design Conference on Physical Education as an Area of Scholarly Study and Research, followed by the Physical Education Theoretical
Structure Project in 1969. The conference participants included scholars
whose work provided the foundation for the development of curriculum
theory in physical education. Two early issues of *Quest* (Vol. 2—The Art
and Science of Human Movement, 1964, and Vol. 9—The Nature of a
Discipline, 1967) described some of these efforts to develop a theoretical
structure for the field. Two books from the period are classics in physical
education curriculum theory literature: Brown and Cassidy (1963), *Theory
in Physical Education*, and Metheny (1968), *Movement and Meaning*. The
AAHPER project culminated in the publication of a report, *Tones of Theory*,
written by Celeste Ulrich and John Nixon (1972). Many current pedagogical scholars have limited knowledge of this period of theoretical activity;
however, Ann Jewett, a coauthor of several books with John Nixon, and
a participant in the 1969 conference, has built upon this early work to
develop a program of research in the area of curriculum theory.

The second significant event in the development of pedagogy as an
area of study was the publication of the *Handbook of Research on Teaching*
(Gage, 1963) by the American Educational Research Association. The
Handbook proposed the use of scientific methods to study teaching, and
fostered increasing use of systematic observation of classroom behavior.
Although physical education was not mentioned in the *Handbook* and it

went relatively unnoticed by most physical educators, the publication provided a major stimulus within education to research on teaching that began to influence the training of some doctoral students in physical education.

One of the leaders who helped to spread that influence in physical education was John Nixon, a colleague at Stanford of the *Handbook* editor, Nate Gage. Nixon played a central role in the founding of pedagogy as an area of scholarly inquiry. A participant in the theory conferences, he had coauthored the report *Tones of Theory*, and he was later invited to contribute a chapter to the *Second Handbook of Research on Teaching* (Nixon & Locke, 1973).

Organization

Although pedagogical research flourished in the 1970s, unlike scholars in other emerging areas in exercise and sport science, pedagogy researchers did not create a new organization to support their work. Perhaps because of their commitment to the improvement of practice, most retained their affiliation with AAHPERD, presenting and publishing their research through that organization. As part of the restructuring of AAHPERD in the mid-1970s, the National Association for Sport and Physical Education (NASPE) was created. In response to the emergence of disciplinary research, NASPE created a number of academies intended to serve scholars in the subdisciplines. In 1975 Sally Robinson, who had studied curriculum with Ann Jewett, was appointed the first chair of the NASPE Curriculum and Instruction Academy. Another of Jewett's students, Linda Bain, made the C&I Academy's first keynote presentation on the topic of the hidden curriculum.

The creation of the NASPE Curriculum and Instruction Academy provided some support for scholars in the field, but the Academy membership consisted primarily of physical education teachers, not pedagogy researchers. For that reason, the Academy programming tended to emphasize practical application rather than pedagogical research.

The other organization that provided support for pedagogy researchers was the Association internationale des écoles superieures d'education physique (AIESEP). Led by the efforts of Maurice Pieron from the University of Liege in Belgium and John Cheffers from Boston University, AIESEP held meetings beginning in 1977 that included sessions on research on teaching (Pieron & Cheffers, 1982).

Although AAHPERD and AIESEP both provided some support for pedagogy researchers, the field received little recognition in the exercise and sport science research community. Lacking a separate organization and retaining their ties to practitioners, pedagogy scholars struggled to gain visibility and acceptance as a legitimate area of research.

It was only in the early 1980s that several events signalled progress in the acceptance of pedagogy as a recognized area of scholarly inquiry. Perhaps the most significant was the publication in 1981 of a new journal, the *Journal of Teaching in Physical Education* (*JTPE*). The initiation of *JTPE* greatly increased the dissemination of pedagogy research, which had been limited previously to a few research studies published each year in the *Research Quarterly for Exercise and Sport* (*RQES*) and summary discussions or theoretical articles published in *Quest*. *JTPE* was begun by two assistant professors, Mark Freedman of Rutgers and Mike Metzler of Iowa State University, who were recent graduates of Daryl Siedentop's doctoral program at Ohio State. Frustrated by the lack of publication outlets for pedagogy research, Freedman and Metzler borrowed start-up money and served as editors and publishers of *JTPE* for its first two years. In 1983 *JTPE* was purchased by Human Kinetics, which continues to publish and distribute the *Journal*.

The second major event in the early 1980s was the CIC Big Ten Symposium on Research on Teaching in Physical Education, held at Purdue University in 1982 (Templin & Olson, 1983). The Committee on Institutional Cooperation (CIC), composed of the major research universities in the Big Ten athletic conference plus the University of Chicago, had initiated an earlier project in 1964 designed to identify the body of knowledge in physical education (Ziegler & McCristal, 1967). The 1964 project had identified six major areas of knowledge: sociology of sport and physical education; administrative theory; history, philosophy, and comparative physical education and sport; exercise physiology; biomechanics; and motor learning and sport psychology. Despite the central role that teaching had played in the history of the field, pedagogy was not included. The decision, nearly 20 years later, for the CIC Big Ten project to sponsor a symposium on teaching in physical education was hailed by pedagogical researchers as a welcomed sign of legitimacy. The inclusion of AIESEP's program on pedagogical research in the 1984 Olympic Scientific Congress in Eugene, Oregon, was further evidence of sport pedagogy's acceptance by the scholarly community in exercise and sport science (Pieron & Graham, 1986).

An additional observation on the politics of the emerging field of study seems in order. The original CIC Big Ten project was organized by men who served as deans, directors, and department heads in those universities. Women were not included until men's and women's programs began to be merged in the 1970s, possibly explaining in part the inclusion of administrative theory but the exclusion of curriculum and instruction, since the latter in the 1960s was primarily an area of scholarly interest to women.

Women were included when the CIC Big Ten symposium on pedagogy was held in 1982, but gender politics still influenced the field. The focus of the symposium was on teaching and teacher education, areas in which men and women conducted research, but most of the early leaders were male. The area of curriculum, dominated by Jewett and her mostly female students, was not included. This exclusion did not appear to be the result of overt sexism but a reflection of the discomfort of those in the dominant natural science paradigm with a form of scholarship unfamiliar to most men, and grounded in the heritage of women's physical education (Bain, 1991; Ulrich, 1979). The curriculum group proceeded separately, holding a series of biennial curriculum theory conferences sponsored by the University of Georgia beginning in 1979 and continuing through 1991.

Two separate but overlapping scholarly communities existed within the field of pedagogy. One, led primarily by men, used natural science methods to study teaching and teacher education. The other, led primarily by women, extended the work of early female movement theorists to build curriculum theory. The separation of the two groups reflects the ways in which the social construction of knowledge interacts with the social construction of gender. However, developments during the 1980s began to lessen the distinction between the two communities.

The 1980s were a period of expansion and accomplishment for pedagogy researchers who produced significant bodies of research related to teaching, teachers, teacher education, and curriculum. A number of doctoral programs provided specialized training in pedagogical research, disseminated through publications and conferences.

As the area became more established, researchers felt a greater need for an organization devoted to their particular needs as scholars. Rather than start an independent organization, they decided to form a special-interest group within the American Educational Research Association (AERA) for research on learning and instruction in physical education (SIG-PE). In 1986 Lynn Housner, then at New Mexico State University, gathered a group of about 30 researchers interested in creating a SIG; in 1995 membership stood at 109. The SIG sponsors a few programs at the AERA annual conference and holds a one-day "invisible college" meeting one day before AERA meetings.

Although many educators view physical education as a marginal subject area, affiliation with AERA has provided some legitimacy to physical education pedagogy research within the educational research community. Although physical education was omitted from the third edition of the *Handbook of Research on Teaching* (Wittrock, 1986), more recent handbooks of research on teacher education and curricular research have included it (Bain, 1990b; Steinhardt, 1992).

The invisible college held by the AERA SIG has also provided opportunities for interaction that were not feasible within the structure of the AAHPERD convention. Those interactions have contributed to improved dialogue among scholars from different research traditions. Perhaps the most significant outcome of the creation of the AERA SIG has been to provide a direct connection to the educational research community, which has been the major source of ideas and methods for pedagogical research in physical education.

Development

Three publications in the early 1970s launched the growth of pedagogy as an area of study and set the directions for its development throughout the decade. *Quest 15* (Educational Change in the Teaching of Physical Education, 1971) and *Quest 18* (Teaching Teachers, 1972) brought the developments within the area of pedagogy to the attention of the field. Of particular influence were articles by William Anderson (1971) on "Descriptive-Analytic Research on Teaching" and by Daryl Siedentop (1972) on "Behavior Analysis and Teacher Training." Much of the research conducted in the 1970s reflected the approaches these papers described. Martin Burlingame's (1972) paper, "Socialization Constructs and the Teaching of Teachers," also produced an important line of research, but teacher socialization research did not receive much attention until the 1980s. An article by Jewett and her colleagues also introduced the conceptual framework that was to serve as the basis for her curriculum research (Jewett, Jones, Luneke, & Robinson, 1971).

The third of these publications, in 1973, was John Nixon and Larry Locke's chapter in the *Second Handbook of Research on Teaching*, which provided guidance and structure to those undertaking research in this fledgling field. Locke (1977, 1984) continued to be a strong influence within the field for the next two decades.

In the 1970s, the positivist paradigm that modeled research on natural science methods was the most widely accepted approach to pedagogical research. Researchers assumed that through the use of objective observation they could discover causal relationships governing human behavior (Dunkin & Biddle, 1974). Most of the pedagogical research of the time fell within two dominant strands. One was descriptive-analytic research that used systematic observation instruments to describe events in physical education classes. William Anderson was a leading figure in the development of this research. He and a group of graduate students at Columbia initiated a videotape data bank project in 1971 that led to a series of research studies (Anderson & Barrette, 1978). Another significant body of descriptive work utilized the Cheffers' Adaptation of the Flanders' Interaction Analysis System (CAFIAS) to describe the interactions between teachers and students in sport and physical education (Cheffers, 1972). The popularity of descriptive-analytic research is evidenced by the large number of observation systems that were created for use in physical education settings (Darst, Mancini, & Zakrajsek, 1983).

Much of the early descriptive-analytic work described events in physical education classes without attempting to link those events to student outcomes. However, a number of pedagogy researchers based their work on the process-product model of research on teacher effectiveness, in which the goal is to identify teacher behaviors that relate to student learning outcomes. In one line of work heavily influenced by movement education and by Muska Mosston's (1966) description of a spectrum of teaching styles, researchers examined the effects of teaching styles on student outcomes such as motor performance and creativity. This work differed from earlier method-A-versus-method-B studies, in that it was theoretically based and researchers used systematic observation instruments to describe the teaching variables.

One of the problems in applying the process-product model in physical education was the difficulty of measuring student learning. In an attempt to address this problem, a number of researchers became interested in the concept of academic learning time in physical education (ALT-PE). The assumption of ALT-PE research is that the time that a student is engaged in relevant tasks is a direct predictor of learning and therefore is appropriate as a substitute variable for outcome measures (Dodds & Rife, 1983). As the body of descriptive-analytic research on teaching began to accumulate, it provided, within limitations, support for what is called the direct model of effective teaching (Siedentop, 1983).

While many researchers were using descriptive-analytic research to describe physical education classes and to identify patterns of effective teaching, another group was studying how to train teachers to use methods that were deemed effective. Daryl Siedentop and his graduate students from Ohio State University were leaders in this second strand of pedagogical research, conducting research on the use of behavior modification principles to modify teacher behavior (Siedentop, 1981, 1986). They identified a number of training strategies that involved manipulation of environmental contingencies in order to change specific teaching behaviors.

Although a number of researchers made important contributions in this early period, the work of Anderson and Siedentop had considerable influence on the development of pedagogy as an area of study. In addition to working with large numbers of doctoral students, both Anderson (1980) and Siedentop (1983) published textbooks that helped to disseminate more widely in the field information about systematic observation of teaching and behavior modification techniques. Siedentop also published a newsletter, *The Bulletin Board*, that provided for informal networking among pedagogy scholars.

Meanwhile, Ann Jewett and her students continued their curriculum research, first at the University of Wisconsin and later at the University of Georgia, focusing on the construction and validation of a conceptual framework they called the Purpose Process Curriculum Framework (PPCF) (Jewett & Mullan, 1977). Although this work emphasized theory construction more than description of the teaching process, it remained within the positivist paradigm (Jewett & Bain, 1987). However, the PPCF work was not viewed as pedagogical research by many other researchers in the United States, perhaps because it did not emphasize systematic observation of instruction.

Scholarship

Most of the strands of pedagogical research in physical education were heavily influenced by scholarship in education. The individuals and doctoral programs that provided leadership for pedagogy research were located at universities where the physical education department was housed in, or had significant relationships with, strong colleges of education. The concepts of process-product research and systematic observation of teaching came from education. Many of the most widely used observation instruments (CAFIAS, ALT-PE) were modifications of instruments developed for observations in classroom research. Although its roots were in education, sport pedagogy began to develop its own body of research and community of scholars.

The CIC Big Ten Symposium symbolized the acceptance of sport pedagogy as a legitimate area of scholarly inquiry, but the importance of the meeting was substantive as well as symbolic. The symposium marked the transition of pedagogy from reliance on a dominant paradigm based on natural science methods to a multiple paradigm field. Hal Lawson's closing presentation at the symposium raised the issue of paradigms, and critiqued the dominant positivist paradigm employed in research on teaching. He argued for the inclusion of a second paradigm, which he called research on teachers:

> This means that colleagues interested in research on teaching will search for *causes* while colleagues in a paradigm for research on teachers may be satisfied with *reasons* . . . ; researchers on teaching will look for generalizable laws derived from replicated findings, while researchers on teachers will look for time-bound forms of understanding that are often situation- and person-specific; researchers on teaching may be in pursuit of a true science, while researchers on teachers may be content with good scholarship, only some of which is scientific. (Lawson, 1983a, pp. 352-353)

While some of the others at the meeting had presented research that employed *qualitative* rather than *quantitative* research methods, it was Lawson who articulated the rationale for the shift to multiple paradigms.

That shift proceeded throughout the next decade. The change moved unevenly and with conflict, but it proceeded. Often the debate centered on the relative merits of quantitative and qualitative research methods, in some cases using the perspective of positivism to evaluate both. Gradually some scholars began to question the assumptions of positivism and to propose alternative views (Schempp, 1987).

The primary alternative that emerged employed qualitative research methods to focus on understanding the meaning of human behavior within a particular social and historical context. In many ways, this work was a natural extension of the early descriptive-analytic research. However, rather than rely on systematic observation that "counts" behaviors using category systems developed by the researcher, this research used qualitative methods, such as interviews and extensive unstructured observations, to describe the complexity of the situation and the perceptions of teachers and students.

The publication in 1986 of a *JTPE* monograph on naturalistic inquiry indicated the growing interest in this qualitative approach (Earls, 1986). The 1989 publication in *RQES* of a tutorial on qualitative research marked wider acceptance of such research, not only by pedagogy researchers but by the field of exercise and sport science (Locke, 1989). Locke and his colleagues at the University of Massachusetts built a highly visible doctoral program that emphasized qualitative research in teacher education. Anderson (1994) and his colleagues conducted a series of qualitative case studies, "Data Bank II," describing outstanding physical education programs. As many doctoral programs began to include training in qualitative as well as quantitative methods, an increasing number of qualitative research studies were published.

Another approach, *critical* research, also began to emerge in the 1980s, but it has had much less impact on pedagogical research in North America. Proponents of this paradigm seek to understand contextual constraints on human behavior and to use this information to empower those being researched. This form of research combines scholarship and advocacy, and is usually grounded in one of three theoretical perspectives: feminism, neomarxism, or empowering pedagogy (Lather, 1986). Within North America a few pedagogy scholars, primarily women who have been influenced by feminist thought, have begun to take a critical stance in their work (Bain, 1990a, 1990c; Dewar, 1990, 1991; Griffin, 1989). Although relatively few of their North American colleagues have adopted the critical perspective, a small network of critical scholars from English-speaking countries has emerged (Kirk & Tinning, 1990; Sparkes, 1992).

The shift from a dominant positivist paradigm to multiple paradigms for pedagogical research was accompanied by a certain amount of conflict, perhaps most clearly exemplified by the debate in *JTPE* between Schempp (1987, 1988) and Siedentop (1987). Recent articles in both *JTPE* and *Quest* have called for collegiality and dialogue rather than "paradigm wars"

(Sparkes, 1991; O'Sullivan, Siedentop, & Locke, 1992). Despite some evidence of continuing tensions, there seems to be a recognition that multiple paradigms will coexist for the foreseeable future.

Present and Future

As pedagogy research enters its third decade, the body of knowledge within the area is growing in complexity and depth. Pedagogy research is based on multiple paradigms or perspectives. The research is characterized by greater theoretical sophistication and a range of research methods. Groups of scholars have established ongoing programs of research that have resulted in a cumulative body of knowledge.

Knowledge Base

Pedagogical research has produced an expanding body of knowledge of increasing complexity and depth. Those interested in descriptive-analytic and behavioral research on teaching and teacher education have expanded their research to include more variables related to context and content (Siedentop & Eldar, 1989; Housner, 1990). Research within this tradition now includes studies of teachers' thoughts and feelings as well as behaviors. Two of the most notable examples are research on teacher cognitions and decision-making (Griffey & Housner, 1991), and research on teacher expectations (Martinek, 1989). In addition to quantitative studies, descriptive research often employs qualitative research methods that describe the complexity and context of the teaching situation.

There is a growing body of research focusing on the socialization of teachers (Lawson, 1983b, 1983c; Stroot, 1993; Templin & Schempp, 1989). This topic had been included in *Quest 18* (Burlingame, 1972; Pooley, 1972), but little socialization research was conducted until research on teachers and qualitative research methods gained acceptance.

Although research on teaching, teachers, and teacher education has received most of the attention, pedagogy scholars also have continued curriculum research. During the 1980s, Jewett and her students shifted to an interpretive perspective for much of the curriculum research they were conducting (Jewett & Bain, 1987). This shift is particularly evident in the work of Ennis related to teachers' goals and value orientations (Ennis, 1987, 1992a, 1992b). The expansion of pedagogical research to include paradigms appropriate to curriculum research, and the increased interest in questions related to expertise in subject matter, have somewhat closed the historical gaps among teaching, teacher education, and curricular research.

The body of pedagogical research from the critical perspective within North America continues to be relatively limited. Thus far it has focused primarily on issues related to the hidden curriculum and to gender (Bain, 1990a; Griffin, 1989). Given the conservatism of those who enter the field of physical education (Sage, 1980), it seems unlikely that critical research will attract large numbers of researchers. However, the complex social issues confronting public education in the US may stimulate greater attention to the issues raised by critical theorists.

Relationship of Research and Practice

Pedagogy scholars have had an ongoing commitment to the improvement of school physical education programs. Kate Barrett, George Graham, Don Hellison, Betty Logsdon, Muska Mosston, Robert Pangrazi, and others have focused their work on the publication of textbooks and other materials designed to help teachers build quality programs. These publications involved considerable scholarship, and their impact on the field has been notable. This work builds on and is complemented by the growing body of pedagogical research.

However, neither the textbooks nor the research seems to be able to address the growing concern over the quality—and perhaps the survival—of school physical education (Dodds & Locke, 1984). Pedagogy scholars have an overt commitment to the improvement of practice but have had little success in affecting the quality of school physical education programs. Nevertheless, Harris (1993) indicates that pedagogy scholars have been more effective than their colleagues in the biophysical sciences and the behavioral/sociocultural sciences in addressing professional competencies. However, she suggests that pedagogy scholars have given more attention to technical pedagogical competency than to critical/reflective knowledge and skills.

Pedagogy scholars differ in how they view the relationship of research and practice (Mitchell, 1993). Positivists see the goal of research as creating a knowledge base of lawlike generalizations, then disseminating that information to teachers. Others, viewing knowledge as socially constructed and context specific, see the task of researchers as working with teachers to generate knowledge that is useful in a particular setting. Their perspective is reflected in a growing interest in *action research*, in which researchers and practitioners collaborate to improve practice (Martinek & Schempp, 1988). William Anderson, for example, has developed a collaborative model of action research in which he and his doctoral students work with local school districts to improve physical education programs (Anderson, 1987, 1988). Don Hellison (1985, 1992, 1995) has established a research program in which he and his graduate students work with "at-risk" youth to identify ways of building social responsibility in physical education.

These projects represent a major change in the view of how research affects practice. Instead of conducting value-free research with the aim of accumulating knowledge and later disseminating that knowledge to teachers, these programs attempt to incorporate the improvement of practice into the research as it is being conducted. Although action research has a long history in educational research, such projects were generally not accepted as real science by researchers in the positivist paradigm. However, the acceptance of multiple paradigms has permitted pedagogy scholars to make a case for action research as legitimate scholarly work. This possibility has been strengthened by societal pressures on research universities to conduct research of greater social relevance, and by the subsequent efforts within higher education to broaden definitions of scholarship (Boyer, 1990).

The growing interest in action research may foster greater attention to critical research, since this approach can be used to empower research participants (Carr & Kemmis, 1986). However, most of the action research in physical education has addressed technical or practical concerns rather than the emancipatory issues of interest to critical theorists (Grundy, 1987).

One of the primary challenges confronting physical education teachers in the United States is how to provide effective instructional programs for diverse student populations. The responsibility of teacher educators is to prepare new teachers for that task and to support the work of teachers in the field. The changing reality in schools may shape the future of pedagogical research.

Educational researchers from all research paradigms are attempting to deal with issues related to diversity and equity. Although the approaches differ, each is giving greater attention to the effects of culture and social context on individual behavior. Historically, both the training of teachers and research on instruction were grounded in psychological theories and constructs, but much greater attention is now being given to social science and cultural studies. This attention seems likely to continue the shift within physical education pedagogy from "pure" behavioral research to social-psychological, interpretive, and critical approaches. It may also foster increased interaction with scholars from sport sociology and sport history.

Where Does Pedagogy Fit?

Much pedagogical research has its roots in the field of education and has been influenced by theories and methods from the educational research community. This close connection to education has raised questions about the relationship of sport pedagogy to education and to kinesiology or exercise and sport science. The theoretical debate has practical consequences such as in what department physical education pedagogy scholars will be located (or whether such specialists are even necessary), and how physical education teacher education programs will be designed.

The primary argument for the need for pedagogy scholars with expertise in physical education is based on a concept that Shulman (1987) labeled *pedagogical content knowledge*. He suggested that such knowledge is an important component of teacher expertise, and described it as "the blending of content and pedagogy into an understanding of how particular topics, problems, or issues are organized, represented, and adapted to the diverse interests and abilities of learners, and presented for instruction" (p. 8).

The implication of pedagogical content knowledge is that teacher educators must be concerned with how teachers learn and process subject matter, as well as with their mastery of teaching methods (Ball & McDiarmid, 1990; Vickers, 1987). The problem that follows is the difficulty of defining what constitutes appropriate subject-matter preparation for physical education teachers (see *Quest 42* [3]). As the body of knowledge has expanded in the subdisciplines of exercise and sport science, faculty have struggled over the relevance of disciplinary knowledge to the professional preparation of teachers. The issue has become more complex as exercise and sport science departments have expanded their programs to include professional training for roles other than teaching.

Ellis (1988) posits that physical education lies at the intersection of the health enhancement industry, which seeks to improve people's health, and the leisure industry, which seeks to improve the quality of life. Lawson and Stroot suggest that physical education teachers are "caught between the social life worlds of two institutions: education and sport" (Lawson & Stroot, 1993, p. 439). Bain (1988) proposes that Ellis's model be expanded to include not only health and leisure but also education, which seeks to help people understand the world and themselves. This composite model depicts a field with professional practice at the intersection of three social institutions, focusing on movement as it relates to health, leisure, and education.

According to this model pedagogical research in physical education must move beyond education as the sole source of theories and research questions. The research needs to include not only effective teaching methods but also issues related to defining and enhancing health and the quality of life. Health, leisure, and sport issues have implications for research on teaching, teachers, teacher education, and curriculum.

One effect of a broader perspective may be to focus attention on questions about the meanings of movement, sport, and exercise in our society, and how those meanings affect program design and instruction in a variety of settings, including (but not limited to) schools. Many children and adults learn sports and exercise in community sports programs, recreational centers, and corporate fitness centers. However, instructors in these nonschool settings generally have not been formally trained in pedagogy, and little pedagogical research has been conducted in these programs. Broadening the scope of pedagogical inquiry will not only provide information about these programs but may also provide insights useful in improving school physical education.

A model that draws on health, leisure, and sport research may also enable pedagogy researchers to reframe questions about the quality of school physical education programs. One effect of the broader perspective might be to address structural barriers to quality school programs, rather than focusing only on the effectiveness of individual teachers. Another effect might be to focus attention on the linkages between school physical education programs and other health and leisure services, increasingly important because of the emerging trend to link schools with family services and health care agencies to provide integrated services to children and their families.

Conclusion

As pedagogy has evolved over the past 20 years, scholarship in the field has grown in complexity and depth. Once dominated by the positivist paradigm, the field now utilizes multiple paradigms and perspectives.

Despite this progress, problems exist. Many young pedagogy scholars are employed in labor-intensive positions as teacher educators in colleges and universities that provide little time or support for their research. Pedagogical research has yet to influence school physical education programs significantly, and there is continuing tension in the relationship of pedagogy to the other subdisciplines of kinesiology or exercise and sport science.

Concerns about the future of school physical education have created considerable uncertainty regarding the future of pedagogy research. If school physical education programs disappear, then so will teacher education programs and jobs for pedagogy scholars. It seems certain that sport and exercise will continue to be significant elements of the culture of the United States and that instruction will continue to be provided to youth and adults in sports programs and exercise centers, if not in schools. What is less clear is what role pedagogy scholars will play if instructional programs shift from schools to other settings such as park districts, youth sports programs, or commercial enterprises. Currently, instructors or coaches in these programs do not receive formal pedagogical training, and few pedagogical scholars have conducted research in settings other than schools. A clear challenge to pedagogy researchers is to establish the relevance of their work to these programs.

Pedagogy touches each of the subdisciplines within exercise and sport science. That breadth, combined with the complexity and value-laden nature of the instructional process, creates a certain "messiness" to the development of research in the area. But those qualities also position the area of pedagogy to play a key role in the future of the field.

References

Anderson, W.G. (1971). Descriptive-analytic research on teaching. *Quest,* **15**, 1-8.

Anderson, W.G. (1980). *Analysis of teaching physical education.* St. Louis: Mosby.

Anderson, W.G. (1987). Five years of program development: A retrospective. In G.T. Barrette, R.W. Feingold, C.R. Rees, & M. Pieron (Eds.), *Myths, models, & methods in sport pedagogy* (pp. 123-134). Champaign, IL: Human Kinetics.

Anderson, W.G. (1988). A school-centered collaborative model for program development. *Journal of Teaching in Physical Education, 7*(3), 176-183.

Anderson, W.G. (1994). Building and maintaining outstanding physical education programs. *Journal of Physical Education, Recreation and Dance,* **65**(7), 22-48.

Anderson, W.G., & Barrette, G.T. (Eds.) (1978). What's going in gym: Descriptive studies of physical education classes. *Motor Skills: Theory into Practice Monograph,* **1**.

Bain, L.L. (1988). Beginning the journey: Agenda for 2001. *Quest,* **40**(2), 96-106.

Bain, L.L. (1990a). A critical analysis of the hidden curriculum in physical education. In D. Kirk & R. Tinning (Eds.), *Physical education, curriculum and culture: Critical issues in the contemporary crisis* (pp. 23-42). London: Falmer Press.

Bain, L.L. (1990b). Physical education teacher education. In W.R. Houston (Ed.), *Handbook of research on teacher education* (pp. 758-781). New York: Macmillan.

Bain, L.L. (1990c). Visions and voices. *Quest,* **42**(1), 1-12.

Bain, L.L. (1991). Knowledge as contested terrain. *Quest,* **43**(2), 214-217.

Ball, D.L., & McDiarmid, G.W. (1990). The subject-matter preparation of teachers. In W.R. Houston (Ed.), *Handbook of research on teacher education* (pp. 437-449). New York: Macmillan.

Boyer, E.L. (1990). *Scholarship reconsidered.* Princeton, N.J.: Carnegie Foundation for the Advancement of Teaching.

Brown, C., & Cassidy, R. (1963). *Theory in physical education.* Philadelphia: Lea & Febiger.

Burlingame, M. (1972). Socialization constructs and the teaching of teachers. *Quest,* **18**, 40-56.

Carr, W., & Kemmis, S. (1986). *Becoming critical: Education, knowledge and action research.* London: Falmer Press.

Cheffers, J. (1972). *The validation of an instrument designed to expand the Flanders' System of Interaction Analysis to describe non-verbal interaction, different varieties of teacher behavior and pupil response.* Unpublished doctoral dissertation, Temple University, Philadelphia.

Darst, P.W., Mancini, V.H., & Zakrajsek, D.B. (1983). *Systematic observation instrumentation for physical education*. Champaign, IL: Leisure Press.

Dewar, A. (1990). Oppression and privilege in physical education: Struggles in the negotiation of gender in a university programme. In D. Kirk & R. Tinning (Eds.), *Physical education, curriculum and culture: Critical issues in the contemporary crisis* (pp. 67-100). London: Falmer Press.

Dewar, A. (1991). Feminist pedagogy in physical education: Promises, possibilities and pitfalls. *Journal of Physical Education, Recreation and Dance*, **62**(6), 68-71, 75-77.

Dodds, P., & Locke, L.F. (1984). Is physical education in American schools worth saving? Evidence, alternatives, judgment. In N. Struna (Ed.), *Proceedings, National Association for Physical Education in Higher Education, Vol. 5* (pp. 76-90). Champaign, IL: Human Kinetics.

Dodds, P., & Rife, F. (Eds.) (1983). Time to learn in physical education: History, completed research, and potential future for academic learning time in physical education. *Journal of Teaching in Physical Education Monograph 1*.

Dunkin, M., & Biddle, B. (1974). *The study of teaching*. New York: Holt, Rinehart & Winston.

Earls, N. (Ed.) (1986). Naturalistic inquiry: Interactive research and the insider-outsider perspective. *Journal of Teaching in Physical Education Monograph*, **6**(1).

Ellis, M.J. (1988). *The business of physical education*. Champaign, IL: Human Kinetics.

Ennis, C.D. (1987). Properties of purpose concepts in an operational middle-school curriculum. *Journal of Teaching in Physical Education*, **6**(3), 287-300.

Ennis, C.D. (1992a). Curriculum theory as practiced: Case studies of operationalized value orientations. *Journal of Teaching in Physical Education*, **11**(4), 358-375.

Ennis, C.D. (1992b). The influence of value orientations in curriculum decision making. *Quest*, **44**(3), 317-329.

Gage, N.L. (Ed.) (1963). *Handbook of research on teaching*. Chicago: Rand McNally.

Griffey, D.C., & Housner, L.D. (1991). Differences between experienced and inexperienced teachers' planning decisions, interactions, student engagement, and instructional climate. *Research Quarterly for Exercise and Sport*, **62**(2), 196-204.

Griffin, P. (1989). Gender as a socializing agent in physical education. In T.J. Templin & P.G. Schempp (Eds.), *Socialization into physical education: Learning to teach* (pp. 219-233). Indianapolis: Benchmark Press.

Grundy, S. (1987). *Curriculum: Product or praxis?* London: Falmer Press.

Harris, J.C. (1993). Using kinesiology: A comparison of applied veins in the subdisciplines. *Quest*, **45**(3), 389-412.

Hellison, D. (1985). *Goals and strategies for teaching physical education*. Champaign, IL: Human Kinetics.

Hellison, D. (1992). If Sargent could see us now: Values and program survival in higher education. *Quest*, **44**(3), 398-411.

Hellison, D. (1995). *Teaching responsibility through physical activity*. Champaign, IL: Human Kinetics.

Henry, F. (1964). Physical education as an academic discipline. *Journal of Health, Physical Education and Recreation*, **37**(9), 32-33.

Housner, L.D. (1990). Selecting master teachers: Evidence from process-product research. *Journal of Teaching in Physical Education*, **9**(3), 201-226.

Jewett, A.E., & Bain, L.L. (Eds.) (1987). The Purpose Process Curriculum Framework. *Journal of Teaching in Physical Education Monograph*, **6**(3).

Jewett, A.E., Jones, L.S., Luneke, S.M., & Robinson, S.M. (1971). Educational change through a taxonomy for writing physical education objectives. *Quest*, **15**, 32-38.

Jewett, A.E., & Mullan, M. (1977). *Curriculum design: Purposes and processes in physical education teaching-learning*. Reston, VA: AAHPERD.

Kirk, D., & Tinning, R. (Eds.) (1990). *Physical education, curriculum and culture: Critical issues in the contemporary crisis*. London: Falmer Press.

Lather, P. (1986). Issues of validity in openly ideological research: Between a rock and a soft place. *Interchange*, **17**(4), 63-84.

Lawson, H.A. (1983a). Paradigms for research on teaching and teachers. In T.J. Templin & J.K. Olson (Eds.), *Teaching in physical education* (pp. 339-358). Champaign, IL: Human Kinetics.

Lawson, H.A. (1983b). Toward a model of teacher socialization in physical education: The subjective warrant, recruitment, and teacher education (Part I). *Journal of Teaching in Physical Education*, **2**(3), 3-16.

Lawson, H.A. (1983c). Toward a model of teacher socialization in physical education: Entry into schools, teachers' role orientations, and longevity in teaching (Part 2). *Journal of Teaching in Physical Education*, **3**(1), 3-15.

Lawson, H.A., & Stroot, S.A. (1993). Footprints and signposts: Perspectives on socialization research, *Journal of Teaching in Physical Education*, **12**(4), 437-446.

Locke, L.F. (1977). Research on teaching physical education: New hope for a dismal science. *Quest*, **28**(1), 2-16.

Locke, L.F. (1984). Research on teaching teachers: Where are we now? *Journal of Teaching in Physical Education Monograph 2*.

Locke, L.F. (1989). Qualitative research as a form of scientific inquiry in sport and physical education. *Research Quarterly for Exercise and Sport*, **60**(1), 1-20.

Martinek, T.J. (1989). The psycho-social dynamics of the Pygmalion phenomenon in physical education and sport. In T.J. Templin & P.G. Schempp (Eds.), *Socialization into physical education: Learning to teach* (pp. 199-217). Indianapolis: Benchmark Press.

Martinek, T.J., & Schempp, P.G. (Eds.) (1988). Collaboration for instructional improvement: Models for school-university partnerships. *Journal of Teaching in Physical Education Monograph*, **7**(3).

Metheny, E. (1968). *Movement and meaning*. New York: McGraw-Hill.

Mitchell, M.F. (1993). Linking teacher educators, knowledge, and the quality of practice in schools. *Journal of Teaching in Physical Education*, **12**(4), 399-412.

Mosston, M. (1966). *Teaching physical education*. Columbus, OH: Charles E. Merrill.

Nixon, J.E., & Locke, L.F. (1973). Research on teaching physical education. In R.M.W. Travers (Ed.), *Second handbook of research on teaching* (pp. 1210-1242). Chicago: Rand McNally.

O'Sullivan, M., Siedentop, D., & Locke, L.F. (1992). Toward collegiality: Competing viewpoints among teacher educators. *Quest*, **44**(2), 266-280.

Pieron, M., & Cheffers, J. (Eds.) (1982). *Studying the teaching in physical education*. Liege, Belgium: Association Internationale des Écoles Superieures d'Education Physique.

Pieron, M., Cheffers, J., & Barrette, G. (1990). *An introduction to the terminology of sport pedagogy*. Liege, Belgium: International Committee of Sport Pedagogy and Association Internationale des Écoles Superieures d'Education Physique.

Pieron, M., & Graham, G. (Eds.) (1986). *Sport pedagogy*. Champaign, IL: Human Kinetics.

Pooley, J.C. (1972). Professional socialization: A model of the pre-training phase applicable to physical education students. *Quest*, **18**, 57-66.

Sage, G.H. (1980). Sociology of physical educator/coaches: Personal attributes controversy. *Research Quarterly for Exercise and Sport*, **51**(1), 110-121.

Schempp, P.G. (1987). Research on teaching in physical education: Beyond the limits of natural science. *Journal of Teaching in Physical Education*, **6**(2), 111-121.

Schempp, P.G. (1988). Exorcist II: A reply to Siedentop. *Journal of Teaching in Physical Education*, **7**(2), 78-81.

Shulman, L.S. (1987). Knowledge and teaching: Foundations of the new reform. *Harvard Educational review*, **57**(1), 1-22.

Siedentop, D. (1972). Behavior analysis and teacher training. *Quest*, **18**, 26-32.

Siedentop, D. (1981). The Ohio State University supervision research program summary report. *Journal of Teaching in Physical Education* (Introductory issue), 30-38.

Siedentop, D. (1983). *Developing teaching skills in physical education*. Mountain View, CA; Mayfield.

Siedentop, D. (1986). The modification of teacher behavior. In M. Pieron & G. Graham (Eds.), *Sport pedagogy* (pp. 3-18). Champaign, IL: Human Kinetics.

Siedentop, D. (1987). Dialogue or exorcism? A rejoinder to Schempp. *Journal of Teaching in Physical Education, 6*(4), 373-376.

Siedentop, D., & Eldar, E. (1989). Expertise, experience, and effectiveness. *Journal of Teaching in Physical Education, 8*(3), 254-260.

Sparkes, A.C. (1991). Toward understanding, dialogue, and polyvocality in the research community: Extending the boundaries of the paradigms debate. *Journal of Teaching in Physical Education, 10*(2), 103-133.

Sparkes, A.C. (Ed.) (1992). *Research in physical education and sport: Exploring alternative visions.* London: Falmer Press.

Steinhardt, M.A. (1992). Physical education. In P.W. Jackson (Ed.), *Handbook of research on curriculum* (pp. 964-1001). New York: Macmillan.

Stroot, S. (Ed.) (1993). Socialization into physical education. *Journal of Teaching in Physical Education Monograph, 12*(4).

Templin, T.J., & Olson, J.K. (Eds.) (1983). *Teacing in Physical Education.* Champaign, IL: Human Kinetics.

Templin, T.J., & Schempp, P.G. (Eds.) (1989). *Socialization into physical education: Learning to teach.* Indianapolis: Benchmark Press.

Ulrich, C. (1979). Tones of theory revisited. In A.E. Jewett & C. Norton (Eds.), *Proceedings of the Curriculum Theory Conference in Physical Education* (pp. 3-13). Athens, GA: University of Georgia.

Ulrich, C., & Nixon, J. (1972). *Tones of theory.* Washington, D.C.: American Association for Health, Physical Education and Recreation.

Vickers, J.N. (1987). The role of subject matter in the preparation of teachers in physical education. *Quest, 39*(2), 179-184.

Wittrock, M.C. (1986). *Handbook of research on teaching.* New York: Macmillan.

Zeichner, K.M. (1983). Alternative paradigms of teacher education. *Journal of Teacher Education, 34*(3), 3-9.

Ziegler, E., & McCristal, K. (1967). A history of the Big Ten body of knowledge project. *Quest, 9*, 79-84.

3

Adapted Physical Activity and Education

Claudine Sherrill
Texas Woman's University at Denton
Karen P. DePauw
Washington State University

Worldwide, *adapted physical activity* is the umbrella term that encompasses exercise, physical education, recreation, dance, sport, fitness, and rehabilitation for individuals with impairments across the lifespan (DePauw & Doll-Tepper, 1989; Porretta, Nesbitt, & Labanowich, 1993; Sherrill, 1993). In school settings, such terms as *adapted, special,* or *developmental* physical education are typically used. The term *adapted physical activity* may refer to a program, process, or practice (Doll-Tepper, Dahms, Doll, & von Selzam, 1990; Dunn & Fait, 1989; Winnick, 1995); a service-oriented profession (American Association for Health, Physical Education, and Recreation, 1973; Kiphard, 1983; Morisbak, 1990; Sherrill, 1988d); or a scholarly subdiscipline or discipline (Broadhead, 1981, 1984; DePauw & Sherrill, 1994; Sherrill, 1982, 1988d, 1993; Winnick, 1995).

Adapted physical activity historically has been associated with impairment, disability, or handicap. Definitions of the World Health Organization (1980) help clarify the types of individual differences addressed.

- **Impairment**—any disturbance of, or interference with, the normal structure and function of the body
- **Disability**—the loss or reduction of functional ability and/or activity
- **Handicap**—a condition produced by societal and environmental barriers

Illustrative conditions that often require adapted physical activity services are autism, blindness, deafness, serious emotional disturbance, mental

▼

A Chronology of Adapted Physical Activity

Early Foundations: 1830s-1970s

<u>Year</u> <u>Event</u>

1840   Per Henrik Ling's theory and practice of medical gymnastics was published. Central Institute of Gymnastics (CIG) in Sweden was well established as academic center for training in medical gymnastics.

1885   Baron Nils Posse, a graduate of CIG, began introducing Swedish gymnastics (medical and educational) into the Boston public schools and hospitals.

1889   Boston Normal School of Gymnastics was founded to train teachers in Swedish gymnastics; later became Wellesley College's Department of Health and Physical Education and remained a center for teacher training in medical gymnastics, which evolved into correctives.

1889   Dudley Allen Sargent, MD, reported that teacher training in his system required work in "physical diagnosis, methods of prescribing exercise for the individual, physical exercise in the treatment of spinal curvature . . . "

1899   Public schooling for students with physical disabilities began with opening of a school for "crippled children" in Chicago.

1905   Therapeutics Section of the American Physical Education Association (APEA) was formed with Baroness Rose Posse as first chair.

1908   Dudley Allen Sargent, MD, emphasized that all teachers of physical education in the public schools should have training in remedial and corrective gymnastics, physical diagnosis, and massage.

1909   R. Tait McKenzie, MD, described physical education for individuals with deafness, blindness, and mental retardation in *Exercise in Education and Medicine*. These persons were mostly served in residential institutions.

1917   First major polio epidemic of the century ended, with thousands of individuals paralyzed.

1918   World War I increased awareness of disability. Individuals who served in medical branches of the armed forces established private practice in physical therapy and/or accepted teaching positions in corrective physical education.

1920s   Battle of the systems ended, with sports dominating the newly emerged American system for students with good fitness and Swedish medical gymnastics, now called correctives, continuing for students diagnosed as needing exercise for medical or orthopedic reasons.

1921   American Physiotherapy Association was founded, but many practitioners identified dually with AAHPER's Therapeutics Section because of initial training in physical education and employment in correctives.

1922   Special education was established well enough in the public schools to support the formation of the International Council for the Education of Exceptional Children, renamed the Council for Exceptional Children (CEC) in 1958.

1928   First textbooks that used term *corrective physical education* were published.

1930   Josephine Rathbone, trained in Swedish gymnastics at Wellesley, began 30 years of teaching correctives, relaxation, massage, and anatomy and kinesiology at Teachers College, Columbia University. Many other universities followed Rathbone's curriculum.

1934   First edition of Rathbone's *Corrective Physical Education* was published; this served as major textbook for correctives through seven editions, until the 1960s.

1939   *Sports for the Handicapped* by George T. Stafford of the University of Illinois was published. This was first indicator of trend away from corrective exercise toward sports as appropriate school programming for individuals with disabilities.

1946   Therapeutics Section of AAHPER established a committee to study needs of individuals with disabilities and recommend guidelines for appropriate programming.

1946   Corrective therapy began with formation of the Association for Physical and Mental Rehabilitation. Name was changed to American Corrective Therapy Association in 1967 and to American Kinesiotherapy Association in 1983.

1952   Change of terminology from *correctives* to *adapted physical education* was recommended by AAHPER Committee established in 1946. Concurrently, a new philosophy was adopted to support teaching of diversified activities.

1952   American Physical Therapy Association formally ended its 30-year cooperative relationship with AAHPER's Therapeutics Section, and the conflict intensified between AAHPER members with a therapeutics/correctives perspective vs. those with an education/sports perspective.

1953 American College of Sports Medicine was founded, which attracted members associated with the therapeutics/correctives movement.

1954 First textbook entitled *Adapted Physical Education*, by Arthur Daniels, was published. Included chapters on all conditions except mental retardation and learning disabilities.

1957 First Children's Physical Development Clinic started by Warren Johnson at the University of Maryland.

1958 Adapted Physical Education Section of AAHPER was created with Janet Wessel as first chair; Therapeutics Section continued to serve professionals with major interest in correctives and rehabilitation.

1958 Federal government authorized the first grants to universities and state education agencies for training personnel in mental retardation. This revitalized special education as a profession and called the attention of all professions to mental retardation.

1959 G. Lawrence Rarick (with Robert J. Francis) published classic research study revealing that children with mental retardation were two to four years behind peers in motor performance.

1960 First International Games for Disabled (wheelchair athletes only) held in Rome; founding of first international organization for wheelchair sports in England.

1960 Hollis Fait published first textbook (since that of R. Tait McKenzie) to include chapter on mental retardation.

1963 Federal legislation amended to encompass all disabilities served by special education.

1963 Julian Stein published extensive review of literature on motor function and physical fitness of individuals with mental retardation. Thus, a knowledge base on physical education and mental retardation was acknowledged.

1964 Buttonwood Farms—Temple University Project was funded 1964 through 1976 by the National Institute of Mental Health (NIH) to conduct short-term, intensive summer training programs in physical education for students with mental retardation or emotional disturbance for college and university teachers. Contemporary leaders like Joseph Winnick and John Dunn gained early experience here.

1965 AAHPER Project on Recreation and Fitness for the Mentally Retarded was established at national headquarters, beginning a 16-year service to membership. Name changed in

1968 to Unit on Programs for the Handicapped. Julian Stein directed this office from 1966 to 1981, exerting tremendous influence on service delivery and personnel preparation.

1966   Hollis Fait changed title of second edition of his textbook to *Special Physical Education*, thereby starting an advocacy movement for a name change of adapted physical education.

1967   First federal legislation (**PL 90-170**) was enacted that authorized funding specifically for personnel training and research in physical education and recreation for individuals with disabilities.

1967   Seminars for college and university teachers on "physical education and recreation for the handicapped" were sponsored by Joseph P. Kennedy, Jr. Foundation in New York, West Virginia, Utah, and Texas. These influenced Winnick, Auxter, Dunn, Sherrill, and many others to change adapted physical education course content and start clinics or practica.

1968   Special Olympics was created, and the AAHPER-Kennedy Foundation Special Fitness awards were begun, thus beginning era of strong advocacy for mental retardation HPER services.

1968   First master's degree specialization in adapted physical education enrolled students; this program was founded by Joseph Winnick at SUNY in New York.

1969   First federal funds received to support university graduate programs in physical education and recreation for the handicapped. Nine universities started graduate specialization training with these funds.

1970   Series of regional institutes on personnel preparation in adapted physical education were cosponsored by AAHPER (Julian Stein) and the Bureau of Education for the Handicapped (William Hillman). Report published in 1973.

1971   Survey shows 24 universities are offering graduate specializations designated as physical education for the handicapped or adapted, special, or developmental physical education.

1973   International Federation of Adapted Physical Activity (IFAPA) was founded in Quebec City, Canada, by Clermont Simard and colleagues.

1973   National Ad Hoc Committee on Physical Education and Recreation for the Handicapped was formed by BEH project directors at AAHPER Conference in Minneapolis.

1975   Ad hoc committee became the National Consortium on Physical Education and Recreation for the Handicapped

(NCPERH); in 1992 the name was changed to National Consortium for Physical Education and Recreation for Individuals with Disabilities (NCPERID)

1975   **PL 94-142**, the Education for All Handicapped Children Act, was enacted that required physical education instruction for all children as part of the special education process.

1976   The Olympiad for the Physically Handicapped was held in Canada after the Olympics. Athletes with amputations and blindness competed for the first time, marking the beginning of the modern Paralympics and the need to generate sports knowledge on these conditions.

1977   Regulations to implement **PL 94-142** were published, and federal funding guidelines emphasized in-service training on operationalization of the law.

1978   The Amateur Sports Act (**PL 95-606**) recognized disability sport organizations and events as part of the U.S. Olympic Committee structure.

1979   U.S. Olympic Committee (USOC) organized Committee for Handicapped in Sports, now named Committee on Sports for the Disabled (COSD). Adapted physical education specialists become increasingly aware of emerging knowledge base of disability sports.

Organization of the Discipline: 1980s

Year   Event

1980   Bureau of Education for Handicapped (BEH) in Washington, DC, became Office of Special Education Programs (OSEP). Federal funding by the agency continued to support university training.

1981   Declared the "International Year of the Disabled" by the United Nations; began "International Decade of the Disabled."

1981   New AAHPERD guidelines (competencies) on adapted physical education personnel preparation published.

1984   Two scholarly journals began publication: *Adapted Physical Activity Quarterly* and *Palaestra*.

1985   Adapted Physical Activity Council (APAC) of AAHPERD formed by merger of the Therapeutics Council of ARAPCS and the Adapted Physical Education Academy of NASPE.

1986   Historic Strategies for Change in Adapted Physical Activity Conference held in Jasper, Canada. Canadians consider this conference the most important date in their APA history.

1988   First unified Paralympics held in Korea with all kinds of physical disabilities included; first time Paralympics held in same facilities as the Olympics.

1989   7th International Symposium of IFAPA held in Berlin with record attendance of over 700; Gudrun Doll-Tepper was symposium chair; *adapted physical activity* first officially defined. This symposium marks the revitalization of IFAPA movement.

Development of the Discipline: 1990s

Year   Event

1990   Two major laws enacted that changed disability terminology and knowledge base, the Individuals with Disabilities Education Act (**PL 101-476**) and the Americans With Disabilities Act (**PL 101-336**).

1990   Twenty-one general textbooks available for use in adapted physical education classes. Books with the most editions were Dunn and Fait (1989, 6th ed.), Auxter and Pyfer (1985, 4th ed.), and Sherrill (1986, 3rd ed.).

1990   Graduate level textbooks on *Problems in Movement Control* (Reid) and *Problems in Movement Skill Development* (Sugden & Keogh) published.

1991   European Master's Degree Program in Adapted Physical Activity began in Leuven, Belgium.

1992   Founding editor of *Adapted Physical Activity Quarterly*, Geoffrey Broadhead, completed eight-year term. Greg Reid became new editor in January 1992.

1992   Greg Reid hosted conference in Canada to begin organization of North American Federation of Adapted Physical Activity (NAFAPA).

1992   Paralympics held in Barcelona, after which International Paralympic Committee (IPC) became governing body for Paralympic movement.

1994   North American Federation of Adapted Physical Activity (NAFAPA) founded, constitution passed, and officers elected at conference hosted by Gail Dummer at Michigan State University. Dale Ulrich elected first president.

1995   Eight general textbooks in adapted physical education seriously competing for market, all with two or more editions; three with four or more editions. Many specialized textbooks emphasizing particular topics available.

R. Tait McKenzie

Josephine Rathbone

Arthur Daniels

H. Harrison Clarke

David Auxter

Julian Stein

William Hillman

Evelyn Davies

Louis Bowers

Geoffrey Broadhead

Hollis Fait

John Dunn

Joseph Winnick

retardation, orthopedic impairment, specific learning disability, traumatic brain injury, and other health impairments like asthma, diabetes, and obesity. Approximately 43 million individuals in the United States have one or more of these conditions severe enough to be documented in census counts. The overall percentage of the population with these conditions increases with age: about 10 percent of all children and adolescents; about 30 percent of young and middle-aged adults; and about 50 percent of persons beyond the age of 65.

Changing Terminology, Philosophy, and Definitions

Terminology for adapted physical activity has varied considerably during the 20th century, causing considerable confusion about the nature, scope, and longevity of this profession and emerging discipline (see table 3.1). Each change in terminology reflects major shifts in philosophy, service delivery patterns, and personnel preparation. A brief summary of these changes follows, to provide insight into the whole before addressing specific historical periods.

Changing Philosophies

Until the 1950s the dominant philosophical model was medical or therapeutic, and service delivery was directed toward individuals with medical

Table 3.1 Synonyms for Adapted Physical Activity and Names of Organizations

Until 1920s	Swedish, medical, curative, or corrective gymnastics; Therapeutics Section or Council of APEA/AAHPERD from 1905-1985.
1920s-1950s	Corrective or individualized physical education, which was often split into two branches: (a) corrective or orthopedic and (b) medical, remedial, modified, or limited.
1950s	Struggle between therapeutic (rehabilitative) and educational (sport) orientations for dominance. *Adapted physical education* became official AAHPER term in 1952, but had strong opposition from many Therapeutics Section members. In 1958, AAHPER added the Adapted Physical Education Section to help resolve the power struggle.
1960s, 1970s	*Adapted physical education* challenged as term of choice by strong advocacy for *developmental physical education* (H. Harrison Clarke, 1963) and for *special physical education* (Hollis Fait, 1966). Also terms from legislation like *physical education for the handicapped* further complicated the terminology issue.
1980s	*Adapted physical activity* became umbrella term of choice with 1985 merger of Therapeutics Council and Adapted Physical Education Academy into the *Adapted Physical Activity Quarterly* from 1984 onward, and the growth of the International Federation of Adapted Physical Activity (IFAPA), founded in 1973.

or orthopedic conditions that could be ameliorated or corrected through individually prescribed exercises and massage. This approach to exercise was lifespan, and professionals (including physicians, therapists, and educators whose main interest was medical and corrective exercise, initially called gymnastics) delivered services in private practice and both school and nonschool settings. Many professionals were dually trained in physical education and physical therapy.

From the 1950s through the 1970s, various philosophies competed for dominance until gradually the school-based adapted physical education model superseded others. Advocates of the American system of sports, dance, and aquatics sought to broaden programming from prescriptive exercises to diversified activities adapted or modified to meet the widely different needs of individuals, many of whom had not previously attended public schools. Special education legislation, funding, and philosophy encouraged development of a knowledge base about the psychomotor abilities of individuals in specific federally funded categories (e.g., mental retardation, deafness, and orthopedic impairments). Concurrently, models evolved that stressed roles, tasks, and competencies needed to provide generic physical education services to *all* students (e.g., planning, assessment, prescription, teaching, and evaluation). These models were classified, respectively, as categorical and generic approaches.

Professionals from the 1950s through the 1970s included individuals with correctives and medical backgrounds, individuals dually trained in special education and physical education, and individuals trained in the new graduate specializations programs of the 1970s, variously called adapted, developmental, or special, or designated as physical education for the handicapped. Employment was primarily in schools, and emphasis was on the age group specified by special education legislation, birth to age 21. A few individuals continued to seek dual physical therapy and education training, but physical therapy separated from its various parent disciplines, and became clearly distinct from adapted physical education.

From the 1980s onward, adapted physical activity gradually became the umbrella term of choice, as many service delivery and employment patterns emerged. The pendulum moved back to lifespan service delivery as legislation emphasized the importance of helping individuals make the transition from school-based physical education to lifelong community-oriented sport and recreation involvement. The trend toward integration and inclusion also increased awareness that adapted physical education services and support systems were needed in the mainstream.

Emphasis from the 1980s onward gradually shifted, from instruction in separate classes for particular categories of disability with presumed characteristics, to generic roles, tasks, and competencies that linked service delivery to assessment, and recognized the uniqueness of each individual regardless of category of disability and placement. Professionals today have diverse backgrounds that draw from many disciplines. Increasingly, specialists have completed master's or doctoral studies in crossdisciplinary adapted physical activity, blending medical, educational, social sciences, and human rights concerns.

Changing Definitions

Many definitions have competed for prominence during each era. Following are a few of the better-known definitions that demarcate specific philosophies.

Medical gymnastics, the first widely used term, was defined as "exercises—either passive, assistive, active, or resistive—prescribed by a physician or medical gymnast, with a view of restoring health to diseased parts, or developing certain parts of the body" (Nissen, 1892, pp. 1-2, citing Ling, 1840). The word *gymnastics* was replaced with *exercises* in the early 1900s. These exercises were originally categorized as *medical* or *remedial* (restoring health) and *corrective* (developing certain parts of the body), but gradually correctives became the broad term of choice (Lippitt, 1923; Rathbone, 1934; Stafford, 1928).

Correctives originally meant therapeutic exercise based on the Swedish gymnastics systems, but numerous definitions and synonyms evolved. Fait (1966, p. 3) stated, "Corrective physical education and remedial physical education are terms used for programs that emphasize the change or improvement in function or structure by means of selected exercises." In contrast, Rathbone and Hunt (1965, pp. 2-3) emphasized,

> "Correctives" is not a narrow field. The scope of the work is much greater than most people envision. It is not just a few exercises for specific muscles, or a method of training a person to stand in perfect balance. . . . The scope of "correctives" involves consideration of the individual at different stages in development, and includes every known physiological and psychological aid to bring a person to a higher level of accomplishment.

Adapted physical education was officially defined by AAHPER (Committee on Adapted Physical Education) in 1952:

> Adapted physical education is a diversified program of developmental activities, games, sports, and rhythms suited to the interests, capacities, and limitations of students with disabilities who may not safely or successfully engage in unrestricted participation in the vigorous activities of the general physical education program.

Sherrill (1976) was one of the first to delete the "separate class placement" concept from this definition and to propose that adapted physical education services should be made available to any student with psychomotor problems, regardless of setting. Sherrill (1976, p. 4) stated, "It [adapted physical education] is the science of analyzing movement, identifying problems in the psychomotor domain, and developing instructional strategies for remediating problems and preserving ego strength."

Recently the National Consortium for Physical Education and Recreation for Individuals with Disabilities (1995, p. 194) defined *adapted physical education* as follows:

1. The art and science of assessment and prescription within the psychomotor domain to ensure that an individual with a disability has access to programs designed to develop physical and motor fitness, fundamental motor skills and patterns, and skills in aquatics, dance, and individual and group games and sports so that the individual can ultimately participate in community-based leisure, recreation, and sport activities and as such, enjoy an enhanced quality of life.
2. A diversified program of physical education having the same goals and objectives as regular physical education, but modified when necessary to meet the unique needs of each individual.

Contemporary Definitions of Adapted Physical Activity

Contemporary definitions of adapted physical activity vary depending on whether reference is being made to a program, process, or practice, or to the profession and emerging discipline. Controversy has not yet been resolved as to whether adapted physical activity is interdisciplinary (Doll-Tepper et al., 1990; Winnick, 1995) or crossdisciplinary (DePauw & Sherrill, 1994; Sherrill, 1993). Following Franklin Henry (1964), who recommended the development of a crossdisciplinary approach to graduate physical education, the authors of this chapter subscribe to the crossdisciplinary perspective. Contemporary *adapted physical activity* is thus defined as crossdisciplinary theory and practice related to the lifespan physical activity of individuals with psychomotor needs who require particular expertise in such processes as adaptation, ecological task analysis, integration, inclusion, and empowerment.

Current Status

Adapted physical activity services, delivered in both mainstream and separate settings in many kinds of job roles, no longer address only individual differences associated with disability. Instead, concern has broadened to focus on the complex relationships between people with and without disabilities, and all of the barriers and affordances in their environments that influence physical activity opportunity and participation. Underlying this focus are several emerging theories (Sherrill, 1995); foremost among these are physical activity ecosystem theory and adaptation theory. *Ecosystem theory* pertains to all of the variables and dynamical systems that impact an individual with psychomotor problems in continuous interaction with other individuals and the everchanging environment, both physical and social. *Adaptation theory* refers to the continuous, dynamic, interactional, multidirectional processes by which individuals and the environment reciprocally change one another to empower lifespan physical activity and wellness.

Professional and Disciplinary Status

The professional and disciplinary status of adapted physical activity is evidenced by a number of professional organizations, the publication of scholarly journals, and the evolution of graduate studies and research. The International Federation of Adapted Physical Activity (IFAPA), founded in 1973, holds biennial conferences that attract 600 to 800 participants who share scholarly products. A branch of IFAPA, the North American Federation of Adapted Physical Activity (NAFAPA), regularly brings scholars from the United States and Canada together to share research.

In the United States, the Adapted Physical Activity Council (APAC) within the American Alliance for Health, Physical Education, Recreation and Dance (AAHPERD) and the National Consortium for Physical Education and Recreation for Individuals with Disabilities (NCPERID) both advance theory and practice. Publication of two scholarly journals began in 1984: *Adapted Physical Activity Quarterly* and *Palaestra: The Forum of Sport, Physical Education, and Recreation for the Disabled*. Since the late 1960s, graduate specializations in adapted physical activity or education have been operative in several U.S. universities (Dunn & McCubbin, 1991; Sherrill, 1988b).

Research has become increasingly theoretical (DePauw, 1992; Reid, 1990, 1992), and the critical mass now permits extensive, scholarly reviews of literature (Crocker, 1993; Reid, 1993; Shephard, 1993). Graduate level textbooks that stress problems and issues are appearing (Reid, 1990; Sherrill, 1988; Sugden & Keogh, 1990; Wade, 1986). Moreover, a growing number of organizations, agencies, and school districts employ adapted, special, or developmental physical education specialists as administrators, consultants, and direct service delivery personnel, typically with graduate degrees in adapted physical education or activity. Undergraduate preparation in adapted physical education is available to prospective teachers through separate courses or through infusion of content into regular education courses (DePauw & Goc Karp, 1994; Winnick, 1972, 1986).

Services Provided

Overall, from 10 to 30 percent of the population benefits directly from adapted physical activity services in a variety of settings. Many other individuals with impairments like asthma, obesity, and coordination/ fitness difficulties benefit from adaptation theory although they have not been formally diagnosed as having an impairment, disability, or handicap. Research is not yet available to document whether theories pertaining to psychomotor growth, development, and function of individuals considered average or above are applicable to individuals with particular disabilities or impairments. However, many academic specializations have historically recognized the wisdom of giving equal attention to normalcy and pathology in evolving theory and practice central to understanding human performance (Roy, 1990; Stelmach, 1987).

The continuing knowledge explosion forces specialization while challenging professionals to remain ever mindful of commonalities and the need for crossdisciplinary collaboration. This chapter describes the history of adapted physical activity as an academic specialization seeking recognition as an emerging discipline, with strong roots both within and outside of exercise and sport science. This history is presented in three periods: (a) Early Foundations, 1830s to 1970s; (b) Organization of the Discipline, 1980s; and (c) Development of the Discipline, 1990s.

Early Foundations: 1830s-1970s

The evolution of adapted physical activity theory has been strongly influenced by medicine, physical education, special education, psychology, sociology, counseling, and human rights legislation. Most adapted physical education textbooks trace beginnings to medical gymnastics in Sweden in the 1830s, but recently more attention has been given to special education roots, which began with sensory-motor training experiments in France in the 1800s (Broadhead, 1981), and the impact of psychosocial and behavioral research (Crocker, 1993; DePauw & Goc Karp, 1992; Rizzo & Vispoel, 1991; Sherrill, 1993; Tripp & Sherrill, 1991).

Reviews of research from 1930 to 1990 (Broadhead, 1986; Pyfer, 1986) indicate a gradually broadened focus from structural and functional physical problems within the "normal" population to the broad spectrum of individual differences that require application of adaptation theory. Evolution of theory has been limited over the years by the populations served in mainstream universities, schools, and medical settings. Until the 1950s attention centered primarily on postures, health impairments, and physical disabilities, because individuals with mental retardation and conditions of blindness and/or deafness were isolated in residential facilities.

The formation of the Therapeutics Section of the American Physical Education Association (APEA) in 1905 documents the long, rich history of the profession now known worldwide as adapted physical activity or education (Sherrill, 1988b). Baronness Rose Posse, a leader in the Swedish gymnastics movement, was the first chair of the Therapeutics Section (Lee & Bennett, 1985), after which history is lost until R. Tait McKenzie, MD, assumed chairmanship in 1917 after his service as APEA president from 1912 to 1916.

R. Tait McKenzie (1867-1938), professor at McGill University in Canada until 1904 and at the University of Pennsylvania thereafter, was the first to describe physical education for students with mental and/or sensory impairments (McKenzie, 1909, 1915, 1923). The creation of AAHPERD's R. Tait McKenzie Award in 1968, annually given to members who have made significant contributions outside the normal scope of the profession, attests to the leadership of McKenzie in advocating physical activity for everyone. Interestingly, the highest honor to professionals from the Canadian Association for HPER is also named after McKenzie.

The foundations of adapted physical activity, prior to its emergence as a discipline in the 1980s, included (a) medical gymnastics/correctives/ therapeutics, (b) special education influences, and (c) various adapted physical education perspectives. Following is a brief account of their contributions to our knowledge base.

Medical Gymnastics/Correctives/Therapeutics

The period from the 1830s to the 1950s included *medical* or *curative gymnastics* (Gulick, 1890; Ling, 1840); *corrective, individualized,* or *therapeutic gymnastics* (Drew, 1922; Lippitt, 1923); and *corrective exercise* or *physical education* (Hawley, 1937; Lowman, Colestock, & Cooper, 1928; Rathbone, 1934; Stafford, 1928; Stafford & Tappan, 1927). Factors influencing this period were (a) the changing nature of students in schools and colleges; (b) controversy about the dominance of medical or educational models; (c) the poliomyelitis epidemics of 1915-1917, 1944, and 1952; and (d) World Wars I and II.

Medical Gymnastics.   Medical gymnastics (exercise or calisthenics for restoration of health and/or development of the body) can be traced to Per Henrik Ling of Sweden, who divided physical activity into four branches: medical, educational, military, esthetical (Ling, 1840; Nissen, 1892). Luther Halsey Gulick, MD (1865-1918), famous American physical education pioneer, also divided exercise/gymnastics into branches (curative, educative, recreative), but noted that "hard and fast lines cannot be drawn . . . as frequently it will be found that exercise belongs to two or more classes at once" (Gulick, 1890, p. 59). *Medical gymnastics* was the term of choice until the 1920s, when school-based physical education was divided into two branches: (a) regular and (b) corrective, therapeutic, remedial, or rehabilitative.

Per Henrik Ling (1776-1839) is acknowledged as the founder of medical gymnastics and hence as the father of adapted physical education. Ling, who started the Central Institute of Gymnastics (CIG) in Stockholm, Sweden, was the first to apply anatomy and physiology scientifically in the development of a systematic exercise system for prevention and treatment of physical defects and disease (Leonard, 1923; McKenzie, 1909). According to Ling (1840), each muscle group should be exercised daily in a particular order; degree of difficulty (i.e., progression) should be adapted to individual needs. Exercises could be done with or without apparatus, although the use of stall bars, climbing ladders, poles, ropes, balancing boards, and an exercise table or plinth were recommended. Today's emphasis on balancing activities (as well as abdominal and arm/shoulder strength) can be traced directly to Ling. This system used no music or rhythmic accompaniment; exercises were performed to verbal commands and counting by the instructor. Ling was not a physician, but subsequent directors of CIG studied medicine (Lars Gabriel Branting) or were physicians (Truls Johan Hartelius).

Part of Ling's historical significance lies in his careful selection of successors who, as faculty of the CIG, attracted physicians and others from all parts of the western world. Hjalmar Ling (1820-1886), Per Henrik's son, applied the principles of medical gymnastics to educational gymnastics, and by the 1880s CIG courses were offered in both educational and medical gymnastics. The Gymnastic Teacher's Course (one year of full-time study) was a prerequisite for acceptance into medical gymnastics training, which required a second full year of study, although prescribed work was sometimes shortened for physicians (Leonard, 1923).

Nils Posse (1862-1895), a graduate of CIG, was recruited by philanthropist Mary Hemenway in 1885 to introduce Swedish gymnastics into the Boston public schools and to become the first director of the Boston Normal School of Gymnastics, founded in 1889 (Leonard, 1923). This teacher training facility for women later became Wellesley College's Department of Health and Physical Education. Posse also opened his own training school, wrote several books (1890, 1891, 1894), and founded the *Posse Gymnasium Journal*. After Posse's early death in 1895, his wife Rose vigorously continued efforts to integrate Swedish gymnastics into Boston educational and medical circles.

Other Scandinavians particularly influential in establishing Swedish gymnastics in the northeastern United States were Hartvig Nissen (1855-1924) and William Skarstrom, MD (1869-1951). Nissen, the vice-consul of Norway and Sweden, was mentored by Edward Mussey Hartwell, MD, director of the gymnasium at Johns Hopkins University in Baltimore and later of the Boston public schools. Skarstrom, mentored by Amy Morris Homans, taught at the Boston Normal School of Gymnastics, 1899-1903; Teacher's College, Columbia University, 1903-1912; and Wellesley College from 1912 on. Nissen (1892) and Skarstrom (1909) both authored influential books that presented Swedish gymnastics concepts. Many women leaders influenced by Skarstrom, including Senda Berenson of Smith College and Josephine Rathbone of Teacher's College, Columbia University, applied Swedish gymnastics concepts throughout their careers (Leonard, 1923; Rathbone, 1989).

From the late 1800s to the 1920s, Swedish gymnastics competed for dominance with the exercise systems created by physician Dudley A. Sargent (1849-1924) of Harvard University, physician Edward Hitchcock (1828-1911) of Amherst College, and the German Turnvereins. This era is often called the *battle of the systems* (Weston, 1962). Regardless of the exercise system advocated, the emphasis was on health and fitness.

By the 1920s, a distinctly American system of sports, dance, and aquatics was replacing the old exercise systems (Leonard, 1923; Schwendener, 1942). This program, however, was not considered appropriate for individuals labeled as *crippled*, who increasingly attended public schools and colleges from 1899 on, or for individuals with posture or health problems that physicians believed could be corrected through specific, prescribed exercise. Educational and medical gymnastics, therefore, evolved respectively into *regular* and *corrective* physical education.

Corrective Gymnastics.   Lillian Curtis Drew (1922) and Louisa Lippitt (1923), directors of departments of corrective gymnastics at Teachers College, Columbia University, and the University of Wisconsin, respectively, were among the first leaders to use the term *correctives*. Lippitt (1923) explained that some schools divided services into two branches: (a) correctives or orthopedics, which aimed to correct postural defects, paralysis, and conditions caused by malnutrition; and (b) medical or remedial exercise, which aimed to relieve health problems, menstrual disorders, and other conditions that prevented participation in vigorous activity.

Whereas the professional preparation of regular physical educators began to change from a medical to an educational model in the 1920s, correctives specialists continued to identify with medicine. Many individuals became interested in disability through service in World War I in the U.S. Army Reconstruction Department, which in 1918 created training and jobs for new careers in physiotherapy and occupational therapy. Subsequently, the American Physiotherapy Association was founded in 1921, and one-year training programs (approximately 1,200 hours of theory and practice) were created to supplement bachelor's degrees in either physical education or nursing (Beard, 1961; Hazenhyer, 1946). This type of advanced training, a viable alternative to completion of a medical degree, attracted many young physical education professionals who subsequently were employed in either school or hospital settings.

Corrective Exercise and Physical Education. The correctives philosophy, dominant from the 1920s to the early 1950s, evolved as a merger of medical gymnastics and therapeutic/rehabilitative activities found effective in the treatment of World War I veterans and subsequently generalized to persons with physical disabilities of all ages. Charles Lowman and George Stafford, leaders in the correctives movement, wrote the first textbooks entitled *Corrective Physical Education* in 1928 (Lowman et al., 1928; Stafford, 1928); Josephine Rathbone's subsequent textbook *Corrective Physical Education* dominated professional preparation from the 1930s through the 1950s. Lowman was a physician, whereas Stafford and Rathbone considered themselves dual correctives/physical therapy professionals. All lived and studied, at least for a while, in the Boston area, where they were exposed to medical gymnastics.

Charles Lowman, MD (1879-1977), director of the orthopedic clinic at the University of Southern California Medical School and orthopedic consultant for the Los Angeles School System, credited Joel Goldthwait and other orthopedists in the Boston area with helping him understand the relationship between medicine and corrective physical education. A prolific writer, Lowman produced *Corrective Physical Education for Groups* (1928), *Balance Skills in Physical Education* (1935), *Technique of Underwater Gymnastics* (1937), *Therapeutic Use of Pools and Tanks* (1952), *Underwater Therapy* (1961), and *Postural Fitness* (1960). Our knowledge base about the scientific use of aquatics as exercise began with Lowman. Likewise, the early exemplary program of remedial physical education in Los Angeles public schools can be traced to Lowman's students.

George Stafford (1894-1968), both a physical therapist and correctives specialist, became interested in these areas through service in the World War I Army Reconstruction Department. Subsequently he practiced physical therapy in Boston from 1919 to 1923, taught correctives at the University of Illinois from 1923 until retirement, and acted as a civilian consultant for the U.S. Army Reconditioning Program, the U.S. Navy Rehabilitation Program, and the Veterans Administration during and after World War II. Stafford's several books included *Practical Corrective Exercises* (1927, with Tappan), *Preventive and Corrective Physical Education* (1928), and *Sports for the Handicapped* (two editions, 1939 and 1947).

Stafford's doctoral degree at New York University in 1937 brought him into contact with leaders in the recreation and playground movement like Jay B. Nash, and encouraged his pioneer advocacy of sports as appropriate correctives content. Harlan G. Metcalf (1929, 1934), who also influenced Stafford, taught correctives at the Ohio State University and conducted the earliest known research on public school correctives (i.e., that only 25% used formal exercise, 29% used mimetic exercise, 16% used game situations, and 44% used a combination of all three types of activities). Stafford (1939) also pioneered in integrating students with physical disabilities into regular physical education. Leadership of the University of Illinois in the wheelchair sports movement can be traced partly to Stafford, who is recognized as the major force in moving correctives away from its original medical gymnastics roots toward sports and recreation.

Josephine Rathbone (1899-1989), who learned medical gymnastics from Skarstrom at Wellesley College and from Boston physicians, continued the traditions of individualized assessment and exercise prescription as director of correctives at Wellesley College (1925-1930) and at Teacher's College, Columbia University (1930-1960). Concurrently she provided leadership for the emerging physical therapy profession, creating a training program at Columbia University (1939-1949), and serving as vice-president of the American Physical Therapy Association from 1930 to 1932. Rathbone's *Corrective Physical Education* (1934) endured through seven editions (Rathbone & Hunt, 1965), influencing more professionals than any other text. She also extended correctives to include relaxation, stress reduction, and mental health strategies.

Although influenced by common roots, Rathbone and Stafford became polar opposites in philosophy. Rathbone taught kinesiology (called exercise analysis) and anatomy/physiology as well as correctives, and believed that strong preparation in medical aspects was essential to learning the combined roles of therapist/educator. Stafford, in contrast, moved away from physical therapy goals and emphasized that school personnel should be responsible for education, not therapy or treatment. He was the first to use the term *adapted sports* and to describe pedagogy for adapting physical activity (Stafford, 1939, 1947).

Special Education Influences

Adapted physical activity also has roots in special education, which traces its history back to physicians and church leaders in residential facilities in the early 1800s. The parent discipline of special education is psychology, particularly the separate branches of individual and developmental psychology that emerged in the late 1800s (Hallahan & Kauffman, 1978; Hutt & Gibby, 1965; Robinson & Robinson, 1965; Sloan & Stevens, 1976). Early practices pertaining to the education of individuals with sensory, mental, and physical disabilities in the United States came from trial-and-error pedagogy in residential schools, individual and developmental psychology, and perceptual-motor theorizing. Special education began to evolve as a profession and discipline in the 1950s when federal legislation supported the shift from residential to public-school education.

Origins in Residential Schools. Of the various disabilities served by special education, deafness and blindness were the first to be addressed. Thomas Hopkins Gallaudet (1787-1851), a minister, founded the first residential school in the United States in 1817, the American School for the Deaf in Hartford, Connecticut. The deaf community honored him in 1856 by naming its first institution of higher education Gallaudet College. This facility, now a university located in Washington, DC, has a long history of excellent physical education and sport, as do most residential schools for students who are deaf. Samuel Gridley Howe (1801-1876), an 1824 graduate of Harvard Medical School, established the Perkins School for the Blind near Boston in the early 1830s, and helped create a similar residential facility for people with mental retardation in Massachusetts in 1848. These two schools, the first of their kind, both provided physical training.

Edward Seguin (1812-1880), a physician and friend of Howe, is the best known leader in the residential school movement for individuals with mental retardation (Sloan & Stevens, 1976). Author of *Idiocy and Its Diagnosis and Treatment by the Physiological Method* (1846), translated into English in 1866, Seguin received his early training in France from Jean Marc Itard (1775-1838), a physician often cited as the originator of special education theory because of his innovative sensory training of an adolescent boy called Victor, the Wild Boy of Aveyron, variously described as autistic, deaf-mute, or mentally retarded.

Maria Montessori (1870-1952), the first woman physician in Italy, is recognized as a special education pioneer also in that she emphasized methodical education of the senses from infancy on for all children, but especially those with mental retardation (Hallahan & Kauffman, 1978). Her 1912 classic, *The Montessori Method*, when translated into English, supported Seguin's physiological method which today would be considered sensory or sensory-motor.

The first physical educator to write about serving individuals in residential facilities was R. Tait McKenzie, MD, whose 1909 book *Exercise in Education and Medicine* described deafness, blindness, and mental retardation and activities appropriate for each population. McKenzie's sources were interviews with physical educators and physicians employed by residential schools in Pennsylvania: Edward Allen at the Overbrook School for the Blind; Grace Green at the Institute for Deaf-Mutes at Mount Airy; and Martin Barr, MD, director of a facility for people with mental retardation at Elwyn, and author of *Mental Defectives* (1905). Barr was the first since Seguin to publish a book on mental retardation (Sloan & Stevens, 1976).

Development of Individual Psychology.   Many scholars in the 1800s created and administered tests to better understand their students. Whereas the best known of these individuals in physical education is Dudley A. Sargent, MD (1849-1924) of Harvard University, the best known in psychology and special education is Sir Francis Galton (1822-1911), of England. In the 1840s, Galton administered to over ten thousand volunteers tests of "height, weight, span, breathing power, strength of pull and squeeze, quickness of blow, hearing, seeing, color sense, and other personal data" (Boring, 1950, p. 487). These results, and those of several other studies published in *Inquiries into Human Faculty and Its Development* (1883) and *Natural Inheritance* (1889), led to recognition of Galton as the founder of *individual psychology*.

Individual psychology, or the study of individual differences, is obviously an important foundation of both special education and adapted physical activity. Closely associated with psychology, assessment theory began to evolve in the early 1900s as James Cattell (Princeton University in New Jersey), Alfred Binet (France), and Lewis Terman (Stanford University in California) sought to develop an intelligence test that could predict and/or explain school performance. Standardization of the Stanford-Binet IQ test and similar others has contributed to the information base on educational diagnosis and placement, but scholars continue to work on assessment approaches (American Association on Mental Retardation, 1992; Sherrill, 1993) that are more holistic, comprehensive, and accurate.

Emergence of Developmental Psychology.   Developmental psychology also emerged in the late 1800s as scholars became interested in how children and adolescents learn, grow, and function. Arnold Gesell (1880-1961), a physician who directed the Yale University Clinic of Child Development in New Haven, Connecticut, from 1911 to 1948, is generally recognized as the founder of developmental psychology (Salkind, 1985). Gesell wrote extensively on both normal and abnormal growth and development, stimulating the subsequent creation of a broad body of knowledge (Clark & Whitall, 1989) that, with periodic revision based on new research and theories, forms the motor development emphasis within adapted physical activity.

Special education, as well as adapted physical activity, has relied heavily on residential facilities for knowledge about the motor development and motor learning of individuals with disabilities. Many of today's university professors trace their first knowledge about individuals with disabilities to volunteer work in residential facilities, institutions which also supplied subjects for the first research.

Perceptual-motor theory and practice also had its origins in residential facilities. Alfred A. Strauss (a neurologist) and Heinz Werner (a developmental psychologist) left Germany to escape Hitler, accepted positions at the Wayne County Training School in Northville, Michigan, in the late 1930s, and began to apply gestalt psychology and perception theory to the remediation of mental retardation and brain injury, an initiative that evolved into perceptual-motor theory (Kephart, 1960; Strauss & Kephart, 1955). The resulting pedagogical trend strongly influenced early special education and adapted physical activity programming, particularly for children with mental retardation and specific learning disabilities.

Public School Classes and Perceptual-Motor Training.   Public schooling for students with orthopedic disabilities began in Chicago in 1899, but this trend progressed very slowly. Education in separate classes or schools was the practice, and regular education remained largely unaware of students with disabilities, who received little or no physical education instruction until the 1960s.

Large cities began to serve a few children with mental retardation in public school special classes in the 1930s, but these programs attracted little attention until the election of President John F. Kennedy, whose older sister Rosemary was mentally retarded. Kennedy's appointment of the first President's Panel on Mental Retardation in 1961 brought national awareness to the poor quality of many residential facilities and the need to expand special education in the public schools.

Meanwhile, psychologists like Marianne Frostig of Los Angeles and Newell Kephart of Purdue University in Indiana added to the body of knowledge begun by Itard, Seguin, and Montessori, by advocating the use of fine and gross motor activities to improve visual and auditory perception, cognition, and various academic abilities. According to Hallahan and Cruickshank (1973), perceptual-motor training was the most popular method from 1936 through 1970 for educating children with learning problems. Particularly popular were obstacle courses, balance boards and beams, trampolines, scooterboards, tunnels, exercise sequences like "angels in the snow," and visual tracking activities. Initially these activities were used mainly by special education teachers in self-contained classrooms for children with mental retardation and learning disabilities; physical educators were not employed in special education settings until the 1970s, when universities began to graduate teachers dually trained in special education and physical education.

Perceptual-motor theory and practice evolved through the contributions of many disciplines: psychology (Marianne Frostig and Newell Kephart), optometry (Gerald Getman), occupational therapy (A. Jean Ayes), special education (Ray Barsch), and physical education (Bryant J. Cratty). These individuals not only produced books and articles for teachers and parents (e.g., Cratty, 1967, 1969a,b; Frostig & Maslow, 1970; Kephart, 1960) but traveled widely, lecturing and giving workshops to conference, university, and parent groups. Many of the gross motor activities advocated (e.g., balance beams, scooterboards, exercise sequences) had been used in regular physical education for years to achieve goals of physical development, fitness, and fun, but had never before been conceptualized as specific approaches to improving mental function. Thus, the 1960s and 1970s are remembered as the era when various theories were posited and tested concerning the efficacy of different systems of perceptual-motor training in improving perception, cognition, and motor function of special education children.

The works of Kephart (1960) and Cratty (1967, 1969a,b) were particularly influential, although the underlying premises guiding their contributions were entirely different. Kephart (1960) believed that movement was the basis of the intellect and that perceptual-motor activities contributed directly to global academic abilities. In contrast, Cratty, a physical education professor at the University of California at Los Angeles, believed that perceptual-motor activities developed motor abilities but would contribute to academic success only when pedagogy specifically emphasized the academic skills to be reinforced. Cratty published over 30 books on perceptual-motor development and training from the 1960s through the 1980s, used by both special educators and physical educators.

As special education matured as a profession and discipline, however, new pedagogical strategies gradually replaced perceptual-motor training as an approach to improving academic success. In 1983, the classical meta-analysis of Kavale and Mattson revealed that perceptual-motor training was not an effective special education intervention technique. Perceptual-motor training, as a means of improving motor performance, continues to be used in physical education settings.

Initial Special Education Legislation.   The year 1958 was a major landmark in special education in that **PL 85-926** authorized federal funds for strengthening and/or creating university programs to train personnel to teach children with mental retardation (MR). Also, the International Council for the Education of Exceptional Children, founded in New York in 1922, changed its name in 1958 to the Council for Exceptional Children (CEC). The CEC continues to be the major governing organization of special education today, and the 1950s are considered the decade of initial recognition as a profession and discipline (Burke, 1976; Hallahan & Kauffman, 1978). Many adapted physical education specialists hold membership in both CEC and AAHPERD.

The 1950s also marked the beginning of special education funding of research on the motor function of children with mental retardation. G. Lawrence Rarick, a physical education professor at the University of Wisconsin and the University of California at Berkeley, began funded research inquiry that extended over 20 years. The first study (Francis & Rarick, 1959) indicated that children with mental retardation were two to four years behind their normal peers in motor performance, creating a strong rationale for extending special education funding to include personnel preparation in physical education and recreation.

Linkage of Physical Education with Special Education.   The 1960s are known for federal legislation that linked the special education and physical education professions, first to prepare personnel to teach children with mental retardation and later to serve all disabilities. Some universities created double majors in special education and physical education, whereas others approved specializations variously called physical education for the handicapped or adapted, special, or developmental physical education. Initially, training was categorical, meaning that courses and sometimes specializations were developed for each disability category (e.g., mental retardation, deafness, orthopedic impairments). Later, many different personnel preparation patterns evolved, and emphasis was given increasingly to generic roles, tasks, and competencies in broad areas like assessment, curriculum development, and service delivery.

From 1967 onward, personnel training funds were earmarked specifically for "physical education and recreation for the handicapped," but the money was essentially controlled by special education. In 1975, **PL 94-142**, the Education for All Handicapped Children Act, officially designated instruction in physical education as a component of the legal definition of special education. Although good from a funding standpoint, this designation tended to exacerbate the identity crisis of adapted physical education as a profession and emerging discipline.

Adapted Physical Education Perspectives

The foundations for adapted physical education as a crossdisciplinary profession strengthened from the 1940s through the 1970s, as leaders in correctives and therapeutics broadened their perspectives to encompass special education and related fields. Also during this period, adapted physical education became closely allied with therapeutic recreation because federal law always referred dually to "physical education and recreation for the handicapped."

Conflict Between Correctives and Adapted Physical Education.

World War II changed physical education programming significantly in schools and colleges from correctives to adapted physical education (Daniels, 1954; Stafford, 1947). Experience with Army Reconditioning and Air Forces and Navy Rehabilitation programs led members of the Therapeutics Section of AAHPER to establish a committee in 1946 to study needs of individuals with disabilities, and to recommend guiding principles for appropriate programming. In 1952 this committee issued the first official definition of *adapted physical education* (Committee on Adapted Physical Education, 1952), thereby changing emphasis from correctives for individuals with physical disabilities and health impairments to diversified programs of developmental activities, games, sports, and rhythms for anyone who could not safely or successfully participate in regular physical education.

Leaders with three different philosophies served on the committee that recommended this momentous change: (a) Arthur Daniels (Ohio State University), H. Harrison Clarke (Springfield College), and Cy Morgan (Army Medical Corps; also part-time George Washington University), whose backgrounds were regular physical education but influenced by World War II veterans' needs; (b) Josephine Rathbone (Teachers College, Columbia) and Catherine Worthington (Stanford University), correctives/physical therapy specialists; and (c) George Stafford (University of Illinois), who had strongly advocated changing from correctives to adapted sport since 1939.

The decision to change the name and service delivery approach of their specialization was strongly resisted by Rathbone, Worthington, and others who identified with both correctives and physical therapy and wanted to keep the two professions together. However, the year 1952 marked the last time that the American Physical Therapy Association (founded in 1921) met cooperatively with AAHPER's Therapeutics Section. Other factors in the separation of the two professions were the maturation of physical therapy as an independent profession in the 1940s (Beard, 1961; Hazenhyer, 1946) and the subsequent competition for jobs and influence between correctives and physical therapy professionals. The 1944 poliomyelitis epidemic, considered the worst in history, coupled with reconditioning needs of war veterans, had led to creation of four-year university degrees in physical therapy, so that persons interested in orthopedics no longer identified dually with physical education, as they had done since the 1880s.

The Therapeutics Section of AAHPER continued to support the combined therapy/education role and to encourage development of the rehabilitation and sports medicine movements. Rathbone and husband Peter Karpovich, an exercise physiology professor at Springfield from 1927 to 1960, particularly promoted the term *rehabilitation* in opposition to *adapted physical education* and helped to found the American College of Sports

Medicine in 1953, which gradually attracted members with interests similar to those in the old correctives/therapeutics movement. Rathbone also helped to found the Association for Physical and Mental Rehabilitation in 1946, called the American Corrective Therapy Association from 1967 to 1983, and now the American Kinesiotherapy Association.

From the 1930s through the 1960s, correctives and adapted physical education struggled for dominance; they finally were blended by a new generation of leaders who sought to meet special education challenges. Rathbone's text *Corrective Physical Education* was last published in 1965, strong evidence that many university professors continued to teach the familiar correctives and to emphasize the role of exercise in postures and health of all persons (Rathbone & Hunt, 1965). A survey of teacher training requirements in the early 1960s reported that 17 percent of men's departments and 22 percent of women's departments still called their required courses corrective physical education; 39 percent of men's departments and 35 percent of women's departments used either adapted physical education or combined adapted/correctives terminology; while approximately 40 percent of male and female departments required no course (Hooley, 1964; Wheeler & Hooley, 1969).

Rathbone's influence was monumental because Teachers College, Columbia University, attracted large numbers of graduate students from 1930 to 1960 who later became university teachers. Evelyn Davies, a physical therapist and correctives/adapted leader, completed her doctorate in 1950 and served as director of Indiana University's adapted physical education program from 1958 to 1982; Claudine Sherrill completed her doctorate in 1961, the same year she began teaching kinesiology and adapted physical education at Texas Woman's University in Denton. Davies, in turn, taught such contemporary authors as Jean Pyfer (Auxter, Pyfer, & Huettig, 1993) and Janet Seaman (Seaman & DePauw, 1989), whereas Sherrill taught such authors as Karen DePauw (DePauw & Gavron, 1995), Luke Kelly (Wessel & Kelly, 1986), and James Rimmer (1993). Davies, Sherrill, and their students have tended to blend correctives and adapted physical education perspectives (i.e., the medical and educational models) together, whereas many other adapted physical education leaders have identified mainly with special education concerns.

Early Adapted Physical Education.   Although 1952 was the date of the publication of the AAHPER report *Guiding Principles for Adapted Physical Education*, which presented a new definition and philosophy for school programming, AAHPER's Adapted Physical Education Section was not formed until 1958 (Sherrill, 1988). Janet Wessel, a professor at Michigan State University, was appointed the first chair of this Section, after which officers were elected. Wessel, a licensed physical therapist, had completed physical education degrees (MA and PhD) at Wellesley College and University of Southern California, respectively. Her background was a blend of the old correctives and new adapted physical education, with considerable expertise in curriculum design and program evaluation. Subsequently, she became known for her strong advocacy of adapted physical education within the emerging special education profession, and the creation of instructional systems known by such acronyms as I CAN (Individualize instruction, Create social leisure competence, Associate all learnings, Narrow the gap between theory and practice) and ABC (Achievement-Based Curriculum) instructional systems (Wessel, 1976, 1977; Wessel & Kelly, 1986).

From the 1950s through the 1970s, many special education teachers reached out to regular physical educators for help in conducting motor activity. While cooperative relationships were developing spontaneously in the public schools, many university professors began to organize campus practica or clinics to meet the needs of special populations, while concurrently providing new experiences for undergraduate students enrolled in adapted physical education courses.

Warren Johnson, University of Maryland, began the first Children's Physical Development Clinic in 1957 (Johnson, 1971), thus deserving recognition as the leader in promoting adapted physical education learning through practica and clinics, today an important part of adapted physical education personnel preparation as well as community service. Among the many students of Johnson who became leaders and started similar programs were Louis Bowers, now at the University of South Florida; Glenn Roswal, Jacksonville State University in Alabama; Ernie Bundschuh, University of Georgia; and Joseph Huber, Bridgewater State University in Connecticut.

A course in adapted physical education was generally required of undergraduate students in universities of high quality, but the preparation of faculty who taught such courses varied widely. Such individuals identified with *both* the Therapeutics and Adapted Physical Education Sections of AAHPERD, and gradually the differences between the two structures seemed to be forgotten. In 1986, the two structures were merged and named the Adapted Physical Activity Council (APAC).

The Knowledge Explosion.   The changing nature of the public school population, special education legislation, and expanded awareness of physical educators resulted in the publication of ten competing textbooks from 1954 to 1970. Of these, only Fait's (Dunn & Fait, 1989) and Auxter's (Auxter, Pyfer, & Huettig, 1993) texts are used today, but Daniels' text (later Daniels & Davies, 1975, 3rd ed.) is important from an historical perspective. Also significant were the works of Julian Stein, published by the American Association for Health, Physical Education, and Recreation (1968 a,b,c and many others until 1981), the motor development research of G. Lawrence Rarick and colleagues, and the perceptual-motor books of Bryant J. Cratty.

Arthur Daniels (1906-1966), who taught at the University of Illinois (1934-1942), The Ohio State University (1945-1957), and Indiana University (1957 until retirement) was the first to write a book entitled *Adapted Physical Education* (1954). Radically different from all previous texts, it included chapters on body mechanics problems, amputations, rheumatic fever, cardiac conditions, cerebral palsy, epilepsy, poliomyelitis, visual and auditory handicaps, and other conditions requiring special services. Of all of the adapted physical education leaders, even to the present, Daniels was the only one to serve as an AAHPERD president (1961-1962) other than R. Tait McKenzie (1912-1916). Daniels was closely associated with Evelyn Davies, who became coauthor of his textbook.

Hollis Fait (1918-1984), who taught at the University of Connecticut and became interested in clients at nearby Mansfield State Training School, was the first textbook author to include a chapter on mental retardation (Fait, 1960) and on learning disabilities (Fait, 1972; chapter written by Sherrill). Fait also was one of the first to publish research combining physical education and mental retardation concerns (Fait & Kupferer, 1956) and to receive a grant from the Joseph P. Kennedy, Jr. Foundation for work in this combined area (Dunn, 1986). On the second edition of his text, Fait (1966) changed the title from *adapted* to *special physical education* in recognition of the value of aligning more closely with the special education profession. He remained a strong advocate for this term and was instrumental in many schools and colleges naming their programs special physical education. Fait was also a strong influence on John Dunn, now Dean of the College of Health at the University of Utah. Dunn began his university teaching career at the University of Connecticut (1972-1975), became Fait's coauthor (Dunn & Fait, 1989; Fait & Dunn, 1984), and directed adapted physical education programming at Oregon State University from 1975 to 1995.

David Auxter (1927-   ), now retired after 21 years of teaching adapted physical education at Slippery Rock University in Pennsylvania, is the only one of the original Arnheim, Auxter, and Crowe (1969) trio who remained with the text. Auxter is especially important because he is the first of the many authors/leaders to have formal training in special education and mental retardation (doctoral degree in 1965 from Boston University). Although his degree work was equally distributed between special and physical education, Auxter traces his contributions to legislation, advocacy, and community-based programming theory to mentor Burton Blatt, a well-known special education pioneer.

Julian Stein (1925-   ), director of the Project on Recreation and Fitness of the Mentally Retarded (1966-1968) and of the Unit on Programs for the Handicapped (1968-1981), both housed at AAHPERD headquarters, was undoubtedly the most prolific creator and disseminator of knowledge that adapted physical education has ever known. During the years 1966 to 1981, Stein wrote, edited, or supervised 110 books (all published under the AAHPERD byline rather than his name), as well as numerous articles and research studies. These works, which covered all aspects of individual differences, service delivery, and personnel preparation, strongly influenced the evolution of adapted physical education as a profession and crossdisciplinary specialization.

Stein completed doctoral work at George Peabody College in Nashville in 1966. While he elected many courses in special education, psychology, and guidance and counseling, his major was physical education. His interest in individuals with disabilities dated back to undergraduate work at George Washington University in Washington, DC, with Cy Morgan, around 1949 and 1950. Morgan, who worked with Art Daniels and H. Harrison Clarke on AAHPERD's decision-making activities in the 1950s about adapted physical education, wrote no books but exerted considerable influence through Stein and other students at George Washington, Ithaca, and George Peabody.

G. Lawrence Rarick (1911-1995) and Bryant Cratty (1929-   ), mentioned previously in conjunction with special education influences, contributed strongly to the motor behavior emphasis that has always characterized personnel preparation in adapted physical activity. Rarick's research, almost all federally funded, is reviewed in many sources (Bruininks, 1974; Rarick, 1973, 1980; Rarick, Dobbins, & Broadhead, 1976). Rarick also influenced many doctoral students (e.g., Geoffrey Broadhead, Vernal Seefelt, Harriet Williams, Gail Dummer), who became productive researchers in motor behavior; Broadhead, the most prolific writer, integrated motor behavior, special education, and physical education concerns. Highly respected as a researcher and scholar, Broadhead became the first editor of the *Adapted Physical Activity Quarterly* in 1984. Cratty contributed through books in motor behavior (including both motor development and motor learning) and perceptual-motor remediation and courses taught at the University of California at Los Angeles. In addition to over 30 textbooks on aspects of motor behavior, Cratty authored *Adapted Physical Education for Handicapped Children and Youth* (1980) and *Adapted Physical Education in the Mainstream* (1989).

Beginning of Graduate Specialization.   At the State University of New York (SUNY) at Brockport in the mid-1960s, Joseph Winnick, a new faculty member who had recently completed his doctoral degree at Temple University under Donald Hilsendager, developed the first master's level specialization. The first students in the SUNY program, enrolled in 1968, received no federal funding but Winnick soon became known as a grant writer, researcher, and scholar of excellence. The SUNY program continues to be one of the strongest master's level specializations, and Winnick's textbook, *Adapted Physical Education and Sport* (2nd ed., 1995) is widely used.

By 1971, 24 universities offered graduate specializations designated as physical education for the handicapped or adapted, special, or developmental physical education (Ersing & Wheeler, 1971). Of these, 19 were receiving federal grant money under Public Law **(PL) 90-170**, the Mental Retardation Facilities and Community Mental Health Centers Construction Act, passed in 1967. Strongly impacting the availability of this grant money was the Joseph P. Kennedy, Jr. Foundation and various members of the Kennedy family, who began advocacy of recreation, fitness, and physical education for individuals with mental retardation early in the 1960s (Hillman, 1986; Lapriola, 1972; Shriver, 1983; Winnick, 1986).

This advocacy was operationalized by the Kennedy Foundation's (a) funding of an office at AAHPER headquarters in 1965 to create nationwide awareness of the needs of special populations and to stimulate action on their behalf, (b) funding of regional teacher training seminars on "physical education for the handicapped" in 1967, and (c) insistence that federal laws funding special education personnel preparation also earmark monies for physical education and recreation leadership training. Concurrently pressure was exerted on the Bureau of Education for the Handicapped (BEH), the government agency responsible for funding priorities and decisions, to employ a staff member specifically to oversee physical education and recreation concerns. William Hillman and Julian Stein, employed by BEH and AAHPER(D) respectively, subsequently directed most of their efforts toward creating and shaping a nationwide system of graduate level personnel preparation.

The initiative began with finding professors willing and able to learn grant writing and legislation and to convince curriculum committees at their respective universities to approve a new graduate specialization. The decision for adapted physical education to become a graduate rather than an undergraduate specialization was made by government officials and advisors who established funding guidelines. Most university professors were content with this direction because they believed specialization should be based on strong undergraduate preparation in regular physical education. This belief can be traced back to the curricular organization of Ling's followers at CIG in Sweden in the late 1800s.

Pioneer programs that remain operative, and the names of those who initiated them between 1969 and 1972, are the Ohio State University (Walter Ersing), Indiana University (Evelyn Davies), Texas Woman's University (Claudine Sherrill), State University of New York at Brockport (Joseph Winnick), University of Utah (O.N. Hunter and Joan Moran), Slippery Rock State University (David Auxter), University of Connecticut (Hollis Fait), and Wisconsin State University of LaCrosse (Lane Goodwin). Directors of these programs (in parentheses) were major shapers of the knowledge base that evolved. Also instrumental in shaping the new specialization were G. Lawrence Rarick (University of California at Berkeley) and Janet Wessel (Michigan State University), researchers whose productivity generated the largest sums of BEH grant funds from 1970 to 1980.

Growth of the Knowledge Base. Professors in the newly created graduate specializations synthesized information from many sources (correctives, adapted physical education, kinesiology/biomechanics, physical and occupational therapy, special education, medicine, human development, psychology, counseling) to produce a knowledge base. Much energy was spent also in refining grant-writing skills because lengthy proposals and reports were required annually to continue program funding. Although the government expected universities gradually to assume fiscal responsibility for these new academic programs, few administrators showed an inclination to do so.

Most of the early graduate specializations included several courses taught in the special education department, a practice based on the belief that special education theory was essential to adapted physical education. Grant guidelines, the same for adapted and special education writers, required that course content should match competencies to perform such roles as teacher, administrator, or researcher and such services as assessment, educational diagnosis and placement, instruction, and program evaluation. Because no guidelines existed for professional preparation in adapted physical education, several regional institutes were sponsored by AAHPER and BEH in 1971 and 1972 to determine standards and future directions (American Association for Health, Physical Education, and Recreation, 1973; Ersing, 1972; Winnick, 1972). Julian Stein (1969) was the acknowledged leader of these efforts to shape early professional preparation.

The greatest impact on knowledge to be taught, however, was **PL 94-142**, the Education for All Handicapped Children Act, passed in 1975 and operationalized by rules and regulations in the *Federal Register* in 1977. **PL 94-142**, now amended as Part B of the Individuals With Disabilities Education Act (IDEA), mandated five rights that changed the nature of public schooling for children with disabilities:

- Free education regardless of severity of disability
- Appropriate education agreed on by a multidisciplinary committee, including parents, and guided by a written individualized education program (IEP)
- Nondiscriminatory testing, evaluation, and placement procedures
- Instruction in the least restrictive environment
- Procedural due process of the law

PL 94-142 specified that these rights applied in physical education instruction, which was defined as an integral part of special education.

Leaders in obtaining the inclusion of physical education in **PL 94-142** and determining implementation approaches were Julian Stein, AAHPERD; William Hillman, BEH; David Auxter, Slippery Rock State College, Pennsylvania; and William Chasey, director of a BEH grant awarded to the National Consortium on Physical Education and Recreation for the Handicapped (NCPERH), an advocacy organization founded in 1973. Others directly involved in this effort through NCPERH were Janet Wessel, Michigan State University; Louis Bowers, University of South Florida; Leon Johnson, University of Missouri; Claudine Sherrill, Texas Woman's University; Joseph Winnick, State University of New York at Brockport; and John Dunn, Oregon State University. Collectively these individuals worked almost a decade to shape what is now variously known as **PL 94-142** or IEP theory.

Sherrill (1976), Wessel (1977), and Winnick (1979) wrote first editions of textbooks incorporating this theory, while earlier authors revised subsequent editions (Arnheim, Auxter, & Crowe, 1977, 3rd ed.; Fait, 1978, 4th ed.). Tremendous emphasis was placed on assessment and evaluation theory, with efforts directed primarily toward development of tests appropriate for individuals with disabilities of different ages. Other leaders focused attention on expansion and revision of the 1971 and 1972 AAHPER adapted physical education competencies and state-level teacher certification, licensure, and endorsement (DePauw, 1979; DePauw & Bundschuh, 1988; French, Jansma, & Winnick, 1978; Hurley, 1981). In 1978 Louisiana became the first state to require for employment a teacher certification in adapted physical education (Broadhead & Brunt, 1982).

New emphasis also was placed on requiring all undergraduate majors to take courses in adapted physical education and to become knowledgeable about implementation of **PL 94-142**. The clinic or practicum instructional approach, begun by Warren Johnson in the 1950s, was widely adopted as a means of acquainting university students with special populations. In addition to supplementing content in theory classes, these clinics provided much needed community service, and brought university teachers into continuous contact with parents, special educators, and related services personnel, such as occupational and physical therapists.

Illustrative of professors in the 1970s who began outstanding interdisciplinary programs of this nature is Janet Seaman of California State University at Los Angeles, a master therapeutic recreation specialist as well as an adapted/correctives leader. Seaman, now executive director of the American Association of Active Lifestyles and Fitness (AAALF) of AAHPERD, was one of the first to emphasize the communication and interaction competencies needed to function effectively in interdisciplinary and crossdisciplinary settings (Seaman & DePauw, 1982; Seaman & Heilbuth, 1988). Seaman was also instrumental in California's becoming one of the first states to establish credentialing standards for adapted physical education.

Early Research. Early research in adapted physical education evolved through individual initiative (e.g., Auxter, 1966; Corder, 1966; Fait & Kupferer, 1956; Keogh & Oliver, 1968; Londeree & Johnson, 1974; Oliver, 1958, 1960; Pyfer & Carlson, 1972; Smith & Hurst, 1961; Stein, 1965) and through federal funding, either directly or through the AAHPER(D) Unit on Programs for the Handicapped (e.g., Brace, 1968; Broadhead, 1972; Chasey & Wyrick, 1971; Francis & Rarick, 1959; Rarick, Widdop, & Broadhead, 1970; Rarick, Dobbins, & Broadhead, 1976). This research focused primarily on development, function, and performance of individuals with disabilities (especially mental retardation) and the efficacy of various programs in facilitating change.

Also well funded by the federal government was field-based or curricular research. Best known for this type of research were Janet Wessel of Michigan State, Thomas Vodola of the New Jersey public schools, John Dunn of Oregon State, Joseph Winnick and Frank Short of the State University of New York (SUNY) at Brockport, and Louis Bowers of the University of South Florida. Wessel (1976, 1977, 1983) blended assessment, curriculum, and instructional design theory to produce the *I CAN* curriculum, a comprehensive instructional system based on qualitative assessment of motor skills. Vodola (1973, 1976, 1978) developed *Project ACTIVE*, an individualized diagnostic-prescriptive motor and physical fitness curriculum with norms and an in-service teacher-training program. Dunn (1980, 1983) blended behavior management theory with physical education programming for individuals with severe disability, thereby creating the *Data Based Gymnasium* curriculum. Winnick and Short (1982, 1984, 1985) created and tested a fitness assessment model called *Project UNIQUE* for individuals with physical or sensory impairments. Bowers (1975, 1979) first directed a Play Learning Center and Demonstration Project for Handicapped Children, 1974 to 1977, and later developed the *I'M SPECIAL* videotape and videodisc series, from 1979 on. The *I'M SPECIAL* videotape series, widely used by state departments of education and universities in preservice and in-service training, included 15 tapes that described good adapted physical education programming in compliance with **PL 94-142**. Steve Klesius, also of the University of South Florida, has worked closely with Bowers on these projects. These and other products of field-based research, mostly created in the 1970s, are described in detail by Ersing (1988) and Churton (1984 a,b).

Several reviews of early research literature (Broadhead, 1981, 1983; Bruininks, 1974; Rarick, 1980, 1983; Sherrill, 1988c; Stein, 1983) substantiate that a huge body of adapted physical education knowledge had been amassed before the 1980s, when several adapted physical educators began to conceptualize their knowledge base as a subdiscipline or discipline (Broadhead, 1984; Eason, Smith, & Caron, 1983; Sherrill, 1982).

Obstacles and Breakthroughs to the Emerging Profession/Discipline

Two major obstacles to the emerging profession/discipline were lack of awareness and/or poor or neutral attitudes of regular physical educators, and the lack of technological and methodological resources. Major breakthroughs were technological advances, legislation, the success of the disability sport movement, and support and mentoring of scholars from regular physical education.

Attitudes and Lack of Awareness.   The major obstacle that adapted physical education has struggled to surmount is society's attitude toward people with disabilities and the professionals who choose to serve them (DePauw, 1990; Rizzo & Davis, 1991; Tripp & Sherrill, 1991). Historically, individuals who are different in appearance and/or behavior (like all minority groups) have been subjected to discrimination, prejudice, and rejection. Association with such people (social or professional) carries the risks of marginality in that it distances physical educators from mainstream issues and concerns as well as the professional/disciplinary power structure.

Mainstream physical education has evidenced little interest in disability and/or individual differences that limit physical activity potential. While most individuals profess belief in high quality physical education for all, the constraints within typical employment ecosystems tend to perpetuate attitudes of neutrality and passivity toward adapted physical activity as an emerging profession/discipline.

In the 1970s the linkage of adapted physical education to special education, psychology, and sociology (through legislation and shared concerns for social minorities) placed demands on adapted physical education leaders that few of their colleagues understood or appreciated. Failing to find empathy within their departments, some adapted physical educators began critical thinking about crossdisciplinary roots and the development of theory to examine beliefs and practices. Others further distanced themselves from colleagues by becoming increasingly involved in legislation, advocacy, and other concerns traditionally outside the physical education domain. Almost all spent huge amounts of time writing grants to fund their personnel preparation and research programs.

Lack of Technological and Methodological Resources.   Before the computer era, dissemination of research findings, collaborative thinking, and interactive theory building were limited. Networking among universities was not yet a common practice, and adapted physical education scholars had little contact with others of similar interests. Knowledge building proceeded in parallel tracks at different universities, with much duplication and little sharing. Crosscultural communication was limited also with much confusion about terminology, philosophy, and method (Doll-Tepper, 1990). Limited federal funds meant inadequate resources to support all programs, and adapted physical educators were forced to compete repeatedly against each other with regard to who could write the best grants and document the most results. Mechanisms, strategies, and models to promote cooperation and community were not yet operationalized.

Assessment of individual differences and program efficacy was complicated by lack of appropriate instruments, inadequate knowledge of small sample statistics, and failure to understand environmental variables that affect test results. Specialized equipment for communication and mobility was not yet sophisticated enough to permit persons with severe disability to reveal their true potential. Traditional quantitative research methodology was hampered by an inability to find appropriate sample sizes, and qualitative research design was seldom included in professional preparation.

Major Breakthroughs.   Technological advances in computers, laboratory and field equipment, wheelchair design, and communication devices enhanced development of the knowledge base. Refinement of various kinds of media enabled university students and the general public to see and hear individuals with disabilities in new ways. Likewise, new emphasis on building, vehicle, and community accessibility increased the travel and visibility of individuals with disabilities, which in turn promoted awareness of needs and rights.

The enactment of **PL 94-142** in 1975 was a major breakthrough in the shaping of the adapted physical education profession. In compliance with the law, specialists prepared to teach special education children and consulted with regular educators, who increasingly began to serve students with disabilities in regular programs. The law also allocated several million dollars for personnel preparation in physical education.

The disability sport movement was also a breakthrough; athletes with disabilities and their coaches began to develop a "methods and materials" body of knowledge specific to sports for different kinds of disabilities. Wheelchair basketball began in the late 1940s, followed by Special Olympics for persons with mental retardation in 1968. Individuals with cerebral palsy, visual impairments, and amputations began serious national and international sports competition in the 1970s, intensifying the need for personnel preparation in adapted physical education, to include methods and materials for teaching and coaching various disability sports (DePauw & Gavron, 1995; Sherrill, 1986).

More important than anything else, however, was the modeling of positive attitudes by established mainstream leaders like G. Lawrence Rarick. Of the early grant writers and program directors, Rarick was the only one respected enough by the mainstream academic community to

have been elected a Fellow of the prestigious American Academy of
Physical Education prior to 1980. An acknowledged scholar in motor
development, Rarick was mentored in doctoral studies by Charles H.
McCloy (1886-1954) at the State University of Iowa. Thereafter, Rarick
taught at Boston University (1943-1950), the University of Wisconsin
(1950-1968), and the University of California at Berkeley (1968-1979). Rarick's dependable presence at adapted physical education meetings
throughout the 1970s heightened the self-esteem of everyone present.
Likewise, his leadership in extending motor development research to
special populations offered insight into a future when collaborative research between regular and adapted physical educators might become
a reality.

Organization of the Discipline: 1980s

By the early 1980s, some professionals were beginning to conceptualize
their knowledge base as a subdiscipline or discipline (Broadhead, 1981,
1984; Eason, Smith, & Caron, 1983; Sherrill, 1982). Numerous factors contributed to the creation of a discipline.

   The human rights movement of the 1960s and 1970s, which culminated
in **PL 94-142**, led to the realization that a body of crossdisciplinary knowledge was needed (a) to protect human rights; (b) to promote understanding of individual differences and environmental variables that affect
movement success, lifespan wellness, and social acceptance; and (c) to
initiate and maintain selected processes and services. Clearly the scholarly
inquiry in adapted physical education focused on populations, issues,
and concerns not typically addressed in regular physical education. The
need for holistic approaches to service delivery and empowerment led
adapted physical education professors to draw content from the many
subdisciplines of physical education (e.g., biomechanics, exercise physiology, motor learning) as well as special education (e.g., mental retardation,
orthopedic impairments, blindness) and other related areas. To synthesize
and apply such content, it appeared that personnel preparation needed
to become more and more crossdisciplinary. Concurrently, it was evident
that unifying theories and themes were essential to formalize a discipline
uniquely focused on individual and ecosystem differences associated with
psychomotor problems.

Major Events in Organization of a Discipline

Three events initially brought together individuals who began to focus
more and more, over the next decade, on the disciplinary nature of
adapted physical education/activity: (a) a doctoral/postdoctoral seminar

at Texas Woman's University in 1979 that culminated in a textbook entitled *Leadership Training in Adapted Physical Education* (Sherrill, 1988d); (b) the Third International Symposium of Adapted Physical Activity, held in New Orleans in 1981; and (c) publication of scholarly journals, beginning in 1984.

Conceptualization of the Emerging Discipline. Claudine Sherrill (1934-) and Karen DePauw (1949-   ), professor and doctoral student, respectively, in 1979, cooperatively planned and conducted an advanced summer school seminar on future directions of adapted physical education as a profession and academic discipline. BEH funding permitted Texas Woman's University to bring leaders (Julian Stein, Joseph Winnick, Janet Seaman, Jean Pyfer, and Lane Goodwin) to campus, each for several days, to stimulate critical thinking among approximately 20 doctoral and postdoctoral students concerning the nature of adapted physical education. The December 1967 *Quest* entitled *The Nature of a Discipline* was required reading, and every seminar participant prepared a paper on whether or not adapted physical education met the criteria of a discipline set forth by Nixon (1967).

Subsequently, several seminar participants wrote chapters for a textbook on leadership training, which were revised several times before publication in 1988. Other persons contributed to the book also; when finished, it represented the efforts of 35 individuals from all parts of the United States. The thinking and sharing of Stein, Winnick, Seaman, Pyfer, Goodwin, Sherrill, DePauw, and doctoral/postdoctoral students contributed significantly to the beginning conceptualization of adapted physical education as a profession and discipline.

International Linking and Sharing. Robert L. Eason (1942-   ), professor at the University of New Orleans and vice-president of the International Federation of Adapted Physical Activity (IFAPA) from 1981 to 1983, was executive chairman of the first symposium of IFAPA to emphasize theory and result in scholarly, published proceedings (Eason, Smith, & Caron, 1983). This was also the time that a large number of adapted physical education leaders in the United States became aware of the existence of IFAPA, which had been founded in Quebec City in 1973. As founder and first president, Clermont Simard, Laval University in Quebec City, was instrumental in selection of *adapted physical activity* as the preferred terminology for the new profession. He was assisted, of course, in this decision by IFAPA board members from several countries.

Two papers presented at the Third IFAPA Symposium in 1981 included theory in their titles (Dunn, 1983; Fait, 1983) and several introduced theory that would become increasingly significant with passing years. Noteworthy among these were discussions of adaptation theory by Ernest Kiphard (1983) of Germany and of ecological theory by Walter Davis

(1983) of Kent State University in Ohio. The Third IFAPA Symposium and its excellent proceedings represent a particularly significant landmark in shaping disciplinary awareness and responsibility.

Publication of Scholarly Journals.   In 1983, Rainer Martens, owner-founder of Human Kinetics, brought Geoffrey Broadhead, Claudine Sherrill, and Herberta Lundegren to Champaign, Illinois, for several days to discuss the founding of a new journal, *Adapted Physical Activity Quarterly*. These individuals selected 11 adapted physical education, 1 special education, and 6 therapeutic recreation leaders to comprise their editorial board. Adapted physical education leaders selected were Denis Brunt, Karen DePauw, John Dunn, G. Lawrence Rarick, Greg Reid, Janet Seaman, Julian Stein, David Sugden, Dale Ulrich, Thomas Vodola, and Joseph Winnick. Various criteria guided the selection process, including (a) scholarly productivity as evidenced by publication of research-based articles and (b) geographical representation. Of the 11 physical educators, one was from Canada (Reid) and two were from Great Britain (Brunt and Sugden).

Broadhead (1937-   ), professor at Louisiana State University and later dean of the School of Physical Education, Recreation, and Dance at Kent State University in Ohio, was named founding editor of *Adapted Physical Activity Quarterly*, and served in this capacity from 1984 until 1992. Sherrill and Lundegren were associate editors with primary responsibility for physical education and recreation, respectively. Broadhead, a doctoral student of G. Lawrence Rarick at the University of Wisconsin, was reared in England and had taught on two continents, established many international contacts, and published extensively in the areas of motor ability and assessment (e.g., Broadhead, 1972; Rarick et al., 1970, 1976). Lundegren (1931-   ), of Pennsylvania State University, was respected for scholarly leadership in both recreation and physical education (Farrell & Lundegren, 1983).

The *Adapted Physical Activity Quarterly* (*APAQ*) was conceptualized as "a scholarly outlet for practitioners and theorists alike" (Broadhead, 1984, p. 1). The focus was broad and multidisciplinary, with the expectation that professionals from many areas would contribute manuscripts on physical activity for special populations. Standards for publication were high, challenging the emerging adapted physical activity discipline to upgrade writing and research skills and to give more attention to theory.

Palaestra: The Forum of Sport, Physical Education, and Recreation for the Disabled also began publication in 1984, offering a second multidisciplinary, scholarly journal for building a strong knowledge base. Owner-editor David Beaver, a professor at Western Illinois University in Macomb and a leader in the Paralympic sport movement, brought together a large editorial board that included physicians and athletes with disability as well as physical education, sport, and recreation leaders. This journal, focusing more on practice than theory, has been particularly successful over the years in promoting a sense of community among individuals who work with special populations. Julian Stein became increasingly involved with *Palaestra*, thereby continuing the leadership and mentoring begun in AAHPERD's Unit on Programs for the Handicapped.

Comparative Influences of Parent Disciplines

In shaping their discipline, adapted physical activity leaders drew heavily upon the parent disciplines of physical education and special education, both of which have roots in medicine, psychology, sociology, and counseling. Most of the adapted physical education professors in the 1980s had completed fairly extensive course work in special education, although their doctoral degrees were in physical education or exercise and sport science subspecializations. Likewise, many maintained membership in the professional organizations of both disciplines.

A continuing dilemma in the 1980s was acceptance and/or inclusion by the parent disciplines (DePauw & Goc Karp, 1994; Rizzo & Davis, 1991; Sherrill, 1988b). Illustrative of exclusion are AAHPERD's decision in 1984 to close the Unit on Programs for the Handicapped, which had provided services since 1965, and the decision in 1986 of the advisory committee for *Research Quarterly for Exercise and Sport* to eliminate the section called "Activities for Special Populations." Physical education structures, including many academic departments in universities, seemed to support adapted physical activity only as long as it generated external funds. This problem mirrors, to a large extent, the actions of society in general.

Leaders have encouraged infusion of content on special populations into regular education courses and textbooks for almost three decades (DePauw & Goc Karp, 1994; Rizzo & Davis, 1991; Sherrill, 1988d; Stein, 1969; Winnick, 1986), but little progress has been made. Continued exclusion (whether conscious or unconscious) and low prioritization are hurtful in many ways.

The problems of adapted physical activity parallel those of its special education parent and promote common concerns. Both specializations receive much of their impetus from laws that provide federal funds. These laws, however, limit disciplinary evolution in that they focus on service delivery to school-aged individuals and refer specifically to education. Implementation of laws that receive low priority from mainstream society leaves little time and energy for basic research, networking, collegiality, and shaping a discipline.

Although not a parent discipline, therapeutic recreation (also called recreation for special populations) deserves recognition as a parallel profession/discipline. The language of federal law, since the 1960s, has been *physical education and recreation for the handicapped* (now individuals with disabilities). The relationship between physical education and recreation is both cooperative and competitive, adding still another complex dimension to disciplinary concerns.

Important Steps in Organizing the Discipline

One step in organizing a discipline is agreement on a name and focus. Universal consensus is, of course, impossible but the trend seems to favor adoption of *adapted physical activity* as an umbrella term that will support lifespan perspectives and the employment of professionals in many diverse settings with all age groups. The term was first used in 1973 when the International Federation of Adapted Physical Activity (IFAPA) was formed in Canada. It was further supported in the naming of the *Adapted Physical Activity Quarterly* in 1984 and of the Adapted Physical Activity Council (APAC) of AAHPERD (the merger of five separate structures) in 1985. Several persons participated in the selection of the APAC name (DePauw, 1986), but John Dunn and Karen DePauw were particularly influential. In the 1990s, the prestigious professional preparation program at the Ohio State University was renamed adapted physical activity (Porretta et al., 1993), and Sherrill renamed her textbook *Adapted Physical Activity, Recreation, and Sport: Crossdisciplinary and Lifespan* (4th ed., 1993).

Another step in organizing a discipline is understanding its criteria or distinguishing elements (Nixon, 1967), along with agreement by leaders that a body of knowledge and practices meets these criteria. The events described earlier—Texas Woman's University doctoral/postdoctoral seminar, 1981 IFAPA symposium and proceedings (Eason et al., 1983) that highlighted theory, and the creation of scholarly journals—document early efforts to specify an identifiable domain for adapted physical activity, a unique conceptual and syntactical structure, and procedural and declarative knowledge.

Also important in organizing a discipline is the support of universities in offering graduate degrees, promoting research, and creating and preserving knowledge. This process is well documented in the United States (Dunn & McCubbin, 1991; Sherrill, 1988a,e; Spirduso & Lovett, 1987), Europe (Van Coppenolle, 1993), and Asia (Yabe & Hong, 1994). Spirduso and Lovett (1987) noted that adapted physical education ranked seventh among academic specializations in sports science degrees granted in the United States. Ranked above adapted physical education were exercise physiology, administration, professional preparation, biomechanics, and motor learning/control. Ranked below it were history and philosophy, general physical education, sport psychology, motor development, bioscience, sport sociology, and measurement and evaluation.

Watershed Events and/or Historical Landmarks

Watershed events in the 1980s that particularly supported the organization of an adapted physical education discipline included international symposia held every two years; reauthorizations of federal funding, which generally required much advocacy; growing sense of community among individuals involved in these endeavors; and the recognition that adapted physical education had amassed a substantial history with many time-tested scholarly works.

International Symposia. In addition to historical landmarks already described, IFAPA symposia in London (1983), Toronto (1985), Brisbane (1987), and Berlin (1989) each comprised historical landmarks in the sharing of knowledge and the creation of an international community of scholars. The Berlin symposium was particularly significant in that 800 participants from 45 countries attended and almost 300 presentations (oral, poster, workshop formats) were made (Doll-Tepper et al., 1990). Revision of the bylaws was begun, with emphasis on formalizing representation from all regions of the world.

The theme of the 1989 symposium was *Adapted Physical Activity: An Interdisciplinary Approach*; several keynote speakers focused on terminology, concepts, premises, methods, and procedures (Doll-Tepper et al., 1990). This symposium marked the first time that leaders had been assigned to examine disciplinary aspects of adapted physical activity. Members of the executive and scientific committees responsible for symposium direction and content included Gudrun Doll-Tepper (Germany), Karen DePauw (USA), Jean-Claude De Potter (Belgium), Robert J. Price (England), Hermann Rieder (Germany), and Adri Vermeer (Netherlands).

The foresight of these leaders and especially of Doll-Tepper, symposium director, was extremely valuable in helping adapted physical activity people begin to think of themselves as a discipline. The symposium planning committee defined *adapted physical activity* as "movement, physical activity, and sports in which special emphasis is placed on the interests and capabilities of individuals with limiting conditions, such as the disabled, health impaired, or aged" (Doll-Tepper et al., 1990, preface). Sherrill (1990), a keynote speaker, resolved that *adapted physical activity* was "an interdisciplinary body of knowledge directed toward the identification and solution of psychomotor problems throughout the total lifespan . . . advocacy of exercise and sport for all persons . . . attitudes, skills, and habits that will facilitate social integration of persons with disability with family members and significant others" (pp. 23-26).

Federal Funding and Advocacy Concerns. In the United States, thus far, federal funding has been essential to the continued acceptance of responsibility by universities for preparing adapted physical activity personnel. Funding is based on the reauthorization of laws approximately every three years. Hence, reauthorizations of **PL 94-142** in 1983, 1986, and 1990 constitute major historical landmarks (Churton, 1987; Hillman, 1986; Sherrill & Hillman, 1988).

Officers and members of the National Consortium on Physical Education and Recreation for the Handicapped (NCPERH) were especially instrumental in maintaining physical education funding. NCPERH presidents in the 1980s who spearheaded these efforts were John Dunn (1981), Ernie Bundschuh (1983), Louis Bowers (1985), Michael Churton (1987), and John Hall (1989). Out of their work and the efforts of NCPERH presidents of the 1970s (Leon Johnson, 1975; Claudine Sherrill, 1977; Joseph Winnick, 1979) has evolved legislative, advocacy, and grant-writing theory. This body of knowledge is recognized in a growing number of textbooks and lists of competencies.

Time-Tested Works.   A discipline is "characterized by a substantial history and a publicly recognized tradition exemplified by time-tested works" (Nixon, 1967, p. 47). Hence, the focus on history at the 1985 AAHPERD conference and the publication of this history in the April 1986 *APAQ* comprise significant historical landmarks. Likewise, the inclusion of several chapters on history in *Leadership Training in Adapted Physical Education* (Sherrill, 1988a,b,e) was a landmark.

Time-tested works in the 1980s included several textbooks published as second editions (Eichstaedt & Kalakian, 1987; Seaman & DePauw, 1989); third editions (Daniels & Davies, 1985; Sherrill, 1986), fifth editions (Auxter & Pyfer, 1985), and sixth editions (Dunn & Fait, 1989). Time-tested works also included the growing body of research (see references in Rarick, 1980) that guided the design of new studies; for example, Joseph Winnick adapted techniques used by Rarick (on individuals with mental retardation) to individuals with physical or sensory impairments, in the development of Project UNIQUE (Winnick & Short, 1982, 1984, 1985).

Political/Sociocultural Factors

Other factors contributed to the emerging discipline of adapted physical activity in the 1980s and 1990s:

1. The United Nations' declaration of the years 1981 through 1992 as the "International Decade of the Disabled" and events stimulated by increasing worldwide awareness and concern: the International Symposium on Physical Education and Sport Programs for the Physically and Mentally Handicapped, held at College Park, Maryland, in November 1982 (Stein, 1986); activities culminating in creation of the 1987 *European Charter for Sport for All: Disabled Persons* (DePauw & Doll-Tepper, 1989); and Canada's national conference in 1986 that resulted in the 1988 conference *The Jasper Talks: Strategies for Change in Adapted Physical Activity in*

Canada (Canadian Association for Health, Physical Education, and Recreation, 1988). This latter conference was co-chaired by Ted Wall, McGill University, and Robert Steadward, University of Alberta, who emerged as pioneer leaders in the adapted physical activity and disability sport movement in Canada.

2. Legislation that included passages on physical education and recreation for individuals with disabilities and/or specified equal access for all people (e.g., reauthorizations of the Education for All Handicapped Children Act of 1975; the Rehabilitation Act of 1973; the Amateur Sports Act of 1978; the Americans With Disabilities Act of 1990).

3. The impact of the Special Olympics, Deaf Sports, and Paralympics movements and increased worldwide awareness that individuals with disabilities may wish to become elite athletes, have the capacity, and deserve the right to equal access (DePauw & Gavron, 1995; Sherrill, 1986; Steadward, 1996). This, in turn, heightened the demand for a scientific knowledge base.

4. The increasing market for adapted physical activity literature, as evidenced by companies willing to publish specialized journals and books. Interacting with this factor were increased scholarly productivity and changing expectations for doctoral students and young professionals (i.e., "publish or perish").

The political/sociocultural factors and conditions of the 1980s heightened awareness of the needs and rights of social minorities; concurrently, health and wellness research made available a substantial mass of knowledge based on data collected primarily from white, middle-class males without impairments or disabilities. The need to extend this knowledge to include all kinds of individual differences challenged adapted physical activity leaders to examine the nature of their specialization and to focus more intensely on its development as a discipline.

Development of the Discipline: 1990s

The 1990s are a time of development. A growing number of leaders recognize the need to balance professional and disciplinary training in higher education and to broaden perspectives from school-based service delivery to multiple roles in a variety of settings.

Key Figures and Roles

Many individuals are contributing to the evolution of adapted physical activity as a discipline, through leadership as officers of key organizations, editors and associate editors of journals, organizers of conferences, and shapers of higher education curricula that stress theory and research. Others contribute primarily through publication of theory-testing and theory-generating works and/or papers that analyze current issues and trends critically or examine philosophy.

Many of the individuals mentioned in earlier sections of this history have played multiple roles in shaping our discipline, especially persons serving as editors and associate editors of scholarly journals (i.e., Geoffrey Broadhead, Claudine Sherrill, Herberta Lundegren, Greg Reid, Dale Ulrich, David Beaver, and Julian Stein). These individuals have guided development of the adapted physical activity knowledge base by insisting on high standards to meet criteria for publication and mentoring many new or emerging researchers and theorists. In 1995, a history of the first ten years of the *Adapted Physical Activity Quarterly* (Reid & Broadhead, 1995) reported that 290 articles had been published, representing 386 authors. Of these authors, only 45 had published three or more articles. Individuals publishing seven or more articles were Sherrill, Dunn, Reid, Winnick, and DePauw.

Faculty employed in universities that offer doctoral level specialization in adapted physical education/activity significantly influence the evolution of a discipline, directly and through their outstanding graduates. Long-term faculty at five universities have been particularly instrumental in this regard: Texas Woman's University (Claudine Sherrill, Jean Pyfer, Ron French); Indiana University (Dale Ulrich, Paul Surburg); Oregon State University (John Dunn, Jeff McCubbin, Douglas Collier); the Ohio State University (Paul Jansma, David Porretta); and the University of Virginia (Luke Kelly, Martin Block). Texas Woman's University, Indiana University, and Oregon State University have traditionally graduated the most doctoral students (Dunn & McCubbin, 1991). The Ohio State University, however, has the longest history of professional preparation leadership. Beginning with Harlan Metcalf (1929) and Arthur Daniels (1954), strong early Ohio State faculty included Donald K. Mathews (Mathews, Kruse, & Shaw, 1962), Ruth Wheeler (Wheeler & Hooley, 1969), and Walter Ersing (1972, 1988). The University of Virginia has a relatively new doctoral specialization compared to the other four universities.

The Texas Woman's University (coeducational at the graduate level) is noteworthy in that each of its adapted physical education faculty has authored or coauthored a major textbook. Claudine Sherrill and Jean Pyfer trace their academic roots directly to the correctives emphasis of Rathbone and lifelong interest in motor development and the neurological bases of motor control. Additionally, Sherrill has been involved in the disability sports movement since the 1980s and has conducted considerable research on the psychosocial aspects of adapted physical activity. Ron French traces his academic roots to Keogh and Cratty at the University of California at Los Angeles and to extensive work in special education and behavior management. This triad of professors places special emphasis on critical thinking, professional leadership, and development of generic competencies for noncategorical service delivery.

From 1980 to 1995, Texas Woman's University conferred 41 doctoral degrees with specialization in adapted physical education, almost twice the number of any other university. Among the graduates who have authored or coauthored textbooks are Karen DePauw, Luke Kelly, Jim Rimmer, Carol Huettig, and Jo Ellen Cowden. These, as well as other graduates, have pioneered in the disciplinary growth of adapted physical activity.

Numerous individuals, with diverse academic backgrounds, have contributed substantially in the 1990s to the disciplinary status of adapted physical activity. Particularly outstanding in multiple roles are Greg Reid, Joseph Winnick, Gudrun Doll-Tepper, Karen DePauw, and John Dunn. DePauw, Reid, and Winnick exemplify leaders in editorial and research roles, whereas Doll-Tepper and DePauw (1996) have excelled in organizational leadership. Dunn has been active in all roles associated with leadership.

Greg Reid, associate editor of *APAQ* from 1990 to 1991 and editor from 1992 through 1996, has repeatedly emphasized the importance of theory in designing research (Reid, 1989, 1990, 1992, 1993). Professor and chair of the physical education department at McGill University, Canada, Reid organized and conducted the first joint adapted physical activity conference of Canada and the United States in October 1992, thereby providing the foundation for organizing the North American Federation of Adapted Physical Activity, this continent's counterpart to the European Association for Research Into Adapted Physical Activity. Reid is well-known for research in motor behavior.

Joseph Winnick, at the State University of New York (SUNY) at Brockport from 1965 to present, and editor of *Adapted Physical Education and Sport* (1990, 2nd ed. in 1995), has mentored many of today's leaders as master's candidates (Luke Kelly, Garth Tymeson), as young faculty members (Paul Jansma, Ron French, Frank Short), and as authors and researchers (see Winnick, 1995). Winnick has been federally funded for research on fitness of special populations (Project UNIQUE and offshoots) since the 1970s, thereby modeling the dual role of researcher-professor and emphasizing the importance of in-depth, long-term, intensive scholarly inquiry. Although SUNY does not offer a doctoral specialization in adapted physical education, its master's level concentration (the first in the world) has created many outstanding specialists and serves as a prototype for other programs.

Gudrun Doll-Tepper of Freie Universität of Berlin and Karen DePauw of Washington State University were president and president-elect, respectively, of the International Federation of Adapted Physical Activity from 1993 to 1995. Concurrently Doll-Tepper served on the board of

directors and acted as 1994 conference director of the Association Internationale des Écoles Superieurs d' Education Physique (AIESEP), and De-
Pauw was president of the National Association for Physical Education in
Higher Education (NAPEHE). Both have advocated strongly for adapted
physical activity as a discipline through scholarly writing and speaking,
conference planning, and influence as an officer. Doll-Tepper has been a
member of the IFAPA board of directors since 1981. Doll-Tepper and
DePauw, along with Sherrill, have been particularly active in applying
sociocultural theories to adapted physical activity, and advocating for
procedural knowledge of integration, inclusion, and infusion.

John Dunn has provided leadership as a scholar, researcher, teacher-
trainer, and officer of many organizations during his tenure at three
universities: University of Connecticut with Hollis Fait (1972-1975); Oregon State University as director of adapted physical education graduate
training (1975-1995); University of Utah as Dean of the College of Health
(1995). Dunn became Fait's co-author of *Special Physical Education* (5th
ed.) in 1984 and senior author of the text in 1989. Dunn, along with Karen
DePauw, provided the major leadership for merger of the Therapeutics
Council and Adapted Physical Education Academy into the Adapted
Physical Activity Council in 1985. Dunn served as chair of both of these
structures before their merger and as the president of NCPERID, thus
becoming the only leader to hold all three major offices. He is best known
for research in curriculum and pedagogy for individuals with severe disability.

Key Organizations

Several professional organizations attempt to meet needs: (a) American
Alliance for Health, Physical Education, Recreation and Dance; (b) the
National Consortium for Physical Education and Recreation for Individuals With Disabilities, named NCPERH until 1992; and (c) the International
Federation of Adapted Physical Activity and its regional affiliates, including the North American Federation for Adapted Physical Activity (NA-
FAPA), founded in 1994. The histories of each of these organizations,
woven into this chapter, reflect the need to address marginal groups or
social minorities generally conceptualized as special populations. Mainstream organizations typically give only token attention and acceptance
to individuals who are considerably different from the norm. This low
prioritization has required networking of experts whose main research,
teaching, and service delivery interests center on specific individual and
ecosystem differences and interactions.

**American Alliance for Health, Physical Education, Recreation,
and Dance.** This organization, under various names, has provided
networking opportunities since the establishment of the Therapeutics

Section in 1905. However, the placement of the Section in relation to other structures changed numerous times, reflecting confusion about its parent discipline and target population. The Therapeutics Section was assigned to the Physical Education Division from 1937 to 1942, to the Health Education Division from 1942 to 1949, and thereafter to the General Division until reorganization in the 1970s placed it in the Association for Research, Administration, Professional Councils, and Societies (ARAPCS), now called the AAALF.

The Adapted Physical Education Section, founded in 1958, in contrast, was identified with the Physical Education Section until the 1970s and then with the National Association for Sport and Physical Education (NASPE).

The current structure, the Adapted Physical Activity Council (APAC), was created in 1985 by the merger of Therapeutics and Adapted Physical Education and assigned to ARAPCS, where it was mentored by executive director Ray Ciszek until his retirement in 1994. The name of ARAPCS changed in 1993 to the American Association for Active Lifestyles and Fitness (AAALF); since October 1994 Janet Seaman has been its executive director. Although superbly qualified in all the areas encompassed by AAALF, Seaman is particularly well-known in adapted physical education. She is senior author of *The New Adapted Physical Education: A Developmental Approach* (Seaman & DePauw, 1982, 1989) and a pioneer in the advocacy of interagency and crossdisciplinary collaboration. Seaman's (1995) most recent book pertains to fitness assessment and inclusion. Prior to joining the AAHPERD staff, Seaman had taught adapted physical education and served in various administrative capacities at the California State University of Los Angeles (CSULA) for 22 years. She is the first individual identified with adapted physical education to work at national headquarters since Julian Stein's leadership there from 1965 to 1981.

Julian Stein is associated with several structures within AAHPERD headquarters, and many consider him the most outstanding mentor that adapted physical education has ever had.

- Chairman of the Task Force on Recreation and Fitness for the Mentally Retarded (1965-66)
- Director of the Project on Recreation and Fitness for the Mentally Retarded (1966-68)
- Executive Director of the Unit on Programs for the Handicapped (1968-81)

During tenure in these positions, Stein traveled widely, conducting workshops and consulting. Concurrently, he published and disseminated over 100 books on various aspects of adapted physical education, advocated legislation, and mentored many faculty members in universities around the world. In 1989 AAHPERD formally recognized Stein's many contributions by giving him the R. Tait McKenzie Award and calling him the "father of contemporary adapted physical activity in the world today."

National Consortium for Physical Education and Recreation for Individuals With Disabilities (NCPERID). This organization began in 1973 as an ad hoc committee of grant directors and formally incorporated as a consortium in 1975. Its purpose was to promote, stimulate, encourage, and conduct professional preparation and research; leaders achieved this purpose largely through working with the Bureau of Education for the Handicapped (BEH), which became the Office of Special Education Programs (OSEP) in 1980. These Washington, DC, structures were responsible for administering grants authorized by the federal government, and physical education and recreation leaders soon learned it was prudent to guide and monitor the distribution of monies allocated to their professions. NCPERID members thus were active in grants review and evaluation and in advocacy for legislation supportive of its purpose.

Two federal government employees have been particularly helpful in working with NCPERID: Bill Hillman from 1967 to the early 1980s, when he retired, and Martha Bokee thereafter. Hillman and Bokee thus tend to be associated, respectively, with BEH and OSEP.

Hillman, a therapeutic recreation specialist, and Louis Bowers, an adapted physical educator, are acknowledged as the founding fathers of NCPERID (Sherrill, 1988), although Joseph Winnick, Leon Johnson, John Nesbitt, and Joan Moran served as co-chairs in the years before incorporation. Thereafter, the presidency alternated between physical education and recreation leaders until 1991, when the membership agreed to elect the best qualified leader each year, regardless of specialization (see table 3.2). Each of these individuals contributed immeasurably to the development of adapted physical education by assuring that federal funding was equitably distributed, that legislation for human rights was enacted, and that directions and trends for personnel preparation and research were clearly communicated to BEH and OSEP employees and grant writers.

NCPERID has received two federal grants to enhance personnel preparation. The first, from 1975 to 1978, was entitled "A Training Program in Special Education for State Education Directors of Physical Education and Special Education." This grant supplied funds and personnel to enhance nationwide inservice training concerning the **PL 94-142** mandate that all students with disabilities should receive physical education instruction in the least restrictive environment possible. The second grant, from 1992 to 1997, has focused on the establishment of national standards to guide adapted physical education instruction in the least restrictive environment possible. The second grant, from 1992 to 1997, has focused on the establishment of national standards to guide adapted physical education personnel preparation and employment (Kelly, 1992; National Consortium for Physical Education and Recreation for Individuals With Disabilities, 1995). These standards, written in learning objectives format, are categorized into 15 content areas essential to adapted physical education service delivery. Plans are underway to develop protocol for determining whether practitioners have adequate knowledge in each of these areas.

Table 3.2   Physical Education Presidents of the National Consortium for Physical Education and Recreation for Individuals With Disabilities

Year	President	Location
1975	Leon Johnson	University of Missouri
1977	Claudine Sherrill	Texas Woman's University
1979	Joseph Winnick	SUNY at Brockport
1981	John Dunn	Oregon State University
1983	Ernie Bundschuh	University of Georgia
1985	Louis Bowers	University of South Florida
1987	Michael Churton	Appalachian State University North Carolina
1989	John Hall	University of Kentucky
1991	Luke Kelly	University of Virginia
1992	Jeff McCubbin	Oregon State University
1994	Gail Webster	Kennesaw State College, Georgia
1997	David Porretta	Ohio State University

Note. Recreation professionals served as president during even years until 1991, when bylaws were changed to two-year terms with all members eligible to hold the presidency.

International Federation of Adapted Physical Activity (IFAPA).
Founded in 1973 in Quebec City, Canada, this organization began in 1977 to hold symposia every other year. Illustrative proceedings include those edited by Doll-Tepper, Dahms, Doll, and von Selzam (1990) and Eason, Smith, and Caron (1983). The mission of IFAPA is to initiate, encourage, and coordinate national, regional, and international functions (both governmental and nongovernmental) that pertain to sport, dance, aquatics, exercise, fitness, and wellness for individuals of all ages with disabilities or special needs. IFAPA is officially linked with several other international governing bodies, including the International Paralympic Committee (IPC) and the International Council of Sport Science and Physical Education (ICSSPE).

The IFAPA Board includes elected representatives from seven regions of the world: Africa, Asia, Central and South America, Europe, Middle East, North America, and Oceania. Through these representatives, IFAPA is striving to establish adapted physical activity service delivery, personnel preparation, and research in every country of the world. Since 1994, the *Adapted Physical Activity Quarterly* (*APAQ*) has served as the official journal of IFAPA.

Sport Organizations.   Organizations related to Deaf Sport, Special Olympics, and Paralympics have also evolved knowledge important in adapted physical activity (Steadward, Nelson, & Wheeler, 1994). Deaf sport was formally organized in 1924 and continues to hold its international competitions separate from those of other organizations. Special Olympics, initiated in 1968, serves only athletes with mental retardation. The Paralympic movement began in 1960 with wheelchair sport but has subsequently expanded to include all disabilities except deafness. The Paralympics parallel the Olympics in that summer and winter games are held quadrennially in the same year and country as the Olympics. The International Coordinating Committee (ICC) of the World Sports Organizations for the Disabled was the governing body from 1984 to 1992. The International Paralympic Committee (IPC) was established in 1989 but did not become the governing organization until after the Paralympic Games in Barcelona in 1992.

Athletes with spinal cord injuries, postpolio, and amputations comprise most of the Paralympic competitors. Athletes with blindness were invited into the Paralympics in 1976, and ambulatory athletes with cerebral palsy, stroke, and traumatic brain injury were added in 1980. Athletes with cerebral palsy in wheelchairs and those with *les autres* conditions (i.e., other locomotor impairments like dwarfism and multiple sclerosis) did not compete until 1984. The 1996 Paralympics in Atlanta marked the first time that athletes with learning difficulties were allowed to participate, but inclusion of this group continues to be debated. The international organization that provides for athletes with learning disabilities is not Special Olympics but the International Sport Federation for Persons With Mental Handicaps (INASFMH), founded in the Netherlands in 1986.

The term *disability sport* is preferred over *adapted sport* in the Paralympic movement. Separate organizations exist for each disability because equipment, sports, rules, strategies, equity classifications, training, and medical concerns vary, each comprising a separate body of knowledge (see table 3.3). Adapted physical activity specialists are expected to collaborate with each organization and to provide research to guide training and coaching practices.

Present and Future

Beliefs about the rights and needs of persons with impairments and disabilities have changed over the centuries. Likewise beliefs about the nature and scope of adapted physical activity have changed and will continue to change. This continuous state of flux causes widespread individual differences in the ways that leaders perceive adapted physical activity. However, there is growing consensus that all persons (regardless of age, gender, impairment, social class, race/ethnicity) should have equal access

Table 3.3 Major Disability Sport Organizations in 1996

AAAD	American Athletic Association for the Deaf
DAAA	Dwarf Athletic Association of America
DS/USA	Disabled Sports/USA, previously National Handicapped Sports
NWBA	National Wheelchair Basketball Association
SOI	Special Olympics International
USABA	United States Association for Blind Athletes
USCPAA	United States Cerebral Palsy Athletic Association
USLASA	United States Les Autres Sports Association
WS-USA	Wheelchair Sports USA, previously National Wheelchair Athletic Association

to physical activity opportunity and resources, and that programming should be inclusive and least restrictive. Crossdisciplinary knowledge is needed now, more than ever before, about individual and environmental variables that affect achievement of active, healthy lifestyle, productive employment, and rich, satisfying leisure.

New, Creative Approaches

New approaches to organizing and synthesizing adapted physical activity knowledge are needed. One such approach calls for dividing this knowledge into declarative, procedural, and affective components. *Declarative* knowledge refers to factual information (biological, sociological, psychological) about individual differences traditionally designated as impairments, disabilities, and handicaps, and environmental variables that affect movement success, lifespan wellness, acceptance, integration, and inclusion. *Procedural* knowledge refers to understandings about processes (e.g., adaptation, normalization, socialization, inclusion, self-actualization, transition, empowerment) and services (planning, assessment, placement, instruction, counseling, coaching, evaluation, advocacy) delivered in a variety of settings. *Affective* knowledge refers to understanding and appreciation of self and others in relation to social minorities and the ecosystems of diversity. Affective knowledge encompasses beliefs, attitudes, behavioral intentions, and advocacy actions.

This approach to organizing knowledge supports the contemporary definition of adapted physical activity presented earlier in this chapter: crossdisciplinary theory and practice related to lifespan physical activity of individuals with psychomotor needs who require particular expertise in such processes as adaptation, ecological task analysis, integration, inclusion, and empowerment. This expertise can come from an adapted physical education specialist or a regular physical educator.

The trend toward integration and inclusion of all individuals into regular physical education and recreation settings creates more diversity than the average professional with four years of undergraduate training can handle. This is particularly true in schools where class sizes exceed 25. In the future, team teaching and regular consultant help will become common practice. Adapted physical education specialists will be employed routinely in team teaching and consultant roles and will work together side by side, sharing the same facilities and resources. Additionally, adapted physical educators will collaborate more with parents and families in the development of home-school physical activity programs and will be employed increasingly in community agencies that provide lifespan exercise, fitness, sport, and recreation programs accessible to everyone.

Athletes with disabilities will increasingly earn advanced degrees in adapted physical activity and find employment in all kinds of settings. They will teach, coach, and counsel individuals with and without disabilities and become more visible in all walks of life. Legislation may be needed to assure access to jobs, but meaningful contact between individuals with different strengths and weaknesses will eventually lead to acceptance and appreciation.

A continuing problem that needs resolution is quality control of adapted physical activity professionals. Only 14 states have defined an endorsement or certification in adapted physical education (National Consortium for Physical Education and Recreation for Individuals With Disabilities, 1995), although leaders have worked toward this goal in nearly every state. Leaders have also worked toward the goal of an adapted physical education specialist in every school district, who serves partly in an administrative and consultant role to regular and special educators as well as to other adapted physical activity professionals in the school system and community. Much time and effort is still needed to help the general public understand the potential contributions of adapted physical activity service delivery and to know the difference between it and occupational and physical therapy.

Current Developments

Other developments appear to be defining the immediate and/or long-range history of the discipline:

1. The European Master's Degree Program in Adapted Physical Activity, begun in September 1991, at the Institute of Physical Education in Leuven, Belgium. This program, now the result of cooperation among over 20 European universities, offers insights into new ways to use resources and is encouraging networking and sharing. The fierce competition among grant writers in the United States needs study with the introduction of new paradigms to promote cooperation.

2. Continued funding of graduate-level adapted physical education leadership training programs by the U.S. government and advocacy for higher education institutions and other agencies to increase fiscal commitment to this specialization (Dunn & McCubbin, 1991; Sherrill, 1988).

3. Continued documentation of the need for diversified, well-qualified professionals with doctoral degrees in adapted physical activity (Dunn & McCubbin, 1991) and progress toward the creation of standards to guide professional preparation (Kelly, 1992) and postdoctoral contributions to the discipline (Lavay & Lasko-McCarthey, 1992; Reid, 1993).

4. Gradual shifting of emphasis in the specialization from school-based to lifespan perspectives and improvement of quality of research and textbooks, particularly with regard to inclusion of theories (Sherrill, 1993).

5. New understandings that the energies of leaders should be more equitably balanced between professional concerns (roles and competencies) and disciplinary needs (theories and conceptual frameworks).

6. Publication of advanced, specialized textbooks and collections of scholarly papers with emphasis on theory and theorizing. Works by Reid (1990) and Sugden and Keogh (1990) illustrate this trend.

7. Closer collaboration between leaders in Canada and the United States as evidenced by the formation of the North American Federation of Adapted Physical Activity in 1994.

8. Increased networking between adapted physical activity and sport leaders of many nations. In January 1994, the *Adapted Physical Activity Quarterly* officially became an international journal, thereby encouraging identification and sharing of resources around the world. In August 1996, many adapted physical activity specialists presented research at the Third Paralympic Congress in Atlanta.

Future Relationship to Exercise and Sport Science

Adapted physical activity will remain closely associated with exercise and sport science and will contribute significantly to broadening the scope of its various subdisciplines to include the full range of individual differences. Undergraduate study in exercise and sport science will continue to serve as the foundation for a graduate specialization in adapted physical activity that merges knowledge from many areas both within and outside of the kinesiology domain. There will be more collaboration among scholars, more concern about the ethics and morality of inclusion and exclusion, and more emphasis on social justice and equity.

Adapted physical activity may act as a catalyst and a conscience in promoting scholarly inquiry into marginality of all kinds. Commonalities among ethnic group, senior citizen, gender, and disability/impairment issues will increasingly be recognized, and scholars who today focus narrowly on one population will use their combined expertise to strengthen such subdisciplines as sport sociology, sport psychology, pedagogy, philosophy, and history.

The long, rich history of adapted physical education/activity as the crossdisciplinary partner of mainstream exercise and sport science substantiates the need for parallel patterns of scholarly inquiry and specialization similar to those represented by special education and regular education and by the Olympics, Paralympics, and Special Olympics. Specialization, however, should not mean fragmentation. The future will bring more joint research and theorizing, more joint application, and more collaboration, as leaders create new paradigms and explore alternative strategies for facilitating equal access, integration, inclusion, and infusion.

Implications of Further Specialization

Further specialization in adapted physical activity may occur within declarative, procedural, and affective knowledge components but many leaders believe that today's first priority should be critical, creative thinking and decision making about philosophy and future directions as both a profession and a scholarly discipline. Consensus that adapted physical activity doctoral students should complete an academic specialization in at least one other area (e.g., special education, biomechanics, motor learning, sociology) is leading to a new generation of university faculty with crossdisciplinary research interests and skills.

Adapted physical activity will be proactive in regard to the ever-changing knowledge base of exercise and sport science. Further specialization, however, must be balanced at the doctoral level and beyond with seminars, coursework, and projects that promote crossdisciplinary integration, application, and discovery.

References

American Association for Health, Physical Education, and Recreation (1968a). *Physical activities for the mentally retarded*. Washington, DC: Author.

American Association for Health, Physical Education, and Recreation (1968b). *Programming for the mentally retarded in physical education and recreation*. Washington, DC: Author.

American Association for Health, Physical Education, and Recreation (1968c). *Special fitness test manual for mildly mentally retarded persons*. Washington, DC: Author.

American Association for Health, Physical Education, and Recreation (1973). *Guidelines for professional preparation programs for personnel involved in physical education and recreation for the handicapped*. Washington, DC: Author.

American Association on Mental Retardation. (1992). *Mental retardation: Definition, classification, and systems of supports* (9th ed.). Washington, DC: Author.

Arnheim, D., Auxter, D., & Crowe, W. (1969, 1977). *Principles and methods of adapted physical education*. St. Louis: Mosby.

Auxter, D. (1966). Strength and flexibility of differentially diagnosed educable mentally retarded boys. *Research Quarterly, 37*, 455-461.

Auxter, D., & Pyfer, J. (1985). *Principles and methods of adapted physical education and recreation* (5th ed.). St. Louis: Mosby.

Auxter, D., Pyfer, J., & Huettig, C. (1993). *Principles and methods of adapted physical education and recreation* (7th ed.). St. Louis: Times Mirror/ Mosby.

Barr, M.W. (1905). *Mental defectives* cited in M.W. Barr (1905). Classification of mental defectives. *Journal of Psycho-Asthenics, 9*(2), 35.

Beard, G. (1961). A review of the first forty years in terms of education, practice, and research. *Physical Therapy Review, 41*(12), 843-861.

Boring, E.G. (1950). *A history of experimental psychology* (2nd ed.). New York: Appleton-Century-Crofts.

Bowers, L. (1975). *Play learning centers for preschool handicapped*. BEH Research and Demonstration Project Report. University of South Florida, Tampa.

Bowers, L. (1979). Toward a science of playground design: Principles of design for play centers for all children. *Journal of Physical Education and Recreation, 50*, 51-53.

Brace, D.K. (1948). Motor learning of feeble-minded girls. *Research Quarterly, 19*, 269-275.

Brace, D.K. (1968). Physical education and recreation of mentally retarded pupils in public schools. *Research Quarterly, 39*, 779-782.

Broadhead, G.D. (1972). Gross motor performance in minimally brain injured children. *Journal of Motor Behavior, 4*, 103-111.

Broadhead, G.D. (1981). Time passages in adapted physical education. In G.A. Brooks (Ed.). *Perspectives on the academic discipline of physical education* (pp. 234-252). Champaign, IL: Human Kinetics.

Broadhead, G.D. (1983). Research directions in adapted physical activity. In R.L. Eason, T.L. Smith, & F. Caron (Eds.). *Adapted physical activity: From theory to application* (pp. 329-341). Champaign, IL: Human Kinetics.

Broadhead, G.D. (1984). Birth of a journal. *Adapted Physical Activity Quarterly, 1*, 1-2.

Broadhead, G.D. (1986). Adapted physical education research trends: 1970-1990. *Adapted Physical Activity Quarterly, 3*, 104-111.

Broadhead, G.D., & Brunt, D. (1982). Physical education training implications of a public law about handicapped children. *American Corrective Therapy Journal*, **36**, 9-13.

Bruininks, R.H. (1974). Physical and motor development of retarded persons. In N.R. Ellis (Ed.). *International Review of Research in Mental Retardation* (pp. 209-261). New York: Academic Press.

Burke, P.J. (1976). Personnel preparation: Historical perspective. *Exceptional Children*, **43**, 144-147.

Canadian Association for Health, Physical Education, and Recreation (1988). *Jasper Talks: Strategies for change in adapted physical activity in Canada*. Ottawa, Canada: Author.

Chasey, W.C., & Wyrick, W. (1971). Effects of a physical developmental program on psychomotor ability of retarded children. *American Journal on Mental Deficiency*, **75**, 566-570.

Churton, M.W. (1984a). I'M SPECIAL review, Part I. *Adapted Physical Activity Quarterly*, **1**(1), 89-94.

Churton, M.W. (1984b). I'M SPECIAL review, Part II. *Adapted Physical Activity Quarterly*, **1**(4), 332-336.

Churton, M.W. (1987). Impact of the Education of the Handicapped Act on adapted physical education: A 10-year overview. *Adapted Physical Activity Quarterly*, **4**, 1-8.

Clark, J.E., & Whitall, J. (1989). What is motor development? The lessons of history. *Quest*, **41**, 183-202.

Clarke, H.H., & Clarke, D.H. (1978). *Developmental and adapted physical education (2nd ed.)*. Englewood Cliffs, NJ: Prentice Hall.

Committee on Adapted Physical Education (1952). Guiding principles for adapted physical education. *Journal of Health, Physical Education, and Recreation*, **23**, 15.

Corder, W. (1966). Effects of physical education on the intellectual, physical, and social development of educable mentally retarded boys. *Exceptional Children*, **32**, 357-364.

Cratty, B.J. (1967). *Developmental sequences of perceptual-motor tasks: Movement activities for neurologically handicapped and retarded children and youth*. Freeport, NY: Educational Activities, Inc.

Cratty, B.J. (1969a). *Motor activity and the education of retardates*. Philadelphia: Lea & Febiger.

Cratty, B.J. (1969b). *Perceptual-motor behavior and educational processes*. Springfield, IL: Charles C. Thomas.

Cratty, B.J. (1980). *Adapted physical education for handicapped children and youth*. Denver: Love.

Cratty, B.J. (1989). *Adapted physical education in the mainstream* (2nd ed.). Denver: Love.

Crocker, P.R.E. (1993). Sport and exercise psychology and research with individuals with disabilities: Using theory to advance knowledge. *Adapted Physical Activity Quarterly*, **10**(4), 324-335.

Daniels, A.S. (1954). *Adapted physical education*. New York: Harper & Row.

Daniels, A.S., & Davies, E.A. (1975). *Adapted physical education* (3rd ed.). New York: Harper & Row.

Davis, W.E. (1973). An ecological approach to perceptual-motor learning. In R.L. Eason, T.L. Smith, & F. Caron (Eds.). *Adapted physical activity: From theory to application* (pp. 162-171). Champaign, IL: Human Kinetics.

DePauw, K.P. (1979). Nationwide survey of professional preparation in adapted physical education. *California Association for Health, Physical Education, and Recreation Journal/Times*, **42**(2), 28.

DePauw, K.P. (1986). Merger of special populations programs within the American Alliance for Health, Physical Education, Recreation and Dance. *Adapted Physical Activity Quarterly*, **3**(2), 139-141.

DePauw, K.P. (1990). Sport, society, and individuals with disabilities. In G. Reid (Ed.). *Problems in movement control* (pp. 319-337). New York: Elsevier Science.

DePauw, K.P. (1992). Current international trends in research in adapted physical activity. In T. Williams, L. Almond, & A. Sparkes (Eds.). *Sport and physical activity: Moving towards excellence* (pp. 221-228). London: E & FN SPON.

DePauw, K.P., & Bundschuh, E. (1988). Vintage years: Competency, certification, and licensure in adapted physical education. In C. Sherrill (Ed.). *Leadership training in adapted physical education* (pp. 290-300). Champaign, IL: Human Kinetics.

DePauw, K.P., & Doll-Tepper, G. (1989). European perspectives on adapted physical activity. *Adapted Physical Activity Quarterly*, **6**, 95-99.

DePauw, K.P., & Gavron, S. (1995). *Disability and sport*. Champaign, IL: Human Kinetics.

DePauw, K.P., & Goc Karp, G. (1992). Framework for conducting pedagogical research in teaching physical education to include diverse populations. In T. Williams, L. Almond, & A. Sparkes (Eds.). *Sport and physical activity: Moving towards excellence* (pp. 243-248). London: E & FN SPON.

DePauw, K.P., & Goc Karp, G. (1994). Integrating knowledge of disability throughout the physical education curriculum: An infusion approach. *Adapted Physical Activity Quarterly*, **11**(1), 3-13.

DePauw, K.P., & Sherrill, C. (1994). Adapted physical activity: Present and future. *Physical Education Review*, **17**(1), 6-13.

Doll-Tepper, G. (1990). Controversies and current tendencies in physical education and sport for the mentally retarded: An international comparison. In A. Vermeer (Ed.). *Motor development, adapted physical activity, and mental retardation* (pp. 78-84). Basel, Switzerland: Karger.

Doll-Tepper, G., Dahms, C., Doll, B., & von Selzam, H. (Eds.) (1990). *Adapted physical activity: An interdisciplinary approach*. Berlin: Springer-Verlag.

Doll-Tepper, G., & DePauw, K.P. (1996). Theory and practice of adapted physical activity: Research perspectives. *Sport Science Review, 5*(1), 1-11.

Drew, L.C. (1922). *Individual gymnastics: A handbook of corrective and remedial gymnastics*. Philadelphia: Lea & Febiger.

Dunn, J.M. (1980). *A data-based gymnasium*. Monmouth, OR: Instructional Development Corporation.

Dunn, J.M. (1983). Physical activity for the severely handicapped: Theoretical and practical considerations. In R.L. Eason, T.L. Smith, & F. Caron (Eds.). *Adapted physical activity: From theory to application* (pp. 63-73). Champaign, IL: Human Kinetics.

Dunn, J.M. (1986). The life and influence of Hollis Francis Fait on adapted (special) physical education. *Adapted Physical Activity Quarterly, 3*, 156-166.

Dunn, J.M., & Fait, H. (1989). *Special physical education: Adapted, individualized, developmental* (6th ed.). Dubuque, IA: Brown.

Dunn, J.M., & McCubbin, J.A. (1991). Preparation of leadership personnel in adapted physical education. *Adapted Physical Activity Quarterly, 8*(2), 128-135.

Eason, R.L., Smith, T.L., & Caron, F. (Eds.). (1983). *Adapted physical activity: From theory to application*. Champaign, IL: Human Kinetics.

Eichstaedt, C.B., & Kalakian, L.H. (1987). *Developmental/adapted physical education: Making ability count* (2nd ed.). Minneapolis: Burgess.

Ersing, W. (1972). Current directions of professional preparation in adapted physical education. *Journal of Health, Physical Education, and Recreation, 43*(8), 78-79.

Ersing, W. (1988). Program models in adapted physical education: Implications for teacher training. In C. Sherrill (Ed.). *Leadership training in adapted physical education* (pp. 191-198). Champaign, IL: Human Kinetics.

Ersing, W., & Wheeler, R. (1971). The status of professional preparation in adapted physical education. *American Corrective Therapy Journal, 25*(4), 111-118.

Fait, H. (1960). *Adapted physical education*. Philadelphia: Saunders.

Fait, H. (1966). *Special physical education* (2nd ed.). Philadelphia: Saunders.

Fait, H. (1972). *Special physical education* (3rd ed.). Philadelphia: Saunders.

Fait, H. (1978). *Special physical education* (4th ed.). Philadelphia: Saunders.

Fait, H. (1983). Evaluation of motor skills of the handicapped: Theory and practice. In R.L. Eason, T.L. Smith, & F. Caron (Eds.). *Adapted physical activity: From theory to application* (pp. 172-179). Champaign, IL: Human Kinetics.

Fait, H., & Dunn, J. (1984). *Special physical education* (5th ed.). Philadelphia: Saunders.

Fait, H., & Kupferer, H. (1956). A study of two motor achievement tests and its implications in planning physical education activities for the mentally retarded. *American Journal of Mental Deficiency, 60*, 729-732.

Farrell, P., & Lundegren, H.M. (1983). *The process of recreation programming* (2nd ed.). New York: Wiley.

Francis, R.J., & Rarick, G.L. (1959). Motor characteristics of the mentally retarded. *American Journal of Mental Deficiency*, **63**, 792-811.

French, R.W., Jansma, P., & Winnick, J.P. (1978). Preparing undergraduate regular physical educators for mainstreaming. *American Corrective Therapy Journal*, **32**, 43-48.

Frostig, M., & Maslow, P. (1970). *Movement education: Theory and practice.* Chicago: Follett.

Galton, F. (1883). *Inquiries into human faculty and its development.* London: Macmillan.

Galton, F. (1889). *Natural inheritance.* London: Macmillan.

Grover, M., & Christaldi, J. (1966). *A practical program of remedial physical education.* Philadelphia: Lea & Febiger.

Gulick, L.H. (1890). Physical education: A new profession. *Proceedings of the American Association for the Advancement of Physical Education*, Ithaca, NY, pp. 59-66. Included in A. Weston (1962, pp. 145-149).

Hallahan, D.P., & Cruickshank, W.M. (1973). *Psychoeducational foundations of learning disabilities.* Englewood Cliffs, NJ: Prentice Hall.

Hallahan, D.P., & Kauffman, J.M. (1978). *Exceptional children.* Englewood Cliffs, NJ: Prentice-Hall.

Hawley, G. (1937). *The kinesiology of corrective exercise.* Philadelphia: Lea & Febiger.

Hazenhyer, I.M. (1946). A history of the American Physiotherapy Association. *Physiotherapy Review*, **26**(1), 3-14.

Henry, F.M. (1964). Physical education—An academic discipline. *67th Proceedings: Annual Meeting of the National College Physical Education Association for Men*, 6-9.

Hillman, W.A. (1986). The role of the federal government in adapted physical education. *Adapted Physical Activity Quarterly*, **3**, 124-126.

Hooley, A.M. (1964). *A study of certification and course work practices in the preparation of teachers for the area of adapted physical education.* Unpublished manuscript, Bowling Green State University, Bowling Green, OH.

Hurley, D. (1981). Guidelines for adapted physical education. *Journal of Physical Education, Recreation, and Dance*, **52**, 43-44.

Hutt, M.L., & Gibby, R.G. (1965). *The mentally retarded child: Development, education, and treatment* (2nd ed.). Boston: Allyn & Bacon.

Jansma, P., & French, R. (1994). *Special physical education: Physical activity, sports, and recreation* (2nd ed.). Englewood Cliffs, NJ: Prentice Hall.

Johnson, W. (1971). Children's physical development clinic. In American Association for Health, Physical Education, and Recreation (Ed.). *The best of challenge*, Volume 1 (pp. 102-103). Washington, DC: AAHPER.

Kavale, K., & Mattson, P.D. (1983). One jumped off the balance beam: Meta-analysis of perceptual-motor training. *Journal of Learning Disabilities*, **16**, 165-173.

Kelly, E.D. (1965). *Adapted and corrective physical education* (4th ed.). New York: Ronald Press. (Earlier editions in 1928, 1950, 1958 with G. Stafford as senior author)

Kelly, L.E. (1993). Adapted physical education national standards: A call for action. *Palaestra,* **10**(1), 15-18.

Keogh, J.F., & Oliver, J.N. (1968). A clinical study of physically awkward educational subnormal boys. *Research Quarterly,* **39**, 301-307.

Kephart, N.C. (1960). *The slow learner in the classroom.* Columbus, OH: Merrill. (Second ed., 1971)

Kiphard, E. (1983). Adapted physical education in Germany. In R.L. Eason, T.L. Smith, & F. Caron (Eds.). *Adapted physical activity: From theory to application* (pp. 25-32). Champaign, IL: Human Kinetics.

Lapriola, E.M. (1972). *The Joseph P. Kennedy, Jr. Foundation and its role in physical education and recreation for the mentally retarded.* Unpublished master's thesis, University of Maryland, College Park.

LaVay, B., & Lasko-McCarthey, P. (1992). Adapted physical activity research: Issues and recommendations. *Adapted Physical Activity Quarterly,* **9**, 189-196.

Lee, M., & Bennett, B. (1985). Alliance centennial—100 years of health, physical education, recreation, and dance. *Journal of Physical Education, Recreation, and Dance,* **56**(4), 17-67.

Leonard, F.E. (1923). *A guide to the history of physical education.* Philadelphia: Lea & Febiger.

Ling, P.H. (1840). *General principles of gymnastics.* Edited by C.A. Georgii and P.J. Liedbeck, and published one year after Ling's death. Described in F.E. Leonard (1923, p. 155).

Lippitt, L. (1923). A manual of corrective gymnastics. New York: Macmillan.

Logan, G. (1964). *Adaptations of muscular activity.* Dubuque, IA: Brown.

Londeree, B.R., & Johnson, L.E. (1974). Motor fitness of TMR vs EMR and normal children. *Medicine and Science in Sports,* **6**, 247-252.

Lowman, C., Colestock, C., & Cooper, H. (1928). *Corrective physical education for groups.* New York: Barnes.

Mathews, D.K., Kruse, R., & Shaw, V. (1962). *The science of physical education for handicapped children.* New York: Harper & Brothers.

McKenzie, R.T. (1909, 1915, 1923). *Exercise in education and medicine.* Philadelphia: Saunders.

Melograno, V., & Loovis, E.M. (1991). Status of physical education for handicapped students: A comparative analysis of 1980 and 1988. *Adapted Physical Activity Quarterly,* **8**, 28-42.

Metcalf, H.G. (1929). Status of special adaptive corrective procedures in colleges and larger universities. *American Physical Education Review,* **34**, 208.

Metcalf, H.G. (1934). *The establishment in the public schools of educational procedures for children with physical defects.* Unpublished PhD dissertation, New York University.

Morisbak, I. (1990). Adapted physical education: The role of the teacher and pedagogical practices. In G. Doll-Tepper, C. Dahms, B. Doll, & H. v. Selzam (Eds.) *Adapted physical activity: An interdisciplinary approach* (pp. 235-243). Berlin: Springer-Verlag.

National Consortium for Physical Education and Recreation for Individuals with Disabilities. (1995). *Adapted physical education national standards*. Champaign, IL: Human Kinetics.

Nissen, H. (1892). *ABC of Swedish educational gymnastics*. New York: Educational Publishing.

Nixon, J.E. (1967). The criteria of a discipline. *Quest* (Monograph IX, Winter), 42-48.

Oliver, J.N. (1958). The effect of physical conditioning exercises and activities on the mental characteristics of educationally subnormal boys. *British Journal of Educational Psychology, 28*, 155-165.

Oliver, J.N. (1960). The effect of physical conditioning on the sociometric status of educationally subnormal boys. *Physical Education, 52*, 38-40.

Porretta, D.L., Nesbitt, J., & Labanowich, S. (1993). Terminology usage: A case for clarity. *Adapted Physical Activity Quarterly, 10*(2), 87-96.

Posse, N. (1890). *The Swedish system of educational gymnastics*. Boston: Lee and Shepard.

Posse, N. (1891). *Handbook of school gymnastics of the Swedish system*. Boston: Lothrop, Lee, & Shepard.

Posse, N. (1894). *The special kinesiology of educational gymnastics*. Boston: Lee and Shepard.

Pyfer, J. (1986). Early research concerns in adapted physical education, 1930-1969. *Adapted Physical Activity Quarterly, 3*, 95-103.

Pyfer, J., & Carlson, B.R. (1972). Characteristic motor development of children with learning disabilities. *Perceptual and Motor Skills, 35*, 291-296.

Rarick, G.L. (1973). Motor performance of mentally retarded children. In G.L. Rarick (Ed.). *Physical activity: Human growth and development* (pp. 225-256). New York: Academic Press.

Rarick, G.L. (1980). Cognitive-motor relationships in the growing years. *Research Quarterly for Exercise and Sport, 51*(1), 174-192.

Rarick, G.L. (1983). Summary of pedagogy sessions. In R.L. Eason, T.L. Smith, & F. Caron (Eds.). *Adapted physical activity: From theory to application* (pp. 325-328). Champaign, IL: Human Kinetics.

Rarick, G.L., Dobbins, D.A., & Broadhead, G.D. (1976). *The motor domain and its correlates in educationally handicapped children*. Englewood Cliffs, NJ: Prentice Hall.

Rarick, G.L., Widdop, J.H., & Broadhead, G.D. (1970). The physical fitness and motor performance of educable mentally retarded children. *Exceptional Children, 37*, 509-519.

Rathbone, J. (1934). *Corrective physical education*. Philadelphia: Saunders.

Rathbone, J. (1989). *My twentieth century*. Springfield, MA: Springfield College Press.

Rathbone, J., & Hunt, V. (1965). *Corrective physical education* (7th ed.). Philadelphia: Saunders.

Reid, G. (1989). Ideas about motor behavior research with special populations. *Adapted Physical Activity Quarterly, 6*, 1-10.

Reid, G. (Ed.) (1990). *Problems in movement control: Advances in psychology.* Amsterdam: North-Holland.

Reid, G. (1992). Editorial on theory, exchange, and terminology. *Adapted Physical Activity Quarterly, 9*, 1-4.

Reid, G. (1993). Motor behavior and individuals with disabilities: Linking research and practice. *Adapted Physical Activity Quarterly, 10*(4), 359-370.

Reid, G., & Broadhead, G.D. (1995). *APAQ* at Ten: A documentary analysis. *Adapted Physical Activity Quarterly, 12*(2), 103-112.

Rimmer, J.H. (1993). *Fitness and rehabilitation programs for special populations.* Dubuque, IA: Brown & Benchmark.

Rizzo, T.L., & Davis, W.E. (1991). The functional exclusion of adapted physical education. *Journal of Physical Education, Recreation, and Dance, 62*, 53-55.

Rizzo, T.L., & Vispoel, W.P. (1991). Physical educators' attributes and attitudes toward teaching students with handicaps. *Adapted Physical Activity Quarterly, 8*, 4-11.

Robinson, N.M., & Robinson, H.B. (1965). *The mentally retarded child: A psychological approach.* New York: McGraw-Hill.

Roy, E.A. (1990). The interface between normality and pathology in understanding motor function. In G. Reid (Ed.). *Problems in movement control* (pp. 3-30). New York: Elsevier Science.

Salkind, N.J. (1985). *Theories of human development* (2nd ed.). New York: Wiley.

Schwendener, N. (1942). *A history of physical education in the United States.* New York: Barnes.

Seaman, J.A. (Ed.) (1995). *Physical best and individuals with disabilities: A handbook for inclusion in fitness programs.* Reston, VA: American Alliance for Health, Physical Education, Recreation and Dance.

Seaman, J.A., & DePauw, K.P. (1982). *The new adapted physical education: A developmental approach.* Palo Alto, CA: Mayfield.

Seaman, J.A., & DePauw, K.P. (1989). *The new adapted physical education: A developmental approach* (2nd ed.). Palo Alto, CA: Mayfield. (1st ed. in 1982)

Seaman, J.A., & Heilbuth, L. (1988). Competencies needed to function in the interdisciplinary arena. In C. Sherrill (Ed.). *Leadership training in adapted physical education* (pp. 162-168). Champaign, IL: Human Kinetics.

Seguin, E. (1846). *Idiocy and its diagnosis and treatment by the physiological method.* Translated into English in 1866.

Shephard, R.J. (1993). Research including persons with disabilities: Practical issues and contributions to knowledge of exercise physiology. *Adapted Physical Activity Quarterly*, **10**(4), 336-345.

Sherrill, C. (1976, 1981, 1986). *Adapted physical education and recreation: A multidisciplinary approach.* Dubuque, IA: Brown.

Sherrill, C. (1982). Adapted physical education: Its role, meaning, and future. *Exceptional Education Quarterly*, **3**(1), 1-9.

Sherrill, C. (Ed.) (1986). *Sport and disabled athletes.* Champaign, IL: Human Kinetics.

Sherrill, C. (1988a). Contemporary adapted physical education teacher training: A history beginning with 1967. In C. Sherrill (Ed.). *Leadership training in adapted physical education* (pp. 43-62). Champaign, IL: Human Kinetics.

Sherrill, C. (1988b). Evolution of a profession: History and contributions of organizations. In C. Sherrill (Ed.). *Leadership training in adapted physical education* (pp. 63-84). Champaign, IL: Human Kinetics.

Sherrill, C. (1988c). Instructional accountability in adapted physical education: A review of research. In C. Sherrill (Ed.). *Leadership training in adapted physical education* (pp. 265-285). Champaign, IL: Human Kinetics.

Sherrill, C. (Ed.) (1988d). *Leadership training in adapted physical education.* Champaign, IL: Human Kinetics.

Sherrill, C. (1988e). Personnel preparation in adapted physical education: Early history. In C. Sherrill (Ed.). *Leadership training in adapted physical education.* (pp. 23-42). Champaign, IL: Human Kinetics.

Sherrill, C. (1990). Interdisciplinary perspectives in adapted physical activity. In G. Doll-Tepper, C. Dahms, B. Doll, & H. v. Selzam (Eds.). *Adapted physical activity: An interdisciplinary approach* (pp. 23-28). Berlin: Springer-Verlag.

Sherrill, C. (1993). *Adapted physical activity, recreation and sport: Crossdisciplinary and lifespan* (4th ed.). Dubuque, IA: Brown & Benchmark.

Sherrill, C. (1995). *Adaptation theory: The essence of our profession and discipline.* Keynote speech at 10th International Symposium of Adapted Physical Activity, Beitostolen, Norway.

Sherrill, C., & Hillman, W. (1988e). Legislation, funding, and adapted physical education teacher training. In C. Sherrill (Ed.). *Leadership training in adapted physical education* (pp. 85-104). Champaign, IL: Human Kinetics.

Shriver, E.K. (1983). Third international symposium on adapted physical activities. In R.L. Eason, T.L. Smith, & F. Caron (Eds.). *Adapted physical activity: From theory to application* (pp. 3-9). Champaign, IL: Human Kinetics.

Skarstrom, W. (1909). *Gymnastic kinesiology.* Springfield, MA: Bassette.

Sloan, S., & Stevens, H.A. (1976). *A century of concern: A history of American Association on Mental Deficiency 1876-1976*. Washington, DC: American Association on Mental Deficiency.

Smith, J.R., & Hurst, J.G. (1961). The relationship of motor abilities and peer acceptance of mentally retarded children. *American Journal of Mental Deficiency, 66*, 81-85.

Spirduso, W.W., & Lovett, D.J. (1987). Current status of graduate education: Program demography. *Quest, 39*(2), 129-141.

Stafford, G.T. (1928). *Preventive and corrective physical education*. New York: Barnes.

Stafford, G.T. (1939, 1947). *Sports for the handicapped*. New York: Prentice Hall.

Stafford, G.T., & Tappan, E.A. (1927). *Practical corrective exercises*. Champaign, IL: Bailey and Himes.

Steadward, R.D. (1996). Integration and sport in the paralympic movement. *Sport Science Review, 5*(1), 26-41.

Steadward, R.D., Nelson, E., & Wheeler, G. (eds.). (1994). *Vista '93: The outlook*. Edmonton, AB: Rick Hansen Centre.

Stein, J. (1963). Motor function and physical fitness of the mentally retarded. *Rehabilitation Literature, 24*, 230-263.

Stein, J. (1969). Professional preparation in physical education and recreation for the mentally retarded. *Education and Training of the Mentally Retarded, 4*, 101-108.

Stein, J. (1983). Bridge over troubled waters—research review and recommendations for relevance. In R.L. Eason, T.L. Smith, & F. Caron (Eds.) *Adapted physical activity: From theory to application* (pp. 189-198). Champaign, IL: Human Kinetics.

Stein, J. (1986). International perspectives: Physical education and sport for participants with handicapping conditions. In C. Sherrill (Ed.). *Sport and disabled athletes* (pp. 51-64). Champaign, IL: Human Kinetics.

Stelmach, G.E. (1987). The cutting edge of research in physical education and exercise science: The search for understanding. *American Academy of Physical Education Papers. No. 20* (pp. 8-25). Champaign, IL: Human Kinetics.

Stone, E.B., & Deyton, J.W. (1951). *Corrective therapy for the handicapped child*. New York: Prentice Hall.

Strauss, A.A., & Kephart, N. (1955). *Psychopathology and education of the brain-injured child*. New York: Grune & Stratton.

Sugden, D.A., & Keogh, J.F. (1990). *Problems in movement skill development*. Columbia: University of South Carolina Press.

Tripp, A., & Sherrill, C. (1991). Attitude theories of relevance to adapted physical education. *Adapted Physical Activity Quarterly, 8*, 12-27.

Van Coppenolle, H. (1993). The European master's degree in adapted physical activity: Training program and research projects. *Abstracts.*

9th International Symposium on Adapted Physical Activity (p. 98). Yokohama, Japan.

Vodola, T. (1973). *Individualized physical education for the handicapped child.* Englewood Cliffs, NJ: Prentice Hall.

Vodola, T. (1976). *Developmental and adapted physical education: A competency-based teacher training manual.* Oakhurst, NJ: PROJECT ACTIVE.

Vodola, T. (1978). *ACTIVE research monograph: Competency-based teacher training and individualized-personalized physical activity.* Oakhurst, NJ: Township of Ocean School District.

Wade, M.G. (Ed.). (1986). *Motor skill acquisition of the mentally handicapped.* Amsterdam: North-Holland.

Walker, L. (1963). *Physical education for the exceptional child.* Dubuque, IA: Brown.

Wessel, J.A. (1976). *I CAN instructional resource materials: Primary skills.* Northbrook, IL: Hubbard.

Wessel, J.A. (Ed.) (1977). *Planning individualized education programs in special education.* Northbrook, IL: Hubbard.

Wessel, J.A. (1983). Quality programming in physical education and recreation for all handicapped persons. In R.L. Eason, T.L. Smith, & F. Caron (Eds.). *Adapted physical activity: From theory to application* (pp. 35-52). Champaign, IL: Human Kinetics.

Wessel, J.A., & Kelly, L. (1986). *Achievement-based curriculum in physical education.* Philadelphia: Lea & Febiger.

Weston, A. (1962). *The making of American physical education.* New York: Appleton-Century-Crofts.

Wheeler, R.H., & Hooley, A.M. (1969). *Physical education for the handicapped.* Philadelphia: Lea & Febiger.

Wheeler, R.H., & Hooley, A.M. (1976). *Physical education for the handicapped* (2nd ed.). Philadelphia: Lea & Febiger.

Winnick, J.P. (1972). Issues and trends in training adapted physical education personnel. *Journal of Health, Physical Education, and Recreation,* **43**(8), 75-78.

Winnick, J.P. (1979). *Early movement experiences and development: Habilitation and remediation.* Philadelphia: Saunders.

Winnick, J.P. (1986). History of adapted physical education: Priorities in professional preparation. *Adapted Physical Activity Quarterly,* **3**, 112-117.

Winnick, J.P. (Ed.) (1990, 1995). *Adapted physical education and sport.* Champaign, IL: Human Kinetics.

Winnick, J.P., & Short, F.X. (1982). *The physical fitness of sensory and orthopedically impaired youth.* Project UNIQUE final report. Brockport: State University of New York.

Winnick, J.P., & Short, F.X. (1984). The physical fitness of youngsters with spinal neuromuscular conditions. *Adapted Physical Activity Quarterly,* **1**, 37-51.

Winnick, J.P., & Short, F.X. (1985). *Physical fitness testing of the disabled: Project UNIQUE*. Champaign, IL: Human Kinetics.

World Health Organization (1980). *International classification of impairments, disabilities, and handicaps: A manual of classification relating to the consequences of disease*. Geneva, Switzerland: Author.

Yabe, K., & Hong, Y.J. (1994). Adapted physical education, health, and fitness in Asian countries. *Physical Education Review, 17*(1), 58-67.

Chronology of Major Textbooks

1890   Posse, N. *The Swedish system of educational gymnastics*

1892   Nissen, H. *ABC of Swedish educational gymnastics*

1909   McKenzie, R.T. *Exercise in education and medicine* (2nd and 3rd eds., 1915, 1923)

1916   Nissen, H. *Practical massage and corrective exercise*

1922   Drew, L.C. *Individual gymnastics: A handbook of corrective and remedial gymnastics*

1927   Stafford, G., & Tappan, E.A. *Practical corrective exercises*

1928   Stafford, G. *Preventive and corrective physical education* (ed. in 1934, 1938, 1946, 1948, 1950, 1958)

1928   Lowman, C., Colestock, E., & Cooper, H. *Corrective physical education for groups*

1934   Rathbone, J. *Corrective physical education* (7 editions, last in 1965 by Rathbone and Hunt, V.)

1939   Stafford, G. *Sports for the handicapped* (2nd ed., 1947)

1954   Daniels, A. *Adapted physical education: Principles and practices of physical education for exceptional students* (2nd ed., Daniels & Davies, 1965; 3rd ed., 1975)

1958   Stafford, G., & Kelly, E. *Preventive and corrective physical education* (3rd ed., author change)

1960   Fait, H. *Adapted physical education* (2nd ed., 1966, *Special physical education*; 3rd-6th eds., 1972, 1978, 1984, 1989)

1962   Matthews, D., Kruse, R., & Shaw, V. *The science of physical education for handicapped children*

1963   Clark, H.C., & Clarke, D. *Developmental and adapted physical education* (2nd ed., 1978)

1964   Logan, G. *Adaptations of muscular activity*

1965   Daniels, A., & Davies, E. (1965). *Adapted physical education* (2nd ed., author change)

1965   Kelly, E. *Adapted and corrective physical education* (4th ed.); title and author change. Reprinted in 1980.

1966   Mueller, G., & Cristaldi, C. *A practical program of remedial physical education*

1966   Fait, H. *Special physical education* (2nd ed., previously titled *Adapted Physical Education*)

1969   Arnheim, D., Auxter, D., & Crow, W. *Principles and methods of adapted physical education* (2nd & 3rd eds. with these authors; 4th ed., Crowe, Auxter, & Pyfer, 1981)

1969   Wheeler, R., & Hooley, A. *Physical education for the handicapped* (2nd ed., 1976)

1973   Vodola, T. *Individualized physical education for the handicapped*

1974   Geddes, D. *Physical education for individuals with handicapping conditions* (2nd ed., 1978)

1976   Sherrill, C. *Adapted physical education and recreation: A multidisciplinary approach* (2nd-5th eds., 1981, 1986, 1993, 1997)

1977   Wessel, J. *Planning individualized education programs in special education: With examples from I CAN physical education*

1977   Vannier, M. *Physical activities for the handicapped*

1979   Winnick, J. *Early movement experiences and development: Habilitation and remediation*

1980   Cratty, B.J. *Adapted physical education for children and youth* (2nd ed., 1990)

1981   Crowe, W., Auxter, D., & Pyfer, J. *Principles and methods of adapted physical education and recreation* (4th ed.; title change; Arnheim was senior author of earlier editions)

1982   French, R., & Jansma, P. *Special physical education* (2nd ed., 1994)

1982   Kalakian, L., & Eichstaedt, C. *Developmental/adapted physical education: Making ability count* (2nd ed., 1987, Eichstaedt senior author)

1982   Miller, A., & Sullivan, J. *Teaching physical activities to impaired youth: An approach to mainstreaming*

1982   Seaman, J., & DePauw, K. *The new adapted physical education: A developmental approach* (2nd ed., 1989)

1982   Wiseman, D. *A practical approach to adapted physical education*

1983   Masters, L., Mori, A., & Lange, E. *Adapted physical education: A practitioner's guide*

1984   Fait, H., & Dunn, J.M. *Special physical education* (5th ed., author change)

1985   Arnheim, D., & Sinclair, W. *Physical education for special populations: Developmental, adapted, and remedial approach*

1985   Auxter, D., & Pyfer, J. *Adapted physical education and recreation* (5th ed.; earlier senior authors were Arnheim [1st-3rd eds., 1969, 1973, 1975]) and Crowe [4th ed., 1981])

1985   Folio, R. *Physical education programming for exceptional learners*

1987   Eichstaedt, C., & Kalakian, L. *Developmental/adapted physical education: Making ability count* (2nd ed., author change)

1989   Dunn, J.M., & Fait, H. *Special physical education: Adapted, individualized, developmental* (6th ed., author change)

1990   Winnick, J. (Ed.) *Adapted physical education and sport* (2nd ed., 1995)

1990   Horvat, M. *Physical education and sport for exceptional students*

1990   Cratty, B.J. *Adapted physical education in the mainstream* (2nd ed., title change)

1993   Auxter, D., Pyfer, J., & Huettig, C. *Principles and methods of adapted physical education and recreation* (7th ed., author change)

1993   Sherrill, C. *Adapted physical activity, recreation, and sport: Crossdisciplinary and lifespan* (4th ed., title change)

1994   Block, M.E. *A teacher's guide to including students with disabilities in regular physical education*

1994   Jansma, P., & French, R. *Special physical education: Physical activity, sports, and recreation* (2nd ed., author change)

1994   Rimmer, J.H. *Fitness and rehabilitation programs for special populations*

Note. Second and subsequent editions are listed by date only when authors or titles change.

4

Sport Sociology

George H. Sage
The University of Northern Colorado

Sociology of sport as a distinct field of study emerged in the late 1960s, but diverse and uncoordinated intellectual processes that had been underway for over a century laid the framework for the development of this academic specialty and its subsequent evolution over the past 30 years. This chapter provides an overview of the history of sport sociology.[1] It identifies key participants, describes milestone events, and examines issues and the prospects for greater knowledge and understanding in sport sociology. The focus is on developments in North American sport sociology (scholars in the United States and Canada maintain a close connection): Although there is a European tradition antedating formation of organized sport sociology in North America, and a growing interest in sport sociology throughout the world, summarizing the field's international developments would exceed the space allocated.

Early Foundations of Sport Sociology

A theory about the social significance of sporting practice was firmly embedded in the British private secondary boarding school system (the so-called Great Public Schools) as early as the mid-1800s. According to the theory of what came to be known as *athleticism*, sporting experiences developed valuable social qualities and manly virtues. School sports, British historian J.A. Mangan (1986) asserted, "were the wheel around which moral values turned. They were the pre-eminent instrument for the training of a boy's character" (p. 18). Like so many ideas and practices of the British upper class, athleticism and its accompanying character-building theme were imported to North America; character development has been proclaimed as a goal and an outcome for organized sports in North America for over a century.

▼

A Chronology of Sport Sociology

Early Foundations

Year	Event
1899	Publication of *The Theory of the Leisure Class* by Thorstein Veblen
1907	Publication of *Games of the North American Indians* by Stewart Culin
1921	Publication of treatise *Soziologie des Sports* by Heinz Risse
1953	Publication of *Sports in American Life* by Frederick Cozens and Florence Stumpf

Organization: Toward a Unified Sociology of Sport

Year	Event
1964	Creation of the International Committee for Sport Sociology
1965	Publication of article "Toward a Sociology of Sport" by Gerald Kenyon and John Loy
1968	Big Ten Symposium with the topic of Sociology of Sport
1976	First North American sport sociology journal, *Review of Sport and Leisure*
1978	Formation of the North American Society for the Sociology of Sport

Development: Emergence of Scholarly Organizations

Year	Event
1980	First North American Society for the Sociology of Sport Conference, held in Denver, Colorado
1984	*The Sociology of Sport Journal* is begun by NASSS and published by Human Kinetics Publishers

---

Diverse Voices in the Formation of an Academic Specialty

Sport as a social phenomenon attracted numerous social and behavioral scientists in the latter nineteenth and early twentieth centuries. Indeed, an international bibliography compiled under the direction of Gunther

(Left to right) George Sage, Gerald Kenyon, and John Loy

Gerald Kenyon receiving the first
Distinguished Service Award at the
1993 Conference of the North
American Society for the Sociology
of Sport, Ottawa, Ontario, Canada

Luschen (1980) at the University of Illinois identified 2,583 scholarly articles in journals, anthologies, and proceedings, and 723 books dealing with the sociology of sport, all of which were published prior to 1978. The bibliography included only materials in standard professional journals and books accessible in libraries, and all citations employed sociological concepts or involved data from social research or appropriate studies.

Before there was a distinct specialty of sport sociology, the nature and social functions of play, games, and sports were probed by some of the most noted psychologists, historians, anthropologists, philosophers, physical educators, and sociologists. No attempts will be made here to identify all of them or their work. Instead, what follows is a selective synopsis of some of the more renowned scholars' works in which the social aspects of play, games, and sports were either the main focus or a significant part.

Philosophers Friedrich Schiller (1875) and Herbert Spencer (1873) were proponents of a theory that play functioned to expel "surplus energy" that built up during periods of inactivity. Karl Groos (1901) advanced the notion that play served as a social preparation for practices one would enact later in life. Psychologist G. Stanley Hall (1920) saw play of children as a recapitulation of the evolution of life, or ontogeny repeating phylogeny. Moritz Lazarus (1883) and George Thomas White Patrick (1916) proposed that play serves a restorative function, enabling individuals to recuperate from the accumulated fatigue of daily living. Sigmund Freud, founder of psychoanalysis during the latter part of the 19th century, believed that children act out and repeat problematic situations in play in order to master them (1955, 1959, 1963). In the mid-twentieth century psychiatrist Erik Erikson (1940, 1941, 1943, 1963) was influential in emphasizing the importance of infant and child play in the process of socialization. Developmental psychologist Jean Piaget (1951, 1965) formulated a sophisticated theory in which playful activities had important functions in the various developmental stages children pass through on their way to adulthood. Social psychologist George H. Mead's (1934) social development theory proposed an important role for play in the development of self: In the first stage of self-development, play has an important role in learning role-taking; in the second stage, games play an important role in acquiring notions of a generalized "other." Historian Johan Huizinga's *Homo Ludens* (1955) analyzed the play element within every aspect of culture, and concluded that the play element has been lost in modern sports. Roger Caillois's *Man, Play and Games* (1961) classified games into four major types and attempted to demonstrate that basic themes of culture can be deduced from the study of play and games.

While playful activities were the focus of many analysts, the study of games and sports and their social significance and functions has also attracted the attention of numerous scholars over the past century. German sociologist Max Weber's attention focused on games as a serious pursuit of education under feudalism for cultivating appropriate abilities and qualities of character in feudal societies. Anthropologist Stewart Culin (1907) studied the games and culture of Native Americans; *Games of the North American Indians* stands as a classic of ethnographic data on Native-American games. Empirical data of anthropologist John Roberts and his colleagues (Roberts, Sutton-Smith, & Kendon, 1963) and psychologist Brian Sutton-Smith and his colleagues (Sutton-Smith, Roberts, & Rozelka, 1963) demonstrated that the types of games played in a culture reflect the inherent values in that culture, while at the same time serving to teach certain attitudes and values.

Thorstein Veblen (1899), an early critic of modern sporting practices, argued in *The Theory of the Leisure Class* that sports represented a regression to barbarism and were marks of an "arrested development of man's moral nature" (p. 256). Following Veblen, other noted social scientists wrote on sport as a social phenomenon. Sociologist W.I. Thomas published an article in the *American Journal of Sociology* in 1901 titled "The Gaming Instinct." Another sociologist, William Graham Sumner (1906), in his book, *Folkways*, included a chapter on "Popular Sports, Exhibitions, and Drama." Both saw connections between sport and social behavior. In his influential book, *The Sociology of Teaching*, educational sociologist Willard Waller (1932) wrote about the role of sports in American high schools; for him, sports in the schools served as an effective instrument of social control.

Bicycle enthusiast and social scientist Norman Triplett's (1898) analysis of pacemaking and competition among bicyclists is hailed by some observers as the first empirical study of sport sociology (Luschen, 1980). Other early social psychological analyses of sport were G.T.W. Patrick's 1903 article in the *American Journal of Psychology* on "The Psychology of Football," and George Elliot Howard's article "Social Psychology of the Spectator," which appeared in the *American Journal of Sociology* in 1912.

Although it is always risky to identify a given piece of writing as being the first of its kind, according to Wohl (1966), in 1921 Heinz Risse published in Germany the first treatise titled *The Sociology of Sport* (*Soziologie des Sports*). Unfortunately, there was no immediate follow-up to this work. Indeed, it was not until 1963, when Peter McIntosh published his very influential *Sport in Society*, that a volume focusing on the social significance of sport received widespread notice. Several North Americans who became the first-generation sport sociologists consider McIntosh's volume as the most influential book in guiding their career toward this field of study.

Physical Education and the Social Aspects of Play, Games, and Sports

Few North American physical educators have devoted their careers to a study of the social aspects of sport. Since its beginnings as a discipline and profession in the mid-nineteenth century, scholarship in American physical education has had a strong biophysical science orientation. The reasons are fairly obvious when one is familiar with the development of this field: All of the early leaders were academically trained in medicine, and early college physical educators, such as Edward Hitchcock at Amherst College, Dudley Allen Sargent at Harvard, William G. Anderson at Yale, and Delphine Hanna of Oberlin College, were all MDs—physicians as well as physical educators. It was perfectly natural for them to emphasize the biophysical sciences as they molded the development of physical education.

The biophysical model for physical education was challenged at the beginning of this century by "The New Physical Education" curriculum, introduced by Thomas Wood and Clark Hetherington, and carried forward into the 1920s and 1930s by Jesse Feiring Williams and Rosalind Cassidy. It gave a privileged position to "social development," and was firmly based on a belief that games and sport experiences provide a rich environment for the socialization of the individual and the development of personal/social characteristics. Unfortunately, neither Wood nor Hetherington nor any of their disciples followed up with a program of empirical research using social research methodology.

There were some exceptions to this picture, however. Charles Cowell (1935, 1958) at Purdue University published a few empirical studies between 1935 and 1960, and a book by two physical educators, Frederick Cozens and Florence Stumpf (1953), entitled *Sports in American Life* must be considered a pioneer effort to examine the social role of sport in American society. But most physical educators were content to evangelize about the "social development" objective of games and sports. They were actually more interested in justifying programs of physical education than they were of studying the broad scope of social behavior in sport contexts, and they did not attempt to develop a basic subject matter in sport sociology.

Organization: Toward a Unified Sociology of Sport

It was not until the early 1950s that a combination of several events served as an impetus in the formalization of the academic specialty of the sociology of sport. At this time, two West German scholars made pleas for the development of a sociology of sport. Their essays, "Toward a Sociology of Sport" by Popplow (1951) and "Sociology of Sport" by Plessner (1952), were persuasive ground-breaking efforts on behalf of sport sociology, but they actually made little stir in North America. The catalyst for a unified field of sport sociology in North America came in the mid-1960s when Gerald Kenyon and John Loy (1965) authored the first programmatic statement of a need for a sociology of sport. Their short article, entitled "Toward a Sociology of Sport," was published in the May 1965 issue of the *Journal of Health, Physical Education, and Recreation*. Other position papers and calls for a sociology of sport followed, such as "The Study of Sport as an Element of Culture" by Daniels (1966) and "A Sociology of Sport: On Becoming a Sub-discipline" by Kenyon (1969b). These writings served to stimulate and/or support more formalized efforts that were beginning to take place, such as conferences and meetings, publications, scholarly societies, and university courses in sport sociology.

Conferences and Other Meetings

Whenever a topic of intellectual curiosity attracts a group of interested persons, they typically organize meetings to get acquainted with each other, establish social ties, and share their ideas and work. The first significant organizational development for the sociology of sport began in June 1964 when an International Committee for Sport Sociology (ICSS), composed of representatives from both physical education and the social sciences, was created by the UNESCO-affiliated International Council for Sport and Physical Education (ICSPE). It subsequently became an official research committee of the International Sociological Association (ISA). In 1966 the ICSS sponsored its first seminar, in Cologne, Germany, with an invited group of around 50 participants. "Small Group Research in Sport" was the focus of the seminar.

Since 1966 the ICSS has sponsored numerous international seminars, symposia, international workshops, and conference sessions, several in conjunction with World Congresses of the ISA and several in conjunction with Olympic Games. It has successfully maintained an international membership with a diversity of research interests. By doing so, it has served as a social bridge and intellectual cement consolidating a community of sport sociologists throughout the world. In 1994 the name of the ICSS was changed to the International Sociology of Sport Association (ISSA). According to Luschen (1980), there were fewer than 20 practicing sociologists of sport prior to 1970; 1994 the ISSA was comprised of approximately 250 full and corresponding members.

Scholarly/professional organizations in North America began including sport sociology sessions in their programs in the mid-1960s. The American Association for Health, Physical Education, and Recreation (AAHPER) (the name was changed to the American Alliance for Health, Physical Education, Recreation and Dance [AAHPERD] in 1979) sponsored its first program on the sociology of sport in 1966; Gerald Kenyon, John Loy, and Cyril White were the keynote speakers. During the next few years the annual meetings of AAHPER usually included a session devoted to the sociology of sport. In the mid-1970s AAHPER underwent a major restructuring, one outcome of which was the creation of what are called "academies." A major function of the academies is to organize sessions at the annual meetings of AAHPERD related to particular areas of scholarly inquiry and professional concerns. In 1976 a Sociology of Sport Academy was founded by AAHPER to coordinate and promote the study of sport sociology.

At its annual meeting in 1968 in Boston, the American Sociological Association (ASA) sponsored a luncheon roundtable discussion on the sociology of sport, led by Charles Page of the University of Massachusetts. Since 1968 the ASA and its regional affiliates have sponsored sessions regularly on the sociology of sport at their annual meetings.

In 1970 the Canadian Association for Health, Physical Education, and Recreation (CAHPER) sponsored a seminar on sociology of sport, held at McMaster University. At that seminar a committee was established to prepare a special issue for the *CAHPER Journal* devoted to sport sociology. That special issue was published in February 1971. CAHPER also sponsored the publication of a set of monographs titled *CAHPER Sociology of Sport Monograph Series*, composed of over a dozen topics relevant to sport sociology. The series was initiated by the Sociology of Sport Committee of CAHPER in response to a need expressed by individuals who were teaching courses in the sociology of sport in Canadian universities.

As the sociology of sport inched its way into higher education in the United States, the greatest support for this field of study was shown by faculty and graduate students at Big Ten universities. In November 1968 at the University of Wisconsin, a major symposium on the sociology of sport was held under the auspices of the Committee for Institutional Cooperation (CIC), composed of one member from each of the Big Ten universities and the University of Chicago. Over 50 participants were in attendance. The conference proceedings were edited by Kenyon and published under the title of *Aspects of Contemporary Sport Sociology* (Kenyon, 1969a). A second CIC symposium on the sociology of sport was held ten years later at the University of Minnesota in April 1978; the proceedings were published under the title *The Dimensions of Sport Sociology* (Krotee, 1979).

Several other notable conferences during the late 1960s and early 1970s focused on issues relevant to sport sociology. In 1967 the University of Illinois hosted an international workshop on the "Cross-Cultural Analysis of Sport and Games," sponsored by the UNESCO Committee on the Sociology of Sport. At the State University of New York, College at Brockport, in 1971, a conference titled "Symposium on Sport and Social Deviancy" dealt with cheating, gambling, political activism, and racism (Landers, 1976). In 1972 three prominent conferences were held: A symposium on problems associated with "Athletics in America" took place at Oregon State University (Flath, 1972), "Sport in a Changing World" was the title of a symposium held at the University of Wisconsin, Madison, and a "Conference on Women and Sport" was held at Pennsylvania State University (Harris, 1972).

New Publication Resources

As interest and scholarship begin to grow in any field of study, publications are created to allow scholars to discuss mutual concerns, issues, and problems, as well as share theoretical ideas and research findings. Early development of sport sociology in North America was facilitated by various publications. The first newsletter and the first journal dealing specifically with the sociology of sport were sponsored by the ICSS. In January 1966 the ICSS began publication of a newsletter called simply *The Bulletin*. Its purpose was to keep its members abreast of current activities and developments in sport sociology; it also provided information about actions taken by the ICSS board of directors.

The first North American sport sociology newsletter, titled the *Sport Sociology Bulletin*, began in 1972 under the editorship of Benjamin Lowe and ceased publication in 1977. Shortly after the North American Society for the Sociology of Sport (NASSS) was formed in 1978 (to be described below), it began publishing a professional newsletter; the first issue of the *NASSS Newsletter* appeared in December 1978, edited by Andrew Yiannakis. In 1982 Lee Vander Velden assumed the editorship of the *NASSS Newsletter* and has retained that position ever since.

Newsletters could not fulfill the publication needs of increasing numbers of sport sociologists and were superseded by scholarly journals. In 1966 the ICSS began publication of a journal, the *International Review of Sport Sociology* (*IRSS*); it was published in Poland under the editorship of Andrzej Wohl. At the beginning it was an annual publication, but this format was changed in 1973 when it became a quarterly. Wohl remained as editor-in-chief until 1984, when Kurt Weis from the Federal Republic of Germany assumed this position. At that time the official title of the journal was changed to the *International Review for the Sociology of Sport*, and a German publisher was acquired. Weis was replaced by Klaus Heinemann, also of the Federal Republic of Germany, in 1988. Authorship of the articles of the *IRSS* has been truly international, with as many as 10 countries sometimes represented in a single issue.

The first sport sociology journal published in North America was the *Review of Sport and Leisure*, first published in 1976, edited by Benjamin Lowe. Several other journals devoted exclusively to sociology of sport emerged in the late 1970s and 1980s. In 1976, Arena, the Institute for Sport and Social Analysis, a creation of Richard E. Lapchick, began publication of the *Arena Newsletter* and the *Journal of Sport and Social Issues* (*JSSI*). Richard Lapchick edited both for the first two years. In 1978 the *Arena*

Newsletter was replaced with a quarterly titled *Arena Review*. James H. Frey became the editor of the *JSSI* beginning in 1978, while the *Arena Review* used a series of guest editors.

Although the founders of NASSS in 1978 aspired from their first organizational meeting to sponsor a journal, it was not until 1984 that their aspirations reached fruition with the first issue of the *Sociology of Sport Journal*, with Human Kinetics Publishers as the publisher and Jay Coakley as editor. The *Sociology of Sport Journal* is a quarterly, publishing empirical, theoretical, and position papers as well as reviews and critical essays.

Articles about the social aspects of sport have been published in a wide variety of sociological journals over the past 20 years. Also, the *Annual Review of Sociology* has published two review articles about sport sociology. In 1980 Gunther Luschen authored a review titled "Sociology of Sport: Development, Present State, and Prospects" and in 1991 James Frey and D. Stanley Eitzen's review was titled "Sport and Society." An annual publication titled *Exercise and Sport Sciences Reviews* has published a number of reviews on sport sociology topics over the years. Two physical education publications have frequently published articles on sport sociology. *Quest*, a publication of the National Association for Physical Education in Higher Education, has been a popular publishing outlet for sport sociologists over the years, and the *Research Quarterly for Exercise and Sport*, an AAHPERD journal, has often published empirical research in sport sociology. During the late 1970s and early 1980s the Sport Studies Research Group in the School of Physical and Health Education at Queen's University in Canada published some excellent critical and theory-oriented work in a series titled "Working Papers in the Sociological Study of Sports and Leisure."

With any new field of inquiry, as it begins to grow and courses are offered on that subject, anthologies are published to bring the literature together, since the written materials that do exist on that subject are typically scattered through many diverse publications. Such was the case for sport sociology. Beginning in 1969 with Loy and Kenyon's *Sport, Culture, and Society* and Sage's (1970) *Sport and American Society* one year later, more than a half dozen books of readings appeared in the next few years (Ball & Loy, 1975; Eitzen, 1979; Gruneau & Albinson, 1976; Hart, 1972; Stone, 1972; Talamini & Page, 1973; Yiannakis, McIntyre, Melnick, & Hart, 1976).

There were no textbooks devoted exclusively to sport sociology prior to 1970. Cozens and Stumpf's (1953) *Sports in American Life*, Boyle's (1963) *Sport: Mirror of American Life*, McIntosh's (1963) *Sport in Society*, and Natan's (1958) *Sport and Society* all examined the social role of sport in society, and there were also physical education textbooks that examined the significance of sport in society, such as Cratty's (1967) *Social Dimensions of Physical Activity* and Ulrich's (1968) *The Social Matrix of Physical Education*, but none of these books was written specifically as a textbook for sociology of sport courses. Although the first books written specifically as textbooks for sport sociology classes appeared in the mid-1970s (Edwards, 1973; Ibrahim, 1975; Nixon, 1976), the year 1978 was a benchmark year because several sport sociology texts were published in that one year (Coakley, 1978; Eitzen & Sage, 1978; Loy, McPherson, & Kenyon, 1978b; Snyder & Spreitzer, 1978).

Sport was not the subject of a chapter in any of the most popular introductory sociology texts prior to 1975. By the late 1970s introductory sociology texts began to include topics on sport and leisure. Smith and Preston's (1977) *Sociology: An Introduction* had an entire chapter entitled "Leisure and Sport." By the early 1990s several introductory sociology texts included a chapter on sport and leisure.

While the anthology and textbook literature was expanding rapidly during the 1970s, academics, sport journalists, and former athletes supplied a prolific volume of literature about various social dimensions of sport (Axthelm, 1970; Dickey, 1974; Edwards, 1969; Hoch, 1972; Lipsyte, 1975; Meggyesy, 1971; Scott, 1971; Shaw, 1972; Shecter, 1970, to name only a few). One of America's most noted novelists, James Michener (1976), even wrote on sport as a social phenomenon in his book *Sports in America*. While these works were primarily reportorial, autobiographical, or essay rather than empirical research oriented, they made significant contributions in promoting the study of sport as an intellectual enterprise.

A major contribution to the preservation of and access to the literature in sport sociology was made in the early 1970s when the University of Waterloo established the unique and valuable computerized information retrieval system for the Sociology of Leisure and Sport (SIRLS). When the University of Waterloo sold the SIRLS collection to the Sport Information Resource Centre (SIRC) in Gloucester, Ontario, Canada, in the early 1990s, SIRLS contained over 17,000 references in the sociology and social psychology of sport and leisure.[2]

Development: Emergence of Scholarly Organizations

It was at the 1978 CIC symposium at the University of Minnesota that the participants assembled in the foyer of Mayo Memorial Auditorium just before the symposium ended and discussed the need for founding a scholarly society for sport sociology in North America. During the discussion, a consensus emerged that such an organization was needed, and a name was agreed upon; the new society would be called the North American Society for the Sociology of Sport (NASSS). A steering committee was established and entrusted with the tasks of developing a newsletter, beginning a membership drive, planning a conference, publishing the proceedings, and considering the feasibility of founding a journal. Andrew Yiannakis, assisted by James Bryant and James Frey, organized the first NASSS conference held in Denver in 1980; NASSS conferences have been held annually ever since. Susan Greendorfer, the first NASSS treasurer, was instrumental in handling the tasks associated with getting the business affairs of NASSS, especially membership matters, established. Membership in NASSS has grown slowly but steadily, increasing from 130 in 1982 to 325 in 1996.

Sociology of Sport Courses in Higher Education

If one were to browse through the physical education offerings in a randomly selected group of college and university catalogs before 1960, one would discover there were no courses titled "sport sociology." Nor is there a listing for this course in the section of catalogs where sociology courses are listed. However, by 1970—a mere ten years later—sport sociology courses could be found in many physical education departments as well as in a few sociology departments.

The emergence of sport sociology courses in North America was grounded in three separate but interrelated trends that occurred in higher education: (1) a shift in perspective in physical education from teacher preparation toward a discipline of human movement, (2) an enormous expansion in higher education during the 1960 decade, and (3) the fragmentation of knowledge in higher education (Chubin, 1976; Lynton, 1987; Massengale, 1987).

Prior to the mid-1960s physical education in higher education was focused exclusively on the pedagogical (although it was not called that at the time) concerns of preparing teachers. But physical education, as well as other departments with an applied professional emphasis, came under increasing pressure (even threats that departments would be eliminated) to demonstrate a basic academic body of knowledge (Sage, 1984).

Physical educators had to respond to these challenges or face an uncertain future at some universities. As a result, the physical education literature throughout the 1960s was filled with programmatic essays— purporting to show that physical education was indeed an academic discipline and articulating the conceptual and theoretical foundations of it. These events set in motion a paradigm shift in physical education. Graduate emphasis in physical education shifted from the preparation of persons with a broad background in education to the preparation of young scholars whose training was linked to an established academic discipline and to the study of exercise and sport. This group took as its model the academic disciplines, not the professional schools, so the focus on the analysis of exercise and sport turned to disciplinary concepts and theories, and methods of empirical research, rather than the preparation of physical education teachers. Younger scholars in turn distanced themselves from teacher preparation, creating a major shift in intellectual perspective in physical education. New specialized subdisciplines arose, such as sport sociology (Sage, 1991).

Concurrent with the unrest in physical education there was massive growth throughout higher education. The 1960s was a dynamic decade for American higher education: Higher education enrollments increased some 130 percent, and the number of full-time faculty in higher education increased 140 percent (National Center for Educational Statistics, 1983). PhD recipients increased 244 percent (United States Bureau of Census, 1975). These conditions provided a fertile environment for new fields of study, and sport sociology became one of those new fields.

While specialization is the hallmark of modern science, and academic specialization was well underway in North American higher education before 1960, this decade witnessed an acceleration of the fragmentation of knowledge into numerous scientific specialties (Chubin, 1976); sociology did not escape the scientific fragmentation process. In the early 1970s several sociologists attempted to identify the numerous subfields into which sociology had become divided (Borgardus, 1973; Stehr & Larson, 1972). The number of specialties ranged from 20 to 33. Sport sociology was just one of many subfields into which sociology had proliferated. By 1986, 249 (2%) of 13,000 members of the American Sociological Association declared leisure/sport/recreation as one of their areas of interest—not a large number, to be sure, but considerable growth by earlier standards.

Scientific trends are not random processes. Several events in higher education, and physical education and sociology in particular, in the late 1960s and early 1970s coalesced to inspire college courses in sport sociology, and eventually graduate specialization in this academic specialty.

Knowledge Production in the Sociology of Sport

The nature of knowledge—its creation and uses—has been at issue throughout the short history of sport sociology. Sport sociology has relied upon sociology for its philosophy of science, and from its beginnings the general field of sociology has been characterized by diverse theoretical and methodological perspectives. Despite over a hundred years of debate it remains a discipline with several theoretical paradigms vying for hegemony within the field as a whole, as well as within its subfields (Ritzer, 1992; Turner, 1990a).

As in most scientific specialties, much of the work of early leaders in the sociology of sport involved establishing the intellectual boundaries of the specialty and making initial research probes. An inevitable part of establishing a new specialty's boundaries is that someone acknowledged as its leader sets the theoretical and methodological agenda and others join in support for it. For the sociology of sport, Gerald Kenyon, then of the University of Wisconsin, quickly emerged as spokesperson, largely through his programmatic speeches at various national conventions, hosting of a Big Ten symposium on the sociology of sport, joint editorship of the first anthology on the sociology of sport, and sponsorship of a group of graduate students at Wisconsin who were destined to become the vanguard in the first generation of sport sociologists. Kenyon was instrumental in defining the scope and task of the emerging field of sport sociology by clarifying definitions and concepts, mapping out theoretical and methodological frameworks, and suggesting favorable areas of future research in the sociology of sport.

Early Epistemological Boundaries

In a series of publications between 1965 and 1969, Kenyon emphatically situated the sociology of sport firmly within the positivistic perspective of science. Sociology was defined as the "study of social order" (Kenyon & Loy, 1965, p. 24) and "sport sociology . . . is a value-free social science" (p. 25); the function of the sport sociologist "is not to shape attitudes and values but rather to describe and explain them" (p. 25; see also Kenyon, 1969b). It is clear that Kenyon was asserting that the scientific legitimacy of sport sociology was tied to what he thought was the appropriate model of sociology, namely the positivist, empirical-analytical paradigm of the established sciences.[3]

There are several quite understandable reasons for Kenyon's scientific orientation. First, in the period following World War II and continuing up to the early 1970s a positivistic vision for sociology was preeminent under the general conceptualization of structural-functionalism. In this view, analysis is concerned with the interrelations among social phenomena in general; more particularly, there is an emphasis upon the use of operational concepts, quantitative mathematical techniques, and "value-free" inquiry and analysis (Giddens, 1987; Turner, 1990a). Kenyon was merely embracing the mainstream sociology orientation of that era. Second, the theoretical and methodological orientation of physical education was (and still is) overwhelmingly grounded in the positivist/natural science tradition. This was the only orientation toward scholarship taught in many graduate programs of physical education, and it was undoubtedly the model that Kenyon learned and internalized as a graduate student in physical education. Third, Kenyon's early career was spent as a faculty member at the University of Wisconsin, at a time when both the physical education department (the department in which he was employed) and the sociology department were bastions of positivist research. Although this observation surely oversimplifies the reasons for Kenyon's orientation, because many influences go into contouring one's outlook at any one time, it probably accounts for many of his inclinations and preferences.

Ironically, Kenyon was making his stand for a positivist science orientation for sport sociology just when this particular approach to sociology was being subjected to devastating and convincing criticism within sociology. During the late 1960s and early 1970s, as part of the unrest and turmoil directed against all of the social institutions and intellectual traditions, sociology witnessed a massive attack on functionalism (e.g., Gouldner, 1970; also see Bernard, 1983).

A number of efforts have been made to review and analyze the theoretical and methodological trends in sport sociology after the initial boundaries and directions were mapped out (e.g., Coakley, 1987; Frey & Eitzen, 1991; Loy, Kenyon, & McPherson, 1980; Loy, McPherson, & Kenyon, 1978a; Luschen, 1980; Luschen & Sage, 1981; MacAloon, 1987; Sage, 1979, 1981, 1982, 1987; Snyder & Spreitzer, 1979). Kenyon (1986) made the most systematic analysis of the topical distribution of the body of sport sociology literature produced up to the mid-1980s. Over 7,000 papers, articles, and monographs were subjected to his analysis, using the SIRLS data base at the University of Waterloo. In his analysis of theoretical material in the literature, Kenyon said that "the significance of theory, no matter how you 'cut it,' is not great in sport sociology literature, whether explicitly or implicitly, or whether as general theory or theory in more contained forms" (p. 15). Coakley (1987) came to essentially the same conclusion from his review of the research; he declared:

Much of the research in sociology of sport has been neither cumulative nor theory-based, nor has it been dedicated to theory development. . . . This is true of the field as a whole, but it is especially true of work done in the U.S. This is not to say that theory has not informed some of the work done by American sport sociologists, but little of their research has grown directly out of concern for theory testing or theory development in sociology. (p. 70)

More recently, Frey and Eitzen (1991) noted that "the most serious charge against sport sociology is that the theoretical development is relatively weak" (p. 518).

Despite conclusions that theory generation and testing have not been central to knowledge production in sport sociology, a review of the cumulative literature of the past three decades suggests that much of the sport sociology research has been firmly in the traditions of positivistic science.[4] The specific studies need not concern us here; suffice it to say that the findings constitute a massive data base about the relationship of a wide variety of variables and sport. Emphasis has been on the accumulation of social facts[5] using empirical techniques for objectively collecting information that is verifiable and "value neutral." Sparks (1985) observed that the "penetration of positivist science into the fabric of sport studies and physical education research has generally been met with widespread support" (p. 2) and that "knowledge, as such, has come to equate with a precise set of factual assertions about people and the world, sharply distinguished from the dominant images, meanings, and values of cultural life" (p. 1). Nevertheless, knowledge about the social aspects of sport has been advanced substantially by this research. To charge that research is positivistic and functionalist does not make it worthless (as criticisms of this sort of scholarship sometimes subtly imply), because certain important questions are addressed by this approach to knowledge.

Alternative Approaches to Knowledge Production

As noted previously, beginning in the late 1960s and continuing through the 1980s new winds swept through the social disciplines. Positivism, and its companion in sociology, functionalism, came under severe critical scrutiny and debate (Bernard, 1983; Giddens, 1977). A growing criticism was leveled at positivist conceptions of knowledge, and functionalism as a model for sociological knowledge came under heavy attack as attention turned to other epistemologies. The targets for the critics were the positivist science framework, the value-free posture that was typically espoused, the political conservatism that appeared to be present in this orientation, and its tendency to ignore the symbolic meanings inherent to social relations (Sewart, 1978; Stockman, 1983).

A diverse group of antinaturalistic, interpretivist, and critical research traditions of social thought, often employing qualitative rather than quantitative methods, challenged the hegemony of the positive science orientation as a way to understand and pursue knowledge accumulation in social science. Important work grounded in feminist theories was present within all of these alternative approaches. Turner (1985) called these competing paradigms "loosely assembled congeries of concepts that sensitize and orient researchers to certain critical processes. . . . [They] are typically more skeptical about the timeless quality of social affairs . . ." (p. 25). Their main contention was that the positivistic/functionalist schemes tended to exaggerate consensus, stability, and integration to the point of essentially disregarding conflict, change, and disorder (see also Giddens, 1977, 1984). According to the alternative perspectives, the study of social organization and behavior requires a concern with meanings and values within cultural settings that are part of an historical process. Society is viewed as a dynamic system of conflicting and competing parts with individuals struggling to meet basic human needs.

In sport sociology, adherents of the alternative theoretical orientations proposed that not only is the positivist value-free position a myth that deludes us into believing something that cannot exist, but it ignores

responsibilities that sport sociologists have as social critics, even reformers. Moreover, they claimed that to focus only on "functions" is to ignore
class, gender, and racial exploitation, unequal power relations, and other
injustices and social phenomena that serve to maintain the status quo (e.g.,
Beamish, 1981; Gruneau, 1983; Harris, 1981; Ingham, 1979; Sparks, 1985).

An interpretivist vector among the alternative research traditions that
predated World War II began to attract renewed support in the 1970s
and early 1980s. Having roots in phenomenology, symbolic interactionism, and hermeneutics, it challenged the scientific notions of explanation, prediction, and control with interpretive notions of understanding,
meaning, and action. Interpretive thought generally rejected the claim
that sociology can be a science in the same sense as the natural sciences.
Instead, "interaction and negotiations in social situations through which
people reciprocally define expectations about appropriate behaviors" was
featured (Popkewitz, 1984, p. 41; also see Berger and Luckman, 1967;
Blumer, 1969; Rabinow & Sullivan, 1979; Schutz, 1972).

Over the past decade and a half, a solid interpretive research tradition
has arisen in sport sociology. Investigators have examined sport cultures
with a variety of theoretical and methodological approaches emphasizing
interpretive and symbolic aspects of human social actions. Here research
processes emphasize interpretation based on direct observation of social
actions, investigator participation in the ongoing social life of interest in
the research, and discussions of particular social meanings with the persons being studied.

Focusing on various aspects of play, games, and sports, scholars working in the interpretive research tradition have broadened the sense of
acceptable methods for sport sociology. Interpretivist thought has made
compelling contributions to sport sociology knowledge, and it has been
useful in opening up sports issues. Some of the best work in recent years
has been grounded in this tradition (e.g., Fine, 1979, 1987; Klein, 1986
and 1993).

In the research models of positivism and interpretivism, sports occupy
a rather isolated position from the structurally unequal and conflict-ridden
society of which they are—in real life—thoroughly a part. Positivist and
interpretivist models make it difficult to fashion a discourse that historically situates and socially links these internal dynamics to the larger
political, economic, and ideological context; they do not address central
questions of power and dominance.

Meanwhile, another tradition of social inquiry—that inspired by Karl
Marx—began to grow in popularity throughout the social sciences, and
has grown among sport sociologists. In the late 1960s Marxian theory
began to make significant inroads into American sociological theory (Jay,
1984; Turner, 1990b). As it began to take off in various directions, the
problem became what to call it: Marxism, neo-Marxism, conflict theory,
critical theory, cultural studies, and so on. Although Marx may have

been the most important founding figure of critical social scholarship, the development of critical social work did not end with him; thus the various terms. In this chapter, I have opted to use the word "critical" accompanied by various other words and terms, even though I recognize that there *are* differences in meanings for these various terms, and there *are* individual preferences that differ from mine.

Critical scholarship has long been a part of sociology's intellectual tradition, but during the past 25 years it has been revitalized as a response to and an interpretation of the social relations which underlie social class inequality, sexism, racism, and other types of social and economic oppression and injustice in North American society. The past two decades have seen a surge of interest in this theory of knowledge (Agger, 1991; Fay, 1987; Kellner, 1989; Wexler, 1991).

The most salient departure for critical social thought from both positivist and interpretivist research traditions is the attempt to understand the *conditions* in which social knowledge is created. In particular, a critical orientation to knowledge treats "what counts as knowledge" as problematic, thus facilitating research into the *ways* in which knowledge is socially organized, transmitted, and assessed. Moreover, far from being neutral, inquiry into society is viewed as involving unresolved questions about power, values, and other social affairs that represent deep divisions within a dynamic system of conflicting and competing parts (Agger, 1992a, 1992b; Morrow, 1991, 1994; Ray, 1993).

Such an outlook brings structures of power and large-scale social dynamics onto center stage; more importantly, it emphasizes that the intent of research is not *just* to describe and interpret the dynamics of a society, but to consider the ways in which the process of social formation can be improved and made more democratic, socially just, and humane. Making problematic the nature of values, customs, and tradition in everyday life increases "the possibility of human agency in providing for a social transformation that creates new social structures and emancipatory conditions" (Popkewitz, 1984, p. 17). Critical inquiry is therefore distinct from the other traditions in adopting a more activist role; unlike researchers of the other traditions who seek to understand the significance of the past and present, critical theorists aspire to transform the present to produce a different (better) future, and thus a better social world (Fay, 1987). On this point, Leonard (1990) noted "the link between social theory and political practice is perhaps the defining characteristic of critical theory, for a critical theory without a practical dimension would be bankrupt on its own terms" (p. 3).

In parallel with critical trends in the social disciplines, scholarship in sport sociology has increasingly focused on critical analyses during the 1980s and 1990s. For critical social thought, sports are interpreted as cultural, economic, and social sites inextricably tied to issues of power and control. Nothing that goes on in sports is fully independent of its historical and social context; indeed, sports are viewed as an important part of a complex structure of legitimation through which dominant social groups are given sanction, and through which privileged social and cultural ideologies are recreated, maintained, and continuously built (Foley, 1990; Gruneau, 1983; Hall, Slack, Smith, & Whitson, 1991; Sage, 1990). Critical social inquiry applied to sport relates sport to general facets of social organization, enabling one to obtain more coherent and comprehensive insights about institutional arrangements and cultural values in a society and the place of sporting activities within it.

Present and Future of Sport Sociology

Early definitions and boundary mappings tended to constrain sociology of sport to the domain of sociology proper, which tended to limit interdisciplinary analysis. Much of the diverse and critical theoretical and methodological knowledge production that has been gaining momentum over the past decade situates sport sociology within a broader framework of what many call "sport studies."

From Restricted Sport Sociology Perspectives to Broader Sport Studies

Sport studies is a variegated set of approaches that draw concepts, theories, and methods from all of the social sciences, and even the humanities (Harris, 1989). Accordingly, the boundaries for studying sport cross all of the social sciences and are not restricted to any one of them. Moreover, since these approaches view sport as a form of popular culture, and thus a mode in which ideas, values, and beliefs may be transmitted, some consider the orientation as coalescing with the cultural studies tradition (Donnelly & Young, 1985; Hollands, 1984).

Because there is no single or static version of cultural studies, it is difficult to define cultural studies with any degree of precision; indeed, Agger (1992a) claims that while cultural studies is an activity of critical theory, "cultural studies resists programmatism—a definitive methodology and a discrete list of critical topics. . . . Thus, there is no single static version of cultural studies, applicable across, or from within, each and every discipline" (pp. 2, 19). Its diversity and flexibility are its epistemological attributes. Nevertheless, cultural studies is a blending of critical theories that moves its attention to ideology—how it is created, signified, and reproduced, and the mechanisms by which it survives and succeeds in shaping consciousness. Indeed, one of the attributes of the intellectual vitality of cultural studies is its interdisciplinary diversity. The major disposition, however, is that positive science orientations for knowledge generation are eschewed (Agger, 1992b; Grossberg, Nelson, & Treichler, 1992).[6]

Scholars on the forefront of the recent sport studies movement have emphasized its fusion of materialist and culturalist perspectives for developing a comprehensive model to analyze the relations of dominance and subordination simultaneously contoured along class, race, and gender lines (Birrell, 1989). They have deepened understanding of the symbolic and cultural significance and meanings of play, games, and sports. The new literature arising from this approach is more critical, contextual, and evaluative (e.g., Andrews, 1993; Andrews & Loy, 1993; Gruneau, 1983; Hall et al., 1991; Ingham & Loy, 1993; Sage, 1990). In spite of important contributions by sport studies researchers, there has been a notable absence of analyses of racial relations as they intersect with class and gender relations, as well as their relatively autonomous realms (Birrell, 1989).

The size and rate of growth in the new sport studies literature make any global treatment impossible. A number of recent studies in the growing sport studies literature are grounded in social/cultural history (e.g., Adelman, 1986; Donnelly & Young, 1985; Gruneau, 1983; Gruneau & Whitson, 1993; Haley, 1978; Hardy, 1981; Hardy & Ingham, 1984; Harris & Park, 1983; Hoberman, 1984, 1992; Klein, 1991; Lenskyj, 1986; MacAloon, 1981; Mangan & Park, 1987; O'Hanlon, 1980). Others are grounded in such diverse theoretical and methodological approaches as symbolic interactionism, cultural anthropology, hermeneutics, and semiology (e.g., Donnelly & Young, 1988; Duncan, 1986; Duncan & Hasbrook, 1988; Harris, 1983; Klein, 1986, 1993; Lever, 1983).

Feminist Studies and Sport

Intellectual endeavors in the behavioral and social sciences during the past 20 years have emphasized the reality that the social positions, behaviors, and culture of males and females are socially problematic, and should be not only explained but questioned. Considerable attention has been devoted to gender in the recent literature of the social sciences. Feminist scholarship has become a field of study that dramatically reworks traditional understandings of social life by focusing on gender inequalities and injustices while uncovering sexist biases in popular and intellectual views of women (Benhabib & Cornell, 1987; Fraser, 1989; Harding, 1986). Woman-centered research has as one of its goals women's empowerment and the transformation of social relations between the sexes. Because traditional theoretical and methodological approaches in the social sciences are viewed as perpetuating gender bias, feminist research has emphasized transitional epistemologies, where multiple standpoints are employed to analyze, understand, and transform the system that subordinates women (Harding, 1986).

Feminist scholarship increasingly incorporates issues of gender into the central debates about sport. Feminist scholars recognize that sport plays a significant role in the reproduction of a patriarchal social order and therefore has the potential to play a critical role in the transformation of that order (Birrell, 1989; Hall, 1985, 1988; Lenskyj, 1986). Sport sociologists contributing to feminist theory and research have used a wide variety of traditions for knowledge production; Hall (1993) observed that there has been a "noticeable shift from . . . the atheoretical distributive research of sociology, to more theoretically informed relational analyses within cultural studies" (p. 62). Feminist scholarship in sport has also moved beyond the traditional accounts that portray sport as merely an oppressive male preserve. Recent feminist contributions have been made to the analysis of gender as a social and cultural construction; indeed, because sport is grounded in physical practice, it is especially fertile ground for the analysis of the construction of gender relations (Duncan, 1990; Birrell, 1988; Birrell & Cole, 1990; Lenskyj, 1986; Messner, 1992; Smith, 1992; Theberge, 1993).

One recent offshoot of feminist scholarship takes a profeminist sport studies approach to studying men and masculinity. It focuses on the social construction of masculinity, male and female social relations, and their linkages to institutional patriarchy, thus foregrounding gender in studies of men and sport. Messner (1990) has argued that studies of masculinity and sport correspond more closely to reality if they are "grounded in an inclusive feminism which utilizes multiple standpoints that take into account the intersections of class, race, gender, and other forms of domination and subordination" in the sporting world (p. 136; see also Messner, 1992; Messner & Sabo, 1990, 1994).

Basic Versus Applied Sociology of Sport

The dilemma over the purposes and uses of sociology dates back to the work of classical European sociologists such as Durkeim, Weber, and Marx, but the debate over pure sociological pursuit of knowledge versus action in sociology may be seen many times in the work of American sociologists such as Summer, Ward, Davis, Mills, and many others. Today there are diverse notions about the relation of sociological theory to policy making, political commitment, and actions within general sociology (Huey-tsyh & Rossi, 1992; Rossi, 1980; Whyte, 1982).

In sport sociology cogent arguments have been advanced for a basic research approach. For example, it has been suggested that the sport situation is an excellent research setting for verifying general sociological propositions and developing sociological models and theories. It has also been proposed as having good potential for generating and verifying substantive theories about the social and cultural significance of sport.

On the other hand, some argue for an applied or action-oriented sport sociology devoted to acquiring knowledge for more effective administration, marketing, and promotion of sports and/or the more humanistic understanding of sport, including ferreting out and exposing illegal and unethical practices in sport (for a discussion of various perspectives on this debate, see Yiannakis & Greendorfer, 1992).

Many who are skeptical about applied social research charge that the so-called "applied" role of scientists often becomes one of legitimating social practices by providing "objective facts" to justify courses of action. Questions about the values underlying these courses of action are believed to be beyond the scope of science and are therefore left unexamined (Carr & Kemmis, 1986). The most scathing indictment against applied sport sociology is directed at research, conducted by academicians in the service of gathering data about sports practices, whose major purpose is helping corporations and sport organizations find new ways to make more money. According to the critics of this type of applied sport sociology, scientific results that simply specify more effective courses of action from less effective ones—not whether or not they should be allowed to occur—are in danger of legitimating the dominant forms of sport and addressing only "technical" and marketing issues (Ingham & Donnelly, 1990; Sage, 1992; Whitson, 1984).

Rapprochement Between the Sociology of Sport and Physical Education

It is ironic that the connection between sport sociology and physical education has been strained for the past 25 years, because the most articulate initial thrusts for a sociology of sport came from persons trained in physical education, and the primary location for most persons teaching and doing research in sport sociology has been in departments of physical education. There are at least two main reasons for the disharmony between physical education and sport sociology. In his early programmatic essays Kenyon went to great lengths to distance sport sociology from physical education: "I cannot conceive of sport sociology and physical education as one and the same things. . . . Just as sociology is not social work, neither is sport sociology motor therapy (Kenyon, 1969b, p. 166) . . . . Sport sociology . . . does not endeavor to . . . find support for the so-called 'social development' objective of physical education . . . the sport sociologist is neither a spreader of gospel, nor an evangelist for exercise" (p. 172). While Kenyon was willing to grant that some of the findings of sport sociology "might well be useful to the physical educator" (p. 178), and that the sport sociologist might "benefit from an exposure to a wide array of physical activities and sport" (pp. 178-179), he cautioned that there was potential for such "exposure" to cause the sport sociologist to become "a devoted apologist for exercise" and "there is a danger of contaminating one's objectivity" (p. 179). One can readily imagine the atmosphere that such statements might create for sport sociologists working in departments of physical education.

Another issue that has tended to trouble relations between sport sociology and physical education was described by Hollands (1984): "The very structure of sport study in North America ironically pairs the social critic [sport sociologist] with those very individuals in sport science whose professional ideology reinforces ahistorical and functionalist approaches to the subject" (p. 73).

It is easy to see, then, that the role of sport sociologists in departments of physical education can become paradoxical. On the one hand, scholars who study cultural practices are in an ideal location for studying these phenomena because sporting practices are cultural practices. On the other hand, critical analyses, especially when they are directed toward sport, are often discounted as unscientific by colleagues whose orientation is the positivist science model; worse, some colleagues, and students taking courses in sport sociology, perceive social critiques of sports as being anti-sport, even unpatriotic, and thus having no legitimate place in the physical education course offerings.

Sport Sociology and the Future

Over the past 30 years the sociology of sport has emerged as a distinct academic specialty, and its roots are firmly embedded in departments of physical education (and in departments with names such as kinesiology, exercise science, or sport studies) and sociology. Its intellectual boundaries are extending throughout the social sciences and are part of a growing sport studies tradition.

In 1980, in their review of the emergence and development of the sociology of sport, Loy, Kenyon, and McPherson (1980) concluded that "the sociology of sport has yet to be perceived as a legitimate subfield within either physical education or sociology owing to factors associated with critical mass, academic status, and ideological orientations" (p. 106). Although no monumental developments have taken place for sport sociology since that statement was written, there has been a growing community of scholars working in this subfield. The academic status of the subfield is now more firmly established, especially through the growing popular and scholarly literature (if not through the number of academic positions in higher education), and theoretical work is assuming a more central position in sport sociology research.

There is also increasing recognition, by broad public and professional constituencies, that sports are important cultural practices closely related to events in society at large. More and more sport sociologists are being consulted by various public and professional groups and asked to share their research and insights, on everything from ethnicity and the World Cup, to violence among groups of male athletes, to eating disorders among women. There also seems to be a growing understanding that sport and other forms of physical activity are linked to the social relations of everyday life, which underlie social class inequality, sexism, racism, and other forms of oppression and discrimination.

Given these developments of the past two decades, there are promising signs that the sociology of sport will continue to grow as a fertile field of study. Beyond that, there seem to be increasing opportunities for sport sociology to play a role in interpreting the reciprocal influences of sport in society and society in sport.

Notes

1. I am indebted to John Loy for his two excellent essays on the history of sport sociology (Loy, 1980; Loy et al., 1978a).
2. The Sport Information Resource Centre is the largest depository in the world for collecting and disseminating information in sport, physical education, physical fitness, and sports medicine.
3. Over the years there has been an abundance of criticism about Kenyon's positivist bias. My comments about Kenyon's theoretical orientation are not meant to be judgmental but rather descriptive.
4. I am certainly not suggesting that *all* first generation sport sociologists had this orientation; indeed, there were a number of notable exceptions.
5. A term popularized by Emile Durkheim (1938) to indicate a category of phenomena distinct from individual characteristics. Social facts are characterized by external constraint: They exist outside any given individual, and they place constraints on an individual's behavior.
6. The relationships among cultural studies, critical theory, poststructuralism, and postmodernism are too complex and controversial to discuss here. To illustrate, Agger (1991) has argued "for the compatibility (if not the outright identity) of critical theory, poststructuralism, and postmodernism" (p. 20), and he has authored a recent book titled *Cultural Studies as Critical Theory* (Agger, 1992a).

References

Adelman, M. (1986). *A sporting time: New York City and the rise of modern athletics, 1820-70*. Urbana, IL: University of Illinois Press.

Agger, B. (1991). *A critical theory of public life: Knowledge, discourse, and politics in an age of decline.* New York: Falmer Press.

Agger, B. (1992a). *Cultural studies as critical theory.* Washington, DC: Falmer Press.

Agger, B. (1992b). *The discourse of domination: From the Frankfurt school to postmodernism.* Evanston, IL: Northwestern University Press.

Andrews, D.L. (1993). Desperately seeking Michel: Foucault's genealogy, the body, and critical sport sociology. *Sociology of Sport Journal,* **10,** 148-167.

Andrews, D.L., & Loy, J.W. (1993). British cultural studies and sport: Past encounters and future possibilities. *Quest,* **45,** 255-276.

Axthelm, P. (1970). *The city game.* New York: Harper & Row.

Ball, D.W., & Loy, J.W. (Eds.) (1975). *Sport and social order.* Reading, MA: Addison-Wesley.

Beamish, R. (1981). The materialist approach to sport study: An alternative prescription to the discipline's methodological malaise. *Quest,* **33,** 55-71.

Benhabib, S., & Cornell, D. (Eds.) (1987). *Feminism as critique.* Minneapolis: University of Minnesota Press.

Berger, P.L., & Luckman, T. (1967). *The social construction of reality.* New York: Doubleday.

Bernard, T.J. (1983). *The consensus-conflict debate: Form and content in social theories.* New York: Columbia University Press.

Birrell, S. (1988). Discourses on the gender-sport relationship: From women in sport to gender relations. In K.B. Pandolf (ed.). *Exercise and Sport Sciences Reviews, Volume 16* (pp. 459-502). New York: Macmillan.

Birrell, S. (1989). Racial relations theories and sport: Suggestions for a more critical analysis. *Sociology of Sport Journal* **6,** 212-227.

Birrell, S., & Cole, C.L. (1990). Double fault: Renée Richards and the construction and naturalization of difference. *Sociology of Sport Journal,* **7,** 1-21.

Blumer, H. (1969). *Symbolic interactionism.* Englewood Cliffs, NJ: Prentice Hall.

Borgardus, E.S. (1973). Twenty-five years of American sociology: 1947 to 1972. *Sociology and Social Research,* **57,** 145-152.

Boyle, R.H. (1963). *Sport: Mirror of American Life.* Boston: Little, Brown.

Caillois, R. (1961). *Man, play and games.* New York: Free Press.

Carr, W., & Kemmis, S. (1986). *Becoming critical: Education, knowledge and action.* Philadelphia: Falmer Press.

Chubin, D.E. (1976). The conceptualization of scientific specialties. *The Sociological Quarterly,* **17,** 448-476.

Coakley, J. (1978). *Sport in society: Issues and controversies.* St. Louis: Mosby.

Coakley, J. (1987). Sociology of sport in the United States. *International Review for the Sociology of Sport,* **22,** 63-79.

Cowell, C.C. (1935). An abstract of a study of differentials in junior high school boys based on the observation of physical education activity. *Research Quarterly, 6,* 129-136.

Cowell, C.C. (1958). Validating an index of social adjustment for high school use. *Research Quarterly, 29,* 7-18.

Cozens, F., & Stumpf, F. (1953). *Sports in American life.* Chicago: University of Chicago Press.

Cratty, B.J. (1967). *Social dimensions of physical activity.* Englewood Cliffs, NJ: Prentice Hall.

Culin, S. (1907). *Games of the North American Indians.* Twenty-Fourth Annual Report of the Bureau of American Ethnology, Washington, DC.

Daniels, A. (1966). The study of sport as an element of culture. *International Review of Sport Sociology, 1,* 153-165.

Dickey, G. (1974). *The jock empire.* Radnor, PA: Chilton.

Donnelly, P., & Young, K.M. (1985). Reproduction and transformation of cultural forms in sport: A contextual analysis of rugby. *International Review for the Sociology of Sport, 20,* 20-38.

Donnelly, P., & Young, K. (1988). The construction and confirmation of identity in sport subcultures. *Sociology of Sport Journal, 5,* 223-240.

Duncan, M.C. (1986). A hermeneutic of spectator sport: The 1976 and 1984 Olympic games. *Quest, 38,* 50-77.

Duncan, M.C. (1990). Sports photographs and sexual differences: Images of women and men in the 1984 and 1988 Olympic Games. *Sociology of Sport Journal, 7,* 22-43.

Duncan, M.C., & Hasbrook, C.A. (1988). Denial of power in televised women's sports. *Sociology of Sport Journal, 5,* 1-21.

Durkheim, E. (1938). *The rules of sociological method.* (S.A. Solvay & J.H. Mueller, Trans.). (8th ed.). New York: Free Press.

Edwards, H. (1969). *The revolt of the Black athlete.* New York: Free Press.

Edwards, H. (1973). *Sociology of Sport.* Belmont, CA: Dorsey Press.

Eitzen, D.S. (1979). *Sport in contemporary society: An anthology.* New York: St. Martin's Press.

Eitzen, D.S., & Sage, G.H. (1978). *Sociology of American sport.* Dubuque, IA: Brown.

Erikson, E.H. (1940). Studies in the interpretation of play: Part 1: Clinical observations of play disruption in young children. *Genetic Psychology Monograph, 22,* 557-671.

Erikson, E.H. (1941). Further exploration in play construction: Three spatial variables and their relation to sex and anxiety. *Psychological Bulletin, 38,* 748. (Abstract)

Erikson, E.H. (1943). Observations on the Yurok: Childhood and world image. *American Archeological and Ethnology, 35,* 257-302.

Erikson, E.H. (1963). *Childhood and society* (2nd ed.). New York: Norton.

Fay, B. (1987). *Critical social science: Liberation and its limits.* Ithaca, NY: Cornell University Press.

Fine, G.A. (1979). Preadolescent socialization through organized athletics: The construction of moral meanings in Little League baseball. In M.L. Krotee (Ed.), *The dimensions of sport sociology* (pp. 79-105). Champaign, IL: Leisure Press.

Fine, G.A. (1987). *With the boys: Little League baseball and preadolescent culture*. Chicago: University of Chicago Press.

Flath, A. (Ed.) (1972). *Athletics in America*. Corvallis, OR: Oregon State University Press.

Foley, D.E. (1990). *Learning capitalist culture deep in the heart of Tejas*. Philadelphia: University of Pennsylvania Press.

Fraser, N. (1989). *Unruly practices: Power, discourse, and gender in contemporary social theory*. Minneapolis: University of Minnesota Press.

Freud, S. (1955). *The cases of "Little Hans" and the "Rat Man"* Vol. 12, Complete Works. London: Hogarth.

Freud, S. (1959). *Beyond the pleasure principle*. New York: Bantam.

Freud, S. (1963). *Jokes and their relations to the unconsciousness*. New York: Norton.

Frey, J.H., & Eitzen, D.S. (1991). Sport and society. In W.R. Scott & J. Blake (Eds.), *Annual Review of Sociology, Vol. 17* (pp. 503-522). Palo Alto, CA: Annual Reviews.

Giddens, A. (1977). *Studies in social and political theory*. New York: Basic Books.

Giddens, A. (1984). *The constitution of society*. Berkeley: University of California Press.

Giddens, A. (1987). *Social theory and modern sociology*. Stanford, CA: Stanford University Press.

Gouldner, A.W. (1970). *The coming crisis of Western sociology*. New York: Basic Books.

Groos, K. (1901). *The play of man*. New York: Appleton.

Grossberg, L., Nelson, C., & Treichler, P. (1992). Cultural studies: An introduction. In L. Grossberg, C. Nelson, and P. Treichler (Eds.), *Cultural studies* (pp. 1-22). London: Routledge & Kegan Paul.

Gruneau, R. (1983). *Class, sports, and social development*. Amherst, MA: University of Massachusetts Press.

Gruneau, R., & Albinson, J. (Eds.) (1976). *Canadian sport: Sociological perspectives*. Reading, MA: Addison-Wesley.

Gruneau, R., & Whitson, D. (1993). *Hockey night in Canada: Sport, identities and cultural politics*. Toronto: Garamond Press.

Haley, B. (1978). *The healthy body and Victorian culture*. Cambridge, MA: Harvard University Press.

Hall, A., Slack, T., Smith, G., & Whitson, D. (1991). *Sport in Canadian society*. Toronto: McClelland & Stewart.

Hall, G.S. (1920). *Youth*. New York: Appleton.

Hall, M.A. (1985). Knowledge and gender: Epistemological questions in the social analysis of sport. *Sociology of Sport Journal, 2*, 25-42.

Hall, M.A. (1988). The discourse of feminism. *Sociology of Sport Journal*, **5**, 330-340.

Hall, M.A. (1993). Gender and sport in the 1990s: Feminism, culture, politics. *Sport Science Review*, **2**, 48-68.

Harding, S. (1986). *The science question in feminism*. Ithaca, NY: Cornell University Press.

Hardy, S. (1981). The city and the rise of American sport: 1820-1920. In D.I. Miller (Ed.), *Exercise and sport sciences reviews, Volume 9*. Philadelphia: Franklin Institute.

Hardy, S., & Ingham, A. (1984). Games, structures, and agency: Historians on the American play movement. *Journal of Social History*, **17**, 285-301.

Harris, D. (Ed.) (1972). *Women and sport: A national research conference*. Pennsylvania State University, College of Health, Physical Education and Recreation.

Harris, J.C. (1981). Hermeneutics, interpretive cultural research, and the study of sports. *Quest*, **33**, 72-86.

Harris, J.C. (1983). Interpreting youth baseball: Players' understandings of attention, winning, and playing the game. *Research Quarterly for Exercise and Sport*, **54**, 330-339.

Harris, J.C. (1989). Suited up and stripped down: Perspectives for sociocultural sport studies. *Sociology of Sport Journal*, **6**, 335-347.

Harris, J.C., & Park, R.J. (1983). *Play, games, & sports in cultural contexts*. Champaign, IL: Human Kinetics.

Hart, M. (Ed.) (1972). *Sport in the socio-cultural process*. Dubuque, IA: Brown.

Hoberman, J. (1984). *Sport and political ideology*. Austin: University of Texas Press.

Hoberman, J. (1992). *Mortal engines: The science of performance and the dehumanization of sport*. New York: Free Press.

Hoch, P. (1972). *Rip off the big game*. New York: Doubleday.

Hollands, R.G. (1984). The role of cultural studies and social criticism in the sociological study of sports. *Quest*, **36**, 66-79.

Howard, G.E. (1912). Social psychology of the spectator. *American Journal of Sociology*, **18**, 33-50.

Huey-tsyh, C., & Rossi, P. (Eds.) (1992). *Using theory to improve program and policy evaluations*. New York: Greenwood Press.

Huizinga, J. (1955). *Homo Ludens*. Boston: Beacon.

Ibrahim, H. (1975). *Sport and society*. Long Beach, CA: Hwong.

Ingham, A. (1979). Methodology in the sociology of sport: From symptoms of malaise to Weber for a cure. *Quest*, **31**, 187-215.

Ingham, A.G., & Donnelly, P. (1990). Whose knowledge counts? The production of knowledge and issues of application in the sociology of sport. *Sociology of Sport Journal*, **7**, 58-65.

Ingham, A.G., & Loy, J.W. (Eds.) (1993). *Sport in social development*. Champaign, IL: Human Kinetics.

Jay, M. (1984). *Marxism and totality: The adventures of a concept from Lukacs to Habermas.* Berkeley: University of California Press.

Kellner, D. (1989). *Critical theory, Marxism, and modernity.* Baltimore: Johns Hopkins Press.

Kenyon, G.S. (1969a). *Aspects of contemporary sport sociology.* Chicago: The Athletic Institute.

Kenyon, G.S. (1969b). A sociology of sport: On becoming a sub-discipline. In R.C. Brown & B.J. Cratty (Eds.), *New perspectives of man in action* (pp. 163-180). Englewood Cliffs, NJ: Prentice Hall.

Kenyon, G.S. (1986). The significance of social theory in the development of sport sociology. In C.R. Rees & A.W. Miracle (Eds.), *Sport and social theory* (pp. 3-22). Champaign, IL: Human Kinetics.

Kenyon, G.S., & Loy, J.W. (1965). Toward a sociology of sport. *Journal of Health, Physical Education and Recreation, 36,* 24-25, 68-69.

Klein, A.M. (1986). Pumping irony: Crisis and contradiction in bodybuilding. *Sociology of Sport Journal, 3,* 112-133.

Klein, A.M. (1991). *Sugarball: The American game, the Dominican dream.* New Haven, CT: Yale University Press.

Klein, A.M. (1993). *Little big men: Bodybuilding subculture and gender construction.* Albany: State University of New York Press.

Krotee, M. (Ed.) (1979). *The dimensions of sport sociology.* Champaign, IL: Leisure Press.

Landers, D.M. (Ed.) (1976). *Social problems in athletics.* Urbana: University of Illinois Press.

Lazarus, M. (1883). *Uber die Reize des Spiels* (Concerning the fascination of play). Berlin: Dummler.

Lenskyj, H. (1986). *Out of bounds: Women, sport and sexuality.* Toronto: Women's Press.

Leonard, S.T. (1990). *Critical theory in political practice.* Princeton, NJ: Princeton University Press.

Lever, J. (1983). *Soccer madness.* Chicago: University of Chicago Press.

Lipsyte, R. (1975). *SportsWorld: An American dreamland.* New York: Quadrangle.

Loy, J.W., & Kenyon, G.S. (Eds.) (1969). *Sport, culture, and society.* New York: Macmillan.

Loy, J.W., Kenyon, G.S., & McPherson, B.D. (1980). The emergence and development of the sociology of sport as an academic specialty. *Research Quarterly for Exercise and Sport, 51,* 91-109.

Loy, J.W., McPherson, B.D., & Kenyon, G.S. (1978a). *The sociology of sport as an academic specialty: An episodic essay on the development and emergence of an hybrid subfield in North America.* Vanier City, ON: University of Calgary Press.

Loy, J.W., McPherson, B.D., & Kenyon, G.S. (1978b). *Sport and social systems.* Reading, MA: Addison-Wesley.

Luschen, G. (1980). Sociology of sport: Development, present state, and prospects. In A. Inkeles, N.J. Smelser, & R.H. Turner (Eds.), *Annual Review of Sociology, Vol. 6* (pp. 315-347). Palo Alto, CA: Annual Reviews.

Luschen, G., & Sage, G.H. (Eds.) (1981). *Handbook of social science of sport*. Champaign, IL: Stipes.

Lynton, E.A. (1987). *New priorities for the university*. San Francisco: Jossey-Bass.

MacAloon, J. (1981). *This great symbol: Pierre de Coubertin and the origins of the modern Olympic games*. Chicago: University of Chicago Press.

MacAloon, J. (1987). An observer's view of sport sociology. *Sociology of Sport Journal, 4*, 103-115.

Mangan, J.A. (1986). *The games ethic and imperialism*. New York: Viking Penguin.

Mangan, J.A., & Park, R.J. (Eds.) (1987). *From "fair sex" to feminism: Sport and the socialization of women in the industrial and post-industrial eras*. Totowa, NJ: F. Cass.

Massengale, J.D. (Ed.) (1987). *Trends toward the future in physical education*. Champaign, IL: Human Kinetics.

McIntosh, P. (1963). *Sport in society*. London: C.A. Watts.

Mead, G.H. (1934). *Mind, self and society*. Chicago: University of Chicago Press.

Meggyesy, D. (1971). *Out of their league*. New York: Paperback Library.

Messner, M.A. (1990). Men studying masculinity: Some epistemological issues in sport sociology. *Sociology of Sport Journal, 7*, 136-153.

Messner, M.A. (1992). *Power at play: Sports and the problem of masculinity*. Boston: Beacon Press.

Messner, M.A., & Sabo, D.F. (Eds.) (1990). *Sport, men, and the gender order: Critical feminist perspectives*. Champaign, IL: Human Kinetics.

Messner, M.A., & Sabo, D.F. (1994). *Sex, violence & power in sports: Rethinking masculinity*. Freedom, CA: Crossing Press.

Michener, J. (1976). *Sports in America*. New York: Random House.

Morrow, R.A. (1991). Critical theory, Gramsci and cultural studies: From structuralism to poststructuralism. In P. Wexler (Ed.), *Critical theory now* (pp. 27-69). New York: Falmer.

Morrow, R.A. (1994). *Critical theory and methodology*. Thousand Oaks, CA: Sage.

Natan, A. (1958). *Sport and society*. London: Bowes and Bowes.

National Center for Educational Statistics. (1983). *Digest of Educational Statistics*. Washington, DC: U.S. Department of Education.

National Research Council. (1983). *Survey Report 1982: Doctoral recipients from United States Universities*. Washington, DC: National Academy Press.

Nixon, H. (1976). *Sport and social organization*. New York: Bobbs-Merrill.

O'Hanlon, T. (1980). Interscholastic athletics, 1900-1940: Shaping citizens for unequal roles in the modern industrial state. *Educational Theory*, **30**, 89-103.

Patrick, G.T.W. (1903). The psychology of football. *American Journal of Psychology*, **14**, 104-117.

Patrick, G.T.W. (1916). *The psychology of relaxation*. Boston: Houghton Mifflin.

Piaget, J. (1951). *Play, dreams and imitation in childhood*. New York: Norton.

Piaget, J. (1965). *The moral judgment of the child*. New York: Free Press.

Plessner, H. (1952). Soziologie des sports. *Deutsche Universitätszeitung, 7*, 9-11, 12-14, 22-23.

Popkewitz, T.S. (1984). *Paradigm and ideology in educational research*. New York: Falmer Press.

Popplow, U. (1951). Zu einer soziologie des sports. *Sports und leibeserziehung*, **11**, 2-4.

Rabinow, P., & Sullivan, W.M. (Eds.) (1979). *Interpretive social science: A reader*. Berkeley: University of California Press.

Ray, L.J. (1993). *Rethinking critical theory*. Newbury Park, CA: Sage.

Ritzer, G. (1992). *Contemporary sociological theory* (3rd ed.). New York: McGraw-Hill.

Roberts, J.M., Sutton-Smith, B., & Kendon, A. (1963). Strategy in games and folk tales. *Journal of Social Psychology*, **61**, 185-199.

Rossi, P.H. (1980). The presidential address: The challenge and opportunities of applied social research. *American Sociological Review*, **45**, 889-904.

Sage, G.H. (1970). *Sport and American society*. Reading, MA: Addison-Wesley.

Sage, G.H. (1979). The current status and trends of sport sociology. In M.L. Krotee (Ed.), *The dimensions of sport sociology* (pp. 23-31). Champaign, IL: Leisure Press.

Sage, G.H. (1981). Sport sociology, normative and nonnormative arguments: Playing the same song over and over and . . . . In S.L. Greendorfer & A. Yiannakis (Eds.), *Sociology of sport: Perspectives* (pp. 7-13). Champaign, IL: Leisure Press.

Sage, G.H. (1982). Sociocultural aspects of physical activity: Significant research traditions, 1972-1982. In H. Eckhert (Ed.), *The academy Papers, No. 16* (pp. 59-66). Reston, VA: AAHPERD.

Sage, G.H. (1984). The quest for identity in college physical education. *Quest*, **36**, 115-121.

Sage, G.H. (1987). Pursuit of knowledge in sociology of sport: Issues and prospects. *Quest*, **39**, 255-281.

Sage, G.H. (1990). *Power and ideology in American sport: A critical perspective*. Champaign, IL: Human Kinetics.

Sage, G.H. (1991). Paradigms, paradoxes, and progress: Reflections and prophecy. In R.J. Park & H.M. Eckert (Eds.), *New possibilities, new paradigms?* (pp. 154-161). American Academy Papers, No. 24. Champaign, IL: Human Kinetics.

Sage, G.H. (1992). Beyond enhancing performance in sport: Toward empowerment and transformation. In R.W. Christina & H.M. Eckert (Eds.), *Enhancing human performance in sport: New concepts and developments* (pp. 85-95). American Academy Papers, No. 25. Champaign, IL: Human Kinetics.

Schiller, F. (1875). *Essays, aesthetical and philosophical*. London: Bell.

Schutz, A. (1972). *The phenomenology of the social world*. London: Heinemann.

Scott, J. (1971). *The athletic revolution*. New York: Free Press.

Sewart, J.J. (1978). Critical theory and the critique of conservative method. *American sociologist, 13*, 15-22.

Shaw, G. (1972). *Meat on the hoof: The hidden world of Texas football*. New York: St. Martin's Press.

Shecter, L. (1970). *The jocks*. New York: Paperback Library.

Smith, R., & Preston, F. (1977). *Sociology: An introduction*. New York: St. Martin's Press.

Smith, Y.R. (1992). Women of color in society and sport. *Quest, 44*, 228-250.

Snyder, E.E., & Spreitzer, E. (1978). *Social aspects of sport*. Englewood Cliffs, NJ: Prentice Hall.

Snyder, E., & Spreitzer, E. (1979). Sport sociology and the discipline of sociology: Present status and speculations about the future. *Review of Sport and Leisure, 4*, 10-29.

Sparks, R.E.C. (1985). Knowledge structures in sport and physical education. *Sociology of Sport Journal, 2*, 1-8.

Spencer, H. (1873). *The principles of psychology*. New York: Appleton.

Stehr, N., & Larson, L.E. (1972). The rise and decline of areas of specialization. *American Sociologist, 7*, 5-7.

Stockman, N. (1983). *Antipositivist theories of the sciences*. Boston: D. Reidel.

Stone, G.P. (Ed.) (1972). *Games, sport and power*. New Brunswick, NJ: Transaction Books.

Sumner, W.G. (1906). *Folkways*. Boston: Ginn.

Sutton-Smith, B., Roberts, J.M., & Rozelka, R. (1963). Games involvement in adults. *Journal of Social Psychology, 60*, 15-30.

Talamini, J., & Page, C. (1973). *Sport and society*. Boston: Little, Brown.

Theberge, N. (1993). The construction of gender in sport: Women, coaching, and the naturalization of difference. *Social Problems, 40*, 301-313.

Thomas, W.I. (1901). The gaming instinct. *American Journal of Sociology, 6*, 750-763.

Triplett, N. (1898). The dynamogenic factors in pacemaking and competition. *American Journal of Psychology, 4*, 507-533.

Turner, J.H. (1985). In defense of positivism. *Sociological Theory, 3*, 24-30.

Turner, J.H. (1990a). *The structure of sociological theory* (5th ed.). Belmont, CA: Wadsworth.

Turner, J.H. (1990b). The past, present, and future of theory in American sociology. In G. Ritzer (Ed.), *Frontiers of social theory: The new syntheses* (pp. 371-391). New York: Columbia University Press.

Ulrich, C. (1968). *The social matrix of physical education*. Englewood Cliffs, NJ: Prentice Hall.

United States Bureau of Census. (1975). *Historical statistics of the United States*. Washington, DC: United States Government Printing Office.

Veblen, T. (1899). *The theory of the leisure class*. New York: Macmillan.

Waller, W. (1932). *The sociology of teaching*. New York: Wiley.

Wexler, P. (Ed.) (1991). *Critical theory now*. New York: Falmer.

Whitson, D. (1984). Sport and hegemony: On the construction of the dominant culture. *Sociology of Sport Journal, 1*, 64-78.

Whyte, W.F. (1982). The presidential address: Social inventions for solving human problems. *American Sociological Review, 47*, 1-13.

Wohl, A. (1966). Conception and range of sport sociology. *International Review of Sport Sociology, 1*, 5-15.

Yiannakis, A., & Greendorfer, S.L. (Eds.) (1992). *Applied sociology of sport*. Champaign, IL: Human Kinetics.

Yiannakis, A., McIntyre, T.D., Melnick, M.J., & Hart, D.P. (1976). *Sport sociology: Contemporary themes*. Dubuque, IA: Kendall/Hunt.

5

Sport History

Nancy L. Struna
University of Maryland

Sport history is a field of scholarly inquiry with multiple and often intersecting foci, including exercise, the body, play, games, athletics, sports, physical recreations, health, and leisure. Its contributors come from many academic homes, and their interests intersect with and are influenced by currents of thought in the broader realms of exercise and sport science as well as other disciplines. Two elements do, however, serve as boundaries for the research of sport historians. One is human movement. We all explore the human agents of movement, movement as cultural performance or social practice, and the various forms of movement (even of animals) that were meaningful to human beings. The second boundary is one that contours all history: time. Sport historians examine change, or the lack of it, over time.[1]

The subdiscipline of sport history has changed in substantive ways, especially in recent decades. Two changes in particular are the subjects of this essay: the "who" and the "what," or the writers and the subjects. Before the 1960s scholars in departments of history produced most of the research and writing, while members of what has become exercise and sport science, or kinesiology, focused more narrowly on activities and individuals who had some role in shaping their own field. In the next 20 years the relative contributions of people from both fields reversed, and by the 1980s many of the leading sport historians were located in departments of exercise and sport science. Simultaneously, scholars from other fields began to investigate sport, broadly conceived, as did people who would not call themselves sport historians. Today, therefore, the sport history community is an immensely varied one, and the history of sport has acquired substantial recognition and significance well beyond the walls of both exercise and sport science and history.

A parallel, and certainly not coincidental, change took place in the body of knowledge about sport in history. Through the 1970s researchers

A Chronology of Sport History

Early Foundations

Year | Event

1886   History of physical education stimulated by Edward Hartwell, with *Physical Training in American Colleges and Universities*

1905   Fred Leonard published "The first introduction of the Jahn gymnastics into America"

1917   History of sport addressed by Frederick Paxson in "The Rise of Sport"

1929   The first "new" social history to incorporate sport history: John A. Krout, *Annals of American Sport*

1940   Foster R. Dulles published a popular history, *America Learns to Play*

Organization of the Subdiscipline

Year | Event

1951   John R. Betts completed his seminal dissertation, "Organized Sport in Industrial America," in the History Department at Columbia University

1960   The CPEA established a History of Sport section

1964   Guy Lewis completed his seminal dissertation, "The American Intercollegiate Football Spectacle, 1869-1917," in the Department of Physical Education at the University of Maryland

1971   Ohio State University hosted the first Big Ten Symposium on sport history

1973   The North American Society for Sport History (NASSH) held its initial conference

Development of the Subdiscipline

Year | Event

1970s   The "take-off" phase for sport history in departments of physical education

1974   NASSH published the first *Journal of Sport History*

1978   Analytic history, and the modernization paradigm, boosted by Allen Guttmann's *From Ritual to Record: The Nature of Modern Sport*

1980s   Modernization paradigm gradually eclipsed by multiple historical and multidisciplinary approaches

| 1990s | Analytical and synthetic books became significant publication trend; specialists in many academic homes contributed to sport history research; sport history incorporated broadly in academicians' research and popular writing |

labored primarily in the domain of organized, competitive, physical contests. Their interests lay in describing and explaining human experiences in those forms, the institutional "evolution" of organized sport, and the programs in which sport and exercise figured. Since then we have come to understand that organized, competitive, physical contests constitute a type of sport, "modern" sport, which was constructed by a particular set of people at a particular time. This understanding, in turn, has provoked a wider range of questions, not only about how and why this historical type, "modern sport," came to be, but also about the making and significance of prior practices, about practices and conceptions of exercise and health, about the multiple contexts in which games and exercises and physical training existed, and about the sources of variance in experiences over time. Indeed, the larger shift has been to understand past experiences on their own terms, rather than on ours, and to employ multiple frames to make sense of the many dimensions of past experiences.

As the 21st century approaches, sport history is a vibrant and diverse subdiscipline. This narrative, however, will not tell the entire "story" of the subdiscipline. Three limits in particular warrant comments. First, this chapter focuses on the history of sport in the United States, as written primarily by citizens of the United States. Thus, unfortunately, it ignores Americans doing other topics and non-Americans doing U.S. history. Second, the literature on which this chapter draws is published primarily by academics and, as time progresses, in book form. Textbooks, presentations, some very fine syntheses (e.g., Baker, 1982; Gorn & Goldstein, 1993; Guttmann, 1988; Mandell, 1984), and the rich works by nonacademic historians such as Robert W. Henderson (1947) are not included. Many are invaluable contributions to the literature, but covering them would require far more space than this work permits.

Finally, this chapter will not convey the international dimensions of the scholarly study of sport history. Americans who write about the history of sport are really contributors to what is a much larger—indeed, a global—scholarly enterprise, and many of us have drawn on the works of colleagues around the world. Moreover, in many countries where sport and physical culture are significant socially and culturally, scholars have organized societies dedicated to expanding and communicating knowledge about sport in history. In turn, members of these national and continental associations, including those in North America, are linked within

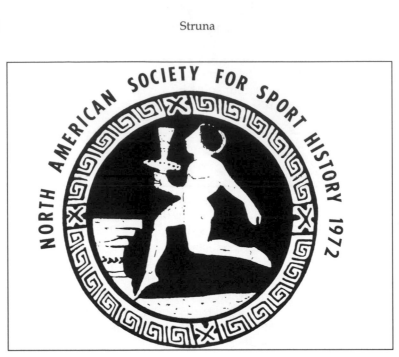

North American Society for Sport History seal

Allen Guttmann   David Voigt

Roberta Park

The first NASSH Council with honorary president, Seward Staley. From left: Ron Smith, Alan Metcalfe, Mary Lou Remley, Seward Staley, Marvin Eyler, Betty McCue, Guy Lewis, and Bruce Bennett.

a global scholarly organization, the International Society for the History of Physical Education and Sport. Unfortunately, this chapter does that international community of scholars no justice.

Early Foundations

Long before sport history constituted a subdiscipline in the United States, there were people "doing" the history of sport. Among the earliest was Frederic Paxson, whose "The Rise of Sport" (1917) remains a classic. Paxson was a student of Frederick Jackson Turner, who had revolutionized American historiography with "The Significance of the Frontier in American History" in 1893 (1963). Turner had argued that the physical frontier was the conditioning, distinguishing dimension of American life; unlike Europeans, Americans had always had land, usually to the West, to which they could move. The frontier was significant economically, militarily, and psychically; it had a "releasing" effect, which later historians transformed into a "social safety valve" argument. By Paxson's time the continental frontier had formally closed and, he suggested, for millions of urban citizens a "new" one emerged in its stead: organized sport, primarily of the athletic variety. He proceeded to describe the participatory habits of his generation and, in the process, to lay the foundation both for the "sport as social safety valve" theory that generations of sport studies scholars have employed, and for the "evolutionary rise of sport" approach that dominated sport history into the 1980s.

In the aftermath both of Paxson's article and the "great war," an entire school of historians began to address the sport and recreational pursuits of Americans. These were the "new" social historians of the interwar years, who were responsible for two distinctive multivolume series, *The History of American Life* and *The Pageant of America*. Each series, in varying degrees, made an effort to incorporate material about the physical activities in which many generations of Americans had engaged. John Allen Krout's *Annals of American Sport* (1929) was one volume in the latter series, and it typified the strengths and the weaknesses of the lot. Krout described a range of games and contests, from the "amusements" and "pastimes" of early Americans to the highly organized contests of their late 19th- and early 20th-century descendants. His work drew from original research and from the many antiquarian studies that local amateur historians had published. The result was a chronicle that ordered activities over time but did not explain them in time. But then, to these early social historians there was little need for explanation; the framework of social evolution provided it.

These early efforts were significant on two counts. First, they represented a shift in American historiography; the subjects of historians were no longer just wars and politics and "high culture," but ordinary people doing ordinary things, like playing. Indeed, one of the subthemes in these volumes was that ordinary people spent a good deal of time, time that was important to them, in sports and recreations. Second, the authors of both series uncovered, or resurrected, information about sports and games, and made it available for public consumption. The timing was propitious. In the 1920s, which later historians dubbed the first "golden age" of sport, the interest of ordinary Americans in organized sports and recreation was at an all-time high. Importantly as well, it was a literate, populist public, living for the first time in a "mass" society. Many citizens were intrigued by the achievements both of "great men" and of ordinary people who demonstrated extraordinary achievements, many of them physical in nature. Americans wanted not only to see Babe Ruth but also to read about the sports and games and about the performers who were his—and their—predecessors.

These series apparently had one other effect as well. Historians could now look for theses and dissertation subjects in the world of ordinary life and sports. A number did. Most notable perhaps were Jesse Steiner's *Americans at Play* (1933) and Jennie Holliman's *American Sports 1785-1835* (1931). Steiner was a student at Columbia University, which was and remained an active center for sport and recreation history research. One of the most influential works that came from Columbia in subsequent years was *America Learns to Play* (1940), by Foster Rhea Dulles, who extended Paxson's generally positive appraisal of the "rise" of organized (read "modern") sport. For him the matter was not just that the evolution of sport paralleled the industrialization and urbanization of America, or even that sports replaced the frontier as a safety valve. Rather, modern sports and other forms of recreation made for a "more satisfying life for the masses" (p. 99) as America left behind its simple rural life and moved headlong into the complex, industrial, international present.

America Learns to Play was also a large-scale defense of popular sporting practice. Although not an apologia for the interests of ordinary people in sports and games, it did attempt both to rationalize and justify those interests and to establish the larger social and cultural significance of recreations. In so doing, it served as a counterpoint to the works of other historians, who directed their most vehement criticisms at the dehumanizing impacts of modernizing, industrializing society to be sure, but who were also not entirely satisfied with the directions of contemporary sports and recreations. Arnold Toynbee (1935), an English scholar, and Lewis Mumford (1934), a New Yorker, both had published critiques in the 1930s. Neither author, however, had as substantial an effect on the systematic, academic study of sport and play in the past as did a Dutch historian, Johan Huizinga.

Huizinga initially published *Homo Ludens. A Study of the Play-Element in Culture* as Adolf Hitler was driving to consume all of Europe in 1939 (paperback edition, 1955). This context is critical, for although *Homo Ludens* argued that play was foundational to civilization, it was also sharply critical, even condemnatory, of contemporary organized sports. Huizinga disliked the regimentation of contemporary organized sport; the use of sports as instruments of propaganda via mass demonstrations dismayed him. American colleges used them this way, and so did the Olympics, the last of which had taken place in Berlin in 1936 and in which Hitler had taken great pride. The problem for Huizinga was not just the overt politicalization of organized sports. Indeed, this phenomenon was actually an indicator of something more profound. In organized sports, according to Huizinga, the creative, humanizing, energizing "essence" of the "play-quality" and the play spirit had been lost. Faced with a continent and its great civilizations about to be destroyed, he saw no future.

Over the years *Homo Ludens* has become obligatory reading for many students in sport studies in general and sport history in particular. At least through the 1970s Huizinga's analysis of play, if not his criticism of organized sport, shaped and sharpened many academic debates and monographs about the nature of play, games, and sport. In fact, his analysis of play was (and remains) the bedrock of both the idealists' and the positivists' hierarchical classification schemes. The book was not translated and widely available in English until 1949, however, so its impact on Americans was minimal until the early 1950s. Importantly as well, World War II interrupted the scholarly study of sport in the past, and virtually no work of significance appeared in the 1940s. Not until 1951 would another substantive scholarly inquiry be completed.

The interwar years constituted a significant foundational period in the history of sport. As a part of the broader movement to reconstruct the histories of ordinary people—to break the constraining bonds of their own predecessors' myopic institutional and "great men" approaches—historians had at least put sports and games and other physical recreations on the stage of history, albeit usually in a corner. To be sure, however, it was not just organized, public sports and recreations that gained the attention of members of the academic community in the 1920s and 1930s. This history of physical training-become-physical education was also emerging, via members of departments of physical education.

The history of physical education began much as did the history of sport, with an article here and there. Some early leaders, such as Luther H. Gulick (1890), had argued that well-prepared physical educators should be knowledgeable about history, as well as psychology and physiology, but his call did not result in a mass movement to employ the methods and questions of history. None of his contemporaries appeared as consciously committed to a particular explanatory framework as Paxson was, but some of them were interested in keeping "what had happened" alive and in employing historical understandings in the shaping of policy and programs. For example, Edward M. Hartwell's *Physical Training in American Colleges and Universities* (1886) and the published report of the physical training conference held in Boston in 1889 (Barrows, 1890) both discussed past movements in exercise, gymnastics, and other physical training activities. These works, in turn, set the stage for the more extensive historical research after the turn of the century. Hartwell (1905) himself completed a history of physical training, and Fred Leonard, a student of Delphine Hanna at Oberlin College, followed suit. Leonard (e.g., 1905, 1915) wrote several pieces about early leaders in the physical training movement, exercise programs, and intercollegiate athletics. Then in 1923 he published a textbook-like *Guide to the History of Physical Education*, dedicated to Hartwell and far broader in scope than anything else in print, such as Harriet Ballintine's *The History of Physical Training at Vassar College, 1865-1915* (n. d.). The redoubtable R. Tait McKenzie took the lead in revising the *Guide* in 1927.

Over the next two decades a number of books emerged, intended primarily for courses in the foundations of the rapidly developing profession of physical education, which included sections devoted to history. In 1926 Emmett Rice published a slim but potent volume, *A Brief History of Physical Education*. A year later Dorothy Ainsworth, apparently aiming in part to correct the male-dominated perspective evident in her predecessors' books, wrote *A History of Physical Education in Colleges for Women* (1930). Thereafter articles that either contained some history or were prepared to chronicle the "rise" of institutional physical education proliferated, even if they did not quite become staples, in the *American Physical Education Review*. The effect was significant. In 1942 Norma Schwendener published the popular *History of Physical Education in the United States*.

Several features are intriguing about these early efforts at writing the history of physical education. One is their timing, especially in comparison to the works of historians and other students of society. These were contemporary works, even to the point of shared publication dates; it seems likely that the history of physical education was reaping the benefits of a generation of Americans who had grown up with institutionalized sports, games, and exercises, as earlier generations either had not, or had not to the same extent. Certainly the public and institutional political interest in physical education was greater than it had been; physical education programs were increasing in number and in terms of the population served in the interwar years.

A second point involves the writers themselves. None of these people apparently had any substantial formal training in the discipline of history; in this respect, they were like other physical educators who investigated biological and social phenomena. Graduate, disciplinary training among physical educators did not become entrenched until after World War II. Consequently, whether they were about physiology or history, the studies published by emergent physical education researchers reflected the limits of their preparation. The books on history from this period were descriptive chronicles: Events unfolded; connections and explanations were left untold.

Although the content of their work is not surprising, what is striking is the fact that Leonard, or Rice, or Schwendener, or anyone else, attempted to write a history before World War II. They did so with little support from their departments or from colleagues in departments of history. The latter were probably not even aware of the physical educators' interests. None of the historians' works on sport indicate knowledge of this emergent field and its relationships to sports and recreations. The early historians of physical education also had no formal networks, although they may have corresponded with one another. In effect, they produced what they did in an academic vacuum, with all of the hindrances that confront latter-day historians of sport and physical education and none of the informal or formal intellectual exchanges and networks. The wonder thus is not that they wrote chronicles but that they wrote about the past at all.

Organization of the Subdiscipline

In the aftermath of World War II, two not entirely unrelated movements altered the context for the historical study of sport. One was the near explosion of popular interest in organized sports, which bore directly on college programs in physical education and athletics. Millions of GIs matriculated at colleges and universities, where they swelled the rosters of athletic teams and took part in physical activity classes and intramurals. Moreover, many women, whose public presence in work and play spaces had altered dramatically during the war, were not inclined to return to pre-war patterns. Inside as well as outside of colleges, they constituted a rising proportion of producers and consumers of organized, public sports.

Physical educators could not have ignored this popular interest in organized sport, even had they so desired, and many had no such interest. Male and female physical educators had served in the war, often in positions where they used their expertise in physical training and sport. As they returned to civilian life and either reclaimed or took up new positions as college faculty members, they also augmented their curricula, both for majors and the general student population, with more organized sport experiences. This is not to suggest, of course, that physical education curricula had not incorporated organized sports in the past. Indeed, as Guy Lewis (1969a) maintained, university and college physical training/ education programs had offered instruction in athletic sports since the 1890s. It is to suggest, however, that sports became increasingly prominent within physical education.

The study of the history of physical education was not unaffected by this turn. In 1953 three men—Deobold Van Dalen, Elmer Mitchell, and Bruce Bennett—published *A World History of Physical Education*, which exceeded all of its predecessors in scope. It had, on the one hand, an international flavor, as befit the times. Moreover, in keeping with their positions in universities where intercollegiate athletics and participatory sport experiences figured prominently, the men demonstrated a keen interest in ancient societies, especially Greece, wherein the "roots" of amateur athletics presumably existed. They focused, too, on the institutional bases for sports, particularly in schools and churches in which they saw long-running resemblances to modern practices. Indeed, in *A World History of Physical Education*, physical education/training and sport emerged as distinguishable, but nonetheless related, phenomena with long histories.

Another perspective on the significance of sport as a serious historical enterprise emerged from the University of Illinois. Here, even before the war, Seward Staley had argued that sport should be the core of physical education (1939), as well as that physical education majors should complete a course in the history of sport (1937). He returned to these themes in the post-war years as he began his own research on historical references to sport in English language publications, and as he began to attract graduate students who wanted to study sport as an historical subject.[2] A dean with extensive administrative duties in a large college, Staley was not a prolific author; yet, as will be seen, he did leave his mark on sport history.

The altered post-war climate also affected the discipline of history, which underwent a paradigm shift in the wake of the Allied victory over Nazism and the emergence of the Cold War. Progressive history, which the "new" social historians of the 1920s and 1930s had constructed, gave way to the writing of "consensus" history, the second movement noted earlier. As Peter Novick (1988) and other analysts of American historiography have noted, consensus history was a fundamentally conservative movement. What was significant in American history, consensus historians maintained, was what bound rather than separated Americans; hence they focused on topics such as abundance, institutions, and common interests such as the defense of freedom.

One consensus historian also took sport as his subject. In 1951 John Rickard Betts completed a seminal dissertation, "Organized Sport in Industrial America," at what remained the academic center of historians for the scholarly study of sport, Columbia University under the tutelage of John A. Krout. The choice of this topic was not illogical, although it was a bit daring for an historian. In post-war America, organized sports were theoretically conservative, even though experiences in sport might be liberating for individuals. Institutions, such as colleges, schools, and even the federal bureaucracy, trumpeted sports as bastions of democracy, and sport victories as symbols of institutional and national prowess. In the context of the Cold War especially, victories by American athletes were particularly meaningful. They displayed and reinforced American prowess, habits of industry, and the positive effects of democratic living, which contrasted markedly with life under authoritarian regimes. Moreover, as contemporary physical educators maintained, participation in sport "taught" longstanding American ideals: fair play, teamwork, industry, and personal and social discipline. In the late 1940s and 1950s, in short, organized sport was a worthy matter for the common interest—and a defensible subject for a consensus historian.

In turn, "Organized Sport in Industrial America" was, like *America Learns to Play* before it, a defense of modern organized sport. Yet it was something more as well—an important transitional work. Betts picked up where the earlier generation of "new" social historians had stopped, by locating an array of sports and recreations popular among various generations of Americans. Moreover, he adapted their evolutionary framework and produced the most comprehensive account to date of the "rise" of organized sport. However, he saw a dynamism in the movement from relatively simple games and pastimes to complex, highly organized contests that no one before had acknowledged. For Betts, the "rise" of sport (specifically, modern athletic contests) did not mean a simple "unfolding." Rather, he argued, modern sports were the products of two processes that had actually determined the shape of modern America: industrialization and urbanization.

Many of us have since criticized Betts's histories (e.g., Struna, 1985; Adelman, 1983). Both his dissertation and the articles he drew from it (1953a, 1953b), as well as later pieces such as the influential "Mind and Body in Early American Thought" (1968), were descriptive, narrative histories. They illustrated rather than analyzed the connections between sport forms and larger social and economic processes, and they focused narrowly on middle-class practices. Yet, none of us could fail to acknowledge the importance and impact of Betts's works. As had no one before, John R. Betts staked out a claim for the significance of modern sports. In his mind, sports were not isolated, idiocratic activities meaningful simply to individuals; they were substantive social and cultural phenomena that affected American society. Importantly as well, in developing this argument Betts located sport, and sports, within the context of social, economic, and cultural movements. Thus, he grounded the history of sport within the larger frame of American history and thereby provided subsequent historians with a conceptual template.

In the 1960s a number of academicians and popular writers, especially journalists, joined Betts as shapers of the emergent subdiscipline. Most authors treated sport, or particular sports, as a developing, evolving phenomenon—indeed, an institution—within American historical experience. A case in point was organized baseball, which received extensive treatment from Harold Seymour (1959-1971) and David Voigt (1966-1970). A broader view of American sport, and perhaps a more compelling one at the time, appeared in *Sport—Mirror of American Life* (1963), written by Robert H. Boyle, an editor for *Sports Illustrated*. As had Betts, Boyle detailed a number of sporting experiences, but he concentrated less on their long-term evolution than on their place and representativeness in 20th-century life. For Boyle, the critical element in the story was the extent to which sport, and sports, reflected both the course and the content of Americans' experience. Thereafter, the passive mirror theory profoundly affected many histories, as well as contemporary discussions of sport; along with evolution, it sufficed as the basis for explanation for years to come.

Through the mid-1960s, people like Betts and Boyle dominated the writing of the history of sport, both in quantitative and qualitative terms. Yet, neither historians nor journalists had made as much of their advantage as they might have. For certain, they had not taken substantive steps either to promote the history of sport or to bring order to their knowledge. There was thus a void, which at least in part was an organizational one. Reenter Seward Staley and his contemporaries in departments of physical education.

One of Staley's goals had been the creation of an organization that would promote the systematic historical study of sport by physical educators. An independent organization lay some years in the future, but the construction of an interim body began in 1960. In that year 63 members of the College Physical Education Association (the CPEA, soon renamed the National College Physical Education Association for Men, NCPEAM) presented their executive council with a petition requesting recognition of a new section or subgroup, with its own program rights (CPEA, 1961). Importantly as well, Marvin Eyler, who had completed his doctorate under Staley, published a paper that outlined "The Nature and Status of Historical Research Pertaining to Sports and Physical Education" (Eyler, 1960). The proponents of the history of sport, it seems, were well prepared to state their case. Still, in an initial mail vote, the council failed to authorize the section. Staley, Eyler, and Earle Ziegler, among others, however, did not let the matter languish. At the annual business meeting, they brought the section proposal before the general membership. Staley's motion received a positive vote, and the History of Sport section came into existence (Berryman, 1973).

The creation of the History of Sport section within the CPEA/NCPEAM was an important step in the promotion of the historical study of sport among physical educators, especially men. It provided historians of sport and of physical education with a forum where they could share their research, and the NCPEAM annual *Proceedings* became an important publication outlet. Significantly as well, the section meetings enabled historians of sport and of physical education to join in the defense of the profession against the challenges about its nonacademic nature leveled by James Conant (1963).

No history of a subdiscipline to which physical educators have contributed can ignore James Conant, the president of Harvard University. As most readers are aware, Conant charged that physical education was not academic and did not warrant recognition either for the field's practitioners as academics or of their classes for academic credit. Thereafter, his attack elicited responses from physical educators, most notably Franklin Henry (1964); it may have encouraged physical educators to make programs more rigorous and to emphasize the importance of knowledge of and about movement. Yet, whether Conant's charges, and the subsequent intellectual and political parrying, had the transformative impact on the subdisciplines that some people have attributed to this episode remains a question.[3] Certainly, it does in the case of the history of sport.

It seems clear that even before 1963 some physical educators who would be historians of sport had begun to do two things that analysts of this critical era have either ignored or downplayed. Either by reading history or, more formally, by completing course work in departments of history, some people had begun to steep themselves in the content and methods of the discipline of history. Consequently, even as Conant spoke, dissertations influenced by Betts's template were in progress. In contrast to earlier (and more than a few contemporary) chronicles and antiquarian studies, these were "real" histories, narrative works that described, *and* made some effort to account for, change or the lack of it over time in human experiences in sport.

One of the earliest figures in this historical knowledge-making movement from within physical education was Guy Lewis, a doctoral student of Marvin Eyler's at the University of Maryland. Courses in history were central to Lewis's program, a fact reflected in his dissertation. Completed in 1964, "The American Intercollegiate Football Spectacle, 1869-1917" was a fairly comprehensive history of the "rise" and "development" not just of a distinctive American version of a centuries-old game, but also of a sport that acquired substantial institutional and, indeed, cultural significance. In its day Lewis's dissertation was a landmark much as John Betts's had been.

The argument here is not that a subdiscipline hinged on one work. Rather, the suggestion is that the preparation of physical educators in the discipline of history both preceded the Conant challenge and helps to account for the increasing numbers of histories for which people like Guy Lewis were responsible. Lewis himself remained an influential historian of sport for more than a decade. His subsequent articles on collegiate sports (1967, 1969b), the impact of World War I on American sporting life (1973), and the significance of sports on youth culture in the 20th century (1977) expanded historians' understandings of American sport and American society. They were also chapters in the expanding "book" on the history of sport and physical education to which other physical educators were contributing. John Lucas had begun his lifelong work on the Olympic movement (e.g., 1962, 1973a, 1980), and Betty Spears, hers on women's contributions to sport and physical education (e.g., 1972, 1976, 1986). In "The Making of Round Hill School," Bruce Bennett (1965) moved beyond earlier efforts to determine the "roots" of physical training/education programs by examining an activity—gymnastics— within the site and milieu of a school. Ellen Gerber (1971, 1972, 1975) also investigated the roots and the "rise" of physical education as she focused on central figures and critical institutions in the past of physical education and, eventually, on the intersection of physical education and sports in the experiences and control of intercollegiate athletics by women physical educators in the early 20th century.

Beyond augmenting the body of knowledge, the presentations and publications by these people, as well as many others both in and outside of physical education, may have had another important and perhaps unintended effect as the decade of the 1960s came to a close. They laid bare the limits of the CPEA/NCPEAM section, two of which were particularly critical. First, the section had never been an encompassing body. Only rarely had section programs drawn historians of sport who were not physical educators. Nor did women have access to the meetings, even though a number of them were visible and influential proponents of the history of sport and physical education. In addition to Gerber and Spears, their ranks included Betty McCue, Mary Lou Remley, and Marianna Trekell. Finally, the section had not effectively challenged the perception of nonhistorically inclined physical educators that historical inquiry was not research—at least not like that done in other subfields. Through 1972 the history of sport section coexisted with the research section of NCPEAM. This relationship, in turn, encouraged a simple conclusion: Only independence would alter historians' second-class status.

Importantly, some members of the history of sport section realized the limits of their structure, and along with nonmembers, they moved to overcome them. Four pivotal years, 1968 to 1972, produced important linkages among historians of sport and physical education who were located in departments of physical education, both internationally and within the United States across disciplines. From Ohio State and the University of Illinois, respectively, Bruce Bennett and Earle Ziegler partici- pated in the First International Seminar on the history of Physical Educa- tion and Sports, held in Israel in 1968. Two years later Americans joined in the First Canadian Symposium on the History of Sport and Physical Education, and then in the First Asian Seminar on the History of Sport and Physical Education. In 1971 Ohio State University was the site of a Big Ten Symposium on the History of Sport and Physical Education. At the end of that year Guy Lewis, Marvin Eyler, and several of the latter's graduate students at the University of Maryland worked with John Betts to arrange a history of sport program for the American Historical Association conference in Boston.

One step remained: the formation of a new organization, the North American Society for Sport History (NASSH), which was broader in mem- bership, both in demographic and geographic terms, than the "old"

NCPEAM section had ever been. Not coincidentally, the initial meeting of the steering committee in 1972 was held in Windsor, Ontario, for a number of people in Canadian universities—especially Maxwell Howell, Alan Metcalfe, and Gerald Redmond—were partners with citizens of the United States in this venture. Moreover, scholars from outside of physical education were prominent figures at the first conference, held at Ohio State University the following year. The NASSH council acknowledged the work of John Betts by naming one of three honorary addresses after him.[4] It then invited one of the foremost historians of baseball, David Voigt, from Albright College in Pennsylvania, to give the inaugural Betts lecture. Voigt, and baseball history, have remained central to the work and the working of NASSH ever since (Eyler, 1982; Lucas, 1973b).

The establishment of NASSH was an important event in this watershed era in the "making" of sport history. More than simply signaling the rising academic interest in the history of sport, especially but not only in departments of physical education, NASSH was the product of a critical mass of scholars, a mass that had not existed in any of the contributing fields even a decade earlier. These scholars, in turn, now had an organization in which they could hone their historical skills and at whose conferences they could converse with other researchers. This was no small achievement. Nor was the fact, which gradually became clear, that the history of physical education was subsumed within the broader history of sport.

Development of the Subdiscipline

Since 1973 the North American Society for Sport History has operated as a facilitating body, if not quite an engine, for the production of the knowledge upon which the claims and the recognition of subdisciplines rest. Participation via research presentations at the annual conferences has risen, from 37 papers at the first meeting (Lucas, 1973b), to a three-day program with multiple, parallel sessions (Bouchier, 1994; NASSH, 1995). This pattern, in turn, corresponds with the general membership increase, from 171 (Lucas, 1973b) initially to nearly 1,000 two decades later (Smith, 1993). Importantly as well, NASSH instigated a scholarly journal, the *Journal of Sport History*, in 1974. Under the able editorships of Alan Metcalfe, Jack Berryman, Steven Riess, and Joseph Arbena, the *Journal* has drawn submissions from scholars in many disciplines and remains the preeminent refereed publication outlet in the field. Indeed, the last time the American Historical Association conducted a survey of historical journal users, it reported that the *Journal of Sport History* was the seventh most frequently cited historical journal among the hundreds published in the United States (AHA, 1985).

The continuity that has been critical to the success of the *Journal* has also characterized the membership and the leadership of NASSH itself. Many current members are also charter members, and over the years they have been joined by newcomers, many of whom are by now long-time NASSHites. Significantly as well, the original steering committee implemented what may be a distinctive office-holding scheme among academic organizations and one that surely has contributed to organizational stability and the maintenance of institutional memory: Most officers serve six years, two each as president-elect, president, and past-president. The exception is the secretary-treasurer; NASSH has had only one, Ronald Smith, from Penn State. Assisted by his wife, Sue, Ron Smith has borne the responsibility for maintaining the organization's financial affairs, among other duties, and has assisted all of the presiding officers, beginning with Marvin Eyler.

Organizational continuity and stability should not, however, be translated as stasis. Over the years NASSH has drawn, and retained, people from many academic fields; in so doing, it has secured a dynamic supply of organizational interest and intellectual energy. Its members have also undertaken a number of tasks to promote research and teaching in the subdiscipline. The recognition and encouragement of graduate students, to whom the organization has always been committed, formalized in 1985 when the council set aside a special conference session for the best research paper submitted by a graduate student. Shortly thereafter, NASSH initiated an annual book award, which had the dual intent of encouraging and recognizing scholarly books. Since the inception of the award, publishers, especially university and other academic presses, have submitted increasing numbers of the monographs that are so vital to the historians' craft.

Thus, the North American Society for Sport History has been and remains both a force in the promotion of the history of sport and the central forum for sport historians on this continent. Indeed, its members, who now come from around the world, have used it as a vehicle for the making and meeting of a vibrant scholarly community. Other organizations, to be sure, afford opportunities for research presentations. In the United States alone, the premier historical societies, the American Historical Association and the Organization of American Historians, often have conference sessions devoted to sport history, as do the American Studies Association and the American Alliance for Health, Physical Education, Recreation and Dance, among others. None, however, encourages the concentrated discussion and debate about sport history like NASSH, and for sport historians, this is no small matter. Unlike researchers in laboratory sciences, they labor primarily as individuals, as do other historians. Consequently, the intellectual exchanges that occur at conferences and in the pages of the *Journal* broaden and deepen the interests and skills of individuals and affect the course and content of knowledge.

It is probably not coincidental, then, that the other major dimension of the subdiscipline's history—the body of knowledge—altered substantially in the years after NASSH came into existence. Many of the producers of this expanding knowledge were, and are, NASSH members, and more than a few have acknowledged the significance of the NASSH community for their work (e.g., Riess, 1984). Still, the two histories are separable, so this narrative will return to the history of the body of knowledge, or at least some of its major trends and representative works.[5]

If there was a "take-off" stage in the body of knowledge in sport history, it was the decade of the 1970s. University courses in sport history in departments of physical education and history proliferated, sustained by a flurry of research activity in which two trends dominated. One resembled the historiography of prior years. Many researchers focused on locating past experiences in, and tracing the roots of, particular sports and, to a lesser extent, the profession of physical education. Thus, much of this literature was descriptive and uncritical, both of sources and of longstanding suppositions and myths. Yet, it also added breadth and depth to the historical map, especially of activities that had existed earlier or in more complex forms than was once thought and of the experiences of previously underexplored eras and people, especially African Americans and women (e.g., Freedman, 1978; Jable, 1974; McKinney, 1976; Remley, 1973).

The second approach—or better, set of approaches—was more visibly critical. One genre actually consisted of critiques, primarily of modern sports as forms of experience, and it owed much to the social unrest that pervaded American society and sport in the late 1960s and 1970s. Although not classical histories of sport, many of these works discussed past experiences, and they did influence sport historians. This was particularly true of books written by people who had either worked within sports or observed mainstream sports people and organizations for years, including the works of sociologists such as Harry Edwards (1969) and Paul Hoch (1972) and the more significant books by journalists, notably Robert Lipsyte (1975) and Leonard Koppett (1981). Considered collectively, their analyses challenged some of the "sacred truths" that academics and ordinary people alike had abided, especially that sport organizations were bastions of democracy and that sport was the social safety valve par excellence, as well as a source of social mobility.

The other critical approach drew not only from the unsettlement of contemporary America but also from a related movement within the discipline of history: the abandonment of the consensus paradigm. Actually, there were several approaches, for as society fractured in the late 1960s and early 1970s, so did the writing of history. No single framework emerged as a dominant one, and historians pursued several conceptual schemes. One was yet another "new" social history approach, which brought to the fore demographic variations in experience and quantitative methods and which, in time, influenced some sport historians.[6] There was also an emergent urban paradigm, one of the earliest exemplars of which was Dale Somers's *The Rise of Sports in New Orleans* (1972). In the vein of Paxson and Betts, Somers maintained that modern athletic sports rooted and evolved in a distinctive setting, the industrializing cities of late 19th- and early 20th-century America. Such places encouraged both the necessary interests on the part of participants, especially for health and catharsis, and the necessary conditions underlying organized, formalized competitions (e.g., facilities, transportation, and population concentrations). Finally, and especially after the publication of Robert Wiebe's *The Search for Order* (1967), a third framework, focusing on the countervailing forces of social order/control and divisiveness, offered sport historians a distinctive set of questions about the functioning of sport in society. Among the first to employ this analytical approach was Steven Riess (1974, 1980b).[7] Building on the works of earlier baseball historians, Riess argued that once major league baseball was armed with a myth-based ideology, it became a force in uniting and controlling various segments of American society in the early 20th century.[8]

In their day the works of Somers and Riess were important contributions to the literature—model narrative and analytic histories, respectively. For all the breadth and depth of the coverage they provided, however, they were not revolutionary works, nor were they as dissimilar from many of the descriptive articles as the prior discussion might suggest. Both books manifested the persisting interest of sport historians in the evolution of modern sport, and beyond that, the conceptualization of sport as an institution. In fact, as the works of other leading scholars suggested, this dual "rise of sport" and "sport as institution" approach characterized mainstream historiography through the 1970s. It was especially evident in the histories of particular sports like baseball (e.g., Crepeau, 1980; Smith, 1975; Voigt, 1976), bicycling (Harmond, 1971; Tobin, 1974), and intercollegiate activities (Lewis, 1972; Smith, 1972, 1981; Westby & Sack, 1976). In the case of organizations such as athletic clubs (Jable, 1979; Wettan & Willis, 1976; Willis & Wettan, 1975), the critical questions were who the members were and how these evolving institutions were organized and functioned. Some scholars also framed movements as evolving processes, the outcomes of which were formalized cores of attitudes, behaviors, and relationships. Certainly this was the case with subcommunity development via clubs in the mid-19th century (Rader, 1977), with the Olympics (Lucas, 1980; Mandell, 1971, 1976), and with women's involvement in sport and physical activity (e.g., Gerber, 1975; Park, 1978; Twin, 1978, 1979). Even biographers of prominent sports figures, who are themselves signifiers of institutional status, contributed to this literature (Roberts, 1979).

Despite its popularity, the evolutionary, institutional approach to the history of sport had certain limits. One constraint owed to the linearity engendered by the evolutionary model. The approach assumed "growth," or development, which not only acquired a positive value connotation often noted as "progress" but also prevented researchers from seeing the lack of change and the persistence of residual practices. A second set of limits involved the conceptualization of sport and the relationship between sport and society. "Sport," as well as particular sports, was commonly conceived of as a unity, if not quite a uniform and preformed object. Moreover, the dominant relationship between sports and society was a simple, unidirectional one. Society affected sports, and "sport" *itself* was another arm, another dimension of society. In short, in the guise of evolutionary, institutional history, the mirror theory was alive and well.

Even before the end of the decade, however, some sport historians who were discontented with the limits of the evolutionary-institutional approach had begun to work with and through alternative frameworks. One of these was "modernization," which Allen Guttmann initially explored in *From Ritual to Record: The Nature of Modern Sport* (1978). In one sense *From Ritual to Record* belonged to an older genre of philosophical and sociological analyses of the relationships among phenomena such as play, games, and sports. Using historical experiences (as opposed to primarily contemporary ones), as well as insights from anthropology, Guttmann identified seven characteristics that distinguished modern from premodern sports. This analysis, however, was only a stepping-off point; it enabled him to argue that the search for the "roots" of modern sports in earlier times was not nearly as meaningful as was the quest to understand the construction of modern sport in the context of a particular time and set of conditions. For Guttmann, a professor of American studies at Amherst College and one of the most prolific sport historians of the past quarter-century (e.g., 1984, 1986, 1988, 1991, 1992, 1994), the central questions thus became how and why modern sports emerged when they did, and what their significance was within the larger frame of American culture and values. Moreover, and following Max Weber, Guttmann emphasized the formative context shaped by the rational scientific world view of the 19th century. In so doing, he moved historical causality away from inevitability and the "large" external forces that many sport historians had stressed.

From Ritual to Record was primarily a theoretical work that included several empirically grounded chapters. What the modernization scheme still required was employment in a monograph, and that was in the making as a dissertation in the department of physical education (now kinesiology) at the University of Illinois. There Melvin Adelman (1980) completed what was the most extensive examination to date of change over time in the sporting life of a city. Once refined and published as *A Sporting Time: New York City and the Rise of Modern Athletics, 1820-1870* (1986), Adelman's analysis became a classic, on several counts. First, drawing on Guttmann's work as well as those of Richard Brown and Eric Dunning, he established that modernization provided a more vibrant framework than had previous paradigms for examining change over time. In particular, it permitted Adelman to examine the dynamic interplay between sport forms/people and the sites and processes of urban society. More fully than did earlier works, *A Sporting Time* illustrated the dynamic role that sports and physical recreations had in the shaping of urban life. The world of sport thus ceased to be simply a "mirror" on society and became a social force. Second, Adelman moved back the timing of the emergence of modern characteristics by at least three decades, from mid-century to the 1820s, which was no insignificant achievement. His dating suggested a different relationship between the modernizing of sports and the processes affecting urban life, such as commercialization, industrialization, and subcommunity formation. Finally, even though he did not do a comparative study, Adelman did support the contentions of historians that modern sports were primarily an urban phenomena, and that New York City was a particularly important site.

Modernization was not, however, without its own limits, discussed at length elsewhere (Gorn, 1990; Gruneau, 1980; Mrozek, 1983a; Stearns, 1980; Struna, 1985), but several are worth restating. A positivist construction, modernization tended to focus on structures and processes at the expense of the human beings who made them. Thus, it was helpful in exploring the "big picture," but it was less adequate for allowing one to examine what the making of that scene involved. It deemphasized interactions among people, acts of resistance, tension between groups, and the meanings of things like prowess, the body, and victory for ordinary life and social relations. Moreover, and in part because it, too, was a linear scheme, modernization failed to account for the persistence of some practices. Finally, the model worked best with urban, male, middle-class people, who were the dominant constructors of the rational scientific world view that was central to the process it framed.

Thus, modernization was not a panacea for the conceptual problems of sport historians. *A Sporting Time* established the value of social scientific models for historical inquiries, to be sure, but it also encouraged researchers to think about the limits of such frameworks. Indeed, it brought into stark relief the larger intellectual dilemma confronted by all historians: the matter of trying to reconcile the quest for historical understanding, which takes the form of *generalizations*, from the primary data on historical experience, which appear as multiple *particulars*.

As were historians more generally, sport historians struggled to resolve this issue in the late 1970s and 1980s; one of the results was the emergence of other alternatives to the flaccid evolutionary-institutional approach. Particularly significant were the historical works that elevated human agency, which differed from the investigations of modernizationists in a number of ways, not the least of which was that they viewed sport as both process and site of human social activity rather than as a product of external forces. They also conceived of the makers of sport, and the making of sports, as constitutive agents in the larger historical drama of society-making. One early, provocative work in this vein was Stephen Hardy's *How Boston Played: Sport, Recreation, and Community, 1865-1915* (1982). Drawing on the work of Louis Wirth, Hardy proposed that sport could be framed as a structure, a social organization, and a value system or state of mind; all were necessary for examining changes over time in human interests and actions and, ultimately, in the relationships between modern sport and its urban setting. In the case of Boston, Hardy employed all three, and the result was an analytic history that revealed the multiple experiences of, as well as the tensions and contradictions among, many Bostonians. Importantly too, he made a strong case for the significance of social class and a range of demographic differences in sporting experiences.

Some of these differences, which are critical for accounting for different historical experiences, received expanded treatment in the works of other historians. Roy Rosenzweig (1983), for instance, framed his investigation about class and ethnicity broadly as he examined work and leisure, instead of just organized sport. He found an intense commitment to longstanding practices, even residual forms, among the ethnic workers of Worcester, Massachusetts, until after the turn of the century, when they both adapted and adopted other more modern, commercial sports and recreations. Ted Vincent (1981), in contrast, focused on modern, organized, and, in fact, institutionalized sports, but he emphasized the agency of the players, some of whom came from the working class. He argued that such sports were the product not of a dominant class (owners and their supporters) but of both players and owners. Finally, Elliott Gorn (1986) produced an enlightening and provocative study of prizefighting among a previously underexamined segment of the population. Unlike earlier histories of particular sports, Gorn's *The Manly Art* located fighting-become-boxing quite fully within the lives, rhythms, and relations of the antebellum, urban, male working class. Ethnic, racial, and gender divisions both fed and were fueled by their battles until after the Civil War, when accommodations with the sensibilities and structures of other classes occurred. At no point, however, did Gorn reduce his version of the modernizing process to inevitability.

Gorn's book, and to a lesser extent Hardy's, represented a significant achievement at another level as well. Many previous full-length histories of sport had displayed a presentist perspective that owed much to their evolutionary, institutional framework. *The Manly Art*, however, attempted to understand the past on its own terms, a goal that had become more pronounced within the larger discipline of history (Kammen, 1980). Consequently, it constructed change over time on the basis of what the experiences were and meant to the people who lived them. Thus, as had Adelman earlier, Gorn demonstrated the significance of sport in society, as well as the intersections of sport and social histories.

Another approach that emerged in the mid-1980s also contributed to this goal of understanding the past on its own terms. In fact, it was an intellectual kin to Gorn's "sport as experience" approach. Influenced by anthropology and cultural history, this was the "sport as performance" framework, which consisted of analyses of cultural symbols, myths, rites, festivals, and value systems. The first book-length treatments of sport as a performance medium and, hence, culture creating and signifying phenomenon were John MacAloon's *This Great Symbol: Pierre de Coubertin and the Origins of the Modern Olympic Games* (1981) and Donald Mrozek's *Sport and American Mentality, 1880-1910* (1983b). Each focused on the social construction of sports as multilayered, multi-meaning performances. In so doing, they reintroduced to sport historiography the cultural history and hermeneutic strains that had lain dormant for years.

The influences that bore on MacAloon's and Mrozek's works also help to account for another set of inquiries that became visible in sport history in the 1980s. The questions and methods of cultural history and anthropology especially had particular significance for research on health, the body, the construction of gender relations, and sports medicine. To be sure, historians of physical education had addressed some of these topics but primarily as dimensions of institutional development and programs. They had not framed them as core cultural matters, let alone as the subjects of significant historical movements or as constitutive features of the historical sport experiences. Among the earliest book-length accounts of changes in the cultural bases and interests in health and fitness was James Whorton's *Crusaders for Fitness: The History of American Health Reformers* (1982). Subsequently, and encouraged by contemporary interests in health and fitness as well as with the support of a public museum, Harvey Green (1986) described 19th- and early 20th-century programs and popular devices for health and fitness and the place of sports therein.[9]

The increasing visibility of historical studies of health and physical exercise within sport history has altered the scope and the content of the subdiscipline in several ways. First, in marked contrast to the days when scholars concentrated on organized sports, women and the historical construction of gender have emerged as viable and visible agents in history-making—rather than primarily as "Joanie-come-lately's" to men's practices—via these topics. A number of scholars (e.g., Verbrugge, 1988; Vertinsky, 1990; and the authors in Berryman & Park, 1992) have contributed to this literature. The result is a far broader view of women's historical experiences, many of which differed from men's, and of the important role that sports and other physical performances had in shaping relationships between men and women.

Second, and not unrelated, systematic investigations of topics once considered tangential to sport have added to our understanding of the complexity and cultural significance in the past not only of sport experiences but also of physical culture more generally. On this point the work of Roberta Park (1977, 1984, 1986, 1987a, 1987b, 1987c, 1987d, 1989, 1991) is instructive. A hermeneuticist trained in anthropology and physical education, as well as cultural and intellectual history, Park has investigated a range of cultural and attitudinal intersections among sport, health, exercise, and physical training in the late 19th and early 20th centuries. In particular, she has explored the ways in which views of the body affected the forms of sport that people constructed; how these perceptions and constructions affected notions of manliness, femininity, and gender relations; and how biological thought affected athletics and vice versa. Not coincidentally, as well, in her efforts to understand the past on its own terms, Park has succeeded in integrating the subhistories of physical education and exercise science within sport history.

The scholarship of people like Park and Gorn, as well as Guttmann, Hardy, Adelman, and others (e.g., Levine, 1985; Rader, 1984; Roberts, 1983; Roberts & Olson, 1989; Tygiel, 1983) who wrote significant historical works, encourages one final comment about directions in the 1980s. Despite their many differences, one sees in the works of these people a common thread that was important in opening up, in expanding—indeed, in transforming—the body of knowledge in sport history. In the 1980s as never before, scholars began to cross the boundaries of traditional history, to fertilize their work with perspectives and methods adapted from other disciplines. The influence of anthropology has already been noted, and economics also had some bearing on some scholars. Even more important perhaps was sociology. History and sociology had never been antagonistic, to be sure, as the works on social control and modernization suggest. However, the relationship became more vibrant as sport historians worked to ask different questions and more questions about different groups and eras. By the middle of the decade, the influences of American sociologists of leisure such as John Kelly and of European and British social theorists and historical sociologists (and social historians)—especially Anthony Giddens, Antonio Gramsci, E. P. Thompson, and Raymond Williams—were particularly acute (e.g., Hardy and Ingham, 1984; Struna, 1986). More recently, postmodernism and feminist theories have informed the scholarship of historians (e.g., Peiss, 1990; Vertinsky, 1990).

It is difficult, if not impossible, to assess the effects of any one change in scholarly practice on a subdiscipline, and in sport history between the 1970s and 1980s, there were many changes. Still, one must at least suspect that this cross-fertilization of sport history with other disciplines and other fields in history was immensely important. As the process occurred in the hands, and heads, of leading scholars such as Adelman, Hardy, Guttmann, Park, Rader, and Riess, among others, it provoked different questions, deeper questions about experiences in the past, as well as more thoughtful, critical reading of the evidence (the data) in context. Importantly as well, the infusion of ideas and methods from other disciplines and historical subfields encouraged sport historians to challenge and debate one another's conclusions and positions (e.g., Adelman, 1989; Gelber, 1983; Goldstein, 1989). Some of this activity had occurred earlier, as in the discussions of the social control and anti-social control advocates. The intellectual impact, however, was limited, in part because the adversaries were coming to the fray with similar assumptions about what history and sport were. This was not the case in the 1980s, when positivists and hermeneuticists, modernizationists and materialists, and proponents of different social classes as critical agents in sports were all active, producing their own histories and reacting to those of others, especially via commentaries and book reviews. Their dialogue and debate thus amounted to an internal dynamism that may help to account for the rapid "development" of the subdiscipline in the 1980s.

Present and Future of the Subdiscipline

Today, sport history remains a dynamic subdiscipline, in many senses of the word. Dialogue, debate, and even some instances of healthy conflict occur at NASSH meetings and in research sessions at the conferences of other scholarly organizations. Book reviews remain appropriately critical, and criticism is now seen as a vital skill of sport historians. It is essential for asking sound and powerful questions, for interrogating evidence, and for producing more rigorous analyses and syntheses. Importantly as well, sport historians have continued to expand their conceptions of sport and their conceptions of the contexts in which sport as site, experience, performance, cultural system, and institutions needs to be investigated.

Some recent books illustrate the topical and contextual breadth that the subdiscipline has achieved. Ronald A. Smith filled a longstanding gap in the literature on the history of intercollegiate athletics and their significance in the larger institutional development of American colleges, with his *Sports & Freedom: The Rise of Big-Time College Athletics* (1988). Bruce Kuklick combined local, urban, and cultural histories in his distinctive analysis of the changing "place" (in cultural, geographical, and social terms) of a ball park in *To Every Thing A Season: Shibe Park and Urban Philadelphia, 1909-1976* (1991). Ann Fabian examined what many people have believed was (and remains) a ubiquitous practice in the history of sport, as well as American life and thought more generally: gambling. Her *Card Sharps, Dream Books, & Bucket Shops: Gambling in 19th-Century America* (1990) is a model history of ideas about gambling and the American economy. Matt Cartmill has also addressed in monographic form another set of practices—hunting—which historians have ignored, at least in part because it does not readily fit modern conceptions of sport. *A View to a Death in the Morning: Hunting and Nature Through History* (1993) is a fine cultural history of a practice, and in fact a way of life, that has probably figured more prominently in the histories of high and folk cultures than has a modern sport like baseball. One recent anthology also stands out, in part because it incorporates historical experiences in sport history as one dimension of a larger realm of experience: leisure. *For Fun and Profit: The Transformation of Leisure into Consumption* (1990), edited by Richard Butsch, enables the reader to understand changes in the sporting goods industry, and women's experiences in the context of changes in other dimensions of popular culture. A broader framing of historical sporting experiences within the labor-leisure nexus emerges in my own *People of Prowess: Sport, Leisure, and Labor in Early America* (Struna, 1996). Beyond looking at an underresearched period, this book in part argues that Britons and American colonists once viewed sports as forms of labor, and not until the mid-18th century did a particular segment of American society either conceive of leisure as a separable realm of experience or locate sports therein. These differing social locations, in turn, affected the formalizing, commercializing, and signifying processes by which people transformed particular practices.

These recent works point to a set of trends that signifies the healthy, dynamic state of the subdiscipline today. First, scholars who would not call themselves sport historians are investigating the history of sports and producing valuable works. Bruce Kuklick, for example, is a professor of humanities, and Matt Cartmill is a biological anthropologist; both men, and others, have made much of the intersections between the history of sport and their other intellectual labors. Second, the scope of sport history is still expanding, as scholars seek to understand the intersections of sports and health, labor and leisure, social resistance movements, and even political economies. Third, sport history is being incorporated within other kinds of history. This latter practice is particularly pronounced in social histories of work and laborers, in scholarship on saloons and drinking, in cultural histories of concepts and practices such as honor, and in histories of regions or groups of people. As historians move to tell larger stories and recognize the place of sports in people's lives, they cannot avoid incorporating information that is germane to the subdiscipline of sport history. But this, of course, was what the first "new" social historians were saying in the 1920s.

These recent trends appear to be having effects similar to those wrought by the disciplinary cross-fertilization in the 1980s. They are enriching the subdiscipline by producing new knowledge, encouraging different questions and bodies of evidence, and augmenting the intellectual agenda of sport historians, an agenda that, as Steven Riess (1990) and others have suggested, is already broad—and becoming more so by the minute. In addition to ongoing work with particular sports, scholars are investigating groups of people and periods that remain either unexamined or incompletely examined. They are also concentrating on topics such as the body, health, ethnicity, and business; on critical constructions like gender, race, and social class that were heavily influenced by physical performance and perceptions; and on the interplay between the making of sports and the making of social relations, society, and culture writ large. In all, our agenda is now more vibrant and of greater significance than ever before, both to other subdisciplines in exercise and sport science and to other disciplines.

A Final Thought

Two decades ago Jack Berryman (1973) posed a question that captured a contemporary concern: whither sport history? The query was really two-pronged: Would sport history develop as a subdiscipline, or would it be subsumed within social history? Subsequent years, of course, resolved both matters, with a resounding yes and no, respectively. In the future, however, we may be asking a variant of Berryman's question: whither sport historians, and sport history, in departments of exercise/ sport science or kinesiology? Even now the number of practicing sport historians has diminished. Many scholars who contributed to the field in the 1970s and 1980s have retired, and more will follow shortly. Only a few of these people are being replaced, as departments choose either to abandon sport history or to assign other faculty to teach history courses who have little or no preparation in history. Moreover, in the face of few jobs and insufficient access to mentors and the range of experiences required for adequate preparation in asking good questions and interrogating evidence, the number of potential sport historians—graduate students—has also contracted.

These trends should be alarming, not just to sport historians but to all exercise scientists and sport studies scholars. Exercise and sport science has a long tradition of multiple subfields that have thrived on internal cross-fertilization, even as they have benefited from exchanges with other fields. Exercise and sport scientists focus on common human movement phenomena—exercise, sport, the body, health. All are biological and sociocultural entities, and they require understanding that only a vibrant, and whole, multidimensional field of study can produce. Consequently, the loss of one set of perspectives and research directions diminishes the vitality and viability of the larger academic enterprise. This, in turn, raises the possibility that the remaining subdisciplines would no longer constitute a distinctive field of study. Instead, they might appear as arms of other disciplines to which they could easily be reattached. Indeed, astute university administrators could rephrase Berryman's "sport history as social history" question. Sport psychology as applied psychology? Biomechanics as biomedical engineering? Exercise physiology as applied biology? Why not?

Perhaps Benjamin Franklin had it right after all. Faced with a divide-and-conquer strategy engineered by the British, he warned his mates in the Continental Congress: "We had better all hang together, or we shall most assuredly hang separately."

Notes

Acknowledgment: The author thanks Marvin Eyler and Roberta Park for the information and ideas they provided for portions of this chapter. Neither, however, knows exactly how I employed their suggestions.

1. Implicit in this statement are two points that I should make explicit. First, historians attempt to describe and analyze their subjects as adequately as possible; hence, in situ, or in context. The basic types of history, narratives and analyses, both involve description and analysis, although in varying degrees. Second, histories should not be confused with other types of writing about the past, such as chronicles (which order events in time) or antiquarian studies (which identify past things, absent context and a focus on change over time).

2. Staley's works remain unpublished, although they are in the hands of an academic press. Marvin Eyler, who probably knew him best, has indicated that Staley essentially completed two major bibliographies, one on English-language books on the history of sport (classified and annotated, approximately 6,500 entries), and the other on English-language books on biographies of sportsmen (also classified and annotated, approximately 7,500 entries).

3. No one, to my knowledge, has fully analyzed this episode. Moreover, as Roberta Park reminds us, physical educators had already begun to enhance the scholarly study and status of the field.

4. The other addresses honored Staley and Howell, the influential Australian who worked in both Canada and the United States.

5. Many fine published review essays more adequately discuss the literature in sport history than does this chapter: See, for example, Adelman, 1983; Hardy, 1981; Hardy & Ingham, 1983; Park, 1983; Rader, 1979; Riess, 1980a, 1990; Struna, 1985. Recently the *Journal of Sport History* published a series of topically framed review essays, an apparent necessity given the expansion of the literature over the last decade: See Gerlach, 1994; Park, 1994; Riess, 1994; Sammons, 1994; Vertinsky, 1994.

6. The impact of demographic studies and social science history more generally was more evident early in Canadian histories.

7. The publication date (1980) of Riess's book, *Touching Base*, is misleading. It drew from his dissertation (1974), and he had previously published some of the chapters or parts of chapters as articles in the 1970s.

8. In time these latter two paradigms merged, with the effect that many studies had an urban focus and some incorporated social order/control or anti-control themes.

9. These are but two illustrations of what is a rich body of literature on the history of health and fitness, which also intersects with the history of medicine. Green's book contains a number of factual errors.

References

Adelman, M.L. (1980). *The development of modern athletics. Sport in New York City, 1820-1870*. Unpublished doctoral dissertation, University of Illinois, Urbana.

Adelman, M.L. (1983). Academicians and American athletics: A decade of progress. *Journal of Sport History*, **10**, 80-106.

Adelman, M.L. (1986). *A sporting time: New York City and the rise of modern athletics, 1820-1870*. Urbana: University of Illinois Press.

Adelman, M.L. (1989). Baseball, business and the work place: Gelber's thesis reexamined. *Journal of Social History*, **23**, 283-302.

AHA (1985). American Historical Association *Newsletter*, **23**, 4, 12-13.

Ainsworth, D. (1930). *A history of physical education in colleges for women*. San Diego: Barnes.

Baker, W.J. (1982). *Sports in the Western world*. Lanham, MD: Rowman & Littlefield.

Ballintine, H.I. (n. d.). *The history of physical training at Vassar college, 1865-1915*. Poughkeepsie, NY: Lansing & Bros.

Barrows, I.C. (Ed.) (1890). *Physical training. A full report of the papers and discussion of the conference held in Boston in November, 1889*. Boston: George H. Ellis.

Bennett, B.L. (1965). The making of Round Hill school. *Quest*, **4**, 1, 53-63.

Berryman, J.W. (1973). Sport history as social history? *Quest*, **20**, 1, 65-73.

Berryman, J.W., & Park, R.J. (Eds.) (1992). *Sport and exercise science. Essays in the history of sports medicine*. Urbana: University of Illinois Press.

Betts, J.R. (1951). *Organized sport in industrial America*. Unpublished doctoral dissertation, Columbia University, New York.

Betts, J.R. (1953a). Sporting journalism in nineteenth-century America. *American Quarterly*, **5**, 1, 39-56.

Betts, J.R. (1953b). The technological revolution and the rise of sport, 1850-1900. *Mississippi Valley Historical Review*, **40**, 231-256.

Betts, J.R. (1968). Mind and body in early American thought. *Journal of American History*, **54**, 787-805.

Bouchier, N. (Ed.) (1994). *Proceedings* of the North American Society for Sport History 22nd annual conference. Hamilton, ON: NASSH.

Boyle, R.H. (1963). *Sport—Mirror of American life*. Boston: Little, Brown.

Butsch, R. (Ed.) (1990). *For fun and profit. The transformation of leisure into consumption.* Philadelphia: Temple University Press.

Cartmill, M. (1993). *A view to a death in the morning: Hunting and nature through history.* Cambridge, MA: Harvard University Press.

Conant, J.B. (1963). *The education of American teachers.* New York: McGraw-Hill.

CPEA (1961). *Proceedings* of the 64th annual meeting of the College Physical Education Association. Washington, DC: AAHPER.

Crepeau, R.C. (1980). *Baseball. America's diamond mind, 1919-1941.* Orlando: University Presses of Florida.

Dulles, F.R. (1940). *America learns to play. A history of popular recreation.* New York: Appleton-Century-Crofts.

Edwards, H. (1969). *The revolt of the Black athlete.* New York: Free Press.

Eyler, M.H. (1960). The nature and status of historical research pertaining to sports and physical education. In W.R. Johnson (Ed.), *Science and medicine of exercise and sports* (pp. 647-662). New York: Harper & Row.

Eyler, M.H. (1982). NASSH, history and sport historians: Seward Staley honor address presented at the North American Society for Sport History annual conference, May.

Fabian, A. (1990). *Card sharps, dream books, & bucket shops: Gambling in 19th-century America.* Ithaca, NY: Cornell University Press.

Freedman, S. (1978). The baseball fad in Chicago, 1865-1870: An exploration of the role of sport in the nineteenth century city. *Journal of Sport History,* **5,** 2, 42-64.

Gelber, S. (1983). Working at playing: The culture of the workplace and the rise of baseball. *Journal of Social History,* **16,** 3-20.

Gerber, E.W. (1971). *Innovators and institutions in physical education.* Philadelphia: Lea & Febiger.

Gerber, E.W. (1972). The ideas and influences of McCloy, Nash, and Williams. In B.L. Bennett (Ed.), *The history of sport and physical education* (pp. 85-100). Chicago: The Athletic Institute.

Gerber, E.W. (1975). The controlled development of collegiate sport for women, 1923-1936. *Journal of Sport History,* **2**(1), 1-28.

Gerlach, L.R. (1994). Not quite ready for prime time: Baseball history, 1983-1993. *Journal of Sport History,* **21,** 103-37.

Goldstein, W. (1989). *Playing for keeps: A history of early baseball.* Ithaca, NY: Cornell University Press.

Gorn, E.J. (1986). *The manly art: Bare-knuckle prize fighting in America.* Ithaca, NY: Cornell University Press.

Gorn, E.J. (1990). Doing sports history. *Reviews in American History,* **18,** 1, 27-32.

Gorn, E.J., & Goldstein, W. (1993). *A brief history of American sports.* New York: Hill & Wang.

Green, H. (1986). *Fit for America. Health, fitness, sport and American Society.* New York: Pantheon Books.

Gruneau, R. (1980). Freedom and constraint. The paradoxes of play, games, and sports. *Journal of Sport History, 7*, 3, 68-86.

Gulick, L.H. (1890). Physical education: A new profession. *Proceedings of the American association for the advancement of physical education, Cambridge and Boston.* Ithaca, NY: Andrus and Church.

Guttmann, A. (1978). *From ritual to record: The nature of modern sport.* New York: Columbia University Press.

Guttmann, A. (1984). *The games must go on: Avery Brundage and the Olympic movement.* New York: Columbia University Press.

Guttmann, A. (1986). *Sports spectators.* New York: Columbia University Press.

Guttmann, A. (1988). *A whole new ball game: An interpretation of American sports.* Chapel Hill: University of North Carolina Press.

Guttmann, A. (1991). *Women's sports: A history.* New York: Columbia University Press.

Guttmann, A. (1992). *The Olympics.* Urbana: University of Illinois Press.

Guttmann, A. (1994). *Games and empires: Modern sports and cultural imperialism.* New York: Columbia University Press.

Hardy, S. (1981). The city and the rise of American sport, 1820-1920. *Exercise and Sport Sciences Reviews, 9*, 183-219.

Hardy, S. (1982). *How Boston played: Sport, recreation, and community, 1865-1915.* Boston: Northeastern University Press.

Hardy, S., & Ingham, A. (1983). Games, structures, and agency: Historians on the American play movement. *Journal of Social History, 17*, 285-302.

Hardy, S., & Ingham, A. (1984). Sport, structuration, subjugation, and hegemony. *Theory, Culture, and Society, 2*, 85-103.

Harmond, R. (1971). Progress and flight: An interpretation of the American cycle craze of the 1890s. *Journal of Social History, 5*, 235-57.

Hartwell, E.M. (1886). *Physical training in American colleges and universities.* Circulars of Information of the Bureau of Education, No. 5, 1885. Washington, DC: U.S. Government Printing Office.

Hartwell, E.M. (1905). On physical training. *Report of the commissioner of education for the year 1903* (pp. 721-757). Washington, DC: Government Printing Office.

Henderson, R.W. (1947). *Ball, bat and bishop: The origin of ball games.* New York: Rockport Press.

Henry, F.M. (1964). Physical education—An academic discipline. In *Proceedings of the 67th annual meeting of the National College Physical Education Association for Men* (pp. 6-9). Washington, DC: AAHPER.

Higham, J. (1973). *History: Professional scholarship in America.* New York: Harper & Row.

Hoch, P. (1972). *Rip off the big game: The exploitation of sports by the power elite.* New York: Anchor.

Holliman, J. (1931). *American sports 1785-1835.* Durham, NC: Seeman Press.

Huizinga, J. (1955). *Homo ludens. A study of the play-element in culture.* Boston: Beacon Press.

Jable, J.T. (1974). Pennsylvania's early blue laws: A Quaker experiment in the suppression of sports and amusements, 1682-1740. *Journal of Sport History,* **1**, 2, 107-21.

Jable, J.T. (1979). The birth of professional football: Pittsburgh athletic clubs ring in professionals in 1892. *Western Pennsylvania Historical Magazine,* **62**, 136-47.

Kammen, M. (Ed.) (1980). *The past before us: Contemporary historical writing in the United States.* Ithaca, NY: Cornell University Press.

Koppett, L. (1981). *Sports illusion, sports reality: A reporter's view of sports, journalism, and society.* Boston: Houghton Mifflin.

Krout, J.A. (1929). *Annals of American sport.* New Haven, CT: Yale University Press.

Kuklick, B. (1991). *To every thing a season: Shibe park and urban Philadelphia, 1909-1976.* Princeton, NJ: Princeton University Press.

Leonard, F.E. (1905). The first introduction of the Jahn gymnastics into America. *Mind and Body,* **12**, 193-98, 217-23, 249-54, 281-87, 313-19, 345-51.

Leonard, F.E. (1915). *Pioneers of modern physical training* (2nd ed.). New York: Association Press.

Leonard, F.E. (1923). *A guide to the history of physical education.* Philadelphia: Lea & Febiger.

Levine, P. (1985). *A. G. Spalding and the rise of baseball: The promise of American sport.* New York: Oxford University Press.

Lewis, G. (1964). *The American intercollegiate football spectacle, 1869-1917.* Unpublished doctoral dissertation, University of Maryland, College Park.

Lewis, G. (1967). America's first intercollegiate sport: The regattas from 1852 to 1875. *Research Quarterly,* **38**, 2, 637-47.

Lewis, G. (1969a). Adoption of the sports program, 1906-39: The role of accommodation in the transformation of physical education, *Quest,* **12**, 1, 34-46.

Lewis, G. (1969b). Theodore Roosevelt's role in the 1905 football controversy. *Research Quarterly,* **40**, 2, 717-24.

Lewis, G. (1972). Enterprise on the campus: Developments in intercollegiate sport and higher education, 1875-1939. In B.L. Bennett (Ed.). *The history of sport and physical education* (pp. 53-56). Chicago: The Athletic Institute.

Lewis, G. (1973). World War I and the emergence of sport for the masses. *Maryland Historian,* **4**, 2, 109-22.

Lewis, G. (1977). Sport, youth culture and conventionality. *Journal of Sport History,* **4**, 2, 129-50.

Lipsyte, R. (1975). *Sportsworld. An American dreamland.* New York: Quadrangle/New York Times.

Lucas, J.A. (1962). *Baron Pierre de Coubertin and the formative years of the modern international Olympic movement.* Unpublished doctoral dissertation, University of Maryland, College Park.

Lucas, J.A. (1973a). The modern Olympic games. Fanfare and philosophy, 1896-1972. *Maryland Historian,* **4,** 2, 71-88.

Lucas, J.A. (Ed.) (1973b). *Proceedings* of the 1st North American Society for Sport History annual conference. University Park, PA: NASSH.

Lucas, J.A. (1980). *The modern Olympic games.* New York: Barnes.

MacAloon, J. (1981). *This great symbol: Pierre de Coubertin and the origins of the modern Olympic games.* Chicago: University of Chicago Press.

Mandell, R.D. (1971). *The Nazi Olympics.* New York: Macmillan.

Mandell, R.D. (1976). *The first modern Olympics.* Berkeley: University of California Press.

Mandell, R.D. (1984). *Sport: A cultural history.* New York: Columbia University Press.

McKinney, G.B. (1976). Negro professional baseball in the upper South in the guilded age. *Journal of Sport History,* **3,** 3, 273-80.

Mrozek, D.J. (1983a). Some thoughts on indigenous Western sport: Moving beyond the model of modernity. *Journal of the West,* **22,** 1, 3-19.

Mrozek, D.J. (1983b). *Sport and American mentality, 1880-1910.* Knoxville: University of Tennessee Press.

Mumford, L. (1934). *Technics and civilization.* New York: Harcourt Brace Jovanovich.

NASSH (1995). North American Society for Sport History 24th annual conference program.

Novick, P. (1988). *That noble dream: The 'objectivity question' and the American historical profession.* Cambridge, England: Cambridge University Press.

Park, R.J. (1977). The attitudes of leading New England transcendentalists toward healthful exercise, active recreations and proper care of the body, 1830-1860. *Journal of Sport History,* **4,** 1, 34-60.

Park, R.J. (1978). 'Embodied selves': The rise and development of concern for physical education, active games, and recreation for American women, 1776-1865. *Journal of Sport History,* **5,** 2, 5-41.

Park, R.J. (1983). Research and scholarship in the history of physical education and sport: The current state of affairs. *Research Quarterly for Exercise and Sport,* **54,** 2, 93-103.

Park, R.J. (1984). Boys into men—State into nation: Rites of passage in student life and college athletics, 1890-1915. In B. Sutton-Smith & D. Kelly-Byrne (Eds.), *The masks of play* (pp. 51-62). Champaign, IL: Leisure Press.

Park, R.J. (1986). Hermeneutics, semiotics, and the nineteenth-century quest for a corporeal self. *Quest,* **38,** 1, 33-49.

Park, R.J. (1987a). Biological thought, athletics and the formation of a 'man of character', 1830-1900. In J.A. Mangan & J. Walvin (Eds.),

Manliness and morality. Middle-class masculinity in Britain and America 1800-1940 (pp. 7-34). New York: St. Martin's Press.

Park, R.J. (1987b). Muscle, mind and *agon*: Intercollegiate debating and athletics at Harvard and Yale, 1892-1909. *Journal of Sport History,* **14**, 3, 263-85.

Park, R.J. (1987c). Physiologists, physicians, and physical educators: Nineteenth century biology and exercise, *hygienic and educative. Journal of Sport History,* **14**, 1, 28-60.

Park, R.J. (1987d). Sport, gender and society in a transatlantic Victorian perspective. In J.A. Mangan & R.J. Park (Eds.), *From 'fair sex' to feminism: Sport and the socialization of women in the industrial and post-industrial eras* (pp. 58-93). London: F. Cass.

Park, R.J. (1989). Healthy, moral, and strong: Educational views of exercise and athletics in nineteenth-century America. In K. Grover (Ed.), *Fitness in American culture. Images of health, sport, and the body, 1830-1940* (pp. 123-68). Amherst: University of Massachusetts Press.

Park, R.J. (1991). Physiology and anatomy are destiny!?: Brains, bodies, and exercise in nineteenth century American thought. *Journal of Sport History,* **18**, 1, 31-63.

Park, R.J. (1994). A decade of the body: Researching and writing about the history of health, fitness, exercise and sport, 1983-1993. *Journal of Sport History,* **21**, 59-82.

Paxson, F.L. (1917). The rise of sport. *Mississippi Valley Historical Review,* **4**, 143-68.

Peiss, K. (1990). Commercial leisure and the 'woman question.' In R. Butsch (Ed.), *For fun and profit. The transformation of leisure into consumption* (pp. 105-117). Philadelphia: Temple University Press.

Rader, B.G. (1977). The quest for subcommunities and the rise of American sport. *American Quarterly,* **29**, 355-69.

Rader, B.G. (1979). Modern sports: In search of interpretations. *Journal of Social History,* **13**, 307-21.

Rader, B.G. (1984). *In its own image. How television has transformed sports.* New York: Free Press.

Remley, M.L. (1973). Women and competitive athletics. *Maryland Historian,* **4**, 2, 88-94.

Rice, E.A. (1926). *A brief history of physical education.* New York: Barnes.

Riess, S.A. (1974). *Professional baseball and American culture in the progressive era. Myths and realities, with special emphasis on Atlanta, Chicago, and New York.* Unpublished doctoral dissertation, University of Chicago, Chicago.

Riess, S.A. (1980a). Sport and the American dream: A review essay. *Journal of Social History,* **14**, 295-304.

Riess, S.A. (1980b). *Touching base: Professional baseball and American culture in the progressive era.* Westport, CT: Greenwood Press.

Riess, S.A. (Ed.) (1984). *The American sporting experience*. Champaign, IL: Leisure Press.

Riess, S.A. (1990). The new sport history. *Reviews in American history*, **18**, 3, 311-25.

Riess, S.A. (1994). From pitch to putt: Sport and class in Anglo-American sport. *Journal of Sport History, 21*, 138-184.

Roberts, R. (1979). *Jack Dempsey, the Manassa mauler*. Baton Rouge: Louisiana State University Press.

Roberts, R. (1983). *Papa Jack. Jack Johnson and the era of White hopes*. New York: Free Press.

Roberts, R., & Olson, J. (1989). *Winning is the only thing: Sports in America since 1945*. Baltimore: Johns Hopkins University Press.

Rosenzweig, R. (1983). *Eight hours for what we will: Workers and leisure in an industrial city, 1870-1920*. Cambridge, England: Cambridge University Press.

Sammons, J.T. (1994). "Race" and sport: A critical, historical examination. *Journal of Sport History, 21*, 203-78.

Schwendener, N. (1942). *A history of physical education in the United States*. New York: Barnes.

Seymour, H. (1959-71). *Baseball*. 2 vols. New York: Oxford University Press.

Smith, L.T. (1975). *The American dream and the national game*. Bowling Green, OH: Bowling Green University Popular Press.

Smith, R.A. (1972). Commercialism in college athletics, 1920-1940: A case study. *Proceedings* of the 75th annual meeting of the National College Physical Education Association for Men (pp. 81-87).

Smith, R.A. (1981). Harvard and Columbia and a reconsideration of the 1905-06 football crisis. *Journal of Sport History, 8*, 3, 5-19.

Smith, R.A. (1988). *Sports & freedom: The rise of big-time college athletics*. New York: Oxford University Press.

Smith, R.A. (1993). Unpublished secretary-treasurer's annual report, presented at the North American Society for Sport History annual conference, May.

Somers, D. (1972). *The rise of sports in New Orleans*. Baton Rouge: Louisiana State University Press.

Spears, B. (1972). Influences on early professional physical education curriculums in the United States. *Proceedings* of the 2nd Canadian Symposium on the history of sport and physical education (pp. 86-103).

Spears, B. (1976). Women in the Olympic games: An unresolved problem. In P.J. Graham & H. Ueberhorst (Eds.), *The modern Olympics*. Champaign, IL: Leisure Press.

Spears, B. (1986). *Leading the way: Amy Morris Homans and the beginnings of professional education for women*. Westport, CT: Greenwood Press.

Staley, S.C. (1937). The history of sport: A new course in the professional training curriculum. *Journal of Health, Physical Education and Recreation, 8*, 522-25, 570-72.

Staley, S.C. (1939). *Sports education*. New York: Barnes.

Stearns, P. (1980). Modernization and social history: Some suggestions and a muted cheer. *Journal of Social History, 14*, 189-210.

Steiner, J. (1933). *Americans at play*. New York: McGraw-Hill.

Struna, N.L. (1985). In "glorious disarray": The literature of American sport history. *Research Quarterly for Exercise and Sport, 56*, 3, 151-60.

Struna, N.L. (1986). The formalizing of sport and the formation of an elite: The Chesapeake gentry, 1650-1720s. *Journal of Sport History, 13*, 3, 212-34.

Struna, N.L. (1996). *People of prowess: Sport, leisure, and labor in early Anglo-America*. Urbana: University of Illinois Press.

Tobin, G.A. (1974). The bicycle boom of the 1890s: The development of private transportation and the birth of modern tourism. *Journal of Popular Culture, 7*, 838-49.

Toynbee, A.J. (1935). *A study of history*. Vol. 4 of 12 vols. (1934-61). London: Oxford University Press.

Turner, F.J. (1963). *The significance of the frontier in American history*. Ed. by H.P. Simonson. New York: Frederick Ungar. (Orig. pub. 1893.)

Twin, S.L. (1978). *Jack and Jill: Aspects of women's sports history in America, 1870-1940*. Unpublished doctoral dissertation, Rutgers University, New Brunswick, NJ.

Twin, S.L. (Ed.) (1979). *Out of the bleachers: Writings on women and sport*. Old Westbury, NY: Feminist Press.

Tygiel, J. (1983). *Baseball's great experiment: Jackie Robinson and his legacy*. New York: Oxford University Press.

Van Dalen, D.B., Mitchell, E.D., & Bennett, B.L. (1953). *A world history of physical education*. Englewood Cliffs, NJ: Prentice Hall.

Verbrugge, M. (1988). *Able-bodied womanhood: Personal health and social change in nineteenth-century Boston*. New York: Oxford University Press.

Vertinsky, P. (1990). *The eternally wounded woman: Women, exercise and doctors in the late nineteenth century*. Manchester, England: Manchester University Press.

Vertinsky, P. (1994). Gender relations, women's history and sport history: A decade of changing enquiry, 1983-1993. *Journal of Sport History, 21*, 1-58.

Vincent, T. (1981). *Mudville's revenge: The rise and fall of American sport*. New York: Seaview Books.

Voigt, D.Q. (1966-70). *American baseball*. 2 vols. Norman: Oklahoma University Press.

Voigt, D.Q. (1976). *America through baseball*. Chicago: Nelson-Hall.

Westby, D.L., & Sack, A.L. (1976). The commercialization and functional rationalization of college football: Its origins. *Journal of Higher Education, 47*, 625-47.

Wettan, R.G., & Willis, J.D. (1976). Social stratification in the New York athletic club: A preliminary analysis of the impact of the club on amateur sport in the late 19th century. *Canadian Journal of History of Sport and Physical Education, 7,* 1, 41-53.

Whorton, J.C. (1982). *Crusaders for fitness: The history of American health reformers.* Princeton, NJ: Princeton University Press.

Wiebe, R. (1967). *The search for order, 1877-1920.* New York: Hill & Wang.

Willis, J.D., & Wettan, R.G. (1975). Social stratification in New York City's athletic clubs, 1865-1915. *Journal of Sport History, 3,* 1, 45-76.

6

Philosophy of Sport

R. Scott Kretchmar
The Pennsylvania State University

This chapter is about the evolution of sport philosophy in North America during the twentieth century. It includes an analysis of three periods of academic development, a history of the Philosophic Society for the Study of Sport, an assessment of the current status of the subdiscipline in relationship to its parent disciplines (primarily philosophy and education), and speculation about its future.

Early Foundations

Since 1900 sport philosophy has progressed through three periods. The first one was dominated by an eclectic, philosophy-of-education approach, the second by an interest in the relative strengths of competing philosophic systems or schools of thought, and the third by the categories and methods of a parent discipline. Each new philosophic stage of development was a reaction to and, in some ways, an improvement upon its predecessor. Even so, this development did not assure consistent growth for this area of research and study. Ironically in recent years, the youthful and relatively sophisticated brand of sport philosophy has turned out to be less visible and influential than its less capable parents. Now as the end of the twentieth century approaches, faint signs suggest that yet another period is about to begin.

Period 1: (The Eclectic, Philosophy-of-Education Approach) 1875–1950

The intellectual heritage of contemporary sport philosophy in North America can be traced most directly to the progressive education movement, a period of educational ferment and experimentation that lasted

▼

A Chronology of Philosophy of Sport

Early Foundations

Year	Event
1875	Dawn of progressive education and foundation for activity, play, and health curricula in the schools
1890–1910	Publication of seminal texts for progressive education by such scholars as J. Dewey, G. Stanley Hall, W. James, and E.L. Thorndike
1910	Development of the "New Physical Education" by T.D. Wood
1927	Publication of J.F. Williams' *The Principles of Physical Education*, the dominant text of the period
1950	Rise of the comparative systems approach following works by J.S. Brubacker and J.D. Butler
1961–1964	Publication of major "systems" volumes in physical education by such authors as E.C. Davis and E.F. Zeigler

Organization of the Subdiscipline

Year	Event
1965	Emergence of Illinois (Zeigler), Ohio State (Kleinman), and the University of Southern California (Metheny & Slusher) as dominant graduate centers, and Brockport (Fraleigh) as a visible undergraduate institution involved in promoting the philosophy of sport
1972	First meeting of the Philosophic Society for the Study of Sport (Boston)
1973	First independent meeting of the Philosophic Society for the Study of Sport; constitution ratified (Brockport)
1974	Volume 1 of the *Journal of the Philosophy of Sport* published; R. Osterhoudt, editor

Development of the Philosophy of Sport

Year	Event
1965–1968	Publication of early discipline oriented literature by E. Metheny, H. Slusher, and P. Weiss
1972	Publication of the most popular discipline-oriented anthology by E. Gerber

1972–1982	Period of rich contributions to the literature, considerable progress on a variety of activity-related philosophic topics
1990	Concerns emerge about isolation of the discipline, the inability to attract and retain parent-discipline philosophers, and the small number of contributors to the literature
1996	Indication of possible move to a post-disciplinary period

from approximately 1875 to the mid-1950s (Cremin, 1961). At the start of this period, progressive reformers took aim at a 19th-century educational system that emphasized rote memorization, required the same learning experiences for all, and focused on the three R's to the near exclusion of everything else. In an age of growing social problems brought on, in part, by industrialization and urbanization, and at a time when scientific advancement began to provide evidence about the importance of individual differences, personal motivation, and satisfaction, the biological roots of all life and learning, stimulus-response bonds, the emotions, and psychophysical holism,[1] this rigid brand of pedagogy came under ever-increasing fire. People like William James in *The Principles of Psychology* (1897) and *Talks to Teachers on Psychology* (1899), Edward L. Thorndike in *Animal Intelligence* (1898), and John Dewey in *The School and Society* (1899) attacked pedagogical traditions that placed order over freedom, work over play, effort over interest, prescription over election, and intellectual content over a broader range of subjects that prepared human beings for what Herbert Spencer (1860) had earlier called "complete living" (p. 31).

With G. Stanley Hall's (1900) insistence that the school be made to fit the child rather than the other way around (a form of naturalism that elevated the status of play, dance, and games), and Thorndike's redefinition of mind as the "total response of the organism to its environment" (Cremin, 1961, p. 112), the way was cleared for the rise of physical education in the schools. Even though physical activity had long been thought to have some health-related instrumental value, very few educators appreciated the ways in which sport, games, play, and exercise might dramatically improve the entirety of human life—both instrumentally and, more importantly, intrinsically. Physical education philosophers were needed to analyze and articulate the possibilities of something that would be called "The New Physical Education." Thomas D. Wood (*Health and Education*, 1910), Clark Hetherington (*School Programs in Physical Education*, 1922), Jesse Feiring Williams (*The Principles of Physical Education*, 1927), Wood and Rosalind Cassidy (*The New Physical Education*, 1927), Charles McCloy (*Philosophical Bases for Physical Education*, 1940), and J. B. Nash (*Physical Education: Interpretation and Objectives*, 1948) answered the call.

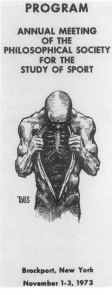

1973 program for
the Annual Meeting
of the Philosophical
Society for the Study
of Sport

Thomas D. Wood

Warren P. Fraleigh

Jesse F. Williams

Paul Weiss

Earle Zeigler

Shenobu Abe

The most original thinker of these progressive era educators was undoubtedly Wood, even though he received less credit than others who
later were to use many of his ideas.[2] While it was Hetherington who gave
the new physical education its name, Wood was the first to sketch its
outlines. Nevertheless a third individual, Jesse Feiring Williams, was
probably the most influential sport philosopher of this period. His *Principles of Physical Education* endured for eight editions and affected physical
education thinking and practice for at least two generations. Williams's
optimistic and ambitious educational agenda attracted legions of followers. Hetherington, Wood, Nash, and McCloy, however, were not among
them. In fact none of these individuals much liked one another and well-
publicized disagreements came to characterize this period. For example,
many practitioners were compelled to pick sides between McCloy's "education of the physical" (a position that focused on health and other biological objectives) and Williams's "education through the physical" (a
philosophy of effecting positive social change and personal growth in
movement "laboratories").

In truth, the positions of the dominant philosophers of this period
differed only marginally. While each maintained distinctive emphases—
Hetherington: mind-body wholeness, balance among physical education
objectives, and play; Williams: social responsibility and moral values;
Wood and Cassidy: natural interests and inclinations, activity in the out-
of-doors, and the integration of physical education with other subjects;
McCloy: organic objectives, strength, and vigor; and Nash: recreation,
and a balanced and full life—they were more nearly alike than different.
They all saw human beings as wholly biological organisms and regarded
themselves as nondualists. Aware of the pressing societal needs of their
time, each of them promoted education for responsible citizenship. They
all honored individual differences. They all distrusted rote exercise and
saw great value in sport, dance, play, and games. Every one of them
viewed physical activity settings as powerful laboratories for learning.
Most importantly, however, they were all engaged in the same project—an
attempt to describe physical education as an integral part of overall human
education from elementary school through postsecondary education.

In order to bring physical education into the early 20th-century educational mainstream, they all had to produce some philosophy. Implicitly
or explicitly, they had to make claims about the nature of humankind
(e.g., the role played by competition or play in the development of children), features of the good life (e.g., the importance of winning, of health,
of friendship among teammates and opponents), and the rights and
wrongs of ethics (e.g., proper behavior toward officials, the virtues that
might be taught through sport, play, and games). But these individuals
were more educationists than philosophers; their passion was the improvement of teaching and learning, not the acquisition of philosophic
insight, and the stimulus for their work came more from the discoveries

of science than any philosophic advances. Predictably, they left themselves open to a number of philosophic criticisms. Their subject matter was narrow. They were more interested in sport, dance, exercise, play, and games as vehicles for education than as phenomena in their own right. Accordingly, they produced little knowledge about the nature and promise of these activities apart from their role in schooling.

To compound problems created by the selection of a narrow subject matter, they proceeded to do relatively little of any philosophic significance with it. For example, typical analyses of holism often read like introductions to physiological psychology, not thoughtful discussions of the philosophic errors committed by the likes of Plato, who elevated contemplation over nonsedentary activity and believed in the immortality of the soul, or Descartes, who radically separated persons into two irreconcilable parts—an immaterial mind and a material body. In Nash's (1931) edited work, *Interpretations of Physical Education: Mind-Body Relationships*, only 2 of 17 chapters were even marginally philosophic in nature. And Williams, for all his clever verbiage about the hand being as much brain as body, and thinking being as surely physical as mental, never (to this writer's knowledge) provided a philosophic analysis of holism; such an investigation would have taken him into a discussion of how performers' thinking in sport does not so much precede movement or otherwise patch itself onto activity, as become an inherent part of it. He did not even engage the insightful nondualistic writings of his primary philosophic mentor, John Dewey (see, e.g., *Soul and Body*, 1886). In short, these writers did not appear comfortable with the philosophic writings and methods of their day. While they did some philosophy, they did a great deal else.

The soundness of their reasoning can be questioned on many fronts. It is not at all clear that they overcame the limits and errors of mind-body dualism. While abandoning an outdated notion of an eternal soul in a material body and touting the biological interrelatedness of the human organism and its functions, these writers remained solidly within the language and some of the traditions of dualism (Gerber, 1966). For example, the previously noted phrase used by Williams, "education through the physical," raised questions for later nondualists. Is the physical aspect of students in a gymnasium to be used as a means to get at something more important, such as mental or moral capacities of these youngsters? If movement professionals are responsible for education somehow related uniquely to the physical, are there others who focus on something called "education through the mental"? Some answers to the first question portrayed the physical active life as a mere means to other more valuable experiences; answers to the second issue suggested that some educators tend to the (inferior) body, while others take care of the more intellectual (and more important) aspects of students.

A number of the progressive education philosophers' conclusions about what should and should not stand as the prime objectives of physical education had a doctrinaire flavor to them, due in large measure to their unwillingness to examine initial assumptions about the nature of the good life—about what values should take priority over other values, about the highest ends of humankind—that is, to do what most trained, careful philosophers would have attempted to accomplish. The goodness of America, democracy, capitalism, and competition were, for these writers, largely givens. If readers happened to agree with these and other unexamined assumptions, subsequent deductions about the role of physical education would be seen as acceptable, perhaps even inspiring. For instance, if fun and individuality (values embraced by several of these writers) are two of the highest ends of life, then certain emphases on spontaneous play, the freedom to pursue personal interests, and flexible learning sequences generally make sense. However, as noncontroversial as some of this reasoning may appear, the granting of initial assumptions, philosophically speaking, is asking a great deal. Examining the assumptions led to a realization that many conclusions in this literature were reached more by conscious or unconscious stipulation than by careful argument.

A common contemporary criticism of these writers is that they promised too much; they raised expectations about the benefits of physical activity far beyond the profession's ability to produce and document them. While there is surely more than an element of truth to such a charge, this problem arose largely from an empirical miscalculation, not a philosophic one. From a philosophic standpoint, the complaint about these writers is more fundamental. It is not that they promised too much, but that they did not argue skillfully for what they were promising. Thus, they may have been promising the wrong things.

For all of these difficulties, however, the work of Wood and Cassidy, Hetherington, Williams, McCloy, and Nash did much to inspire physical educators for over 40 years. Their writings and presentations were comprehensible, optimistic, and practical, based on some of the best scientific insights of the period and compatible with the pragmatic, scientific spirit of that age. Importantly, they helped to generate a golden era of physical education during which physical activity was required in most programs at most levels of education, and was also integrated with intramurals and athletics. But their partial successes were not enough to prevent a new group of philosophers from emerging on the scene and taking the philosophy of sport in a very different direction.

Period 2: (The Systems Approach) 1950–1965

Some might argue that this is actually a later phase of the previous eclectic, philosophy-of-education period because the themes, categories, and interests of this time, as then, were dominated by the concerns of education, not philosophy. The systems approach could be seen simply as a variation on the same theme, as another way to identify physical education as an important element in general schooling.

However, the two most important systems philosophers, Elwood Craig Davis[3] (*The Philosophic Process in Physical Education*, 1961; *Philosophies Fashion Physical Education*, 1963) and Earle F. Zeigler (*Philosophical Foundations for Physical, Health, and Recreation Education*, 1964), broke with the procedures of the educationist era in significant ways, and their products were unmistakably different.

The terms "systems" refers to schools of philosophic thought, the so-called "isms," such as idealism, realism, and naturalism. The most common procedure used by systems philosophers was to describe and compare schools of thought, for example, to put idealism up against realism. Yet, there were other ways in which systems philosophy proceeded. The focus could be placed on recurring problems (e.g., the mind-body debate), great philosophers (e.g., Plato, Aristotle, Kant), the history of philosophy (e.g., the transition from idealism to existentialism in twentieth-century Europe), and the branches of philosophy (e.g., axiology, epistemology, and metaphysics). While all of these approaches, singly and in combination, were utilized in the literature of this period, it was the method of examining comparative schools of thought that was most popular. Both Davis and Zeigler devoted large portions of their texts to juxtaposing and evaluating such systems as naive naturalism, experimentalism, realism, and idealism.

The procedure used for systems comparisons was straightforward. First, the main elements of the positions themselves were described. The key philosophers who belonged to these schools of thought were identified and their central ideas laid out. Second, the basic concepts and positions of the systems were related to education in general. Third, deductions were drawn relative to the field of physical education. In this process, recommendations regarding such practical concerns as staffing, curriculum, and teaching methodology were deduced. Finally, the strengths and weaknesses of the systems were compared, particularly as they related to the vested interests of physical education. For example, a strength of naive naturalism for activity teachers was its simplicity, its emphasis on taking play cues from children in developing a curriculum. Some realistic philosophers, however, highlighted the complexity of life and doubted the capacity of children's natural impulses to lead them into sufficient learning activities. They concluded the physical education curricula should not be developed on models of youthful play, or at least not solely on such criteria.

This systems-comparison approach signaled an advance over the efforts of writers from the philosophy-of-education period for several reasons. It focused on philosophy—from start to finish the comparative systems books were about philosophers, philosophic ideas, and philosophic methods—and it incorporated a broad range of philosophic insights and speculations. These books mentioned nearly all the major philosophers from the parent discipline of philosophy (not education) and their positions, and they allowed readers to pick and choose from among them. Such volumes were to include samples from the "best philosophy that has been thought and written" (Davis, 1961, p. 18). This approach reflected a degree of philosophic sophistication. Unexamined assumptions, faulty reasoning, unsubstantiated speculations—many of the potential pitfalls of philosophy—were, to a degree, avoided in these books.

This period, however, was short-lived, and the quick demise of systems philosophy was related to its shortcomings. Both the validity and utility of the schools-of-thought approach were questioned. If philosophers categorized as existentialists, for example, disagree with one another on important matters, and their points of differences are as significant as their points of agreement, how valid (it was asked) is it to place them all in the same school of thought? Indeed, some existentialists were atheists and described an arbitrary sporting world populated by absurd heroes; others were theists and painted sport in the colors of courageous joy. Some feared human relationships and thus favored individual sports or lonely exercise; others saw human community as the source of much that is good in life and consequently supported group play.

The quality of scholarship that produced this work was questioned for at least two reasons. First, the physical education literature mimicked previous works in educational philosophy. For example, Brubacker's (1950) *Modern Philosophies of Education* and Butler's (1957) *Four Philosophies* appeared around the middle of the century and were heavily utilized by physical education philosophers to formulate the content and style of their own later works. Second, the fact that preexisting categories were superimposed on physical education led to questions about whether or not the right questions were being asked. Some suggested that a complex field like physical education and the unique practices of sport, dance, exercise, games, and play that comprised much of its content should have more influence on the philosophic approaches used to unravel its mysteries. The emerging disciplinary philosophers, for example, wanted to cut more directly to the hunt by asking, "Are competition and play compatible and, if so, how?" They saw the systems question (e.g., "What is a realist's attitude toward play and competition?") as unnecessarily circuitous.

The systems approach was also experienced by some as too encyclopedic and thus, overwhelming. (How many philosophers and systems could one keep track of at the same time?) For others it was tedious. (Were there no more lively ways to do philosophy than trudge through one system after another?) For yet others it was frustrating. (How does one make progress by reviewing systems, each with its own similar list of strengths and weaknesses? Whose answers are better? How is anyone to come to closure on important questions like the value of sport?) On all of these counts, the comparative systems literature often left the reader wondering.

Finally, the frame of reference during this period was still education. Sport philosophers had not yet broken loose to look at human beings as people, not primarily students, or examine sport, exercise, games, play, dance, human movement, competition, and the like on their own terms, not primarily as means to educational ends. In sum, the comparative systems approach provided limited returns on its investment. It would be replaced quickly by another stage in sport philosophy.

Organization of the Subdiscipline

In 1970, at the end of the systems period, no organization existed for philosophers of sport and no specialized journal stood ready to publish their research. Talk about forming a society and founding a publication, by necessity, began at a variety of other professional meetings, among them, the American Association for the Advancement of Science Conference (Texas, 1968), the Meeting of the National College Physical Education Association for Men (Portland, Oregon, 1970), the Olympic Scientific Congress (Munich, Germany, August 1972), and the Sport and Ethics Symposium (Brockport, New York, October 1972).

At the Munich congress, Warren Fraleigh and Paul Weiss agreed to form a steering committee for the formation of a scholarly society, a group that would include two philosophers (Weiss and Richard Zaner) and two physical educators (Fraleigh and Ellen Gerber). It was determined that the recommendations of this group would be discussed at the ethics symposium later that fall in Brockport.

Support from conferees at Brockport led to the first official meeting of the newly formed Philosophic Society for the Study of Sport (PSSS) in Boston, Massachusetts, on December 28, 1972, at the Eastern Division conference of the American Philosophic Association. Weiss was elected first president of the PSSS, Fraleigh the president-elect, Frances Keenan the secretary-treasurer, and Michel Bouet, Scott Kretchmar, Hans Lenk, and Earle Zeigler members-at-large. Fraleigh was named chair of a constitution committee that also included Pat Gallasso, Gerber, James Keating, and Seymour Kleinman. The first full conference of the PSSS took place in Brockport, November 1–3, 1973, and, at that time, the new constitution was ratified. This initial meeting was cosponsored by the Center for Philosophic Exchange, a nonprofit organization that provided administrative and financial, if not also important moral, support during the early years of the Society.[4]

The Society immediately founded a scholarly publication, the *Journal of the Philosophy of Sport*. The first issue was published in 1974 under the editorship of Robert Osterhoudt; he was succeeded by Harold VanderZwaag in 1976, who in turn was replaced two years later by Klaus Meier, who would hold this position for over 16 years.

The mission of the Philosophic Society for the Study of Sport was printed on the inside cover of its first program and read as follows: "The primary purpose of the Society is to foster interchange and scholarship among those interested in the scholarly study of sport. The Society is conceived as international in its membership and program." The term "sport" was interpreted broadly to include many forms of human movement, but to focus on dance, exercise, play, and games, as well as competitive sport. The term "scholarly study" in the mission statement proved more contentious. Some wanted scholarship to be defined broadly and hoped that the Society would sponsor contributions related to pedagogy and a variety of practical concerns. Others, and these turned out to be in the majority, favored a brand of scholarship that lay closer to the discipline of philosophy itself, that was to be of the highest quality, and that would pass muster on standards traditionally used by the parent discipline. Consequently, most of the papers delivered at Society meetings, and the vast majority of articles included in the *Journal*, were focused on basic research, with relatively little attention paid to practical application. Papers on teaching and learning in educational settings were virtually nonexistent.

Most of the scholarly activity in North America after 1970 can be traced to four spheres of influence, three of them graduate centers and the fourth an undergraduate mecca for early employment, curricular growth, and professional dialogue. Most philosophers of sport at this time were graduates of one of three institutions: the University of Illinois (Zeigler), the University of Southern California (Metheny & Slusher), and The Ohio State University (Kleinman). These programs so dominated the field that it is difficult today to find a practicing American sport philosopher who had not studied at one of these institutions or with an individual who had been there.

The fourth sphere of influence was the State University of New York— College at Brockport. In the early 1970s, under the deanship of Fraleigh, this institution hired at different times a remarkable total of ten discipline-oriented philosophers of sport.[5] At one time the Brockport curriculum included six different courses devoted exclusively to philosophic content and inquiry. Perhaps most importantly, this college served as a center for stimulation, dialogue, and (as noted above) organizational work that culminated in the founding of the PSSS.

The efforts of the Society and its journal produced, or at least contributed to, a number of successes. The PSSS attracted a membership approaching 200 at its peak. A high-quality refereed journal served to communicate philosophic sport research around the globe. A substantial body of knowledge on such topics as the nature of sport, sport aesthetics, and ethical behavior in sport was produced in little over 25 years.[6] Considerable progress—arguably to the point of reaching near consensus—was achieved on such questions as the following: Is sport art? What is the relationship between competition and cooperation? Is competitive activity, per se, good? Can people cheat and still be playing the same game, let alone win it? Does playing a game well require the use of intelligence and, if so, in what specific ways? What does a person know when he or she plays a game, and how is that knowledge like and unlike insights encountered in the so-called academic fields of study? What are the relationships among sport, games, and play? Is sport more valuable when it is conducted in the spirit of play than when it is not? Are games trivial activities? Many other questions on which considerable research progress has been made could be added to the list.

In addition, a number of philosophers, some of them highly respected in the parent discipline, became members of the Society and contributed journal articles or conference papers. International membership grew with strong representation from such countries as England, Germany, Norway, Australia, Canada, and Japan. If never a large organization, the Society has enjoyed a dedicated core membership. It has held annual meetings since 1972 in five different countries and on three continents, and the *Journal* recently published its 20th anniversary issue.

Development of the Philosophy of Sport

The intellectual energy that undergirded the organization of the Philosophic Society for the Study of Sport in the early 1970s, spawned its journal, and led to the development of graduate programs was already on the rise at the end of the systems period, producing a new style of philosophic thinking that persists to the present day.

Period 3: (The Disciplinary Approach) 1965–Present

Two major shifts occurred at the start of what is called the disciplinary period. First, philosophers of sport began to produce new philosophic research, using the tools of philosophy, generating insights about such topics as sport and games and their relationship to human development, liberation, achievement, and happiness. In contrast to the eclectic philosophers of education, they took their primary cues from the discipline of philosophy, not science. In contrast to the philosophers of the comparative systems approach, they attempted to do actual research much like many scholars in the parent discipline. To copy, borrow, translate, apply, or deduce from already completed analyses of "real philosophers," while often a good starting place, was no longer sufficient.

Second, these writers made a relatively clean break from pedagogical concerns. Attention shifted from movement in an education setting to, simply, movement itself, opening new vistas of inquiry. The relatively narrow preoccupation with how sport fit the schools was now broadened to thoughts about how sport fit human life.

Early progress was decidedly uneven. The groundbreaking analyses of Metheny (*Connotations of Movement in Sport and Dance*, 1965; and *Movement and Meaning*, 1968), Slusher (*Man, Sport, and Existence*, 1967) and Weiss (*Sport: A Philosophic Inquiry*, 1969) were about as different as they possibly could be. Metheny, interested primarily in movement as a way of knowing and expressing human intelligence, focused on the individual, on personal idiosyncratic experience, and on a variety of movement forms, but particularly dance. Weiss, the first modern philosopher to write a book-length work on sport and the only one of the three who would play a significant role in the later development of the sub-discipline,[7] was nearly the opposite. He was interested in excellence, not knowledge; in universal conceptions of success, not personal experience; and in sport, not dance. Metheny was a radical holist; Weiss something of a Platonic dualist. Metheny was interested in describing intentional human movement as a form of insightful and meaningful activity for all people; Weiss saw sport as a realm where primarily youth and males might achieve excellence. Weiss engaged easily in speculative metaphysics; Metheny avoided them.

Metheny received criticism for leaning too heavily on the philosophers of symbolic thinking, specifically Cassirer (1944) and Langer (1942) and their dubious epistemological theories.[8] She also adopted a curious and confusing terminology to describe the workings of intelligence in human movement. Her discussions of kinescepts, kinestructs, and kinesymbols proved, for many, more mystifying than enlightening. While a number of lay professionals in teacher education and other movement vocations felt she was onto something important, they were unable to negotiate successfully her language and analyses. This difficulty foreshadowed a problem that plagues sport philosophy even to the present day.

Weiss, a well-known philosopher already in his sixties when he wrote *Sport: A Philosophic Inquiry*, was an idealist and thus not in the mainstream of research in the parent discipline. While his analysis of sport turned out to be fairly straightforward and not overly speculative, it still generated considerable criticism. Some wondered about his singular emphasis on excellence as the prime value in sport, his seemingly dualistic recommendation that mind was needed to guide the body in skillful performance, and his tendency to focus primarily on male capabilities in sport.

Slusher, influenced by certain brands of European existential philosophy, provided a third book-length analysis of physical activity, and a markedly distinctive one at that. He examined sport for its capacity to promote personal authenticity, freedom, responsibility, and other values championed in the existential literature. His ambitious volume included insights from Heidegger to Marcel and from Sartre to Jaspers. Yet, this book probably received the heaviest criticism of any—both from inside and outside the profession. Concerns ranged from the accuracy of Slusher's interpretations of the existential literature to his writing style.

Nevertheless, whatever the philosophic merits of their work, Metheny, Weiss, Slusher, and a host of others who played pioneering roles stimulated a new generation of scholars and a new way of thinking and writing philosophically about sport. Research was no longer limited to educational philosophy, the content of human movement was regarded as legitimate and interesting subject matter for serious philosophic inquiry, some philosophers from the parent discipline began to write about sport, and the quality of work from inside physical education reached ever higher levels. Whether for better, worse, or some of each, the new disciplinary approach was underway.

Problems During the Disciplinary Period. During this time all has not gone well with the sport philosophy generally or the Philosophic Society and its journal specifically. Perhaps most disturbing is the fact that philosophy courses have disappeared from many undergraduate physical education curriculums, and just under 90 percent of those that remain are taught by individuals with little interest or training in sport philosophy (Edwards, 1987). Some attribute this decline to the esoteric turn taken by sport philosophers during the disciplinary period, and the resultant difficulty among lay persons in understanding their work. Others say that it is due to the expansion of scientific content and the lesser perceived importance of philosophy. Still others think that it is due to increasing fiscal pressures experienced during the 1970s and 1980s and the inability of departments to afford sport philosophers in a profession that generally sees physiology and biomechanics as more essential. Fraleigh (1989) summarized the current state of affairs when he wrote that the profession "lacks comprehension and respect of the need for competent, rigorous courses and research in philosophy of physical education and sport" (p. 10).

Related to the invisibility of philosophy in the undergraduate curriculum, and the practice of using unqualified and disinterested faculty to teach the existing courses, is the lack of production of new scholars. Because there is little demand, very few graduate programs support philosophy concentrations, and very few graduates emerge each year (King & Bandy, 1987). Currently to this writer's knowledge, the only North American programs that currently accept philosophy of sport PhD students are University of Idaho, The Ohio State University, the University of Western Ontario, The Pennsylvania State University, Purdue University, and The University of Tennessee. The only graduate programs that have at least two specialists active in the discipline are Western Ontario (Meier and Angela Schneider) and Tennessee (Morgan and Joy DeSensi).

The number of different scholars actively involved in producing research during the disciplinary period has been relatively small. Meier (1984) showed that only 46 North American authors published two or more scholarly articles in the philosophy of sport from 1963 to 1983. More shocking is the fact that almost 50 percent of all the scholarly journal literature during this period was produced by only ten authors.

The small number of specialists in this area is due not only to the weak demand for them, or the reluctance of graduate programs to produce them, but also to the inability of early Society members to attract and retain philosophers from the parent discipline. While philosophers like Weiss, Zaner, and Kuntz were instrumental in founding the PSSS, their involvement, and that of others who followed, was generally short-lived and erratic. Most of the sustaining work of the Society was provided by individuals from physical education, even though seven presidents of PSSS have been philosophers, and in spite of the fact that some philosophers have made notable and consistent contributions to the disciplinary movement.[9]

This uneven participation may be due in part to the reluctance of traditional philosophers to approach subjects that are seen as too mundane or problems that are thought to be too applied. For example, one leading philosopher in the United States, upon being asked to provide support for a joint philosophy/physical education conference, responded spontaneously, "There are absolutely no interesting problems in the philosophy of sport." While this reaction is extreme, it may point to an historic unwillingness among philosophers to deal with what they may see as trivial matters like sport, games, and play. This view would help to explain the complaints of some previous sport philosophers that their department heads were unwilling to provide travel support to PSSS conferences, or award any credit for research published in the *Journal of the Philosophy of Sport*.

While some of this history is disturbing, a final verdict regarding the disciplinary movement in sport philosophy is still difficult to reach. In spite of the relatively small numbers of scholars involved and the low demand for its pedagogical and research products, the philosophic subdiscipline has maintained a strong refereed journal along with a steady and dedicated membership. As noted earlier, considerable progress has been made on a number of research problems, and while only modest inroads have been made in the parent discipline, the fact remains that since 1969 over ten texts have been written by disciplinary philosophers on such topics as sport, games, and play.[10]

The Present and Future
of the Philosophy of Sport

Earlier in this chapter I traced three evolutionary phases in the philosophy of sport—the eclectic philosophy-of-education, systems, and disciplinary approaches. It is possible that sport philosophy is on the verge of another shift, one that is being driven by changes in philosophy, physical education, and society at large. These changes include new attitudes toward science, skepticism, and philosophy as a commodity of the marketplace.

In some ways the promise of science, and the unrealistic optimism that accompanied its early phases, has run its course. Science will not solve all the world's problems—some of its harsher critics would say that it may not even be able to solve many of them—not because science or scientists are inept, but rather because the traditional reductionistic model on which science has operated cannot, in principle, produce a complete understanding of human behavior or fully predict it (see, e.g., MacIntyre, 1984). Worse yet, science done in the absence of moral research and reflection is dangerous. What can be done is not always what should be done, and a growing realization is emerging that "should" questions need the attention of specialists in philosophy and nonspecialists alike (Bellah, Madsen, Sullivan, Swidler, & Tipton, 1991).

A growing disenchantment with the skeptical spirit that typifies much scientific inquiry also seems to be on the horizon. Oversimplified, the hard-nosed empirical attitude that is the target of some ire can be portrayed as follows: If it cannot be logically demonstrated, measured, or otherwise physically observed, it is not worth talking about. In physical education, some think that this attitude led to a curriculum top-heavy in courses like physiology, biomechanics, experimental psychology, motor learning, and other scientific bases of movement, but far too light in philosophy, ethics, history, and literature.

This science-adulating perspective affected philosophy, too. It heavily influenced John Dewey and his pragmatic, test-it-first orientation to truth and falsity. Dewey in turn heavily influenced early twentieth-century philosophers of physical education, and we are still the bearers of much of that heritage. In the parent discipline of philosophy, the skepticism of science helped to produce logical positivism and language analysis, two exceedingly dry, overly careful, and often difficult-to-read philosophic approaches. It became apparent to some that these ways of doing philosophy produced limited returns (see, e.g., MacIntyre, 1984; Bloom, 1987) and turned the parent discipline into a narrow field of study dominated by philosophical technologists.

Today some indicators suggest that philosophy is returning to Aristotle's marketplace, where educated people with inquiring minds, common sense, a thirst for truth, and normal language abilities can communicate fruitfully with one another and make philosophic progress on practical human problems. At recent PSSS meetings, for example, more talks addressed day-to-day concerns in simple terms, and fewer technical papers were in evidence.

All this may be signaling the arrival of a fourth historic period in modern sport philosophy, distinguished from its predecessors by its lesser

concern for the categories, terminology, and standards of the parent discipline. It would not be as serious or pretentious, nor would it be as interested in meeting external disciplinary criteria for success. It would be
more interdisciplinary, more flexible, more interested in sport and other
forms of human movement, still rigorous but more fun-loving. It would
be more inclined to involve educationists and others with very practical
interests in sport philosophy. In short, it would be more comfortable with
its differences from the parent discipline. Perhaps this age will be called
the post-disciplinary period.

The terminology of the present time implies dependency. As a so-called
subdiscipline, the legitimacy of sport philosophy is more derived than
inherent. Any glory it might display is more reflected than self-generated.
The tendency, therefore, has been to think that good sport philosophy is
nothing more than a variation on good philosophy!

If a post-disciplinary period comes about, this relationship of dependency will be lessened, not eliminated. To be sure, the insights of philosophers and the categories and methods of traditional philosophy will still
have to be studied, respected, and utilized. But so will the analyses of a
variety of scholars who use nontraditional methodologies ranging from
literary interpretation to poetry, from dance to Olympic-level athletic
participation. Scholars will be encouraged to take different roads toward
a common destination—one of solving the fascinating philosophic questions posed by human involvement in sport, dance, exercise, games,
and play.

Notes

1. Psycho-physical holism in this period was grounded in the scientific
   understanding that biology is the foundation of all. Thinking, in
   other words, is ultimately a product of biology, and no other-
   worldly "ghost in the machine" is required to account for
   human reflection.
2. This information came from personal letters written by Jesse F.
   Williams and Rosalind Cassidy to Bruce L. Bennett dated November
   26, 1949, and July 25, 1951, respectively. Bennett (February 1983)
   graciously shared these letters with me. Williams wrote that "Wood
   was my source." Cassidy indicated that both Williams and Hetherington owed much of their early stimulation to Wood.
3. Davis's book, more than Zeigler's, anticipated the subsequent shift
   to the disciplinary period. When Harper revised the Davis text, it
   became even more focused on thinking philosophically and less
   oriented toward a mechanical application of preexisting systems
   (Harper, Miller, Park, & Davis, 1977).

4. Prior to the founding of the *Journal of the Philosophy of Sport*, a number of articles on sport and related topics were published in the Center's journal, *Philosophic Exchange*.

5. This group, all of whom received PhDs in the philosophy of sport, included Jan Fetters (Ohio State), Fraleigh (Ohio State), Meier (Illinois), Steven Mosher (Massachusetts), Keenan (Illinois), Kretchmar (USC), Osterhoudt (Illinois), Ken Ravizza (USC), Ginny Studer (Ohio State), and Carolyn Thomas (Ohio State).

6. The journal itself published over 125 articles from 1974 through 1993, and well over 20 books on sport philosophy were written during this time. Osterhoudt (1991) in his compendium on sport philosophy cites nearly 1,000 references, the vast majority of which were published in the disciplinary period.

7. Metheny was nearing retirement and was always suspicious of what she saw as the trickery of philosophers in the parent discipline. Slusher, in apparent response to the criticisms aimed at *Man, Sport, and Existence*, left philosophy altogether, earned a law degree, and became a successful sport agent. Ironically, given the fact that their works were often cited and some of their students became active in sport philosophy, neither Metheny nor Slusher ever spoke at a meeting of the Philosophic Society for the Study of Sport or published a single article in the *Journal of the Philosophy of Sport*.

8. A primary criticism focused on relationships between the two objects of consciousness that such a philosophy required—the thing-in-itself and the thing-as-symbol.

9. At the same time that Metheny, Slusher, and Weiss were publishing their book-length essays, physical educators like Warren Fraleigh, Sy Kleinman, and Ellen Gerber and philosophers like Bernard Suits, Richard Zaner, and James Keating were producing their own research. Gerber's (1972) anthology, in fact, proved to be the most widely used volume in the disciplinary period. Earle Zeigler, at the University of Illinois, was active both in continued writing and the mentoring of graduate students who would later assume important leadership roles in the disciplinary movement. Becky Seidel at Kent State University and VanderZwaag at the University of Massachusetts were also producing graduate students early in the disciplinary period.

10. This includes Drew Hyland (2), James Keating, Joe Mihalich, Michael Novak, Robert Simon (2), Bernard Suits, Paul Weiss, and Spencer Wertz (2), among others.

References

Bellah, R.N., Madsen, R., Sullivan, W.M., Swidler, A., & Tipton, S.M. (1991). *The good society*. New York: Knopf.

Bloom, A. (1987). *The closing of the American mind.* New York: Simon & Schuster.

Brubacker, J.S. (1950). *Modern philosophies of education* (2nd ed.) New York: McGraw-Hill.

Butler, J.D. (1957). *Four philosophies* (Rev. ed.). New York: Harper & Row.

Cassirer, E. (1944). *An essay on man.* New Haven, CT: Yale University Press.

Cremin, L.A. (1961). *The transformation of the school: Progressivism in American education, 1876–1957.* New York: Vintage Books.

Davis, E.C. (1961). *The philosophic process in physical education.* Philadelphia: Lea & Febiger.

Davis, E.C. (Ed.) (1963). *Philosophies fashion physical education.* Dubuque, IA: Brown.

Dewey, J. (April 1886). Soul and body. *The Bibliotheca Sacra, XLIII,* 239–63.

Dewey, J. (1899). *The school and society.* Chicago: University of Chicago Press.

Edwards, W.H. (1987). *The philosophy course in physical education: A survey of its current state and role in undergraduate professional preparation curriculum.* Unpublished manuscript.

Fraleigh, W.P. (1989). *The demise of philosophy in physical education.* A paper delivered at the Earle Zeigler Symposium, London, ON.

Gerber, E.W. (1966). *Three interpretations of the role of physical education, 1930–1960: Charles Harold McCloy, Jay Bryan Nash and Jesse Feiring Williams.* Unpublished doctoral dissertation, University of Southern California.

Gerber, E.W. (Ed.) (1972). *Sport and the body: A philosophical symposium.* Philadelphia: Lea & Febiger.

Hall, G.S. (1900). Child-study and its relation to education. *The Forum, XXIX,* 700.

Harper, W.A., Miller, D.M., Park, R.J., & Davis, E.C. (1977). *The philosophic process in physical education* (3rd ed.). Philadelphia: Lea & Febiger.

Hetherington, C. (1922). *School programs in physical education.* Yonkers-on-Hudson, NY: World Book.

James, W. (1897). *The principles of psychology.* New York: Appleton.

James, W. (1899). *Talks to teachers on psychology and to students on some of life's ideals.* New York: Holt Rinehart & Winston.

King, H.A., & Bandy, S.J. (1987). Doctoral programs in physical education: A census with particular reference to the status of specialization. *Quest, 39,* 153–162.

Langer, S.K. (1942). *Philosophy in a new key: A study in the symbolism of reason, rite, and art.* New York: Mentor Books.

Lewis, C.S. (1947). *The abolition of man.* New York: Macmillan.

MacIntyre, A. (1984). *After virtue: A study in moral theory* (2nd ed.). South Bend, IN: University of Notre Dame.

McCloy, C.H. (1940). *Philosophical bases for physical education.* New York: Appleton-Century-Crofts.

Meier, K.V. (1984). A meditation on critical mass in the philosophy of sport. *Journal of the Philosophy of Sport, X,* 8–20.

Metheny, E. (1965). *Connotation of movement in sport and dance.* Dubuque, IA: Brown.

Metheny, E. (1968). *Movement and meaning.* New York: McGraw-Hill.

Nash, J.B. (Ed.) (1931). *Interpretations of physical education: Mind-body relationships, Volume I.* New York: Barnes.

Nash, J.B. (1948). *Physical education: Interpretations and objectives.* New York: Barnes.

Osterhoudt, R.G. (1991). *The philosophy of sport: An overview.* Champaign, IL: Stipes.

Slusher, H.S. (1967). *Man, sport and existence: A critical analysis.* Philadelphia: Lea and Febiger.

Spencer, H. (1860). *Education: Intellectual, moral, and physical.* New York: Appleton.

Thorndike, E.L. (1898). *Animal intelligence.* New York: Hafner.

Weiss, P. (1969). *Sport: A philosophic inquiry.* Carbondale: Southern Illinois University.

Williams, J.F. (1927). *The principles of physical education* (8th ed., 1964). Philadelphia: Saunders.

Wood, T.D. (1910). *Health and education, Part I.* (9th yearbook of the National Society for the Study of Education.) Chicago: University of Chicago Press.

Wood, T.D., & Cassidy, R. (1927). *The new physical education: A program of naturalized activities for education toward citizenship.* New York: Macmillan.

Zeigler, E.F. (1964). *Philosophical foundation for physical, health, and recreation education.* Englewood Cliffs, NJ: Prentice Hall.

7

Motor Behavior[1]

Jerry R. Thomas
Arizona State University

The researches of many commentators have already thrown much darkness on this subject, and it is probable that, if they continue, we shall soon know nothing at all about it.

Attributed to
Mark Twain

Introduction

Simply stated, the goal of this chapter is to provide an accurate history of the field of motor behavior—defined to include motor control, development, and learning—while avoiding throwing "much darkness" on it. Although this history includes work of the past century, the emphasis will be on the past three decades, the time frame that includes the development of the more general field of exercise and sport science. Developing this historical account began with locating as many original reports and other materials as possible, writing to several people[2] who have played major roles in motor behavior research, and gathering their responses to a series of questions. The focus was on

- graduate programs,
- scholars,
- scholarly societies and organizations, and
- journals and books.

Motor behavior is defined in a broad sense and as it is typically used in the United States: "... an area of study stressing primarily the principles of human skilled movement generated at a behavioral level of analysis"

▼

PART I. A Chronology of Motor Control and Learning

Early Foundations of Motor Control and Learning

Year	Event
1846–1892	Beginnings of motor control—spring-like quality of muscles, relation between brain electrical activity and movement
1897, 1899	Beginnings of motor skills research—Bryan and Harter's research on telegraphy
1903	Woodworth's book, *Le Mouvement*
1910–1935	Five themes of motor skill research—knowledge of results, distribution of practice, transfer of training, retention, and individual differences
1927, 1932	Thorndike's Law of Effect—influenced learning and knowledge of results research
1930–1937	Beginnings of motor skills research in physical education—Griffith and McCloy
1940	Influence of World War II on motor skill research, particularly on pilot training; Gibson work on perception
1943	Hull's *Principles of Behavior*—influenced research on motor skills practice
1948	Craik's ideas on the human brain as a computer; Bartlett—practice, the results of which are known, makes perfect
1953	Fleishman—abilities affect motor performance at different points in learning; Merton's work on muscle spindles regulating movement
1954	Fitts's Law about the relation between movement speed and accuracy
1959	Henry's advocacy for skills being specific, not general in nature

Emergence of the Discipline of Motor Control and Learning

Year	Event
1960	Henry and Rogers publish "memory drum" paper—first real theory from motor behavior

1964	Henry's academic discipline paper influenced the development of motor behavior as a discipline; Cratty publishes first motor learning textbook
1965–1971	Henry, Hubbard, and Slater-Hammel begin producing the first generation of motor behavior doctoral graduates
1966–1969	Series of theoretical papers about motor skill are published by Adams; Adams and Dijkstra; Keele; Pew; Posner; Posner and Konick; and Schmidt
1967	Establishment of North American Society for Psychology of Sport and Physical Activity; Bernstein's work on coordination published in English translation
1968	Singer publishes outstanding text in motor learning that is widely recognized and provides structure to the field
1969	Dick Schmidt establishes the *Journal of Motor Behavior*

Development of Motor Learning and Control

Year	Event
1971	Adams publishes closed-loop theory in *JMB*; Welch and Henry publish paper on individual differences
1973	Schutz and Roy publish "Absolute Error: The Devil in Disguise" in *JMB*; Kroll's work on fractionating reaction time; Landers and Landers publish modeling paper
1975	Schmidt publishes schema theory, the most cited paper in motor learning and control; Spirduso's work on fitness and reaction time in aging subjects; Singer's paper on trial-and-error learning; Stelmach, Kelso, and Wallace publish paper showing movement information has short-term component
1975–1976	Stelmach holds conference at University of Wisconsin and edits *Motor Control: Issues and Trends*—structures research area
1977–1978	Stelmach organizes symposium followed by edited book, *Information Processing in Motor Control and Learning*—set future research agenda
1979	Paper by Kelso, Southard, and Goodman in *Science* advocating dynamical systems as a model; Shea and Morgan's paper on practice and contextual interference

1980	Magill's undergraduate text, *Motor Learning: Concepts and Applications*—really good first text for undergraduates; Allard and Starkes publish work on motor expertise
1981	Paper in *JMB* by Kelso, Holt, Rubin, & Kugler providing theory and data on dynamical systems
1982	Christina's work on response complexity paradigm; Schmidt's *Motor Control and Learning*—first graduate textbook to cover field
1984	Outstanding summary of KR literature—Salmoni, Schmidt, and Walter
1987	Adams publishes outstanding paper on history of motor skills research; French and Thomas publish paper relating knowledge, skill, and performance in motor expertise
1988	Abernethy publishes motor expertise paper using more ecologically valid approach to perception
1991	Rosenbaum publishes *Human Motor Control*
1993	Starkes and Allard edit first book on motor expertise, *Cognitive Issues in Motor Expertise*; McCullagh publishes excellent review paper on observational (modeling) learning
1995	Kelso publishes *Dynamic Patterns: The Self-Organization of Brain and Behavior*

▼

PART II. A Chronology of Motor Development

Early Foundations of Motor Development

Year	Event
1797–1906	Baby biographies—descriptions of day-to-day changes in young infants
1859–1877	Darwin's theories about human evolution and their role in shaping behavior
1876	Galton suggests twin studies as a means of evaluating the role of heredity and environment
1928	Gesell's book, *Infancy and Human Growth*

1935	McGraw's studies of Jimmy and Johnny; Bayley's development of the California Infant Scale of Motor Development; Dennis's study of influence of deprivation on motor development
1937	Wild's dissertation on overhand throwing—approach to analysis yields stages and defines a model to be used for over 50 years
1940	Dennis and Dennis paper on Hopi Indian children restricted to cradle boards; Espenschade's paper on motor performance, growth, and maturation establishes model used for 20 years
1956–1962	Studies on growth, strength, and motor performance by Clarke and Harrison, Rarick and Thompson establish model used for 30 years
1960	Espenschade's chapter summarizes motor outcome and performance work since Wild's dissertation
1959–1975	Perceptual-motor programs claiming influence for movement on intellectual function (e.g., Delacato, Kephart); debunked by Kavale and Mattson (1983), Seefeldt (1974), Thomas and Thomas (1986)

Emergence and Development of the Discipline of Motor Development

Year	Event
1967–1973	Publication of four books—Connolly's *Mechanisms of Motor Skill Development*, Espenschade and Eckert's *Motor Development*, Rarick's *Physical Activity: Human Growth and Development*, Wickstrom's *Fundamental Motor Patterns*
1971	DeOreo and Wade's paper on children's balance
1974	Carron and Bailey publish paper on variation in performance associated with maturation; Malina, Hamill, and Lemeshow paper on racial/ethnic factors and motor performance
1975	Malina's book on *Growth and Development: The First Twenty Years* published
1976	Wade's review on motor learning and control theories applied to children
1977	Papers by Roberton and Halverson; Roberton; Safrit; and Roberts on overhand throwing; Thomas and Bender's paper on neo-Piagetian models and children's motor development

1978	Newell and Kennedy paper on age differences in speed of processing
1979	Malina's paper on the role of physical activity in growth and maturation
1980	Thomas review on cognitive factors in children's motor skill development; Barclay and Newell paper on working memory processes and children's motor performance
1982	Edited book by Kelso and Clark, *The Development of Movement Control and Co-ordination*—application of dynamical systems approach to children
1984	Gallagher and Thomas paper on development of control processes in children's motor performance
1985	Thomas and French meta-analysis on gender differences in motor performance
1986	Eaton and Enns meta-analysis on the role of physical activity in growth; Haywood's text *Life Span Motor Development* provides good structure for an undergraduate course
1987	Thelen's paper on the history and role of motor development in psychology; Payne and Isaacs provide a second good undergraduate textbook
1989	What is motor development? Series of papers in *Quest* by Clark and Whitall; Roberton; and Thomas and Thomas
1991	Thelen and Ulrich's monograph on dynamical systems applied to motor development; Malina and Bouchard provide an outstanding text, *Growth, Maturation, and Physical Activity*
1993	Thomas, Thomas, and Gallagher's review on developmental factors in children's skill acquisition
1994	Clark provides an excellent chapter overview of motor development from a dynamical systems view

(Schmidt, 1988, p. 17). Used in this general way, motor behavior encompasses:

- motor control—an area of study dealing with the understanding of the neural, physical, and behavioral aspects of movement (Schmidt, 1988);

G. Lawrence Rarick

Franklin M. Henry

George E. Stelmach

Anna Espenschade

Waneen Spirduso

Richard Schmidt

Jane Clark

- motor development—changes in motor behavior over the life span and the process(es) which underlie these changes (Clark & Whitall, 1989; Motor Development Academy, 1980); and
- motor learning—an area of study focusing on the acquisition of skilled movements as a result of practice (Schmidt, 1988).

Sport psychology, even though sharing many of the original roots and paradigms of motor behavior, is not included in this definition. The delimiting of motor behavior in this way is accepted in North America but differs considerably from other parts of the world (e.g., Germany) where sport psychology would be an all-inclusive term that subsumes motor behavior. It is worthwhile to note that this chapter is delimited to the history of motor behavior in the United States, but probably has some relevance to Canada. Thus, by its very nature it is "nearsighted" because much significant work has been done in Europe, Russia, Australia, and other parts of the world. That work is only discussed as it impacts motor behavior in the United States.

Part I. Motor Control and Learning

In the following section the history of motor control and learning is described together because their evolution is similar. (Motor development is discussed separately.) Adams (1987) wrote an excellent historical review of research in the learning, retention, and transfer of human motor skills and his division of the area into three historical periods is used (although these divisions are similar to those used earlier by Irion, 1969): Early Period, 1880–1940; Middle Period, 1940–1970; and Present Period, 1970 to the present. The use of 1940 as the first dividing date is commonly agreed upon because of the surge of research activity, conducted primarily by psychologists, associated with World War II, particularly emphasizing questions about pilot training for the military. Beginning about 1970 there was a new surge and a shift toward more theoretical research models coinciding with the development of the discipline—the study of human physical activity—and one of its subdisciplines, motor behavior.

Early Foundations of Motor Control and Learning

While it is undeniably true that here, as in other situations, want of identifiable ancestry can be an embarrassment, it is also true that the field of motor skills probably owes some of its vitality to just that deficiency. A founder tends to define the field of discourse, to set the methods of investigation, to identify the problems to be solved, and, all too often, to bequeath a legacy of sterility as well. . . . The field of motor skills does not suffer from a lack of variety or imaginativeness. Indeed, the approaches are so extremely various that there is some difficulty in defining just what the field of motor skills is. (Irion, 1969, pp. 1–2)

The history of this field has seen a number of name changes, although "motor control and learning" seems to have current acceptance (e.g., Schmidt, 1988). However, Adams (1987) has used the term "human motor skills," as have a number of previous individuals doing reviews of the area (e.g., Irion, 1969). This term reflects the strong association of the field with experimental psychology and human factors. Other terms like "motor learning and performance" (e.g., Singer, 1968) and "psychology of motor learning" (e.g., Oxendine, 1968) have been used. The upcoming review will reveal that exercise and sport science (or, if you prefer, kinesiology or physical education) has played a major role in this area only since about 1970. When the current period (1970 to the present) is discussed, the influence of useful theories (e.g., Adams, 1971; Henry & Rogers, 1960; Keele, 1968; Kelso & Tuller, 1984; Pew, 1966; Schmidt, 1975) to the generation of research in motor learning and control will be the focus, much of this work coming from exercise and sport scientists who frequently published in the *Journal of Motor Behavior*, but also in *Research Quarterly for Exercise and Sport, Journal of Experimental Psychology* (Human Learning, Memory and Cognition, and Human Perception and Performance sections since *JEP* was subdivided) and other journals.

Early Period, 1880–1940

Where is the beginning of research in motor control and learning? This question is problematic because most of the early work on motor skills focused on other questions (e.g., solving industrial problems—safety, efficiency). For example, Bryan and Harter's (1897, 1899) research on telegraphy involved expert and novice performers in the use of Morse code. They reported learning curves and plateaus (this work has not withstood replication; see Adams, 1987) as well as the differing characteristics of expert and novice performers. This line of research could be identified as leading to later work in both motor learning and motor expertise (Abernethy & Sparrow, 1992; Lee & Swinnen, 1993), yet the focus of the research was on neither topic. Schmidt (1988) identified some of the earliest studies involving motor skills as those of Bowditch and Southard (1882) in the use of vision in hand movements; Fullerton and Cattell (1892) in force reproducibility; Judd (1908) in transfer of learning in dart throwing; and Leuba (1909) in limb positioning accuracy. However, the

"motor" part of each of these studies was only incidental to other purposes—typically, introspection that might lead to understanding the mind
(Abernethy & Sparrow, 1992; Schmidt, 1988). The first research that really
focused on motor skills per se may have been Woodworth's (1899) study
identifying principles of rapid arm and hand movements. In fact Noble
(1968) suggested that Woodworth's book (1903), *Le Mouvement*, and his
earlier monograph should represent the founding of the field of motor
skills research. However, Woodworth's work did not receive much attention until Ammons (1958) identified its significance. Thus, while Woodworth's research may have been the first that really focused on motor
skills, labeling him as the founding father does not seem useful because
his work was not the basis for subsequent research.

Sporadic research, mostly from psychology, using motor skills as outcome measures but focusing on objectives other than understanding
skilled action, continued throughout the early twentieth century (e.g.,
typing skills—Bean, 1912; Book, 1925; Swift & Schuyler, 1907; time-and-
motion studies—Stimpel, 1933). Thorndike (1927, 1932) developed his
Law of Effect, which had tremendous impact on later motor learning
research. His idea—that out of many responses, those that are rewarded
become stronger, are selected most often, and therefore, "learned"—is
the basis for much of the subsequent work in knowledge of results (Adams, 1987). Along with the knowledge of results theme developed from
Thorndike's research, Adams suggested that the underpinnings of four
other themes were developed during this period: distribution of practice
(Doré & Hilgard, 1938; Ebbinghaus, 1885/1964; Gentry, 1940; Hunter,
1929; Lorge, 1930); transfer of training (Hunter, 1929; Judd, 1908; McGeoch,
1931; Whipple, 1928; Woodworth, 1938); retention (Hollingworth, 1909;
McGeoch & Melton, 1929; Swift, 1905; Swift & Schuyler, 1907; Tsai, 1924);
and individual differences (Kincaid, 1925; Reed, 1931; Thorndike, 1908).
Indeed, even now the two most frequently used undergraduate textbooks
(Magill, 1993; Schmidt, 1991) are still partly organized around those major
themes. One additional item of importance was Tolman's (1932) distinction between performance and learning, a phenomenon that is still sometimes overlooked in current research.

A small amount of research from the measurement of sport and athletic
performance could be classified in motor behavior (e.g., McCloy, 1934,
1937). Probably the first laboratory in motor skills and sport research in
physical education in the United States was established by Coleman R.
Griffith at the University of Illinois in 1925 (University of Illinois Board
of Trustees, 33rd Report, 1924–1926, May 16, 1925, p. 227 as cited in Kroll,
1982) for studying the psychological and physiological aspects of athletics.
Griffith (1930) reported on this laboratory in *Research Quarterly* and listed
an interesting set of about 30 research studies that were underway. Several
of these are topics of interest to motor behavior today:

- Origin and development of timing and pace as related to learning plateaus
- Effect of nicotine on learning
- Muscular coordination in shooting baskets
- Effects of fear on learning
- Reaction time of all entering freshmen (at U of I)
- Thinking processes during critical decisions in sport
- Types of errors in throwing
- Effects of muscular tension on skill
- Reaction time in grade school children
- Sex differences in motor skills

In addition Griffith (1930) reported devising tests and apparatus for this laboratory to measure: reaction time to muscular load; baseball ingenuity; muscular tension and relaxation; serial reaction time; steadiness, muscular coordination, and learning ability; all types of reaction time; and mental alertness (paper and pencil test). Two subsequent research papers were published (Jackson, 1933; McCristal, 1933) reporting experiments from this laboratory. Griffith might be considered the first motor behavior researcher within physical education, but he is often considered that for sport psychology, too. However, work from this laboratory has had little subsequent impact on motor behavior.

A related area that had considerable influence on motor control is the physiological and neurological bases of movement. The "spring-like" qualities of muscle, a major topic of interest in recent years in motor control, was reported by Blix (1892–1895) and Weber (1846) before the beginning of the twentieth century. The discovery that the brain produced electrical impulses (Fritsch & Hitzig, 1870) led to investigations of the relation between brain electrical activity and movement control (Beevor & Horsely, 1887, 1890; Ferrier, 1888). Sherrington's (1906) research on neural control, in which he (and co-workers) classified electrical responses to stimuli given at the extremities, led to many classical concepts still useful in describing how the nervous system controls muscles and movements (Abernethy & Snyder, 1992; Schmidt, 1988): reciprocal innervation, final common path, muscle tension and length, and proprioception. Work evaluating electrical activity in brain structures and what happens when they are damaged, often using simple movements as the response variable, continued through the 1920s and 1930s (e.g., Adrian & Buytendijk, 1931; Herrick, 1924; Holmes, 1939).

Research workers in the two areas, motor behavior and neurophysiology, showed little concern for, or interest in, the research in the associated area (Schmidt, 1988). The focus of the work in motor behavior was on complex movements like typing and telegraphy, with little interest shown in either the biomechanical or neurological bases for the movements. The neurophysiological researchers were interested in the neural mechanisms and damage to them, with little concern for complex movements or even the nature of the simple movements (e.g., speed, accuracy, pattern) they studied. The only place where the two areas were being integrated in the 1930s and 1940s was in Russia—Bernstein's work on locomotion. However, this research was not known in the United States until it was translated into English in the 1960s (Bernstein, 1947, 1967); therefore, its influence is discussed under the Present Period.

Middle Period, 1940–1970

The most important influence with regard to motor behavior in this period was the research conducted in conjunction with World War II. Because of the need to select and train military personnel, particularly pilots, considerable money and support were provided for research on the motor skills related to piloting aircraft. While much of the research had an applied bent because of its military connections, the general themes from the early period still persisted (Adams, 1987): knowledge of results, distribution of practice, transfer of training, retention, and individual differences. However, the relative importance of these themes varied somewhat, due to the practical nature of the military's needs and evolving theories—Hull's (1943) *Principles of Behavior*, the growth of behaviorism (Skinner, 1953), and Gibson's (1940) work on perception.

Craik's (1948) ideas concerning the similarities between the human brain and a computer had a profound influence and eventually led to other theories involving concepts such as short-term and long-term memory (e.g., Atkinson & Shiffrin, 1968). These theories of cognitive function were important in the development at the end of this period of the first real theories about aspects of motor behavior: memory drum theory (Henry & Rogers, 1960); sensory feedback in movement (Adams, 1968) and subsequently, closed-loop theory (Adams, 1971); motor control (Keele, 1968); short-term motor memory (Adams & Dijkstra, 1966; Posner & Konick, 1966); attention and movement control (Posner, 1969); anticipation and timing in motor performance (Schmidt, 1968); and practice and automaticity (Pew, 1966).

During this middle period Thorndike's (1927, 1932) work continued to influence motor skills research on knowledge of results. With regard to Thorndike, Adams (1987) suggested that a real tribute exists when a researcher's ideas have as much impact after his death as during his lifetime. Research on knowledge of results (KR) focused on both the associative (either habit strength or informational) and motivational (goal setting) explanations. Nearly everyone was convinced that giving knowledge of results at the end of a movement sequence was the way to learn skills (Adams, 1987). As Bartlett (1948) said, "The common belief that 'practice makes perfect' is not true. It is practice *the results of which are known* that makes perfect" (p. 86). Manipulation of knowledge of results, including varying KR withdrawal schedules as well as KR delay schedules, began during this time. Also, the point where KR was given during the inter-trial interval, time between the end of one trial and the beginning of the next, was used to evaluate the influence of delaying KR, as well as how much time was needed to process KR.

Hull's (1943) book, *Principles of Behavior*, was very influential on the distribution of practice research. This work was summarized by Adams (1987):

- More time between trials produces better performance (e.g., Adams, 1954).
- Responses that require greater work result in poorer performance (e.g., Bilodeau, 1952; Bilodeau & Bilodeau, 1954).
- Following massed practice longer rest periods result in bigger gains or reminiscence (e.g., Ammons, 1947; Irion, 1949).

Work on transfer of training was done with pilots. Questions of particular importance were (Adams, 1987): When pilots learn to fly on one aircraft and transfer to another, is performance adversely affected (negative transfer); then, what happens to performance if the pilot returns to the first aircraft (retroactive interference)? Of course researchers hoped that training transferred in a beneficial way and that retroactive interference did not occur. However, that was not the case (Lewis, McAllister, & Adams, 1951). Additional transfer topics of note were the fact that verbal pretraining positively transferred to a motor response (e.g., McAllister, 1953), and that part-task training worked sometimes (e.g., Briggs & Naylor, 1962) but not as well as whole-task training (e.g., Adams & Hufford, 1962; Briggs, Naylor, & Fuchs, 1962).

Most retention work focused on applied topics such as "warm-up" decrements, the idea that nonspecific warm-up enhances subsequent motor performance (e.g., Adams, 1952; Irion, 1948); late in this time period, more theoretical work began: short-term motor retention (e.g., Adams & Dijkstra, 1966; Posner & Konick, 1966); retroactive and proactive interference (e.g., Boswell & Bilodeau, 1964; Posner, 1967; Stelmach, 1970); attention demand (e.g., Ascoli & Schmidt, 1969; Stelmach, 1969); and long-term retention (e.g., Fleishman & Parker, 1962; Meyers, 1967).

One of the areas of greatest interest during the 1940–1970 period, because of the funding from the U.S. military, was individual differences in motor skills, particularly pilot selection and training (Adams, 1987). Motor tests were useful in increasing the prediction of written tests, but written tests still were given more weight (Melton, 1947). The U.S. Air Force began the Human Resources Research Center in 1948 (Adams, 1987); a very prolific researcher from this group was E.A. Fleishman from the Perceptual and Motor Skills Research Laboratory. His work is well known to most motor skills researchers (Fleishman, 1953, 1956; Fleishman & Hempel, 1956; for a summary see Fleishman, 1972). His findings about different abilities affecting motor performance at different points in learning were logical and well received. However, his analytical techniques have been criticized in recent years, calling some of his findings into question (Alvares & Hulin, 1972; Bechtoldt, 1962; Corballis, 1965; Humphreys, 1960). In addition there was some work within physical education on individual differences. During the early period McCloy (1934, 1937) had proposed the concept of "general motor ability," the concept that athletic talent was generalizable across sports. Henry (1959, 1968) actively disputed the notion of general motor ability during this time period; he was a strong advocate for the specificity of skills and their lack of transfer across motor and athletic tasks.

In addition to these standard themes, the research on humans in performance situations led to the emergence of new areas—human factors, ergonomics, and engineering psychology (Schmidt, 1988). Fitts (1954) presented his findings about the relations among movement time, movement extent, and accuracy in hand movements, leading to the first "real" law about movement, called Fitts' Law. This law suggests a relation between movement speed and accuracy (Schmidt, 1988, p. 269) such that:

$$MT = a + b[Log_2 (2A/W)]$$

where MT = average movement time; A = amplitude of the movement; W = target width; a = intercept on Y-axis; b = regression weight.

Of particular note to our field at the end of this time period was Franklin Henry's (PhD in psychology) memory drum theory (Henry & Rogers, 1960), a first for the field of motor behavior: a theory explaining movement, proposed by researchers in physical education. Henry and his students had a profound impact on the development of motor behavior (more on this later). In addition Henry's (1964) paper, "Physical Education: An Academic Discipline," set the stage for the development of the study of human physical activity and the emergence of motor behavior as a subdiscipline within physical activity, apart from the discipline of psychology.

"As in the early period, the neural control and motor behavior scientists were oblivious to each other, but important contributions were being made in neural control that would later be important in joining the two areas" (Schmidt, 1988, p. 13). For example, Merton's (1953) work about muscle spindles regulating movement still seems reasonable, at least generally. In particular Merton's neural control work was among the first to measure movements in connection with the neurophysiological processes (Schmidt, 1988). The finding that joint receptors (Skoglund, 1956) responded only at certain joint angles was also important, although this work now seems less useful because most joint receptors seem to be active only at the extremes of joint angles (Burgess & Clark, 1969). Research on the "spring-like" quality of muscle continued during this period (Schmidt, 1988) and began to attract the attention of researchers in motor control and behavior (Rack & Westbury, 1969).

Development of the Discipline of Motor Control and Learning (1970 to present)

Most of the remaining sections in this chapter will be devoted to this time period, because the discipline that focuses on the study of human physical activity developed, with motor behavior becoming an active subdiscipline while maintaining relations with psychology and neuroscience; and motor behavior expanded significantly with theoretical developments, new emphases in PhD programs, new journals, changes in older journals, and increased funding support for research. Later in this chapter these issues (important individuals, new journals, doctoral programs, etc.) will be discussed in greater detail; however, making sense of the growth of research in this field is nearly impossible without an overview of what occurred in the areas of motor control and learning.

Emergence of the Discipline
of Motor Control and Learning

Two papers by Franklin Henry had a profound influence. His "memory drum" paper (Henry & Rogers, 1960) provided a useful theory about the role of cognitive activity in motor control and learning that could be tested empirically. Second, his paper on physical education as an academic discipline (Henry, 1964) set the stage for the development of a discipline, the study of human physical activity, from what had previously been a teaching area within education, namely, physical education.

However, Henry was not alone in his endeavors in motor control and learning. Alfred "Fritz" Hubbard at the University of Illinois (also, Jack Adams in the Department of Psychology there) and Arthur Slater-Hammel at Indiana University had a significant impact on the development of motor control and learning, particularly with their preparation of doctoral students and the research programs of Henry and Adams. In fact the three have often been called the "three Hs of motor behavior." John Lawther at Pennsylvania State University was also one of the early influential motor learning leaders. While Henry probably had the most influence, thus Schmidt's (1988, p. 12) labeling of him as the "father of motor behavior research in physical education," the three Hs produced a number of graduate students who have impacted motor control and learning since then.[3] As you will note in the subsequent research review in this section, this first generation of doctoral students, and their doctoral students (the second generation), account for a major part of the research in motor learning and control during this period.

The three Hs, but particularly Slater-Hammel, who was the first president (1967–1969), were also major players in the founding of the North American Society for Psychology of Sport and Physical Activity, in 1967. This academic society was a place for the presentation of current scholarly work, discussion of ideas, and networking of faculty and doctoral students in motor control and learning, motor development, and sport psychology.

Finally, two of the first-generation doctoral students and their actions played a significant role in the development of motor control and learning as a coherent subdiscipline particularly at the beginning of this period. Dick Schmidt, in addition to being one of the major researchers and theorists in motor control and learning since 1970, founded the *Journal of Motor Behavior* (*JMB*) in 1969. This journal has been the major outlet for the field in the United States and Canada, although John Whiting's founding of the *Journal of Human Movement Studies* a year later (1970) in England also served as a significant research outlet; also in recent years *Research Quarterly for Exercise and Sport* has played a significant role. *JMB* found a really important niche in the field, because at the beginning of this period *Research Quarterly* (became *Research Quarterly for Exercise and Sport* in 1980) had more of an applied perspective, while the *Journal of Experimental Psychology* was not focused on motor behavior and publishing in it was very difficult (Schmidt, personal communication, July 20, 1993).

A second major factor was a series of conferences and subsequent edited books organized by George Stelmach. The first book resulting from these conferences was Stelmach (1976), *Motor Control: Issues and Trends*. As Stelmach said in the preface (p. ix):

> . . . emphasis has shifted to the processes intervening between the stimulus and response. With this changing scene, investigators began to perform experiments that utilized behavior techniques that examined such topics as feedback as a regulating agent, the internal representation of sensory information, and the development of a perceptual trace. These efforts quickly demonstrated the benefits of an interdisciplinary approach since it was realized that the neurophysiologist had to relate his findings to behavior. Likewise, the behaviorist realized his need to link his findings to the neuromechanisms that underlie motor control.

This book was quickly followed by a symposium (in 1977) that Stelmach organized at the University of Wisconsin—Madison, also resulting in an edited book, Stelmach (1978), *Information Processing in Motor Control and Learning*. These two books contained chapters by the major researchers in motor control and learning that summarized and set the stage for future research. Maybe of equal importance, as Schmidt said in a personal communication (July 20, 1993), both ". . . really highlighted the cross-disciplinary nature of motor behavior."

Finally, the second-generation doctoral students produced by Schmidt (e.g., Robert Christina, John Shea, Howard Zelaznik) and Stelmach (e.g., Scott Kelso, Charles Worringham) have continued to influence the direction of motor behavior research. This group, together with other major scholars (e.g., Walter Kroll, Richard Magill, Karl Newell, Robert Singer, Waneen Spirduso) and many of their students (e.g., Les Carlton, Mark Fischman, Timothy Lee, Gilmore Reeve), have developed a legitimate subdiscipline of motor control and learning within the field that grew from physical education to the study of human physical activity.

Research Direction and Activity

Two interrelated factors have influenced research directions and activity since 1970. Of course these factors are closely related to the changes that occurred at the end of the previous period.

First, a new breed of motor behavior scholar was being developed in what were then physical education departments, particularly by the three Hs, Henry at University of California—Berkeley, Hubbard (and Adams) at the University of Illinois, and Slater-Hammel at Indiana University. This new breed was well trained in the sciences, with a strong experimental psychology flavor. They used careful laboratory experimentation, good experimental designs, and quantitative statistical procedures.

Second, for the first time the motor control and learning area developed its own theories about skill acquisition and control. Previously, the motor skills area had used general learning theories from psychology (e.g., Hull, 1943; Thorndike, 1932), and adapted them to motor skills. At the end of the middle period researchers began to publish papers that proposed specific theoretical views about motor control and learning—Adams (1968) on sensory feedback in movement; Adams and Dijkstra (1966) and Posner and Konick (1966) on short-term motor memory; Keele (1968) on motor control; Posner (1969) on attention and movement control; Pew (1966) on practice and automaticity; and Schmidt (1968) on anticipation and timing in motor performance. This theorizing led to the first real theories of motor control and learning.

Research in the Present Period.   The general categories used in the previous two periods are not used to organize the research in the present period. While they are still somewhat useful, the organizational categories around which the major graduate text (Schmidt, 1988) and the two most used undergraduate texts (Magill, 1993; Schmidt, 1991) are developed seem more valid: motor control and motor learning. In this structure motor control includes cognitive views on topics like attention, motor programs, neuromotor activity, and individual differences. In addition, motor control includes action systems research focusing on cyclic stability and entrainment, perturbation and coordinative structures, phase transitions in continuous actions, and scaling factors in actions. Motor learning includes feedback and knowledge of results, retention and transfer, and practice conditions.

The period since 1970 could be called the "motor control and learning theory period." Research in this area was difficult to publish unless it was theory-based.

Closed-Loop Theory   Jack Adams (1971) started theory-based research in this period with his paper in *JMB* titled "A Closed-Loop Theory of Motor Learning." Basically, this paper explained the way that increasing movement control was acquired in slow and discrete movements, mostly on linear positioning tasks—the movement of a handle down a near-frictionless track to a specific position, usually without the assistance of vision. Closed-loop theory explained how feedback was used to update the cognitive representation of the movement so that the next performance trial would be better. The concept of a "closed loop" is used to describe this model because it is like the thermostat on a furnace. Heat in the house is adjusted by the thermostat's comparing the desired temperature with the current temperature and turning the furnace on or off based on this comparison. Adams proposed that learning motor skills was a closed-loop system: In memory the cognitive representation of the location was compared with the current location and the movement was adjusted until they matched. Feedback in the form of error information allowed the central representation of the position to be updated for the next performance.

An analysis by Abernethy and Sparrow (1992) showed that Adams's (1971) closed-loop theory was the most popular theory tested in *JMB* between its publication and 1977 averaging three to four papers per year. Particularly significant papers testing aspects of closed-loop theory are in table 7.1.

Researchers noted several problems with closed-loop theory. In particular closed-loop theory was not very useful in explaining the fast ballistic and continuous movements used in sport and other motor tasks; the fact that very rapid movements are clearly being produced without the use of feedback to working memory for adjustments during the movement; and how response variability is used to adapt to a changing performance situation. Researchers, especially Schmidt (1975), began to address these problems.

Error Scores   Just at this time when closed- and open-loop theories were being debated, tasks were often of the type yielding error scores (e.g., linear and curvilinear position, anticipation-timing). An error score can be considered in many ways:

Table 7.1   Papers Testing Aspects of Closed-Loop Theory

Variation of proprioceptive and visual feedback
    Adams, Goetz, & Marshall, 1972; Adams, Gopher, & Lintern, 1977.

Stability of performance when knowledge of results is withdrawn
    Adams et al., 1977; Newell, 1974.

Number of acquisition trials and ability to estimate performance
    Adams et al., 1972; Adams et al., 1977; Newell, 1974; Schmidt & White, 1972.

Influence of withdrawal of knowledge of results on continued performance
    Adams et al., 1972; Adams et al., 1977; Newell, 1974; Schmidt & White, 1972;
    Williams, 1974; but for a different finding see Newell, 1976b.

Influence when a task was interpolated in the inter-trial interval
    Boucher, 1974; Magill, 1973, 1977; Schendel & Newell, 1976; Shea & Upton,
    1976.

Influence of manipulating the acquisition conditions on memory states
    Christina & Merriman, 1977; Christina & Anson, 1981.

- The absolute deviation from target disregarding whether the error is short/long or fast/slow, called absolute error (AE)
- The deviation from the target with a plus or minus sign indicating the nature of the error, called constant error (CE)
- The standard deviation of the errors within a single subject's several trials, called variable error (VE)
- Other variations: total error ($\sqrt{CE^2 + VE^2}$); absolute constant error, the averaging of several trials for one subject's CE and then dropping the plus/minus sign (| CE |)

Each of the error terms has been suggested to have specific meaning and to be useful under certain circumstances (Schmidt, 1988).

Schutz and Roy (1973) published an important paper, "Absolute Error: The Devil in Disguise," which not only impacted error measurement practices but also generated a useful controversy and discussion (Henry, 1974, 1975; Newell, 1976a; Roy, 1976; Schutz, 1977) about the appropriate measurement and analysis of error scores.

Open-Loop Theory   Although one must acknowledge that Adams never proposed closed-loop theory to handle rapid ballistic movements, the failure of closed-loop theory on the previously described issues led Schmidt (1975) to publish what may be the most significant paper during this period, "A Schema Theory of Discrete Motor Skill Learning." This paper, with subsequent adjustments of the theory (Schmidt, 1976, 1980, 1982), was the first from the new generation of scholars. Schmidt (personal communication, July 20, 1993) indicated that he took the best aspects of Adams's (1971) closed-loop theory and combined them with Schmidt's own adjustment to the idea of motor programs (e.g., see Keele, 1968), the "generalized motor program." Schmidt suggested that, rather than every movement having a motor program, movements fell in classes and used a generalized motor program to control them. For example, throwing a ball would be controlled by a generalized motor program regardless of whether the ball was a softball or a baseball, and whether the throw was from third to first base or from center field to home plate.

Abernethy and Sparrow's (1992) analysis of theories tested in *JMB* between 1969 and 1987 indicates that Schmidt's schema theory was the most tested theory, averaging six to seven papers per year from its publication in 1975 to 1985. In fact, his is the only paper in motor control and learning (and likely the field of human physical activity) to be listed as a "Citation Classic" in *Current Contents* (Social and Behavioral Sciences ISI, **15** (25), June 20, 1983, p. 20); *Current Contents* indicated that the paper had been cited in over 155 publications as of 1983—current estimates are over 500 citations (Lai & Shea, 1995).

Schema theory (Schmidt, 1975) suggested that open-loop movements (movement without, or with very limited, feedback) could exist in the same model with a closed-loop system. Thus, the "general motor program" could run off a very rapid movement without the use of feedback as well as slower movements using feedback (for a summary of the KR literature, see Salmoni, Schmidt, & Walter, 1984). The general motor program did this by setting relative phasing (timing) and maybe relative force requirements for a general class of movements. Memory representations of both fast and slow movements are updated with feedback. Problems with schema theory relate to where the general motor program comes from, how the rules to govern movement develop, and how a movement is done the first time (Adams, 1987; Schmidt, 1988). Particular findings of note on schema theory are in table 7.2.

Table 7.2 Findings of Note Relative to Schema Theory

Practicing a variety of movement outcomes within the same movement class resulted in a "better" schema
　　For a summary, see Shapiro & Schmidt, 1982; but for another view, see van Rossum, 1990.

Separation of the response recognition schema from the recall schema
　　Zelaznik, Shapiro, & Newell, 1978.

Motor learning may be mostly rule learning
　　Schmidt, 1988.

Novel movements can be produced better with more variable practice
　　Schmidt, 1977.

Error should not be detected following slow movements
　　Schmidt & White, 1972.

Schmidt and colleagues (Schmidt, Zelaznik, Hawkins, Frank, & Quinn, 1979) attempted some "midcourse" corrections of schema theory to explain the speed-accuracy trade-off described early in Fitts's (1954) work. These corrections were labeled as an impulse-variability model and suggested the relation between movement errors and the force and duration applied to a limb movement (for reviews, see Hancock & Newell, 1985; Schmidt, Sherwood, Zelaznik, & Leikind, 1985).

A Paradigm Crisis?   The first real suggestion of a paradigm crisis in motor control and learning—in Kuhn's (1970) terms, revolutionary science—was the emergence of "dynamical systems" (or "action systems"). This view is grounded "in the belief that movement kinematics are *not* represented centrally (in a motor program, plan, schema, or any other form) but are rather an emergent property of the dynamics of the underlying motor system, and hence should be understood in terms of the collective physical properties of the functional muscle groups involved in any particular action" (Abernethy & Sparrow, 1992, p. 24). The first attempt at explaining movement control in this way, called the mass-spring model, was by Asatryan and Fel'dman (1965), and more recently Polit and Bizzi (1978) tried to apply the principles, but the model proved to have limited explanatory power (Abernethy & Sparrow, 1992).

Dynamical Systems   The emergence of a more complete theory for dynamical systems had much to do with Scott Kelso's, one of George Stelmach's PhD students, work with Michael Turvey at the Haskin's Laboratories in New Haven, Connecticut, and Hermann Haken at Florida Atlantic University. This work led to a series of papers (e.g., Haken, Kelso, & Bunz, 1985; Kelso, 1981; Kelso & Schoner, 1988; Kelso, Holt, Rubin, & Kugler, 1981; Kugler, Kelso, & Turvey, 1982) proposing how a dynamical systems model was a better explanation of motor control than cognitive views that depended on a central memory representation for the movement. For a comparison of a cognitive view and a dynamical systems view of motor control and learning, see table 7.3, developed by Abernethy and Sparrow (1992).

Dynamical systems models are based (Turvey, 1977) on the principles of modern physics and theoretical biology, combined with the conceptual views on coordination (Bernstein, 1967) and perception (Gibson, 1979). The basic view rejects the man-machine (actor-environment) division of more cognitive views and calls for an ecological and holistic view of human action (Abernethy & Sparrow, 1992). According to Abernethy and Sparrow, the dynamical systems approach addresses a number of the problems of open- and closed-loop systems of motor control:

- The fact that total body actions involve a large number of joints and muscles acting together that require control from the nervous system, called the degrees of freedom problem (Kelso, Buchanan, DeGuzman, & Ding, 1993; Turvey, Fitch, & Tuller, 1982)

Table 7.3   Dimensions of Contrast Between the "Movement Systems" and "Dynamical Systems" Approaches in Motor Control and Learning

Dimensions of contrast	Movement systems approach	Dynamical systems approach
Alternative label	Information-processing Computational Representational	Dynamical Emergent Direct
Philosophical origins	Belief in the man-machine metaphor. Implicit support of the actor-environment dualism.	Belief in ecological realism. Explicit support of actor-environment synergy.
Origin of theoretical explanation and model	Computer science and engineering	Modern physics and theoretical/comparative biology.
Direction of exploratory logic	Improved explanatory power by adding sophistication and intelligence to the computational model.	Improved explanatory power by seeking more fundamental process.
Nearest psychology subdicipline	Cognitive psychology	Ecological psychology
Movement organization and control mode	Top-down, hierarchical control acting via prescription.	Bottom-up heterarchical control acting through coordinative structures.
Solution to the control of multiple degress of freedom	Generalized motor programs structured and stored centrally.	Coordinative structures that self-assemble the dynamical properties of the motor system.
Relationship of control mode to kinematics	A priori planning resulting in desired kinematics. Organization and assembly prescribed from overriding plan.	Kinematics as an a posteriori consequence of the self-organization and self-assembly of muscle collectives.
Central representation of desired movement	Present	Absent
Translation mechanism	Essential to convert abstract plan to *language* of muscle.	Not necessary; all control is in common environmental units.

(continued)

Table 7.3   *(continued)*

Dimensions of contrast	Movement systems approach	Dynamical systems approach
Role of muscle	Subserviently carries out control commands specified centrally.	Determines movement form and phase interactions through dynamics.
Temporal organization of movement	Temporal features of kinematics metered out through an intrinsic time-keeping device.	Temporal features of kinematics arise as an emergent property through preservation of invariant phase angular relationships between effectors.
Relationship of perception	Independent serial processes, with perception preceding action (separate stages as revealed by Sternberg's addictive factors method).	Perception and action as tightly coupled processes, functionally and evolutionally inseparable. Perception in units of action and vice versa.
Perceptual model supported	Computational model (e.g., Marr, 1982)	Direct perception model of Gibson (1979)
Explanation of learning	Improved information-processing strategies (and, with development, increased processing capacities).	Increased attunement to essential invariants and control over context-conditioned variability.
Role of memory in learning	Fundamental to improve strategy formation and long-term skill acquisition.	Minimal role in learning. Many deny memory processes per se because of necessity to invoke representation.
Type of experimental paradigm advocated	Laboratory work on contrived movements historically favored, but naturalistic work ultimately desirable.	Ecological validity essential. Study of natural actions prescribed.
Units of measurement	Information measured mathematically with respect to stimulus/ task uncertainty and difficulty.	Essential information described in units scaled to the actor.

This table used with permission from Abernethy and Sparrow (1992), pp. 28-29.

- Alternatives to a cognitive representation for invariant features controlling actions (Kelso, 1986; Kelso et al., 1992; Kelso & Tuller, 1984)
- Scaling features, physical and perceptual, of actions (Haken, Kelso, & Bunz, 1985; Kugler et al., 1982; Thelen, Skala, & Kelso, 1987; Turvey & Carello, 1986)

A look at the data reported by Abernethy and Sparrow (1992) indicates that from 1981 through 1987, two to four papers per year were being published in *JMB* using dynamical systems as a model. Since schema theory was on a downward trend in a number of papers from about 1984 to 1987, the evidence suggests that a paradigm crisis might exist in motor control and learning. An interesting aside is Abernethy's (personal communication, August 1993) analysis of types of tasks used as dependent measures in research reported in *JMB* between 1969 and 1987. For the most part studies testing cognitive theories of motor control and learning have used contrived laboratory tasks such as linear positioning, while the use of natural actions is a basic premise of dynamical systems theories.[4] Abernethy reported that from 1970 to 1985 about 10 percent of the studies in *JMB* used natural actions, but the increase was to just under 50 percent in 1987. Contrived movements were used in 85 percent or above of the studies through 1985 but dropped to just over 50 percent in 1987. Abernethy and Sparrow (1992) provide an interesting account of what these changes in the basic philosophy and tasks underlying different theories may mean for motor control and learning, as well as potential ways toward a resolution of a paradigm crisis. Even though individual researchers argue for or against the various theories, the total field should applaud the fact that scientific research in motor control and learning has matured enough to experience a potential paradigm crisis.

Motor Control   The area of motor control cannot be separated from the previous discussions; however, specific areas can be identified around which research in motor control in the current period is organized. Motor control is just as its sounds: "How do we move?" (Rosenbaum, 1991, p. 3). Two important issues are, how is movement controlled and stability maintained? There are both physiological and psychological dimensions to this question. Rosenbaum makes clear the important questions to ask by the structuring of his book:

- **The degrees of freedom problem**: Movements are very complex involving many muscles and joints; how do we coordinate all those potential components (degrees of freedom)?
- **The serial order problem**: How is the sequence of our movement behaviors controlled?
- **The perceptual-motor integration problem**: How is information from the environment used to plan and adjust movements?
- **The skill acquisition problem**: How do we get better at skilled motor behavior?

Table 7.4   Categories of Frequent Interest in Motor Control

Gait patterns in locomotion
  Alexander, 1984; Lee, Lishman, & Thompson, 1982; Shapiro, Zernicke, Gregor, & Diestel, 1981; Thelen, 1983.

Stability and balance
  Lee & Lishman, 1975; Nashner, Woollacott, & Tuma, 1979; Stelmach, Populin, & Mueller, 1990; Stelmach, Phillips, DiFabio, & Teasdale, 1989; Teasdale, Stelmach, & Breunig, 1991; Woollacott, Debu, & Mowatt, 1987.

Reaching and grasping
  Carlton, 1981; Castiello, Stelmach, & Lieberman, 1993; Jeannerod, 1984; Kelso, Putnam, & Goodman, 1983; Larish & Stelmach, 1982; Marteniuk, MacKenzie, Jeannerod, Athenes, & Dugas, 1987; Meyer, Abrams, Kornblum, Wright, & Smith, 1988; Schmidt, Zelaznik, Hawkins, Frank, & Quinn, 1979; Stelmach, Teasdale, & Phillips, 1992; Stelmach, Teasdale, Phillips, & Worringham, 1989; von Hofsten, 1979, 1980; Wallace & Newell, 1983; Wing, Turton, & Fraser, 1986; Zelaznik, Hawkins, & Kisselburgh, 1983; Zelaznik, Schmidt, & Gielen, 1986.

Reaction time
  Anson, 1982; Carlton, Carlton, & Newell, 1987; Proctor, Reeve, Weeks, Dornier, & Van Zandt, 1991; Reeve, Proctor, Weeks, & Dornier, 1992; Rosenbaum, Kenny, & Derr, 1983; Zelaznik & Hahn, 1985.

Coordination and timing
  Abrams, Meyer, & Kornblum, 1990; Corcos, 1984; Fleury & Bard, 1985; Gentner, 1987; Haken, Kelso, & Bunz, 1985; Keele, Pokorny, Corcos, & Ivry, 1985; Kelso, Southard, & Goodman, 1979; Roy & Elliott, 1986; Stelmach & Nahom, 1992; Stelmach, Amrhein, & Goggin, 1988.

Of course motor control issues apply to all skilled movements, from speaking to painting to nailing to where most of the interest from exercise and sport science lies. Within the field, interest in aspects of motor control have included the categories shown in table 7.4.

Other Important Research Areas in the Current Period.   While it is not necessary in this chapter to cover all areas of research interests, six areas not specifically mentioned in the previous sections need attention because they have generated considerable interest among prominent scholars. The first is practice. Practice effects were of interest in the middle years but seemed to fall out of favor as a limited number of useful theories were available for explanation. Interest increased with the advent of schema theory (Schmidt, 1975) and its predictions about the value of variable practice. However, the biggest impetus to studying practice came from Shea's work (e.g., Shea & Morgan, 1979) interpreting Battig's (1979) ideas about contextual interference. Soon controversy developed as Magill and his student, Tim Lee, challenged Shea's interpretation (Lee & Magill, 1983). As described in the next section, that controversy continues.

The second area of sustained interest arose from memory drum theory (Henry & Rogers, 1960). This theory suggested that the complexity of the response was related to movement planning time before the response. Christina (for a review, see his 1992 paper) and his students have been particularly active in the current period in investigating the complexity effect.

The third area is the use of cognitive strategies to enhance motor performance. While this area may also be represented in the history of sport psychology, the view taken here is different. A major researcher in this area has been Robert N. Singer. In particular his work (with his students and colleagues) has focused on the role of cognitive processes in learning motor skills and identifying strategies that can be used to enhance the effectiveness of these processes, reviewed by Singer in 1992.

The fourth area is the work on special populations in motor control, especially problems associated with aging. Clearly, two leaders in this area have been George Stelmach and Waneen Spirduso. Stelmach's work has centered on two particular problems: postural and coordination control (e.g., Stelmach, Amrhein, & Goggin, 1988); and reaching and grasping movements in Parkinson's patients (Stelmach, Teasdale, Phillips, & Worringham, 1989). Spirduso's (e.g., 1975) work has focused on reaction time and movement time as it relates to fitness level in aging populations.

The fifth area is reaction time, especially focused by Kroll (1973) and his colleagues as they fractionated reaction time into pre-motor and motor time. This idea continues to be quite useful in looking at speed of processing for motor control.

The sixth area, individual differences, is listed as much for the lack of interest during the current period as for any other reason. Individual differences are important and have received a lot of attention during the two previous time periods; however, little work focusing on individual differences in motor learning and control has occurred in recent years.

Practice One of the benefits of Schmidt's (1975) schema theory was a renewed interest in some aspects of learning, particularly practice (for a review, see Chamberlin & Lee, 1993; and Lee & Genovese, 1988, as well as numerous responses to their paper in the same issue). His concept was that variable practice within movement class resulted in an increased ability to make a novel response. However, schema theory did not address the best way to understand and develop practice schedules (Magill, 1993). One way of considering practice schedules was introduced by Battig (1979) and called contextual interference. "Contextual interference refers to the finding that practice of multiple tasks in a random (high contextual interference) practice schedule results in greater retention and transfer than when tasks are practiced in a blocked practice schedule (low contextual interference) in which practice of one task is completed before practice on a different task is given" (Shea & Wright, 1991, p. 293).

The research on contextual interference has been developed around two basic theoretical explanations within a cognitive processing model. The first is that random practice is beneficial because it results in more elaborate and deep processing of the information (e.g., Shea & Morgan, 1979; Shea & Wright, 1991; Shea & Zimmy, 1983). The alternate explanation is called reconstruction and suggests that during random practice the motor program is forgotten and must be reconstructed each time from memory, resulting in better retention and transfer (c.g., Lee & Magill, 1983; Lee & Weeks, 1987; Magill & Hall, 1990).

Response Complexity   Henry and Rogers (1960) originally proposed and provided supporting data that simple reaction time was increased when the movement was more complex, because time is required to select (in memory) and "read out" the program specifications for movements that are not well learned; well-learned or automatic responses do not require this "programming time." The time period required is between when the signal for a response is detected and when the beginning of fast ballistic movements occur. Christina (1992) has recently described his 15-year research program and other work in this area investigating the complexity effect. Particular points of interest to note here involve

- the difficulties in establishing a research paradigm (e.g., Christina, Fischman, Vercruyssen, & Anson, 1982; Henry, 1980; Klapp, Wyatt, & Lingo, 1974; Marteniuk & MacKenzie, 1981);
- increasing complexity by adding more movement parts (e.g., Christina, Fischman, Lambert, & Moore, 1985; Christina & Rose, 1985; Fischman, 1984); and
- the accuracy hypothesis, which was that, rather than the number of movement parts being the determinant of simple reaction time, the accuracy demands of the movement were the critical feature. This work incorporates Fitts's (1954) index of movement difficulty into the complexity effect (e.g., Sidaway, 1991; Sidaway, Christina, & Shea, 1988).

Cognitive Processes Enhancement of Motor Performance   While much of the work in motor learning and control over the past hundred years has focused on cognitive factors in motor control and learning, the intent of the work reported here is to understand the cognitive processes involved, and discover ways to enhance the operation of these processes so that motor performance is improved. Singer and Gaines (1975) provided evidence that trial-and-error learning, as compared to prompted learning, reduced the acquisition rate across motor performance trials, but enhanced transfer. This finding was supported and extended to the positive effects of a more general concept—discovery learning—on learning, retention, and transfer (Singer & Pease, 1976). Reviews of this work for instruction (Singer, 1977) and strategy use (Singer & Gerson, 1981) have been published. From this and other work, Singer and his students developed and tested a five-step program—readying, imaging, focusing, executing, and evaluating—that assisted the learner in the acquisition, retention, and transfer of gross motor skills (Singer & Suwanthada, 1986; Singer, De-Francesco, & Randall, 1989; Singer, Flora, & Abourezk, 1989).

Special Populations In addition to Stelmach's early leadership and research in the development of motor behavior as a subdiscipline (described previously), he has provided a model of the blending of theory and practice, using a population with specific needs and problems: aging citizens. For example, his work has covered topics such as:

- coordination in aging populations (e.g., Stelmach & Nahom, 1992; Stelmach, Amrhein, & Goggin, 1988; Teasdale, Stelmach, Breunig, & Meeuwsen, 1991; Worringham, Stelmach, & Martin, 1987);
- posture and balance in aging populations (e.g., Stelmach, Populin, & Mueller, 1990; Stelmach, Phillips, DiFabio, & Teasdale, 1989; Teasdale, Stelmach, & Breunig, 1991); and
- movement problems in Parkinson's patients (e.g., Castiello, Stelmach, & Lieberman, 1993; Stelmach, Teasdale, & Phillips, 1992; Stelmach, Worringham, & Strand, 1986; Stelmach, Teasdale, Phillips, & Worringham, 1989; Teulings & Stelmach, 1991).

Spirduso has been particularly active in evaluating the influence of aging and fitness level on motor control. Her two papers in the *Journal of Gerontology* (Spirduso, 1975; Spirduso & Clifford, 1978) sparked considerable interest in an important gerontology question: Can increased levels of exercise delay the loss in motor function seen in aging populations? Subsequent reviews of this and other work (Spirduso, 1980; Spirduso & MacRae, 1990) have provided valuable insight into this issue, and research is ongoing (see Thomas, Landers, Salazar, & Etnier, 1994, for a review).

Using Fractionated Reaction Time in Motor Control Reaction time has been a popular dependent measure in studying the influence of many variables (e.g., fatigue, movement planning) on motor control. Weiss (1965) fractionated reaction time by using EMG to subdivide the reaction time interval into the time between the stimulus and the beginning of muscle contraction—pre-motor time—and the time from the beginning of muscle contraction to the beginning of the movement—motor time. Schmidt and Stull (1970), studying muscular tension and fractionated reaction time, and Kroll (1973), studying the influence of fatigue on fractionated reaction time, demonstrated the value of this technique to motor control. This work led to a number of subsequent studies where fractionated reaction time was used as an indicator of the speed with which the nervous system moved a stimulus through processing to the site of the movement; studies looked at joint displacement (Wyrick & Duncan, 1974); practice effects (Clarkson & Kroll, 1978); fatigue (Kamen, Kroll, Clarkson, & Zigon, 1981; Kroll, 1974; Morris, 1977; Stull & Kearney, 1978);

and age and activity level (Clarkson, 1978). The study of processing time
as indicated by pre-motor time continues to be an important indicator in
cognitive processing models.

Individual Differences in Motor Performance   Individual differences was
an important category of motor skills research during the previous two
time periods of this review. However, the interest in this area has not
been as great during the current period. Yet, regardless of whether motor
control and learning are viewed from a cognitive control perspective or
from a dynamical systems view, individuals do differ in the control and
learning of movements. The few studies that have focused on individual
differences were heavily influenced by Henry's (1959) and Jones's (1969)
research and writing from the previous period. Examples of work during
this period include Boswell and Spatz's (1975) study of reminiscence;
Thomas and Halliwell's (1976) evaluation of Jones's (1969) ideas about
superdiagonal form; and Keele and Hawkins's (1982) review of individual
differences and high level skill. However, individual differences can be
considered from other perspectives such as variation in relations among
motor control mechanisms (e.g., Keele, Pokorny, Corcos, & Ivry, 1985),
age differences (e.g., Thomas, 1980), or sex differences (e.g., Thomas &
French, 1985) in performance. From that perspective much more work
has been done in recent years.

Research Achievements

Achievements in scholarship can be considered from the perspective of
the researcher involved and the publications produced. In the following
sections, I attempt to identify significant scholars and works that affect
the nature of motor control and learning.

Major Researchers.   Of course, identifying the major researchers in
the motor control and learning area is somewhat controversial. The following list represents nothing more than this author's opinions about the
value, frequency, and nature of contributions to the scholarly literature.
This list is delimited to the current period and does not list several individuals who had influence in ways other than through their research program. Because of the nature and focus of the chapter, the individuals are
from the exercise and sport science (or kinesiology) area. However, a few
individuals from other areas who could not be omitted are mentioned at
the end of the list. The following list is in alphabetical order except for
the first listing. The reason Franklin Henry is listed first should be obvious
by now.

Franklin M. Henry—"Doc" Henry, who died on September 13, 1993,
has been called the "father of motor behavior in physical education"
(Schmidt, 1988), an appropriate designation. He spent his academic career
as professor at the University of California, Berkeley, where he retired in

1971. A check of *Citation Index* (ISI) shows that in 1992, over 20 years after his retirement, his work was still cited over 30 times. Many of his contributions—he had over 120 publications—have been described in previous sections of this chapter. No doubt his memory drum theory (Henry & Rogers, 1960) was his most important contribution to theory and research in motor control and learning, while his paper on the development of the academic discipline (Henry, 1964) had impact world wide. However, his greatest legacy might be his graduate students and their students who continue to have impact. Henry was a Fellow in the American Academy of Kinesiology and Physical Education, and was honored with the Hetherington Award of 1972. He was the first "Distinguished Scholar" of the North American Society for Psychology of Sport and Physical Activity, and received the "Honor Award" from the American College of Sports Medicine in 1975 (see Henry's chapter in Abernethy & Snyder, 1992, for greater detail about his work).

Robert W. Christina—Christina (Schmidt's first doctoral student), doctorate from the University of Maryland, is currently Dean of the School of Health and Human Performance at the University of North Carolina at Greensboro; however, most of his scholarly record was compiled during 17 years as a faculty member at Pennsylvania State University. In particular, his scholarly contributions on the mechanisms underlying anticipatory timing behavior (see Christina, 1976) and the issue of response complexity (see Christina, 1992, for a review), much of the latter based on Henry's memory drum theory, are significant. He has also been an advocate for applied research in motor learning (Christina, 1989). Christina produced a number of graduate students who are active scholars in motor control and learning. He is a former President of both the American Academy of Kinesiology and Physical Education and the North American Society for Psychology of Sport and Physical Activity, as well as a former C.H. McCloy Lecturer (Research Consortium, AAHPERD).

J.A. Scott Kelso—One of the second generation of doctoral students (his doctoral mentor was George Stelmach at the University of Wisconsin, who was one of Henry's students), he is professor and Director of the Center for Complex Systems at Florida Atlantic University, but he did much of his work at Haskin's Laboratory in New Haven, Connecticut. Kelso's main contribution has been in the development and promotion of dynamical systems (e.g., 152 references to his work in the 1992 *Citation Index*) as a view of motor control and learning (e.g., Kelso & Tuller, 1984; Kelso, Southard, & Goodman, 1979). If a paradigm crisis currently exists in motor control and learning, Kelso's promotion of dynamical systems is largely responsible (see Kelso's chapter in Abernethy & Snyder, 1992, or his new 1995 book, *Dynamic Patterns: The Self-Organization of Brain and Behavior*, MIT Press, for more details about his work).

Walter Kroll—Kroll, doctorate from Indiana University with Arthur Slater-Hammel, is professor at the University of Massachusetts, Amherst, and is a long-time contributor to the study of physical activity. Kroll is difficult to classify because he has contributed across a number of areas. Some of his work on motor control, particularly with regard to fractionated reaction time, was reviewed previously. However, he has made contributions in exercise physiology (Clarkson, Katch, Kroll, Lane, & Kamen, 1980) and biomechanics (Kroll, Bultman, Kilmer, & Boucher, 1990), as well as the crossing of biomechanics with motor control (Ives, Kroll, & Bultman, 1993). His book *Graduate Study and Research in Physical Education* (1982) was instrumental in shaping the discipline of physical activity. He has produced a number of PhD students who continue to contribute to the knowledge base. Kroll was active very early in the development of the North American Society for Psychology of Sport and Physical Activity, and is a former President of the Research Consortium (AAHPERD), a former Alliance Scholar (AAHPERD), and a Fellow in the American Academy of Kinesiology and Physical Education.

Richard A. Magill—Magill, another second-generation scholar (doctoral work with Robert N. Singer at Florida State University), is professor at Louisiana State University. His most notable scholarly contributions have been in the area of the influence of practice, particularly from a contextual interference perspective, on motor learning (see Magill & Hall, 1990, for a review). He also has one of the current best-selling undergraduate textbooks (Magill, 1993) in motor learning and control. He is a former President of the North American Society for Psychology of Sport and Physical Activity and is a Fellow in the American Academy of Kinesiology and Physical Education.

Karl M. Newell—Newell, doctorate from the University of Illinois, is professor and head of the Department of Exercise and Sport Science at Pennsylvania State University, a recent move; most of his scholarly work was done over a 20-year career as a faculty member and then department head at the University of Illinois. His work has spanned both the cognitive view of motor development, control and learning (e.g., Newell & Kennedy, 1978), and dynamical systems (Newell, 1985) and is often cited (e.g., 96 references to his work in the 1992 issue of *Citation Index*). He is a former coeditor of the *Journal of Motor Behavior* and a Fellow in the American Academy of Kinesiology and Physical Education. He had been an active advocate to use "kinesiology" as the name for the discipline (Newell, 1990).

Richard A. Schmidt—Schmidt, doctorate from the University of Illinois, is professor at the University of California, Los Angeles. Schmidt was also a faculty member at the Universities of Maryland, Michigan, and Southern California. Much has been written previously in this chapter about his contributions. He has maintained an active research program in motor learning and control for 25 years (for example, a check of the 1992 issue of *Citation Index* shows 161 references to his work). Schema theory (Schmidt, 1975) was the first theory developed from the new scholars in the current period, and stimulated a major research initiative in motor learning and control. His graduate textbook (Schmidt, 1988) has not only been the leading text in the discipline, but has shaped motor learning and control. His new undergraduate text (Schmidt, 1991) is also having significant impact. He has prepared a number of doctoral students, including Christina, who also appears on this list. Schmidt is a former President of the North American Society for Psychology of Sport and Physical Activity and has been named one of its five "Distinguished Scholars." He is a Fellow in the American Academy of Kinesiology and Physical Education. He was the founding and long-time editor of the *Journal of Motor Behavior.*

Robert N. Singer—Singer, doctorate from Ohio State University, is currently professor and chair at the University of Florida; however, much of the research reported is from his 20 years at Florida State University. As detailed in the previous section on cognitive processes and motor learning and control, his contributions have been in developing ways to enhance the learning, retention, and transfer of applied motor skills (see Abernethy & Snyder, 1992, for a summary). Singer published a number of books, but an early influential textbook, *Motor Learning and Human Performance* (1968), is in its third edition and was listed as one of the 20 outstanding educational books in 1968. Singer has also been active in the sport psychology area and has produced excellent doctoral students in both fields. He is a leader in the International Society for Sport Psychology, previously serving as President, and is a Fellow in the American Academy of Kinesiology and Physical Education.

Waneen W. Spirduso—Spirduso, doctorate from the University of Texas, is professor and former department chair at the University of Texas. As indicated previously, her major scholarly line that has influenced motor learning and control is the interaction of aging and level of physical fitness on motor control (see Spirduso & MacRae, 1990, for a summary). She has produced a number of doctoral students in motor control. Spirduso has been professionally active, previously serving as President of the North American Society for Psychology of Sport and Physical Activity. She is a Fellow and former President of the American Academy of Kinesiology and Physical Education. Spirduso is an exemplary model for women scholars in an area where few women have been active.

George E. Stelmach—Stelmach, doctorate from the University of California, Berkeley, with Franklin Henry, is professor at Arizona State University; however, much of his research and production of doctoral students was done during a 17-year period at the University of Wisconsin. As previously indicated, Stelmach was very influential in setting the directions of motor control and learning in the 1970s. He has been a prolific author (*Citation Index* shows over 70 references to his work in 1992) and is probably the most highly funded scholar in motor control and learning.

His work with aging and special populations is a model for good science that is externally supported. He has produced a number of doctoral students (Kelso being one of the most influential) and has trained many "post-docs." In addition to the symposia and conferences he organized in the United States, his international conferences and papers have had significant impact world wide, particularly in Europe. Stelmach is a Fellow in the American Academy of Kinesiology and Physical Education and has received many international awards and honors.

In addition to the previous list, a number of other scholars have had a significant influence and deserve mention (see table 7.5) and probably would be on other people's list (or a list completed a few years from now).

A number of scholars from outside of the field called exercise and sport science (or kinesiology) have focused much of their careers on motor control and learning, and have been a major influence on the directions of research in the current period. These individuals can easily be identified from the reference list of this paper but a few should at least be listed: J.A. Adams, E.A. Bilodeau, E.A. Fleishman, A.L. Irion, S.W. Keele, L.M. Nashner, C.E. Nobel, M.I. Posner, D.A. Rosenbaum, and M.T. Turvey.

Table 7.5   Other Motor Control and Learning Scholars From the U.S. and Other Countries

---

United States

   L.G. Carlton, University of Illinois, is a productive scholar in the visual control of movement.

   A.M. Gentile, Columbia University, has contributed much to motor learning, particularly insightful explanations of task constraints.

   T.G. Reeve, Auburn University, has been particularly influential in recent years with research into the role of control processes in motor skill.

   J.B. Shea, Florida State University (formerly at Pennsylvania State University and the University of Colorado), contributed greatly to understanding the role of practice on motor skill acquisition.

   C.A. Wrisberg, University of Tennessee, studies the role of knowledge of results in motor learning and control.

   H.N. Zelaznik, Purdue University, is a productive scholar in the motor control area, particularly in motor programming.

Other countries

   Australia—B. Abernethy, D.J. Glencross, and J. Summers.

   Canada—T.D. Lee and R.G. Marteniuk.

   England—H.T.A. Whiting, J. Annett, S. Henderson, D. Lee, P. Macleod, L. Shaffer, and A. Wing.

   Europe—P. Beck, R. Bootsma, H. Heuer, M. Jeannerod, J. Paillard, J. Requin, S. Swinner, and C. von Hofsten.

   New Zealand—D.G. Russell, L. Williams, and G. Anson.

Table 7.6 Influential Textbooks in Motor Control and Learning

Cratty, B.J. (1964, several subsequent editions). *Movement behavior and motor learning.* Philadelphia: Lea & Febiger. This was the first book in the field.

Lawther, J.D. (1968). *The learning of physical skills.* Englewood Cliffs, NJ: Prentice-Hall. Popular early book for undergraduates.

Magill, R.A. (1980; 4th ed., 1993). *Motor learning: Concepts and applications.* Dubuque, IA: Brown. Probably the most influential undergraduate textbook during the 1980s; along with Schmidt, 1991, it continues as a leader in the field.

Oxendine, J.B. (1968, several subsequent editions). *Psychology of motor learning.* New York: Appleton-Century-Crofts. An influential early textbook.

Rosenbaum, D.A. (1991). *Human motor control.* San Diego, CA: Academic Press. Written by a person outside the field, it is the most influential textbook in motor control.

Sage, G.H. (1971; 2nd ed., 1977). *Introduction to motor behavior: A neuropsychological approach.* Reading, MA: Addison-Wesley. The first text in motor behavior to take a biological approach.

Schmidt, R.A. (1982; 2nd ed., 1988). *Motor control and learning: A behavioral emphasis.* Champaign, IL: Human Kinetics. The most influential graduate textbook in the field.

Schmidt, R.A. (1991). *Motor learning & performance: From principles to practice.* Champaign, IL: Human Kinetics. With Magill, 1993, one of two leading undergraduate textbooks.

Singer, R.N. (1968, several subsequent editions). *Motor learning and human performance: An application to physical education skills.* New York: Macmillan. Probably the most influential of the early textbooks.

Major Textbooks from Motor Learning and Control. A number of books, particularly scholarly ones, have already been identified. However, textbooks also shape the field, and the need for textbooks in motor learning and control has existed since the late 1960s. Most of these have been undergraduate textbooks because one or more courses have been regularly included in what might be called the "core" of human physical activity (e.g., see Corbin & Eckert, 1990). Table 7.6 provides a list of influential textbooks in motor control and learning.

Part II. Motor Development

Contemporary developmental psychology is . . . the science of the strange behavior of children in strange situations with strange adults for the briefest possible periods of time.

Bronfenbrenner (1977, p. 513)

If you wish to understand the relation between the developing
person and some aspect of his or her environment, try to budge
the one, and see what happens to the other.

Bronfenbrenner (1977, p. 518)

We rarely take the time to keep our experimental hands off a
behavior long enough to make systematic descriptive observations
in naturalistic settings of the several dimensions and circumstances
of the behavior we wish to study. . . . much of our research represents a nearly blind run into a forest of behavior to study the
growth of a single tree. . . . Developmental psychologists should
accord description the esteem other disciplines do because much
has been learned at its hand: consider the theory of evolution, the
plate theory of continental drift, and our knowledge of the early
evolution of *Homo sapiens*. Paleontology, geology, and astronomy
seem to be alive and well without manipulating fossils, continents,
or heavenly bodies.

McCall (1977, pp. 336–337)

When reading the quandary (examples above) in which developmental
psychology finds itself (where motor development's historical roots are
located; however, the area of biology also contributed to the early roots
of motor development), as well as the discussion (e.g., Newell, 1990;
Thomas, 1987) about the organization, structure, and name of our discipline—the study of human physical activity—it is no surprise to see
the question: What is motor development (*Quest*, **41**, special feature, pp.
179–234)? While most motor development scholars are likely to agree
with the following definition of motor development—changes in motor
behavior over the lifespan and the process(es) which underlie these
changes (Clark & Whitall, 1989; Motor Development Academy, 1980, also
given at the beginning of this chapter)—the inclusion of motor development as a subset of motor behavior,[5] as is done here, is controversial
(Clark & Whitall, 1989; Roberton, 1989; Thomas & Thomas, 1989). In
fact a careful evaluation of the previous definition suggests that motor
behavior (and, some would argue, all of the discipline of the study of
human physical activity) should be a subset of motor development (e.g.,
Smoll, 1982).

The above discussion is not a trivial issue when writing a chapter like
this one, because it directly impacts what should be included. If Thomas
and Thomas's (1989) or Smoll's (1982) definition (the two are very different
but have the same impact in terms of what to include) were to be accepted,
then nearly anyone using a developmental perspective should be included. For example, while Stelmach and Spirduso (see previous section
on motor control and learning) would not classify themselves as motor
development researchers, their perspective on aging would suggest that

they be included here. The time point at which this becomes critical is the current period, 1970 to the present. For inclusion during that period, a rather arbitrary definition of motor development will be used—scholars who label themselves and their work "motor development."

Regardless of this issue, however, the editors of this book have assigned motor development to be reviewed as part of the history of motor behavior. While there is considerable common theoretical and empirical ground among some scholars of motor development and motor control and learning (see Clark & Whitall, 1989, and Thomas & Thomas, 1989, for examples), this commonality has generally happened since about 1970 with the advent of the discipline of physical activity and its subdisciplines. As you will note in the subsequent sections, before 1970 there was little in common between motor development and motor control and learning, except that both have their historical roots in psychology—motor development in developmental psychology, and motor control and learning in experimental psychology.

Early Foundations of Motor Development

The history of motor development will be divided into four time periods as previously used by Clark and Whitall (1989): precursor period (1787–1928), maturational period (1928–1946), normative/descriptive period (1946–1970), and process-oriented period (1970–present).

Precursor Period (1787–1928)

Clark and Whitall (1989) called this period the precursor because "much of the foundation was established for contemporary developmental psychology and motor development . . ." (p. 185), although Roberton (1989) uses the label "child development" rather than "developmental psychology." In fact, a quotation from Irion (1969) used previously, about definitive methodologies that are established early having a limiting effect, has a serious impact on motor development. It was during this period that the descriptive observation was begun that has been so prevalent and, some would argue, limiting (obviously not McCall, 1977).

The precursor period established what has come to be called the "baby biographies" (e.g., Tiedemann, 1787, as cited by Borstelmann, 1983; Pestalozzi, as cited by De Guimps, 1906; Shinn, 1900). These observers described, usually in their own or a friend's baby, the day-to-day changes in reflexes, movements, and feeding behaviors of young babies; these descriptions are examples of the description of the products of development rather than the developmental process (Clark & Whitall, 1989). However, observing motor development was not the main purpose of this work; rather, these observers were interested in insights the baby's motor behavior provided into intelligence and cognitive development.

Dixon and Lerner (1984) pointed out Darwin's (1859, 1871, 1877) important role in development with his theories about the evolution of humans and the role of the environment in shaping behavior. Galton (1876) suggested that twin studies were a good way to evaluate the role of heredity and environment in human behavior if twins could be provided with different opportunities and experiences. Because they would have a common hereditary influence (of course this is only true with identical twins), differences and commonalities in behavior could be determined.

Maturational Period (1928–1946)

This period saw more activity related to motor development, and provided the groundwork for much of the field, even into the present period. Clark and Whitall (1989) suggested that the publication of Gesell's (1928) book, *Infancy and Human Growth*, should appropriately mark the beginning of this period. Gesell, and also McGraw (1935, 1939), with her studies of Johnny and Jimmy, provided a view of the role of biology in children's maturation. Their careful and thorough descriptions of the behavioral sequences that occur in infants and young children are classic, and remain accurate and often cited in current motor development texts (e.g., Haywood, 1993; Payne & Isaacs, 1995). These early developmentalists used this evaluation of the products of motor behavior to infer the biological processes that cause maturation, an unusual research strategy given that behaviorism was beginning to flourish (Hull, 1943).

While Gesell and McGraw were doing similar work with twins during this period, they often did not agree. McGraw (1939) indicated that she undertook her study to analyze changes in performance with growth, and to evaluate the effects of training on these performances, "because of the current pediatric and psychiatric notion that infants should not be overstimulated and because of a general assumption following a co-twin study by Dr. Gesell (1929) that the immature nervous system of the infant is unresponsive to practice effects and that development during infancy is essentially a matter of neural maturation" (McGraw, 1939, p. 1).

Thus, while McGraw and Gesell are often considered together as maturationalists, their views were very different (Thelen, 1987). Both were influenced from biology (e.g., Coghill, 1929); however, McGraw (1969) used behavior to track the development of the human nervous system. She evaluated the influence of maturation on one twin (no practice) while the other twin received practice (McGraw, 1935). This approach allowed her to see the interaction between endowment and opportunity. Gesell (1954) was more interested in the general form and nature of organisms (morphology). He sought general and theoretical principles of growth inferred from the movements he observed in young children. Thelen (1987, p. 13) summarizes the difference: "This contrast, I believe, is a reflection of two very distinct traditions in biology in general—the more commonly accepted reductionist view, which posits that biological organization can be understood in terms of a central directing agency, and the perhaps less well known *systems view*, which holds that living organisms are characterized by the time-space dimension of their interrelated parts." Thus, Thelen suggests that the current paradigm crisis, discussed later in this section, between a cognitive and dynamical systems view of movement control in motor development (paralleling the one in motor control and learning) had the groundwork established by McGraw and Gesell's contrasting views during the maturational period.

A number of scales for movement assessment of infants were developed during this period, Bayley's of 1935 being the best known—modifications are still in use today. In this study she developed "The California Infant Scale of Motor Development" that included 76 items providing descriptive norms for movements from 0.2 months to 50.0 months of age.

Two classic field studies by Dennis (1935; Dennis & Dennis 1940) evaluated the role of maturation in motor development. Dennis (1935) and his wife raised two fraternal twin girls, not their own, in their home from 36 days after birth to 428 days of age. While the twins were provided a healthy diet and living circumstance, their opportunities to practice reaching, sitting, and standing were severely restricted. The restrictions delayed the onset of reaching and grasping, sitting alone, and standing with help when compared to norms for similar children. Dennis felt this study supported the premise that more than maturation drives development. The second study (Dennis & Dennis, 1940) compared Hopi Indian children restricted to a cradleboard for the first year of life, to Hopi Indian children who were not restricted. While Hopi Indian children were slightly slower in walking than other comparison groups (other Native American and White groups), the children restricted to the cradleboard were no slower in walking than those not restricted. However, the children who were on the cradleboards did have some opportunities to move about, particularly toward the end of the constrainment period. Dennis and Dennis concluded the restrictions were not drastic enough to influence walking.

The final two studies discussed during this period had significant impact on motor development during the next two periods: Wild's (1937) dissertation and subsequent paper (1938) on overhand throwing established a model for evaluating movement patterns that still persists. Her purpose was "to determine how children of successive age levels use their bodies when they execute a hard overhand throw" (Wild, 1938, p. 20). She used motion pictures with a distance scale and a clock in the view field to record the throwing movements. She determined throwing velocities and classified throwing movements into four stages that were generally age related, and these are still commonly used (e.g., Payne & Isaacs, 1995). Espenschade's (1940) work established a model that was used quite extensively during the next period (normative/descriptive) when she evaluated the relations among measures of motor performance, growth, and maturity. These approaches to measuring the development of fundamental movement forms and performance outcomes are a major theme for work in the next two periods, particularly Espenschade and Eckert at the University of California at Berkeley; Glassow, Rarick, Halverson, and Roberton at the University of Wisconsin; Keogh at UCLA; and Seefeldt, Haubenstricker, and Branta at Michigan State University.

This period was critical because subsequent work in the motor development field seemed "trapped" in a maturational view using descriptive methodology (Clark & Whitall, 1989) mainly developed during this period. While the work completed was carefully done and of considerable value, the limitation in approach and methodology probably reduced the impact of the motor development area. A second factor reducing the influence of motor development was the loss of interest in motor development by developmental psychology at the end of this period, an interest that has only returned in a limited way in the current period (Thelen, 1987).

Normative/Descriptive Period (1946–1970)

Because developmental psychologists had lost their interest in motor development at the end of the last period, what little research was conducted during this period was by physical educators with an interest in children (Clark & Whitall, 1989). Much of the work focused on growth, strength, and motor performance in children (e.g., Asmussen & Heeboll-Nielsen, 1955; Clarke & Harrison, 1962; Clarke, Irving, & Heath, 1961; Rarick & Oyster, 1964; Rarick & Smoll, 1967; Rarick & Thompson, 1956; Seils, 1951).

Another theme was to describe the performance outcomes of movement (e.g., Espenschade, Dable, & Schoendube, 1953; Dohrman, 1964; Grieve & Gear, 1966; Hellebrandt, Rarick, Glassow, & Carns, 1961; Hindley, Filliozat, Klackenberg, Nicolet-Meister, & Sand, 1966; Hutinger, 1959) as well as the movement itself (e.g., Hellebrandt, Rarick, Glassow, & Carns, 1961) following the tradition of Wild (1938). This work was summarized by Espenschade (1960) in terms of movement product—outcome measures like speed and distance. This period could also be described as the "unpublished period" when evaluating fundamental motor skills, as much of the motor development work failed to appear in scholarly journals (see table 7.7).

Motor development might well have died out as a field if not for the work of Espenschade, Glassow, and Rarick during this period (Motor Development Academy, 1980). Their research work, and the establishment

Table 7.7   Unpublished Thesis/Dissertation Work on Fundamental Motor Skills During the Normative/Descriptive Period

Walking and running
  Beck, 1966; Clouse, 1959; Dittmer, 1962; Fortney, 1964.
Jumping
  Felton, 1960; Halverson, 1958; Johnson, 1957; Wilson, 1945.
Throwing
  Deach, 1950; Ekern, 1969; M. Hanson, 1965; S. Hanson, 1961; Jones, 1951;
  Singer, 1961.
Catching
  Bruce, 1966; Deach, 1950; Victors, 1961; Warner, 1952; Williams, 1968.

of doctoral programs in motor development at the University of Wisconsin (Glassow and Rarick) and the University of California at Berkeley (Espenschade), kept the field alive within physical education. While the focus changed from its developmental psychology emphasis of understanding the influence of maturation to the physical education emphasis of how to improve children's motor behavior (Clark & Whitall, 1989), the area was maintained as viable research interest. This allowed motor development to be included when the discipline of the study of physical activity was emerging in the mid- to late 1960s (Thomas, 1990; Thomas & Thomas, 1989).

One other area of research interest emerged from educational psychology during this period: perceptual-motor development. This was the idea that motor skills could be used in some way to improve academic/intellectual performance in certain groups of children. The concept came from observations in clinical settings that children with intellectual problems, slow learners, and intellectually handicapped also tended to have motor problems. A number of individuals proposed that improving motor skills would improve academic/intellectual performance (e.g., Delacato, 1959, 1963—neurological organization; Kephart, 1960—Purdue perceptual-motor training program).

Physical educators wanted to support this notion because it provided a justification for children's physical education programs beyond the typical objectives of skill and fitness development (Thomas & Thomas, 1986). While a number of programs were developed within physical education for normal and special children, research began to show that, while the relationship between cognitive and motor skills was present under certain circumstances (e.g., Ismail, Kane, & Kirkendall, 1969; Thomas & Chissom, 1972), training programs using motor skills did not improve intellectual/academic function (e.g., Thomas, Chissom, Stewart, & Shelley, 1975; for a review, see Seefeldt, 1974). A meta-analysis of this literature by Kavale and Mattson (1983) summarized the findings from this research:

Training is *ineffective* for any type of measure, program, subject group, or age level. While this area was not very useful as a research direction, it did focus attention on cognitive factors in the development of children's movement skills, an area that fits nicely in the present period because of similar interest in motor control and learning.

Emergence and Development of the Discipline of Motor Development (1970–present)

The absolute beginnings of this time period vary somewhat. As is obvious from the previous section, the perceptual-motor training area carried over into the beginning of this period. The publication of four books at the beginning of this period makes a good demarcation point:

- Connolly (1970a), *Mechanisms of Motor Skill Development*, brought a cognitive focus to motor skill development similar to motor control and learning.
- Espenschade and Eckert (1967), *Motor Development*, provided the first complete coverage for the area although Rarick (1952, 1961) had previously published a text locally at the University of Wisconsin.
- Rarick (1973a), *Physical Activity: Human Growth and Development*, provided a detailed look at the influence of growth on motor performance and of physical activity on growth.
- Wickstrom (1970), *Fundamental Motor Patterns*, provided a description of most fundamental movement patterns from the research base of the second and third periods.

The different nature of these four books explains the dilemma at the beginning of this chapter—what is motor development and how broadly should it be conceived? Connolly's (1970a) book focused attention on the cognitive aspects of skill development and works nicely with the beginnings of cognitive theories for motor skill acquisition (e.g., Adams, 1971; Schmidt, 1975). Espenschade and Eckert (1967) take more of a maturational overview of what motor development had been in the previous two periods, tracing the development of skills, mostly outcomes of movements, across infancy, childhood, adolescence, and adulthood, and into aging populations (the first book to advocate a lifespan approach). Rarick's (1973a) edited book was unique in developing a very broad view of motor development including diverse topics: effect of exercise on growth and development of muscle tissue, bone and joint structures, strength and power, physical work capacity, and body composition; age changes in motor skills; sex and age differences in motor learning; growth and motor performance; psychosocial factors in children's motor performance; and competitive sports for children. Wickstrom (1970) provided a detailed description of each fundamental motor skill (e.g., jumping, throwing, striking) with stages and performance measures, much in the tradition of Wild's (1938) work. Reading any single one of these four books provides nearly independent views of what constitutes motor development.

Research Directions and Activities

Given this perspective, the current period will be divided into four themes:

- The influence of growth on motor performance
- The development of fundamental movements and related performance measures
- Cognitive factors influencing skill acquisition across age
- Dynamical systems as an explanation for motor development

The first two themes clearly relate to work in the previous two periods, maturational and normative/descriptive. The third and fourth themes are more closely tied to developments in motor control and learning during this period, although the first two can and have been related to dynamical systems.

The Influence of Growth on Motor Performance.   An interesting observation is that the book that set the stage for this work and the most current and useful book in this area are both by the same author and the most influential person in the area, Robert M. Malina. They are Malina (1975), *Growth and Development: The First Twenty Years*, and Malina and Bouchard (1991), *Growth, Maturation, and Physical Activity*. Malina did doctoral work with Rarick at the University of Wisconsin; his line of work, and much of this general area, follows the Rarick traditions established in the previous period (e.g., Rarick & Oyster, 1964; Rarick & Smoll, 1967). The research literature in this area can generally be organized around topics like those in table 7.8 (Malina & Bouchard, 1991).

Development of Fundamental Movements and Related Performance Measures.   As previously indicated, the model for studying fundamental movements and their performance outcomes was established by Wild (1938). Wickstrom (1970, 1st ed.) provided a summary of this previous work. Most of the published research during this period on fundamental movements has been from Roberton and Halverson at the University of Wisconsin, and Seefeldt and Haubenstricker at Michigan State University. While the approaches of these scholars were similar with regard to establishing the levels (much like the idea of stages) of fundamental movement that children passed through as they grew and acquired skill, their way of establishing those levels was different. Seefeldt and Haubenstricker (1982) continued with the analysis of the complete

Table 7.8   Research Topics for Growth and Motor Performance

Variations in performance associated with age and sex
  Beunen, Malina, Ostyn, Resnon, Simons, & Van Gerven, 1983; Bouchard, Mal-
  ina, Hollmann, & Leblanc, 1976, 1977; Branta, Haubenstricker, & Seefeldt,
  1984; Haubenstricker & Seefeldt, 1986; Krahenbuhl, Skinner, & Kohrt, 1985;
  Mirwald & Bailey, 1986; Morris, Williams, Atwater, & Wilmore, 1982; Nel-
  son, Thomas, & Nelson, 1991; Nelson, Thomas, Nelson, & Abraham, 1986;
  Rarick, 1973b; Seefeldt & Haubenstricker, 1982; Smoll & Schutz, 1990;
  Thomas & French, 1985; Thomas & Thomas, 1988; Thomas, Nelson, &
  Church, 1991.

Variation in performance associated with maturation
  Beunen & Malina, 1988; Beunen, Ostyn, Resnon, Simons, & Van Gerven,
  1976; Bouchard, Leblanc, Malina, & Hollmann, 1978; Bouchard, Malina, Hollmann, & Leblanc, 1976; Carron & Bailey, 1974; Malina, Beunen, Wellens, &
  Claessens, 1986.

Physical activity as a factor in growth and maturation
  Eaton & Enns, 1986; Eaton & Yu, 1989; Malina, 1979, 1983a, 1983b; Malina &
  Buschang, 1985; Malina & Roche, 1983; Malina, Little, Shoup, & Buschang,
  1987.

Racial/ethnic and social (health, family) factors influencing motor performance
  Erbaugh & Clifton, 1984; Lee, 1980; Malina, 1988; Malina & Buschang, 1985;
  Malina & Roche, 1983; Malina, Hamill, & Lemeshow, 1974; Milne, Seefeldt, &
  Reuschlein, 1976; Schnabl-Dickey, 1977; Thomas & French, 1985; Thomas &
  Thomas, 1988; Thomas, Nelson, & Church, 1991.

movement, much in the tradition of Wild (1938). Roberton (1982) developed a component model where the movement (e.g., overhand throwing)
was considered according to the actions of certain body components (e.g.,
arm action, trunk rotation, leg action). Both approaches were valuable
when considered in light of their intention: to aid teachers and coaches
in the analysis of children's movement patterns. However, the shortcomings of this approach are that the descriptions of the actions are qualitative
in nature rather than being quantified using typical biomechanical analysis techniques. Thus, while they are extremely useful for teachers/coaches,
they are not as useful as ways to evaluate the changes in fast ballistic
movements associated with the influences of biology and practice
(Thomas, Thomas, & Gallagher, 1993). Table 7.9 provides categories and
research studies looking at fundamental movements and their outcome
measures. In addition to the work published in refereed journals, the
extensive work on fundamental movements by Seefeldt and Haubenstricker at Michigan State University has been presented in chapter form
(Branta, Haubenstricker, & Seefeldt, 1984; Haubenstricker & Seefeldt,
1986) and a summary of the work of Roberton and Halverson appears in
Thomas (1984).

Table 7.9   Research Categories of Fundamental Skills

Throwing
Halverson, Robertson, & Langendorfer, 1982; Halverson, Roberton, Safrit, & Roberts, 1977; Nelson, Thomas, Nelson, & Abraham, 1986; Nelson, Thomas, & Nelson, 1991; Roberton, 1977, 1978; Roberton, Halverson, Langendorfer, & Williams, 1979; Thomas, Michael, & Gallagher, 1994.

Walking/running
Fortney, 1983; Roberton & Halverson, 1988.

Kicking
Elliot, Bloomfield, & Davies, 1980.

Jumping
Poe, 1976.

Catching
Isaacs, 1980; Morris, 1976; Payne, 1982, 1985; Payne & Koslow, 1981.

Hopping
Halverson & Williams, 1985.

Considerable work has been completed on various types of skilled behavior in children:

- Balance (e.g., DeOreo & Wade, 1971; Drowatzky & Zuccato, 1967; Shumway-Cook & Woollacott, 1985; Williams, Fisher, & Tritschler, 1983; Woollacott, Debu, & Mowatt, 1987)
- Reaction time in children (e.g., Eckert & Eichorn, 1977; Elliot, 1972; Thomas, Gallagher, & Purvis, 1981)
- Anticipation-timing in children (e.g., Haywood, 1977; Haywood, Greenwald, & Lewis, 1981; Payne, 1988; Thomas, Gallagher, & Purvis, 1981; Wade, 1980, 1982; Williams, 1985)
- Forward roll (e.g., Williams, 1980, 1987)
- Tapping (e.g., McCracken, 1983; Salmoni, 1983; Schellenkens, Kalverboer, & Scholten, 1984).

Cognitive Factors Influencing Skill Acquisition Across Age.   The previous two sections represent a continuation into the current period of both the maturation and descriptive aspects of motor development, and provide important studies that contribute to the knowledge base. However, the drastic changes that occurred during the current period are discussed in this section, on cognitive factors, and the next, on dynamical systems. These new approaches certainly represent paradigm shifts in motor development.

The area of cognitive factors influencing motor development research came from two directions. First, psychology in general was moving to a cognitive model to explain human behavior. This model caught on quickly in motor control and learning with the influence of Adams (1971) and Schmidt (1975). Certainly the researchers in motor learning and control also influenced research in motor development, but the single most influential event may have been Connolly's (1970a) edited book, *Mechanism of Motor Skill Development*. The publication of this book represented a suggested approach to studying skill development as well as a renewed interest of developmental psychologists in motor development (Clark & Whitall, 1989), although the bus to motor development was not very crowded with developmental psychologists then, nor is it now. The long-term research program in cognitive factors was by Thomas (for a review see Thomas, 1992, or Thomas, Thomas, & Gallagher, 1993) and his students at Louisiana State University (he is now at Arizona State University), using paradigms from developmental psychology to evaluate the influence of cognitive factors on children's motor skill acquisition.

The research on cognitive factors during this period tended to follow one of two models (see table 7.10): the application of approaches from developmental psychology for studying cognitive development to motor skills (for findings and potential directions, see Thomas, 1980); or the use of motor control and learning theories with children (for findings and potential directions, see Wade, 1976).

An interesting point to note is that several of the research papers cited in this subsection of motor development are from individuals previously identified in the motor control and learning section; indeed, several of these individuals were among the group listed as most influential (Kelso, Newell, and Schmidt). The focus of these individual's work with children was to understand the cognitive processes that change across childhood and adolescence as they influence changes in motor behavior (Clark & Whitall, 1989).

Dynamical Systems as an Explanation for Motor Development. Just as there may be a paradigm crisis in motor control and learning between cognitive processing and dynamical systems, this same potential crisis is present in the motor development area. An important contribution in bringing the dynamical systems view to motor development was the book edited by Kelso and Clark (1982), *The Development of Movement Control and Co-ordination*. In particular the chapter by Kugler, Kelso, and Turvey (1982) on the control and coordination of naturally developing systems was influential. Thelen, a developmental psychologist who had maintained a sustained interest in motor development (see Thelen, 1987), has been a major research leader with her work on coordination and control of movement in young infants (for reviews see Thelen, 1986, 1988; Thelen & Ulrich, 1991). Her work and that of several other significant motor development scholars, particularly Clark (for reviews, see Clark, 1995; Clark & Phillips, 1991), have suggested that a dynamical systems view of skill development has advantages over a more cognitive view for areas such as

Table 7.10   Research on Cognitive Factors in Children's Skill Acquisition

---

Use of cognitive theories from developmental psychology
Age influences motor performance (in the speed of cognitive processing):
Burton, 1987; Clark, 1982; Connolly, 1970b; Dunham & Reid, 1987; Gallagher & Thomas, 1980; Kerr, 1985; Kerr, Blanchard, & Miller, 1980; Newell & Kennedy, 1978; Nicholson, 1982; Salmoni & Pascoe, 1979; Thomas, Gallagher & Purvis, 1981; Thomas, Mitchell, & Solmon, 1979; reviews of this work offer varying hypotheses to explain the findings (e.g., Chi & Gallagher, 1982; Dempster, 1988; Kail, 1988).

Perceptual development influences motor performance:
Thomas & Thomas, 1987; Williams, 1983; Williams, Temple, & Bateman, 1979.

Working memory processes (rehearsal, labeling, organization, intention) develop across childhood and adolescence and influence motor performance:
Barclay & Newell, 1980; Corlett & Dickinson, 1983; Dayan & Thomas, 1994; Gallagher & Thomas, 1984, 1986; Reid, 1980; Sudgen, 1978, 1980; Thomas, Thomas, Lee, Testerman, & Ashy, 1983; Weiss & Klint, 1987; Winther & Thomas, 1981; summaries of this approach are provided by Newell and Barclay (1982); Thomas, (1980, 1984); and Thomas, Thomas, and Gallagher (1993).

Use of a neo-Piagetain model of development explains changes in motor performance across age:
Gerson & Thomas, 1977, 1978; Thomas & Bender, 1977; Todor, 1979.

Application of motor control and learning theories to children
The applications have come mostly from Adams's (1971) closed-loop theory and Schmidt's (1975) schema theory, and evaluating how children may respond differently according to age level (for a review, see Shapiro & Schmidt, 1982). Typical topics include

- the differential influence on children of feedback, particularly knowledge of results:
Gallagher & Thomas, 1980; Hay, 1979; Newell & Carlton, 1980; Newell & Kennedy, 1978; Thomas, Mitchell, & Solmon, 1979.
- development of schema to control movements:
Carson & Wiegand, 1979; Gerson & Thomas, 1977; Kelso & Norman, 1978; Moxley, 1979; Wrisberg & Mead, 1981.

- locomotion and gait (e.g., Berger, Quintern, & Dietz, 1984; Bril & Breniere, 1992; Clark & Phillips, 1993; Clark, Whitall, & Phillips, 1988; Forrsberg, 1985; Thelen, 1986; Thelen & Fisher, 1982; Thelen, Skala, & Kelso, 1987; Whitall, 1991);
- jumping (e.g., Clark, Phillips, & Petersen, 1989); and
- coordination and timing (e.g., Burton, 1986; Thelen, Ulrich, & Niles, 1987; Thelen, Kelso, & Fogel, 1987; Whitall, 1989).

Recent books by Woollacott and Shumway-Cook (1989) and Thelen and Smith (1994), monographs by Thelen and Ulrich (1991) and Clark (1994), and a chapter by Whitall and Clark (1991) provide excellent overviews of the developmental work done within dynamical systems.

Research Achievements

Achievements in scholarship can be considered from the perspective of the researcher involved and the publications produced. In the following sections, I attempt to identify significant scholars and work that impact the nature of motor development.

Scholars from the Current Period of Motor Development.   The following list represents individuals making exceptional contributions to the scholarly literature during the current period. The list is in alphabetical order except for Rarick, who has made tremendous contributions over the previous and current period, as well as training two of the other individuals on the list.

G. Lawrence Rarick—Rarick, doctorate from the State University of Iowa, was professor emeritus at the University of California at Berkeley and a long-time professor at the University of Wisconsin. His scholarly and active motor development career began just at the end of the descriptive/maturational period (for a review, see Rarick, 1992). He maintained an active research program in the 1950s, 1960s, and 1970s, in areas such as the influence of maturation, age, and sex on motor performance (e.g., Rarick & Oyster, 1964; Rarick & Smoll, 1967; Rarick & Thompson, 1956) as well as motor development in handicapped children (e.g., Rarick, Rapaport, & Seefeldt, 1966; Rarick, Wainer, Thissen, & Seefeldt, 1975). As previously indicated, his edited book, *Physical Activity: Human Growth and Development* (1973a), was one of the most significant contributions to the field. He maintained active doctoral programs at both Madison and Berkeley and trained two other members of this list, Malina and Seefeldt. Rarick is a former Alliance Scholar (AAHPERD), Distinguished Scholar of the North American Society for Psychology of Sport and Physical Activity, and a Fellow in the American Academy of Kinesiology and Physical Education.

Jane E. Clark—Clark, doctorate from the University of Wisconsin (with Lolas Halverson), is professor at the University of Maryland. While her preparation was more in the maturation/descriptive mode with some cognitive processing, she has made the transition to a dynamical systems perspective. The book she edited with Kelso, *The Development of Movement Control and Co-ordination* (Kelso & Clark, 1982) really served to move a significant number of motor development scholars into the dynamical systems camp. Her work over the past ten years in this area has been excellent (for a summary see Clark, 1995; Clark & Phillips, 1991) and is often cited (28 citations as indicated by *Citation Index* in 1992). Clark is actively producing excellent PhD students from Maryland. She is a former chair of the Motor Development Academy (AAHPERD), former President of the Research Consortium (AAHPERD) as well as the North American Society for Psychology of Sport and Physical Activity, and is a Fellow in the American Academy of Kinesiology and Physical Education.

Robert M. Malina—Malina, doctorates from both the University of Wisconsin (with Rarick) and the University of Pennsylvania (in anthropology with Wilton Krogman), was a long-time professor at the University of Texas at Austin. As indicated previously, he is the premier scholar in the field of growth and development over the past 25 years. He has produced many publications that are often cited (68 citations as indicated by *Citation Index* in 1992). In addition to refereed publications in excellent journals both within and external to the field, he has produced two books that have profoundly influenced growth and development: Malina (1975), *Growth and Development: The First Twenty Years*, and Malina and Bouchard (1991), *Growth, Maturation, and Physical Activity*. He maintained an active doctoral program at Texas. Malina is a former editor of *Human Biology*, a former Alliance Scholar (AAHPERD), and a Fellow and former President of the American Academy of Kinesiology and Physical Education.

Mary Ann Roberton—Roberton, doctorate from the University of Wisconsin (with Lolas Halverson), is now professor and Director of the School of HPERD at Bowling Green State University. However, her major contributions were made as a long-time faculty member at the University of Wisconsin, where she worked closely with Lolas Halverson (recently deceased, who could also appear on this list as she made significant contribution from the 1950s onward). Her rather unique approach to the understanding of fundamental movements involved looking at the development of the components of the movements (arm action, leg action) rather than the total movement. She also developed a series of techniques for validation of movement sequences (for reviews of this work, see Roberton, 1982, 1989; Roberton & Halverson, 1984). She is a former Chair of the Motor Development Academy (AAHPERD) and former President of the North American Society for Psychology of Sport and Physical Activity.

Vern Seefeldt—Seefeldt, doctorate from the University of Wisconsin (with Rarick), is professor emeritus at Michigan State University. Much of the work by Seefeldt and his long-time colleagues, Haubenstricker and Branta, on longitudinal analysis of fundamental motor skills has been presented as conference papers. However, an excellent summary of this work is in *Exercise and Sport Sciences Reviews* (1984). In addition to this work Seefeldt has been a long-time leader in the development of youth sport programs, and established the Institute for the Study of Youth Sport (with funding from the Michigan legislature) as a research and training program at Michigan State. An example from that work is his editing the *Handbook for Youth Sports Coaches* (1987). He is a Fellow in the American Academy of Kinesiology and Physical Education, former chair of the

Motor Development Academy (AAHPERD), and an active member of the Youth Sport Coalition (AAHPERD).

Jerry R. Thomas—Thomas, doctorate from the University of Alabama, is professor at Arizona State University. However, he was a long-time faculty member at Louisiana State University, where many of his scholarly contributions were made. He has maintained an active research program (31 citations to his work in *Citation Index*, 1992) in cognitive factors in children's skill acquisition (for a review, see Thomas, 1992) as well as the development of gender differences in children's motor performance (for a summary see Thomas & Marzke, 1992). His more recent focus has been on the development of expertise in children's sport performance (for a review, see Abernethy, Thomas, & Thomas, 1993). His book with J.K. Nelson, *Research Methods in Physical Activity* 3rd ed., 1996, is the leading one in the field. He maintained an active doctoral program at LSU and continues a program at ASU. He is a former Alliance Scholar (AAHPERD), President of the Research Consortium (AAHPERD), and Editor-in-Chief of *Research Quarterly for Exercise and Sport*. He was President of the North American Society for Psychology of Sport and Physical Activity, and is a Fellow and former president of the American Academy of Kinesiology and Physical Education.

Of course the above list is somewhat arbitrary, and significant individuals have been omitted—Halverson has already been identified as one. Others who would appear on other people's list or on future lists include Kathleen Haywood at the University of Missouri at St. Louis, Jack Keogh (retired) at UCLA, Frank Smoll at the University of Washington, Beverly Ulrich and David Gallahue at Indiana University, Michael Wade at the University of Minnesota, Harriet Williams at the University of South Carolina, and Marjorie Woollacott at the University of Oregon. If the list were not restricted to our field, certainly Kevin Connolly from University of Sheffield (England) and Esther Thelen from Indiana University would appear on it; if not restricted to the United States, Donald Bailey from the University of Saskatchewan in Canada and David Sudgen from the University of Leeds (England) would be included. In addition several individuals from motor learning and control who appear on that list have contributed to motor development, including Scott Kelso, Karl Newell, and Richard Schmidt.

Major Textbooks Influencing Motor Development.   In addition to the list of significant scholarly books already mentioned in this section that have impacted motor development during this period, textbooks listed in table 7.11 have also been valuable in shaping the field.

Part III. Looking Across Motor Behavior

In this final part, I provide a brief look at research in motor behavior that is difficult to assign to either motor control and learning or motor

Table 7.11   Influential Textbooks in Motor Development

Corbin, C.B. (Ed.) (1980). *A Textbook of Motor Development* (2nd ed.). Dubuque, IA: Brown.

Eckert, H.M. (1987). *Motor Development* (3rd ed.). Indianapolis: Benchmark.

Gallahue, D.L. (1989). *Understanding Motor Development* (2nd ed.). Indianapolis: Benchmark.

Haywood, K.M. (1993). *Life Span Motor Development* (2nd ed.). Champaign, IL: Human Kinetics.

Keogh, J., & Sugden, D. (1985). *Movement Skill Development*. New York: Macmillan.

Payne, V.G., & Isaacs, L.D. (1995). *Human Motor Development: A Lifespan Approach* (3rd ed.). Mountain View, CA: Mayfield.

Ridenour, M.V. (Ed.) (1978). *Motor Development: Issues and Applications*. Princeton, NJ: Princeton Books.

Thomas, J.R. (Ed.) (1984). *Motor Development During Childhood and Adolescence*. Minneapolis: Burgess.

Williams, H.G. (1983). *Perceptual and Motor Development*. Englewood Cliffs, NJ: Prentice Hall.

---

development. In addition I have provided an overview of doctoral programs, organizations, and journals that have been important in motor behavior.

Research Crossing Motor Control, Learning and Development—Observational Learning and Expertise

Obviously from looking at the reviews of the present period (1970 onward), several topics have been of interest in motor control and learning and motor development (e.g., schema theory, cognitive processes in motor performance). However, two general themes have generated substantial research, yet are hard to classify according to motor control and learning or development: observational learning (or modeling) and motor expertise.

Observational Learning

Adams (1987), in his review of the history of motor skills, adds observational learning as a new category during the present period. Where observation learning is best included—motor behavior or sport psychology—is debatable. While the acquisition of skills is often the focus of observational learning, much of the work has been done either in a development model (e.g., Martens, Burwitz, & Zuckerman, 1976; Weiss, 1983; Weiss, Ebback, & Rose, 1992) or in studies using social learning theory (Bandura, 1977) which has typically been used as a theory for research in social psychology of sport (e.g., McCullagh, 1986; Weiss, Ebback, & Rose, 1992). In fact observational learning work has been done by sport psychologists (e.g., Gould & Roberts, 1981; Landers & Landers, 1973; McCullagh, 1986; Weiss, 1983; Weiss, Ebback, & Rose, 1992) and researchers in motor control and learning (e.g., Pollock & Lee, 1992; Weeks, 1992) making it difficult to clearly assign it to a subdiscipline. A recent excellent review of observational learning has been completed by McCullagh (1993).

Motor Expertise

The development of motor expertise is the second topic that has clearly overlapped motor control, development, and learning as well as other subdisciplines (e.g., exercise physiology, sport psychology, biomechanics, and pedagogy) within the study of human physical activity. This work most often uses an expert-novice model[6] and has fallen into two general categories:

- Perceptual and anticipation factors in expert performance (e.g., Abernethy, 1988; 1990a, 1990b; Abernethy & Russell, 1987; Allard & Starkes, 1980; Starkes, 1987; Starkes & Allard, 1983)
- Differences between experts and novices in cognitive factors (e.g., knowledge, decision-making) in sport performance (e.g., Abernethy, 1992; Allard, Graham, & Paarsalu, 1980; French & Thomas, 1987; McPherson & Thomas, 1989; Starkes, Deakin, Lindley, & Crisp, 1987; Starkes, Caicco, Boutilier, & Sevsek, 1990).

A recent overview of expertise across many areas of motor skill (e.g., sport and youth sport, video game playing, microsurgery and surgical skill, speech production) appeared in an edited volume by Starkes and Allard (1993), *Cognitive Issues in Motor Expertise*.

Influence of Doctoral Programs

Doctoral programs have had major influences on the direction of motor behavior. Not only have they prepared the doctoral faculty and scholars, but they have provided a significant source of the research productivity in the United States. Doctoral programs and the most important mentors in these programs are described for motor control and learning and for motor development. These programs are limited to the field of the study of human physical activity, although certainly psychology and other academic fields have had significant impact.

Motor Learning and Control

Some programs have varied over time in their impact, while others have maintained their position. Three programs were important in the middle period (1940–1970) and carried over into the current period (1970 onward):

• University of California at Berkeley—Probably enough has been said about this program and the impact of Franklin Henry. He trained a number of the first-generation scholars in motor control and learning. However, this program has not been as active in motor control and learning since Henry's retirement in 1971.

• University of Illinois—This program under Alfred Hubbard's direction produced a number of the first-generation scholars. Productive work continued through the current period under the direction of Karl Newell. However, it is currently unclear what will happen at the U of I with Newell's departure to Pennsylvania State University.

• Indiana University—This was one of the early active doctoral programs under the direction of Arthur Slater-Hammel. However, this program has not been as influential in recent years.

The following programs have become active doctoral programs in the current period:

• UCLA—Richard Schmidt is the important mentor in this program and has been for a significant time period. However, the kinesiology area has changed at UCLA and Schmidt is now in psychology. The impact of this change on future doctoral education is unclear.

• Florida State University—Robert Singer was the active mentor in this productive program through much of this period. However, whether FSU will continue its activity in motor control and learning is unclear with Singer's departure to the University of Florida.

• Louisiana State University—This program has become and continues as an active producer of doctorates over the past 15 years with the advent of Richard Magill as a senior scholar and mentor.

• Pennsylvania State University—This program was quite important in doctoral education under the direction of Robert Christina; John Shea joined the program in the early 1980s. Both are now gone, but Karl Newell has arrived and is likely to continue the traditional contributions of PSU in this area.

• University of Texas at Austin—The work of Waneen Spirduso has provided the impetus for the development of the program at UT and her leadership there continues.

• University of Wisconsin—The program was a major player throughout this period under the mentorship of George Stelmach. However, Stelmach is now at Arizona State University and UW has not appointed a senior scholar to replace him; thus, the continued influence of this program is unclear.

Motor Development

Just as in motor control and learning, two programs in motor development were influential early (from about 1950 into the current period) while most of the programs in the study of human physical activity became active during the current period. Two early programs were the following:

• University of California at Berkeley—Anna Espenschade and Helen Eckert were influential in this program in the 1950s and 1960s. With Rarick's arrival from Wisconsin, the influence continued into the 1970s, but with his retirement, Berkeley no longer plays a major role in doctoral education in motor development.

• University of Wisconsin—Ruth Glassow and Larry Rarick were early mentors although Rarick later moved to Berkeley. Halverson became active in the 1960s and worked into the 1980s. Roberton also became an active mentor in the late 1970s and 1980s. However, Halverson retired (and is recently deceased) and Roberton moved to Bowling Green State University. Wisconsin has not replaced either with senior scholars, although they have hired younger scholars. Thus, the future of doctoral training in motor development at UW is unclear.

Programs that have developed in the current period include the following:

• Indiana University—Under the long-time direction of David Gallahue, and with the recent development of Beverly Ulrich (along with Esther Thelen in psychology), the program at IU seems to be "up and coming" in motor development.

• Louisiana State University—Jerry Thomas was instrumental in developing the program at LSU and it was a productive doctoral program in the late 1970s and 1980s. However, he has now moved to Arizona State University and LSU has chosen not to continue with a specialization in motor development.

• University of Maryland—This program was not active in motor development until the mid- to late 1980s with the advent of Jane Clark. However, UM now seems to be an "up and coming" program in motor development.

• Michigan State University—Vern Seefeldt (with his colleagues John Haubenstricker and Crystal Branta) has maintained an active doctoral program since the mid-1970s.

• University of Texas at Austin—The program in motor development at UT is based on the mentorship of Robert Malina. However, most of his students have been prepared through physical anthropology. He has now moved to Michigan State University; thus, the future of the UT at Austin program is uncertain.

Organizations and Journals in Motor Control, Learning, and Development

Several organizations and journals have influenced the development of both motor control and learning and motor development. These generally cross the two areas and in some instances also cross sport and exercise psychology (e.g., North American Society for Psychology of Sport and Physical Activity).

Organizations

Two organizations from exercise and sport science have been important for motor behavior—North American Society for Psychology of Sport and Physical Activity and the Motor Development Academy (AAHPERD). Of course motor behavior scholars have participated in a number of organizations outside the field (e.g., American Psychological Association, Society for Child Development).

North American Society for Psychology of Sport and Physical Activity. The major scholarly organization for motor control and learning and motor development is the North American Society for Psychology of Sport and Physical Activity. This society has three subsections: motor development, motor learning and control, and sport psychology. It has been a major site for the presentation of research, theoretical papers, and invited speakers from allied fields. In addition, graduate students have been actively involved in this group; thus, recruitment of doctoral students has frequently occurred at the annual meeting. Because the history of NASPSPA overlaps sport psychology, the details of the development of NASPSPA are presented in the chapter by D. Gill (this volume), "History of Sport and Exercise Psychology." Table 7.12 provides a list of the former Presidents, Distinguished Scholars, and Early Career Scholars from NASPSPA who were from motor behavior.

Motor Development Academy (AAHPERD). The Motor Development Academy is one of the largest academies of the National Association for Sport and Physical Education, an association in the American Alliance for Health, Physical Education, Recreation and Dance. This group was first provided the opportunity to participate in the AAHPERD national

Table 7.12   List of NASPSPA Presidents, Distinguished Scholars, and Early Career Scholars From Motor Behavior*

Presidents
   A.T. Slater-Hammel (1967-69)
   B.J. Cratty (1969-71)
   Waneen W. Spirduso (1976-77)
   Richard Schmidt (1977-78)
   Harriet Williams (1978-79)
   Robert Christina (1979-80)
   Ronald Marteniuk (1980-81)
   Richard Magill (1984-85)
   Mary Ann Roberton (1986-87)
   Michael Wade (1987-88)
   Craig Wrisberg (1988-89)
   Jerry Thomas (1990-91)
   Gil Reeve (1991-92)
   Jane Clark (1992-93)
   Karl Newell (1994-95)

Distinguised Scholars
   Franklin Henry (1981)
   G. Lawrence Rarick (1981)
   Jack Adams (1989)
   Richard Schmidt (1992)

Early Career Scholars
   Les Carlton (1986)
   Peter Hancock (1987)
   Beverly Ulrich (1992)
   Stephan Swinnen (1993)

*This does not include individuals from sport psychology.

program in 1980 in Detroit. The first elected Chair of the Motor Development Academy was Lolas Halverson in 1979. In addition to organizing a program each year at AAHPERD, the MDA publishes a newsletter and promotes the growth of motor development within the field of physical education. Former chairs of the MDA are listed in table 7.13.

Journals

Two scholarly journals, *Journal of Motor Behavior* and *Research Quarterly for Exercise and Sport*, have been most influential in the field of motor behavior, committed to publishing quality research studies within learning, control, and development. Their editorial boards have strong scholars and their annual list of reviewers includes the best scholars in motor behavior. In addition scholars from motor behavior have published in

Table 7.13   Former Chairs of the Motor Development Academy

Lolas Halverson (1979-80)
John L. Haubenstricker (1980-81)
G. Lawrence Rarick (1981-82)
Mary Ann Roberton (1982-83)
Charles Corbin (1983-84)
Vern Seefeldt (1984-85)
Jane Clark (1985-86)
Crystal Branta (1986-87)
Steve Langendorfer (1987-88)
David Gallahue (1988-89)
Kathleen Williams (1989-90)
Harriet Williams (1990-91)
Beverly Ulrich (1991-92)
Gregory Payne (1992-93)
Jere Gallagher (1993-94)

research journals within parent disciplines. For example, papers from motor behavior scholars can regularly be found in *Child Development, Developmental Psychology, Human Performance, Journal of Experimental Child Psychology, Journal of Experimental Psychology: Human Learning and Memory, Journal of Experimental Psychology: Human Perception and Performance, Psychological Bulletin*, and *Psychological Review*, to name a few.

Journal of Motor Behavior.   Richard Schmidt (most of this information is based on a personal communication from Schmidt, July 1993) was the founding editor of *JMB*. His father, Allen Schmidt, was a printer and publisher. In a discussion with his father, Dick indicated his perceived need for a new journal in this area. He and his father had a meeting with Clifford Morgan, founding editor of *Psychonomic Science*, and received a number of tips about procedures to follow. The initial price was $8 for a subscription. To quote Schmidt (personal communication, July 1993), "We wanted it to be cheap to subscribe to, quick in reviewing, and especially with no page charges. . . . We were determined not to make any money on it, which really p____ off my dad. But I was a real anti-capitalist in those days, so I won that battle. We never took any money out of it and it was a real low-budget operation." They began *JMB* with the first volume in 1969. Schmidt solicited an outstanding editorial board helped by his connection with Jack Adams at the University of Illinois and Adams's agreement to serve on the board. Schmidt served as editor for 12 years and provided outstanding leadership and direction to a journal that was shaping the field of motor behavior.

Schmidt sold *JMB* to Heldref Publications (Washington, DC) and beginning with Volume 13 in 1981, J.A.S. Kelso, R.G. Marteniuk, and K.M.

Newell became tri-editors. To quote Kelso, Marteniuk, and Newell (1981, inside front cover) about Schmidt:

> That a young freshly graduated doctoral student could inspire and sustain the creation of a new interdisciplinary journal is a remarkable achievement. This is particularly so in light of a lull in research activity in motor behavior in the late 1960s. Indeed, the development of the Journal through its initial years has to be both a factor in, and a reflection of, a general revival of interest in motor skills in the 1970s. The field of motor behavior owes much to the foresight and determination of Schmidt in promoting the Journal.

Since 1981, *JMB* has had tri-editors: Kelso, Marteniuk, and Newell until 1986, when Alan Wing replaced Newell. In 1988, Wynne Lee replaced Kelso, and in 1990 Howard Zelaznik replaced Marteniuk. The current tri-editors are Wynne Lee, Howard Zelaznik, and Melvyn Goodle.

Research Quarterly for Exercise and Sport.   *RQES*, a publication of the American Alliance for Health, Physical Education, Recreation and Dance, was established in 1930 as *Research Quarterly*, a name it retained until 1980, when the name and format were changed such that sections were established within *RQES* to reflect its cross-disciplinary nature. Two of these sections relate directly to motor behavior: Growth and Motor Development, and Motor Control and Learning. *RQES* has published papers in growth and motor development, and motor control and learning, for over 60 years including the "memory drum" paper by Henry and Rogers (1960) that may well be the most highly cited paper ever from *RQES*. While not as influential as *JMB* in establishing the directions of research in motor behavior, *RQES* has served two particularly important roles—it provided an outlet more likely to reach allied areas because of its cross-disciplinary nature, and it reached a more applied audience than *JMB*.

   RQ had Elmer Mitchell as its first editor and he continued from 1930 until 1943. From 1943 to 1965, *RQ* had a managing editor from AAHPER and a board of editors. Beginning in 1965 *RQ* went back to a scholarly editor, selecting Carolyn Bookwalter, who served until 1969. John Mitchem was editor from 1969 to 1974, Gladys Scott from 1974 to 1977, Margaret Safrit from 1977 to 1980, Harold Falls from 1980 to 1983, Jerry Thomas from 1983 to 1989 (the first editor from the motor behavior area), James Morrow from 1989 to 1993, Maureen Weiss from 1993 to 1996, and the current editor, Richard Magill (the second from motor behavior). Many of the individuals listed in this chapter have served as section editors in either motor control and learning or growth and motor development.

Relation of Motor Behavior
to the Study of Human Physical Activity

The area of motor behavior has been active since the mid-1960s as a subdiscipline of the study of human physical activity. The activity in motor behavior has been of several types: developing an area of inquiry (this paper), as well as the content for undergraduate and graduate courses within the study of human physical activity (see textbooks listed in motor control and learning and motor development); and maintaining relations with allied areas within the discipline (e.g., biomechanics, physical education pedagogy) and in allied disciplines (e.g., psychology, neuroscience).

That the previous statements are true is evidenced by the standard inclusion of courses in motor behavior as part of the undergraduate major of kinesiology (or exercise and sport science) and opportunities to specialize in motor behavior at the graduate level. Faculties in allied disciplines recognize the value of motor behavior faculty with joint appointments to their discipline, and submit requests for joint appointments to physical activity. Work from motor behavior is published not only in physical activity scholarly journals but also in journals from parent disciplines. Granting agencies regularly fund the research programs of scholars in motor behavior.

The sub-areas of motor behavior—motor control, motor learning, and motor development—appear increasingly to overlap in research focus. Both the cognitive and dynamical-systems views of motor skill performance and acquisition are influencing this common interest. Whether the view of skill control and learning is developmental or within a single age group, the questions, theories, and methodologies share common features. In addition, many of the procedures using the kinematic and neurobiological measurements of movement process and outcome bring motor behavior and biomechanics to common approaches and cross-disciplinary questions. I consider this commonality a good feature and one that will lead to better theories and research in the future. After all, humans perform complex movements within the context of their environment. Motor behavior scholars must increasingly adopt ecologically valid paradigms to study these features of motor performance.

Thus, motor behavior seems to have a solid and valuable place within the discipline of the study of human physical activity, as well as in the larger academic community. In addition to being valued within the field, motor behavior knowledge is useful in physical and occupational therapy, leisure studies, medicine, neuroscience, psychology, and physiology.

Notes

1. My thanks to Robert Christina, Jane Clark, Richard Schmidt, and Vern Seefeldt for reviewing this chapter and making many helpful

suggestions. However, any errors of fact, omission, and judgment are mine.

2. My thanks to the following for their comments, suggestions, and recollections: Bruce Abernethy, University of Queensland, Australia; Jack Adams, retired, University of Illinois; Robert Christina, University of North Carolina-Greensboro; Jane Clark, University of Maryland; Helen Eckert, retired, University of California at Berkeley; Denis Glencross, recently deceased, Curtin University of Technology, Perth, Australia; Franklin Henry, recently deceased, University of California at Berkeley; Alfred Hubbard, recently deceased, University of Illinois; Scott Kelso, Florida Atlantic University; Walter Kroll, University of Massachusetts; Lawrence Rarick, recently deceased, University of California at Berkeley; Richard Schmidt, UCLA; Vern Seefeldt, retired, Michigan State University; Frank Smoll, University of Washington; and Michael Wade, University of Minnesota.

3. Franklin Henry's students included Ronald Marteniuk and George Stelmach; Fritz Hubbard's students included Richard Schmidt (Jack Adams also contributed significantly); Slater-Hammel's students included Walter Kroll.

4. This point is really debatable; for example, a number of cognitive-based studies use reaching and grasping as a task—obviously a natural movement—while finger wiggling has been used within dynamical systems. Scott Kelso's (personal communication, June 27, 1994) point is a good one: It makes sense to decompose or reduce movements to something simpler; the trick in making this reduction is not to destroy the very phenomenon you are trying to understand.

5. Vern Seefeldt's paper, "This is Motor Development," at this 1989 Motor Development Academy meeting defined motor development as it is functionally used in this chapter, a subset of motor behavior.

6. For a critique of the work on motor expertise, see Abernethy, Thomas, & Thomas, 1993.

References

Abernethy, B. (1988). The effects of age and expertise upon perceptual skill development in a racket sport. *Research Quarterly for Exercise and Sport*, **59**, 210–221.

Abernethy, B. (1990a). Anticipation in squash: Differences in advance cue utilization between experts and novice players. *Journal of Sport Sciences*, **8**, 17–34.

Abernethy, B. (1992). Visual search strategies and decision-making in sport. *International Journal of Sport Psychology*, **22**, 189–210.

Abernethy, B., & Russell, D.G. (1987). Expert-novice differences in an applied selective attention task. *Journal of Sport Psychology, 9,* 326–345.

Abernethy, B., & Snyder, C.W. (1992). Fundamentals of experimentation. In C.W. Snyder & B. Abernethy (Eds.), *The creative side of experimentation: Personal perspectives from leading researchers in motor control, motor development, and sport psychology* (pp. 3–30). Champaign, IL: Human Kinetics.

Abernethy, B., & Sparrow, W.A. (1992). The rise and fall of dominant paradigms in motor behavior research. In J.J. Summers (Ed.), *Approaches to the study of motor control and learning.* Amsterdam: Elsevier Science.

Abernethy, B., Thomas, K.T., & Thomas, J.R. (1993). Strategies for improving understanding of motor expertise (or mistakes we have made and things we have learned!!). In J.L. Starkes & F. Allard (Eds.), *Cognitive issues in motor expertise* (pp. 317–356). Amsterdam: Elsevier Science.

Abrams, R.A., Meyer, D.E., & Kornblum, S. (1990). Eye-hand coordination: Oculomotor control in rapid aimed limb movements. *Journal of Experimental Psychology: Human Perception and Performance, 16,* 248–267.

Adams, J.A. (1952). Warm-up decrement in performance on the pursuit-rotor. *American Journal of Psychology, 65,* 404–414.

Adams, J.A. (1954). Psychomotor performance as a function of intertrial rest interval. *Journal of Experimental Psychology, 48,* 131–133.

Adams, J.A. (1968). Response feedback and learning. *Psychological Bulletin, 70,* 486–504.

Adams, J.A. (1971). A closed-loop theory of motor learning. *Journal of Motor Behavior, 3,* 111–149.

Adams, J.A. (1987). Historical review and appraisal of research on the learning, retention, and transfer of human motor skills. *Psychological Bulletin, 101,* 41–74.

Adams, J.A., & Dijkstra, S. (1966). Short-term memory for motor responses. *Journal of Experimental Psychology, 71,* 314–318.

Adams, J.A., & Hufford, L.E. (1962). Contributions of a part-task trainer to the learning and relearning of a time-shared flight maneuver. *Human Factors, 4,* 159–170.

Adams, J.A., Goetz, E.T., & Marshall, P.H. (1972). Response feedback and motor learning. *Journal of Experimental Psychology, 92,* 391–397.

Adams, J.A., Gopher, D., & Lintern, G. (1977). Effects of visual and proprioceptive feedback on motor learning. *Journal of Motor Behavior, 9,* 11–22.

Adrian, E.D., & Buytendijk, F.J.J. (1931). Potential changes in the isolated brainstem of goldfish. *Journal of Physiology, 71,* 121–135.

Alexander, R.M. (1984). Walking and running. *American Scientist, 72,* 348–354.

Allard, F., Graham, S., & Paarsalu, M.E. (1980). Perception in sport: Basketball. *Journal of Sport Psychology, 2,* 14–21.

Allard, F., & Starkes, J.L. (1980). Perception in sport: Volleyball. *Journal of Sport Psychology, 2*, 22–33.

Alvares, K.M., & Hulin, C.L. (1972). Two explanations of temporal changes in ability-skill relationships: A literature review and theoretical analysis. *Human Factors, 14*, 295–308.

Ammons, R.B. (1947). Acquisition of motor skill: II. Rotary pursuit performance with continuous practice before and after a single rest. *Journal of Experimental Psychology, 37*, 393–411.

Ammons, R.B. (1958). *Le mouvement*. In G.S. Seward & J.P. Sweard (Eds.), *Current psychological issues: Essays in honor of Robert S. Woodworth* (pp. 146–183). New York: Holt Rinehart & Winston.

Anson, J.G. (1982). Memory drum theory: Alternative tests and explanation for the complexity effects on simple reaction time. *Journal of Motor Behavior, 14*, 228–246.

Asatryan, D.G., & Fel'dman, A.G. (1965). Functional tuning of the nervous system with control of movement or maintenance of a steady posture. *Biophysics, 10*, 925–935.

Ascoli, K.M., & Schmidt, R.A. (1969). Proactive interference in short-term motor retention. *Journal of Motor Behavior, 1*, 29–36.

Asmussen, E., & Heeboll-Nielsen, K. (1955). A dimensional analysis of physical performance and growth in boys. *Journal of Applied Physiology, 7*, 593–603.

Atkinson, R.C., & Shiffrin, R.M. (1968). Human memory: A proposed system and its control processes. In K.W. Spence & J.T. Spence (Eds.), *The psychology of learning and motivation* (Vol. 2, pp. 89–195). New York: Academic Press.

Bandura, A. (1977). *Social learning theory*. Englewood Cliffs, NJ: Prentice Hall.

Barclay, C., & Newell, K. (1980). Children's processing of information in motor skill acquisition. *Journal of Experimental Child Psychology, 30*, 98–108.

Bartlett, F.C. (1948). The measurement of human skill. *Occupational Psychology, 22*, 83–91.

Battig, W.F. (1979). The flexibility of human memory. In L.S. Cermak & F.I.M. Craik (Eds.), *Levels of processing in human memory* (pp. 23–44). Hillsdale, NJ: Erlbaum.

Bean, C.H. (1912). The curve of forgetting. *Archives of Psychology, 3*, 1–45.

Bechtoldt, H.P. (1962). Factor analysis and the investigation of hypotheses. *Perceptual & Motor Skills, 14*, 319–342.

Beck, M. (1966). *The path of the center of gravity during running in boys grades one to six*. Unpublished doctoral dissertation, University of Wisconsin, Madison.

Beevor, C.E., & Horsely, V. (1887). A minute analysis (experimental) of the various movements produced by stimulating in the monkey different regions of the cortical centre for the upper limb as defined by Professor Ferrier. *Philosophical Transactions, 178*, 153.

Beevor, C.E., & Horsely, V. (1890). A record of the results obtained by electrical excitation of the so-called motor cortex and internal capsule in the orangutan. *Philosophical Transactions, 181*, 129.

Berger, W., Quintern, J., & Dietz, V. (1984). Afferent and efferent control of stance and gait: Developmental changes in children. *Electroencephalography and Clinical Neurophysiology, 66*, 244–252.

Bernstein, N. (1967). *The co-ordination and regulation of movements.* Oxford, England: Pergamon Press.

Bernstein (Bernshtein), N.A. (1947). *On the structure of movements.* Moscow, USSR: State Medical Publishing House.

Beunen, G., & Malina, R.M. (1988). Growth and physical performance relative to the timing of the adolescent spurt. *Exercise and Sport Sciences Reviews, 16*, 503–540.

Beunen, G., Malina, R.M., Ostyn, M., Renson, R., Simons, J., & Van Gerven, D. (1983). Fatness, growth and motor fitness of Belgian boys 12 through 20 years of age. *Human Biology, 55*, 599–613.

Beunen, G., Ostyn, M., Renson, R., Simons, J., & Van Gerven, D. (1976). Skeletal maturation and physical fitness of girls aged 12 through 16. *Hermes, 10*, 445–457.

Bilodeau, E.A. (1952). Decrements and recovery from decrements in a simple work task with variation in force requirements at different stages of practice. *Journal of Experimental Psychology, 44*, 96–100.

Bilodeau, I.M., & Bilodeau, E.A. (1954). Some effects of work loading in a repetitive motor task. *Journal of Experimental Psychology, 48*, 455–467.

Blix, M. (1892–1895). Die Lange und Spannung des Muskels. *Skandinavische Archiv Physiologie, 3*, 295–318; *4*, 399–409; *5*, 150–206.

Book, W.F. (1925). *The psychology of skill.* New York: Gregg.

Borstelmann, L.J. (1983). Children before psychology. In W. Kessen (Ed.), *Handbook of child psychology: Vol. I. History, theory, and methods* (4th ed., pp. 1–140). New York: Wiley.

Boswell, J.J., & Bilodeau, E.A. (1964). Short-term retention of a simple motor task as a function of interpolated activity. *Perceptual & Motor Skills, 18*, 227–230.

Boswell, J.J., & Spatz, Jr., K.C. (1975). Reminiscence: A rich source of individual differences. *Journal of Motor Behavior, 7*, 1–7.

Bouchard, C., Leblanc, C., Malina, R.M., & Hollmann, W. (1978). Skeletal age and submaximal working capacity in boys. *Annals of Human Biology, 5*, 75–78.

Bouchard, C., Malina, R.M., Hollmann, W., & Leblanc, C. (1976). Relationships between skeletal maturity and submaximal working capacity in boys 8 to 18 years. *Medicine and Science in Sports, 8*, 186–190.

Bouchard, C., Malina, R.M., Hollmann, W., & Leblanc, C. (1977). Submaximal working capacity, heart size and body size in boys 8–18 years. *European Journal of Applied Physiology, 36*, 115–126.

Boucher, J.-L. (1974). Higher processes in motor learning. *Journal of Motor Behavior, 6*, 131–137.

Bowditch, H.P., & Southard, W.F. (1882). A comparison of sight and touch. *Journal of Physiology, 3*, 232–254.

Branta, C., Haubenstricker, J., & Seefeldt, V. (1984). Age changes in motor skills during childhood and adolescence. *Exercise and Sport Sciences Reviews, 12*, 467–520.

Briggs, G.E., & Naylor, J.C. (1962). The relative efficiency of several training methods as a function of transfer task complexity. *Journal of Experimental Psychology, 64*, 505–512.

Briggs, G.E., Naylor, J.C., & Fuchs, A.H. (1962). *Whole versus part training as a function of task dimensions.* Port Washington, NY: U.S. Naval Training Device Center, Technical Report NAVTRADEVCEN 950-2, 18 February. (as cited in Adams, 1987)

Bril, B., & Breniere, Y. (1992). Postural requirements and progression velocity in young walkers. *Journal of Motor Behavior, 24*, 105–116.

Bronfenbrenner, U. (1977). Toward an experimental ecology of human development. *American Psychology, 32*, 513–531.

Bruce, R. (1966). *The effects of variations in ball trajectory upon the catching performance of elementary school children.* Unpublished doctoral dissertation, University of Wisconsin, Madison.

Bryan, W.L., & Harter, N. (1897). Studies in the physiology and psychology of the telegraphic language. *Psychological Reviews, 4*, 27–53.

Bryan, W.L., & Harter, N. (1899). Studies on the telegraphic language: The acquisition of a hierarchy of habits. *Psychological Reviews, 6*, 345–375.

Burgess, P.R., & Clark, F.J. (1969). Characteristics of knee joint receptors in the cat. *Journal of Physiology, 203*, 317–335.

Burton, A.W. (1986). The effect of age on relative timing variability and transfer. *Journal of Motor Behavior, 18*, 323–342.

Burton, A.W. (1987). The effect of number of movement components on response time. *Journal of Human Movement Studies, 13*, 231–247.

Carlton, L.G. (1981). Processing visual feedback information for movement control. *Journal of Experimental Psychology: Human Perception and Performance, 7*, 1019–1030.

Carlton, L.G., Carlton, M.J., & Newell, K.M. (1987). Reaction time and response dynamics. *Quarterly Journal of Experimental Psychology, 39A*, 377–360.

Carron, A.V., & Bailey, D.A. (1974). Strength development in boys from 10 through 16 years. *Monographs of the Society for Research in Child Development, 39* (Serial No. 157).

Carson, L.M., & Wiegand, R.L. (1979). Motor schema formation and retention in young children: A test of Schmidt's schema theory. *Journal of Motor Behavior, 11*, 247–251.

Castiello, U., Stelmach, G.E., & Lieberman, A. (1993). Temporal dissociations in the prehension pattern in Parkinson's disease patients. *Neuropsychologia, 4*, 395–402.

Chamberlin, C., & Lee, T. (1993). Arranging practice conditions and designing instruction. In R.N. Singer, M. Murphey, & L.K. Tennant (Eds.), *Handbook of research on sport psychology* (pp. 213–241). New York: Macmillan.

Chi, M.T.H., & Gallagher, J.D. (1982). Speed of processing: A developmental source of limitation. *Topics of Learning and Learning Disabilities*, **2**, 23–32.

Christina, R.W. (1976). Proprioception as a basis of anticipatory timing behavior. In G.E. Stelmach (Ed.), *Motor control: Issues and trends* (pp. 187–199). New York: Academic Press.

Christina, R.W. (1989). Whatever happened to applied research in motor learning? In J. Skinner et al. (Eds.), *Future directions in exercise and sport science research* (pp. 411–422). Champaign, IL: Human Kinetics.

Christina, R.W. (1992). The 1991 C.H. McCloy Research Lecture: Unraveling the mystery of the response complexity effect in skilled movements. *Research Quarterly for Exercise and Sport*, **63**, 218–230.

Christina, R.W., & Anson, J.G. (1981). The learning of programmed- and feedback-based processes controlling the production of a positioning response in two dimensions. *Journal of Motor Behavior*, **13**, 48–64.

Christina, R.W., Fischman, M.G., Lambert, A.L., & Moore, J.F. (1985). Simple reaction time as a function of response complexity: Christina et al. (1982) revisited. *Research Quarterly for Exercise and Sport*, **56**, 316–322.

Christina, R.W., Fischman, M.G., Vercruyssen, M.J.P., & Anson, J.G. (1982). Simple reaction time as a function of response complexity: Memory drum theory revisited. *Journal of Motor Behavior*, **14**, 301–321.

Christina, R.W., & Merriman, W.J. (1977). Learning the direction and extent of a movement: A test of Adams' closed-loop theory. *Journal of Motor Behavior*, **9**, 1–9.

Christina, R.W., & Rose, D.J. (1985). Premotor and motor reaction time as a function of response complexity. *Research Quarterly for Exercise and Sport*, **56**, 306–315.

Clark, J.E. (1982). Developmental differences in response processing. *Journal of Motor Behavior*, **14**, 247–254.

Clark, J.E. (1994). Motor development. *Encyclopedia of Human Behavior* (Vol. 3). New York: Academic Press.

Clark, J.E. (1995). Dynamical systems perspective on gait. In R.L. Craik & C.A. Oatis (Eds.), *Gait analysis: Theory and application*. St. Louis: Mosby.

Clark, J.E., & Phillips, S.J. (1991). The development of intralimb coordination in the first six months of walking. In J. Fagard & P.H. Wolff (Eds.), *The development of timing control and temporal organization in coordinated action* (pp. 245–257). New York: Elsevier Science.

Clark, J., & Phillips, S.J. (1993). A longitudinal study of intralimb coordination in the first year of independent walking: A dynamical systems analysis. *Child Development*, **64**, 1143–1157.

Clark, J.E., Phillips, S.J., & Petersen, R. (1989). Developmental stability in jumping. *Developmental Psychology, 25*, 929–935.

Clark, J.E., & Whitall, J. (1989). What is motor development?: The lessons of history. *Quest, 41*, 183–202.

Clark, J.E., Whitall, J., & Phillips, S.J. (1988). Human interlimb coordination: The first 6 months of independent walking. *Developmental Psychobiology, 21*, 445–456.

Clarke, H.H., & Harrison, J.C.E. (1962). Differences in physical and motor traits between boys of advanced, normal, and retarded maturity. *Research Quarterly, 33*, 13–25.

Clarke, H.H., Irving, R.N., & Heath, B.H. (1961). Relation of maturing, structural, and strength measures to the somatotypes of boys 9 through 15 years. *Research Quarterly, 34*, 449–460.

Clarkson, P.M. (1978). The effect of age and activity level on simple and choice fractionated response time. *European Journal of Applied Physiology, 40*, 17–25.

Clarkson, P.M., Katch, F.I., Kroll, W., Lane, R., & Kamen, G. (1980). Regional adipose cellularity and reliability of adipose cell size determination. *American Journal of Clinical Nutrition, 33*, 2245–2252.

Clarkson, P.M., & Kroll, W. (1978). Practice effects on fractionated response time related to age and activity level. *Journal of Motor Behavior, 10*, 275–286.

Clouse, F. (1959). *A kinematic analysis of the development of the running pattern of preschool boys.* Unpublished doctoral dissertation, University of Wisconsin, Madison.

Coghill, G.E. (1929). *Anatomy and the problem of behavior.* New York: Macmillan.

Connolly, K.J. (Ed.) (1970a). *Mechanisms of motor skill development.* New York: Academic Press.

Connolly, K.J. (1970b). Response speed, temporal sequencing and information processing in children. In K.J. Connolly (Ed.), *Mechanisms of motor skill development* (pp. 161–188). New York: Academic Press.

Corballis, M.C. (1965). Practice and the simplex. *Psychological Review, 72*, 399–406.

Corbin, C.B., & Eckert, H.M. (1990). *The evolving undergraduate major* (American Academy of Physical Education Papers, No. 24). Champaign, IL: Human Kinetics.

Corcos, D.M. (1984). Two-handed movement control. *Research Quarterly for Exercise and Sport, 55*, 117–122.

Corlett, J.T., & Dickinson, J. (1983). Proactive and retroactive interference in children's motor short-term memory. *Journal of Human Movement Studies, 9*, 21–29.

Craik, K.J.W. (1948). The theory of the human operator in control systems: II. Man as an element in a control system. *British Journal of Psychology, 38*, 142–148.

Darwin, C. (1859). *On the origin of species.* London: John Murray.

Darwin, C. (1871). *Descent of man.* London: John Murray.

Darwin, C. (1877). Biographical sketch of an infant. *Mind, 2,* 285–294.

Dayan, A., & Thomas, J.R. (1994). Intention to remember spatial location in movement: Developmental considerations. *Human Performance, 7,* 37–53.

Deach, D. (1950). *Genetic development of motor skills of children two through six years of age.* Unpublished doctoral dissertation, University of Michigan, Ann Arbor.

De Guimps, R. (1906). *Pestalozzi, his life and work.* New York: Appleton.

Delacato, C. (1959). *The treatment and prevention of reading problems.* Springfield, IL: Thomas.

Delacato, C. (1963). *The diagnosis and treatment of speech and reading problems.* Springfield, IL: Thomas.

Dempster, F.N. (1988). Short-term memory development in childhood and adolescence. In C.J. Brainerd & M. Pressley (Eds.), *Basic processes in memory development: Progress in cognitive development research* (pp. 209–248). New York: Springer-Verlag.

Dennis, W. (1935). The effect of restricted practice upon the reaching, sitting, and standing of two infants. *Journal of Genetic Psychology, 47,* 17–32.

Dennis, W., & Dennis, M.G. (1940). The effect of cradling practices upon the onset of walking in Hopi children. *Journal of Genetic Psychology, 56,* 77–86.

DeOreo, K., & Wade, M.G. (1971). Dynamic and static balancing ability of preschool children. *Journal of Motor Behavior, 3,* 326–335.

Dittmer, J. (1962). *A kinematic analysis of the development of the running pattern of grade school girls and certain factors which distinguish good from poor performance at the observed ages.* Unpublished master's thesis, University of Wisconsin, Madison.

Dixon, R.A., & Lerner, R.M. (1984). A history of systems in developmental psychology. In M.H. Bornstein & M.E. Lamb (Eds.), *Developmental psychology: An advanced textbook* (pp. 1–35). Hillsdale, NJ: Erlbaum.

Dohrman, P. (1964). Throwing and kicking ability of eight-year-old boys and girls. *Research Quarterly 35,* 464–471.

Doré, L.R., & Hilgard, E.R. (1938). Spaced practice as a test of Snoddy's two processes in mental growth. *Journal of Experimental Psychology, 23,* 359–374.

Drowatzky, J.N ., & Zuccato, F.C. (1967). Interrelationships between static and dynamic balance. *Research Quarterly, 38,* 509–510.

Dunham, P., & Reid, D. (1987). Information processing: Effect of stimulus speed variation on coincidence anticipation of children. *Journal of Human Movement Studies, 13,* 151–156.

Eaton, W.O., & Enns, L.R. (1986). Sex differences in human motor activity level. *Psychological Bulletin, 100,* 19–28.

Eaton, W.O., & Yu, A.P. (1989). Are sex differences in child motor activity level a function of sex differences in maturation status? *Child Development*, **60**, 1005–1011.

Ebbinghaus, H. (1885/1964). *Memory: A contribution to experimental psychology*. New York: Dover. (original publication in 1885)

Eckert, H.M., & Eichorn, D.H. (1977). Developmental variability in reaction time. *Child Development*, **48**, 452–458.

Ekern, S.R. (1969). *An analysis of selected measures of the overarm throwing patterns of elementary school boys and girls*. Unpublished doctoral dissertation, University of Wisconsin, Madison.

Elliot, B., Bloomfield, J., & Davies, C. (1980). Development of the punt kick: A cinematographic analysis. *Journal of Human Movement Studies*, **6**, 142–150.

Elliot, R. (1972). Simple reaction time in children: Effects of incentive, incentive shift, and other training variables. *Journal of Experimental Child Psychology*, **13**, 540–557.

Erbaugh, S.J., & Clifton, M.A. (1984). Sibling relationships of preschool-aged children in gross motor environments. *Research Quarterly for Exercise and Sport*, **55**, 323–331.

Espenschade, A. (1940). Motor performance in adolescence, including the study of relationships with measures of physical growth and maturity. *Monographs of the Society for Research in Child Development*, **5** (Serial No. 24).

Espenschade, A. (1960). Motor development. In W.R. Johnson (Ed.), *Science and medicine of exercise and sports* (pp. 439). New York: Harper & Row.

Espenschade, A., Dable, R.R., & Schoendube, R. (1953). Dynamic balance in adolescent boys. *Research Quarterly*, **24**, 270–275.

Espenschade, A., & Eckert, H.M. (1967). *Motor development*. Columbus, OH: Merrill.

Felton, E. (1960). *Kinesiological comparison of good and poor jumpers in the standing broad jump*. Unpublished master's thesis, University of Wisconsin, Madison.

Ferrier, D. (1888). Discussions on cerebral localization. *Transactions of the Congress of American Physicians and Surgeons*, **1**, 337–340.

Fischman, M.G. (1984). Programming time as a function of number of movement parts and changes in movement direction. *Journal of Motor Behavior*, **16**, 405–423.

Fitts, P.M. (1954). The information capacity of the human motor system in controlling the amplitude of movement. *Journal of Experimental Psychology*, **47**, 381–391.

Fleishman, E.A. (1953). Testing for psychomotor abilities by means of apparatus tests. *Psychological Bulletin*, **50**, 243–262.

Fleishman, E.A. (1956). Psychomotor selection tests: Research and application in the United States Air Force. *Personnel Psychology*, **9**, 449–467.

Fleishman, E.A. (1972). On the relation between abilities, learning, and human performance. *American Psychologist, 27,* 1017–1032.

Fleishman, E.A., & Hempel, W.E., Jr. (1956). Factorial analysis of complex psychomotor performance and related skills. *Journal of Applied Psychology, 40,* 96–104.

Fleishman, E.A., & Parker, J.F., Jr. (1962). Factors in the retention and relearning of perceptual-motor skill. *Journal of Experimental Psychology, 64,* 215–226.

Fleury, M., & Bard, C. (1985). Age, stimulus velocity, and task complexity as determinants of coincident timing behavior. *Journal of Human Movement Studies, 11,* 305–311.

Forrsberg, H. (1985). Ontogeny of human locomotor control: I. Infant stepping, supported locomotion and transition to independent locomotion. *Experimental Brain Research, 57,* 480–493.

Fortney, V. (1964). *The swinging limb in running of boys ages seven through eleven.* Unpublished master's thesis, University of Wisconsin, Madison.

Fortney, V.L. (1983). The kinematics and kinetics of the running pattern of 2-, 4-, and 6-year-old children. *Research Quarterly for Exercise and Sport, 54,* 126–135.

French, K.E., & Thomas, J.R. (1987). The relation of knowledge development to children's basketball performance. *Journal of Sport Psychology, 9,* 15–32.

Fritsch, G., & Hitzig, E. (1870). Uber die elektrische Erregbarkeit des Grosshirns. *Archiv Anatomie Physiologie, 37,* 300–322.

Fullerton, G.S., & Cattell, J. (1892). On the perception of small differences. *University of Pennsylvania Philosophical Series,* No. 2.

Gallagher, J.D., & Thomas, J.R. (1980). Effects of varying post-KR intervals upon children's motor performance. *Journal of Motor Behavior, 12,* 41–46.

Gallagher, J.D., & Thomas, J.R. (1984). Rehearsal strategy effects on developmental differences for recall of a movement series. *Research Quarterly for Exercise and Sport, 55,* 123–128.

Gallagher, J.D., & Thomas, J.R. (1986). Developmental effects of grouping and recoding on learning a movement series. *Research Quarterly for Exercise and Sport, 57,* 117–127.

Galton, F. (1876). The history of twins as a criterion of the relative power of nature. *Anthropological Institute Journal, 5,* 391–406.

Gentner, D.R. (1987). Timing of skilled motor performance: Tests of the proportional duration model. *Psychological Review, 94,* 255–276.

Gentry, J.R. (1940). *Immediate effects of interpolated rest periods on learning performance* (Teachers College Contribution to Education, No. 799). New York: Columbia University, Teachers College.

Gerson, R.F., & Thomas, J.R. (1977). Schema theory and practice variability within a neo-Piagetian framework. *Journal of Motor Behavior, 9,* 127–134.

Gerson, R.F., & Thomas, J.R. (1978). A neo-Piagetian investigation of the serial position effect in children's motor learning. *Journal of Motor Behavior, 10*, 95–104.

Gesell, A. (1928). *Infancy and human growth.* New York: Macmillan.

Gesell, A. (1954). The ontogenesis of infant behavior. In L. Carmichael (Ed.), *Manual of child psychology* (2nd ed.) (pp. 335–373). New York: Wiley.

Gibson, E.J. (1940). A systematic application of the concepts of generalization and differentiation to verbal learning. *Psychological Review, 47*, 196–229.

Gibson, J.J. (1979). *The ecological approach to visual perception.* Boston: Houghton Mifflin.

Gould, D., & Roberts, G. (1981). Modeling and motor skill acquisition. *Quest, 33*, 214–230.

Grieve, D.W., & Gear, R.J. (1966). The relationship between length of stride, step frequency, time of swing and speed of walking for children and adults. *Ergonomics, 9*, 379–284.

Griffith, C.R. (1930). A laboratory for research in athletics. *Research Quarterly, 1*(3), 34–40.

Haken, H., Kelso, J.A.S., & Bunz, H. (1985). A theoretical model of phase transitions in human hand movements. *Biological Cybernetics, 51*, 347–356.

Halverson, L.E. (1958). *A comparison of the performance of kindergarten children in the take-off phase of the standing broad jump.* Unpublished doctoral dissertation, University of Wisconsin, Madison.

Halverson, L., Roberton, M.A., & Langendorfer, S. (1982). Development of the overarm throw: Movement and ball velocity changes by seventh grade. *Research Quarterly for Exercise and Sport, 53*, 198–205.

Halverson, L.E., Roberton, M.A., Safrit, M.J., & Roberts, T. (1977). Effect of guided practice on overhand-throw ball velocities of kindergarten children. *Research Quarterly, 48*, 311–318.

Halverson, L.E., & Williams, K. (1985). Developmental sequences for hopping over distance: A prelongitudinal screening. *Research Quarterly for Exercise and Sport, 56*, 37–44.

Hancock, P.A., & Newell, K.M. (1985). The movement speed-accuracy relationship in space-time. In H. Heuer, U. Kleinbeck, & K.-H. Schmidt (Eds.), *Motor behavior: Programming, control, and acquisition* (pp. 153–188). Berlin: Springer-Verlag.

Hanson, M. (1965). *Motor performance testing of elementary school age children.* Unpublished doctoral dissertation, University of Washington, Seattle.

Hanson, S. (1961). *Comparison of the overhand throw performance of instructed and non-instructed kindergarten boys and girls.* Unpublished master's thesis, University of Wisconsin, Madison.

Haubenstricker, J., & Seefeldt, V. (1986). Acquisition of motor skills during childhood. In V. Seefeldt (Ed.), *Physical activity & well-being* (pp. 41–102). Reston, VA: AAHPERD.

Hay, L. (1979). Spatial-temporal analysis of movements in children: Motor programs versus feedback in the development of reaching. *Journal of Motor Behavior, 11,* 189–200.

Haywood, K.M. (1977). Eye movements during coincidence-anticipation performance. *Journal of Motor Behavior, 9,* 313–318.

Haywood, K.M. (1993). *Life span motor development* (2nd ed.). Champaign, IL: Human Kinetics.

Haywood, K.M., Greenwald, G., & Lewis, C. (1981). Contextual factors and age group differences in coincidence-anticipation performance. *Research Quarterly for Exercise and Sport, 52,* 458–462.

Hellebrandt, F.A., Rarick, G.L., Glassow, R., & Carns, M.L. (1961). Physiological analysis of basic motor skills: I. Growth and development of jumping. *American Journal of Physical Medicine, 40,* 14–25.

Henry, F.M. (1959). Reliability, measurement error, and intra-individual difference. *Research Quarterly, 30,* 21–24.

Henry, F.M. (1964). Physical education: An academic discipline. *Proceedings of the 67th Annual Conference of NCPEAM,* 6–9 (reprinted in *Journal of Health, Physical Education and Recreation, 35,* 32–33, 69).

Henry, F.M. (1968). Specificity vs. generality in learning motor skill. In R.C. Brown & G.S. Kenyon (Eds.), *Classical studies on physical activity* (pp. 331–340). Englewood Cliffs, NJ: Prentice Hall. (Originally published in 1958)

Henry, F.M. (1974). Variable and constant performance errors within a group of individuals. *Journal of Motor Behavior, 6,* 149–154.

Henry, F.M. (1975). Absolute error versus "E" in target accuracy. *Journal of Motor Behavior, 7,* 227–228.

Henry, F.M. (1980). Use of simple reaction time in motor programming studies: A reply to Klapp, Wyatt, and Lingo. *Journal of Motor Behavior, 12,* 163–168.

Henry, F.M., & Rogers, D.E. (1960). Increased response latency for complicated movements and a "memory drum" theory of neuromotor reaction. *Research Quarterly, 31,* 448–458.

Herrick, C.J. (1924). Origins and evolutions of the cerebellum. *Archives of Neurology and Psychiatry, 11,* 621–652.

Hindley, C.B., Filliozat, A.M., Klackenberg, G., Nicolet-Meister, D., & Sand, E.A. (1966). Differences in age of walking in five European longitudinal samples. *Human Biology, 38,* 364–379.

Hollingworth, H.L. (1909). The inaccuracy of movement. Archives of Psychology, *13,* 1–87.

Holmes, G. (1939). The cerebellum of man. *Brain, 62,* 1–30.

Hull, C.L. (1943). *Principles of behavior.* New York: Appleton-Century-Crofts.

Humphreys, L.G. (1960). Investigations of the simplex. *Psychometrika, 25,* 313–323.

Hunter, W.S. (1929). Learning: II. Experimental studies of learning. In C. Murchison (Ed.), *The foundation of experimental psychology* (pp. 564–627). Worcester, MA: Clark University Press.

Hutinger, P.W. (1959). Differences in speed between American Negro and White children in performance of the 35-yard dash. *Research Quarterly,* **30,** 366–368.

Irion, A.L. (1948). The relation of "set" to retention. *Psychological Reviews,* **55,** 336–341.

Irion, A.L. (1949). Reminiscence in pursuit-rotor learning as a function of length of rest and amount of pre-rest practice. *Journal of Experimental Psychology,* **39,** 492–499.

Irion, A.L. (1969). Historical introduction. In E.A. Bilodeau & I.M. Bilodeau (Eds.), *Principles of skill acquisition* (pp. 1–31). New York: Academic Press.

Isaacs, L.D. (1980). Effects of ball size, ball color, and preferred color on catching by young children. *Perceptual and Motor Skills,* **51,** 583–586.

Ismail, A.H., Kane, J., & Kirkendall, D.R. (1969). Relationships among intellectual and non-intellectual variables. *Research Quarterly,* **40,** 83–92.

Ives, J.C., Kroll, W.P., & Bultman, L.L. (1993). Rapid movement kinematic and electromyographic control characteristics in males and females. *Research Quarterly for Exercise and Sport,* **64,** 274–283.

Jackson, C.O. (1933). An experimental study of the effect of fear on muscular coordination. *Research Quarterly,* **4**(4), 71–80.

Jeannerod, M. (1984). The timing of natural prehension movement. *Journal of Motor Behavior,* **16,** 235–254.

Johnson, B. (1957). *An analysis of the mechanics of the take-off in the standing broad jump.* Unpublished master's thesis, University of Wisconsin, Madison.

Jones, F. (1951). *A descriptive and mechanical analysis of throwing skills of children.* Unpublished master's thesis, University of Wisconsin, Madison.

Jones, M.B. (1969). Differential processes in acquisition. In E.A. Bilodeau (Ed.), *Principles of skill acquisition* (pp. 141–170). New York: Academic Press.

Judd, C.H. (1908). The relation of special training to general intelligence. *Educational Review,* **36,** 28–42.

Kail, R. (1988). Developmental functions for speeds of cognitive processes. *Journal of Experimental Child Psychology,* **45,** 339–364.

Kamen, G., Kroll, W., Clarkson, P.M., & Zigon, S.T. (1981). Fractioned reaction time in power-trained and endurance-trained athletes under conditions of fatiguing isometric exercise. *Journal of Motor Behavior,* **13,** 117–129.

Kavale, K., & Mattson, P.D. (1983). "One jumped off the balance beam": A meta-analysis of perceptual-motor training. *Journal of Learning Disabilities,* **16,** 165–173.

Keele, S.W. (1968). Movement control in skilled performance. *Psychological Bulletin*, **70**, 387–403.

Keele, S.W., & Hawkins, H.L. (1982). Explorations of individual differences relevant to high level skill. *Journal of Motor Behavior*, **14**, 3–23.

Keele, S.W., Pokorny, R.A., Corcos, D.M., & Ivry, R. (1985). Do perception and motor production share common timing mechanisms?: A correlational analysis. *Acta Psychologica*, **60**, 173–191.

Kelso, J.A.S. (1981). Contrasting perspectives on order and regulation in movement. In J. Long & A. Baddeley (Eds.), *Attention and performance IX* (pp. 437–458). Hillsdale, NJ: Erlbaum.

Kelso, J.A.S. (1986). Pattern formation in multi-degree of freedom speech and limb movements. *Experimental Brain Research Supplement*, **15**, 105–128.

Kelso, J.A.S. (1996). *Dynamic patterns: The self-organization of brain and behavior*. Cambridge, MA: MIT Press.

Kelso, J.A.S., Bressler, S.L., Buchanan, S., DeGuzman, G.C., Ding, M., Fuchs, A., & Holroyd, T. (1992). A phase transition in human brain and behavior. *Physics letters A*, **169**, 134–144.

Kelso, J.A.S., Buchanan, J.J., DeGuzman, G.C., & Ding, M. (1993). Spontaneous recruitment and annihilation of degrees of freedom in biological coordination. *Physics Letters A*, **179**, 364–371.

Kelso, J.A.S., & Clark, J.E. (Eds.) (1982). *The development of movement control and co-ordination*. Chichester, England: Wiley.

Kelso, J.A.S., Holt, K.G., Rubin, P., & Kugler, P.N. (1981). Patterns of human interlimb coordination emerge from the properties of nonlinear, limit-cycle oscillatory processes: Theory and data. *Journal of Motor Behavior*, **13**, 226–261.

Kelso, J.A.S., Marteniuk, R.G., & Newell, K.M. (1981). Editorial note. *Journal of Motor Behavior*, **13**, i.

Kelso, J.A.S., & Norman, P.E. (1978). Motor schema formation in children. *Developmental Psychology*, **14**, 153–156.

Kelso, J.A.S., Putnam, C.A., & Goodman, D. (1983). On the space-time structure of human interlimb coordination. *Quarterly Journal of Experimental Psychology*, **35A**, 347–375.

Kelso, J.A.S., & Schoner, G. (1988). Self-organization of coordinative movement patterns. *Human Movement Science*, **7**, 27–46.

Kelso, J.A.S., Southard, D.L., & Goodman, D. (1979). On the nature of human interlimb coordination. *Science*, **203**, 1029–1031.

Kelso, J.A.S., & Tuller, B. (1984). Converging evidence in support of common dynamical principles for speech and movement coordination. *American Journal of Physiology*, **246**, R928–R935.

Kephart, N. (1960). *The slower learner in the classroom*. Columbus, OH: Merrill.

Kerr, R. (1985). Fitts' law and motor control in children. In J. Clark & H.H. Humphrey (Eds.), *Motor development: Current selected research* (pp. 45–53). Princeton, NJ: Princeton Books.

Kerr, B., Blanchard, C., & Miller, K. (1980). Children's use of sequence information in partially predictable reaction-time sequences. *Journal of Experimental Child Psychology*, **29**, 529–549.

Kincaid, M. (1925). A study of individual differences in learning. *Psychological Reviews*, **32**, 34–53.

Klapp, S.T., Wyatt, E., & Lingo, W. (1974). Response programming in simple and choice reactions. *Journal of Motor Behavior*, **6**, 263–271.

Krahenbuhl, G.S., Skinner, J.S., & Kohrt, W.M. (1985). Developmental aspects of maximal aerobic power in children. *Exercise and Sport Sciences Reviews*, **13**, 503–538.

Kroll, W. (1973). Effects of local muscular fatigue due to isotonic and isometric exercise upon fractionated reaction time components. *Journal of Motor Behavior*, **5**, 81 –93.

Kroll, W. (1974). Fractionated reaction and reflex time before and after fatiguing isotonic exercise. *Medicine and Science in Sports*, **6**, 260–266.

Kroll, W.P. (1982). *Graduate study and research in physical education*. Champaign, IL: Human Kinetics.

Kroll, W.P., Bultman, L.L., Kilmer, W.L., & Boucher, J. (1990). Anthropometric predictors of isometric arm strength in males and females. *Clinical Kinesiology*, **44**, 5–11.

Kugler, P.N., Kelso, J.A.S., & Turvey, M.T. (1982). On coordination and control in naturally developing systems. In J.A.S. Kelso & J.E. Clark (Eds.), *The development of movement control and co-ordination* (pp. 5–78). New York: Wiley.

Kuhn, T.S. (1970). *The structure of scientific revolutions* (2nd ed.). Chicago: University of Chicago Press.

Lai, Q., & Shea, C. (1995). Citations in motor learning and control. *Journal of Sport & Exercise Psychology*, **175**, 568.

Landers, D.M., & Landers, D.M. (1973). Teacher versus peer models: Effect of model's presence and performance level on motor behavior. *Journal of Motor Behavior*, **5**, 129–139.

Larish, D.D., & Stelmach, G.E. (1982). Preprogramming, programming, and reprogramming of aimed hand movements as a function of age. *Journal of Motor Behavior*, **14**, 322–340.

Lee, A.M. (1980). Child-rearing practices and motor performance of Black and White children. *Research Quarterly for Exercise and Sport*, **51**, 494–500.

Lee, D.N., & Lishman, J.R. (1975). Visual proprioceptive control of stance. *Journal of Human Movement Studies*, **1**, 87–95.

Lee, D.N., Lishman, J.R., & Thomson, J. (1982). Regulations of gait in long jumping. *Journal of Experimental Psychology: Human Perception and Performance*, **8**, 448–459.

Lee, T.D., & Genovese, E.D. (1988). Distribution of practice in motor skill acquisition: Learning and performance effects reconsidered. *Research*

Quarterly for Exercise and Sport, **59**, 277–287 (and responses by Ammons, R.B.; Christina, R.W., & Shea, J.B.; Lintern, G.; Magill, R.A.; Newell, K.M., Antoniou, A., & Carlton, L.G.; in the same issue).

Lee, T.D., & Magill, R.A. (1983). The locus of contextual interference in motor skill acquisition. *Journal of Experimental Psychology: Learning, Memory, and Cognition,* **9**, 730–746.

Lee, T.D., & Swinnen, S.P. (1993). Three legacies of Bryan and Harter: Automaticity, variability and change in skilled performance. In J.L. Starkes & F. Allard (Eds.), *Cognitive issues in motor expertise* (pp. 295–315). Amsterdam: Elsevier Science.

Lee, T.D., & Weeks, D.J. (1987). The beneficial influence of forgetting on short-term retention of movement information. *Human Movement Science,* **6**, 233–245.

Leuba, J.H. (1909). The influence of the duration and of the rate of arm movements upon the judgment of their length. *American Journal of Psychology,* **20**, 374–385.

Lewis, D., McAllister, D.E., & Adams, J.A. (1951). Facilitation and interference in performance on the Modified Mashburn Apparatus: I. The effects of varying the amount of original learning. *Journal of Experimental Psychology,* **41**, 247–260.

Lorge, I. (1930). *The influence of regularly interpolated time intervals upon subsequent learning* (Teachers College Contributions to Education, No. 438). New York: Columbia University, Teachers College.

Magill, R.A. (1973). The post-KR interval: Time and activity effects and the relationship of motor short-term memory theory. *Journal of Motor Behavior,* **5**, 49–56.

Magill, R.A. (1977). The processing of knowledge of results information for a serial-motor task. *Journal of Motor Behavior,* **9**, 113–118.

Magill, R.A. (1993). *Motor learning: Concepts and applications* (3rd ed.). Dubuque, IA: Brown.

Magill, R.A., & Hall, K.G. (1990). A review of the contextual interference effect in motor skill acquisition. *Human Movement Science,* **9**, 241–289.

Malina, R.M. (1975). *Growth and development: The first twenty years.* Minneapolis: Burgess.

Malina, R.M. (1979). The effects of exercise on specific tissues, dimensions and functions during growth. *Studies in Physical Anthropology,* **5**, 21–52.

Malina, R.M. (1983a). Human growth, maturation and regular physical activity. *Acta Medica Auxotogica,* **15**, 5–23.

Malina, R.M. (1983b). Menarche in athletes: A synthesis and hypothesis. *Annals of Human Biology,* **10**, 1–24.

Malina, R.M. (1988). Racial/ethnic variation in the motor development and performance of American children. *Canadian Journal of Sport Sciences,* **13**, 136–143.

Malina, R.M., Beunen, G., Wellens, R., & Claessens, A. (1986). Skeletal maturity and body size of teenage Belgian track and field athletes. *Annals of Human Biology,* **13**, 331–339.

Malina, R.M., & Bouchard, C. (1991). *Growth, maturation, and physical activity*. Champaign, IL: Human Kinetics.

Malina, R.M., & Buschang, P.H. (1985). Growth, strength and motor performance of Zapotee children, Oaxaca, Mexico. *Human Biology, 57,* 163–181.

Malina, R.M., Hamill, P.V.V., & Lemeshow, S. (1974). Body dimension and proportions, White and Negro children 6–11 years, United States. *Vita and Health Statistics* (Series 11, no. 143).

Malina, R.M., Little, B.B., Shoup, R.F., & Buschang, P.H. (1987). Adaptive significance of small body size: Strength and motor performance of school children in Mexico and Papua New Guinea. *American Journal of Physical Anthropology, 73,* 489–499.

Malina, R.M., & Roche, A.F. (1983). *Manual of physical status and performance in childhood: Vol. 2. Physical performance.* New York: Plenum.

Marteniuk, R.C., & MacKenzie, C.L. (1981). Methods in the study of motor programming: Is it just a matter of simple vs. choice reaction time? A comment on Klapp et al. (1979). *Journal of Motor Behavior, 13,* 313–319.

Marteniuk, R.G., MacKenzie, C.L., Jeannerod, M., Athenes, S., & Dugas, C. (1987). Constraints on human arm movement trajectories. *Canadian Journal of Psychology, 4,* 365–378.

Martens, R., Burwitz, L., & Zuckerman, J. (1976). Modeling effects on motor performance. *Research Quarterly, 47,* 277–291.

McAllister, D.E. (1953). The effects of various kinds of relevant verbal pretraining on subsequent motor performance. *Journal of Experimental Psychology, 46,* 329–336.

McCall, R.B. (1977). Challenges to a science of developmental psychology. *Child Development, 48,* 333–344.

McCracken, H.D. (1983). Movement control in a reciprocal tapping task: A developmental study. *Journal of Motor Behavior, 15,* 262–279.

McCloy, C.H. (1934). The measurement of general motor capacity and general motor ability. *Research Quarterly, 5* (Suppl. 5), 45–61.

McCloy, C.H. (1937). An analytical study of the stunt type test as a measure of motor educability. *Research Quarterly, 8,* 46–55.

McCristal, K.J. (1933). Experimental study of rhythm in gymnastics and tap dancing. *Research Quarterly, 4*(2), 63–75.

McCullagh, P. (1986). Model status as a determinant of observational learning and performance. *Journal of Sport and Exercise Psychology, 8,* 319–331.

McCullagh, P. (1993). Modeling: Learning, developmental, and social psychological considerations. In R.N. Singer, M. Murphey, &. L.K. Tennant (Eds.), *Handbook of research on sport psychology* (pp. 106–126). New York: Macmillan.

McGeoch, J.A. (1931). The acquisition of skill. *Psychological Bulletin, 28,* 413–466.

McGeoch, J.A., & Melton, A.W. (1929). The comparative retention values of maze habits and of nonsense syllables. *Journal of Experimental Psychology, 12*, 392–414.

McGraw, M.B. (1935). *Growth: A study of Johnny and Jimmy.* New York: Appleton-Century-Crofts.

McGraw, M.B. (1939). Later development of children specially trained during infancy: Johnny and Jimmy at school age. *Child Development, 10*, 1–19.

McGraw, M.B. (1969). *The neuromuscular maturation of the human infant.* New York: Hafner. (Originally published in 1945)

McPherson, S.L., & Thomas, J.R. (1989). Relation of knowledge and performance in boys' tennis: Age and expertise. *Journal of Experimental Child Psychology, 48*, 190–211.

Melton, A.W. (Ed.) (1947). *Apparatus tests: Report No. 4.* Washington, DC: Army Air Forces Aviation Psychology Program Research Reports. Superintendent of Documents, U.S. Government Printing Office. (As reported in Adams, 1987)

Merton, P.A. (1953). Speculations of the servo control of movement. In G.E.W. Wolstenholme (Ed.), *The spinal cord.* London: Churchill.

Meyers, D.E., Abrams, R.A., Kornblum, S., Wright, C.E., & Smith, J.E.K. (1988). Optimality in human motor performance: Ideal control of rapid aimed movements. *Psychological Review, 95*, 340–370.

Meyers, J.L. (1967). Retention of balance coordination learning as influenced by extended lay-offs. *Research Quarterly, 38*, 72–78.

Milne, C., Seefeldt, V., & Reuschlein, P. (1976). Relationship between grade, sex, race, and motor performance in young children. *Research Quarterly, 47*, 726–730.

Mirwald, R.L., & Bailey, D.A. (1986). *Maximal aerobic power.* London, ON: Sports Dynamics.

Morris, A.A. (1977). Effects of fatiguing isometric and isotonic exercise on resisted and unresisted reaction time components. *European Journal of Applied Physiology, 37*, 1–11.

Morris, A.M., Williams, J.M., Atwater, A.E., & Wilmore, J.H. (1982). Age and sex differences in motor performance of 3 through 6 year-old children. *Research Quarterly for Exercise and Sport, 53*, 214–221.

Morris, G.S.D. (1976). Effects ball and background color have upon the catching performance of elementary school children. *Research Quarterly, 47*, 409–416.

Motor Development Academy. (1980). *Journal of Physical Education and Recreation, 51*, 38.

Moxley, S.E. (1979). Schema: The variability of practice hypothesis. *Journal of Motor Behavior, 11*, 65–70.

Nashner, L.M., Woollacott, M., & Tuma, G. (1979). Organization of rapid responses to postural and locomotor-like perturbations of standing man. *Experimental Brain Research, 36*, 463–476.

Nelson, J.K., Thomas, J.R., Nelson, K.R., & Abraham, P.C. (1986). Gender differences in children's throwing performance: Biology and environment. *Research Quarterly for Exercise and Sport, 57*, 280–287.

Nelson, K.R., Thomas, J.R., & Nelson, J.K. (1991). Longitudinal changes in throwing performances: Gender differences. *Research Quarterly for Exercise and Sport, 62*, 105–108.

Newell, K.M. (1974). Knowledge of results and motor learning. *Journal of Motor Behavior, 6*, 235–244.

Newell, K.M. (1976a). More on absolute error, etc. *Journal of Motor Behavior, 8*, 139–142.

Newell, K.M. (1976b). Motor learning without knowledge of results through the development of a response recognition mechanism. *Journal of Motor Behavior, 8*, 209–217.

Newell, K.M. (1985). Coordination, control and skill. In D. Goodman, R.B. Wilberg, & I.M. Franks (Eds.), *Differing perspectives in motor learning* (pp. 295–317). Amsterdam: North-Holland.

Newell, K.M. (1990). Kinesiology: The label for the study of physical activity in higher education. *Quest, 42*, 269–278.

Newell, K.M., & Barclay, C.R. (1982). Developing knowledge about action. In J.A.S. Kelso & J.E. Clark (Eds.), *The development of movement control and co-ordination* (pp. 175–212). Chichester, England: Wiley.

Newell, K.M., & Carlton, L.G. (1980). Developmental trends in motor response recognition. *Developmental Psychology, 16*, 550–554.

Newell, K.M., & Kennedy, J.A. (1978). Knowledge of results and children's motor learning. *Developmental Psychology, 14*, 531–536.

Nicolson, R.I. (1982). Cognitive factors in simple reactions: A developmental study. *Journal of Motor Behavior, 14*, 69–80.

Noble, C.E. (1968). The learning of psychomotor skills. *Annual Review of Psychology, 19*, 203–250.

Oxendine, J.B. (1968). *Psychology of motor learning.* New York: Appleton-Century-Crofts.

Payne, V.G. (1982). Current status of research on object reception as a function of ball size. *Perceptual and Motor Skills, 55*, 953–954.

Payne, V.G. (1985). Effects of object size and experimental design on object reception by children in the first grade. *Journal of Human Movement Studies, 11*, 1–9.

Payne, V.G. (1988). Effects of direction of stimulus approach, eye dominance, and gender on coincidence-anticipation timing performance. *Journal of Human Movement Studies, 15*, 17–25.

Payne, V.G., & Isaacs, L.D. (1995). *Human motor development: A lifespan approach* (3rd ed.). Mountain View, CA: Mayfield.

Payne, V.G., & Koslow, R. (1981). Effects of varying ball diameters on catching ability of young children. *Perceptual and Motor Skills, 53*, 739–744.

Pew, R.W. (1966). Acquisition of hierarchical control over the temporal organization of a skill. *Journal of Experimental Psychology, 71,* 764–771.

Poe, A. (1976). Description of the movement characteristics of two-year-old children performing the jump and reach. *Research Quarterly, 47,* 260–268.

Pollock, B.J., & Lee, T.D. (1992). Effects of the model's skill level on observational motor learning. *Research Quarterly for Exercise and Sport, 63,* 25–29.

Posner, M.I. (1967). Characteristics of visual and kinesthetic memory codes. *Journal of Experimental Psychology, 75,* 103–107.

Posner, M.I. (1969). Reduced attention and the performance of "automated" movements. *Journal of Motor Behavior, 1,* 245–258.

Posner, M.I., & Konick, A.F. (1966). Short-term retention of visual and kinesthetic information. *Organizational Behavior and Human Performance, 1,* 71–86.

Proctor, R.W., Reeve, T.G., Weeks, D.J., Dornier, L., & Van Zandt, T. (1991). Acquisition, retention, and transfer of response-selection skill in choice-reaction tasks. *Journal of Experimental Psychology: Learning, Memory, and Cognition, 17,* 497–506.

Rack, P.M.H., & Westbury, D.R. (1969). The effects of length and stimulus rate on tension in the isometric cat soleus muscle. *Journal of Physiology, 204,* 443–460.

Rarick, G.L. (1952). *Motor development during infancy and childhood.* Madison, WI: College Printing and Typing.

Rarick, G.L. (Ed.) (1973a). *Physical activity: Human growth and development.* New York: Academic Press.

Rarick, G.L. (1973b). Stability and change in motor ability. In G.L. Rarick (Ed.), *Physical activity: Human growth and development* (pp. 201–224). New York: Academic Press.

Rarick, G.L. (1992). Autobiography. In C.W. Snyder, Jr., & B. Abernethy (Eds.), *The creative side of experimentation: Personal perspectives from leading researchers in motor control, motor development, and sport psychology* (pp. 109–124). Champaign, IL: Human Kinetics.

Rarick, G.L., & Oyster, N. (1964). Physical maturity, muscular strength and motor performance of young school-age boys. *Research Quarterly, 35,* 523–531.

Rarick, G.L., Rapaport, L.F., & Seefeldt, V. (1966). Long bone growth in Down's Syndrome. *American Journal of Diseases of Children, 112,* 566–571.

Rarick, G.L., & Smoll, F.L. (1967). Stability of growth in strength and motor performance from childhood to adolescence. *Human Biology, 39,* 295–306.

Rarick, G.L., & Thompson, J.A.J. (1956). Roentgenographic measures of leg muscle size and ankle extensor strength of seven-year-old children. *Research Quarterly, 27,* 321–332.

Rarick, G.L., Wainer, H., Thissen, D., & Seefeldt, V. (1975). A double logistic comparison of growth patterns of normal children and children with Down's Syndrome. *Annals of Human Biology*, **2**, 339–346.

Reed, H.B. (1931). The influence of training on changes in variability in achievement. *Psychological Monographs*, **41** (2, Whole No. 185).

Reeve, T.G., Proctor, R.W., Weeks, D.J., & Dornier, L. (1992). Salience of stimulus and response features in choice-reaction tasks. *Perception and Psychophysics*, **52**, 453–460.

Reid, G. (1980). The effects of motor strategy instruction in the short-term memory of the mentally retarded. *Journal of Motor Behavior*, **12**, 221–227.

Roberton, M.A. (1977). Stability of stage categorizations across trials: Implication for the 'stage theory' of overarm throw development. *Journal of Human Movement Studies*, **3**, 49–59.

Roberton, M.A. (1978). Longitudinal evidence for developmental stages in the forceful overarm throw. *Journal of Human Movement Studies*, **4**, 167–175.

Roberton, M.A. (1982). Describing 'stages' within and across motor tasks. In J.A.S. Kelso & J.E. Clark (Eds.), *The development of movement control and co-ordination* (pp. 293–307). Chichester, England: Wiley.

Roberton, M.A. (1989). Motor development: Recognizing our roots, charting our future. *Quest*, **41**, 213–223.

Roberton, M.A., & Halverson, L.E. (1984). *Developing children—their changing movement: A guide for teachers*. Philadelphia: Lea & Febiger.

Roberton, M.A., & Halverson, L.E. (1988). The development of locomotor coordination: Longitudinal change and invariance. *Journal of Motor Behavior*, **20**, 197–241.

Roberton, M.A., Halverson, L.E., Langendorfer, S., & Williams, K. (1979). Longitudinal changes in children's overarm throw ball velocities. *Research Quarterly*, **50**, 265–264.

Rosenbaum, D.A. (1991). *Human motor control*. San Diego: Academic Press.

Rosenbaum, D.A., Kenny, S., & Derr, M.A. (1983). Hierarchical control of rapid movement sequences. *Journal of Experimental Psychology: Human Perception and Performance*, **9**, 86–102.

Roy, E. (1976). Measuring change in motor memory. *Journal of Motor Behavior*, **8**, 283–287.

Roy, E.A., & Elliot, D. (1986). Manual asymmetries in visually directed aiming. *Canadian Journal of Psychology*, **40**, 109–121.

Salmoni, A.W. (1983). A descriptive analysis of children performing Fitts' reciprocal tapping task. *Journal of Human Movement Studies*, **9**, 81–96.

Salmoni, A.W., & Pascoe, C. (1979). Fitts reciprocal tapping task: A developmental study. In G.C. Roberts & K.M. Newell (Eds.), *Psychology of motor behavior and sport—1978* (pp. 355–386). Champaign, IL: Human Kinetics.

Salmoni, A.W., Schmidt, R.A., & Walter, C.B. (1984). Knowledge of results and motor learning: A review and critical reappraisal. *Psychological Bulletin*, **95**, 355–386.

Schellekens, J.M.H., Kalverboer, A.F., & Scholten, C.A. (1984). The microstructure of tapping movements in children. *Journal of Motor Behavior*, **16**, 20–39.

Schendel, J.D., & Newell, K.M. (1976). On processing the information from knowledge of results. *Journal of Motor Behavior*, **8**, 251–255.

Schmidt, R.A. (1968). Anticipation and timing in human motor performance. *Psychological Bulletin*, **70**, 631–646.

Schmidt, R.A. (1975). A schema theory of discrete motor skill learning. *Psychological Review*, **82**, 225–260.

Schmidt, R.A. (1976). Control processes in motor skills. *Exercise and Sport Sciences Reviews*, **4**, 229–261.

Schmidt, R.A. (1977). Schema theory: Implications for movement education. *Motor Skills: Theory into Practice*, **2**, 36–38.

Schmidt, R.A. (1980). Past and future issues in motor programming. *Research Quarterly for Exercise and Sport*, **51**, 122–140.

Schmidt, R.A. (1982). More on motor programs. In J.A.S. Kelso (Ed.), *Human motor behavior: An introduction* (pp. 189–217). Hillsdale, NJ: Erlbaum.

Schmidt, R.A. (1988). *Motor control and learning: A behavioral emphasis* (2nd ed.). Champaign, IL: Human Kinetics.

Schmidt, R.A. (1991). *Motor learning & performance: From principles to practice*. Champaign, IL: Human Kinetics.

Schmidt, R.A., Sherwood, D.E., Zelaznik, H.N., & Leikind, B.J. (1985). Speed-accuracy trade-offs in motor behavior: Theories of impulse variability. In H. Heuer, U. Kleinbeck, & K.-H. Schmidt (Eds.), *Motor behavior: Programming, control, and acquisition* (pp. 79–123). Berlin: Springer-Verlag.

Schmidt, R.A., & Stull, G.A. (1970). Premotor and motor reaction time as a function of preliminary muscular tension. *Journal of Motor Behavior*, **2**, 96–110.

Schmidt, R.A., & White, J.L. (1972). Evidence for an error detection mechanism in motor skills: A test of Adams' closed-loop theory. *Journal of Motor Behavior*, **4**, 143–153.

Schmidt, R.A., Zelaznik, H.N., Hawkins, B., Frank, J.S., & Quinn, J.T. (1979). Motor-output variability: A theory for the accuracy of rapid motor acts. *Psychological Review*, **86**, 415–451.

Schnabl-Dickey, E.A. (1977). Relationships between parents' childrearing attitudes and the jumping and throwing performance of their preschool children. *Research Quarterly*, **48**, 382–390.

Schutz, R.W. (1977). Absolute, constant, and variable error: Problems and solutions. In D. Mood (Ed.), *The measurement of change in physical education: Proceedings of the Colorado measurement symposium* (pp. 82–100). Boulder: University of Colorado.

Schutz, R.W., & Roy, E.A. (1973). Absolute error: The devil in disguise. *Journal of Motor Behavior, 5*, 141–153.

Seefeldt, V. (1974). Perceptual-motor programs. In J.H. Wilmore (Ed.), *Exercise and sport sciences reviews* (Vol. 2). New York: Academic Press.

Seefeldt, V. (Ed.) (1987). *Handbook for youth sports coaches* Reston, VA: AAHPERD.

Seefeldt, V., & Haubenstricker, J. (1982). Patterns, phases, or stages: An analytical model for the study of developmental movement. In J.A.S. Kelso & J.E. Clark (Eds.), *The development of movement control and coordination* (pp. 309–318). Chichester, England: Wiley.

Seils, L.G. (1951). The relationship between measures of physical growth and gross motor performance of primary grade school children. *Research Quarterly, 22*, 244–260.

Shapiro, D.C., & Schmidt, R.A. (1982). The schema theory: Recent evidence and developmental implications. In J.A.S. Kelso & J.E. Clark (Eds.), *The development of movement control and coordination* (pp. 113–173). Chichester, England: Wiley.

Shapiro, D.C., Zernicke, R.F., Gregor, R.J., & Diestel, J.D. (1981). Evidence for generalized motor programs using gait-pattern analysis. *Journal of Motor Behavior, 13*, 33–47.

Shea, J.B., & Morgan, R.L. (1979). Contextual interference effects on the acquisition, retention, and transfer of motor skill. *Journal of Experimental Psychology: Human Learning and Memory, 5*, 179–187.

Shea, J.B., & Upton, G. (1976). The effects on skill acquisition of an interpolated motor short-term memory task during the KR-delay interval. *Journal of Motor Behavior, 8*, 277–281.

Shea, J.B., & Wright, D.L. (1991). When forgetting benefits motor retention. *Research Quarterly for Exercise and Sport, 62*, 293–301.

Sherrington, C.S. (1906). *The integrative action of the nervous system.* New Haven, CT: Yale University Press.

Shinn, M. (1900). *Biography of a baby.* Boston: Houghton Mifflin.

Shumway-Cook, A., & Woollacott, M.H. (1985). The growth of stability: Postural control from a developmental perspective. *Journal of Motor Behavior, 17*, 131–147.

Sidaway, B. (1991). Motor programming as a function of constraints on movement initiation. *Journal of Motor Behavior, 23*, 120–130.

Sidaway, B., Christina, R.W., & Shea, J.B. (1988). A movement constraint interpretation of the response complexity effect on programming time. In A. Colley & J. Beech (Eds.), *Cognition and action in skilled behavior* (pp. 87–102). Amsterdam: North-Holland.

Singer, F. (1961). *Comparison of the development of the overarm throwing patterns of good and poor performers (Girls).* Unpublished master's thesis, University of Wisconsin, Madison.

Singer, R.N. (1968). *Motor learning and human performance: An application to physical education skills*. New York: Macmillan.

Singer, R.N. (1977). To error not to err: A question for the instruction of psychomotor skills. *Review of Educational Research, 47,* 479–498.

Singer, R.N., DeFrancesco, C., & Randall, L.E. (1989). Effectiveness of a global learning strategy practiced in different contexts on primary and transfer of self-paced motor tasks. *Journal of Sport and Exercise Psychology, 11,* 290–303.

Singer, R.N., Flora, L.A., & Abourezk, T.L. (1989). The effect of a five-step cognitive learning strategy on the acquisition of a complex motor skill. *Journal of Applied Sport Psychology, 1,* 98–108.

Singer, R.N., & Gaines, L. (1975). Effects of prompted and trial-and-error learning on transfer performance of a serial motor task. *American Educational Research Journal, 12,* 395–403.

Singer, R.N., & Gerson, R.F. (1981). Task classification and strategy utilization in motor skills. *Research Quarterly for Exercise and Sport, 52,* 100–116.

Singer, R.N., & Pease, D. (1976). Effect of guided versus discovery learning strategies on learning, retention, and transfer of a serial motor task. *Research Quarterly, 47,* 788–796.

Singer, R.N., & Suwanthada, S. (1986). The generalizability of effectiveness of a learning strategy on achievement in related closed motor skills. *Research Quarterly for Exercise and Sport, 57,* 205–213.

Skinner, B.F. (1953). *Science and human behavior*. New York: Macmillan.

Skoglund, S. (1956). Anatomical and physiological studies of the knee joint innervation in the cat. *Acta Physiologica Scandinavica, 36,* (suppl. 124).

Smoll, F.L. (1982). Developmental kinesiology: Toward a subdiscipline focusing on motor development. In J.A.S. Kelso & J.E. Clark (Eds.), *The development of movement control and co-ordination* (pp. 319–354). Chichester, England: Wiley.

Smoll, F.L., & Schutz, R.W. (1990). Quantifying gender differences in motor performance: A developmental perspective. *Developmental Psychology, 26,* 360–369.

Spirduso, W.W. (1975). Reaction and movement time as a function of age and physical activity level. *Journal of Gerontology, 30,* 335–340.

Spirduso, W.W. (1980). Physical fitness, aging, and psychomotor speed: A review. *Journal of Gerontology, 35,* 850–865.

Spirduso, W.W., & Clifford, P. (1978). Neuromuscular speed and consistency of performance as a function of age, physical activity level and type of physical activity. *Journal of Gerontology, 33,* 26–30.

Spirduso, W.W., & MacRae, P.G. (1990). Motor performance and aging. In. J.E. Birren & K.W. Schaie (Eds.), *The handbook of psychology of aging* (3rd ed.) (pp. 184–197). San Diego: Academic Press.

Starkes, J.L. (1987). Skill in field hockey: The nature of the cognitive advantage. *Journal of Sport Psychology, 9,* 146–160.

Starkes, J.L., & Allard, F. (1983). Perception in volleyball: The effects of competitive stress. *Journal of Sport Psychology, 2,* 22–33.

Starkes, J.L., & Allard, F. (Eds.) (1993). *Cognitive issues in motor expertise,* Amsterdam: Elsevier Science.

Starkes, J.L., Caicco, J., Boutilier, C., & Sevsek, B. (1990). Motor recall of experts for structured and unstructured sequences in creative modern dance. *Journal of Sport and Exercise Psychology, 12,* 317–321.

Starkes, J.L., Deakin, J.M., Lindley, S., & Crisp, F. (1987). Motor versus verbal recall of ballet sequences by young expert dancers. *Journal of Sport Psychology, 9,* 222–230.

Stelmach, G.E. (1969). Prior positioning responses as a factor in short-term retention of a simple motor task. *Journal of Experimental Psychology, 81,* 523–526.

Stelmach, G.E. (1970). Kinesthetic recall and information reduction activity. *Journal of Motor Behavior, 2,* 183–194.

Stelmach, G.E. (Ed.) (1976). *Motor control: Issues and trends.* New York: Academic Press.

Stelmach, G.E. (Ed.) (1978). *Information processing in motor control and learning.* New York: Academic Press.

Stelmach, G.E., Amrhein, P.C., & Goggin, N.L. (1988). Bimanual coordination and aging: Deficits in synchronization and parameterization processes. *Journal of Gerontology, 43,* 18–23.

Stelmach, G.E., & Nahom, A. (1992). Age related motor deficits in driving ability. *Human Factors, 34,* 53–67.

Stelmach, G.E., Phillips, J., DiFabio, R.P., & Teasdale, N. (1989). Age, functional postural reflexes, and voluntary sway. *Journal of Gerontology, 44,* 100–106.

Stelmach, G.E., Populin, L., & Mueller, F. (1990). Postural muscle onset and voluntary movement in the elderly. *Neuroscience Letters, 117,* 188–194.

Stelmach, G.E., Teasdale, N., & Phillips, J. (1992). Response initiation delays in Parkinson disease patients. *Human Movement Science, 11,* 37–45.

Stelmach, G.E., Teasdale, N., Phillips, J., & Worringham, C.J. (1989). Force production characteristics in Parkinson's disease. *Experimental Brain Research, 76,* 165–172.

Stelmach, G.E., Worringham, C.J., & Strand, E.A. (1986). Movement preparation in Parkinson's disease: The use of advanced information. *Brain, 109,* 1179–1194.

Stimpel, E. (1933). Der wurf (The throw). *Neue Psychologische Studien, 9,* 105–138.

Stull, G.A., & Kearney, J.T. (1978). Effects of variable fatigue levels on reaction-time components. *Journal of Motor Behavior, 10,* 223–231.

Sudgen, D.A. (1978). Visual motor short term memory in educationally subnormal boys. *British Journal of Educational Psychology, 48,* 330–339.

Sudgen, D.A. (1980). Movement speed in children. *Journal of Motor Behavior*, **12**, 125–132.

Swift, E.J. (1905). Memory of a complex skillful act. *American Journal of Psychology*, **16**, 131–133.

Swift, E.J., & Schuyleer, W. (1907). The learning process. *Psychological Bulletin*, **4**, 307–310.

Teasdale, N., Stelmach, G.E., & Breunig, A. (1991). Postural sway characteristics under normal and altered visual and support conditions. *Journal of Gerontology*, **46**, 238–244.

Teasdale, N., Stelmach, G.E., Breunig, A., & Meeuwsen, H.J. (1991). Age differences in visual sensory integration. *Experimental Brain Research*, **85**, 691–696.

Teulings, H.L., & Stelmach, G.E. (1991). Control of stroke size, peak acceleration, and stroke duration in Parkinsonian handwriting. *Journal of Movement Studies*, **10**, 315–333.

Thelen, E. (1983). Learning to walk is still an "old" problem: A reply to Zelazo (1983). *Journal of Motor Behavior*, **15**, 139–161.

Thelen, E. (1986). Treadmill-elicited stepping in seven-month-old infants. *Child Development*, **57**, 1498–1506.

Thelen, E. (1987). The role of motor development in developmental psychology: A view of the past and an agenda for the future. In N. Eisenberg (Ed.), *Contemporary topics in developmental psychology* (pp. 3–33). New York: Wiley.

Thelen, E. (1988). Dynamical approaches to the development of behavior. In J.A.S. Kelso, A.J. Mandell, & M.F. Shiesinger (Eds.), *Dynamic patterns in complex systems* (pp. 348–369). Singapore: World Scientific.

Thelen, E., & Fisher, D.M. (1982). Newborn stepping: An explanation for a "disappearing reflex." *Developmental Psychology*, **18**, 760–775.

Thelen, E., Kelso, J.A.S., & Fogel, A. (1987). Self-organizing systems in infant motor development. *Developmental Review*, **7**, 39–65.

Thelen, E., Skala, K.A., & Kelso, J.A.S. (1987). The dynamic nature of early coordination: Evidence from bilateral leg movements in young infants. *Developmental Psychology*, **23**, 179–186.

Thelen, E., & Smith, L.B. (1994). *A dynamical systems approach to the development of cognition and action*. Cambridge, MA: MIT Press.

Thelen, E., & Ulrich, B.D. (1991). Hidden skills: A dynamic systems analysis of treadmill stepping during the first year. *Monographs of the Society of Research in Child Development*, **56** (1, Serial No. 223).

Thelen, E., Ulrich, B.D., & Niles, D. (1987). Bilateral coordination in human infants: Stepping on a split-belt treadmill. *Journal of Experimental Psychology: Human Perception and Performance*, **13**, 405–410.

Thomas, J.R. (1980). Acquisition of motor skills: Information processing differences between children and adults. *Research Quarterly for Exercise and Sport*, **51**, 158–173.

Thomas, J.R. (Ed.) (1984). *Motor development during childhood and adolescence*. Minneapolis: Burgess.

Thomas, J.R. (1987). Are we already in pieces, or just falling apart? *Quest*, **39**, 114–121.

Thomas, J.R. (1990). The body of knowledge: A common core. In C.B. Corbin & H.M. Eckert (Eds.), *The evolving undergraduate major: American Academy of Physical Education Papers* (no. 23) (pp. 5–12). Champaign, IL: Human Kinetics.

Thomas, J.R. (1992). Autobiography. In C.W. Snyder, Jr. & B. Abernethy (Eds.), *The creative side of experimentation: Personal perspectives from leading researchers in motor control, motor development, and sport psychology* (pp. 135–147). Champaign, IL: Human Kinetics.

Thomas, J.R., & Bender, P.R. (1977). A developmental explanation for children's motor behavior: A neo-Piagetian interpretation. *Journal of Motor Behavior*, **9**, 81–93.

Thomas, J.R., & Chissom, B.S. (1972). Relationships as assessed by canonical correlation between perceptual-motor and intellectual abilities for pre-school and early elementary age children. *Journal of Motor Behavior*, **4**, 23–29.

Thomas, J.R., Chissom, B.S., Stewart, C., & Shelley, F. (1975). Effects of perceptual-motor training on pre-school children. *Research Quarterly*, **46**, 505–513.

Thomas, J.R., & French, K.E. (1985). Gender differences across age in motor performance: A meta-analysis. *Psychological Bulletin*, **98**, 260–282.

Thomas, J.R., Gallagher, J.D., & Purvis, G. (1981). Reaction time and anticipation time: Effects of development. *Research Quarterly for Exercise and Sport*, **52**, 359–367.

Thomas, J.R., & Halliwell, W. (1976). Individual differences in motor skill acquisition. *Journal of Motor Behavior*, **8**, 89–99.

Thomas, J.R., Landers, D.M., Salazar, W., & Etnier, J. (1994). Exercise and cognitive function. In C. Bouchard, R.J. Shephard, &. T. Stephens (Eds.), *Physical activity, fitness and health: 1992 proceedings*. Champaign, IL: Human Kinetics.

Thomas, J.R., & Marzke, M. (1992). The development of gender differences in throwing: Is human evolution a factor? In R. Christina & H. Eckert (Eds.), *The academy papers—enhancing human performance in sport* (pp. 60–76). Champaign, IL: Human Kinetics.

Thomas, J.R., Michael, D., & Gallagher, J.D. (1994). Effects of training on gender differences in overhand throwing: A brief quantitative literature analysis. *Research Quarterly for Exercise and Sport*, **65**.

Thomas, J.R., Mitchell, B., & Solmon, M.A. (1979). Precision knowledge of results and motor performance: Relationship to age. *Research Quarterly*, **50**, 687–698.

Thomas, J.R., & Nelson, J.K. (1990). *Research methods in physical activity* (2nd ed.). Champaign, IL: Human Kinetics.

Thomas, J.R., Nelson, J.K., & Church, G. (1991). A developmental analysis of gender differences in health related physical fitness. *Pediatric Exercise Science,* **3,** 28–42.

Thomas, J.R., & Thomas, K.T. (1986). The relation of movement and cognitive function. In V. Seefeldt (Ed.), *Physical activity & well-being* (pp. 443–452). Reston, VA: AAHPERD.

Thomas, J.R., & Thomas, K.T. (1988). Development of gender differences in physical activity. *Quest,* **40,** 219–229.

Thomas, J.R., & Thomas, K.T. (1989). What is motor development: Where does it belong? *Quest,* **41,** 203–212.

Thomas, J.R., Thomas, K.T., & Gallagher, J.D. (1993). Developmental considerations in skill acquisition. In R.N. Singer, M. Murphey, & L.K. Tennant (Eds.), *Handbook of research on sport psychology* (pp. 73–105). New York: Macmillan.

Thomas, J.R., Thomas, K.T., Lee, A.M., Testerman, E., & Ashy, M. (1983). Age differences in use of strategy for recall of movement in a large scale environment. *Research Quarterly for Exercise and Sport,* **54,** 264–272.

Thorndike, E.L. (1908). The effect of practice in the case of a purely intellectual function. *American Journal of Psychology,* **19,** 374–384.

Thorndike, E.L. (1927). The law of effect. *American Journal of Psychology,* **39,** 212–222.

Thorndike, E.L. (1932). *The fundamentals of learning.* New York: Teachers College Press.

Todor, J.I. (1979). Developmental differences in motor task integration: A test of Pascual-Leone's theory of constructive operators. *Journal of Experimental Child Psychology,* **28,** 314–322.

Tolman, E.C. (1932). *Purposive behavior in animals and men.* New York: Century.

Tsai, C. (1924). A comparative study of retention curves for motor habits. *Comparative Psychology Monographs,* **2,** No. 11.

Turvey, M.T. (1977). Preliminaries to a theory of action with reference to vision. In R. Shaw & J. Bransford (Eds.), *Perceiving, acting and knowing* (pp. 211–263). Hillsdale, NJ: Erlbaum.

Turvey, M.T., & Carello, C. (1986). The ecological approach to perceiving-acting: A pictorial essay. *Acta Psychologica,* **63,** 133–155.

Turvey, M.T., Fitch, H.L., & Tuller, B. (1982). The Berstein perspective: I. The problems of degrees of freedom and context conditioned variability. In J.A.S. Kelso (Ed.), *Human motor behavior: An introduction* (pp. 239–252). Hillsdale, NJ: Erlbaum.

Victors, E. (1961). *A cinematical analysis of catching behavior of a selected group of 7- and 9-year-old boys.* Unpublished doctoral dissertation, University of Wisconsin, Madison.

von Hofsten, C. (1979). Development of visually guided reaching: The approach phase. *Journal of Human Movement Studies, 5,* 150–178.

von Hofsten, C. (1980). Predictive reaching for moving objects by human infants. *Journal of Experimental Child Psychology, 30,* 369–392.

Wade, M.G. (1976). Developmental motor learning. In J. Keogh & R.S. Hutton (Eds.), *Exercise Science and Sport Reviews* (Vol. 4). Santa Barbara, Ca: Journal.

Wade, M.G. (1980). Coincidence anticipation of young normal and handicapped children. *Journal of Motor Behavior, 12,* 103–112.

Wade, M.G. (1982). Timing behavior in children. In J.A.S. Kelso & J.E. Clark (Eds.), *The development of movement control and co-ordination* (pp. 239–251). Chichester, England: Wiley.

Wallace, S.A., & Newell, K.M. (1983). Visual control of discrete aiming movements. *Quarterly Journal of Experimental Psychology, 35A,* 311–321.

Warner, A.P. (1952). *The motor ability of third, fourth, and fifth grade boys in the elementary school.* Unpublished doctoral dissertation, University of Michigan, Ann Arbor.

Weber, E. (1846). Muskelbewegung [Muscle movement]. In R. Wagner (Ed.), *Handworterbuch der Physiologie* (Vol. 3, Pt. 2, pp. 1–122). Braunschweig, Germany: Bieweg.

Weeks, D.L. (1992). A comparison of modeling modalities in the observational learning of an externally paced skill. *Research Quarterly for Exercise and Sport, 63,* 373–380.

Weiss, A.D. (1965). The locus of reaction time changes with set, motivation, and age. *Journal of Gerontology, 20,* 60–64.

Weiss, M.R. (1983). Modeling and motor performance: A developmental perspective. *Research Quarterly for Exercise and Sport, 54,* 190–197.

Weiss, M.R., Ebbeck, V., & Rose, D.J. (1992). "Show and tell" in the gymnasium revisited: Developmental differences in modeling and verbal rehearsal effects on motor skill learning and performance. *Research Quarterly for Exercise and Sport, 63,* 292–301.

Weiss, M.R., & Klint, K.A. (1987). "Show and tell" in the gymnasium: An investigation of developmental differences in modeling and verbal rehearsal of motor skills. *Research Quarterly for Exercise and Sport, 58,* 234–241.

Whipple, G.M. (1982). The transfer of training. *Yearbook of the National Society for the Study of Education, 27,* 179–209.

Whitall, J. (1989). A developmental study of the interlimb coordination in running and galloping. *Journal of Motor Behavior, 21,* 392–408.

Whitall, J. (1991). The developmental effect of concurrent cognitive and locomotor skills: Time-sharing from a dynamical perspective. *Journal of Experimental Child Psychology, 51,* 245–266.

Whitall, J., & Clark, J.E. (1991). The development of bipedal interlimb coordination. In S.P. Swinnen, H. Heuer, J. Massion, & P. Casaer

(Eds.), *Interlimb coordination: Neural, dynamical, and cognitive constraints.* New York: Academic Press.

Wickstrom, R. (1970). *Fundamental movement patterns.* Philadelphia: Lea & Febiger.

Wild, M. (1937). *The behavior pattern of throwing and some observations concerning its course of development in children.* Unpublished doctoral dissertation, University of Wisconsin, Madison.

Wild, M. (1938). The behavior pattern of throwing and some observations concerning its course of development in children. *Research Quarterly,* **9**, 20–24.

Williams, H. (1968). *The effects of systematic variation of speed and direction of object flight and of skill and age classifications upon visuo-perceptual judgments of moving objects in three-dimensional space.* Unpublished doctoral dissertation, University of Wisconsin, Madison.

Williams, H., Fisher, J., & Tritschler, K. (1983). Descriptive analysis of static postural control in 4, 6, and 8 year old normal and motorically awkward children. *American Journal of Physical Medicine,* **62**, 12–26.

Williams, H.G. (1983). *Perceptual and motor development.* Englewood Cliffs, NJ: Prentice Hall.

Williams, H.G., Temple, J., & Bateman, J. (1979). A test battery to assess intrasensory and intersensory development of young children. *Perceptual and Motor Skills,* **48**, 643–659.

Williams, I.D. (1974). Practice and augmentation in learning. *Human Factors,* **16**, 503–507.

Williams, K. (1980). The developmental characteristics of a forward roll. *Research Quarterly for Exercise and Sport,* **51**, 703–713.

Williams, K. (1985). Age differences on a coincident anticipation task: Influence of stereotypic or "preferred" movement speed. *Journal of Motor Behavior,* **17**, 389–410.

Williams, K. (1987). The temporal structure of the forward roll: Inter- and intra-limb coordination. *Human Movement Science,* **6**, 373–387.

Wilson, M. (1945). *Development of jumping skill in children.* Unpublished doctoral dissertation, University of Iowa, Iowa City.

Wing, A.M., Turton, A., & Fraseer, C. (1986). Grasp size and accuracy of approach in reaching. *Journal of Motor Behavior,* **18**, 245–260.

Winther, K.T., & Thomas, J.R. (1981). Developmental differences in children's labeling of movement. *Journal of Motor Behavior,* **13**, 77–90.

Woodworth, R.S. (1899). The accuracy of voluntary movement. *Psychological Review,* **3** (Suppl. 2).

Woodworth, R.S. (1903). *Le mouvement.* Paris: Doin.

Woodworth, R.S. (1938). *Experimental psychology,* New York: Holt Rinehart & Winston.

Woollacott, M., & Shumway-Cook, A. (Eds.) (1989). *Development of posture and gait across the lifespan.* Columbia: University of South Carolina Press.

Woollacott, M.H., Debu, B., & Mowatt, M. (1987). Neuromuscular control of posture in the infant and child: Is vision dominant? *Journal of Motor Behavior, 19,* 167–186.

Worringham, C.J., Stelmach, G.E., & Martin, Z.E. (1987). Limb segment inclination sense in proprioception. *Experimental Brain Research, 66,* 653–658.

Wrisberg, C.A., & Mead, B.J. (1981). Anticipation of coincidence in children: A test of schema theory. *Perceptual and Motor Skills, 52,* 599–606.

Wyrick, W., & Duncan, A. (1974). Electromyographical study of reflex, premotor, and simple reaction time of relaxed muscle to joint displacement. *Journal of Motor Behavior, 6,* 1–10.

Zelaznik, H.N., & Hahn, R. (1985). Reaction time methods in the study of motor programming: The precuing of hand, digit, and duration. *Journal of Motor Behavior, 17,* 190–218.

Zelaznik, H.N., Hawkins, B., & Kisselburgh, L. (1983). Rapid visual feedback processing in single-aiming movements. *Journal of Motor Behavior, 15,* 217–236.

Zelaznik, H.N., Schmidt, R.A., & Gielen, C.C.A.M. (1986). Kinematic properties of rapid aimed hand movements. *Journal of Motor Behavior, 18,* 353–372.

Zelaznik, H.N., Shapiro, D.C., & Newell, K.M. (1978). On the structure of motor recognition memory. *Journal of Motor Behavior, 10,* 313–323.

8

Sport and Exercise Psychology

Diane L. Gill
University of North Carolina at Greensboro

Interest in sport psychology is not new. Participants, the public, and the occasional scholar have been intrigued by the mental side of physical activities for some time. Still, the "disciplined" study of sport and exercise psychology emerged in the late 1960s as the overall field began to develop its disciplinary base. Like the scholars in the other subdisciplines, sport psychologists turned away from the traditional practice-oriented physical education and looked to scientific psychology as a model. Within 20 years, academic sport psychologists built a knowledge base and developed an identifiable subdiscipline with professional organizations, journals, and specialized graduate programs. In a typical text (Gill, 1986), sport psychology was described as the scientific study of human behavior in sport and exercise.

Over the last ten years sport psychologists have regained their interest in practice, and in 1995, an accurate definition must encompass the *art*, as well as the science, of exercise and sport psychology. Applied sport psychology has captured the interest of many sport psychologists and the general public. Moreover, both the art and science have moved beyond competitive sport to include the psychological parameters of health-oriented exercise and recreational sport activities.

Like the other subdisciplines, sport and exercise psychology emerged from physical education. In 1984 Wiggins (p. 10) noted, "It is apparent that the growth of sport psychology in both Canada and the United States has been the result of sustained efforts by physical educators." In 1995 his statement is questionable, and by 2005, it likely will be downright incorrect. Several of today's sport psychologists have come from the ranks of general psychology, lacking specific training in either sport and exercise psychology or physical education. For years sport psychologists were

---

▼

A Chronology of Sport and Exercise Psychology

Early Foundations: Precursors of Sport Psychology

<u>Year</u> <u>Event</u>

1898 Triplett's social psychology experiment—examining social influence (competition) on motor performance

1925 Athletic Research Lab established at the University of Illinois with Coleman R. Griffith as director

1949 Warren Johnson's study of pre-game emotion in football—a precursor to later competitive anxiety studies

Organization of the Subdiscipline

<u>Year</u> <u>Event</u>

1965 First International Society of Sport Psychology (ISSP) Congress, Rome

1967 North American Society for the Psychology of Sport and Physical Activity (NASPSPA) officially incorporated

1968 Second ISSP Congress held in Washington, DC

1970 *International Journal of Sport Psychology* begins publication

1973 NASPSPA holds its first independent conference, Allerton, IL

1979 *Journal of Sport Psychology* begins publication

Development: The Art and Science of Sport and Exercise Psychology

<u>Year</u> <u>Event</u>

1985 Association for the Advancement of Applied Sport Psychology (AAASP) formed

1986 AAASP holds its first conference, Jekyll Island, GA

1986 Division 47—Exercise and Sport Psychology becomes an official division of the American Psychological Association

1987 *The Sport Psychologist* begins publication

1989 AAASP approves certification criteria for title "Certified Consultant, AAASP"

---

trained and located in physical education or exercise and sport science departments. They borrowed theories and methods from general psychology, while psychologists ignored sport. Now, many psychologists look to sport as a setting for both research and practice; moreover, many of

Coleman Griffith

Rainer Martens

Bruce Ogilvie

Dan Landers

Tara Scanlan   Dan Gould

today's psychology students wish to pursue graduate work and become tomorrow's sport and exercise psychologists.

Today most sport and exercise psychology scholars identify with the larger discipline of exercise and sport science, and share an understanding of the field. With more people entering the field from psychology, counseling, or other backgrounds, and with increasing specialization within sport and exercise psychology (e.g., psychophysiological, social, applied), the common ground is elusive. These pressures present challenges and opportunities as today's sport and exercise psychologists continue to advance the study of the art and science of human behavior in sport and exercise.

Early Foundations: Precursors of Sport Psychology

Although sport and exercise psychology as a subdiscipline is relatively young, scholarly interest in sport psychology extends further into the past. As long as sport and exercise activities have been around, psychology has played a role. Throughout the history of psychology as a science, a few psychologists have applied their theories to sport and exercise and, as long as scholars have studied physical activity or exercise and sport science, some of those efforts have involved psychological issues.

Early Research: 1890–1920

Early organizations and research in the broader fields of both psychology and physical education developed around the turn of the century, and that early work includes evidence of sport psychology. In earlier histories of the field, both Wiggins (1984) and Ryan (1981) cited an early psychological study of football by G.T.W. Patrick (1903), and reported that G. Stanley Hall, founding president of the American Psychological Association, wrote: "Physical education is for the sake of mental and moral culture and not an end in itself. It is to make the intellect, feelings and will more vigorous, sane, supple, and resourceful" (Hall, 1908, pp. 1015–1016).

The most recognized early psychology research with implications for sport psychology is Norman Triplett's (1898) lab study of social influence and performance, widely cited as the first social psychology experiment. Triplett's work is a foundational benchmark for sport and exercise psychology because his experiment involved a physical task (winding fishing reels), and even more because his experiment was inspired by his observations of sport. Specifically, Triplett, a cycling enthusiast, observed that social influence (pacing machine, competition) seemed to motivate cyclists to better performance, and designed his experiment to test those observations.

Other researchers from both psychology and physical education (often aligned with physical training and medical schools) espoused psychological benefits of physical education and conducted isolated studies of sport psychology issues. George W. Fitz (1895) of Harvard, operating from what may be the first physical education research lab in North America, conducted experiments on the speed and accuracy of motor responses. Wiggins (1984) also cites turn-of-the-century work by William G. Anderson on mental practice; Walter Wells Davis's studies of transfer of training; Robert A. Cummins's investigation of the effects of basketball practice on motor reaction, attention, and suggestibility; and E.W. Scripture's study of character development and sport.

Coleman R. Griffith: 1920–1940

Clearly the first person to conduct systematic sport psychology research and practice, Coleman R. Griffith began his sport psychology work in 1918, as a doctoral student at the University of Illinois, with informal studies on psychological factors in basketball and football. Griffith's work caught the attention of George Huff, director of Physical Welfare for Men at Illinois, and Huff developed plans for an Athletics Research Lab, which was established by the board of trustees at Illinois in 1925 with Griffith as director. Griffith, a prolific researcher, focused on psychomotor skills, learning, and personality, and developed measures and procedures for that research. He taught sport psychology classes and published numerous research articles, as well as two classic texts, *Psychology of Coaching* (1926) and *Psychology and Athletics* (1928). As many current sport psychologists advocate, Griffith did not remain confined in his lab, but ventured into the field to make observations and interview athletes. For example, he used an interview with Red Grange after the 1924 Michigan-Illinois football game, in which Grange noted that he could not recall a single detail of his remarkable performance, to illustrate that top athletes perform skills automatically without thinking about them. Griffith also corresponded with Knute Rockne on the psychology of coaching and motivation. One quotation from that correspondence (Dec. 13, 1924, Rockne reply to Griffith) illustrates strategies of a successful coach, and counters some popular images:

> I do not make any effort to key them up, except on rare, exceptional occasions. I keyed them up for the Nebraska game this year, which was a mistake, as we had a reaction the following Saturday against Northwestern. I try to make our boys take the game less seriously than, I presume, some others do, and we try to make the spirit of the game one of exhilaration and we never allow hatred to enter into it, no matter against whom we are playing. (from the Coleman Griffith Collection, University Archives, University of Illinois at Urbana-Champaign)

When financial constraints closed the Athletics Research Lab in 1932, Griffith continued as a professor of educational psychology (and eventually Provost) at Illinois. Griffith did not totally abandon sport psychology. In 1938 he was hired as team sport psychologist for the Chicago Cubs by Philip Wrigley, and used psychological and research skills to test players and act much like psychological skills consultants today. Griffith always maintained his scientific perspective while recognizing the expertise of coaches and athletes. The concern he voiced in 1925 (pp. 193–194) still holds today:

> A great many people have the idea that the psychologist is a sort of magician who is ready, for a price, to sell his services to one individual or one group of men. Nothing could be further from the truth. Psychological facts are universal facts. They belong to whoever will read while he runs. There is another strange opinion about the psychologist. It is supposed that he is merely waiting until he can jump into an athletic field, tell the old-time successful coach that he is all wrong and begin, then, to expound his own magical and fanciful theories as to proper methods of coaching, the way to conquer overconfidence, the best forms of strategy, and so on. This, of course, is far from the truth, although certain things have appeared in the application of psychology to business and industry to lead to such an opinion.

During the last few years and at the present time, there have been and are many men, short in psychological training and long in the use of the English language, who are doing psychology damage by advertising that they are ready to answer any and every question that comes up in any and every field. No sane psychologist is deceived by these self-styled apostles of a new day. Coaches and athletes have a right to be wary of such stuff.

Griffith's prolific research, publications, and thoughtful insights place him among the most significant figures in the history of sport psychology, and he is widely described as the "father of sport psychology in North America." However, as Kroll and Lewis (1970) note, Griffith was a prophet without disciples, and "father" is really a misnomer. Sport psychology research and practice did not continue after Griffith's pioneering work. Parallel efforts in Germany by R.W. Schulte and in Russia by Peter Roudik and A.C. Puni continued there, but did not influence North America.

1940–1965

From Griffith's time through the late 1960s, when an identifiable sport psychology specialization emerged, sustained sport psychology programs were nonexistent. As Ryan (1981) noted, most physical education texts of the time had sections on psychological aspects, and many physical education objectives were psychological, but research was sporadic. C.H. McCloy (1930) of Iowa examined character-building through physical education, and Walter Miles (1928, 1931) of Stanford conducted studies of reaction time, but other work waited until the post-World War II extension of psychological research on learning and performance.

After World War II several schools developed motor behavior research programs that incorporated some current sport psychology topics. Arthur Slater-Hammel at Indiana, Alfred (Fritz) Hubbard at Illinois, John Lawther at Penn State, and most notably, Franklin Henry at Berkeley (the mentor for many PhDs who went on to shape several subdisciplines) developed research programs focusing on motor learning and performance. In his 1951 book, *The Psychology of Coaching,* Lawther extended his work into applied sport psychology issues as well as learning and performance principles. Warren Johnson's (1949) study of precontest emotion in football is a notable contribution of this time, and a precursor to later studies of competitive emotion.

In the 1960s more texts with psychology issues and information began to appear. Bryant Cratty published *Movement Behavior and Motor Learning* in 1964 and *Psychology and Physical Activity* in 1967; he continued as one of the most prolific sport psychology text authors for several years. In 1968 Robert Singer published the first edition of *Motor Learning and Human Performance,* a text that introduced many undergraduate and graduate physical education students to both motor learning and sport psychology. Bruce Ogilvie and Thomas Tutko published their controversial handbook, *Problem Athletes and How to Handle Them*, in 1966. Their clinical approach and the absence of a scientific framework or supporting evidence led to a cold reception from scholars who were trying to advance the scientific discipline. However, Ogilvie and Tutko's work was popular in the coaching community and foreshadowed similarly oriented applied sport psychology works in the 1980s.

Organization of the Subdiscipline

Sport and exercise psychologists began to organize a recognizable subdiscipline in the late 1960s when a number of individuals developed research programs, graduate courses, and, eventually, specialized organizations and publications. Among the first individuals who identified primarily with sport psychology were those cited in the preceding section, such as Slater-Hammel, Singer, and Cratty, as well as some beginning scholars, such as Rainer Martens, Dan Landers, and William Morgan.

NASPSPA

As these individuals developed sport psychology research lines and graduate programs to train a generation of sport psychology specialists, they began to organize, at first meeting in conjunction with the American Association of Health, Physical Education, and Recreation (AAHPER) (now American Alliance for Health, Physical Education, Recreation and Dance; AAHPERD). Soon they developed plans for a sport psychology organization, and the North American Society for the Psychology of Sport and Physical Activity (NASPSPA) was officially incorporated in 1967. John Loy, one of the early members, described the history of NASPSPA prior to its first independent meeting at Allerton, Illinois, in 1973, and his account is published in those proceedings (Loy, 1974). As Loy noted, a small group met at the Dallas AAHPER conference in 1965 to discuss the possibility of forming a sport psychology organization. Encouraged particularly by Warren Johnson, the group continued discussion at the First International Congress of Sport Psychology held in Rome later that year, and that encouraging meeting led to further discussion at the Chicago AAHPER meetings in 1966. In Chicago a steering committee was formed that agreed to host the 1968 Second International Congress in Washington, DC. The steering committee also began the organizational process and elected NASPSPA's first officers, Arthur Slater-Hammel as president along with vice-presidents Bryant Cratty and Warren Johnson, secretary-treasurer Roscoe Brown, and publication director Gerald Kenyon (see table 8.1 for a list of presidents of NASPSPA and other sport psychology organizations).

NASPSPA held its first meeting on March 8, 1967, at the AAHPER conference in Las Vegas. Along with a business meeting, the program included a scientific session of three papers: (1) "Kinesthetic After-Effects: The Phenomena and Their Implications" by E. Dean Ryan and Richard Nelson, (2) "A Psychologist Looks at the Science and Mythology of Sport" by Richard Bartols, and (3) "The Personality of the Athlete" by Bruce Ogilvie and Thomas Tutko. NASPSPA was officially incorporated on March 13, 1967, just after that meeting, and continued to meet in conjunction with the AAHPER conference until 1972. In two years, at the 1969 meeting in Boston, the business meeting included considerable discussion of possible alternatives for the cumbersome name—an issue that has continued to resurface every four to five years. Nevertheless, NASPSPA has passed 25 years without a consensus for change. The program also expanded greatly in just two years and included an invited lecture by Brian Sutton-Smith, "Games of Two Cultures," as well as eight research papers:

- "Social Reinforcement and Complex Motor Performance" by Glyn Roberts and Rainer Martens (Illinois)
- "Comparison Between the Motor Performance of the Jew and the White Non-Jew" by Menahem Less (Adelphi)
- "Eliminating Plausible Rival Hypotheses" by Rainer Martens (Illinois)
- "Effects of Verbal Suggestion on Muscular Performance: A Case Study" by Warren Johnson (Maryland)
- "The Cathartic Effect of Vigorous Motor Activity" by E. Dean Ryan (UC Davis)
- "Social Facilitation of a Muscular Endurance Task" by Rainer Martens and Daniel Landers (Illinois)
- "Bob Beamon's Collapse at Mexico City" by Ernst Jokl (Kentucky)
- "Pre-match Anxiety in a Group of College Wrestlers" by William Morgan (Missouri)

At the 1972 meeting NASPSPA members took a major step and decided to hold the annual meeting separate from other organizations. As NASPSPA President E. Dean Ryan (1972, p. 1) stated:

It is hoped that the new format will make it possible for the NASPSPA to be the primary meeting for new research and ideas in the area of psychology as it relate[s] to sport and physical activity. This new format should encourage and permit more intimate and intensive academic interchange by the participants, more extensive discussion of theoretical issues, and coordination of research efforts by the membership so we may have fewer "piles of bricks" but more permanent and meaningful structures.

Table 8.1   Presidents of Major Sport Psychology Organizations

Year	NASPSPA	AAASP	ISSP
1965-66			Ferruccio Antonelli
1966-67			
1967-68	Arthur Slater-Hammel		
1968-69			
1969-70	Bryant Cratty		
1970-71			
1971-72	E. Dean Ryan		
1972-73			
1973-74	Rainer Martens		Miroslav Vanek
1974-75	Dorothy Harris		
1975-76	Don Kirkendall		
1976-77	Waneen Spirduso		
1977-78	Richard Schmidt		
1978-79	Harriet Williams		
1979-80	Robert Christina		
1980-81	Ronald Marteniuk		
1981-82	Tara Scanlan		
1982-83	Glyn Roberts		
1983-84	Robert Schutz		
1984-85	Richard Magill		
1985-86	Daniel Landers	John Silva	Robert Singer
1986-87	Mary Ann Roberton		
1987-88	Michael Wade	Ronald Smith	
1988-89	Craig Wrisberg	Robert Weinberg	
1989-90	Diane Gill	Daniel Gould	
1990-91	Jerry Thomas	Lawrence Brawley	
1991-92	Gil Reeve	Michael Sachs	
1992-93	Jane Clark	Charles Hardy	
1993-94	Robert Weinberg	Jean Williams	Denis Glencross
1994-95	Karl Newell	Tara Scanlan	
1995-96	Steve Wallace	Penny McCullagh	

Rainer Martens and colleagues at the University of Illinois hosted the first independent meeting of NASPSPA May 14–16, 1973, at Allerton Park, IL. The Allerton meeting set the format that NASPSPA still follows. The meetings extended over several days, included major invited addresses as well as submitted research papers, and the special setting encouraged discussion before, during, and after sessions. Major addresses were presented in motor learning, social psychology of physical activity, and motor development. The presenters at Allerton included several recognizable motor behavior and sport psychology scholars (many just beginning in the field), such as Richard Schmidt, George Stelmach, Karl Newell, Ann

Gentile, Robert Singer, Glyn Roberts, Rainer Martens, Dorothy Harris, Dan Landers, Tara Scanlan, George Sage, Frank Smoll, and Harriet Williams. The proceedings of that conference were published (Wade & Martens, 1974), marking the start of Human Kinetics Publishers as well as a milestone for sport and exercise psychology. In 1974, NASPSPA again held its meeting with the AAHPERD conference in Anaheim, California, but every year since 1975 NASPSPA has held separate meetings. NASPSPA continued to be the major organizational force in sport and exercise psychology through the 1970s and 1980s; most active researchers and their graduate students joined, the conference drew high quality submissions, and the proceedings included some of the best work in the field.

The NASPSPA organization reflected the overlapping of sport psychology and motor behavior of the 1960s and 1970s. Many of the early sport psychology specialists branched out from motor learning, and NASPSPA included subareas of motor learning, motor development, and social psychology of physical activity (now the sport psychology area). Those three sub-areas remain in NASPSPA, although each has changed and grown more specialized since NASPSPA's foundation.

International Organization

Although NASPSPA clearly was the first and most prominent organization in the development of sport and exercise psychology in North America, international sport psychology also influenced the emerging subdiscipline. In 1965 the International Congress of Sport Psychology in Rome marked the beginning of the International Society of Sport Psychology (ISSP). Miroslav Vanek (1993), a key figure in international sport psychology, reflecting on the development of ISSP, noted that the use of psychology in sport was stimulated in the 1950s by the sovietization of top-level sport. Thus, international sport psychology traditionally has aligned more with performance enhancement of elite athletes (and has a clearer applied psychology foundation) than the more sport and exercise science-oriented discipline in North America. This orientation is reflected in Vanek's citation of a sport psychology session (keynotes by Vanek, Kane, Matsuda) at the 1964 Olympic Congress in Tokyo as a key initial international meeting.

Several sport psychologists from Europe and the Soviet Union were instrumental in forming an international society, including Paul Kunath (East Germany), Peter Roudik (Russia), Miroslav Vanek (Czechoslovakia), Morgan Olsen (Norway), and John Kane (England). However, Ferruccio Antonelli (Italy), founding president of ISSP and organizer of the first International Congress of Sport Psychology in Rome, was the primary organizing force. Antonelli met with Michel Bouet (France) and Jose Cagigal and Jose Ferrer-Hombravella (Spain) at the 1963 Sports Medicine

Congress in Barcelona and decided to hold the first international congress in Rome in 1965. That 1965 meeting included 34 U.S. delegates along with individuals from 16 countries, mainly in Europe (Cratty, 1989). Over a hundred papers were presented, and international scholars became acquainted with one another; this meeting was particularly inspiring to the North Americans, who returned to form NASPSPA. As noted in the previous section, the second international congress was held in Washington, DC, in 1968, cosponsored by NASPSPA and AAHPER. The 878-page proceedings of that congress (Kenyon & Grogg, 1970) includes papers by most of the sport psychology scholars mentioned in this section, and provides a nice overview of the emerging subdiscipline at that time. The international congress has continued to expand and meet every four years since then.

In contrast to North American societies, the international society has been dominated by strong personalities rather than rotating officers. Antonelli, founding president, remained in that role for several years, and in 1970 founded and became editor of the *International Journal of Sport Psychology*, the first sport psychology research journal. At the 1973 congress Vanek was elected as president of ISSP and he continued in that role for three four-year terms. The 1985 congress decided to limit the president to two terms, and Robert Singer of the United States was elected president. Denis Glencross (Australia) was elected president at the 1993 congress.

ISSP not only played a key role in the development of NASPSPA, but also inspired sport psychology organizations in Europe and Canada. The European sport psychology organization, FEPSAC, formed in 1968 and continues as an active international force. Although NASPSPA has had a strong Canadian presence from its initial foundation, and several conferences have been held in Canada, a separate Canadian organization formed and developed in parallel with NASPSPA. Following the 1968 international congress, Bob Wilberg (Alberta) was instrumental in founding the Canadian Society for Psychomotor Learning and Sport Psychology (CSPLSP; now using the French acronym SCAPPS for Societe Canadienne d'Apprentissage Psychomoteur et Psychologie du Sport) in 1969 under the auspices of the Canadian Association for Health, Physical Education, and Recreation. SCAPPS became an independent society in 1977 and, like NASPSPA, holds an annual conference.

Publications

Before organization of the subdiscipline, specialized publications were not needed. Isolated psychology studies related to sports appeared in a variety of psychology journals, but none were really considered sport psychology research at that time. The major research journal used by physical education scholars for sport psychology work was the *Research Quarterly (RQ)*, later renamed *Research Quarterly for Exercise & Sport (RQES)*. The primary research publication of AAHPERD since its foundation in 1930, *RQES* continues to publish sport and exercise psychology research, along with other exercise and sport science work. As research expanded in the late 1960s and 1970s, however, sport psychologists developed specialized publications.

With NASPSPA's annual conference stimulating research activity, sport psychologists sought additional publishing outlets. The *International Journal of Sport Psychology*, which began publishing as the first sport psychology research journal in 1970, never served as the primary source or outlet for North American sport psychology scholars. The *Journal of Motor Behavior (JMB)* began publishing in 1969, and motor behavior scholars of NASPSPA found in it a respected outlet for their research. In the late 1960s and early 1970s *JMB* also included some sport psychology research related to social psychology, such as research on social influence and motor performance. However, as sport psychology diverged from motor behavior into a separate subdiscipline with differing issues, perspectives, and approaches, scholars sought specialized publications.

The most important publication outlet for sport psychology research during the early years was the NASPSPA proceedings, which included the most current research by leading scholars as well as invited addresses on important topics. As noted earlier, proceedings of the 1973 Allerton conference were published (Wade & Martens, 1974) by Human Kinetics Publishers under the title *Psychology of Motor Behavior and Sport*. Proceedings of the 1975 conference hosted by The Pennsylvania State University were published by The Pennsylvania State University Press as *Psychology of Sport and Motor Behavior II*, edited by conference organizers Dan Landers, Dorothy Harris, and Robert Christina (1975). From 1976 to 1980 the conference proceedings were published by Human Kinetics Publishers as *Psychology of Motor Behavior and Sport*. These proceedings did not include all submitted papers, but only papers evaluated favorably by reviewers and selected by the editors. Thus, from 1976 to 1980, *Psychology of Motor Behavior and Sport* was the primary refereed sport psychology publication in North America. At the 1980 executive meeting NASPSPA decided such a publication was no longer needed. The 1980 *Psychology of Motor Behavior and Sport* (Roberts & Landers, 1981) included full texts of major addresses but only abstracts of submitted papers, and all subsequent proceedings consisted of abstracts available at the conference.

One major reason for discontinuing full papers was the 1979 appearance of the *Journal of Sport Psychology (JSP)*. Just as *JMB* served as a publication outlet for the best motor behavior research, *JSP* became available as an outlet for the best sport psychology research. *JSP*, the first journal venture for Human Kinetics Publishers, emerged from NASPSPA, particularly through the work of Rainer Martens and Dan Landers. As Landers (1979, p. 2) noted in his opening editorial statement,

> The inauguration of *JSP* comes with a great sense of accomplishment in satisfying the longstanding need for a specialized sport psychology publication that has a rigorous review process. It is anticipated that *JSP* will provide an outlet for sport psychology information in North America and also internationally. . . . *JSP*'s purpose is to facilitate communication about all facets of sport psychology by publishing original research, major reviews, and theoretical papers.

Indeed, *JSP* (*Journal of Sport & Exercise Psychology*, *JSEP*, since 1988) has served that purpose well. Through Dan Landers' seven-year term, and the subsequent editorial terms of Diane Gill (1985–1990), Jack Rejeski (1991–1994), and current editor Thelma Horn, *JSEP* has been recognized as the leading publication outlet for sport and exercise psychology research (see table 8.2 for list of journals and editors).

Development: The Art and Science of Sport and Exercise Psychology

The emergence and early organization of the sport psychology subdiscipline paralleled the development of NASPSPA. Starting in the late 1960s, sport psychology scholars developed their own research base separate from but related to motor behavior, established graduate programs, held

Table 8.2 Major Sport Psychology Journals, Publication Years, and Editors

Journal title	Years	Editor
International Journal of Sport Psychology	1970-1989	Ferruccio Antonelli
	1989-present	Alberto Cei & John Salmela
Journal of Sport Psychology (became *Journal of Sport and Exercise Psychology*, 1988)	1979-1985	Daniel M. Landers
	1986-1990	Diane L. Gill
	1990-1994	W. Jack Rejeski
	1995-present	Thelma Horn
The Sport Psychologist	1987-1991	Daniel Gould & Glyn C. Roberts
	1992-1995	Robin S. Vealey
	1996-present	Graham Jones
Journal of Applied Sport Psychology	1989-1991	John M. Silva
	1992-1995	Joan L. Duda
	1996-present	Albert V. Carron

successful annual conferences to share research and ideas, developed a respected research journal, and gradually became the largest and most diverse of the three areas within NASPSPA. Some sociology of sport scholars, such as Gerald Kenyon and John Loy, contributed to the early social psychology emphasis, but during the first ten years sport psychologists closely aligned with motor behavior and looked to experimental psychology theories and research models for guidance.

Rainer Martens's (1975) text, *Social Psychology and Physical Activity*, reflects the content and orientation of those years. Major psychological theories (e.g., inverted-U hypothesis, Zajonc's social facilitation theory, Atkinson's achievement motivation theory) framed the content. Most supporting research was from psychology, and the sport psychology work that was cited seldom involved *sport*, but more likely involved experimental tests of psychology theory predictions with laboratory motor tasks such as the rotary pursuit and stabilometer.

By the mid-1980s, ten years after the exciting Allerton conference, sport psychology had indeed grown as promised, but also changed directions. While motor behavior scholars continued to emphasize psychological theories and experimental research, sport psychologists took a different path and moved to more applied issues and approaches. Martens, who ten years earlier was the prototype of an experimental social psychologist, was a leading advocate for change. His 1979 article in the second issue of *JSP*, which had been presented as "From Smocks to Jocks" at the 1978 CPMLSP conference in Toronto, prompted many sport psychologists to turn to more applied research and practical concerns. Martens observed that ten years of sport psychology research, while often theory-based and methodologically sound, told us little about sport behavior. Indeed, most of the research did not involve sport at all, but laboratory tasks that were too far removed from sport to help teachers, coaches, and participants. Martens called for more research in the field, on relevant issues, and with attention to the development of *sport-specific* conceptual models and measures.

Martens's own work on competitive anxiety (Martens, 1977) illustrated that approach. Martens developed a conceptual framework, combining the psychology models of Spielberger and McGrath with his own competition model; defined sport-specific constructs; developed psychometrically sound, sport-specific measures; and conducted systematic research in varied field settings. Martens's competitive anxiety work served as a model for subsequent sport-specific research and measures such as Gill's competitive orientation work (Gill, 1993; Gill & Deeter, 1988); Carron, Widmeyer, and Brawley's (1985) group cohesion work; and Martens's continuing work on competitive anxiety (Martens, Vealey, & Burton, 1990).

Although some continued to emphasize theory-driven, controlled experimental research, many sport psychology scholars pursued applied issues with sport participants. One notable example of this research approach is the work on youth sport coaching by Ron Smith and Frank Smoll of the University of Washington. Smith and Smoll began their work in the late 1970s, took a practical issue (effective coaching in youth sports), conducted systematic observation and field research, developed sport-specific measures and approaches, and eventually developed coach education programs to put their research into practice (e.g., Smith, Smoll, & Curtis, 1979; Smoll & Smith, 1984, 1993). Notably, this research also involved collaboration of an established psychologist (Smith) with a sport and exercise science scholar (Smoll).

Through the 1980s field research and applied issues moved to the forefront of sport psychology. Applied issues also captured the attention of students and the public, making more people aware of the field and bringing more people into the field. Most sport psychology researchers made at least some moves in more applied directions. A few took bigger steps and moved away from research to focus on application of sport psychology in work with athletes. Before 1980, the main application of sport psychology was in physical education, but with the 1980s, application came to imply psychological skills training with elite competitive athletes. This applied focus caught the attention of some psychologists who began to see sport and athletics as a setting for clinical and counseling work.

With more diverse students and psychologists participating in sport psychology organizations and activities, the original NASPSPA structure no longer fit all interests. In particular, many sport psychologists wanted more discussion of applied issues, such as anxiety management techniques or certification of sport psychologists, as well as research information. NASPSPA did not respond to those interests, and in an eventful 1984 business meeting, a spirited discussion was held on the possibility of expanding into such professional issues. In a subsequent mail ballot, the membership voted 2 to 1 to follow the executive committee's recommendation to *not* incorporate professional issues at the conference.

That 1984 decision prompted many of NASPSPA's sport psychologists to consider separate organizations and publications to accommodate applied interests and activities. John Silva was instrumental in calling an organizational meeting at the 1985 NASPSPA conference. An executive board was formed, which then held an organizational meeting at Nags Head, NC, in October 1985, thus marking the beginning of the Association for the Advancement of Applied Sport Psychology (AAASP). At Nags Head the executive board developed plans for AAASP's first conference, as well as AAASP's structure and guidelines. As summarized in the first issue of *AAASP Newsletter* (Winter, 1986):

The purpose of AAASP is to promote the development of psychological theory, research and intervention strategies in sport psychology.

AAASP provides a forum for individuals who are interested in research, theory development, and the application of psychological principles in sport and exercise. AAASP is also concerned with ethical and professional issues relating to the development of sport psychology and to the provision of psychological services in sport and exercise settings. In order to accomplish these goals AAASP incorporates information and expertise from the fields of exercise and sport science and psychology. The Association is comprised of three interrelated sections: intervention/performance enhancement, social psychology, and health psychology.

John Silva became AAASP's first president, and AAASP held its first conference at Jekyll Island, GA, October 9–12, 1986, with James Blumenthal (health), Don Meichenbaum (intervention), Rainer Martens (social), and Bonnie Strickland (Coleman R. Griffith Memorial Lecture) giving invited addresses. That first successful conference got AAASP off to a strong start; AAASP continues to hold an annual conference and maintains the basic structure set in 1985 (see Table 8.1 for list of AAASP presidents). Intervention is the largest interest area within AAASP, but conference sessions, including workshops and colloquia as well as research papers, are also held in social psychology and health psychology, and most AAASP members attend sessions and have interests across all three areas.

Martens's address at that first AAASP conference, like his "smocks and jocks" paper eight years earlier, advocated major changes in sport psychology research and practice, and presented a challenge that many sport psychologists have accepted. Martens criticized sport psychology's unjustified reliance on orthodox science as the primary source of knowledge. Instead, he encouraged sport psychologists to accept more diverse sources of knowledge, and to consider alternative approaches to science, such as idiographic and introspective methods, so that sport psychology might develop truly useful knowledge.

Martens's paper prompted many sport psychology scholars to consider alternative research strategies. One highly regarded scholar, Tara Scanlan, incorporated alternative methods in a typically well planned and carefully conducted research program. A series of articles by Scanlan and her colleagues (e.g., Scanlan, Ravizza, & Stein, 1989; Scanlan, Stein, & Ravizza, 1989) on their in-depth studies of enjoyment and stress in figure skaters provided a model of sound research for other sport psychologists wishing to use alternative methodologies. Martens's (1987b) widely cited paper was published in the inaugural issue of *The Sport Psychologist* (*TSP*). Martens, in consultation with other sport psychologists, developed *TSP* to focus on the emerging applied sport psychology literature and to be complementary to the successful *JSEP*. As the editorial statement of *TSP* (Martens, 1987c, ii) states:

The Sport Psychologist (*TSP*) is published for educational sport psychologists (those who teach psychological skills to coaches and athletes) and for clinical sport psychologists (those who provide clinical services to athletes and coaches with psychological dysfunctions). The journal is also intended for those who teach sport psychology in academic institutions, and for coaches who have training in sport psychology. *TSP* focuses on the professional interests of sport psychologists as these pertain to the delivery of psychological services to coaches and athletes. It is international in scope, receptive to nonscientific methodologies, and refereed.

In his opening publisher's statement in that first issue, Martens noted that *TSP* was both an applied research journal and an interpretive journal, and specifically called for applied research using less traditional methods, offering a publication outlet for the alternative approaches he called for in his paper. *TSP* was endorsed by ISSP, and Dan Gould and Glyn Roberts served as founding coeditors from 1987 to 1991. Gould and Roberts echoed Martens's calls in their opening editorial comment, and they successfully guided *TSP* through its initial years.

With *TSP* focusing on applied research and professional issues, *JSP* received fewer of those submissions, and focused on strong sport psychology research. In 1988, *JSP* added "exercise" to the title (becoming *JSEP*) and more explicitly sought research on health-oriented exercise as well as sport. *JSEP* and *TSP* continue to serve as strong complementary journals. Each makes important contributions to the knowledge base, and most sport and exercise psychologists value both sources of information.

Although *TSP* met many needs for a more applied journal, AAASP also started its own journal, the *Journal of Applied Sport Psychology* (*JASP*), in 1989 with John Silva as editor. *JASP* serves many of the same purposes as *TSP*, and gives applied researchers another outlet. *JASP* also provides AAASP information, publishes major addresses from the conference, and has developed informative theme issues to add to the literature.

The foundation and rapid rise to prominence of AAASP and *TSP* are the most visible indicators of applied sport psychology growth in the 1980s, but some other organizations also added to this movement. As alluded to earlier, several individuals who were trained in traditional psychology programs moved into sport psychology during this time (a very few, such as Ron Smith, had been active sport psychology researchers earlier and remained active), and sport psychology began to appear in psychology literature and conferences. A few psychologists had done isolated applied sport psychology work earlier. Most notably Bruce Ogilvie, whose earlier applied work was not accepted in sport and exercise science in the 1960s, was recognized for those pioneering efforts when applied sport psychology organized in the 1980s. Ogilvie has presented at AAASP and ISSP conferences, published in applied journals, and generally offered his clinical experience and perspective to applied sport psychology organizations and individuals. As a lead-in to a conversation with Bruce Ogilvie in the second *AAASP Newsletter* (Spring, 1986), Straub noted:

> Dr. Bruce Ogilvie, professor emeritus, San Jose State University, is often referred to as the "Father of Applied Sport Psychology." His early work in the 1950s and 1960s paved the way for the current interest in sport psychology. Professor Ogilvie earned his doctoral degree in clinical psychology from the University of London. During his long and distinguished career, he authored many articles and books, worked for college, university, and professional teams. His humanistic style and crisis intervention methods have been emulated by many sport psychologists.

Later in that same conversation, after describing the sport psychology literature, experiences, and individuals that influenced his approach, Ogilvie added:

> As a final comment, I must make reference to trust I have in my clinical intuitions that sometimes defy empirical validation. After testing and consulting with thousands of competitors, things sometimes come together that go beyond your hard data and interview information.

Ogilvie's clinical perspective was a new approach for sport psychology, and through the 1980s more clinically trained psychologists entered sport psychology. The early work of Richard Suinn, a respected clinical psychologist and active member of the American Psychological Association (APA), should also be noted. Suinn's work with Olympic skiers did a great deal to bring sport psychology to public attention. Moreover, he participated in sport psychology organizations, published articles and chapters on his work (e.g., Suinn, 1980), and, as an active APA member, helped sport psychology gain a place in that organization.

Suinn and other psychologists, such as Steve Heyman, helped organize a sport psychology presence within APA, but William Morgan was the most influential person in that movement. After starting as an interest group, Division 47—Exercise and Sport Psychology—became a formal division of APA in 1986. Division 47 brought sport and exercise psychology to the attention of many psychologists otherwise unaware of the field, and also drew some sport and exercise science scholars into that major psychology organization. The first four Division 47 presidents (William Morgan, 1986–1988; Dan Landers, 1988–1990; Steve Heyman, 1990–1992; Dan Kirschenbaum, 1992–1994) include two trained in sport and exercise science and two in clinical psychology. The membership and conference program of Division 47 reflects a similar mix of psychology with sport and exercise science, and includes basic research on sport and exercise behavior as well as more applied and clinical issues.

NASPSPA, AAASP, and Division 47 of APA are the primary sport and exercise psychology organizations, but sport psychology also has a presence in some other exercise and sport science organizations. AAHPERD, which was the site of the initial organization of the discipline, includes a Sport Psychology Academy; many sport psychology scholars, especially those with interests in applications to physical education teaching and coaching, participate in that organization. The American College of Sports Medicine (ACSM), a large and powerful organization dominated by exercise physiology and sports medicine, has expanded its sport psychology constituency and accommodated more sport and exercise psychology scholars and presentations in recent years.

Suinn's early work with skiers in the 1976 Olympics helped the U.S. Olympic Committee (USOC) recognize the potential role of sport psychology. Several other sport psychologists began to work with teams, and in 1983 the USOC established an official sport psychology committee and a registry with three categories of clinical, educational, and research sport psychology. The first systematic assignments were made with the Elite Athlete Project for the 1984 games and the matching of 11 sport psychologists to teams: Bruce Ogilvie (volleyball), Jerry May (alpine skiing), Dan Landers (archery and shooting), John Adderson (boxing), Andrew Jacobs (cycling), Herbert Fensterheim (fencing), Rainer Martens (Nordic skiing), Richard Suinn (women's track and field), Betty Wenz (synchronized swimming), Robert Nideffer (men's track and field), and Michael Mahoney (weight lifting) (Singer, 1992). Other sport psychologists have worked with athletes, coaches, and training programs through the USOC since then, and most notably, in January 1987, the USOC hired Shane Murphy as its first permanent full-time sport psychologist to work at the training center in Colorado Springs.

The highly visible sport psychology presence in the Olympics, and the individual efforts of several psychologists and sport psychology consultants who worked with elite athletes in universities, on professional teams, and in private settings, raised new professional issues for sport and exercise psychology. Conversation at conferences and in graduate student offices abounded with questions such as: Who is a sport psychologist? What training do I need to become a sport psychologist? Must sport psychologists be licensed clinical psychologists? What is the role of the sport psychologist working with athletes, and where does that role cross the role of the coach or the clinician? Such conversations, and often heated debates, were especially prominent at AAASP meetings, and AAASP officers and members expended considerable effort over several years attempting to define and set standards for appropriate sport psychology practice. At the 1989 conference, fellows of AAASP approved the criteria for certification, and in 1991 AAASP began to confer the title "Certified Consultant, AAASP" on qualified candidates. AAASP's certified consultants are *not* licensed psychologists, and the consultant's role is defined as an educational role emphasizing psychological skill training. Although the AAASP certification criteria provide some guidelines, the issues are by no means resolved. Multiple viewpoints are expressed in meetings and publications, and the debates continue.

As applied sport psychology organized and caught the attention of students and the public, applied courses and psychological skills training workshops developed, creating a market for more literature. Few sport psychology texts existed before the 1980s. Cratty's books were widely used, Martens's 1975 *Social Psychology and Physical Activity* served its purpose, and in the mid-1980s Gill (1986) wrote *Psychological Dynamics of Sport* to fit the needs of undergraduate and graduate sport psychology courses. By the late 1980s, however, the market for sport psychology literature extended beyond physical education and graduate sport psychology programs, and many books appeared with an applied focus. Several appeared in the more popular literature with no evidence of sport psychology research or a knowledge base. Applied sport psychology books that *do* reflect knowledge of the field include Robert Nideffer's (1976) *The Inner Athlete* and (1985) *Athlete's Guide to Mental Training*, Dorothy Harris and Bette Harris's (1984) *The Athlete's Guide to Sport Psychology*, Terry Orlick's (1980) *In Pursuit of Excellence* (now 2nd ed., 1990) and (1986) *Psyching for Sport*, Rainer Martens's (1987a) *Coaches Guide to Sport Psychology*, and Jean Williams's (1986) excellent volume *Applied Sport Psychology* (now 2nd ed., 1993), which includes chapters by top applied sport psychologists (e.g., Dan Gould, Robin Vealey, Robert Weinberg, Robert Rotella, Ken Ravizza, and several others mentioned in this section).

Sport and exercise psychology organizations and journals developed because the specialization flourished within exercise and sport science departments. Many of the scholars who organized the discipline in the 1960s and 1970s (e.g., Landers, Martens, Morgan, Singer) developed courses and began specialized graduate programs to train the next generation of sport and exercise psychologists. Sport and exercise psychology grew rapidly through the 1970s and 1980s to become one of the most popular graduate specializations. Today most major PhD programs in exercise and sport science offer a sport and exercise psychology specialization. Undergraduate programs often include a hands-on psychological skills course, as well as a core course based on sport and exercise psychology theory and research. The general core or survey courses at both the graduate and undergraduate levels continue to include the major topics introduced in the early courses, such as personality and individual differences, motivation, stress and anxiety, aggression and moral development, social influence and group dynamics. Specialized graduate programs have expanded greatly and diversified far beyond the survey courses of the early years. Graduate scholars often offer advanced seminars on social, developmental, or psychophysiological sport and exercise psychology, as well as both research and practice-oriented applied courses and supervised experiences.

Interestingly, psychology departments have not incorporated sport and exercise psychology courses at either the undergraduate or graduate level. Many psychologists have moved into sport and exercise settings for research and practice, but the development of the disciplinary knowledge base remains the task of the sport and exercise psychology specialists in exercise and sport science programs.

Summary: A Century of Sport and Exercise Psychology History

The preceding sections reviewed 100 years of events and trends in the development of sport and exercise psychology. The formation of the subdiscipline was preceded by 70 years of isolated studies that retrospectively can be labeled sport psychology. One brief period of identifiable sport psychology work, from 1925 to 1932, punctuated this period when Coleman Griffith conducted his remarkable sport psychology research, writing, and practice. But sport and exercise psychology did not emerge as a subdiscipline until the late 1960s when several scholars with sport psychology interests initiated research meetings and formal organizations. During the next ten years graduate programs and research expanded, creating a knowledge base as well as specialized organizations and publications. During the 1980s the subdiscipline turned toward applied research and practice.

Sport and exercise psychology in the 1990s is much different from the discipline that emerged in the 1960s. The young discipline remained aligned with motor learning and performance, and relied heavily on experimental social psychology theories and research models in the early stages. Sport psychology made a strong move to sport-relevance about ten years later, as research moved to the field and scholars developed sport-specific models and measures to build a more relevant psychology of sport and exercise behavior. Shortly thereafter, with an influx of individuals from psychology and with more direct applied concerns, sport psychologists began to apply information more directly in education and consulting work.

Present and Future

As applied interests continue to expand, academic and research interests also are expanding and changing. Sport and exercise psychologists have responded to the public concern for health and fitness with increased research on health-oriented exercise. Healthy, active lifestyles and preventive or rehabilitative exercise programs involve behaviors, and today's exercise instructors and health professionals recognize the value of the psychological component of exercise and sport science.

Although sport and exercise psychology is not an especially large subdiscipline (e.g., compared to exercise physiology), it is incredibly diverse in both research and practice. Some researchers emphasize theory-based basic research with tight controls, and search for underlying physiological mechanisms; others shun traditional research, using interpretive approaches and searching for experiential knowledge. Some are not concerned with research at all, but seek information on strategies and techniques to educate, consult, or clinically treat sport and exercise participants.

The expansion of sport and exercise psychology organizations and professional journals, each with its own orientation, reflects this diversity. The most visible scholars maintain ties with all major organizations and are familiar with the varied publications. However, keeping up with all developments across the field, attending all conferences, and obtaining all literature is no longer possible for most professionals. Moreover, many sport and exercise psychologists, especially younger professionals just starting in the field, do not have strong ties to all organizations and activities, but align primarily with one aspect of the field and perhaps with other disciplines (e.g., applied sport psychologists associated with clinical psychology, or exercise psychologists aligned with sports medicine or health psychology).

Most likely both the research and practice sides of sport and exercise psychology will remain strong and continue to grow and change in the immediate future. The main question is whether these two sides of the field will grow together or apart. As Martens (1987b) suggested, scholars must conduct sound research, but that research must be relevant and aimed at answering questions about sport and exercise behavior. Sport and exercise psychology practitioners must have a grounding in the research and theory base, including knowledge of the science and the art, but must also incorporate their experiential knowledge as well as listen to participants to help develop and use the knowledge base. Researchers and practitioners, sport and exercise psychologists, physical educators and psychologists, sport psychologists and sport participants, must value the knowledge and skills of each other if, as Martens (1987b) advocated, we once again will have one sport psychology.

Issues related to research and practice or alternative research approaches have profound implications for the subdiscipline, but such debates are not likely to affect the relationship of sport and exercise psychology to the discipline of exercise and sport science. Similar controversies are prominent in other specializations, and the overall discipline accommodates varied options. For example, alternative research approaches in sport and exercise psychology take cues from sociocultural sport studies, and controlled research studies of underlying mechanisms have models in exercise physiology. Professional issues also have counterparts in other applied areas (e.g., athletic training, teacher education). Indeed, sport and exercise psychology likely will develop more alternatives and richer discussion by considering and debating controversial issues within the context of the larger discipline. At the same time, some forces threaten to pull the subdiscipline, or parts of the subdiscipline, away from exercise and sport science.

The areas of the subdiscipline most likely to pull away from exercise and sport science are related to applied sport psychology, and more specifically to professional sport psychology practice. Scholars interested in developing the sport and exercise psychology knowledge base likely will maintain allegiance to exercise and sport science. Research questions, whether on psychophysiological mechanisms of exercise and stress reduction or effective coaching behaviors, reflect a focus on sport and exercise behavior. Research trends through the development of the discipline have moved to more sport and exercise-specific approaches, and more recently to an appreciation of the richer understanding that can be gained through collaborative research across specializations, such as exercise physiology and motor behavior.

In contrast, as applied sport psychologists did more consulting with athletes, they sometimes moved away from exercise and sport science into areas within the province of counselors or clinical psychologists. Psychiatrists, psychologists, and counselors have developed professional programs, established legal and ethical boundaries and guidelines, and demonstrated expertise that sport and exercise psychologists from exercise and sport science cannot match. Determining appropriate professional qualifications depends in part upon the definition of sport psychology practice. If sport psychology practice implies counseling athletes on such issues as eating disorders, depression, substance abuse, or marital problems, professionals should be trained in counseling or clinical psychology. Exercise and sport science knowledge is helpful for a more complete understanding of the athlete, but clinical and counseling skills and knowledge are essential. On the other hand, considerable sport and exercise psychology practice does depend on exercise and sport science knowledge and training. For example, conducting workshops on effective coaching or consulting exercise participants on training demands an understanding of exercise and sport science. Counseling skills, although useful, are not essential.

Sport psychology consulting has captured the attention of the public and many students, but the scope of the field and professional guidelines are not clearly established. In practice, boundaries are blurred. As psychologists with counseling and clinical perspectives and exercise and sport science consultants delineate their areas of professional practice and expertise—as many sport and exercise psychologists are now doing within the major organizations—these issues may be clarified and resolved. Exercise and sport science can make its greatest contribution by offering courses and workshops, consulting with practitioners, and conducting research to help counselors and clinically trained professionals better understand sport and exercise contexts and participants. Sport and exercise psychologists interested in applied work within the traditional scope of exercise and sport science might incorporate some psychology or counseling training, but develop applied training programs that incorporate primary knowledge and skills from the other specializations within exercise and sport science.

Thus, research in sport and exercise psychology likely will remain clearly within the larger field of exercise and sport science. Indeed, ties to other subdisciplines and the larger field seem stronger than in the early development when the subdiscipline relied more heavily on psychology for its theories and research models. Applied professional practice seems to be pulled both by exercise and sport science and by applied psychology or counseling. As professional areas and boundaries are delineated, a clearer applied sport and exercise psychology may develop within the larger discipline of exercise and sport science. Those applied scholars and practitioners within exercise and sport science should maintain ties with clinical psychologists, counselors, and other professionals who share some interests, to enrich both the larger discipline and sport and exercise psychology.

References

Carron, A.V., Widmeyer, W.N., & Brawley, L.R. (1985). The development of an instrument to assess cohesion in sport teams: The Group Environment Questionnaire. *Journal of Sport Psychology, 7*, 244–266.

Cratty, B.J. (1964). *Movement behavior and motor learning.* Philadelphia: Lea & Febiger.

Cratty, B.J. (1967). *Psychology and physical activity.* Englewood Cliffs, NJ: Prentice Hall.

Cratty, B.J. (1989). *Psychology in contemporary sport* (3rd ed.). Englewood Cliffs, NJ: Prentice Hall.

Fitz, G.W. (1895). A local reaction. *Psychological Review, 2*, 37–42.

Gill, D.L. (1986). *Psychological dynamics of sport.* Champaign, IL: Human Kinetics.

Gill, D.L. (1993). Competitiveness and competitive orientation in sport. In R.N. Singer, M. Murphey, & L.K. Tennant (Eds.), *Handbook of research on sport psychology* (pp. 314–327). New York: Macmillan.

Gill, D.L., & Deeter, T.E. (1988). Development of the Sport Orientation Questionnaire. *Research Quarterly for Exercise and Sport*, **59**, 191–202.

Griffith, C.R. (1925). Psychology and its relation to athletic competition. *American Physical Education Review*, **30**, 193–198.

Griffith, C.R. (1926). *Psychology of coaching*. New York: Scribners.

Griffith, C.R. (1928). *Psychology and athletics*. New York: Scribners.

Hall, G.S. (1908). Physical education in colleges. *Report of the National Education Association*. Chicago: University of Chicago Press.

Harris, D.V., & Harris, B.L. (1984). *The athlete's guide to sport psychology: Mental skills for physical people*. Champaign, IL: Leisure Press.

Johnson, W.R. (1949). A study of emotion revealed in two types of athletic sport contests. *Research Quarterly*, **20**, 72–79.

Kenyon, G.S., & Grogg, T.M. (1970). *Contemporary psychology of sport*. Chicago: The Athletic Institute.

Kroll, W., & Lewis, G. (1970). America's first sport psychologist. *Quest*, **13**, 1–4.

Landers, D.M. (1979). Sport psychology today. *Journal of Sport Psychology*, **1**, 2–3.

Landers, D.M., Harris, D.V., & Christina, R.W. (1975). *Psychology of sport and motor behavior II*. University Park, Pennsylvania State University Press.

Lawther, J.D. (1951). *The psychology of coaching*. Englewood Cliffs, NJ: Prentice Hall.

Loy, J.W. (1974). A brief history of the North American Society for the Psychology of Sport and Physical Activity. In M.G. Wade & R. Martens (Eds.), *Psychology of motor behavior and sport*. Champaign, IL: Human Kinetics.

Martens, R. (1975). *Social psychology and physical activity*. New York: Harper & Row.

Martens, R. (1977). *Sport competition anxiety test*. Champaign, IL: Human Kinetics.

Martens, R. (1979). From smocks to jocks. *Journal of Sport Psychology*, **1**, 94–99.

Martens, R. (1987a). *Coaches guide to sport psychology*. Champaign, IL: Human Kinetics.

Martens, R. (1987b). Science, knowledge and sport psychology. *The Sport Psychologist*, **1**, 29–55.

Martens, R. (1987c). Editorial Statement. *The Sport Psychologist*, **1**, ii.

Martens, R., Vealey, R.S., & Burton, D. (1990). *Competitive anxiety in sport*. Champaign, IL: Human Kinetics.

McCloy, C.H. (1930). Character building through physical education. *Research Quarterly*, **1**, 41–61.

Miles, W.R. (1928). Studies in physical exertion: I. A multiple chronograph for measuring groups of men. *American Physical Education Review*, **33**, 379–387.

Miles, W.R. (1931). Studies in physical exertion: II. Individual and group reaction time in football charging. *Research Quarterly*, **2**, 14–31.

Nideffer, R.M. (1976). *The inner athlete*. New York: Crowell.

Nideffer, R.M. (1985). *Athlete's guide to mental training*. Champaign, IL: Human Kinetics.

Ogilvie, B.C., & Tutko, T.A. (1966). *Problem athletes and how to handle them*. London: Pelham Books.

Orlick, T. (1980). *In pursuit of excellence*. Champaign, IL: Human Kinetics.

Orlick, T. (1986). *Psyching for sport*. Champaign, IL: Human Kinetics.

Patrick, G.T.W. (1903). The psychology of football. *American Journal of Psychology*, **14**, 104–117.

Roberts, G.C., & Landers, D.M. (1981). *Psychology of motor behavior and sport—1980*. Champaign, IL: Human Kinetics.

Ryan, E.D. (1972). Message from the President. *Sport Psychology Bulletin*, p. 1.

Ryan, E.D. (1981). The emergence of psychological research as related to performance in physical activity. In G. Brooks (Ed.), *Perspectives on the academic discipline of physical education* (pp. 327–341). Champaign, IL: Human Kinetics.

Scanlan, T.K., Ravizza, K., & Stein, G.L. (1989). An in-depth study of former elite figure skaters: I. Introduction to the project. *Journal of Sport & Exercise Psychology*, **11**, 54–64.

Scanlan, T.K., Stein, G.L., & Ravizza, K. (1989). An in-depth study of former elite figure skaters: II. Sources of enjoyment. *Journal of Sport & Exercise Psychology*, **11**, 65–83.

Singer, R.N. (1968). *Motor learning and human performance*. New York: Macmillan.

Singer, R.N. (1992). United States. In J.H. Salmela, *The world sport psychology sourcebook* (2nd ed.) (pp. 54–60). Champaign, IL: Human Kinetics.

Smith, R.E., Smoll, F.L., & Curtis, B. (1979). Coach effectiveness training: A cognitive-behavioral approach to enhancing relationship skills in youth sport coaches. *Journal of Sport Psychology*, **1**, 59–75.

Smoll, F.L., & Smith, R.E. (1984). Leadership research in youth sports. In J.M. Silva & R.S. Weinberg (Eds.), *Psychological foundations of sport* (pp. 371–386). Champaign, IL: Human Kinetics.

Smoll, F.L., & Smith, R.E. (1993). Educating youth sport coaches: An applied sport psychology perspective. In J. Williams (Ed.), *Applied sport psychology* (2nd ed.) (pp. 36–57). Mountainview, CA: Mayfield.

Suinn, R.M. (1980). *Psychology in sports: Methods and applications*. Minneapolis: Burgess.

Triplett, N. (1898). The dynamogenic factors in pacemaking and competition. *American Journal of Psychology*, **9**, 507–533.

Vanek, M. (1993). On the inception, development and perspectives of ISSP's image and self-image. In S. Serpa, J. Alves, V. Ferreira, & A. Paula-Brito (Eds.), *Proceedings VIII World Congress of Sport Psychology* (pp. 154–158). Lisbon, Portugal: International Society of Sport Psychology.

Wade, M.G., & Martens, R. (1974). *Psychology of motor behavior and sport*. Champaign, IL: Human Kinetics.

Wiggins, D.K. (1984). The history of sport psychology in North America. In J.M. Silva & R.S. Weinberg (Eds.), *Psychological foundations of sport* (pp. 9–22). Champaign, IL: Human Kinetics.

Williams, J.M. (1986). *Applied sport psychology*. Mountainview, CA: Mayfield.

Biomechanics

Jerry D. Wilkerson, PhD
Texas Woman's University

Most professionals agree that *biomechanics,* a term combining *biology* and *mechanics,* deals with the principles and methods of mechanics applied to the study of the structure and functioning of biological systems (Fung, 1968; Hatze, 1974; Lissner, 1967; Wartenweiler, 1973). A reference to biomechanics by Steindler (1935) may have been the first appearance of the term in the physical education literature. This rather simple combination word, *biomechanics,* has occasioned much discussion during the past few decades. Establishing some definitions of the term and several related terms is an important starting point in this summary of the discipline's history as a sport and exercise science.

The term biomechanics is so broad, in fact, that a descriptor is often added, such as *human* biomechanics, *sport* biomechanics, or biomechanical *kinesiology.* Within the context of exercise and sport science, biomechanics is seen as the science that investigates the effects of internal and external forces on human bodies in motion and at rest (Broer & Zernicke, 1979; Brunnstrom, 1972; Contini & Drillis, 1954, 1966; Hay, 1993; LeVeau, 1992; Miller & Nelson, 1973). In borrowing structure from mechanics, however, biomechanics also is influenced by physics, with its two major divisions of *statics* and *dynamics.* Statics is a state of balance, or equilibrium, and dynamics is a state of motion. Within the dynamics division, biomechanics is further broken into *kinematics* and *kinetics.* Kinematics is the study of the geometry of motion, whereas kinetics is the study of the forces that produce motion (Brunnstrom, 1972; Contini & Drillis, 1966).

Historical foundations of biomechanics can be traced to the beginning of civilization. Several articles illuminate this history in detail (Asmussen, 1976; Braun, 1941; Contini & Drillis, 1954; Fung, 1968; Hart, 1925; Hirt, 1955; Rasch, 1958). As the 20th century is closing, a retrospective analysis of this century permits the identification of two important periods in the history of biomechanics: the *kinesiology era* and the *biomechanics era.*

▼

A Chronology of Biomechanics

Early Foundations: The Kinesiology Era

Year	Event
1894	First textbook with "kinesiology" in the title
Late 1800s	Invention of motion-picture photography
1900-1959	Top scholars of kinesiology
Late 1920s	Movement analysis with motion-picture photography
1930s	Use of electromyography (EMG) in research
1959	Invention of electrogoniometer

Organization of the Subdiscipline: The Biomechanics Era

Year	Event
1960s and 70s	Wide utilization of the computer in biomechanics
1970s	High-speed 16-mm motion-picture techniques
1970s	Electronic digitizer
1977	First national teaching symposium
1978	Direct linear transformation (DLT) technique utilized in biomechanics
1980	First guidelines and standards for undergraduate kinesiology
1980s	Video and optoelectronic-based systems
Late 1980s	Pressure distribution devices

Development of Biomechanics

Year	Event
1963	Creation of the Kinesiology/Biomechanics Academy of NASPE
1965	Founding of the International Society of Electromyography
1967	First International Seminar on Biomechanics
1968	Origination of the *Journal of Biomechanics*
1970	First meeting in North America for researchers in biomechanics
1973	Founding of the International Society of Biomechanics (ISB)

1976	Founding of the American Society of Biomechanics (ASB)
1982	Founding of the International Society for Biomechanics in Sport (ISBS)
1985	First issue of the *International Journal of Sport Biomechanics*, now titled the *Journal of Applied Biomechanics*

Early Foundations: The Kinesiology Era

Early in the history of biomechanics in the United States, the science of applying mechanics to human movement was called *kinesiology*. Indeed, until recently the two terms have been used interchangeably. Although European sport scientists did not adopt the word (Nelson, 1989), kinesiology was the preferred term in North America, where physical educators, physical therapists, occupational therapists, and orthopedists have been its primary advocates. According to Atwater (1980), the first appearance of the term might have been in the title of the third edition of a book by Baron Nils Posse entitled *The Special Kinesiology of Educational Gymnastics* in 1894. Of Greek derivation, *kine* means movement or motion, and *logos* means to discourse or to study (Rasch, 1958; Scott, 1963), thus making kinesiology the study of movement. Scott further delimits the definition as the study of human movement within exercise and sport science. The Kinesiology Era spans the first six decades of the 20th century and represents the infancy of biomechanics. The following review of this era is best represented by the three areas of *kinesiology scholars, textbooks and curriculum,* and *research and instrumentation.*

Kinesiology Scholars

The central mission of physical education during the early 20th century was teacher education which, combined with other factors, precluded the development of specializations. Therefore, scholars of this time period, diverse in their interests, can be credited with pioneering efforts in other subdisciplines in addition to biomechanics. However, the work of several of the following scholars who advocated the application of mechanics to human movement paved the way for the development of the biomechanics specialization.

Wilbur P. Bowen (1864-1928). Wilbur Bowen began as a wrestling coach at the University of California at Berkeley and later became a professor of physical education at Michigan State Normal College in Ypsilanti

John M. Cooper

Ruth B. Glassow

Richard C. Nelson

Louis E. Alley

James G. Hay

Anne Elizabeth (Betty) Atwater

Carol J. Widule

(J.M. Cooper, personal communication, October 12, 1995). As a very active professional and charter member of the American Academy of Physical Education, he was interested in kinesiology for two primary reasons. First, he felt that the human body was the most complex of all machines and easily predisposed itself to scientific inquiry. For this and other reasons he felt that there were no problems more fascinating than those posed by kinesiology. Second, he believed that the practical applications of kinesiology were particularly important, specifically those related to muscular functioning. He was a firm believer that "function determines structure" (Bowen, 1912). His work accumulated in one of the first textbooks that could be identified with a kinesiology course.

William Skarstrom, MD (1869-1951).   William Skarstrom, a Swedish doctor who was a strong supporter of the gymnastic programs in physical education at that time, was brought to the United States from Sweden in 1912 by Amy Morris Homans to teach in the Department of Hygiene and Physical Education at Wellesley College (Wells, 1968). Katharine Wells took a 90-hour kinesiology course from him in 1930 and recalls his intense and thorough knowledge of the human body and his particular interest in the study of joints in relation to their structure and function (Wells, 1968). His book *Gymnastic Kinesiology* (1909) reflected his interpretation of kinesiology. Dr. Skarstrom's emphasis that the physical education teacher must have a thorough knowledge of the human body was reflected in the requirements of anatomy and physiology in addition to kinesiology at Wellesley College. His primary focus was functional anatomy and the application of knowledge of joints and muscles to movements that were both gymnastic and athletic. He was particularly thorough in the movements of joints. He demonstrated his interest in his students with his practice of writing long and detailed notes on their papers and his attention to their professional needs even after graduation (Wells, 1968). His contributions are particularly noted in his insistence of scientific knowledge for the teacher of physical education.

Arthur Steindler, MD (1878-1959).   A strong and influential professional during the 1930s outside of physical education was Arthur Steindler, MD. He was a professor at the University of Iowa where he taught graduate kinesiology classes and supervised interns in orthopedic surgery (Atwater, 1980). His lectures and notes accumulated into a book entitled *Mechanics of Normal and Pathological Locomotion in Man* in 1935, the first to use the term biomechanics in the physical education literature. In 1942 he also authored an article in the *Journal of Health, Physical Education and Recreation (JOHPER)* advocating the application of mechanics to the study of human movement by answering two fundamental questions. First, is it possible at all to express human motion in mathematical formulae? Second, if human motion can be analyzed by these means, can it be of any practical benefit? He made a strong argument for positive answers to both questions (Steindler, 1942). Being a physician, he was also deeply interested in the physiology of human movement, and believed that the two most influential events in the field of kinesiology were Sherrington's theory of reciprocal innervation and the all-or-none theory by Henry P. Bowditch (Cooper, 1978). His influence can be traced through many individuals who studied with him, such as M. Gladys Scott.

C.H. McCloy (1886-1959). Charles H. McCloy was born in Marietta, Ohio, and attended Marietta College for both the bachelor's and master's degrees. He served the YMCA for many years in China before returning to the United States to work on his doctorate at Columbia University. A significant player in the field of physical education, he served as the president of the American Association for Health and Physical Education (AAHPE) in 1937 and 1938 and became a charter member of the American Academy of Physical Education (Lee, 1983). During his years at the University of Iowa, McCloy had an important role in the development of scientific inquiry in physical education and specifically the application of mechanics to movement. In 1937, McCloy published an article on the application of mechanics to gymnastics in the *Journal of Physical Education*. In a chapter published in 1960, McCloy summarized his work since the 1920s, which included identification of principles relative to the mechanics of human movement.

Ruth B. Glassow (1891-1988). Many scholars in physical education have recognized the contributions of Ruth Glassow to kinesiology (Atwater, 1980; Cooper, 1978; Remley, 1980; Sloan, 1987, 1989; Widule, 1980). Ruth Glassow was born in 1891 and spent her childhood in Wisconsin. She graduated from high school in 1909 and then completed a two-week institute to get her license to teach. She taught in a one-room school house for several years before attending the University of Wisconsin where she earned a bachelor's degree in 1916 (Sloan, 1987). She taught in the public schools of Gary, Indiana, and several institutions of higher education before attending graduate school, receiving her master's degree from Teachers College, Columbia University, in 1924 (Remley, 1980).

In 1924, Glassow was hired by the University of Illinois and asked to teach a class in kinesiology, since she had taken such a class from Clark Hetherington in her undergraduate study (Cooper, 1978). Her primary concern was to apply the knowledge of kinesiology to the teaching of physical activities. To accomplish this task, it was necessary to design a new course and, with her students she began to classify movements into patterns such as locomotion, throwing, striking, and balance, to which they then applied basic mechanical principles. In 1926, Glassow discussed the application of mechanical principles to movement with Margaret H'Doubler on her way to her new teaching position at Oregon State

College. When she discovered that H'Doubler was applying mechanical principles to her teaching of dance, they decided to meet annually for a week in the summer to discuss their common concerns (Cooper, 1978; Sloan, 1987). This collaboration continued for three summers before Glassow agreed to return to the University of Wisconsin in 1930. She agreed to return only if she could teach kinesiology and did not care if it meant a drop in rank and salary (Remley, 1980). Glassow's ideas culminated in the textbook *Fundamentals of Physical Education* in 1932. She was determined to make knowledge practical and was noted as a pioneer in her use of motion picture film for movement analysis in physical education (Remley, 1980). The Women's Department at the University of Wisconsin had a 16-mm Bell and Howell motion picture camera which provided her with the means to observe human movement in slow motion (Sloan, 1987). She recognized that film at speeds higher than what the eye can photograph could reveal the actual performance details not mentioned in textbook descriptions of skills (Atwater, 1980).

Ruth Glassow was also a pioneer in tests and measurements. In 1938, she and Marion Broer, who had been one of her students, wrote *Measuring Achievement in Physical Education* (Glassow & Broer, 1938b). In 1943, she was given an Honor Award from the American Association of Health, Physical Education, and Recreation (AAHPER) for her work as the chair of the Research Section, which culminated with the organization of the Research Council in 1942 (Sloan, 1989). John Cooper persuaded her prior to her retirement in 1962 to coauthor the second edition of the textbook *Kinesiology* (Cooper & Glassow, 1963). She continued to influence scholars in kinesiology for many years through her previous work and the subsequent editions of the textbook. She is remembered by her students as a great "investor" in them and the profession (Sloan, 1987).

Thomas K. Cureton, Jr. (1902-1993).   Thomas Cureton, Jr., was born and raised in Florida. He was an All-American swimmer from Yale (1901) and graduated from that institution with a BS degree in electrical engineering. After graduation, he was the director of Athletics, Health and Physical Education at Suffield Academy in Connecticut. He received a master's degree in health and physical education from Teachers College, Columbia University, and a PhD from Teachers College, Advanced School of Education in Educational Research, also at Columbia University. Cureton joined the Springfield College faculty first as a chemistry, physics, and mathematics teacher (Cooper, 1978). Later, when he became a professor of health and physical education, he wrote an article in the *Journal of Health and Physical Education (JOHPE)*, advocating the application of physics to physical education activities (Cureton, 1932). During his tenure at Springfield College and then the University of Illinois, he sponsored over 100 graduate student theses and published many articles on the topics of posture and body mechanics in swimming, track and field, and gymnastics. Cureton influenced early research efforts by his work on the mechanics of movement and his many publications such as an article in *Research Quarterly* on the principles of cinematography (Cureton, 1939). In a letter to John Cooper, he said: "After many years (about 50) in various aspects of physical education work, I have always been a strong proponent of kinesiology (including mechanics of sports and activities, and body mechanics) and after teaching this subject for twelve years at Springfield College (1929-1941) I came to Illinois; and at Illinois I continued to teach this course as 'Scientific Analysis of Physical Education Activities and Sports' until 1969—that is a 40-year stint!" (Cooper, 1978, p. 9). Thomas Cureton was an exceptional professional and most likely accredited with pioneering the initial efforts in several subdisciplines, most specifically in the area of fitness.

M. Gladys Scott (1905-1990). M. Gladys Scott, a major force in kinesiology, started as a romance language major at DePauw University but later transferred to the University of Iowa as a physical education major. Upon graduation, she taught briefly in both North and South Dakota. She attended graduate school at the University of Iowa, where she was greatly influenced by Arthur Steindler (Cooper, 1978). Scott was an accomplished professional in more areas than kinesiology. The outcome of her dissertation was the Scott Motor Ability Test which began her efforts in the area of tests and measurements (Cooper, 1978). Additionally, she published with Ester French one of the first test and measurement books for women (Scott & French, 1959). As a member of the Research Council in AAHPER, she and Thomas Cureton coedited a general guide to research methodology (Scott & Cureton, 1949), revised and edited by Scott in 1959. In 1942, Scott wrote a textbook in kinesiology titled *Analysis of Human Motion* (and an accompanying workbook in 1947), which became an extensively utilized textbook in undergraduate kinesiology courses (Scott, 1942, 1947). Her accomplishments were extensive and her efforts as chairperson of the Research Council, editor of *Research Quarterly* and the *Academy Papers*, president of the Central District of AAHPER, and president of the Academy of Physical Education served the profession well (Cooper, 1978).

Katharine F. Wells (1899-1995). In 1924 Katharine F. Wells received a certificate from the Central School of Hygiene and Physical Education in New York, which later became the School of Physical Education of Russell Sage College. Before beginning work on the bachelor's degree, she was awarded a certificate from the Gymnastic People's College of Ollerup, Denmark in 1926. She received her BS degree in 1929 from New York University and her MS degree from Wellesley College in 1934. The doctorate degree was completed in 1946 at the State University of Iowa (University of Iowa). Wells spent the majority of her career at Wellesley

College, where she taught courses in kinesiology and adapted physical education. Her primary interests were in therapeutics and corrective physical education. With encouragement from Eleanor Metheny at Iowa, she developed a laboratory manual for kinesiology in conjunction with her studies for the doctorate, which later evolved into her textbook (Cooper, 1978). *Kinesiology* (1950), a popular textbook for undergraduates, exists today under different authorship (Luttgens, Deutsch, & Hamilton, 1992). She was influenced by Arthur Steindler and C.H. McCloy at the University of Iowa, and credits Steindler with stimulating her interest in kinesiology (Cooper, 1978; K. Luttgens, personal communication, November 1, 1995).

Marion Broer.   Marion Broer was born in Toledo, Ohio, in 1910. She attended the University of Wisconsin at Madison for her first two degrees in higher education (the BS degree in 1933 and the MS degree in 1936) and was greatly influenced by Ruth Glassow during both degrees. Broer began her professional speaking at the Central and Midwest Health, Physical Education, and Recreation meetings in 1936 and 1937 on phases of human motion and body mechanics related to posture (Cooper, 1978). Her primary interests, in fundamental movement patterns, efficiency of motion, and the application of mechanical principles to movement patterns, were a continuation of her work at the University of Wisconsin with Ruth Glassow. Eighteen years after earning her master's degree, Broer completed her doctorate at New York University (Cooper, 1978). She taught at the University of Washington, where she published several textbooks. She is the author of *Introduction to Kinesiology* (1968) and coauthor with Sara Jane Houtz of *Patterns of Muscular Activity in Selected Sport Skills: An Electromyography Study* (1967). Marion Broer made a substantial contribution when she published *Efficiency of Human Movement* in 1960. She produced an accompanying laboratory manual with the third edition of her book in 1973 (Broer 1973a, 1973b). Her strongest premise was that there existed a generality in the mechanics of movement that must be learned by the student of movement (Broer, 1960). She dared to make movement analysis realistic (Cooper, 1978). Marion Broer still teaches exercise and the application of mechanics to daily movement activities to senior citizens at her current residence.

John M. Cooper.   John Cooper was born in 1912 in Kentucky where he remained until high school graduation in 1930. He attended the University of Missouri where he was a basketball player and track runner; his undergraduate work was done in history and he graduated with an AB degree in 1934. As a basketball player, he was credited with inventing the jumpshot in basketball (Fox, 1994). Following this degree, Cooper taught and coached at both the high school and college level. His master's and doctoral degrees were also attained from the University of Missouri, in 1936 and 1946, respectively. He joined the faculty of the University of

Southern California in 1945, where he taught kinesiology and chaired graduate students until 1967. He coauthored the textbook *Kinesiology* with Laurence Morehouse in 1950. When Morehouse moved toward the discipline of exercise physiology, Cooper convinced Ruth Glassow to coauthor the second edition of this book with him (Cooper & Glassow, 1963). Cooper said that Glassow tempered his enthusiasm with her cool logic in their cooperative efforts of the textbook (Cooper, 1978). He believes that one of the highlights of his career was working with Ruth Glassow (Cooper, 1978; J.M. Cooper, personal communications, October 12, 1995). In 1967 Cooper was hired as a professor of physical education and director of graduate studies at Indiana University. The dean of the School of Health, Physical Education and Recreation, Arthur S. Daniels, charged him with the responsibility of developing and expanding the research laboratories and increasing the scientific emphasis on studies at the doctoral level (IDS, 1966). John Cooper served the profession in many endeavors, such as president of the California Association of Health, Physical Education, Recreation and Dance, and president of AAHPER in 1970. He retired from Indiana University in 1982. He is and always will be respected and loved by the many graduate students he has guided over the years.

Textbooks and Curriculum

In the early 1900s the physical education curriculum was still significantly influenced by the various gymnastic systems, and the scientific aspect of physical education was in its earliest beginnings. In addition to the influence of gymnastics, the profession was also shaped and influenced by the medical profession. As in other areas of the college curriculum, kinesiology courses were generally influenced by the textbooks published at that time (see table 9.1). William Skarstrom, MD, combined his interest in gymnastics and science to publish the first scientific treatise titled *Gymnastic Kinesiology* (Skarstrom, 1909). This book and several others in the early 1900s represent the anatomical focus of content with primary emphasis placed on the structural and functional aspects of the human body. The primary sources utilized for examples and illustrations were internal muscular actions relative to basic movements found in gymnastics.

The earliest textbooks identified with a kinesiology course were those written by Wilbur Bowen and Wilhelmine Wright (Bowen, 1912; Wright, 1928). Bowen's text was comprehensive in the structural aspects of the skeletal, nervous, and muscular systems of the body, with some applications to formal gymnastics, industrial movements, and a few sport movements. R. Tait McKenzie was the series editor for Bowen's second edition of the book, when the title was changed to *Applied Anatomy and Kinesiology: The Mechanism of Muscular Movement* (Bowen, 1917). The fourth edition in 1928 changed to reflect the shift in curriculum, decreasing the emphasis

Table 9.1 Textbooks and Laboratory Manuals During the Kinesiology Era

Author	Year	Book Title
Textbooks		
Skarstrom, William	1909	Gymnastic kinesiology
Bowen, Wilbur Pardon	1912	The action of muscles in bodily movement and posture
Wright, Wilhelmine G.	1928	Muscle function
Steindler, Arthur	1935	Mechanics of normal and pathological locomotion in man
Hawley, Gertrude	1940	An anatomical analysis of sports
Scott, M. Gladys	1942	Analysis of human motion: A textbook in kinesiology
Wells, Katharine F.	1950	Kinesiology
Morehouse, Laurence E. and Cooper, John M.	1950	Kinesiology
Lipovitz, Ferdinand John	1952	Basic kinesiology
Bunn, John W.	1955	Scientific principles of coaching
Duvall, Ellen Neall	1959	Kinesiology: The anatomy of motion
Rasch, Philip J. and Burke, Roger K.	1959	Kinesiology and applied anatomy
Laboratory manuals		
Scott, M. Gladys	1947	Kinesiology handbook: A study guide and laboratory manual
Kranz, Leon G.	1948	Kinesiology manual
Glassow, Ruth B.	1950	A laboratory manual for functional kinesiology

on gymnastics and placing more importance on movement skills found in sports, games, and dance (Bowen, 1928). This book, revised by several different authors over the years, might have the longest history as a text (Cooper, 1978); the latest version is by Philip J. Rasch (1989). The textbook by Wilhelmine Wright, designed for students in both kinesiology and physical therapy, was focused on the muscular interactions during human movement.

A classic book in the area of efficiency of work and body dynamics, published by Jules Amar in 1914 but not translated into English until 1920, was *The Human Motor*. This book brought together all the scientific principles of body mechanics as applied to the industrial workplace, and set the standards for human engineering in both the United States and Europe. In 1935, Arthur Steindler came out with his textbook, which incorporated the term *mechanics* in the title (Steindler, 1935). This textbook offered the first formal presentation of basic information on the application of mechanics to internal structures of the human body with a few references to such external mechanics as balance, Newton's laws of motion, center of gravity, and the calculations of external force. His approach to kinesiology, in addition to the traditional structural and mechanical focus of the content, included more physiological mechanics and pathologies. A new edition of this book was published in 1955 under the title *Kinesiology of the Human Body Under Normal and Pathological Conditions* (Steindler, 1955).

Curriculum change from foreign gymnastic systems to sports and games did not go unnoticed by Ruth Glassow. She viewed movement as purposeful and started grouping these new motor skills by purpose or goal, which led to exploring the elements that lead to the accomplishment of these purposes. Glassow and her students began classifying movements into categories and applying the mechanical principles of physics to these movements in the mid- to late 1920s (Sloan, 1987). This work would play a significant role in the basic thinking in the categorization and application of mechanics to sport skills.

In 1940 Gertrude Hawley's *An Anatomical Analysis of Sports*, which followed her 1937 book titled *The Kinesiology of Corrective Exercise*, contained muscular and skeletal analyses of 12 different sports. This textbook demonstrated the link between kinesiology and corrective exercise, which later became known as adapted physical education. Corrective exercise at that time centered around the study of posture and the correction of any abnormalities. A laboratory manual written by Leon G. Kranz in 1948 focused on the structural aspects of the skeletal and muscular systems. This manual exists today with the same general focus and is currently authored by Thompson and Floyd (1994).

In 1942 a major change in textbooks occurred with the publishing of a new textbook titled *Analysis of Human Motion: A Textbook in Kinesiology* by M. Gladys Scott. This book, a benchmark in the traditional framing of the undergraduate kinesiology course content that exists today, was considered the most comprehensive in its approach to anatomical and mechanical analysis of physical activities and the most understandable text at that time (Atwater, 1980; Cooper, 1978). Five years later she published a companion laboratory book (Scott, 1947); the textbook and laboratory manual served kinesiology courses for many years.

The 1950s brought new textbooks and many revisions of previous textbooks to better reflect the addition of mechanical applications to sport, dance, and games. Two textbooks came out in 1950 with the same title. The first of these was *Kinesiology* by Katharine Wells which is presently in its eighth edition and titled *Kinesiology: Scientific Basis of Human Motion* (Luttgens, Deutsch, & Hamilton, 1992). The second book titled *Kinesiology* was authored by Laurence Morehouse and John Cooper. The second edition of this book was with Ruth Glassow (Cooper & Glassow, 1963); the last (fifth) edition was coauthored with Marlene Adrian (Cooper, Adrian, & Glassow, 1982). Additionally, Glassow wrote a laboratory manual for functional kinesiology in 1950. Ferdinand John Lipovitz from LaCrosse State Teachers College, now the University of Wisconsin-LaCrosse, published a book titled *Basic Kinesiology* in 1952. The seventh edition of Wilbur Bowen's textbook, published by Henry A. Stone (1953), included major changes in mechanical principles with a more mathematical approach and additional sport skill applications. This textbook was then published as a first edition by Philip J. Rasch and Roger K. Burke in 1959 with the new title *Kinesiology and Applied Anatomy*.

Several books published outside the traditional content focus and format of this time period were written for specific groups. The textbook for physiotherapists by T. McClurg Anderson detailed sport and industrial movement analysis (Anderson, 1951). Another textbook was published for nursing students by Ellen Neall Duvall (Duvall, 1959). However, the textbook most closely associated with physical education was written by John Bunn, titled *Scientific Principles of Coaching* (Bunn, 1955). His training in engineering and physical education helped him produce a text based completely on the application of mechanical principles to sport movements.

Graduate study in kinesiology was present during the 1930s. Ruth Glassow had chaired several master's theses in the 1930s (Preaseley, 1932; Wild, 1937), and some graduate work in kinesiology had begun under the direction of Thomas Cureton, Jr., at the University of Illinois. However, the beginning of an expanding growth period in graduate programs in kinesiology occurred during the 1940s. The primary schools offering graduate degrees in kinesiology at this time were the University of Illinois, University of Iowa, University of Southern California, Springfield College, and the University of Wisconsin (Atwater, 1980).

Research and Instrumentation

The quantification of movement was greatly hindered by the lack of a recording method to preserve movement until Janssen, an astronomer who utilized a series of pictures to study the transit of Venus, suggested kinematographic pictures to study movement (Rasch, 1958). The lives and interests of two men from different countries, Eadweard Muybridge (1831-1904) and Etienne Jules Marey (1830-1904), brought about motion picture photography. Muybridge from the United States was the first to take a series of successive photographs that could be viewed in fast sequential order to reproduce movement (Braun, 1941). Marey from France advanced this process by taking a series of exposures on one photographic plate, and then enhanced this process further by developing "chronophotography on a ribbon" (Braun, 1941; Contini & Drillis, 1966). This discovery characterizes a very important benchmark in the methodological advancement of biomechanics. Additionally, Marey was the first to attempt direct measurements by equipping his subjects with pressure-recording tambours in the soles of the shoes and a device to measure vertical acceleration of the head during running (Asmussen, 1976).

Refinement of the recording techniques and data reduction methods of Muybridge and Marey was continued by Wilhelm Christian Braune and Otto Fischer in their curiosity about the center of gravity. They were the first to describe the body as segmental organic links (Contini & Drillis, 1966). According to Rasch (1958), their premise was that knowledge of the center of gravity and the positioning of segments was fundamental to the understanding of all resistive forces involved in human movement. Instrumentation was advanced by Willem Einthoven when he developed a string galvanometer in 1906 that was a more sensitive instrument for monitoring action currents (Rasch, 1958).

Interest in efficiency and energy cost was continued by Archibald V. Hill, who with his colleagues investigated the energy cost of running in the 1920s. Hill published two books during this time period, *Muscular Movement in Man* in 1920 and *Living Machinery* in 1927. He distinguished himself as the authority on all aspects of muscular activity (Rasch, 1958).

The first published biomechanical research studies that set the standard for analysis were contributed by Wallace O. Fenn (Cooper, 1978). While working with Eastman Kodak Company, Fenn used motion pictures in calculating velocity, kinetic energy, and muscular power (Braun, 1941). He published an article in 1929 in the *American Journal of Physiology* titled "Mechanical Energy Expenditure in Sprint Running as Measured by Moving Pictures," which could be the first published biomechanical work in the exercise and sport science literature (Fenn, 1929). Fenn published three additional articles on running in 1930 (Fenn, 1930a, 1930b; Fenn & Morrison, 1930). In 1931, he published a summary article on the cinematographic study of sprinters, in *Scientific Monthly* (Fenn, 1931). Another researcher who published in the *American Journal of Physiology* during the 1930s was Frances Hellebrandt, who studied center of gravity and posture (Hellebrandt & Braun, 1939; Hellebrandt, Trepper, Braun, & Elliott, 1938). Other researchers of this period were Herbert Elftman from Columbia University, who studied the function of muscles in relation to the dynamics of walking, and Nicholas Bernstein, a Russian, who assessed walking, running, and jumping (Contini & Drillis, 1954).

Other scholars were conducting studies with the use of motion picture film. Ruth Glassow and several of her students conducted cinematographical studies on sport skills. In 1938, she and one of her students, Marion Broer, developed an apparatus for single-frame viewing of motion picture film without distortion, and published their method in *Research Quarterly* (Glassow & Broer, 1938a). This was the precursor to the Recordak made commercially. Thomas Cureton also conducted cinematographical studies with his students (Atwater, 1980).

The 1940s brought some new researchers to the literature. M. Gladys Scott and Thomas Cureton coedited a general guide to research methodology through the Research Council (Scott & Cureton, 1949). This research guide had three chapters on kinesiology which highlighted several of the researchers in kinesiology at this time: a chapter on methods of research in experimental kinesiology by Alfred Hubbard, Thomas K. Cureton, Jr., Arthur H. Steinhaus, and R.H. Stetson (1949); another chapter on photographical and cinematographical research methods by Ruth B. Glassow, Hubbard, and Freeman Brown (1949); and finally a chapter on research methods in mechanics of sports and physical education activities by Hubbard, Cureton, Laura Huelster, and Louis F. Keller.

Research equipment and methodologies were expanded during the 1950s. Although cinematography remained the primary methodology used to study human motion, there was an increase in the number of studies incorporating electromyography (EMG). This technique had already proven to produce useful results in the 1930s by such people as Hubbard (1939), Hudgins (1939), and Sperry (1939), and in the 1940s by individuals such as Slater-Hammel (1948, 1949). John Basmajian began a career of EMG research in the 1950s, which continued extensively until the 1980s. In addition to using electromyography, Peter Karpovich developed the electrogoniometer in 1959 for measuring instantaneous joint angles (Adrian, 1973). In 1959, M. Gladys Scott edited the revision of *Research Methods in Health, Physical Education, and Recreation*, with two chapters on kinesiology, by C. Etta Walters, John M. Cooper, and Olive Young on kinesiology and activity analysis, and a second chapter by Alfred W. Hubbard on photography (Hubbard, 1959; Walters, Cooper, & Young, 1959). The combination of research methodologies such as EMG, cinematography, electromyography, and electrogoniometry gave biomechanical research a more holistic approach.

Organization of the Subdiscipline: The Biomechanics Era

The 1960s mark the beginning of a new era in the development and growth of biomechanics as a subdiscipline within exercise and sport science. The growth pattern increased exponentially with the creation of scholarly societies and the development of research instrumentation. It was during this era that the term *biomechanics* slowly replaced the term *kinesiology*. The representation of the Biomechanics Era is divided into the subtitles of *textbooks and curriculum* and *research and instrumentation*.

Textbooks and Curriculum

Starting in the 1960s increasing numbers of universities were requiring an undergraduate kinesiology course as a part of their core curriculum. A number of textbooks had been revised at the beginning of the 1960s

(Cooper & Glassow, 1963; Rasch & Burke, 1963; Scott, 1963; Wells, 1960). The mechanical aspects of human performance were beginning to surface in the textbook writing. Course content that covered both the anatomical and mechanical aspects was becoming the norm. Table 9.2 lists all the new textbooks during the Biomechanical Era that stressed both anatomical and mechanical aspects of human movement.

Table 9.2 Anatomical and Mechanical Textbooks of the Biomechanics Era

Author	Year	Book Title
Logan, Gene A. and McKinney, Wayne C.	1970	Kinesiology
Jensen, Clayne R. and Schultz, Gordon W.	1970	Applied kinesiology: The scientific study of human performance
Kelley, David L.	1971	Kinesiology: Fundamentals of motion description
O'Connell, Alice L. and Gardner, Elizabeth B.	1972	Understanding the scientific bases of human movement
Gowitzke, Barbara A. and Milner, Morris	1972	Scientific bases of human movement
Northrip, John W.; Logan, Gene A.; and McKinney, Wayne C.	1974	Introduction to biomechanic analysis of sport
Groves, Richard and Camaione, David N.	1975	Concepts in kinesiology
Higgins, J.R.	1977	Human movement: An integrated approach
Hinson, Marilyn M.	1977	Kinesiology
Kreighbaum, Ellen and Barthels, Katharine M.	1981	Biomechanics: A qualitative approach for studying human movement
Piscopo, John and Bailey, James A.	1981	Kinesiology: The science of movement
Hay, James G. and Reid, J. Gavin	1982	The anatomical and mechanical bases of human motion
Kirby, Ronald and Roberts, John A.	1985	Introductory biomechanics
Enoka, Roger M.	1988	Neuromechanical basis of kinesiology
Adrian, Marlene J. and Cooper, John M.	1989	The biomechanics of human movement
Hall, Susan J.	1991	Basic biomechanics
Bloomfield, John; Ackland, Timothy R.; and Elliott, Bruce C.	1994	Applied anatomy and biomechanics of sport
Hamill, Joseph and Knutzen, Kathleen M.	1995	Biomechanical basis of human movement

Large numbers of new textbooks were generated during the 1970s, with a slow decline from the 1980s until now. At the close of the 1970s, approximately 30 different textbooks were available for undergraduate kinesiology courses. The textbooks were diverse and ranged significantly in content and format.

Teaching symposia in the field helped clarify textbook and curricular standards. At the first national teaching symposium at the University of Illinois in 1977, professionals discussed the differences between the terms *kinesiology* and *biomechanics* (Dillman & Sears, 1978); as a result, the Kinesiology Academy appointed a task force to develop guidelines for undergraduate kinesiology. The outcome was a paper entitled "Guidelines and Standards for Undergraduate Kinesiology," edited by Kathryn Luttgens and published in the February edition of *JOPER* (Kinesiology Academy, 1980). These guidelines have greatly influenced the teaching of kinesiology/biomechanics and have provided guidance in curricular decisions and textbook content. The suggested content has three areas of focus: (a) structural and functional aspects of the neuromuscular system, (b) mechanical applications to human movement, and (c) qualitative analysis techniques and experiences. This traditional content became the rule rather than the exception in the 1980s and fewer textbooks were published that emphasized only structural and functional aspects of human movement. These guidelines, updated, were published in the *Kinesiology Newsletter* in the spring of 1992.

A number of textbooks have been written that focus only on the mechanical aspects of human performance. They became less popular after the guidelines and standards for undergraduate kinesiology/biomechanics were published, but a number of these textbooks are invaluable resources in the mechanics of human movement (see table 9.3). A classic in the mechanics of movement relative to fundamental patterns and efficiency

Table 9.3 Mechanical Textbooks of the Biomechanics Era

Author	Year	Book Title
Broer, Marion R.	1960	Efficiency of human movement
Dyson, Geoffrey H.G.	1962	The mechanics of athletics
Tricker, R.A.R. and Tricker, B.J.K.	1967	The science of movement
Wilt, Fred	1970	Mechanics without tears
Hopper, B.J.	1973	The mechanics of human movement
Krause, J.V. and Barham, Jerry N.	1975	The mechanical foundations of human motion
Barham, Jerry N.	1978	Mechanical kinesiology
Simonian, Charles	1981	Fundamentals of sports biomechanics

Table 9.4   Laboratory Manuals of the Biomechanics Era

Author	Year	Book Title
Harris, Ruth W.	1967	Kinesiology: Workbook and laboratory manual
Widule, Carol J.	1974	Analysis of human motion: Experiences, experiments and problems
Spence, Dale W.	1975	Essentials of kinesiology: A laboratory manual
Donnelly, Joseph E.	1982	Living anatomy
Scheuchenzuber, H. Joseph	1983	Experiments in the mechanics of human movement
Widule, Carol J.	1994	Biomechanical foundations of motor skills with computer applications

of movement was written by Marion Broer (Broer, 1960). Several textbooks, such as the textbook written by John Bunn in 1955, were written for the coach (Dyson, 1962; Hopper, 1973; Wilt, 1970). The textbook by J.V. Krause and Jerry Barham was the first programmed text for the mechanics of human movement (Krause & Barham, 1975).

A few laboratory manuals have been written since the 1960s. The task of writing a laboratory manual has always been difficult due to the type of equipment each instructor has or does not have in order to complete various laboratory experiences. However, with the increasing technology available today, laboratory manuals or software should be more available to the instructor of biomechanics classes without much equipment (see table 9.4). The latest editions of some manuals are primarily for structural biomechanics (Thompson & Floyd, 1994; Donnelly, 1990), whereas others are both mechanical and structural (Harris, 1967; Scheuchenzuber, 1983; Spence, 1975; Widule, 1974). Two instructional aids that demonstrate the technological advances are a new laboratory manual with accompanying software by Carol Widule (1994) and interactive laser disk software by Dave Barlow, which covers structural and functional anatomy (Barlow et al., 1992).

During this time period, several textbooks were published that emphasized the structural and functional anatomy (see table 9.5). Those textbooks designed for kinesiology/biomechanics undergraduate classes were written before the guidelines and standards were published (Barham & Thomas, 1969; Barham & Wooten, 1973; Logan & McKinney, 1970; MacConaill & Basmajian, 1969). The first programmed text for learning kinesiology was written by Barham and Thomas in 1969. A special application of electromyography of selected sport skills was published by Broer and Houtz in 1967.

Table 9.5   Anatomical and Clinical Textbooks of the Biomechanics Era

Author	Year	Book Title
Brunnstrom, S.	1962	Clinical kinesiology
Williams, Marian and Lissner, H.R.	1962	Biomechanics of human motion
Brocr, Marion R. and Houtz, Sara J.	1967	Patterns of muscular activity in selected sport skills: An electromyography study
MacConaill, M.A. and Basmajian, John V.	1969	Muscles and movement: A basis for human kinesiology
Barham, Jerry N. and Thomas, William L.	1969	Anatomical kinesiology: A programmed text
Logan, Gene A. and McKinney, Wayne C.	1970	Anatomical kinesiology
Barham, Jerry N. and Wooten, Edna P.	1973	Structural kinesiology
Frankel, Victor H. and Nordin, Margareta	1980	Basic biomechanics of the skeletal system
Norkin, Cynthia C. and Levangie, Pamela K.	1983	Joint structure and function: A comprehensive analysis
Weineck, Jurgen	1986	Functional anatomy in sports
Soderbery, Gary L.	1986	Kinesiology: Application to pathological motion
Gench, Barbara E.; Hinson, Marilyn M.; and Harvey, Patricia T.	1995	Anatomical kinesiology

Several new textbooks were directed toward physical therapy and the clinical sciences: *Clinical Kinesiology* by Signe Brunnstrom in 1962, with a second edition in 1966; *Biomechanics of Human Motion* by Marion Williams and H.R. Lissner (1962), revised in 1977 and 1992 by Barney LeVeau. Since the 1960s, this type of book has become popular for the clinical sciences; additional titles are probably forthcoming.

A second national teaching symposium was held in Colorado Springs in 1984 (Shapiro & Marett, 1984), and a third was held in 1991 at Iowa State University. The papers presented at this conference were published in a proceedings (Wilkerson, Kreighbaum, & Tant, 1991). The contents were teaching methods, undergraduate curriculum perspectives, computer applications to teaching, theoretical versus clinical foundations, laboratory applications, and graduate curriculum perspectives.

Graduate program growth had spurts of activity, but many believe that this growth was slowed due to the lack of trained researchers and the shortage of well-equipped research laboratories (Hay, 1978; Nelson, 1973). During the 1960s, the term *biomechanics* was becoming recognized as a graduate specialization. Louis Alley, a strong advocate for specializations in physical education, wrote an article in 1966 about the design of a graduate program that trained specialists in the mechanics of human movement (Alley, 1966). James Hay was one of the first graduates of this program under the guidance of Louis Alley. Richard Nelson was attracted to Penn State University in 1964, where he established a laboratory for biomechanical research in 1966, the first to be identified by the term *biomechanics* (Atwater, 1980). Another graduate program and research laboratory was created in the 1960s by John Cooper at Indiana University. The graduate experience at that time was primarily coursework and descriptive research utilizing the very time-consuming methodologies of cinematography and electromyography.

More institutions in the 1970s were offering graduate degrees in biomechanics. In 1978, Hay reported that no less than ten institutions offered a doctoral degree with a biomechanics specialization (Hay, 1978, 1990): the University of Illinois (major advisor, Charles Dillman), Indiana University (John Cooper), the University of Iowa (Louis Alley), the University of Maryland (David Kelley), the University of Massachusetts (Stanley Plagenhoef), the University of Oregon (Barry Bates), Penn State University (Richard Nelson), Purdue University (Carol Widule), Washington State University (Marlene Adrian), and the University of Wisconsin (Elizabeth Roberts).

A number of textbooks have been written for the graduate student (see table 9.6). One of these, the textbook of electromyography, has endured the test of time: *Muscles Alive: Their Functions Revealed by Electromyography* by John Basmajian in 1962. The second edition came out in 1967 and the last edition was coauthored with Claro J. De Luca (Basmajian, 1967; Basmajian & De Luca, 1985). Stanley Plagenhoef's book included computer application programs, and was more suited for graduate teaching (Plagenhoef, 1971). Several other books were aimed at the graduate student population (Grieve, Miller, Mitchelson, Paul, & Smith, 1976; Hay, 1973; Miller & Nelson, 1973; Winter, 1979). Two unique books have been published since 1990: *Dynamics of Human Gait* by Vaughan, Davis, and O'Connor (1992), directed toward the procedures and techniques of three-dimensional gait analysis; and *Three-Dimensional Analysis of Human Movement* by Allard, Strokes, and Blanchi (1995) offers much-needed information about the three-dimensional process and its applications. Three books have been published that summarize the research literature in selected areas of interest. The first of these, edited by Van Gheluwe and Atha, covers a range of topics from muscle elasticity to gymnastics (Van Gheluwe & Atha, 1987). Christopher Vaughan edited the second of these books, summarizing the research on running, swimming, rowing, sculling, speed skating, throwing (in track and field), skiing, tennis, and cycling (Vaughan, 1989). Then in 1993, Mark Grabiner coordinated the writing of *Current Issues in Biomechanics*, covering the literature, problems, and

Table 9.6   Graduate and Instrumentation Textbooks of the Biomechanics Era

Author	Year	Book Title
Basmajian, John V.	1962	Muscles alive: Their functions revealed by electromyography
Plagenhoef, Stanley	1971	Patterns of human motion: A cinemato-graphic analysis
Hay, James G.	1973	The biomechanics of sports techniques
Miller, Doris I. and Nelson, Richard C.	1973	Biomechanics of sport: A research approach
Grieve, D.W.; Miller, Doris I.; Mitchelson, J.P.; Paul, J.P.; and Smith, A.J.	1976	Techniques for the analysis of human movement
Winter, David A.	1979	Biomechanics of human movement
Van Gheluwe, B. and Atha, J. (Editors)	1987	Current research in sports biomechanics
Dainty, David A. and Norman, Robert W.	1987	Standardizing biomechanical testing in sport
Vaughan, Christopher L. (Editor)	1989	Biomechanics of sport
Vaughan, Christopher L.; Davis, Brian L.; and O'Connor, Jeremy C.	1992	Dynamics of human gait
Grabiner, Mark D. (Editor)	1993	Current issues in biomechanics
Allard, Paul; Stokes, Ian A.F.; and Blanchi, Jean-Pierre (Editors)	1995	Three-dimensional analysis of human movement

future research of topics such as mechanics of human motion, basic tissue biomechanics, and neuromotor elements (Grabiner, 1993). The first textbook to explain research procedures, standards, and protocols was also published (Dainty & Norman, 1987).

Research and Instrumentation

Research instrumentation for biomechanical analysis has made significant advancements since the 1960s. The discipline has advanced from hand drawing on graph paper of individual frames of 64-Hz motion picture film to optoelectronic-based systems. Instrumentation has also advanced from very minimal means of measuring kinetic forces to forceplates, sensors, force pressure distribution devices, telemetry accelerometers, goniometers, and electromyography. The most important advancement of instrumentation was the incorporation of the digital computer to both collection and analysis of biomechanical data. This advancement alone has revolutionized biomechanics and made possible data collection and reduction beyond the imagination of researchers of the 1950s.

In the 1960s only a few institutions had access to the state-of-the-art equipment. The equipment of this time was a 16-mm motion picture camera that could take 64 pictures per second with a homemade clock in the picture for recording time on the film. The analysis was a painfully long process of frame-by-frame analysis of the images, in a microfilm reader or commercially produced Recordak. By the end of the 1960s the Recordak was replaced with a Vanguard analyzer adopted from the space program (Hay, 1990), and force platforms were available for some institutions.

The primary focus of many researchers in biomechanics during the 1970s was instrumentation. The most important improvement in cinematography was the design of the LoCam 16-mm motion picture camera, which permitted film rates up to 500 frames per second. The design permitted changes in shutter factors and internal timing lights for accuracy of frame rate and was small enough to take into the field for on-site research. Additionally, the Kistler forceplate had become more common in institutions. This forceplate and other types of strain gauge devices for measuring forces were more readily available at the end of the 1970s and the beginning of the 1980s (Cavanagh, 1978; Matake, 1976). The Vanguard analyzer was replaced with the electronic digitizer, which continued to become more and more sophisticated and eventually interfaced with the computer for more direct input of coordinate data.

A benchmark in methodologies in biomechanics in the mid- to late 1970s was three-dimensional cinematography (Bergemann, 1974; Lindholm, 1974; Miller & Petak, 1973; Shapiro, 1978; Van Gheluwe, 1974, 1978; Walton, 1979, 1981). This advancement was made possible when biomechanics adopted the direct linear transformation (DLT) procedures from the area of civil engineering (Abdel-Azis & Karara, 1971). The DLT technique advanced biomechanics from two-dimensional planar analysis to the more realistic three-dimensional analysis.

The 1980s have brought additional advancements in data processing that have overwhelmingly decreased data reduction time. The data analysis systems that permit the automatic tracking of reflective markers placed on the human body have almost eliminated the need to digitize points from film. Real-time optoelectronic on-line analysis has significantly reduced data reduction time, and the new systems for measuring pressure distribution between the foot and the shoe have advanced research in kinetics.

Research productivity appears to be positively correlated with improvements in research methodology and instrumentation, transforming the research process from a very time-consuming and laborious process to a more automatic procedure with considerably less time commitment.

James Hay (1990) reported research productivity for specific years progressively over time since 1965. He reported only 50 research papers that were predominately theses and dissertations in 1965. In 1975, there were 90 papers and of these one-third were theses and dissertations. The count was 151 research papers in 1985 on sport biomechanics, without the inclusion of theses and dissertations (Hay, 1990). The number of research papers in sport biomechanics for 1995 has not been accumulated at this time, but an increase is expected. This information was acquired from various editions of *A Bibliography of Biomechanics Literature* (Hay, 1981).

The majority of research prior to the 1970s was descriptive in nature (Hay, 1978). However, after the mid- to late 1970s the research in sport biomechanics increased significantly. In addition to research in sport biomechanics in the 1970s, a large amount of research on instrumentation and noise reduction in data was being completed. This preoccupation with instrumentation and data manipulation, probably due to the infancy of the discipline (Hay, 1978), was indicated by the theme "Biomechanics: Techniques of Drawings of Movement and Movement Analysis" of the First International Biomechanics Conference held in Zurich, Switzerland (Hay, 1990; Wartenweiler, Jokl, & Hebbelinck, 1968). This interest in instrumentation and methodology provided the profession with new ways of viewing problems and improved methods for representing the human motion. The topic of noise reduction, or the elimination of error from data, was referred to as data smoothing. Researchers applied numerous mathematical systems such as spline functions and filtering techniques to various types of biomechanical data to reduce errors (McLaughlin, Dillman, & Garner, 1977; Winter, Sidwall, & Hobson, 1974; Wood & Jennings, 1979; Zernicke, Caldwell, & Roberts, 1976). Other popular research topics were movement optimization, computer simulation, and modeling. The most prominent researchers in modeling at this time were Doris Miller and H. Hatze (Hatze, 1976; Miller, 1971, 1975). In addition to the individuals mentioned previously, other researchers in the United States who appeared frequently in the sports biomechanical literature were Gideon Ariel, Barry Bates, Charles Dillman, James Hay, Stanley Plagenhoef, and Juris Terauds.

Citations of biomechanical research have grown significantly each year. Running is one topic popular since the late 1970s. Researchers who have appeared in the literature are too numerous to identify, but one individual who has focused specifically on running is Peter Cavanagh from Penn State University. His research on running (and especially the interfacing of the runner, shoe, and surface) has brought great insights to running.

The diversity of research since the 1980s has been extensive and it would be difficult to mention all the different categories and the key researchers in each. Readers interested in specific areas of research are directed to the many volumes of conference proceedings, abstracts from the biomechanical societies, and such journals as the *Journal of Applied*

Biomechanics, Medicine and Science in Sports and Exercise, and the *Research Quarterly for Exercise and Sport.*

Development of Biomechanics

The development of a discipline is best demonstrated through the creation of scholarly societies, the holding of academic workshops and seminars, and the creation of scholarly journals for publishing. The development of biomechanics from this perspective has been exponential since the 1960s, an active and productive time for the formation of academic societies in biomechanics/kinesiology.

In the early part of this decade several members of AAHPER decided that an organization within this group needed to be formed to promote the academic discipline of kinesiology. A pilot Kinesiology Section was approved by the General Division of AAHPER, and operated during 1963 and 1964 (Atwater, 1980). The chair of the section was Jerry Barham, who described his views on the structure for the discipline of kinesiology in a 1963 article in the *Physical Educator.* The first meeting of this group was at the 1963 AAHPER convention in Minneapolis; the group officially became the Kinesiology Section in 1965. Its name was changed to the Kinesiology Committee in 1972 during the restructuring of AAHPER and in 1974 it became the Kinesiology Academy (Atwater, 1980).

The original intent of the Kinesiology Section was to be broadly focused (Barham, 1963). The Kinesiology Section approved by the national organization was a global entity inclusive of all individuals interested in the scientific study of human movement. Barham (1966) proposed a framework for the discipline of kinesiology which included: (a) anatomical kinesiology, (b) mechanical kinesiology, (c) physiological kinesiology, (d) psychological kinesiology, and (e) maturational or sociological kinesiology. The pilot group planned several major projects. The first project, to sponsor a "Kinesiology" column in the *JOHPER,* became a reality and continued for years, but does not exist today. The second project was to publish a journal. Members of the pilot group formed a board of 17 editors and the first publication, *Kinesiology Review 1968,* came out under the editorship of Alice O'Connell. There were three more editions to follow (Hay, 1974; Widule, 1971, 1973). As other groups were formed such as the exercise physiology, motor development, sport psychology, and sport sociology academies, the focus of the Kinesiology Academy narrowed (Atwater, 1980).

Major strides were made on the international level during this decade. The International Society of Electromyography (ISEK) was formed in 1965. Regional and international meetings were held for members of this group (Basmajian, 1968, 1971), which sponsored the creation of a journal to support the research of its members. *Electromyography* was first published in 1961 at the EMG Laboratory, University of Louvain in Belgium; it is now named *Electromyography and Clinical Neurophysiology*. The second international benchmark in academic societies was the First International Seminar on Biomechanics held in Zurich, Switzerland, in 1967. An official group was not formed at that time, but the proceedings were published in 1968 and edited by Wartenweiler, Jokl, and Hebbelinck. The second seminar was held two years later in Eindhoven, Netherlands, with proceedings published in 1971 under the editorship of Vredenbregt and Wartenweiler (Vredenbregt & Wartenweiler, 1971). Additionally, an international journal named the *Journal of Biomechanics* was originated in 1968. During the first year of publication, several well-known researchers in biomechanics published articles on sport biomechanics (Dillman & Nelson, 1968; Plagenhoef, 1968).

The 1970s witnessed phenomenal growth in academic societies that focused on biomechanics. In 1970, Indiana University hosted the first meeting in North America for researchers from physical education in the area of biomechanics. It was at this meeting, organized by John Cooper with papers presented on selected sport skills and instrumentation (Cooper, 1971), that Richard Nelson presented an overview of biomechanics and proclaimed that the semantic struggle was over between the terms "kinesiology" and "biomechanics" (Nelson, 1971). One of the reasons for this statement was that this was the first meeting in North America which included *biomechanics* in its title. During the summer of 1971, Carol Widule coordinated a biomechanics workshop at Purdue University (Atwater, 1980); other workshops of the same type were held at Penn State University in 1971 and 1972 (Nelson, 1980).

The Third International Seminar on Biomechanics was held in Rome, Italy, in 1971 and resulted in published proceedings (Cerquiglini, Venerando, & Wartenweiler, 1973). The Fourth International Seminar on Biomechanics in 1973 at Penn State University marked the founding of the International Society of Biomechanics (ISB) and the election of Jurg Wartenweiler as its first president (Atwater, 1980; Bates, 1974). Proceedings were published under the editorship of Richard Nelson and Chauncey Morehouse (Nelson & Morehouse, 1974). The focus of this society was broader than sport and physical education, and included all applications of mechanics to biological systems (Hatze, 1974). This group sponsored biennial international congresses as its primary activity for the purpose of sharing information (Nelson, 1980). Subsequent meetings were held in Jyvaskyla, Finland, in 1975 (Komi, 1976), Copenhagen, Denmark, in 1977 (Asmussen & Jorgensen, 1978), and Warsaw, Poland, in 1979 (Morecki, Fidelus, Kedzior, & Wit, 1981). In 1975 in Jyvaskyla, Finland, a group met to consider the founding of an American Society of Biomechanics. At this meeting Juris Terauds moved to form a United States Society of Biomechanics, subject to name change. Representatives from physical education, medicine, ergonomics, biology, and engineering formed the committee that created this society. Representing physical education on this group were John Cooper, James Hay (chair), and David Kaufmann (ASB minutes, July 2, 1975, meeting). In January of 1976 in Chicago, Illinois, the affiliate organization for the United States was founded under the title of the American Society of Biomechanics (ASB) (ASB, minutes, January 15, 1976). The first annual meeting of this society was on October 17–19, 1977, at the University of Iowa in Iowa City, Iowa; the organization has met annually since 1977, with the abstracts of their meetings published in the *Journal of Biomechanics* since 1979.

The Kinesiology Academy continued to offer section meetings at the National Convention each year, publish the newsletter, and solicit articles for the Kinesiology column in *JOHPER*. It was generally felt that a conference was needed to deal with some of the concerns and issues in teaching kinesiology and particularly at the undergraduate level (Atwater, 1980). To meet these needs, Charles Dillman held the First National Conference on Teaching Kinesiology at the University of Illinois in 1977 (Dillman & Sears, 1978), attended by more than 200 professionals who participated in group discussions such as structure and organization of kinesiology/ biomechanics content at the undergraduate level. The results of that discussion were published in the proceedings (Luttgens & Zernicke, 1978).

At the First National Conference on Teaching in Kinesiology in 1977, a discussion occurred pertaining to the distinguishing differences between "kinesiology" and "biomechanics." The general consensus was that "kinesiology does not equal biomechanics, but there was little agreement to the proper name to call the basic course in kinesiology/biomechanics" (Luttgens & Zernicke, 1978, p. 256). At that time, kinesiology ranged from a name of a course to the identifying term or title of a college department. In 1989, after much debate, the Academy of Physical Education changed its name to the Academy of Kinesiology and Physical Education (Charles, 1994). Kinesiology in this context was defined as the overall science of human movement and the appropriate term to describe collegiate preparation in physical education. Since this change, many college and university departments of physical education have changed their names to kinesiology. Therefore, in 1993 the Kinesiology Academy of AAHPERD changed its name to the Biomechanics Academy.

The 1970s was a time for seminars and workshops that strengthened the discipline of biomechanics. The need for more specific biomechanical information within each individual sport became apparent to professionals. The First International Symposium on the Biomechanics of Swimming was held in 1970 (Lewillie & Clarys, 1971) and was followed by additional conferences on this topic (Lewillie & Clarys, 1975; Terauds & Bedingfield, 1979). Numerous papers on sport biomechanics were presented at the International Congress of Physical Activity prior to the Montreal Olympics (Landry & Orban, 1978). In 1978 at the University of Alberta in Canada, an International Congress of Sports Science was conducted and papers were presented on the science of athletics; gymnastics; racquet sports; skiing, skating, and hockey; weight lifting; and other sports, in addition to such topics as the science of cinematography (Terauds, 1978a-g). When the Olympic Scientific Congress was held in 1976 at Quebec City, biomechanics was recognized as an integral part of the science of athletics; all subsequent Olympic Congresses included biomechanics (Nelson, 1989).

The inclusion of biomechanical research papers at the American College of Sports Medicine (ACSM) began in the 1970s. Two oral presentation sessions and some poster opportunities were provided for the biomechanists of this group (Nelson, 1980). Gideon Ariel represented the field of biomechanics on the United States Olympic Committee (USOC) when a well-equipped biomechanics laboratory was included in the Olympic Training Center in Colorado Springs (Nelson, 1980). Ariel also represented biomechanics to the public through popular magazines and television interviews and stories. He made significant strides in educating the public about biomechanics.

During the 1978 International Congress of Sport Sciences held in Edmonton, Alberta, Canada, a group of biomechanics professionals interested in the application of biomechanics to sport began discussion on the need for a biomechanics society specifically dedicated to sport biomechanics and having as its mission bridging the gap between sport biomechanics research and the coaching and teaching of sport. In 1982, the International Society for Biomechanics in Sport (ISBS) was founded in San Diego, California (E. Kreighbaum, personal communication, November 11, 1994). This meeting became the first annual symposium of the ISBS and has had published proceedings each year since (Terauds, 1982). Annual symposia in the 1980s were Colorado Springs in 1984 (Terauds, Barthels, Kreighbaum, Mann, & Crakes, 1984), University of Northern Colorado in 1985 (Terauds & Barham, 1985), Dalhousie University, Nova Scotia, in 1986 (Terauds, Gowitzke, & Holt, 1987), Athens, Greece, in 1987 (Tsrouchas, 1987), Montana State University, Bozeman, in 1988 (Kreighbaum & McNeill, 1990), and Footscray Institute, Melbourne, Australia, in 1989 (Morrison, 1989). In October 1980 a biomechanics conference was sponsored by the Big Ten CIC Physical Education Body of Knowledge Project and the Indiana State Board of Health. This conference, hosted by John Cooper at Indiana University, marked the tenth anniversary of the first biomechanics conference held in the same location. The content of this conference was directed toward biomechanical concerns in sport, measurement, philosophy, history, and teaching (Cooper & Haven, 1980).

The Second National Symposium on Teaching Kinesiology and Biomechanics in Sports was held in Colorado Springs, Colorado, in January of 1984, in conjunction with the 1984 ISBS Symposium. The conference was sponsored by the United States Olympic Committee, Sport Medicine Council, and the Kinesiology Academy of NASPE. The program emulated the first teaching conference, with many programs on teaching, curriculum, laboratory experiences, and computer instruction (Shapiro & Marett, 1984).

Communications among professionals in biomechanics were enhanced through several new options. An international computer communication system entitled BIOMCH-L was developed for on-line messages and announcements in 1988 (Boger & Gielo-Perczak, 1992). The *International Journal of Sport Biomechanics* first appeared in 1985 under the leadership of Richard Nelson (Nelson, 1989); this journal has been renamed the *Journal of Applied Biomechanics* to better reflect the intent of the journal. Biomechanists also found new possibilities for publishing their research in other disciplinary journals. An Olympic Film Archives was begun at the 1984 Los Angeles Olympic Games, established under the direction of the Medical Commission of the International Olympic Committee (Nelson, 1989).

The International Society of Biomechanics continued its biennial meetings with published proceedings throughout the 1980s. The Eighth Congress was held in Nagoya, Japan, in 1981 (Matsui & Kobayashi, 1983). The Ninth and Tenth Congresses were held in Waterloo, Canada, in 1983 (Winter, Norman, Wells, Hayes, & Patla, 1985) and Umea, Sweden, in 1985 (Jonsson, 1987), respectively. The last published proceedings came from the Eleventh Congress in Amsterdam, The Netherlands, in 1987 (deGroot, Hollander, Huijing, & van Ingen Schenau, 1988). The Twelfth Congress was held in Los Angeles, California, in 1989 with proceedings published in the *Journal of Biomechanics* (Huiskes & Brand, 1989).

Previously established organizations continued their conferences. The ISB has held conferences in Australia in 1991, Italy in 1993, and Finland in 1995. The abstracts of presentations since the 1989 meeting in Los Angeles, California, have been published in the *Journal of Biomechanics*. The ISBS has held annual meetings in Czechoslovakia in 1990 (Nosek, Sojka, Morrison, & Susanka, 1990), Iowa in 1991 (Tant, Peterson, & York, 1991), Italy in 1992 (Rodano, Ferrigno, & Santambrogio, 1992), Massachusetts in 1993 (Hamill, Derrick, & Elliott, 1993), Budapest in 1994, and Thunderbay, Canada, in 1995. The Third National Symposium on Teaching Kinesiology and Biomechanics in Sports was held in conjunction with the Ninth International Symposium on Biomechanics in Sports in Ames, Iowa, in 1991 (Wilkerson, Kreighbaum, & Tant, 1991). The Kinesiology Academy continued its activities, such as publishing a newsletter and organizing meetings at the annual national conference of AAHPERD in addition to planning preconference sessions before the national conference. This group changed its name to the Biomechanics Academy in 1993.

Present and Future of Biomechanics

The growing pains and development experienced by the discipline of biomechanics are typical of any scientific discipline. Biomechanics has come from an unrecognized discipline to a well-established discipline nurtured and enhanced by the many diverse specializations that embrace it. Biomechanics has been embraced by the field of exercise and sport science. While the biomechanist is focused on understanding the mechanics of human movement, there exists an expansive diversity of special interests within biomechanics, from muscle mechanics to the mechanics of movement, from the highly skilled to the novice and movements of the daily routine, and from the healthy to the injured. Additionally, topics of instrumentation and equipment as well as multidisciplinary inquiry of human movement are vital to the researcher in biomechanics.

The research of the biomechanist has progressed from the "black box" approach—an approach in which the effects were studied with little or no regard for their underlying causes—to the pursuit of solutions and universal truths (Hay, 1978). According to Nelson (1980), the number of citations in *Index Medicus* has increased exponentially. The organizations representing biomechanics have come from nonexistence to healthy and growing societies and groups, promoting biomechanics through their efforts to motivate and support the activities and research of their members. There are increasing numbers of workshops, seminars, and research conferences for biomechanical scholars to share their research. The application of biomechanics within exercise and sport science has expanded tremendously over its history. New opportunities that were never dreamed of now exist in research and development departments in industry, and in hospitals and clinical laboratories.

Biomechanists today have more opportunities to network and interact with other specialists, affiliated with organizations such as the American Society of Mechanical Engineers, the American College of Sports Medicine, the International Ergonomics Association, and the Human Factors Society. The biomechanics curriculum in colleges and universities has advanced from one course at the undergraduate level that represented all sciences of human movement, to increasing numbers of graduate programs at the master's and doctoral levels with specializations in biomechanics. Technology has developed from naked-eye observations to highly sophisticated motion analyses, facilitated by automated technology with a level of accuracy once thought impossible to achieve. The technological age has affected biomechanics in the most important developmental ways. Without the technological advances, biomechanics would not have grown as it has. Research funding from external grants and contracts has become a reality for biomechanists; the largest source of such funding has been from private companies and industry (Nelson, 1989).

In summary, biomechanics has grown from infancy to adolescence. The science of biomechanics within exercise and sport science has expanded and developed rapidly since the 1960s. If biomechanics continues to grow at the same rate previously seen, the future of this discipline is limitless.

Generally, the prediction of future trends and developments, risky at best, is usually an educated guess based on the current trends or factors already set into motion. Additionally, many times the predictions are based on the expectations and hopes of the predictor. Nevertheless, many factors already set into motion will affect the future of biomechanics. Technological developments will impact the instrumentation and methodologies of biomechanics, freeing biomechanists from being held hostage by their instrumentation. The almost daily improvements in technology, especially computer technology that directly impacts biomechanics, make biomechanical advancement limitless. Computer technology improvements directly impact biomechanics. In addition, John Greaves (1995) predicts a new development called dynamic morphology or shape tracking, where the computer tracks objects or segments by color and shape, a technique which would possibly eliminate the use of reflective markers. He also believes that real-time video now under development will become a reality, due to the expanding base of applications for such technology (Greaves, 1995). We can look forward to even more accurate and efficient means of tracking human motion in the future.

Other instrumentation advancements are also imminent. Computerized sports equipment design, smaller and lighter computer devices to be worn by the performer, smaller and more accurate detection devices in EMG, and improved accelerometers are just a few of the possibilities. The future is bright in instrumentation design, with accompanying methodological advances.

Another future development recommended by a number of professionals is the shift in the subject population that we study and emphasize (Cavanagh, 1989; Nelson, 1989). These professionals and others believe that we should study the average person and their needs in order to enrich their lives. Cavanagh (1989) believes we should abandon the idea that the elite performance represents the ideal style for the average performer to emulate. Additionally, Nelson (1989) feels that greater emphasis on individual characteristics will appear in designing products and in our research efforts. Two specific populations separated out for study in the future are women and the elderly (Cavanagh, 1989; Nelson, 1989), obvious topics, due to lack of previous research on women and the increasing percentage of elderly in the total population.

Recommendations have been made relative to future research directions. Cavanagh (1989) calls for more predictive and correlational model development. Repeated trials are also a new expectation in determining typical performance. Studies that assess the results of altering normal performance, the effects of training, and movement pattern acquisition are a few of the suggested research directions. Another research theme that appears in the literature more frequently is neuromuscular modeling. One of the expressed needs in this research is better assessment of internal force with better biological fidelity. New graphic approaches will facilitate all modeling procedures in the future (Greaves, 1995).

As disciplines continue to split into more and more specializations, the boundaries separating the sciences are dissolving (Stelmach, 1987). Even the sharpness among the subdisciplines within exercise and sport science is becoming less distinct. The answers needed today are multifaceted and appear to be in many layers; the one belief that has the most support by the largest number of professionals is the need for multidisciplinary research efforts (Atwater, 1990; Cavanagh, 1990; Dillman, 1989; Nelson, 1989; Norman, 1989; Winter, 1989). In reality the biomechanist in isolation will not likely make major advances in the holistic problems of performance (Cavanagh, 1989). Nelson (1989) states that the primary objectives of improving human performance and minimizing injury will continue, objectives that could also belong to other subdisciplines within exercise and sport science and could act to solidify a common objective from which future interdisciplinary research efforts might develop.

One of the distinct challenges for us in the administration of multidisciplinary research is to determine the minimum common knowledge base necessary to have effective communications across the subdisciplines (Norman, 1989). This information could be incorporated into the graduate curriculum as core requirements. In addition, other curriculum shifts may become necessary at the graduate level. Students in the future will have access to large amounts of information through such mechanisms as the World Wide Web and other communication systems of the future. Because of this access to information and the continued generation of new information, students will need to be trained in the tools of learning and inquiry for lifelong learning and questioning (Wilkerson, 1991). New scholars in the field must be adaptable, prepared for processing large amounts of information, and able to handle ambiguity.

Future researchers should continue to strive for improved validity in their research. Some researchers have suggested a need for basic research aimed at understanding movement mechanisms and theory development (Norman, 1989). Theoretical research should also facilitate interdisciplinary research. Research in biomechanics will continue toward determining causal relationships and searching for answers on different levels of explanation and understanding. As stated by Winter, "The days of measurement, description, and data smoothing are over" (Winter, 1989, p. 206). The future biomechanists will know what is "normal" and what is "optimal." Baselines for performance will be determined. Through interdisciplinary research, more valid models will be created to answer the questions of "what if . . . ?" With better models, realistic optimization will be possible.

Acknowledgment

The author wishes to thank Drs. Anne E. (Betty) Atwater, Ellen Kreighbaum, Richard Nelson, and Carol Widule for reading the first version of this chapter and making such excellent suggestions for its improvement. Thank you is extended to Drs. Betty Atwater, James Hay, Ellen Kreighbaum, Kathryn Luttgens, Richard Nelson, and Carol Widule for sharing information, pictures, and articles for this publication. A special thank you is given to my mentor, Dr. John Cooper, for all the time he spent on the phone talking to me about the history of biomechanics. Additionally, gratitude is expressed to all the biomechanists of today and those of the past for their contributions to the field of biomechanics.

References

Abdel-Aziz, Y.I., & Karara, H.M. (1971). Direct linear transformation from comparator coordinates into object space coordinates in close-range photogrammetry. *Proceedings of The Symposium on Close-Range Photogrammetry*. Falls Church, VA: American Society of Photogrammetry.

Adrian, M.J. (1973). Cinematographic, electromyographic, and electrogoniometric techniques for analyzing human movement. In J. Wilmore (Ed.), *Exercise and sport science reviews* (Vol. 1). New York: Academic Press.

Adrian, M.J., & Cooper, J.M. (1989). *The biomechanics of human movement*. Indianapolis: Benchmark Press.

Allard, P., Stokes, I.A.F., & Blanchi, J. (Eds.) (1995). *Three-dimensional analysis of human movement*. Champaign, IL: Human Kinetics.

Alley, L.E. (1966). Utilization of mechanics in physical education and athletics. *Journal of Health, Physical Education, and Recreation*, March, 67-70.

Amar, J. (1920). *The human motor*. New York: Dutton.

Anderson, T.M. (1951). *Human kinetics and analyzing body movements*. London: Heinemann Medical.

Asmussen, E. (1976). Movement of man and study of man in motion: A scanning review of the development of biomechanics. In P.V. Komi (Ed.), *Biomechanics V-B* (pp. 23-40). Baltimore: University Park Press.

Asmussen, E., & Jorgensen, K. (Eds.) (1978). *Biomechanics VI-A and VI-B*. Baltimore: University Park Press.

Atwater, A.E. (1980). Kinesiology/biomechanics: Perspectives and trends. *Research Quarterly for Exercise and Sport*, **51**(1), 193-218.

Atwater, A.E. (1990). Biomechanics: An interdisciplinary science. In *American Academy of Physical Education Papers: New Possibilities, New Paradigms?* (Vol. 24, pp. 5-13). Champaign, IL: Human Kinetics.

Barham, J.N. (1963). Organizational structure of kinesiology. *Physical Educator*, **20**(3), 20-121.

Barham, J.N. (1966). Toward a science and discipline of human movement. *Journal of Health, Physical Education, and Recreation,* October, pp. 65-68.

Barham, J.N. (1978). *Mechanical kinesiology.* St. Louis: Mosby.

Barham, J.N., & Thomas, W.L. (1969). *Anatomical kinesiology: A programmed text.* New York: Macmillan.

Barham, J.N., & Wooten, E.P. (1973). *Structural kinesiology.* New York: Macmillan.

Barlow, D.A., Neeves, R.E., Handling, K.A., & Troutman, K.D. (1992). *Dynamics of human anatomy: Interactive videodisc programs.* Philadelphia: Lea & Febiger.

Basmajian, J.V. (1962). *Muscles alive: Their functions revealed by electromyography.* Baltimore: Williams & Wilkins.

Basmajian, J.V. (1967). *Muscles alive: Their functions revealed by electromyography* (2nd ed.). Baltimore: Williams & Wilkins.

Basmajian, J.V. (1968). The present status of electromyographic kinesiology. In J. Wartenweiler, E. Jokl, & M. Hebbelinck (Eds.), *Biomechanics I* (pp. 110-122). New York: S. Karger.

Basmajian, J.V. (1971). Electromyographic analysis. In J.M. Cooper (Ed.), *Selected topics on biomechanics* (pp. 109-117). Chicago: Athletic Institute.

Basmajian, J.V., & DeLuca, C.J. (1985). *Muscles alive: Their functions revealed by electromyography* (5th ed.). Baltimore: Williams & Wilkins.

Bates, B.T. (1974). The fourth international seminar on biomechanics. *Journal of Health, Physical Education and Recreation,* 45(2), 69-70.

Bergemann, B.W. (1974). Three-dimensional cinematography: A flexible approach. *Research Quarterly,* 45, 302-309.

Bloomfield, J., Ackland, T.R., & Elliott, B.C. (1994). *Applied anatomy and biomechanics of sport.* Champaign, IL: Human Kinetics.

Bogert, T.V., & Gielo-Perczak, K. (1992). Letter to the Editor: BIOMCH-L: An electronic mail discussion forum for biomechanics and movement science. *Journal of Biomechanics,* 25(11), 1367.

Bowen, W.P. (1912). *The action of muscles in bodily movement and posture.* Springfield, MA: Bassette.

Bowen, W.P. (1917). *Applied anatomy and kinesiology—The mechanism of human movement.* Philadelphia: Lea & Febiger.

Bowen, W.P. (1928). *Applied anatomy and kinesiology—The mechanism of human movement* (4th ed.). Philadelphia: Lea & Febiger.

Braun, G.L. (1941). Kinesiology: From Aristotle to the twentieth century. *Research Quarterly,* 12, 163-173.

Broer, M.R. (1960). *Efficiency of human movement.* Philadelphia: Saunders.

Broer, M.R. (1968). *An introduction to kinesiology.* Englewood Cliffs, NJ: Prentice Hall.

Broer, M.R. (1973a). *Efficiency of human movement* (3rd ed.). Philadelphia: Saunders.

Broer, M.R. (1973b). *Laboratory experiences: Exploring efficiency of human movement*. Philadelphia: Saunders.

Broer, M.R., & Houtz, S.J. (1967). *Patterns of muscular activity in selected sport skills: An electromyographic study*. Springfield, IL: Charles C. Thomas.

Broer, M.R., & Zernicke, R.F. (1979). *Efficiency of human movement* (4th ed.). Philadelphia: Saunders.

Brunnstrom, S. (1962). *Clinical kinesiology*. Philadelphia: Davis.

Brunnstrom, S. (1966). *Clinical kinesiology* (2nd ed.). Philadelphia: Davis.

Brunnstrom, S. (1972). *Clinical kinesiology* (3rd ed.). Philadelphia: Davis.

Bunn, J.W. (1955). *Scientific principles of coaching*. Englewood Cliffs, NJ: Prentice Hall.

Cavanagh, P.R. (1978). A technique for averaging center of pressure paths from a force platform. *Journal of Biomechanics*, **11**, 487-491.

Cavanagh, P.R. (1989). Biomechanical studies of elite distance runners: Directions for future research. In J.S. Skinner, C.B. Corbin, D.M. Landers, P.E. Martin, & C.L. Wells (Eds.), *Future directions in exercise and sport science research* (pp. 163-179). Champaign, IL: Human Kinetics.

Cavanagh, P.R. (1990). Biomechanics: A bridge builder among the sport sciences. *Medicine and Science in Sports Exercise*, **22**(5), 546-557.

Cerquiglini, S., Venerando, A., & Wartenweiler, J. (Eds.) (1973). *Biomechanics III*. Baltimore: University Park Press.

Charles, J.M. (1994). *Contemporary kinesiology: An introduction to the study of human movement in higher education*. Englewood, CO: Morton.

Contini, R., & Drillis, R. (1954). Biomechanics. *Applied Mechanics Review*, **7**(2), 49-52.

Contini, R., & Drillis, R. (1966). Biomechanics. In H.N. Abramson, H. Liebowitz, J.M. Crowley, & J. Juhasz (Eds.), *Applied Mechanics Surveys* (pp. 161-172). Washington, DC: Spartan Books.

Cooper, J.M. (Ed.) (1971). *Selected topics on biomechanics*. Chicago: Athletic Institute.

Cooper, J.M. (1978). The historical development of kinesiology with emphasis on concepts and people. In C.J. Dillman & R.G. Sears (Eds.), *Proceedings. Kinesiology: A national conference on teaching* (pp. 3-15). Urbana-Champaign: University of Illinois.

Cooper, J.M., Adrian, M., & Glassow, R.B. (1982). *Kinesiology* (5th ed.). St. Louis: Mosby.

Cooper, J.M., & Glassow, R.B. (1963). *Kinesiology* (2nd ed.). St. Louis: Mosby.

Cooper, J.M., & Haven, B. (1980). *Biomechanics: Symposium proceedings*. Indianapolis: Indiana State Board of Health.

Cureton, T.K. (1932). Physics applied to physical education. *Journal of Health and Physical Education*, January, pp. 23-25.

Cureton, T.K. (1939). Elementary principles and techniques of cinemato-graphic analysis as aids in athletic research. *Research Quarterly*, **10**, 3-24.

Dainty, D.A., & Norman, R.W. (1987). *Standardizing biomechanical testing in sport*. Champaign, IL: Human Kinetics.

de Groot, G., Hollander, A.P., Huijing, P.A, & van Ingen Schenau, G.J. (Eds.) (1988). *Biomechanics XI-A and XI-B*. Amsterdam, The Nether-lands: Free University Press.

Dillman, C.J. (1989). Improving elite performance through precise biome-chanical analysis. In J.S. Skinner, C.B. Corbin, D.M. Landers, P.E. Martin, & C.L. Wells (Eds.), *Future directions in exercise and sport science research* (pp. 91-95). Champaign, IL: Human Kinetics.

Dillman, C.J., & Nelson, R.C. (1968). The mechanical energy transforma-tions of pole vaulting with a fiberglass pole. *Journal of Biomechanics*, **1**, 175-183.

Dillman, C.J., & Sears, R.G. (1978). *Proceedings. Kinesiology: A national conference on teaching*. Urbana-Champaign: University of Illinois.

Donnelly, J.E. (Ed.) (1982). *Living anatomy*. Champaign, IL: Human Kinetics.

Donnelly, J.E. (Ed.) (1990). *Living anatomy* (2nd ed.). Champaign, IL: Human Kinetics.

Duvall, E.N. (1959). *Kinesiology: The anatomy of motion*. Englewood Cliffs, NJ: Prentice Hall.

Dyson, G.H.G. (1962). *The mechanics of athletics*. London: University of London Press.

Enoka, R.M. (1988). *Neuromechanical basis of kinesiology*. Champaign, IL: Human Kinetics.

Fenn, W.O. (1929). Mechanical energy expenditure in sprint running as measured by moving pictures. *American Journal of Physiology*, **90**, 343-344.

Fenn, W.O. (1930a). Frictional and kinetic factors in the work of sprint running. *American Journal of Physiology*, **92**, 583-611.

Fenn, W.O. (1930b). Work against gravity and work due to velocity changes in running. *American Journal of Physiology*, **93**, 433-462.

Fenn, W.O. (1931). A cinematographic study of sprinters. *Scientific Monthly*, **32**, 346-354.

Fenn, W.O., & Morrison, C.A. (1930). Frictional and kinetic factors in the work of sprint running. *American Journal of Physiology*, **92**, 583-611.

Fox, S. (1994). *Big leagues: Professional baseball, football, and basketball*. Fair-field, NJ: Morrow.

Frankel, V.H., & Nordin, M. (1980). *Basic biomechanics of the skeletal system*. Philadelphia: Lea & Febiger.

Fung, Y.C. (1968). Biomechanics: Its scope, history, and some problems of continuum mechanics in physiology. *Applied Mechanics Reviews*, **21**(1), 1-20.

Gench, B.E., Hinson, M.M., & Harvey, P.T. (1995). *Anatomical kinesiology.* Dubuque, IA: Eddie Bowers.

Glassow, R.B. (1932). *Fundamentals of physical education.* Philadelphia: Lea & Febiger.

Glassow, R.B. (1950). *A laboratory manual for functional kinesiology.* Madison, WI: Kramer Business Service.

Glassow, R.B., & Broer, M.R. (1938a). A convenient apparatus for the study of motion picture films. *Research Quarterly,* **9**(2), 41-49.

Glassow, R.B., & Broer, M.R. (1938b). *Measuring achievement in physical education.* Philadelphia: Saunders.

Glassow, R.B., Hubbard, A.W., & Brown, F. (1949). Photographical and cinematographical research methods. In M.G. Scott & T.K. Cureton (Eds.), *Research methods applied to health, physical education, and recreation.* Washington, DC: American Association for Health, Physical Education, and Recreation.

Gowitzke, B.A., & Milner, M. (1972). *Understanding the scientific bases of human movement.* Baltimore: Williams & Wilkins.

Grabiner, M.D. (Ed.) (1993). *Current issues in biomechanics.* Champaign, IL: Human Kinetics.

Greaves, J.O.B. (1995). Instrumentation in video-based three-dimensional systems. In P. Allard, I.A.F. Stokes, & J-P Blanchi (Eds.), *Three-dimensional analysis of human movement* (pp. 41-55). Champaign, IL: Human Kinetics.

Grieve, D.W., Miller, D.I., Mitchelson, D., Paul, J.P., & Smith, A.J. (1975). *Techniques for the analysis of human movement.* Princeton, NJ: Princeton Book.

Groves, R., & Camarone, D.N. (1975). *Concepts in kinesiology.* Philadelphia: Saunders.

Hall, S.J. (1991). *Basic biomechanics.* St. Louis: Mosby.

Hamill, J., Derrick, T.R., & Elliott, E.H. (Eds.) (1993). *Proceedings of the XI Symposium of the International Society of Biomechanics in Sports.* Amherst: University of Massachusetts.

Hamill, J., & Knutzen, K.M. (1995). *Biomechanical basis of human movement.* Baltimore: Williams & Wilkins.

Harris, R.W. (1967). *Kinesiology: Workbook and laboratory manual.* Boston: Houghton Mifflin.

Hart, I.B. (1925). *The mechanical investigations of Leonardo daVinci.* London: Chapman & Hall.

Hatze, H. (1974). Letter: The meaning of the term "biomechanics." *Journal of Biomechanics,* **7**, 189-190.

Hatze, H. (1976). Biomechanical aspects of successful motion optimation. In P.V. Komi (Ed.), *Biomechanics V-B* (pp. 5-12). Baltimore: University Park Press.

Hawley, G. (1937). *The kinesiology of corrective exercise.* Philadelphia: Lea & Febiger.

Hawley, G. (1940). *An anatomical analysis of sports*. New York: Barnes.

Hay, J.G. (1973). *The biomechanics of sport techniques*. Englewood Cliffs, NJ: Prentice Hall.

Hay, J.G. (Ed.) (1974). *Kinesiology IV*. Washington, DC: American Association for Health, Physical Education, and Recreation.

Hay, J.G. (1978). Biomechanics: The present and future state of the discipline in the United States and other western countries. In F. Landry & W.A.R. Orban (Eds.), *Biomechanics of sports and kinanthropometry* (pp. 3-10). Miami: Symposia Specialists, Inc.

Hay, J.G. (1981). *A bibliography of biomechanics literature* (4th ed.). Iowa City: The University of Iowa.

Hay, J.G. (1990). Sport biomechanics: A 25-year retrospective. In H-J Menzel and R. Preiss, *Forschungsgegenstant Sport*. (pp. 17-29). Frankfurt: Harry Deutsch Verlag.

Hay, J.G. (1993). *The biomechanics of sports techniques* (4th ed.). Englewood Cliffs, NJ: Prentice Hall.

Hay, J.G., & Reid, J.G. (1982). *The anatomical and mechanical bases of human motion*. Englewood Cliffs, NJ: Prentice Hall.

Hellebrandt, F.A., & Braun, G.L. (1939). Influence of sex and age on the postural sway of man. *American Journal of Physical Anthropology, 24*, 247-260.

Hellebrandt, F.A., Trepper, R.H., Braun, G.L., & Elliott, M.C. (1938). Location of the cardinal anatomical planes passing through the center of weight in young adult women. *American Journal of Physiology, 121*, 465-470.

Higgins, J.R. (1977). *Human movement: An integrated approach*. St. Louis: Mosby.

Hill, A.V. (1920). *Muscular movement in man*. New York: McGraw-Hill.

Hill, A.V. (1927). *Living machinery*. New York: Harcourt, Brace.

Hinson, M.H. (1977). *Kinesiology*. Dubuque, IA: Brown.

Hirt, S. (1955). What is kinesiology? A historical review. *Physical Therapy Review, 35*(8), 419-426.

Hopper, B.J. (1973). *The mechanics of human movement*. Great Britain: Fletcher & Sons, Ltd.

Hubbard, A.W. (1939). An experimental analysis of running and of certain fundamental differences between trained and untrained runners. *Research Quarterly, 10*, 28-38.

Hubbard, A.W. (1959). Photography. In M.G. Scott (Ed.), *Research methods in health, physical education, and recreation* (2nd ed.). Washington, DC: American Association for Health, Physical Education, and Recreation.

Hubbard, A.W., Cureton, T.K., Huelster, L., & Keller, L.F. (1949). Research methods in mechanics of sport and physical education activities. In M.G. Scott & T.K. Cureton (Eds.), *Research methods applied to health, physical education, and recreation*. Washington, DC: American Association for Health, Physical Education, and Recreation.

Hubbard, A.W., Cureton, T.K., Steinhaus, A.H., & Stetson, R.H. (1949). Methods of research in experimental kinesiology. In M.G. Scott & T.K. Cureton (Eds.), *Research methods applied to health, physical education, and recreation*. Washington, DC: American Association for Health, Physical Education, and Recreation.

Hudgins, C.V. (1939). The incidence of muscular contraction in reciprocal movement under conditions of changing loads. *Journal of General Psychology*, **20**, 327-338.

Huiskes, R., & Brand, R.A. (Eds.) (1989). Proceedings of the XII Congress of the International Society of Biomechanics, *Journal of Biomechanics*, **22**(1). (Chairmen: Robert J. Gregor and Ronald F. Zernicke)

Indiana Daily Student (1966). California professor to join I.U. faculty. March 8th.

Jenson, C.R., & Schultz, G.W. (1970). *Applied kinesiology: The scientific study of human performance*. New York: McGraw-Hill.

Jonsson, B. (Ed.) (1987). *Biomechanics X-A and X-B*. Champaign, IL: Human Kinetics.

Kelley, D.S. (1971). *Kinesiology: Fundamentals of motion description*. Englewood Cliffs, NJ: Prentice Hall.

Kinesiology Academy (1980). Guidelines and standards for undergraduate kinesiology. *Journal of Physical Education and Recreation*, February, 19-21.

Kinesiology Academy (1992). Guidelines and standards for undergraduate kinesiology. *Kinesiology Academy Newsletter*, Spring 1992, 3-6.

Kirby, R.F., & Roberts, J.A. (1985). *Introductory biomechanics*. Ithaca, NY: Mouvement.

Komi, P.V. (Ed.) (1976). *Biomechanics V-A and V-B*. Baltimore: University Park Press.

Kranz, L.G. (1948). *Kinesiology manual*. St. Louis: Mosby.

Krause, J.V., & Barham, J.N. (1975). *The mechanical foundations of human motion: A programmed text*. St. Louis: Mosby.

Kreighbaum, E., & Barthels, K.M. (1981). *Biomechanics: A qualitative approach for studying human movement*. Minneapolis: Burgess.

Kreighbaum, E., & McNeill, A. (Eds.) (1990). *Proceedings of the VIth Symposium of the International Society of Biomechanics in Sports*. Bozeman: Montana State University.

Landry, F., & Orban, W.A.R. (Eds.) (1978). *Biomechanics of sports and kinanthropometry*. Miami: Symposia Specialists, Inc.

Lee, M. (1983). *A history of physical education and sports in the U.S.A.* New York: Wiley.

LeVeau, B. (1977). *Williams and Lissner: Biomechanics of human motion* (2nd ed.). Philadelphia: Saunders.

LeVeau, B.F. (1992). *Williams & Lissner's: Biomechanics of human motion* (3rd ed.). Philadelphia: Saunders.

Lewillie, L., & Clarys, J.P. (Eds.) (1971). *Biomechanics of swimming*. Brussels: Universite Libre de Bruxelles.

Lewillie, L., & Clarys, J.P. (Eds.) (1975). *Swimming II*. Baltimore: University Park Press.

Lindholm, L.E. (1974). An opto-electronic instrument for remote on-line movement monitoring. In R.C. Nelson & C.A. Morehouse (Eds.), *Biomechanics IV* (pp. 510-512). Baltimore: University Park Press.

Lipovetz, F.J. (1952). *Basic kinesiology*. Minneapolis: Burgess.

Lissner, H.R. (1967). Biomechanics—What is it? In E.F. Byars, R. Contini, & V.L. Roberts (Eds.), *Biomechanics Monograph* (pp. 1-11). New York: American Society of Mechanical Engineers.

Logan, G.A., & McKinney, W.C. (1970). *Anatomical kinesiology*. Dubuque, IA: Brown.

Logan, G.A., & McKinney, W.C. (1970). *Kinesiology*. Dubuque, IA: Brown.

Luttgens, K., Deutsch, H., & Hamilton, N. (1992). *Kinesiology: Scientific basis of human motion* (8th ed.). Dubuque, IA: Brown & Benchmark.

Luttgens, K., & Zernicke, R.F. (1978). Structure and organization of kinesiology/biomechanics content at undergraduate level. In C.H. Dillman & R.G. Sears (Eds.), *Proceedings. Kinesiology: A national conference on teaching* (pp. 255-257). Urbana-Champaign: University of Illinois.

MacConaill, M.A., & Basmajian, J.V. (1969). *Muscles and movements: A basis for human kinesiology*. Baltimore: Williams & Wilkins.

Matake, T. (1976). On the new force plate study. In P.V. Komi (Ed.), *Biomechanics V-B* (pp. 426-432). Baltimore: University Park Press.

Matsui, H., & Kobayashi, K. (Eds.) (1983). *Biomechanics VIII-A and VIII-B*. Baltimore: University Park Press.

McCloy, C.H. (1937). The organization and teaching of apparatus work and tumbling. *Journal of Physical Education*, March-April, 60-62.

McCloy, C.H. (1960). The mechanical analysis of motor skills. In W.R. Johnson (Ed.), *Science and Medicine of Exercise and Sports*. New York: Harper.

McLaughlin, T.M., Dillman, C.J., & Gardner, T.J. (1977). Biomechanical analysis with cubic spline functions. *Research Quarterly*, **48**, 569-582.

Miller, D.I. (1971). A computer simulation model of the airborne phase of diving. In J.M. Cooper (Ed.), *Selected topics on biomechanics* (pp. 207-215). Chicago: Athletic Institute.

Miller, D.I. (1975). Computer simulation of human motion. In *Techniques for the analysis of human movement* (pp. 69-105). Princeton, NJ: Princeton Book.

Miller, D.I., & Nelson, R.C. (1973). *Biomechanics of sport: A research approach*. Philadelphia: Lea & Febiger.

Miller, D.I., & Petak, K.L. (1973). Three-dimensional cinematography. In C.J. Widule (Ed.), *Kinesiology III* (pp. 14-19). Washington, DC: American Association for Health, Physical Education, and Recreation.

Morecki, A., Fidelus, K., Kedzior, K., & Wit, A. (Eds.) (1981). *Biomechanics VII-A and VII-B*. Baltimore: University Park Press.

Morehouse, L.E., & Cooper, J.M. (1950). *Kinesiology*. St. Louis: Mosby.

Morrison, W.E. (Ed.) (1989). *Proceedings of the VIIth Symposium of the International Society of Biomechanics in Sports*. Victoria, Australia: Footscray Institute of Technology.

Nelson, R.C. (1971). Biomechanics of sport: An overview. In J.M. Cooper (Ed.), *Selected topics on biomechanics* (pp. 31-37). Chicago: Athletic Institute.

Nelson, R.C. (1973). Biomechanics of sport: Emerging discipline. In S. Cerquiglini, A. Venerando, and J. Wartenweiler (Eds.), *Biomechanics III* (pp. 336-341). Baltimore: University Park Press.

Nelson, R.C. (1980). Biomechanics: Past and present. In J.M. Cooper and B. Haven (Eds.), *Proceedings of the biomechanics symposium* (pp. 4-13), Bloomington: The Indiana State Board of Health.

Nelson, R.C. (1989). Biomechanics for better performance and protection from injury. In J.S. Skinner, C.B. Corbin, D.M. Landers, P.E. Martin, & C.L. Wells (Eds.), *Future directions in exercise and sport research* (pp. 5-12). Champaign, IL: Human Kinetics.

Nelson, R.C., & Morehouse, C.A. (Eds.) (1974). *Biomechanics IV*. Baltimore: University Park Press.

Norkin, C.C., & Levangie, P.K. (1983). *Joint structure & function: A comprehensive analysis*. Philadelphia: Davis.

Norman, R.W. (1989). A barrier to understanding human motion mechanisms: A commentary. In J.S. Skinner, C.B. Corbin, D.M. Landers, P.E. Martin, & C.L. Wells (Eds.), *Future directions in exercise and sport science research* (pp. 151-161). Champaign, IL: Human Kinetics.

Northrip, J.W., Logan, G.A., & McKinney, W.C. (1974). *Introduction to biomechanics analysis of sport*. Dubuque, IA: Brown.

Nosek, M., Sojka, D., Morrison, W.E., & Susanka, P. (Eds.) (1990). *Proceedings of the VIIIth Symposium of the International Society of Biomechanics in Sports*. Prague, Czechoslovakia: Conex Company.

O'Connell, A.L. (Ed.) (1968). *Kinesiology Review 1968*. Washington, DC: American Association for Health, Physical Education, and Recreation.

O'Connell, A.L., & Gardner, E.B. (1972). *Understanding the scientific bases of human movement*. Baltimore: Williams & Wilkins.

Peaseley, H.V. (1932). Experimental study of kinesiological factors influencing the learning of the golf drive. Unpublished master's thesis, University of Wisconsin.

Piscopo, J., & Bailey, J.A. (1981). *Kinesiology: The science of movement*. New York: Wiley.

Plagenhoef, S.C. (1968). Computer programs for obtaining kinetic data on human movement. *Journal of Biomechanics*, **1**, 221-234.

Plagenhoef, S. (1971). *Patterns of human motion: A cinematographic analysis*. Englewood Cliffs, NJ: Prentice-Hall.

Posse, B.N. (1894). *The special kinesiology of educational gymnastics* (3rd ed.). Boston: Lothrop, Lee, & Shepard.

Rasch, P.J. (1958). Notes toward a history of kinesiology. Parts I, II, and III. *Journal of the American Osteopathic Association*, **58**: 572-574, 641-644, 713-714.

Rasch, P.J. (1989). *Kinesiology and applied anatomy* (7th ed.). Philadelphia: Lea & Febiger.

Rasch, P.J., & Burke, R.K. (1959). *Kinesiology and applied anatomy*. Philadelphia: Lea & Febiger.

Rasch, P.J., & Burke, R.K. (1963). *Kinesiology and applied anatomy* (2nd ed.), Philadelphia: Lea & Febiger.

Remley, M.L. (1980). Ruth B. Glassow: Teacher-scholar. In M.J. Swoboda & A.J. Roberts (Eds.), *They came to learn, they came to teach, them came to stay*. Madison, WI: Office of Women.

Rodano, R., Ferrigno, G., & Santambrogio, G.C. (Eds.) (1992). *Proceedings of the Xth Symposium of the International Society of Biomechanics in Sports*. Milano, Italy: Edi-Ermes.

Scheuchenzuber, J. (1983). *Experiments in the mechanics of human movement*. Ithaca, NY: Mouvement.

Scott, M.G. (1942). *Analysis of human motion: A textbook in kinesiology*. New York: Meredith.

Scott, M.G. (1947). *Kinesiology handbook: A study guide and laboratory manual*. New York: Appleton-Century-Crofts.

Scott, M.G. (Ed.) (1959). *Research methods in health, physical education, and recreation* (2nd ed.). Washington, DC: American Association for Health, Physical Education, and Recreation.

Scott, M.G. (1963). *Analysis of human motion* (2nd ed.). New York: Meredith.

Scott, M.G., & Cureton, T.K. (Eds.) (1949). *Research methods applied to health, physical education, and recreation*. Washington, DC: American Association for Health, Physical Education, and Recreation.

Scott, M.G., & French, E. (1949). *Measurement and evaluation in physical education*. Dubuque, IA: Brown.

Shapiro, R. (1978). Direct linear transformation method for three-dimensional cinematography. *Research Quarterly*, **49**(2), 197-205.

Shapiro, R., & Marett, J.R. (Eds.) (1984). *Proceedings of second national symposium on teaching kinesiology and biomechanics in sports*. Colorado Springs, CO: United States Olympic Committee.

Simonian, C. (1981). *Fundamentals of sports biomechanics*. Englewood Cliffs, NJ: Prentice Hall.

Skarstrom, W. (1909). *Gymnastic kinesiology*. Springfield, MA: Bassette.

Slater-Hammel, A.T. (1948). Action current study of contraction-movement relationships in golf stroke. *Research Quarterly*, **19**, 164-177.

Slater-Hammel, A.T. (1949). An action current study of contraction-movement relationships in the tennis stroke. *Research Quarterly*, **20**, 424-431.

Sloan, M.R. (1987). Ruth B. Glassow: The cutting edge. In *American Academy of Physical Education Papers* (Vol. 20, pp. 120-128). Champaign, IL: Human Kinetics.

Sloan, M.R. (1989). In memoriam: Ruth Glassow. *Journal of Physical Education, Recreation and Dance*, February, 20-21.

Soderberg, G.L. (1986). *Kinesiology application to pathological motion*. Baltimore: Williams & Wilkins.

Spence, D.W. (1975). *Essentials of kinesiology: A laboratory manual*. Philadelphia: Lea & Febiger.

Sperry, R.W. (1939). Action current study in movement coordination. *Journal of General Psychology*, **20**, 295-313.

Steindler, A. (1935). *Mechanics of normal and pathological locomotion in man*. Springfield, IL: Charles C Thomas.

Steindler, A. (1942). What has biokinetics to offer to the physical educator? *Journal of Health, Physical Education and Recreation*, **13**(9), 507-509, 555-556.

Steindler, A. (1955). *Kinesiology of the human body under normal and pathological conditions*. Springfield, IL: Charles C. Thomas.

Stelmach, G.E. (1987). The cutting edge of research in physical education and exercise science: The search for understanding. In *American Academy of Physical Education Papers* (Vol. 20, pp. 8-25). Champaign, IL: Human Kinetics.

Stone, H.A. (1953). *Applied anatomy and kinesiology—The mechanism of human movement by Wilbur Pardon Bowen* (7th ed.). Philadelphia: Lea & Febiger.

Tant, C.L., Patterson, P.E., & York, S.L. (Eds.) (1991). *Biomechanics in Sports IX: Proceedings of the 9th International Symposium on Biomechanics in Sports*. Ames: Iowa State University.

Terauds, J. (Ed.) (1978a). *Science in athletics*. In *Proceedings of the International Congress of Sport Sciences*. Edmonton, Alberta, Canada. Del Mar, CA: Academic.

Terauds, J. (Ed.) (1978b). *Science in biomechanics cinematography*. In *Proceedings of the International Congress of Sport Sciences*. Edmonton, Alberta, Canada. Del Mar, CA: Academic.

Terauds, J. (Ed.) (1978c). *Science in gymnastics*. In *Proceedings of the International Congress of Sport Sciences*. Edmonton, Alberta, Canada. Del Mar, CA: Academic.

Terauds, J. (Ed.) (1978d). *Science in skiing, skating and hockey*. In *Proceedings of the International Congress of Sport Sciences*. Edmonton, Alberta, Canada. Del Mar, CA: Academic.

Terauds, J. (Ed.) (1978e). *Science in sports*. In *Proceedings of the International Congress of Sport Sciences*. Edmonton, Alberta, Canada, Del Mar, CA: Academic.

Terauds, J. (Ed.) (1978f). *Science in racket sports*. In *Proceedings of the International Congress of Sport Sciences*. Edmonton, Alberta, Canada. Del Mar, CA: Academic.

Terauds, J. (Ed.) (1978g). *Science in weight lifting.* In *Proceedings of the International Congress of Sport Sciences.* Edmonton, Alberta, Canada. Del Mar, CA: Academic.

Terauds, J. (Ed.) (1982). *Biomechanics in sports: Proceedings of the international symposium of biomechanics in sports.* Del Mar, CA: Academic.

Terauds, J., & Barham, J. (Eds.) (1985). *Proceedings of the II Symposium of the International Society of Biomechanics in Sports.* San Diego. Del Mar, CA: Academic.

Terauds, J., Barthels, K., Kreighbaum, E., Mann, R., & Crakes, J. (Eds.) (1984). *Proceedings of the 1st Symposium of the International Society of Biomechanics in Sports.* Del Mar, CA: Academic.

Terauds, J., & Bedingfield, E.W. (Eds.) (1979). *Swimming III.* Baltimore: University Park Press.

Terauds, J., Gowitzke, B.A., & Holt, L.E. (Eds.) (1987). *Proceedings of the III & IVth symposium of the International Society of Biomechanics in Sports. Nova Scotia.* Del Mar, CA: Academic.

Thompson, C.W., & Floyd, R.T. (1994). *Manual of structural kinesiology* (12th ed.). St. Louis: Mosby.

Tricker, R.A.R., & Tricker, B.S.K. (1967). *The science of movement.* New York: American Elsevier.

Tsrouchas, L. (Ed.) (1987). *Proceedings of the Vth Symposium of the International Society of Biomechanics in Sports.* Athens, Greece: Hellenic Sports Research Institute.

Van Gheluwe, B. (1974). A new three-dimensional filming technique involving simplified alignment and measurement procedures. In R.C. Nelson & C.A. Morehourse (Eds.), *Biomechanics IV* (pp. 476-481). Baltimore: University Park Press.

Van Gheluwe, B. (1978). Computerized three-dimensional cinematography for any arbitrary camera setup. In E. Asmussen & K. Jorgensen (Eds.), *Biomechanics VI-A* (pp. 343-348). Baltimore: University Park Press.

Van Gheluwe, B., & Atha, J. (Eds.) (1987). *Current research in sports biomechanics.* New York: Karger.

Vaughan, C.L. (Ed.) (1989). *Biomechanics of sport.* Boca Raton, FL: CRC Press.

Vaughan, C.L., Davis, B.L., & O'Connor, J.C. (1992). *Dynamics of human gait.* Champaign, IL: Human Kinetics.

Vredenbregt, J., & Wartenweiler, J. (Eds.) (1971). *Biomechanics II.* Baltimore: University Park Press.

Walters, C.E., Cooper, J.M., & Young, O. (1959). Kinesiology and activity analysis. In M.G. Scott (Ed.), *Research methods in health, physical education, and recreation* (2nd ed.). Washington, DC: American Association for Health, Physical Education, and Recreation.

Walton, J.S. (1979). Close-range cine-photogrammetry: Another approach to motion analysis. In J. Terauds (Ed.), *Science in biomechanics cinematography* (pp. 69-97). Del Mar, CA: Academic.

Walton, J.S. (1981). Close-range cine-photogrammetry: A generalized technique for quantifying gross human motion. *Dissertation Abstracts International*, **42**, 1526B.

Wartenweiler, J. (1973). Status report on biomechanics. In S. Cerquiglini, A. Venerando, & J. Wartenweiler (Eds.), *Biomechanics III* (pp. 65-72). Baltimore: University Park Press.

Wartenweiler, J., Jokl, E., & Hebbelinck, M. (Eds.) (1968). *Biomechanics*. New York: Karger.

Weineck, J. (1986). *Functional anatomy in sports*. St. Louis: Mosby.

Wells, K.F. (1950). *Kinesiology*. Philadelphia: Saunders.

Wells, K.F. (1960). *Kinesiology* (3rd ed.). Philadelphia: Saunders.

Wells, K.F. (1968). Kinesiology reports: William Skarstrom, M.D., teacher in kinesiology. *Journal of Health, Physical Education, and Recreation*, September, 77-78.

Widule, C.J. (Ed.) (1971). *Kinesiology Review 1971*. Washington, DC: American Association for Health, Physical Education, and Recreation.

Widule, C.J. (Ed.) (1973). *Kinesiology III 1973*. Washington, DC: American Association for Health, Physical Education, and Recreation.

Widule, C.J. (1974). *Analysis of human motion: Laboratory experiences, experiments, and problems*. Lafayette, IN: Balt.

Widule, C.J. (1980). The contributions of Ruth B. Glassow to pedagogical kinesiology. In J.M. Cooper & B. Haven (Eds.), *Biomechanics: Symposium proceedings* (pp. 101-118). Indianapolis: Indiana State Board of Health.

Widule, C.J. (1994). *Biomechanical foundations of motor skills with computer applications*. West Lafayette, IN: Learning Systems, Inc.

Wild, M.R. (1937). The behavior pattern of throwing and some observations concerning its course of development in children. Unpublished master's thesis, University of Wisconsin.

Wilkerson, J.D. (1991). Teaching for competencies in graduate biomechanics. In J.D. Wilkerson, E. Krieghbaum, & C.L. Tant (Eds.), *Teaching kinesiology and biomechanics in sports* (pp. 167-171). Ames: Iowa State University.

Wilkerson, J.D., Kreighbaum, E., & Tant, C.L. (Eds.) (1991). *Teaching kinesiology and biomechanics*. Ames: Iowa State University.

Williams, M., & Lissner, H.R. (1962). *Biomechanics of human motion*. Philadelphia: Saunders.

Wilt, F. (1970). *Mechanics without tears*. Tucson, AR: United States Track and Field Federation.

Winter, D.A. (1979). *Biomechanics of Human Movement*. New York: John Wiley & Sons.

Winter, D.A. (1989). Future directions in biomechanics research of human movement. In J.S. Skinner, C.B. Corbin, D.M. Landers, P.E. Martin, & C.L. Wells (Eds.), *Future directions in exercise and sport resarch* (pp. 201-207). Champaign, IL: Human Kinetics.

Winter, D.A, Norman, R.W., Wells, R.P., Hayes, K.C., & Patla, A.E. (Eds.) (1985). *Biomechanics IX-A and IX-B*. Champaign, IL: Human Kinetics.

Winter, D.A., Sidwall, H.G., & Hobson, D.A. (1974). Measurement and reduction of noise in kinematics of locomotion. *Journal of Biomechanics*, **7**, 157-159.

Wood, J.A., & Jennings, L.S. (1979). On the use of spline functions for data smoothing. *Journal of Biomechanics*, **12**, 477-479.

Wright, W.G. (1928). *Muscle function*. New York: Hoeber.

Zernicke, R.F., Caldwell, G., & Roberts, E.M. (1976). Fitting biomechanical data with cubic spline functions. *Research Quarterly*, **47**, 9-19.

Exercise Physiology

Elsworth R. Buskirk, PhD (*Part I*)
The Pennsylvania State University
Charles M. Tipton, PhD (*Part II*)
University of Arizona

The following chapter has been written in two parts; the authors are key players in the American exercise physiology movement during the times about which each writes. Elsworth Buskirk takes us from classical and European influences in the nineteenth century to the 1940s and the demise of the Harvard Fatigue Laboratory.

Charles Tipton looks at the field's coming into its own after World War II. He argues that it is during this time that exercise physiology becomes more than a subdiscipline of physiology, and its research and discourse gain legitimacy in the academic community.

As with the other subdisciplines discussed in this book, exercise physiology has seen increasing specialization in the last two decades. As the chronology shows, the number of advanced degrees in this field have exploded. Yet the reader will deduce in both articles that the field of exercise physiology has always stressed practical application—from Johnson's study of pre-game emotion in football players to Flair's findings on the health benefits of exercise. The field has not succumbed to academicism even as it has become more systematic in its methodologies.

Part I: Early History in the United States

Perhaps it goes without saying that advances in exercise physiology have followed those in basic physiology, albeit influenced by athletic and other human performance. Thus, the understanding of the impact of various types of exercise on body systems, cellular elements, and so on has provided a driving force for investigators. There is little doubt that numerous

▼

A Chronology of Exercise Physiology

Early Foundations

Year   Event

1855   William H. Byford published a seminal paper on the physiology of exercise.

1861   Edward Hitchcock began the systematic collection of data before and after training regimens at Amherst College.

1891   The American Association for the Advancement of Physical Education was founded which emphasized the importance of exercise physiology to physical education.

1891   George W. Fitz established the first formal research laboratory in physical education in the United States at Harvard University. Physiological responses to exercise were measured at this site.

1898   The first volume of *The American Journal of Physiology* was published due to the efforts of William T. Porter. He also started the Harvard Apparatus Company which encouraged physiological research by providing affordable instruments.

1899-1901   Eugene Darling conducted pre- and posttraining studies on athletes at Harvard University.

1900s   James H. McCurdy initiated physiological research at Springfield College. Later, Peter V. Karpovich developed a teaching and research laboratory at this institution in 1927.

1910   R. Tait McKenzie, the renowned sculptor of sport, published an important book entitled *Exercise in Education and Medicine*.

1923   Arthur H. Steinhaus established a laboratory at George Williams College devoted largely to the teaching and research of exercise physiology.

1925-1929   Archibald V. Hill visited the United States on more than one occasion to interact with American physiologists and to present his important studies on the physiology of skeletal muscle.

1927   The Harvard Fatigue Laboratory was established by Lawrence J. Henderson and G.E. Mayo who appointed David Bruce Dill as director. Before its closing in 1946, this prestigous and productive laboratory demonstrated the scientific importance of exercise physiology investigations, became a model for interdisciplinary research, and had personnel that subsequently established major research programs throughout the United States.

1930s Several textbooks devoted to exercise physiology appeared including revisions of books by F.A. Bainbridge and J.H. McCurdy.

1933 The "Chronic effects of exercise" is authored by Arthur Steinhaus and published in *Physiological Reviews*.

Development of Discipline

Year Event

1948 The American Physiological Society established the *Journal of Applied Physiology* to publish research related to the responses of humans exposed to a variety of stress and environmental conditions that included exercise.

1948 Thomas K. Cureton established the Physical Fitness Research Laboratory at the University of Illinois that graduated highly motivated and capable physical educators in the physiological foundations of fitness.

1954 The American College of Sports Medicine was established for professionals from medicine, physiology, and physical education.

1963 James B. Conant published a scathing indictment of teacher training in the United States with particular emphasis on the lack of scholarship and academic rigor in the physical education graduate programs. He recommended their abolishment.

1964 Physical education and interdisciplinary units in Big Ten and Pac-10 institutions plus Pennsylvania State University begin to implement rigorous PhD degree programs with an emphasis in exercise physiology.

1964 The National Institutes of Health (NIH) established the Applied Physiology Study Section to evaluate the increasing number of proposals seeking federal funding for proposals related to physical fitness, exercise physiology, environmental physiology, and neuromuscular-joint functions.

1969 The American College of Sports Medicine established a new professional journal entitled *Medicine and Science in Sports* with Bruno Balke as its editor-in-chief. The majority of the articles published in the next decade pertained to exercise physiology.

Present and Future of the Discipline

Year Event

1970s National Defense Education Act and NIH programs begin to support pre- and postdoctoral students with a specialty in exercise physiology. In addition, federal funds were awarded to investigators for exercise physiology related research and to institutions for the construction of laboratory facilities.

1970s   Marked increases in PhD programs that offer an academic specialization in exercise physiology. This era was the beginning of departmental name changes to exercise science, exercise and sport sciences, kinesiology, and combinations thereof.

1977   The American Physiological Society established a membership section that included exercise with thermal and environmental physiologists.

1977   The title of the *Journal of Applied Physiology* was changed to include exercise physiology with respiratory and environmental physiology.

1994   International conference on physical activity, fitness, and health in Toronto, Canada, published its comprehensive proceedings which incorporated findings from exercise physiology research into its recommendations for the future.

1996   American Physiological Society will publish its first handbook devoted to exercise physiology. Loring B. Rowell and John T. Shephard will serve as co-editors of this extensive and prestigious publication.

---

budding investigators have been attracted to the field because of their own active lifestyles. Brooks (1981, p. 48) has succinctly stated that "the physiologist amplifies physiological responses by means of exercise." Thus, a theoretical advantage regarding understanding may well occur with such amplification.

Our heritage in the United States with respect to exercise physiology is heavily dependent on the early work, particularly in the eighteenth and nineteenth centuries, in Europe. Nevertheless, there is a significant early history of exercise physiology within the United States emanating both from clinical personnel interested in exercise programs and investigators interested in the bodily responses to exercise and the mechanisms underlying these responses. Fortunately, as science in general and physiology in particular have progressed, so has exercise physiology; this trend is destined to continue (Buskirk, 1981).

Trends and transitions in society shaped the discipline we now know as exercise physiology. Because virtually all of the early investigators were physicians the discipline has been closely linked to medicine. Thus, to understand the early days of the subdiscipline, it will be helpful to look at what medicine's concerns were in those days. In the early part of the century the treatment and prevention of contagious diseases was a major issue. Sanitation was poor and emphasis was placed on providing

Gerard, Bard, and Fenn going to the APS meeting in Atlantic City, 1946

Glenn Cunningham (subject)

Harvard Fatigue Lab group. Left to right: Sid Robinson, C.F. Consolazio, R.E. Johnson, Aste-Salazar, R. McFarland, L.J. Henderson, Bogue, L. Brouha, Jones, and Bruce Dill.

F. Miescher   David Bruce Dill

Archibald V. Hill

C.H. McCloy

William G. Anderson

Clark W. Hetherington

Harvard Fatigue Laboratory reunion, Atlantic City, NJ, 1961. Front, left to right: Pecora, Phillips, F. Consolazio, Barger, W. Consolazio, Zamcheck. Sitting: Forbes, Bock, Dill, Hall, McFarland. Third row: Robinson, Horvath, Knehr, Lee, Riley, Belding, Whittenberger, Johnson, Brouha, Karpovich, Gray, Pace. Far left rear: G. Consolazio, Scholander, Hickan, Pitts.

Thomas K. Cureton

Arthur H. Steinhaus

Peter V. Karpovich

R.E. Johnson

Sid Robinson

Henry L. Taylor

Elsworth Buskirk

Leonard A. Larson

Bruno Balke

Henry J. Montoye

Participants in the meeting held in Bethesda on January 10, 1984. Standing, left to right: Jere H. Mitchell, John T. Shepherd, Loring B. Rowell, Carl V. Gisolfi, Jerome A. Dempsey, Philip D. Gollnick. Seated: Howard F. Morgan, Leo C. Senay, Jr., Alfred P. Fishman, Charles M. Tipton, and H. Lowell Stone.

Erik Hohwu-Christensen

uncontaminated water, sewage disposal, safe foods, rodent elimination, and so on.

Frequently the heads of the university departments of physical education were physicians who also had responsibility for student health. The Turnerverein movement from Europe, principally Germany, was present in our Turner schools with physicians prominent on the faculties, frequently even as presidents. Thus, an orientation toward science, and particularly physiology, was evident.

Social changes also affected this developing field, such as shifts in occupations and some diminution in physical labor. The needs of our military personnel in terms of fitness for service, particularly in the World Wars, promoted an overall interest in physical activity. Throughout, a variety of athletes engaged in several sports focused national interest on their achievements—everything from rowing and cross-country bicycling to boxing and wrestling. Organized sports such as baseball and football began to appear, as did the professional athlete. International games such as the Olympic games stimulated research interest in ways of enhancing performance.

This essay focuses on what might be regarded as major early events and contributors to the formation of the field of exercise physiology. The perspective presented here essentially ends with World War II and the closing of the Harvard Fatigue Laboratory in 1947.

Early Foundations

In the early 1800s, a time when our story really begins in the United States, the core of an exercise training regimen involved real physical sacrifice and adjuncts such as heavy sweating and purging. The major aim was to improve strength and improve the wind but things such as purging and bleeding were deemed necessary to rid the body of noxious material, as was the administration of Glauber's salt, an internal cleanser. Such was the state of affairs in exercise physiology at the beginning of the nineteenth century, for science had dealt with exercise only to a very limited extent (Thom as referenced in Park, 1987a).

Textbooks of physiology began to appear but the inclusion of useful information about exercise was extremely limited (Combe, 1843). Nevertheless, the zeal for competitive sport and rigorous physical recreation was well established, with considerable interaction between Europe and the United States. Empirically gained experience was passed from one group to another and a variety of advisory publications gave counsel to the laity. Park (1987b) has termed his pass-through of empiricism the "persistence of tradition."

During the first half of the nineteenth century classical Greek preventive hygiene still prevailed in medical training, with the six non-naturals that formed part of the "humoral theory" of Hippocrates and Galen becoming virtually the "laws of health" (Withington, 1894; Berryman, 1989). Thus, regular exercise as the non-natural component "motion and rest" became an important component for behavior leading to good health. To this day we have embodied this concept into our "wellness" and "healthy lifestyle" programs.

During the middle of the nineteenth century William H. Byford published an article dealing with the physiology of exercise, but there was little interest in the scientific analysis of exercise. Nevertheless, he encouraged such involvement because he believed exercise's effects upon the economy had not been thoroughly investigated and understood. He wanted to draw the attention of the profession to the importance of further research. Despite Byford's plea it would be several more decades before serious research efforts were undertaken regarding physiology of exercise (Byford, 1855).

A development of some consequence was the popularity of high level athletic competition in the 1800s and early 1900s, and the dedicated training that accompanied it. Physicians of the time viewed as suspect such activity that stressed the body inordinately and thereby severely taxed the athlete's physiological systems. Those physicians who became involved did so at a college or university involved in intercollegiate sport or at an athletic club. Relatively simultaneously physiologists, particularly in Europe, recognized that the study of athletes could provide insights into stress responses, physiological adaptation to regular exercise or training, and the limits of human performance.

The Physical Education Connection

With respect to the origin of scientific emphasis in exercise physiology as applied to physical education, credit should undoubtedly be given Edward Hitchcock, who in 1861 began systematically collecting anthropometric data before and after schedules of physical training. Following the lead of the Englishman Archibald Maclaren and practices instituted by others both in the USA and abroad, Hitchcock merely formalized anthropometrical assessment. Dudley Sargent at Harvard also instituted anthropometric appraisals in 1879. The interest in anthropometry waned, largely because many felt that no real science was involved. The efforts of physiologists began to be recognized, culminating in 1891 when the American Association for the Advancement of Physical Education bestowed honorary membership status upon several scientists, including H.O. Bowditch, a noted physiologist and Dean of the Harvard Medical School. Luther Halsey Gulick, who worked at the YMCA Training School in Springfield, MA, wrote for the Association in 1890 that he believed an understanding both of physiology and medicine was necessary to properly teach gymnastics. He also noted that the opportunity for new and worthy scientific investigation was available in physical education to a greater extent than in any other profession. Because of his beliefs Gulick went on to found the Academy of Physical Education, which required the performance of original research for admission and continuation of research for retention of membership (Kroll, 1982).

Further impetus for the merging of science with physical education was provided in the 1890s by the initiative of Thomas Wood at Stanford university. He established a four-year degree program leading to an undergraduate degree in physical training and hygiene. Physiology of exercise was an important component, as was applied anatomy and physiology (as well as animal physiology). Special investigations were to be undertaken by advanced students, including the testing of physical conditions and specific effects of various exercises upon the nervous system, heart, lungs, and other systems. Collaboration with the Department of Physiology was a significant asset. Sixteen hours of basic science and three hours of investigative effort were part of a 35-hour semester (Kroll, 1982).

A contemporary of Wood was George Fitz, who established the first formal research laboratory in physical education in the United States. In the midst of arguments in support of the many competing systems for the teaching of physical education, he emphasized the need for grounding physical education training in science. The training program he set up at Harvard emphasized the accumulation of scientific knowledge; thus, the Department of Anatomy, Physiology, and Physical Training was housed in the Lawrence Scientific School and offered a four-year BS degree. Fitz was involved with the program from 1891 until 1899 when he resigned, presumably under pressure for limited publishing (Kroll, 1982; Park, 1987a).

Among the aims of the department were:

1. to prepare persons who, with or without subsequent training in medicine, may intend to seek employment as directors of gymnastics or instructors of physical training; and
2. to afford, in the first two years, a suitable general training for young men who may desire afterwards to pursue the study of medicine. Students completing the four-year course could enter the second class at the Medical School and graduate in three years.

The associated laboratory was described as follows: "A large and well-equipped laboratory has been organized for the experimental study of the physiology of exercise. The object of this work is to exemplify the hygiene of the muscles, the conditions under which they act, the relation of their action to the body as a whole affecting blood supply and general hygienic conditions, and the effects of various exercises upon muscular growth and general health" (Fitz 1908). Fitz himself taught elementary physiology and the physiology of exercise, and shared teaching responsibilities with Dudley Sargent for a course in the history of physical education. Sargent was also responsible for applied anatomy, anthropometry, tests and measurements, animal mechanics, and the effects of age and physical training. These topics were to be pursued after the students were well grounded in biology, physics, and chemistry during their first two years. In addition, students were obliged to spend the third year of the program in the Medical School (Kroll, 1982).

In 1900 the title of the department was changed to Anatomy and Physiology with no further reference to physical education. During the program's tenure nine men graduated from the program but none seems to have contributed measurably to the physiology of exercise literature. Although important work in physiology continued at Harvard it was not until the establishment of the Harvard Fatigue Laboratory in 1927 that Harvard refocused on exercise physiology (Kroll, 1982; Park, 1987a).

Fitz was born in New York in 1860 and met his demise in an auto collision with a passenger train in 1934 on Long Island. He was apparently somewhat of a gadgeteer, having developed a three-phase camera, a micromanipulator, and a reaction-to-location apparatus. Some of his publications involving exercise physiology included a study of types of respiratory movements (1894); a location reaction apparatus (1895); the physiological cost of insufficient protective clothing (1914); a clinical study of muscular cramp (1926); a new micromanipulator (1931); and a micromanipulator for pure culture and microchemical work (1934). Fitz's interest in respiratory mechanics as well as body heat exchange and the physiological utility of protective clothing demonstrated a unique capability in human applied physiology that set an example for both his professional peers and students.

In addition to publishing physiologically oriented research he was the author of *Principles of Physiology and Hygiene* (Fitz, 1908). Kroll (1982) has compiled considerable perspective regarding Fitz's contributions; the interested reader should consult his extensive review.

Eugene Darling, a professor at Harvard, was invited by the Harvard Athletic Committee in 1899 to conduct metabolic studies on the Harvard crew to clarify the consequences of overtraining. He later studied members of the football team but could only conclude that modest weight loss produced no ill effects. His related observations on myocardial function yielded the generalized observation that "not size but quality tells in the long run" (Darling, 1899, 1901).

A variety of others, including W.O. Atwater, A.P. Bryant, J.B. Blake, R.C. Larrabee, G. Meylan, W. Savage, and M. Murphy, contributed useful information in the early 1900s about gross metabolism, pulse rate, blood pressure, body temperature, and urinary and bowel excretion. Murphy was regarded as the guru of athletic training, and his book *Athletic Training*, published in 1914, was regarded as applying the best scientific knowledge to the training of athletes. Nevertheless, Murphy recognized that a major reason for the international success of U.S. athletes was the popularity of athletes and the large pool of school, college, and club participants, and not scientific knowledge (Murphy, 1914; Park, 1987a). Although Murphy was not a physician or an investigator in his own right, he had studied medicine for two years at the University of Pennsylvania and had read widely from the scientific literature. Nevertheless, he relied heavily on his observations of athletes responding to his recommendations as a track and football coach at Yale as well as a club trainer. He was selected by the U.S. Olympic Committee to coach both the 1908 and 1912 teams. He held sway in U.S. athletics as the preeminent source of information for nearly 30 years, from 1887 to 1916.

A contemporary of Murphy was Paul Withington, a physician, who published his *Book of Athletics* in 1914. Withington, a wrestler and rower at Harvard, updated N. Bingham's 1895 *Book of Athletics and Out-of-Door Sports* by utilizing several "experts" to provide information about training regimens and techniques for a variety of sports. He himself contributed sections on track and football (Bingham, 1895; Withington, 1914). Ironically, neither Murphy nor Withington made use of the available scientific literature by citing pertinent experimental studies from such journals as the *Boston Medical and Surgical Journal, American Journal of Medical Sciences,* and the *American Journal of Physiology.* Such brief reference was contained in R. Tait McKenzie's book *Exercise in Education and Medicine* (1910) but not to the extent possible or to an important level of scientific enlightenment. His emphasis was on sportsmanship and character-building, together with mental and moral development. Nevertheless, he did mention metabolic cardiovascular and metabolic studies as well as his urinary excretion studies at the 1904 Olympics.

R. Tait McKenzie, most often recognized as a renowned sculptor of sport, earned his MD degree at McGill University in 1892, following the earning of a diploma in physical education from Dudley A. Sargent's Summer School at Harvard's Hemenway Gymnasium. He learned Sargent's system of exercises, and anthropometric assessment, and was exposed to exercise physiology. His sculptures certainly reflected this training. In 1904 as chairman of the Department of Physical Education at the University of Pennsylvania he opened a new gymnasium and opined "the policy of the department may thus be said to contain something of the hospital clinic, a great deal of the classroom and laboratory, and a little of the arena." McKenzie was interested in the effects of exercise on the heart as well as the lifelong impact of strenuous training and athletic competition on the body. He launched efforts in preventive medicine by debunking the notion of "athlete's heart." He had considerable influence on those around him, including Joseph Wolffe and Grover Mueller, who were both instrumental in the founding of the American College of Sports Medicine (Berryman, personal communication; McKenzie, 1910).

The Athletic Research Laboratory, of some significance in exercise physiology, was established at the University of Illinois in 1925 by Coleman Griffith. The program in the laboratory was primarily oriented toward psychology, although it was founded to undertake research on the effects of physical training and athletics on bodily functions. Five hundred square feet of laboratory space was ostensibly devoted to physiology, including a workshop and a rat colony, with animals supplied by the Wistar Institute. Among the testing possibilities were utilization of an apparatus for determining reaction times to various stimuli, including muscular load as well as muscular tension and relaxation. The laboratory went out of existence in 1932, perhaps because the severe economic depression that started in 1929 caused the Athletic Association to withdraw its support. Nevertheless, Griffith went on to bigger things in psychology and administration, eventually becoming provost of the University of Illinois (Donnelly, 1960; Kroll, 1982).

Certainly one of the important personages in exercise physiology, particularly as related to physical education, is Arthur H. Steinhaus, who became the founder in 1923 of the second laboratory devoted to exercise physiology in YMCA-supported schools. In the early 1900s, largely under the leadership of James Huff McCurdy, physiologic research was begun at Springfield College. Later, direction and solidification of a true laboratory were achieved under the direction of Peter Karpovich, who remained active in research until his death. Following the lead of Springfield College, Steinhaus organized a laboratory at Williams College in Chicago and began training students for laboratory-based research. Research on the tension and resilience of human muscles, components of strength, muscular coordination, acid-base balance during exercise, and so on, soon began to appear in publications from the laboratory. Significantly, Steinhaus published two exemplary reviews that had a major impact on exercise physiology, in the 1930s and 1940s. Steinhaus was a philosopher as well as a distinguished investigator, and those interested in gaining perspective on his remarkable insights would be well advised to peruse his book *Toward an Understanding of Health and Physical Education* (1963).

International Union of Physiological Sciences

The First International Congress of the International Union of Physiological Sciences (IUPS) was held in Basel, Switzerland, in 1889. The IUPS was organized by a group of prime movers consisting of H. Kronecker, professor of physiology at Bern; Michael Foster of Cambridge; W.M. Bayliss and E.A. Shafer of London; and Carl Ludwig of Leipzig. Their organizational meeting was held in Ludwig's laboratory in 1888. At the first meeting it was noteworthy that Mosso demonstrated his spring myograph for recording fatigue in human muscles. The initiation of this triennial meeting provided an opportunity for international information exchange and camaraderie that has persisted to this day. Since most of the early U.S. researchers in exercise physiology spent either training or collaborative research time in Europe, the IUPS meetings provided not only opportunities for initial contact but also for furthering collaborative research. Professor H.P. Bowditch of Harvard was appointed as the U.S. representative to the First Congress. Upon organization about 130 members joined IUPS which, according to the available records from the First Congress, included seven members from the U.S. Gerald F. Yeo, professor of physiology at King's College, London, was made honorary secretary of the First Congress, because it was he who had originally suggested the idea for a congress. Frithiof Holmgren, from Upsala, Sweden, was designated president of the First Congress. Although U.S. scientists played only a modest role in the First Congress, they continued participating in subsequent Congresses in important ways, which had an impact on the careers of several of them as related to their activities associated with the physiology of exercise (Fenn, 1968; Whitteridge, 1989).

All of the IUPS congresses were held in Europe until 1929, when the 13th Congress was held in Boston. This congress was a unique affair because there were now 1,700 members and a good many of the Europeans traveled together aboard the S.S. Minnekahda, a chartered one-class ship. An exception were 60 French physiologists who arranged their travel on the S.S. France. The chartered ship was arranged for by A.V. Hill, the renowned British physiologist who has contributed so much to our understanding of the physiology of skeletal muscle. August Krogh, the distinguished Danish physiologist, gave an opening address.

At the two previous congresses, the 1923 congress in Edinburgh and the 1926 congress in Stockholm, former combatants from World War I (22 nations were represented) had bridged over many of their political differences and the Minnekahda experience provided ample opportunity for social interchange. Wives, female physiologists, and about 200 secretaries returning from a European trip enlivened the crossing. Dancing in the evening, shared meals, and deck sports such as shuffleboard and deck tennis helped reduce any residual tensions. As Prohibition was still in force, no alcoholic beverages were served.

The weather was most accommodating and the sea was quite calm, thwarting the expectations of Starkenstein, a pharmacologist from Prague to test his new drug for seasickness with the 400 physiologists on board. He was sighted frequently inspecting the seas from the bridge for an opportunity to start testing.

Nevertheless, talking shop was the main order of each day for the ten days. Orbelli talked about his experiments on the effect of sympathetic stimulation on fatigued muscle. A.V. Hill discussed with the Eggletons their observations regarding "phosphagen" and heat production in muscle; Lundsgaard observed that muscle could contract without freeing lactic acid, which countered the commonly held view of Embden that lactic acid was only liberated after a contraction. Here was an opportunity for the younger scientists to share their views and aspirations with established investigators, for there were no fewer than nine future Nobel Prize winners on board. Thus, the crossing served the function of a pre-congress.

On docking in Boston the entourage was greeted by Walter Cannon, chairman of the Congress Bureau at Harvard. Unfortunately, it was quite warm in the dock barracks, but within an hour everyone was transported to their respective dormitories at Harvard University (Y. Zotterman, *The Minnekahda Voyage* as reported in Fenn, 1968).

Early Physiologists Who Had an Impact on Exercise Physiology

As now, exercise physiology in the late 1800s and early 1900s in the United States derived much of its general impetus from the work that was ongoing in the general field of physiology. In this context several prominent physiologists were instrumental in facilitating the training and support of those interested in pursuing the reactions of bodily systems to exercise. It is fitting that the contributions of these outstanding scientists be mentioned.

Porter. W.T. Porter not only established the first laboratory west of the Atlantic seaboard in 1885 at St. Louis Medical School (now Washington University) but also the Harvard Apparatus Company in 1901. He started the *American Journal of Physiology* in 1898 with his own resources, and originated the Porter Fellowship, which has helped numerous budding young investigators since its initiation. Designing apparatus was a hobby of his and his founding of the Harvard Apparatus Company allowed investigators to obtain instruments that they needed at prices they could afford.

Porter was born in Plymouth, Ohio, in 1862. He had to work to support himself and his education because both parents died before he entered college. He received his degree in medicine from the St. Louis College of Medicine in 1885. Thereafter, he spent a year in three laboratories in Germany before being appointed professor of physiology at his alma mater. His early studies involved intracardiac pressures, effects of coronary ligation, and child growth. In 1893 he was called by Professor Bowditch to the Harvard Medical School; there he continued work on respiration and circulation.

Porter edited the *American Journal of Physiology* until 1914, when he turned over to the American Physiological Society an established journal of high standards. He retired in 1928 but his legacy for exercise physiology includes instrumentation that many early investigators used in their studies, the promotion of laboratory courses in physiology, his setting of high publication standards for a journal in which U.S. scientists could publish their work in exercise physiology, and the establishment of the Porter

Fellowship for young investigators, which continues to this day (Anonymous, *The Physiologist*, 1961).

Howell.   William Henry Howell was a product of Johns Hopkins University, with a background in chemistry and biology, and a student of
Newell Martin. He received his PhD in 1884 in animal physiology. His
thesis involved work on blood coagulation, a topic he stayed with throughout his investigative career. He served on the faculties of Michigan and
Harvard before returning to Johns Hopkins in 1893 as professor of physiology. He encouraged work in the area of exercise physiology, and mentioned that a large Fick Pendulum Myograph was the chief visitor
attraction. A further contribution was the editing in 1896 of the *American
Textbook of Physiology*. In 1905 he prepared his own textbook, which subsequently went through 14 editions and became the main source of written
physiology for American medical students. Following his death the text
was continued under joint authorship for a period of about 40 years.
His original work on the isolation of thrombin and work on heparin, a
compound that he later named, provided considerable understanding of
the coagulation process.

Howell greatly enjoyed sports, which no doubt contributed to his interest in supporting work on exercise physiology. He was said to play
excellent tennis, and good golf, and sailed the Maine coast. During his
later years, after giving up tennis, he became expert at lawn bowling. He
passed away in 1945 but had remained relatively active scientifically,
although severely compromised with a chronic ulcer problem (Anonymous, *The Physiologist*, 1961).

Chittenden.   Russell Henry Chittenden is remembered as the father of
biochemistry in the United States. He was born, raised, and educated in
New Haven, graduating with a PhD from the Sheffield Scientific School
of Yale University in 1875. His PhD was the first, in physiological chemistry, given by an American university. He regarded physiological chemistry as an important part of physiology, with chemistry providing basic
tools for investigators. In 1882, he was appointed professor of physiological chemistry at Yale.

As he and others had done, young people interested in a career in
physiology were obliged to go abroad to further their training, but that
was changed by Chittenden, along with Bowditch at Harvard, and Martin
and Howell at Johns Hopkins. Their development of laboratories in the
United States created excellent opportunities for budding investigators.
Chittenden's own work was on human protein requirements, but his
emphasis on the chemical side of physiology contributed uniquely to the
growing emphasis on physiology in the United States (Anonymous, *The
Physiologist*, 1960). In addition, he provided the impetus for incorporating
biochemical analyses into studies conducted by those investigating various aspects of exercise physiology.

Flint. An exceptional early contribution to exercise physiology was made by Flint (1871), a professor of physiology at the College of Physicians and Surgeons, Columbia University. He doubted the observation that protein was not a fuel supporting muscular exercise—an observation that was based on a lack of increase in nitrogen excretion with exercise, including mountain climbing. Flint and his colleagues studied the famous distance walker Edward Payson Weston before, during, and after a five-day walk covering 317.5 miles. The conclusion, based on body weight change and nitrogen intake and output, was that there is loss of body protein with prolonged heavy exercise—a finding that has been supported by subsequent work (Flint, 1871, 1878).

Early Physiology of Exercise Papers in the American Journal of Physiology

The first volume of the *American Journal of Physiology* was published in 1898 and contained three papers that dealt with the physiology of exercise. The first, a paper by C.C. Stewart (a Fellow in physiology at Clark University), described variations in daily activity among gray rats, a red squirrel, and dogs. Spontaneous activity in a revolving drum was found to be inversely related to barometric pressure among the rats and the squirrel, but the effect on dogs was a direct relationship. The difference was attributed to wildness versus domestication. A rich diet (dog biscuits and water) led to a decrease in spontaneous activity, whereas a plain diet increased it. Alcohol decreased activity among the rats when alcohol was given as a 30 to 60 percent solution. A 20 percent solution had no effect.

The second paper, by R.H. Cunningham (1898) from Columbia, involved the restoration of movement by nerve crossing using ulnar, median, and musculo-spiral nerves in the forelegs of dogs. He concluded that crossing the peripheral portion of the motor nerve of rhythmically contracting muscles to the central portion of the motor nerve of nonrhythmic muscles results in the permanent abolition of the rhythmic action of the former muscles. These results confirmed that central nervous mechanisms do not adjust their impulses to satisfy altered peripheral innervation, as others had concluded. Nevertheless, coordinated volitional movement could be reattained.

The third paper, from the University of Chicago, was by J.C. Welch (1898), on the interrelationships between mental and physical activity. An important conclusion from the hand dynamometer mental task experiments was that the feeling of muscular fatigue sets in much later (15% to 33%) when the muscular activity was accompanied by mental activity. Although many of the other papers contained observations and assessment techniques of consequence to subsequent studies of exercise physiology, these three papers were the only ones in which physical activity was directly involved.

The exercise physiology papers published in the first five volumes of the *American Journal of Physiology* emanated from several university laboratories, most of which were in basic science and chiefly physiology (see table 10.1). With respect to the initiation of journals devoted to physiology that contained important papers on exercise physiology, the *American Journal of Physiology*, started in 1989, held the forefront until 1921 when *Physiological Reviews* was begun. It was not until 1948 that the *Journal of Applied Physiology* was initiated. Thus, the field of physiology was expanding at a rapid rate and those interested in exercise physiology began to have the tools and expertise of all physiologists to support their work.

Energetics

An important feature of early work on energetics was the development and extensive utilization of indirect calorimetry. Accurate chemical determinations of the components of inspired and expired air, chiefly oxygen and carbon dioxide concentrations, became possible, as did accurate measurement of the volume of expired air using volume-collecting devices such as Douglas bags and Tissot spirometers along with gas meters.

Table 10.1 Papers Related to the Physiology of Exercise Published in the First Five Issues of *The American Journal of Physiology*

Volume	Year	Author	Location
1	1898	Stewart, C.C.	Physiology, Clark University
	1898	Cunningham, R.H.	College of Physicians & Surgeons, Columbia University
	1898	Welch, J.C.	Hull Physiological Laboratory, University of Chicago
2	1898-1899	Latimer, C.W.	Physiological Laboratory, Johns Hopkins University
3	1899-1900	Huber, G.C.	Laboratory of Histology, University of Michigan
4	1900-1901	Franz, S.I.	Laboratory of Physiology, Harvard Medical School
5	1901	McCurdy, J.H.	Laboratory of Physiology, Harvard Medical School
	1901	Hough, T.	Biological Laboratory of the Massachusetts Institute of Technology
	1901	Cleghorn, A. and Stewart, C.C.	Laboratory of Physiology, Harvard Medical School

The emphasis upon study of human energy requirements in the early years of the twentieth century was led by the Europeans Carl Voit and Max Rubner, but significant contributions were also made by the U.S. scientists G. Lusk, F.G. Benedict, W.O. Atwater, and E. DuBois. The basic energy values of carbohydrates, proteins, and fats derived by Atwater remain the rough standards we use today, namely 4, 4, and 9 kcal · g^{-1}, respectively. Benedict and his colleagues explored many avenues of energy expenditure during exercise, and DuBois gave us standards for the basal metabolic rate (Bursztein, Elwyn, Askanazi, & Kinney, 1989).

A notable series of investigations on energy expenditure during exercise was carried out by F.G. Benedict and his associates at the Carnegie Nutrition Laboratory in Boston. The results of the studies were published as monographs by the Carnegie Institution of Washington. They used a treadmill extensively and had the first one devoted to research in this country. They also developed a universal respiration apparatus and utilized a Cambridge string galvanometer, together with electrodes on the chest, for recording the heart rate during exercise. Thus, they were able to follow oxygen uptake and carbon dioxide elimination as well as heart rate and rectal temperature. Modern instrumentation facilitates better continuous measurement with less manpower, but accuracy has not been improved to date. Benedict's colleague, Thorne Carpenter, modified the Haldane chemical gas analysis system so that oxygen and carbon dioxide concentrations could be measured very accurately. In addition he prepared meticulous tables for the appraisal of energy transformations. Thus, the contributions from this laboratory provided a solid base in this country for the study of energy turnover during exercise (Benedict & Cathcart, 1913; Benedict & Murschhauser, 1915; Carpenter, 1948).

Complementary contributions were made to an understanding of energetics by investigators in the agricultural sciences in the 1920s, 1930s, and 1940s. Two who worked diligently to clarify the concepts of efficiency of muscular work were S. Brody and M. Kleiber. Brody's contributions were set forth in that exceptional summary of his work published as *Bioenergetics and Growth* in 1945. Brody and his colleagues worked primarily with farm animals, although they studied other mammalian species as well. Their work with ponies and horses established that, for given intensities of work, the efficiencies (gross, net, and absolute) were essentially the same in large Percheron horses, smaller Shetland ponies, and still smaller men. They formulated the concept that efficiency of work is independent of the size of the animal. Their calculations revealed that the efficiency associated with converting energy to physical work was 25 percent for gross, 28 percent for net, and 35 percent for absolute efficiency. In addition to making contributions to our understanding of energy conversions in mammalian species, they also added to the equipment and technological armamentaria available to other scientists.

Kleiber published a review of his work on energetics in a book entitled *Fire of Life* in 1961. Many of his contributions were made much earlier when he became involved with the general issue of body size and metabolism (1932). Among other things, Kleiber calculated the partial efficiency of animal work to be about 23 percent, and came to the conclusion that the conversion of chemical energy to work in the muscle does not go via heat, but that muscle is a chemodynamic machine and not a thermodynamic one. In addition to studies of muscular work efficiency, Kleiber also contributed to our basic understanding of respiratory, metabolic, and heat exchanges.

The Contributions of Hill and Bock

In 1923 A.V. Hill was inaugurated as Joddrell Professor of Physiology at University College, London. His inaugural address, printed in a modified form in *Science* (1925, pp. 294-365), was noteworthy for the guiding principles that have subsequently influenced human physiology, including exercise physiology. Some excerpts follow:

It is strange how often a physiological truth discovered on an animal may be developed and amplified, and its bearing more truly found, by attempting to work it out on man.

Man has proved . . . the best subject for experiments on respiration and on the carriage of gases by the blood, and an excellent subject for the study of kidney, muscular, cardiac, and metabolic function. . . .

The methods . . . are those of biochemistry, of biophysics, of experimental physiology; but there is a special kind of art and knowledge required . . . realizing the limits to which it is wise and expedient to go.

Quite apart from direct physiological research on man, the study of instruments, methods . . . , their . . . standardization . . . , are bound to prove of great advantage to medicine . . . .

Athletics, physical training, flying, working, . . . all require a knowledge of the physiology of man.

The observation of sick men in hospitals is not the best training for the study of normal man at work.

While a visiting lecturer at Cornell, Hill took the opportunity to study the Cornell sprinters, and developed a timing system to measure their acceleration. Hill also visited Arlie Bock's laboratory at Harvard in 1926. Bruce Dill was working there at the time and Hill encouraged Bock and Dill to prepare a third edition of Bainbridge's *The Physiology of Muscular Exercise*, which they did. Dill remarked:

This we did with great profit to ourselves since it gave us a good historical perspective, useful in shaping the program of the Fatigue Laboratory . . . . (Dill, 1980).

No doubt the conversations with Hill also had a bearing on the direction the studies in the Fatigue Laboratory would take. Another American on whom Hill had an impact was Wallace Fenn, who later contributed substantially to our understanding of muscle physiology (Fenn, 1930).

Hill presented a series of lectures at the Lowell Institute in Boston and also at Cornell University. These lectures were published in two monographs in 1927. The steady state of exercise, as well as the factors governing recovery from fatigue, were presented in *Muscular Movement in Man*. The relationship of neuromuscular coordination and cardiorespiratory function to strength, speed, and endurance were described in *Living Machinery*. Hill's pioneering work was well received in the United States and he stimulated, as well as interacted with, many U.S. scientists (Hill, 1927a, 1927b).

Arlie Bock. Arlie Bock, an Iowa farm boy and a Harvard product, received the Harvard Moseley Traveling Fellowship in 1920 to study with Professor Barcroft, the respiratory, high-altitude physiologist, at Cambridge University. That association led to his participation in Barcroft's high-altitude expedition to Peru in 1922. Upon his return to the United States in 1923 he was put in charge of a research laboratory at the Massachusetts General Hospital, which was associated with the Harvard Medical School.

Bruce Dill arrived in Cambridge in 1925 to work with L.J. Henderson as a postdoctoral Fellow in chemistry. Henderson advised Dill to join Bock's team in research on the physicochemical properties of blood. This project fit nicely with Dill's background in physical chemistry and his Stanford study of wheat proteins. Bock had acquired from F.G. Benedict, director of the Boston Nutrition Laboratory, the equipment and skill for the assessment of oxygen uptake during exercise, and Dill also learned these skills. Bock had also instituted arterial puncture techniques, so that gas exchange between lungs and blood could be investigated. Clarence DeMar, who won the Boston Marathon seven times, was a subject for studies of muscular activity, published in the *Journal of Physiology* (London) by Bock, Dill, and others (Bock, van Caulaert, Dill, Fölling, & Hurxthal, 1928a, 1928b).

During the period from 1925 to 1927 when Henderson conceived the Harvard Fatigue Laboratory, Bock played a key role in its formation in the role of advisor and research collaborator, and took an important part in the Laboratory's first study in the desert in 1932.

Bock was renowned for analyzing the gas concentrations of venous and arterial blood. He was adept at the painstaking procedure of equilibrating portions of blood with appropriate gas mixtures to establish the tightly fitted curves that Henderson plotted on his charts. A consummate scientist and a dedicated physician, Bock remained close friends with Dill for 59 years before passing on at age 95 (Dill, 1985).

Organization of the Discipline: Beginning With Harvard

The Harvard Fatigue Laboratory really constitutes a unique spot in the history of exercise physiology in the United States. L.J. Henderson, aided by G.E. Mayo, pulled an influential group of people together and convinced them to back the formation of the Laboratory within the School of Business Administration. Bruce Dill was given the directorship of the Laboratory—a position he held from the opening of its doors in 1927 until they closed in 1947. Under Dill's leadership the Laboratory became an example for several laboratories that have since been initiated, such as the Institute of Environmental Stress established by Steve Horvath at the University of California at Santa Barbara, and the Laboratory for Physiological Hygiene that Ancel Keys developed at the University of Minnesota.

A Shared Philosophy

The Laboratory program reflected Henderson's special interest in man's internal physiological environment, that is, the *milieu intérieur* proposed by Claude Bernard. Henderson's view encompassed the biological and psychological interactions that comprise our physiological responses to stress. Dill shared this philosophy and evidenced the necessary ability to integrate the roles of body systems in their response to life's activities. Dill also had the ability to attract bright, dedicated people to work in the Laboratory. Scientists of various stripes were represented, including physiologists, biochemists, biologists, clinicians, psychologists, psychiatrists, sociologists, and anthropologists.

Several pieces of equipment were routinely utilized in the Laboratory: treadmill, cycle ergometer, Haldane gas analyzer, van Slyke blood gas analyzer, Tissot spirometer, and an electrocardiograph string galvanometer. Special equipment was designed and built as needed (Dill, 1967; Horvath & Horvath, 1973).

The title of the research unit contained the word "fatigue." Chapman (1990) has credited Mayo, who worked on industrial fatigue, with the views that worker fatigue impaired worker productivity and that fatigue should be studied systematically. Henderson followed with the observation that the title Fatigue Laboratory was useful because ''business leaders, engineers, physiologists, and the general public . . . all agree about the importance of fatigue. . . ." Thus, the title seems to have been chosen because of its general interest, and because it did not label research activities along departmental lines (Chapman, 1990).

An important impetus for the Harvard Fatigue Laboratory may well have come from the work of English physiologist Edward Smith who, in the middle of the nineteenth century with relatively crude equipment, measured carbon dioxide output, expiration volume, respiratory and pulse rates, and water output, in human subjects. He studied prisoners sentenced to the hard labor of driving the prison treadmills. By simultaneous measurement of several variables, he established the basic holistic approach subsequently adopted by those in the Fatigue Laboratory. Perhaps he should also be credited with maturation of the British school of physiology, which later produced such luminaries in physiology as William Bayless, Ernst Starling, J.S. Haldane, A.V. Hill, and Joseph Barcroft, all of whom had an impact on the development of exercise physiology (Billings, 1870; Chapman, 1990). Research areas of exercise physiology with which personnel from the Laboratory were involved included maximal oxygen uptake, oxygen debt, substrate metabolism, fitness assessment, blood gas profiles, acid-base balance, and environmental and occupational effects.

The important papers on the physiology of exercise from the Laboratory began to appear in 1928. Over 50 papers on exercise eventually were published during the 20 years of the program's existence. As demonstrated by many of these papers, personnel associated with the Laboratory established exceptional technology and developed considerable insight as to the effects of exercise (plus different ambient conditions) on intact human subjects. Among those who worked in the Laboratory, most have expressed the presence of a great "esprit de corps" developed from working within the Henderson-Dill-Bock-Mayo ambience. The prevailing camaraderie and generous intellectual exchange provided the stage for significant accomplishment, as well as an exemplary laboratory role model for additional generations of exercise physiologists. It was exceedingly unfortunate that Harvard's President Conant in 1947 decreed the demise of the Fatigue Laboratory, largely because he was doubtful of its post-war value (Chapman, 1990; Horvath & Horvath, 1973).

The Closing of the Harvard Fatigue Laboratory

In regard to the closing of the Laboratory, Dill explained philosophically:

> The dissolution of the laboratory and distribution of its assets, the unhappy task of W.H. Forbes, was completed in 1946. While it saddened those of us who had spent happy years there, I do not consider it to have been an irreparable loss to physiology. Successful organisms

have a way of reaching maturity, declining, and dying, but not without perpetuating their kind. So it was with the Fatigue Laboratory. (Horvath & Horvath, 1973)

In the aftermath of the Laboratory's closing many of the people moved on to locations at which they could continue work on the physiology of exercise. Dill and Whittenberger moved to the U.S. Army Chemical Corps Medical Labs in Maryland. Dill later joined Sid Robinson, who had relocated at Indiana University where he established the Human Physiology Laboratory. Whittenberger subsequently returned to Harvard's School of Public Health. C.F. Consolazio joined the U.S. Army Medical Research and Nutrition Laboratory in Denver. R.C. Darling became a prominent professor at Columbia University's Department of Rehabilitation Medicine. Lucien Brouha set up a Fitness Research Unit at the University of Montreal and then moved to the Haskell Laboratory at the DuPont Chemical Company in Delaware. Steve Horvath moved to the physiology department at the University of Iowa, before joining Kaare Rodahl at the Lankenau Hospital's Division of Research for a few years, prior to establishing the Institute of Environmental Stress at the University of California at Santa Barbara. R.E. Johnson became part of the U.S. Army Quartermaster Medical Nutrition Laboratory in Chicago before establishing, with Fred Sargent, the Human Environmental Unit at the University of Illinois. H.S. Belding also became affiliated with the U.S. Army, becoming part of the Quartermaster Climatic Research Laboratory in Massachusetts before moving to the University of Pittsburgh, where he set up the Environmental Physiology Laboratory. Ancel Keys established the Laboratory for Physiological Hygiene at the University of Minnesota, where Henry Taylor subsequently joined him. D.H.K. Lee moved to the USPHS Occupational Health and Training Facility in Cincinnati before moving on to the Quartermaster Environmental Research Laboratory in Massachusetts. Thus, the legacy of Harvard Fatigue Laboratory has been far-reaching, and the contributions of those whose roots emanate from the Laboratory have been exceptional. At this writing only a few survivors remain, including Steve Horvath, Ancel Keys, and R.E. Johnson, all of whom are still active (as of 1996) regarding science. Senior personnel associated with the Harvard Fatigue Laboratory included Edward F. Adolph, Arlie V. Bock, Bruce Dill, Robert C. Darling, Harold T. Edwards, William H. Forbes, Robert E. Johnson, Ross A. McFarland, and John H. Talbott.

Dill's philosophy was expressed in an interesting manner in the introduction of the book *Physiology of Exercise*, written by L.E. Morehouse and A.T. Miller, Jr. (1948):

The reader will be impressed with the arduous experiments upon which our present understanding of the physiology of muscular exercise rests. It is not enough to make neat studies of frogs' nerve-muscle preparations, of swimming rats and of panting dogs. Man himself must be the subject; many of the advances in exercise physiology have come from self-experimentation. The examples of Barry Wood spending Saturday evening in the Fatigue Laboratory studying blood samples collected from himself and his fellow football players during the afternoon, of Sid Robinson running to exhaustion on the treadmill with unheard-of blood lactate concentrations, of Ancel Keys, cold and anoxic, undergoing arterial punctures during six days at 20,000 feet, of Harold Edwards keeping pace on desert sands with a burro, give one a picture of the stuff from which exercise physiologists are made.

Early Textbooks: Exercise Physiology

Perhaps the most influential textbooks of the early twentieth century are those listed below. F.A. Bainbridge's book *The Physiology of Muscular Exercise* first appeared in 1923 and was later revised, but the third edition in 1931 was completely rewritten by A.V. Bock and D.B. Dill, who were then working together in the Harvard Fatigue Laboratory. Their interaction with various European scientists, their interpretation of their investigations, and summaries of their own work were included. In 1924 J.H. McCurdy published the first edition of *The Physiology of Exercise*. He revised it in 1928 and teamed with L.A. Larson for another revision in 1939. E.C. Schneider's book *Physiology of Muscular Activity* also appeared in 1931. This book went through several editions (1939) with Schneider later teaming up with P. Karpovich from Springfield College to keep the book current with investigative work. After Schneider's death, Karpovich continued to revise the book, with Wayne Sinning eventually taking over.

Slightly later (1935) P. Dawson's book *Physiology of Physical Education* joined the parade of works that presented numerous basic observations on the impact of exercise under a variety of conditions. It is remarkable that many of the results and interpretations reported have stood the test of subsequent verification. Nevertheless, the abbreviated spelling detracted from this book's usefulness.

Several other pre-World War II books should also be mentioned, because they had an effect on the education of contemporary and future investigators, as well as teachers. These books include A. Combe (1843), *The Principles of Physiology Applied to the Preservation of Health and to the Improvement of Physical and Mental Education*; A. Flint, Jr. (1878), *On the Source of Muscular Power*; N.W. Bingham, ed. (1895), *The Book of Athletics and Out-of-Door Sports*; R.T. McKenzie (1910), *Exercise in Education and Medicine*; M.C. Murphy (1914), *Athletic Training*; G. Dreyer (1920), *The Assessment of Physical Fitness*; F. Deutsch, E. Kauf, and L.M. Warfield (1927), *Heart and Athletics*; C.H. McCloy (1932), *The Measurement of Athletic*

Power; H.W. Haggard and L.A. Greenberg (1933), *Diet and Physical Efficiency*; and A.G. Gould and J.A. Dye (1935), *Exercise and its Physiology*.

Research Support

In the early years only meager financial support was available, usually through the employing institution or from small grants from foundations or industry. In 1887 the federal government appropriated $300 for a one-room Laboratory of Hygiene in the top floor of the Staten Island Marine Hospital. The unit was kept afloat there until 1938, when a National Institute of Health was created on a 300-acre campus in Bethesda, Maryland. The National Cancer Institute was the first disease-oriented institute formed. Growth continued until 1945, when a significant step was taken by Congress to create the extramural program. The Laboratory of Hygiene, and later the NIH, did virtually nothing to support research in exercise physiology. It was not until the late 1950s and early 1960s, when an ad hoc Study Section of Applied Physiology was converted into a permanent Study Section, that financial support became available. Such support continues to this day, albeit with add-ons to the Study Section such as orthopedics and respiration. Thus, creation of the Study Section of Applied Physiology insured a modicum of broad-based support for exercise physiology for the first time by a branch of the federal government. It is amazing that so much good work was accomplished with the meager resources available prior to World War II.

Part II: A Contemporary Historical Perspective

This chapter is a contemporary perspective on the history of exercise physiology since the end of World War II. According to Webster's new World Dictionary, a historian is a writer of history and/or an authority on history (Neufeld & Guralnik, 1988). Since the author does not possess the academic credentials to warrant such a distinction, this part of the chapter will provide a perspective on the myriad of factors, influences, and interactions that have contributed to the current development and acceptance of exercise physiology in the United States. An insight on the research accomplishment that has occurred in exercise physiology since 1954 can be found, in part, within the *40th Anniversary Lectures*, as published in 1994 by the American College of Sports Medicine (ACSM, 1994) and presented by G.A. Brooks and D.L. Costill in the "Basic Exercise" and "Applied Physiology" lectures, respectively (Brooks, 1994a; Costill, 1994a).

However, it is the position of the author that by the end of World War II, exercise physiology was a subdiscipline of physiology, even though its existence was barely acknowledged by the academic community. Moreover, the research findings, albeit limited, associated with exercise up to that time, had become an integral component of the physiological literature (as Buskirk discusses in Part I of this chapter), and the justification of exercise physiology research was never an issue that required scientific approval. Rather, it was a matter of whether the results of exercise physiology would be accepted by the biological, medical, and educational communities as a legitimate body of scientific knowledge. In this chapter, the emphasis will be on the myriad of factors and interactions that facilitated its emergence (Anonymous, 1948).

Physiology has been defined as the "mother of the biological sciences" and that definition includes exercise physiology. Restated in the terminology of Kroll (1982), exercise physiology is a subdiscipline of physiology that became a discipline within the profession of exercise science, or kinesiology.

From a classical and traditional viewpoint, an exercise physiologist is an individual who, academically prepared as a physiologist by physiology departments, subsequently specializes in exercise physiology as demonstrated by his/her research, teaching, service, or clinical endeavors. However, as elaborated in later sections, the majority of individuals who contributed to the development of the discipline of exercise physiology were not academically prepared in accordance with this classical definition. Thus, the modern description of an exercise physiologist will indicate the individual received his/her physiological backgrounds and foundations from courses provided by either physiology, biology, or cognate departments, while acquiring their exercise physiology training and expertise from departmental and/or interdisciplinary degree programs that included physiology, biology, physical education, kinesiology, exercise science, physical therapy, or combinations thereof. It is of interest that in the 1990 APS "White Paper" on the future of physiology, the point was made that the education, training, and definition of a physiologist could no longer be described or explained by traditional approaches or terminology (Giebisch et al., 1990). The same concept is applicable for exercise physiology.

It is well documented that individuals with MD degrees have made significant contributions to the history of physiology (Fenn, 1963); the same is true for exercise physiology, although the numbers are drastically lower. Some of the physicians associated with the early history who remained active in the contemporary era were R.E. Johnson of the Harvard Fatigue Laboratory and the University of Illinois, E. Simonson of the Laboratory of Physiological Hygiene at the University of Minnesota, and P.V. Karpovich from Springfield College. Later, B. Balke of the School of Aerospace Medicine and the University of Wisconsin, C.B. Chapman and

J.H. Mitchell of University of Texas Southwestern Medical Center, J.O. Holloszy of Washington University, R.J. Shephard of the University of Toronto, P.D. Wagner of the University of California at San Diego, and K. Wasserman of the University of California at Los Angles (UCLA), to name several, made diverse and significant contributions that helped establish the scientific foundations, leadership, and directions for exercise physiology. These same statements are applicable for two MDs from Sweden who, in later decades, greatly influenced North American developments, namely, P.-O. Astrand and B. Saltin.

Because physicians can also be classified as physiologists, cardiologists, internists, and so on, it would be inappropriate to assume that all individuals who contributed to the development of exercise physiology with PhD or equivalent degrees considered themselves exercise physiologists; rather, many preferred to be identified as applied, work, human, environmental, or stress physiologists, or as physical educators. To some, D.B. Dill could be considered the father of contemporary exercise physiology; however, it is evident from his activities and responsibilities at the Harvard Fatigue Laboratory and thereafter that he also could have been classified as a human, work, or environmental physiologist (Horvath & Horvath, 1973). In essence, many of the scientists who contributed to the development of exercise physiology were similar to Dill in their classifications.

Development of the Discipline

Like most disciplines, the evolvement and recognition of exercise physiology was not an orderly or systematic process (Kroll, 1982). For this section, the contemporary era spans the years since World War II that have been empirically classified into three time periods whose beginnings have historical reference points. The first period, labelled the "Embryonic Years," begins with the end of World War II and the demise of the Harvard Fatigue Laboratory (Buskirk, 1996; Horvath & Horvath, 1973), and the creation of the Research Grants Office within the National Institutes of Health (NIH Almanac, 1989). The second period, identified as the "Formative Years," starts with the Conant Report of 1963 (Conant, 1963). The third period, named the "Recognition Years," is associated with the recognition of exercise physiology in 1977 by the American Physiological Society (APS) when they included it in the title of the *Journal of Applied Physiology* (Fishman, 1977) and within the Environmental, Thermal and Exercise Physiology Section (Brobeck, Reynolds, & Appel, 1987; Buckler, 1994).

Readers must realize that when separate events are assigned into defined time periods, the description becomes somewhat artificial because the impact and influence of the various events will have different "half-lives." Consequently, considerable overlap will exist between the various periods as the history of contemporary exercise physiology unfolds with time.

The Embryonic Years (1946-1962)

As was mentioned in the first part of this chapter, the Harvard Fatigue Laboratory was closed in 1946. This "academic blunder" prevented the continuation of the fundamental, productive, collaborative, international, and integrated research projects in environmental and exercise physiology that had been its hallmark between 1927 and 1946 (Horvath & Horvath, 1973). Equally important, it stopped a PhD program at Harvard and the Fatigue Laboratory that had graduated H.L. Taylor (Buskirk, 1992), S.M. Horvath, and S. Robinson (Horvath & Horvath, 1973), while eliminating a promising "feeder" system that provided undergraduates the opportunity to participate in honor projects of the laboratory. In discussing the closure, the Horvaths (1973) concluded (p. 84), "the closing of the Laboratory was a blessing in disguise. . . . Further, it stimulated the remaining staff, as well as those who might have returned, to develop their potentials as leaders on their own in the second and third generation laboratories, as listed. . . ." Individuals affiliated with the Harvard Fatigue Laboratory who earlier had left or would leave to establish programs and laboratories were S.M. Horvath at the Institute of Environmental Stress at the University of California at Santa Barbara, S. Robinson at the Human Physiology Laboratory at Indiana University, R.E. Johnson at the Human Environmental Unit at the University of Illinois, H.S. Belding at the Environmental Physiology Laboratory at the University of Pittsburgh, G.E. Folk, Jr. at the Environmental Laboratory at the State University of Iowa, and D.B. Dill who, after retirement, joined S. Robinson at Indiana University before developing the Applied Physiology Laboratory in Boulder City, Nevada (Horvath & Horvath, 1973).

The Fitness Movement and The University of Illinois. At the time when the Harvard Fatigue Laboratory was being dissolved, the Physical Fitness Research Laboratory at the University of Illinois had been in existence for several years under the direction of T.K. Cureton within the Department of Physical Education (Cureton, 1963; Kroll, 1982). Previously, Cureton had been at Springfield College, a member of a productive faculty whose publications continue to be quoted by current investigators in physical education and exercise science. Physical fitness was a national objective when Cureton arrived from Springfield, and with S.C. Staley's encouragement and the university's board of trustees' approval, the laboratory was established and became an integral component of Cureton's research, graduate, and service programs. Although Cureton's academic background was more in engineering and education than in physiology, he was a confident, energetic, and indefatigable investigator as well as a prolific author with a vision and passion for physical fitness. In fact, to Cureton, physical fitness was "an alternate term" for the physiology of exercise (Cureton, 1964). The collective effect was that he attracted motivated and capable students interested in the measurement and foundations of physical fitness.

The interest in physical fitness by the United States and the American Association for Health, Physical Education, and Recreation continued after World War II, and was reactivated by the Korean War in 1950 and the establishment of the President's Council on Youth Fitness in 1957 (Park, 1988). However, fitness for survival was not the reason for the President's Council; rather, it was a report by H. Kraus and R.P. Hirshland that indicated that 57 percent of American children had failed a "fitness" test (Park, 1988). The report startled the nation, challenged the leadership of physical education departments, motivated mass testing, and facilitated the initiation of fitness programs. Although other institutions besides Illinois established fitness courses, programs, and laboratories, the academic and research programs in physical education, and the presence of Cureton, made this university different from the others. However, the significance of this fact was, first, that many of the University of Illinois graduates (Bernauer, 1994; Cureton, 1963; Mole, 1994; Van Huss, 1994) who were associated with Cureton and the Physical Fitness Research Laboratory during this era (R.V. Ganslen, L.A. Golding, W.W. Heusner, A.W. Hubbard, P.A. Hunsicker, B.H. Massey, E.D. Michael, H.J. Montoye, R.H. Rochelle, N.B. Strydom, and W.D. Van Huss) subsequently assumed responsible research and leadership positions in departments of physical education. Second, most if not all, of these individuals had recognized the importance of exercise physiology and its physiological mechanisms as being essential for the implementation of a fitness program and the interpretations of its results.

The Impact of the YMCA Colleges.   To the author, exercise physiology flourished more as an academic subject because of curriculum requirements in physical education than because it was a course offered by physiology departments. According to Buskirk (1996), Kroll (1982), and Zeigler (1979), in the 1890s exercise physiology was a required subject for students majoring in physical education at Harvard, Stanford, and Oberlin. Although these three institutions did not remain influential in promoting physical education or emphasizing the importance of exercise physiology in the education of teachers and coaches, there were two colleges associated with the preparation of undergraduate and graduate students for careers in the Young Men's Christian Organization (YMCA) and in the teaching of physical education at universities that became known for their emphasis on exercise physiology: George Williams College in Chicago, Illinois, and Springfield College in Springfield, Massachusetts. Even though they had limited research facilities and no PhD programs, these institutions became recognized because of the presence, accomplishments, and personalities of A.H. Steinhaus, PhD at George Williams College, and P.V. Karpovich, MD from Springfield College. Both individuals were well prepared in physiology and the cognate sciences, taught physiology as well as exercise physiology to their students, and had strong convictions. In addition, they were well recognized for their extensive publications in physical education and physiology journals; each had relevant review articles in prestigious physiology journals. In 1948 Karpovich became a coauthor of *The Physiology of Muscular Activity* (Schneider & Karpovich, 1948), which was widely used in exercise physiology courses. Last, both were Fellows in the American Academy of Physical Education (original membership limited to 100 elected Fellows), and founders (with nine others) of the American College of Sports Medicine. Since many of the graduates of these institutions subsequently assumed important leadership positions in universities or in state educational organizations, Steinhaus and Karpovich had a significant impact in establishing exercise physiology as an academic discipline.

The Influence of Physiologists and Physiology Departments. As noted previously, the demise of the Harvard Fatigue Laboratory resulted in the relocation of many of its faculty and staff to other laboratories and universities. Those besides Dill who became contributors to the development of exercise physiology were R.E. Johnson at the University of Illinois, S. Robinson at Indiana University, and S.M. Horvath at the State University of Iowa (before going to the University of California at Santa Barbara). Each established laboratories, continued as prodigious investigators, attracted outstanding faculty members as well as graduate students, taught classes that included exercise physiology concepts, and received federal funding for their programs and facilities. In addition, they provided instruction and research experiences to graduate students in physical education. When Johnson was head of the Department of Physiology, his department provided courses that satisfied the minor requirements of the graduate college for the PhD degree. Not only did this arrangement complement the fitness orientation of the students of T.K. Cureton, it also provided the opportunity for graduate students to increase their understanding of physiology, which in turn encouraged physical and health education students like E.M. Bernauer to secure an MS degree in physiology and a few, such as D. Zarahko and C.M. Tipton, to transfer to physiology for their doctoral training. In 1962 Bernauer joined the Department of Physical Education at the University of California at Davis and subsequently established a human performance laboratory (Bernauer, 1994, Smith et al., 1986).

Before S.M. Horvath moved to Santa Barbara he was located in the Department of Physiology at the State University of Iowa (now the University of Iowa). In the same department was W.W. Tuttle, the first PhD recipient in physiology from Ohio State University (Lessler & Hitchock, 1985). Tuttle taught exercise physiology to physical education students, conducted research on performance, published in physiology and physical education journals, assumed authorship of the Zoethouth's undergraduate textbook of physiology (Tuttle & Schottelius, 1969) and mentored or co-mentored PhD students in physical education (L.E. Morehouse) or physiology (E. Evonuk). After receiving his degree, and at the end of World War II, Morehouse was a Fellow at Harvard University. Before moving to California, where he became established as the first author of an undergraduate exercise physiology textbook widely used in departments of physical education (Morehouse & Miller, 1948), he served as a consultant to the space program, and became a physical education faculty member at UCLA (American Men and Women in Science, 1972). Evonuk left Iowa to direct an arctic aero-medical laboratory before joining the Department of Physical Education at the University of Oregon in the 1960s (Carmack, 1995).

Although A. Keys was associated with the activities of the Harvard Fatigue Laboratory, he left before it closed and became a faculty member of the University of Minnesota, where he established the Laboratory of Physiology and Physical Education in the Stadium, later renamed the Laboratory of Physiological Hygiene (Buskirk, 1992). Keys was instrumental in recruiting H.L. Taylor and E. Simonson to Minnesota (Buskirk, 1992), where they became known, along with Keys, for scholarly activities that included human performance changes during semistarvation, and for the edited text by Simonson (1971) on work capacity and fatigue. Taylor served as the PhD advisor for E.R. Buskirk and L.B. Rowell, who both made significant contributions to the development of exercise physiology by their research publications and their professional activities for NIH, APS, and ACSM (Taylor, Buskirk, & Henschel, 1955; Buskirk, 1992; Rowell, 1993).

During these embryonic years, the physiology department at Ohio State University made available its research facilities for the exercise physiology research projects of D.K. Matthews, who was a research-oriented physical educator, a former student of P.K. Karpovich (Montoye & Washburn, 1980), and a graduate of the University of Illinois (Lessler & Hitchcock, 1985). Later, Matthews would be first author of a textbook in exercise physiology that had a specific orientation for physical education and athletics (Matthews & Fox, 1971; see table 10.3, p. 406).

Near the end of this era, the departments of physiology and medicine at the University of Texas Southwestern Medical Center appointed J.H. Mitchell from the NIH National Heart Institute to their faculty, who instantly became active in the exercise physiology projects of C.B. Chapman, which will be discussed in more detail in a subsequent section. In retrospect, it was evident at this time that a trend was being established, by departments of physiology for preparing individuals for careers in physical education that would require an understanding of physiology and an emphasis on exercise physiology.

Science-Oriented Physical Educators.   In the embryonic years from 1946 to 1962, there were other physical educators deserving mention besides those individuals recognized earlier. One was F.M. Henry of the University of California at Berkeley. Although his formal training was in physiological psychology, he was also well versed in mathematics and experimental design. In fact, his early studies on performance were published in the *Journal of Applied Physiology*. Later he became acknowledged for the concept of exercise specificity (Scheuer & Tipton, 1977). Another prominent physical educator and productive researcher was C.H. McCloy, who left medical school to become a YMCA director before becoming responsible for the graduate program at the State University of Iowa. Not only was he an expert in the use of tests and measurements, but he was also a prolific author on numerous topics that included growth, fitness, and performance, and served as mentor for many distinguished physical educators (Gerber, 1971). Also acknowledged is L.A. Larson of Columbia University, who later moved to the University of Wisconsin. It is unknown to many he had coauthored a physiology of exercise text (McCurdy & Larson, 1939) before World War II, was active in cardiovascular fitness testing, became a founder of the American College of Sports Medicine, and, in the next era, assumed a major leadership role in changing graduate programs in departments of physical education to become more science-oriented and focused. Lastly, G.R. Hearn deserves recognition because he encouraged his physical education doctoral students at Rutgers University and Washington State University to conduct animal exercise physiology experiments to understand physiological mechanisms, despite the fact it was well known that both Cureton and Karpovich believed that animal experimentation had no place or future in physical education research (Tipton, 1993). One of Hearn's students who became renowned for his exercise physiology research with animals was P.D. Gollnick.

The Activities of the American Physiological Society.   In Part I of this chapter, Buskirk has effectively documented the early physiologists who made significant contribution to the establishment of exercise physiology, and has listed the exercise physiology manuscripts published in the first issue of the *American Journal of Physiology* in 1897. The Society approved the publication of the *Journal of Applied Physiology* 51 years later, after receiving a report on the matter from E. Simonson of the University of Minnesota. Simonson emphasized that World War II had stopped the publication of *Arbeitsphysiologie,* and there was no equivalent journal available to publish relevant research (Fenn, 1963). According to the foreword in the first issue (Anonymous, 1948), the intent of the journal was to be a peer-reviewed forum for manuscripts related to the physiological responses of humans exposed to a variety of stress and environmental conditions that included exercise. Unlike most journals, it had no editor or editor-in-chief; rather, it had an editorial board of prominent scientists with ties to exercise physiology that included D.B. Dill, R.E. Johnson, E. Simonson, and A.H. Steinhaus. One individual who later regretted turning down the invitation to be listed was P.V. Karpovich. Although the focus of the journal was on human results, perusal of Volume 1 shows several reports based on animal research.

During the same year the journal was being established, APS endorsed J.D. Hardy's efforts to form an interest group in temperature regulation (Fenn, 1963). This group met yearly at the Federation meetings and had informal, as well as formal, programs (dinners) for interested APS members and guests. The significance of this specific interest group was that it served as the precursor in later years for a section that included exercise physiology.

For many years APS members and sponsored future members presented their research findings at fall and spring meetings of the Society. The fall meeting was a sole function of APS, while the spring meeting was a component of the meetings of the Federation of American Societies for Experimental Biology or FASEB. The advantage of these sessions for exercise physiologists, and the development of the field, was that they provided an established forum for the presentation and discussion of the results, which were published in abstract form in either the *Federation Proceedings* (starting in 1942) or in *The Physiologist* (starting in 1977). It is interesting to note that in 1946, at the 30th FASEB meeting in Atlantic City, there was an exercise session scheduled in the Physiology Section, which had seven papers.

Journals and Texts.   With the exception of the *American Journal of Physiology* and the *Journal of Applied Physiology*, there were few journals available in the United States during this time for the submission of manuscripts that pertained to exercise physiology. One other exception was the physical education journal known as *Research Quarterly*, first published in 1930. This publication of peer-reviewed manuscripts related to physical education research, and included many descriptive exercise physiology studies. According to Kroll (1982), the five most productive institutions whose faculties contributed publications in the *Research Quarterly* during the embryonic years were universities located in California (at Berkeley and Los Angeles), Iowa, and Illinois, as well as from Springfield College.

Summarized in table 10.2 are *Citation Index* results for the number of manuscripts and journals, during select years, that published articles in English under the headings of either exertion or exercise (Booth, 1984). In 1946 the *Citation Index* was not available, but a perusal of available journals by the author for peer-reviewed articles published that year

Table 10.2   Approximate Number of Journals and Their Citations Concerning the Topic of Exertion and Exercise as Modified From Booth (1984)

Year	Subject	Citations	No. of Journals
1946*	Exercise	14	5
1962	Exertion	128	51
1981	Exertion	655	224
1992*	Exertion	890	
1992*	Exercise	3,895	
2002**	Exertion	3,354	963

*Search conducted by Tipton using English titles and Medline facilities when available; see text for discussion.

**As predicted by Booth using exertion as the subject and data from *Index Medicus* between 1962 and 1981.

resulted in five journals with 14 articles. Interestingly, Costill listed the same number of journals in 1954 that he considered were publishing manuscripts in the area of applied exercise physiology (Costill, 1994a). By 1962 Booth listed 51 journals with 128 manuscripts using his exertion criterion.

As noted by Buskirk in part I, *Physiological Reviews* and *The Annual Review of Physiology* were firmly established and acknowledged as journals with invited peer-evaluated reviews. However, between 1946 and 1962 there were less than ten articles published in *Physiological Reviews* that were primarily concerned with the effects of exercise. Several that were appropriate for reference purposes in graduate courses were authored by Grodins (1950), Otis (1954), the symposium on cardiac performance that was chaired by Katz (1954), Asmussen and Nielsen (1955), Passmore and Durnin (1955), Astrand (1956), and Bartley (1957). Moreover, during this same time period, there were only two manuscripts published in the *Annual Review of Physiology* that were related to exercise physiology, one authored by R.E. Johnson (1946) and the other by P.V. Karpovich (1947). One interpretation of this information is that either the editorial boards felt there was insufficient interest or inadequate subject matter to warrant more emphasis on exercise physiology in their journals.

Summarized in table 10.3 are textbooks available and used by instructors of exercise physiology. It is the opinion of the author that either Schneider and Karpovich (1948), or Morehouse and Miller (1948), and their subsequent editions, were required in the majority of the undergraduate

Table 10.3 Select Listing of Textbooks and Reference Sources Available to Students Enrolled in Exercise Physiology Courses Between 1946 and 1976 (See Part I for earlier years.)

Year	Author(s)	Title
1948	Schneider, E.C. & Karpovich, P.V.	*Physiology of Muscular Activity.* Third edition that was revised. Saunders.
1948	Morehouse, L.E. & Miller, A.T., Jr.	*Physiology of Exercise.* Revised several times. Mosby.
1950	Reidman, S.R.	*The Physiology of Work & Play.* Dryden.
1960	Colloquium at Monticello, IL	*Exercise & Fitness.* The Athletic Institute.
1960	Johnson, W.O.	*Science & Medicine of Exercise and Sports.* Harper.
1961	Symposium edited by Spector, H.; Brozek, J.; & Peterson, M.S.	*Performance Capacity.* The Athletic Institute.
1964	Jokl, E.	*Physiology of Exercise.* Thomas.
1966	De Vries, H.A.	*Physiology of Exercise.* Revised several times. Brown.
1967	Ricci, B.	*Physiological Basis of Human Performance.* Lea & Febiger.
1968	Falls, H.B.	*Exercise Physiology.* Academic Press.
1971	Matthews, D.K. & Fox, E.L.	*The Physiological Basis of Physical Education & Athletics.* Revised several times. Saunders.
1976	Edington, D.W. & Edgerton, V.R.	*The Biology of Physical Activity.* Houghton Mifflin.
1976	Wilmore, J.H.	*Athletic Training & Physical Fitness.* Allyn & Bacon.

classes, and likely for some graduate courses as well. However, in 1960 this situation changed with the publication of the text edited by W.R. Johnson entitled *Science and Medicine of Exercise and Sport,* because it contained detailed chapters written by prominent authorities, and was suitable for a graduate course in exercise physiology. Eight years later, H.B. Falls of Southwestern Missouri State University edited a textbook in exercise physiology that was sufficiently advanced for use in graduate courses (Falls, 1968).

The Formation of the American College of Sports Medicine. In 1954, the American College of Sports Medicine (ACSM, 1994) was founded by 11 people who believed that individuals with backgrounds and orientations in medicine, physiology, and physical education should exist in a single professional organization whose purposes were to advance scientific and clinical knowledge, promote informational exchanges, and facilitate interactions among members on subjects related to physical activity and its mechanisms: the evaluation of athletic performance; the care and prevention of athletic injuries; the promotion, testing, and achievement of physical fitness; and various combinations thereof. Besides Karpovich, Larson, and Steinhaus, E. Jokl was a founder. He was a physician from South Africa associated with the Valley Forge Heart Institute in Pennsylvania, and had several publications on topics related to exercise physiology. Later, he became a faculty member in the Department of Physical Education at the University of Kentucky (Jokl, Cluver, Goedvolk, & De Jongh, 1941).

Physiology was designated as a cornerstone of the College, and for many years it was represented by a vice-president. However, it was the interest in exercise physiology that attracted most of the physiologists and many of the physical educators to the organization. In 1962 the College had a total of 514 members, of which 20 percent or more were in the physiology category (Yoder, 1994). Approximately two decades later, ACSM emerged as a significant professional organization in representing sports medicine and exercise science. One factor that contributed to this emergence was the development of, and the interest in, exercise physiology.

Federal Programs and Funding. In 1944 Congress passed the Public Health Service Act, which consolidated and revised existing public health legislation pertaining to programs on the diseases and disabilities of humans and included the authorization of the National Institutes of Health (NIH), to conduct and support research, projects, and fellowships (*NIH Almanac*, 1989). However, legislation passed in 1946 established the Research Grant Office (later the Division of Research Grant Office) in NIH to administer the extramural grant and fellowship programs for biomedical and health-related sciences. Ten years later, in 1956, the Health Research Facilities Act was passed, which authorized a federal matching grant program to public and nonprofit institutions for the construction of health-related facilities (*NIH Almanac*, 1989). By the early 1960s additional legislation had been passed that authorized grants-in-aid to laboratories, universities, and nonprofit organizations, which would strengthen facilities and the teaching, research, and research training programs to prepare the scientists needed for programs in health care and delivery. In 1946 NIH funded 850 grants that totaled approximately $2.5 million, whereas 16 years later the number of total grants and funds expended in direction operations increased by more than 60-fold. It is unknown as to what amount or percentage of these funds were directly related to exercise physiology proposals; however, the changes in the total number of grants and their financial support indicated that health-related research had become a national policy. Although the funding for exercise physiology projects was minimal, it is notable that in 1961 C.B. Chapman at Southwestern Medical School of the University of Texas was funded by the Heart and Lung Institute of NIH for his program project grant entitled "Human Adaptation to Environmental and Exercise Stress." One year later J.H. Mitchell from NIH joined Chapman and participated in his projects. With time, Mitchell became the principal investigator, and it is of interest that this grant is still active today (Mitchell, 1994). Even though few exercise physiologists received NIH postdoctoral support until after 1963, one individual who was successful before this date was P.D. Gollnick of Washington State University, who had received his PhD degree in physical education, with an emphasis in biochemistry and zoophysiology (Tipton, 1993).

Associated with the legislation of 1946, which established the Division of Research Grants Office, was the creation of study sections to evaluate the scientific and technical merit of grant applications. Subsequently, study sections related to hematology, pathology, pharmacology, physiology, and surgery were formed (*NIH Almanac*, 1989). NIH archival records for the Division of Research Grants indicate that the Physiology Study Section received 154 proposals between January 1, 1946, and July 1, 1948, of which 85 percent were approved. Of the projects approved and mentioned, none was directly related to exercise physiology (Mandel, 1994). Although additional study sections were established after these dates, it was not until the next era that proposals related to exercise physiology had a specific section designated for their consideration.

The Formative Years (1963–1976)

In 1961, the former president of Harvard University, J.B. Conant, was asked by leaders in the field of education to study programs designed to prepare teachers. Two years later he published his findings, which became known as the "Conant Report" (Conant, 1963). As discussed in chapter 1, it was a scathing indictment of the teaching training system in the United States, with the graduate programs in physical education being identified as an example of the system at its worst.

Although this report shocked many physical educators, it was no surprise to certain individuals in the Big Ten Conference, and elsewhere, who started discussions in the late 1950s and early 1960s on the quality of their graduate programs and the need to include more rigorous classes in the mathematical, chemical, biological, and physical sciences for graduate students. In fact, the Conant Report intensified and facilitated the efforts of university leaders, such as S.C. Staley (Illinois), L.A. Larson (Wisconsin), L.E. Alley (Iowa), P.A. Hunsicker (Michigan), L. Hess (Ohio State), G.E. Mikles (Michigan State), and A.S. Daniels (Indiana), to upgrade and modify their graduate programs so that in-depth specialization could occur in departments of physical education in a myriad of disciplines that included exercise physiology. In fact, Alley wrote, "Much of the research in physical education is concerned with trivial problems and is of poor quality. In many instances, it appears that the researcher does not know enough about his problem to realize he knows little about it" (Forker, 1984).

PhD Specialization Programs. The specialization emphasis in graduate programs had direct and indirect effects on the emergence of exercise physiology. The direct effects were manifested by departments revamping their graduate entrance requirements to include courses in mathematics, chemistry, biology, and physics, before allowing enrollment in graduate level courses in physiology, exercise physiology, biochemistry, pharmacology, and anatomy (required courses at Iowa and other institutions). Some departments of physical education had their own PhD programs with an orientation in exercise physiology, while others participated in interdisciplinary programs that involved departments of anatomy, biology, biochemistry, physiology, zoology, zoophysiology, or their equivalents. Thus, it was possible at the University of Iowa or Pennsylvania State University (to cite two examples) for an individual to receive a PhD degree in applied physiology, physical education, or physiology with an emphasis in exercise physiology. Another direct effect was the establishment of joint appointments between departments of physical education and science-oriented departments in Colleges of Engineering, Liberal Arts, Medicine, and Veterinary Medicine. Some individuals who received these types of appointments during the Formative Era were S.M. Horvath at the University of California at Santa Barbara, B. Balke and F.J. Nagle at the University of Wisconsin, C.M. Tipton and C.V. Gisolfi at the University of Iowa, J.A. Faulkner at the University of Michigan, P.D. Gollnick at Washington State University, and H.G. Welch at the University of Tennessee. The significance of these appointments should not be ignored because they provided academic credibility and recognition for exercise physiology graduate programs, while serving as a "magnet" for interested students. In addition, they helped to reduce the negative impression created by the Conant Report.

Interestingly, the Conant Report had a delayed effect in changing the science requirements for the undergraduate major in physical education who had an interest in exercise physiology. As a consequence, the majority of the graduate students during this time had to enroll in numerous undergraduate science courses to be eligible for the required courses.

The Influential Graduates of the "Big Three" Institutions. The implementation of specialization programs was not an instantaneous or uniform process. However, the activities and practices of the "Big Three" institutions (Big Ten Conference, Pacific Coast Conference, and Pennsylvania State University) served as effective models for other universities to emulate in their efforts to establish graduate, research, and teaching programs emphasizing exercise physiology.

At the University of Illinois, the influences of R.E. Johnson and his physiology faculty (notably F. Sargent and F.R. Steggedra), and of T.K. Cureton and W.W. Hubbard from the physical education faculty, were still present in the mentoring of graduate students. Individuals from the physiology department deserving of mention were J.E. Greenleaf, who established the Gravitational Research Laboratory at NASA Ames Research Center; P.A. Mole, who joined E.M. Bernauer at the Human Performance Laboratory at the University of California at Davis; and W.A. Kachadorian of NIH. Students of Cureton and/or Hubbard, and their recent addresses, include W.C. Adams of the University of California at Davis, R.A. Berger of Temple University, J.S. Bosco of California State University at Sacramento, D.B. Franks of Louisiana State University, W.L. Haskell of the Stanford Center for Research in Disease Prevention, B.J. Noble of the University of Wyoming, L.B. Oscai of the University of Illinois at Chicago, M.L. Pollock of the University of Florida, P.M. Ribisil of Wake Forest University, and J.S. Skinner, who is currently located at the Exercise and Sport Research Institute at Arizona State University (Bernauer, 1994; Mole, 1994; Tipton, 1994b; Van Huss, 1994). Of this group, Berger and Noble subsequently authored undergraduate textbooks in exercise physiology (Berger, 1982; Noble, 1986).

In the physiology department at Indiana University, S. Robinson with the assistance of R.W. Bullard continued to be productive; subsequently they recruited D.B. Dill to be a research scholar (Horvath & Horvath, 1973). Robinson served as the mentor for C.V. Gisolfi, who was recruited by the University of Iowa, where he remains. Dill served in the same capacity for L.G. Myhre, who is located at the School of Aerospace Medicine in San Antonio, while Bullard served as the advisor for W. Van Beaumont who became a faculty member at St. Louis University (Gisolfi, 1994).

Graduates from the physical education and physiology departments at the University of Iowa, most of whom were under the supervision of C.M. Tipton and C.V. Gisolfi, include K.M. Baldwin of the University of California at Irvine, R.J. Barnard of UCLA, F.W. Booth of the University of Texas Health Science Center at Houston, R.K. Conlee of Brigham Young University, R.T. Dowell of the University of Kentucky, M.L. Foss of the University of Michigan, G.O. Johnson of the University of Nebraska, M.H. Laughlin of the University of Missouri, J.A. Maynard and R.J. Tomanek of the University of Iowa, R.L. Terjung of SUNY-Syracuse, and E.J. Zambraski of Rutgers University. In recent years Foss became an author on the original textbook of Matthews and Fox (Fox, Bowers, & Foss, 1988).

At the time of the Conant Report, H.J. Montoye and J.A. Faulkner were faculty members in the Department of Physical Education at the University of Michigan, under the leadership of P.A. Hunsicker. They recruited H.G. Welch from the physiology department at the University of Florida (mentor was W.N. Stainsby) to improve their exercise physiology program. Later, Welch left Michigan to establish a related program at the University of Tennessee. After several years, Faulkner made an intra-university transfer to the Department of Physiology. However, their graduate program was sufficiently interdisciplinary that students majoring in either physiology or physical education could receive an emphasis in exercise physiology. Individuals who graduated from Michigan and who had an impact on the future developments of exercise physiology were J.K. Barclay of the University of Guelph, G.A. Brooks of the University of California at Berkeley, D.A. Cunningham of the University of Western Ontario, G.J.F. Heigenhauser of McMaster University, W.D. McArdle of Queens College, and L.C. Maxwell of the University of Texas Health Science Center at San Antonio (Faulkner, 1994; Tipton, 1994b; Welch, 1994). Later, McArdle as well as Brooks would become authors of exercise physiology textbooks used by undergraduate and graduate students (McArdle, Katch, & Katch, 1981; Brooks & Fahey, 1984).

In East Lansing, Michigan, W.D. Van Huss and W.W. Heusner formed a strong nucleus that attracted capable graduate students that included B.S. Brown of the University of Arkansas, K.D. Coutts of the University of British Columbia, V.R. Edgerton of UCLA, D.W. Edington of the University of Michigan, M.C. Greenisen of NASA Johnson Space Center in Houston, D. Hanson of Purdue University, R.C. Hickson of the University of Illinois at Chicago, D.R. Lamb of Ohio State University, M.G. Maksud of Oregon State University, R.R. Roy of the Brain Institute at UCLA, and R.O. Ruhling of George Mason University (Edgerton, 1994; Lamb, 1994; Van Huss, 1994). Later, Edington and Edgerton, as well as Lamb, became authors of undergraduate textbooks for exercise physiology students (Edington & Edgerton, 1976; Lamb, 1978).

In Minnesota, H.L. Taylor supervised the teaching of exercise physiology to physical education students, while the department recruited J.A. Alexander, a student of Montoye, to be their exercise physiologist. Later, he was assisted in this role by R.A. Serfass (Serfass, 1994).

As mentioned earlier, D.K. Matthews was a faculty member at Ohio State University, after previously being located at the University of Illinois and Washington State University. Graduates of Ohio State University during this time were R.W. Bowers of Bowling Green University, D.L. Costill of Ball State University, E.L. Fox of Ohio State University, and F.C. Hagerman of Ohio University. Although he was not a student of

Matthews or Fox, H.G. Knuttgen graduated during this period, and later assumed responsibilities at Pennsylvania State University (Bowers, 1994; Costill, 1994b). Matthews is also remembered for his exercise physiology textbook with Fox (Matthews & Fox, 1971), which has undergone several revisions since being published. With the untimely death of Fox several years ago, Bowers became a contributing author (Fox, Bowers, and Foss, 1988). Costill became known for his research and speaking endeavors, and recently combined with Wilmore on an exercise physiology textbook (Wilmore & Costill, 1994).

With B. Balke, F.J. Nagle, and later H.J. Montoye, the physical education faculty at the University of Wisconsin had a strong emphasis in exercise physiology. Early graduates of their program were F.J. Cerny of SUNY-Buffalo, J.T. Daniels of SUNY-Cortland, J.A. Dempsey (who remained at Madison in the Department of Preventive Medicine), N. Gledhill of York University, H.J. Green of the University of Waterloo, E.T. Howley of the University of Tennessee, P.W.R. Lemon of Kent State University, J.D. MacDougall of McMaster University, N.B. Olderidge of the University of Wisconsin at Milwaukee, W.G. Reddan of the University of Wisconsin at Madison, and K.G. Stoedefalke who is located at Pennsylvania State University (Dempsey, 1994; Reddan, 1994; Tipton, 1994b).

In the Big Ten Conference, their implementation of specialty programs occurred within a brief time period, and somewhat in unison. However, this was not the situation with the Pacific Coast Conference, even though the effects were similar. In the physical education department at Washington State University, P.D. Gollnick developed a science-oriented graduate program that prepared individuals for careers in exercise physiology and biochemistry. Graduates during the early years were R.B. Armstrong of Texas A and M, G.J. Bagby of Louisiana State University, C.D. Ianuzzo of the Deborah Research Institute in New Jersey, D.W. King of Washington State University, C.W. Saubert IV of Cleveland Chiropractic College, R.E. Shepherd of Louisiana State University, T.M.K. Song of Thunder Bay, R.G. Soule of Biola College, and A.W. Taylor of the University of Western Ontario. Two other graduates during this time, M. Knudson and W.L. Sembrowich, were on the faculty at the University of Washington before leaving to form their instrument company (Tipton, 1993).

With the presence of H.H. Clarke, P. Seigerseth, and E. Evonuk, the physical education department at the University of Oregon had become recognized for its research emphasis and its orientation toward exercise physiology. Oregon graduates who became active in the field were C.E. Brubaker of the University of Virginia, D.H. Clarke of the University of Maryland, R.R. Pate of the University of South Carolina, P.R. Raven of the University of North Texas Health Science Center at Fort Worth, W.E. Sinning of Kent State University, J.E. Wilkerson (who was on the faculty at Indiana University before entering medical practice), and J.H. Wilmore of the University of Texas (Clarke, 1994; Pate, 1994; Raven, 1994). Of these graduates, Clarke authored a textbook on exercise physiology (Clarke, 1975), Sinning became coauthor and then sole author of the exercise physiology textbook identified with Schneider and Karpovich (1948), while Wilmore became recognized for his research and textbooks on exercise conditioning (Wilmore, 1976) and exercise physiology (Wilmore & Costill, 1994).

In the physiology department at Stanford University Medical School, K. Wasserman supervised the research activities of B.J. Whipp. Later, they united at UCLA, conducted research on the anaerobic threshold as well as in exercise and respiratory physiology, and collaborated on a text concerned with exercise testing before Whipp moved to England (Wasserman et al., 1987).

At Berkeley, F.M. Henry continued to be productive during this time and supervised many students in physical education (Katch, 1994). Two of his students who became active in exercise physiology, and later combined with McArdle to author an exercise physiology textbook, were F.I. Katch and his brother V.L. Katch (McArdle, Katch, and Katch, 1981). They became located at the University of Massachusetts and the University of Michigan, respectively. With the arrival of G.A. Brooks at Berkeley in 1971, exercise physiology at the graduate level became more mechanistic and cellular in its orientation. One PhD who graduated before 1977 was T.P. White, who recently returned to his alma mater after being at the University of Michigan for many years (Brooks, 1994).

Although Morehouse was on the faculty at UCLA, it was the arrival of R.J. Barnard and V.R. Edgerton in the late 1960s that provided the foundation for their graduate program, with an emphasis in exercise physiology, that became prominent after 1977 (Barnard, 1994). At the University of Southern California (USC), A.S. Lockhart served as the mentor of H.A. de Vries, who remained on the faculty. Later he would publish a textbook on exercise physiology for students majoring in physical education and interested in athletic performance (de Vries, 1966). He also served as the advisor for G.M. Adams of California State University at Fullerton and R.A. Wiswell who is located at USC (de Vries, 1994).

The activities at the University of California at Santa Barbara deserve mention even though it is not a member of the Pacific Coast Conference. It was here that S.M. Horvath developed an interdisciplinary PhD program that involved academic units of physical education and/or ergonomics, biology, and engineering. Assisting him in the preparation of graduate students for research careers was B.L. Drinkwater who later moved to Pacific Medical Center in Seattle, Washington. Individuals active in exercise physiology who received their advanced degrees from this program before 1977 were C.A. Dawson of the Medical College of Wisconsin at Milwaukee, M.B. Maron of Northeastern Ohio Universities, E.R. Nadel of the John B. Pierce Foundation in New Haven, and R.R. Wolfe at the University of Texas Health Science Center at Galveston (Horvath, 1994; Nadel, 1994).

The arrival of E.R. Buskirk in 1963 from NIH resulted in the establishment of one of the first research laboratories to be named as a human performance laboratory; E.M. Bernauer of the University of California at Davis also established a research laboratory with the same title in the same year (Smith et al., 1986). As noted earlier, this university, with Buskirk's leadership, established a graduate program in applied physiology that enabled an individual from either physiology or physical education to secure a degree that allowed specialization in exercise physiology. Individuals graduating from this program before 1977 were R.A. Boileau of the University of Illinois, B.A. Franklin of William Beaumont Hospital in Michigan, E.M. Haymes of Florida State University, P.V. Komi of the University of Jyvaskyla in Finland, D.H. Nielsen of the University of Iowa, and C.L. Wells of Arizona State University (Buskirk, 1994).

Since the "Big Three" is an empirical listing, it is obvious that certain institutions and their graduates have been omitted. Even so, the contention still remains that without the graduate programs developed by the universities identified within this classification, the involvement of exercise physiology as an academic discipline would have been drastically delayed and possibly different.

The Influence of Federal Funding for Health-Related Programs. In the years between 1963 and 1976, federal funding for the programs of the National Institutes of Health (NIH) increased approximately 580 percent to a total approaching $840 million (*NIH Almanac*, 1989). Precisely what percent was allocated for proposals related to the acute and chronic effects of exercise is unknown, but it is safe to conclude that it was significantly higher than in the previous era. The rationale was that the emphasis on cardiovascular morbidity and mortality required a knowledge of exercise physiology testing procedures and principles (advocated by Balke & Ware, 1959; Bruce, 1973; Hellerstein et al., 1973; Taylor, Buskirk, & Henschel, 1955; and summarized by ACSM, 1975) that were being followed for diagnostic and evaluative purposes by physicians. In addition, physical activity training programs were being prescribed for rehabilitative and preventive purposes, especially in the area of cardiovascular diseases (Hellerstein, Hirsch, Ader, Greenblott, & Siegel, 1973; Rabb, 1966). The significance of these facts was that a knowledge of exercise physiology was essential to implement and interpret the results of the various intervention programs that had the support of the different institutes within NIH. Although the point is made by Blair, Kohl, and Powell (1987) that the President's Council on Physical Fitness and Sports was the only federal agency at this time seriously interested in the benefits of exercise, they had no financial allocations for research programs, and their concern was more on mass participation than on physiological mechanisms.

A Study Section is a select group of peers who evaluate research grant proposals and advise funding agencies on their respective scientific merit and potential. Although Study Sections had been established in 1946, and E.R. Buskirk and others at NIH had been lobbying for one in environmental and exercise physiology since 1957 (Buskirk, 1994), it was not until 1963 that NIH established an Advisory Committee on Applied Physiology for this purpose (NIH Advisory Committees, 1991). A year later it became an official Study Section with eight members who evaluated 20 research proposals during its first meeting. In 1965 the Division of Research Grants reported that these applications could be categorized as being in areas related to either physical fitness, exercise-work physiology, or neuromuscular and joint function (Mandel, 1994). Most of the proposals were requesting less than $20,000 and the majority (approximately 65%) were approved. With time, this Study Section received applications primarily related to exercise and environmental physiology, orthopaedics, musculoskeletal and respiratory systems, and bioengineering (NIH Advisory Committees, 1991). In fact, the name of the Study Section was changed to Applied Physiology and Bioengineering in 1972 and to the Applied Physiology and Orthopaedics Study Section in 1976. Scientists with a knowledge of exercise physiology who were appointed to the Applied Physiology Study Section during the initial years were S.M. Horvath (the first chairperson), D.B. Dill, E.R. Buskirk, and H.J. Montoye. Other knowledgeable individuals who later served during the formative era (Stewart, 1994) were H.S. Belding, C.G. Blomqvist, R.W. Bullard, F.L. Eldridge, E. Evonuk, P.D. Gollnick, E.H. Gordon, J.O. Holloszy, L.B. Rowell, J. Scheuer, L.C. Senay, Jr., H.L. Taylor, and C.M. Tipton (Stewart, 1994). The establishment of the Applied Physiology Study Section was an important event for the discipline of exercise physiology, because it provided academic credence for exercise physiologists and the opportunity for their proposals to receive critical peer review and insightful commentary on future directions.

The increase in research funding from 1963 to 1976 enabled investigators to support graduate students from their grants, and many exercise physiologists received their advanced education by this means. Because of the increasing need for basic and medical scientists in health care and delivery, legislation enacted in the 1960s provided training grant funds to institutions for the preparation of pre- and postdoctoral students for research, teaching, and service careers in health-related areas. The availability of these funds to institutions had a significant impact on the magnitude and quality of their graduate programs, especially if they were departments of physiology or biochemistry and located within a medical school complex. On the other hand, if the academic unit was not a basic science department with a medical school affiliation, it was unlikely the department received training grant funds to prepare future exercise physiologists. Two exceptions to this point were the PhD programs at the University of California at Santa Barbara and the University of Iowa, as the program directed by Horvath had NIH funds whereas the one supervised by Tipton and Gisolfi had fellowship support from the National Defense Education Act (Horvath, 1994; Tipton, 1994b). Consequently, the NIH predoctoral training grant program between 1963 and 1976 had a limited impact on increasing the numbers of PhDs with an emphasis in exercise physiology.

The need for postdoctoral training in all areas of science was apparent during this time, and the availability of NIH training grant and fellowship programs helped to achieve these goals. Training grants were awarded to institutions that subsequently appointed the trainee, whereas in the fellowship program NIH would award the funds to a specific individual to become a trainee on an approved research proposal with a designated supervisor. The collective effect was an increase in the critical mass of potential researchers for both departments and principal investigators, while providing more research opportunities for new PhDs.

In 1963 postdoctoral training was widely accepted in basic science departments, although the concept was new to physical education units that were establishing specialty programs in exercise physiology. However, this situation changed rapidly because of the availability of training grants and fellowships and the science backgrounds of the faculty responsible for implementing the PhD programs. By the end of 1976, there were three individuals who had established premier postdoctoral training programs that provided new and in-depth scientific experiences for future exercise physiologists to be competitive in an academic environment. They were J.O. Holloszy of Washington University, S.M. Horvath of the University of California at Santa Barbara, and E.R. Buskirk of Pennsylvania State University. Not only did these programs serve as examples and models for other institutions to emulate, they continued to flourish during the next era.

Exercise and The American Public.   During the formative era, there was an increased interest by the American public in exercise, characterized by individual and group running programs that included both men and women, 10K events, marathons, 100-mile endurance events, Iron Man competitions, televised exercise programs, pocket books on exercise that made "the best sellers" list, aggressive commercialism of exercise equipment, and the establishment of health and fitness clubs and centers. Using interest in running as an example, in 1964 there were 124 individuals registered to run the 7.6 miles of the San Francisco "Bay to Breakers" race. Sixteen years later the number was approximately 24,000 and after 21 years, it was 80,000 (Corbin, 1986; Nieman, 1986).

The reasons for this interest are complex, but it was due in part to the perception that physical activity was beneficial in reducing the mortality and morbidity of cardiovascular diseases (Raab, 1966; Wenger, 1994) as well as improving the quality of life; the social acceptance of Bowerman's "jogging" as a desirable form of physical activity (Nieman, 1986); the persuasiveness of K.H. Cooper's texts on the health benefits of aerobic exercise and the simplicity of his aerobic fitness scoring system to be understood by the general public (Cooper, 1968, 1970); and the efforts of AAHPERD and the President's Council on Physical Fitness to increase the exercise habits and fitness levels of children in schools, and the adult population as well (Blair, Kohl, & Powell, 1987; Nieman, 1986; Park, 1988). Associated with this increased public interest and participation was the need for individuals trained in exercise physiology and sports medicine who could explain and interpret the benefits and consequences of physical activity. As a result, exercise science and sports medicine began to emerge as the academic and professional representatives for the exercise movement.

In many communities that sponsored running events, the organizers frequently scheduled symposia featuring presentations by local and national authorities on sports medicine (prevention of injuries), exercise physiology (training principles, problems of dehydration, thermal regulation), and nutritional topics (carbohydrate "loading"). Lay magazines began to publish exercise physiology articles on a multitude of issues, and for a while it was fashionable to wear jogging clothing and shoes for informal purposes.

The Sports Medicine Movement and Activities of the American College of Sports Medicine (ACSM).   Perusal of Booth's data in table 10.2 (see p. 405) suggests that the academic community was as interested in the effects of exercise as the general public during this time (Booth, 1984). Historical scholars can argue whether it was the interest in exercise that facilitated the sports medicine movement or whether the opposite interpretation is correct. In 1963 ACSM had a membership of 639; 13 years later the total was 3,460 (Yoder, 1994). Of this number, approximately one-third were classified either as physiologists (essentially exercise physiologists), physicians, or physical educators. In addition to expanding its membership, ACSM pursued an aggressive strategy to become recognized as the leading professional organization in the United States for sports medicine policy and practice. This strategy included the establishment of regional chapters, the issuance of position statements on performance and health issues (ACSM, 1975, 1976), planning national meetings with diverse programs and prominent speakers, and the publication of a professional journal for its members as well as for the scientific and medical community.

Using the report from the planning committee, which included exercise physiologists (J.A. Faulkner, H.G. Knuttgen, F.J. Nagle, and C.M. Tipton), ACSM appointed B. Balke as the first editor-in-chief of *Medicine and Science in Sports*, which was published as a quarterly starting in 1969 (Nagle et al., 1968; Balke, 1969). In his initial editorial, Balke stated that the purposes of the journal were to disseminate reports pertaining to the biological aspects of exercise and sports, and to publish experimental or clinical studies of medical, physiological, psychological, or sociological interactions between man and the various environments of his chosen sport. When the term "sport" was used, it was Balke's perspective that it included all varieties of physical activity (Balke, 1969). Manuscripts were to be peer reviewed, and E.R. Buskirk was appointed as the Section editor for physiology. Interestingly, A.H. Steinhaus was designated as the Section editor for sociology and psychology and R.J. Shephard for clinical medicine. Exercise physiologists appointed to the editorial board were H.A. de Vries, J.A. Faulkner, S.M. Horvath, H.G. Knuttgen, H.J. Montoye, S. Robinson, and C.M. Tipton. Although the journal was intended to represent the interests of the various disciplines within ACSM, it soon became unofficially known for the manuscripts, review articles, and published symposia that were related to exercise physiology. In fact, between 1969 and 1976, of the approximately 340 articles published, 60 percent were on physiological topics.

APS Membership and the FASEB Meetings.   APS membership requires that the individual demonstrate "training" in physiology or its equivalent, and independence as an experimental investigator. It is a selective process that involves scrutiny by the membership committee and approval by the membership. Total membership in APS was 911 in 1946, 2,498 in 1963, and 3,273 in 1976 (Reynolds, 1976). In 1963, the Society published a PhD training survey from physiology departments located in 68 medical schools and in 20 nonmedical schools (APS, 1963). Although most departments indicated they were preparing their graduates for futures in mammalian, cardiovascular, or endocrine physiology, exercise physiology was not listed as a possibility. However, opportunities still existed for members interested in exercise to present their papers at fall and spring meetings and to organize symposia on topics related to exercise physiology. Unlike other members, exercise physiologists had no sanctioned APS Section that guaranteed input to the program committee, formal meetings, or the scheduling of prominent scientists for after-dinner speeches at FASEB. However, these conditions partly changed in the late 1960s by the scheduling of "exercise mixers" at spring meetings—unofficial APS activities organized by E.R. Buskirk to facilitate interactions and discussions by exercise physiologists. Each year he would designate a topic that was current, solicit speakers and discussion leaders, and schedule a room that allowed a cash bar. The well-received event contained lively discussions, and had between 30 to 150 individuals in attendance. To new or non-APS members, it provided an informal and nonthreatening social and professional environment to become acquainted with the exercise physiology interests and concerns of the Society. One outgrowth of the exercise mixer was that it contributed to the establishment of an APS Section that recognized exercise physiology.

Materials for Exercise Physiology Courses and Name Changes.
For undergraduate students between 1963 and 1976, the later editions of
Morehouse and Miller (1948), Schneider and Karpovich (1948), Karpovich
(1959), Karpovich and Sinning (1948), plus those of de Vries (1966) and
Matthews and Fox (1971), were available and received wide usage. On the
other hand, instructors of graduate classes had limited options and the
texts of Johnson (1960) or Falls (1968) were usually assigned for this purpose.
However, in 1970, Astrand and Rodahl published the first of several editions
of *Textbook of Work Physiology: Physiological Bases of Exercise*, which gained
instant acceptance and use by professors responsible for advanced classes.

Since most course instructors are never satisfied with the material or
perspectives provided within a single text, they have reading assignments
of published papers or chapters from relevant journals or books. Inspection of the contents of *Physiological Reviews* or the *Annual Review of Physiology* during these years indicates that the former had four relevant papers,
or 1.7 percent of the total manuscripts published, whereas the latter had
two papers, or 0.8 percent of the manuscripts that were in print. From
these data one would have to conclude that the editors of these prestigious
review journals continued to have little interest in soliciting exercise physiology manuscripts. Two papers deserving attention by advanced students
were by Bevegard and Shepherd (1967) on the regulation of circulation
during exercise, and by Rowell (1974) on cardiovascular and thermal
responses with stress.

Starting in 1973, the American Association for Health, Physical Education and Recreation, in conjunction with the Franklin Press, initiated the
publication of review articles that specifically pertained to exercise and
sport science, and appointed J.H. Wilmore as its first editor (Robertson,
1995). Its first edition and those that followed until 1977 contained numerous exercise physiology manuscripts, which became assigned readings
for countless students.

The graduate speciality programs that were implemented after the
Conant Report and F.M. Henry's persuasive arguments for a scientific
foundation (Henry, 1964) changed the direction, composition, and viewpoints of the faculty in departments of physical education that offered or
intended to offer PhD degrees. One noticeable effect was their efforts to
change departmental names to better define their new focus and direction,
which included exercise physiology. In 1971 the first academic unit to
change was the Department of Physical Education at the University of
Massachusetts, which became the Department of Exercise Science under
the leadership of H.K. Campney, Jr. (Kroll, 1982). Soon, physical education
departments at UCLA and the University of Washington changed their
names to Department of Kinesiology for the same reasons. Because of the
orientation of this chapter, the Canadian influences and contributions
have been essentially ignored; however, it was during this time period
that Canada was establishing new universities and academic departments

with exercise physiology orientations. Interestingly, many were identified as departments of kinesiology or human kinetics, or by titles that did not include physical education.

Present and Future of the Discipline

Two events occurred during 1977 that were of importance to the discipline of exercise physiology. First, when APS established specialty sections, Environmental, but not Exercise, Physiology was included, even though the program committee had scheduled exercise sessions at the fall and spring meetings (Jackson & Saunders, 1987). However, 31 years after sections had been formed, the Society changed the name of the Environmental Section to become the Environmental, Thermal, and Exercise Physiology Section (later the thermal component was removed from the title). The year 1977 was also the first time that APS surveyed the membership to identify their specialty areas. Out of 4,026 regular members, 18.5 percent listed cardiovascular, 4.2 percent mentioned environmental, and 4.2 percent were classified as muscle or exercise physiologists (APS Membership, 1977). In 1994, out of 7,464 members, 6.3 percent were included within the Environmental and Exercise Physiology Section, and 6.5 percent were listed as having a muscle and exercise specialty. In all probability, the number of exercise physiologists was less than 3 percent of the total.

The second event in 1977 that solidified the recognition of exercise physiology was the title change by APS of the *Journal of Applied Physiology* to the *Journal of Applied Physiology: Respiratory, Environmental and Exercise Physiology*. This change represented the deliberations of their publications committee on how the needs and directions of these specialty areas of physiology could be best fulfilled. Almost a decade later, the publications committee implemented the recommendations from the membership and from a "summit meeting" with ten active investigators on how the *Journal of Applied Physiology: Respiratory, Environmental and Exercise Physiology* could better represent the interests of environmental and exercise physiologists. One recommendation that was implemented was the changing of the title back to the *Journal of Applied Physiology* (Fishman, 1985).

The collective significance of these events was that exercise physiology had finally achieved official recognition as a legitimate specialty area in physiology by the American Physiological Society. This fact not only provided academic credence to the exercise physiologist, but it also enhanced the acceptance of exercise physiology as a major discipline within the profession of exercise science.

Academic Programs

The specialization influence characterized by institutions designated as the "Big Three," combined with the increasing interest in sports medicine and exercise science, continued through most of the Recognition Years with more institutions following their lead and example.

Within the "Big Three," the interdisciplinary PhD program at the University of Iowa, directed by C.M. Tipton and C.V. Gisolfi, received NIH training grant funding, which continued until the middle 80s; new graduate programs were started at UCLA, the University of Washington, Arizona State University, and Purdue University (Barnard, 1994; Skinner, 1994; Tipton, 1994b). The University of California at Davis instituted an interdisciplinary doctoral program in the physiological sciences, and the physical education department became an active participant (Bernauer, 1994; Mole, 1994; Smith et al. 1986). The exercise physiology interests at the University of Arizona became an active component in an animal physiology PhD program in which J.H. Wilmore and F.R. Roby had major roles. Subsequently, this program was eliminated and the university adopted a plan that was modeled after the one followed by UC-Davis. Outside the "Big Three," programs at the universities identified with Ball State, Florida, Florida State, Georgia, Maryland, South Carolina, and Texas became operational and produced graduates who assumed exercise physiology teaching and research responsibilities.

The program at Ball State under D.L. Costill, which had its first graduate in 1980 (W.J. Evans), deserves mention because it was, and continues to be, supported primarily by state funds (Costill, 1994). This is an extremely important consideration because doctoral programs that are heavily dependent upon federal programs are vulnerable to "downsizing" and elimination because of sudden economic and policy changes. Consequently, it is quite probable that by the year 2010 the operational and productive exercise physiology graduate programs will be those that have changed with the times and have been able to be maintained with state financial support.

It is likely that historians will designate the middle of the 1980s as the start of the molecular biology era. However, most exercise science, kinesiology, or physical education departments have been slow to change their PhD curricula or faculty in recognition of this fact, and continue to be systems-oriented. Exceptions to this situation were at UCLA, where the department of kinesiology (later changed to physiological sciences) recruited a molecular biologist to their faculty (Tipton, 1994b), and at the University of Illinois at Chicago, where the exercise physiologists (L.B. Oscai, W.K. Palmer, and R.C. Hickson) have a PhD proposal, with an emphasis in exercise molecular biology, under state review (Oscai, 1994). By the year 2010 and thereafter, the recruitment of molecular biologists to departments of exercise science, kinesiology, and physical education will undoubtedly have increased.

Physiology Departments. In contrast to the departments of physical education, exercise science, or kinesiology that were increasing the number of PhDs with an emphasis in exercise physiology, the situation was different with medical school physiology departments associated with the "Big Three." Because of retirements, faculty departures, and changes of focus, they experienced a decline in the number of individuals interested in exercise physiology. Although the numbers of PhDs produced were markedly lower than in non-physiology departments, there were academic units outside the "Big Three" institutions that graduated students with exercise physiology orientations. Individuals in or associated with physiology departments who served as mentors were K.M. Baldwin of UC-Irvine, F.W. Booth of the University of Texas Medical Center at Houston, R. Foreman of the University of Oklahoma, H.L. Laughlin of the University of Missouri, J.H. Mitchell of the University of Texas Southwestern Medical Center at Dallas, E.R. Nadel of Yale University, P.B. Raven of the University of North Texas Health Science Center, L.R. Rowell of the University of Washington, R.L. Terjung of SUNY-Syracuse, and K. Wasserman and B.J. Whipp of UCLA.

As suggested earlier, physiology and biology departments in the middle of the 1980s recognized the importance and significance of molecular biology to the future of science and medicine and changed their names, faculty, and curriculum accordingly. One of the first scientists with an exercise physiology background who elected to be "retrained" in order to become proficient in molecular biology was F.W. Booth. He also became a spokesperson for the use of molecular biology principles to study the problems in exercise physiology (Booth, 1988, 1991). Another exercise physiologist who repeated the pattern of Booth was K.M. Baldwin. Their students, plus others who have graduated with an understanding of systems physiology and molecular biology, will become the critical mass of the future that will use the principles and concepts of molecular biology to investigate many of the unresolved problems and issues in exercise physiology. By the year 2010, it is conceivable that departments of either physiology or exercise science-kinesiology will have the necessary PhD programs to accomplish this goal.

Postdoctoral Training Opportunities for Exercise Physiologists. What started as a trend in the last era became an expectation for recently graduating PhDs with an emphasis in exercise physiology. Remember that this type of training could occur with an institutional training grant (T) or by individual fellowship (Y) awards. As a general rule, approximately 40 percent of the T awards were allocated for postdoctoral training, while 75 percent of the Y category were for this purpose (*NIH Extramural Trends*, 1994). Although both types were used in the "Recognition Years," it is difficult to know how many of the 4,600 T and the 1,300 Y awards in 1984 or the 4,700 T and 1,700 Y awards in 1983 went to exercise physiologists. In 1984, 219 institutions had received T support; nine years later, the number had increased to 276. These data indicate that a plateauing effect for postdoctoral training had occurred and suggest that this type of award had become more competitive than in previous times.

The institutions that had pioneered postdoctoral training in the last era (UC-Santa Barbara, Pennsylvania State University, Washington University) continued their activities, although the closing of the Environmental Stress Institute at Santa Barbara diminished its impact in the field. However, new postdoctoral opportunities occurred and two examples (in cardiovascular physiology) were at the University of Texas Southwest Medical Center at Dallas, directed by J.H. Mitchell, and at the University of North Texas Health Science Center at Fort Worth, directed by P.B. Raven. With the availability of both T and Y awards, many exercise physiologists were able to receive postdoctoral training at institutions other than those mentioned above. However, none has been so impressive or influential as the one directed by J.O. Holloszy of Washington University; scores of his trainees have assumed responsible positions in academic institutions and have been recognized for their research projects in exercise biochemistry and physiology. When the next chapter is written on the history of exercise physiology, the postdoctoral students of Holloszy, and their accomplishments, will occupy numerous paragraphs.

Funding of Research Projects. When comparing private versus federal funding, the latter source is the most influential and essential, because the differences in amounts and durations provide more security for constancy, diversity, and innovation. This concept does not minimize the value of having funds from the various private organizations representing interests in heart, diabetes, muscular dystrophy, multiple sclerosis, etc., or their short-term importance in initiating new projects or maintaining existing ones. In essence, exercise physiology flourished because of the availability of federal funds for training and research purposes.

In 1977 the operational budget for NIH was slightly more than $1 billion with approximately 80 percent being directed for extramural research (*NIH Almanac*, 1989; *NIH Extramural Trends*, 1994). However, it is unknown how much of this amount actually pertained to exercise physiology. It is a matter of record that many of the individuals mentioned in this chapter had NIH funding on one or more occasions since 1963. Furthermore, in most academic departments it was essential for individuals to have received NIH funding before they could be seriously considered for advancement to the next professorial level. One impressive record of NIH grantsmanship pertains to a program project grant entitled "Human Adaptation to Environmental and Exercise Stress," which was awarded to C.B. Chapman in 1961 at the University of Texas Southwestern Medical Center in Dallas (Mitchell, 1994). Five years later, J.H. Mitchell assumed leadership of the project and was successful in securing renewals until 1997 (Mitchell, 1994). The importance of these facts is that this program project grant, which includes 19 investigators, 10 fellows, and 5 graduate or medical students, is to examine the physiological, biochemical, and molecular processes involved in the reactions of the cardiovascular and skeletal muscle systems to exercise (Mitchell, 1994). This example is mentioned because it reinforces the point raised earlier, that a knowledge of molecular biology and its techniques will be essential to conduct much of the future research in exercise physiology.

The precise role of NIH Study Sections in charting the direction of investigative research in the United States after 1946 is a subject beyond the scope of this chapter, and one that will require extensive analyses of the summary "pink sheets" associated with the submitted proposals. Of the "pink sheets" from the Applied Physiology Study Section that were available for comment, it is of interest that in 1980-81, 29 percent of the 360 proposals reviewed were directly related to exercise physiology, and many of the recommendations to the principal investigators were directed toward cellular and molecular approaches (Tipton, 1994c). In 1983, NIH reorganized, and formed the Respiratory and Applied Physiology Study Section (*NIH Advisory Committees*, 1991).

American College of Sports Medicine (ACSM). The professional and scientific interest in exercise science and sports medicine that began in the 1960s continued during the next decades, although the rate of professional growth was not as rapid as during the Formative Era. This fact was evident, in part, with the change in the number of members within ACSM, which totaled 639 in 1963, 4,418 in 1977, and 14,087 in 1993, with exercise physiologists representing approximately 30 percent of the total (Yoder, 1994). One factor that contributed significantly to the growth of ACSM was the acceptance of graduate students as members, with the franchise to vote in national elections. Traditionally, students represent between 15 and 20 percent of the total membership, and are primarily interested in exercise physiology. This fact, coupled with regional and national programs that have an emphasis on student interest and participation, enabled ACSM to acquire a strong critical mass of exercise physiologists who identified with the College because of its scientific presentations, symposia, and tutorials.

During the Recognition Years, ACSM reorganized its membership categories so that individuals could be professionally classified into either medicine, basic and applied science, or education and allied health (Yoder, 1994). One of the reasons for this change was that the medicine, physiology, and physical education classification did not effectively differentiate or acknowledge exercise physiologists who were in departments of physical education. Also during the Recognition Years, ACSM changed *Medicine and Science in Sports* to become *Medicine and Science in Sports and Exercise* to indicate that the science of exercise, including exercise physiology, was an integral component of the College and its scientific journal (Tipton, 1994a).

As mentioned by Wilmore (1979), ten exercise physiologists, members of the College, met at Pennsylvania State University to examine definitions, certification standards, curricula requirements, and research areas for exercise physiology. However, when their recommendations were presented at a 1979 ACSM board of trustees meeting for possible implementation, it incensed several exercise physiologists in attendance to such an extent that the material was tabled for extinction. It is of interest that the group identified future areas of research to include the need for basic studies and knowledge pertaining to the pharmacological aspects of exercise, exercise effects on disease and aging, membrane mechanisms, molecular aspects of muscle physiology, motor control and recruitment, neuromuscular basis of strength development, exercise effects on the immune system, and the effects of exercise on connective tissue. Sixteen years later, it appears these ten individuals were correct in many of their recommendations.

It was during the end of the Formative Years and the start of the Recognition Years that the College began to establish its professional image and scientific credibility, by using its membership to formulate position statements on physiological problems in exercise and sports. For example, in 1977 a position stand was taken on the use and abuse of anabolic-androgenic steroids (ACSM, 1977), and in 1978 an important statement was made on the recommended quantity and quality of exercise for developing and maintaining fitness in healthy adults (ACSM, 1978). Other subjects covered by ACSM position stands or opinion statements pertain to weight loss, distance running by the female athlete, the effects of alcohol, heat-related illness during distance running (Brooks and Fahey, 1984), and exercise effects on blood pressure (Hagberg, Blair, Ensani, Gordon, Kapan, Tipton, & Zambraski, 1993). This important professional function and service continues today and, in the majority of the positions being published, the results of exercise physiology research are the foundations for the statement.

Course Materials for Students in Exercise Physiology. Unlike the previous eras, there were a plethora of books available to students enrolled in undergraduate classes; many have been cited in the sections dealing with the graduates of the "Big Three" institutions. At the graduate level the comprehensive and revised text of Astrand and Rodahl (1970) became the book required by a large number of instructors. Also during this time the revised text of Johnson (1960) was used, while R.J. Shepherd (1982) and G.A. Brooks and T.D. Fahey (1984) published books that were purchased by many students in advanced courses.

In 1977 ACSM assumed the editorial responsibility for *Exercise and Sport Sciences Reviews*, and reappointed R.S. Hutton of the University of

Washington as editor. This annual text published many review articles in exercise physiology and became a meaningful reference source for students in graduate courses (Robertson, 1995). Twelve years later the College expanded its involvement with the series and provided copies to its members as a component of their membership fees. Individuals besides Hutton who served terms as editors were D.I. Miller of the University of Washington, R.L. Terjung of SUNY-Syracuse, K.B. Pandolf of the U.S. Army Institute of Environmental Medicine, and J.O. Holloszy of Washington University (Robertson, 1995).

Between 1977 and 1994, *Physiological Reviews* and the *Annual Review of Physiology* collectively published approximately 1,200 review manuscripts, of which 2.5 percent directly pertained to exercise physiology. While these statistics suggested that the respective editors continued to have little interest in exercise and its physiological consequences, there were several papers deserving of assignment purposes: articles on training by Clausen (1977); cardiovascular responses by Scheuer and Tipton (1977); ventilatory changes by Dempsey and Forster (1982); and a 1983 annual review series that included temperature effects by Brengelmann, cardiovascular adaptations by Blomqvist and Saltin, sympathetic involvements by Christensen and Galbo, circulatory reflexes by Mitchell and associates, plus coronary changes by Stone. Of interest were two comparative papers by Taylor (1987) and Jones and Lindstedt (1993). Booth and Thomason (1991) produced a manuscript with a molecular orientation, while Fitts (1994) published a paper on muscular fatigue. These articles, plus brief reviews published in *Journal of Applied Physiology and Medicine and Science in Sports and Exercise*, enabled faculty as well as students to be current on relevant topics.

During 1990 the proceedings of the International Conference on Exercise, Fitness, and Health that was held in Toronto were published in a textbook that not only contained a consensus report of the conference, but also 62 separate chapters by 90 acknowledged authorities in exercise physiology, medicine, sports medicine, physical fitness, exercise prescription, and exercise epidemiology (Bouchard, Shepard, Stephens, Sutton, & McPherson, 1990). Four years later, the process was repeated. Interestingly, the selection of the 142 participants-speakers was determined, in part, from the results of a *Citation Index* search for the most productive investigators in a specific subject matter area. The result was the publication of a reference containing 72 chapters on a myriad of topics, a collection that will be worthy of assignment for any advanced course in exercise physiology (Bouchard, Shepard, & Stephens, 1994).

In 1983 APS published a handbook of physiology devoted to muscle function, and a chapter written by Saltin and Gollnick (1983) became an assigned reading for many serious students. In fact, during the 1990s APS exhibited great vigor in publishing their handbook series; one being planned will be devoted to exercise physiology. This specific issue will feature sections devoted to circulation, metabolism, motor control, and respiration, with J.M. Johnson, R.L. Terjung, P.D. Wagner, J.L. Smith, and J.A. Dempsey serving as section editors, while J.T. Shepherd and L.B. Rowell will be the coeditors. It is safe to conclude that this book will become an important reference in the years ahead.

Concluding Remarks

With a contemporary perspective, the selection and interpretation of events can be easily contested, and this chapter is no exception. The research findings that have highlighted the scientific importance of exercise physiology, and reinforced its value to the biological and medical communities, have not been detailed because of space limitations, and because of the belief that exercise physiology was dormant as an academic discipline until various educational, national, social, and professional changes occurred to facilitate its emergence. Accordingly, it was the leadership of departments of physical education, the importance of the exercise science component to the sports medicine movement, the value of exercise prescriptions for clinical and experimental medicine, and the level of federal funding for research and educational programs that enhanced the process. On the other hand it was the conservativeness of departments of physiology, the review standards of the *Journal of Applied Physiology*, and the critical nature of the Applied Physiology Study Section that fostered and maintained scientific credibility. The collective results were professional recognition and the academic establishment of exercise physiology.

This chapter started with the demise of the Harvard Fatigue Laboratory in 1946. No attempt was made to identify the laboratory or laboratories that have assumed its mantle since that time because the bias of the author maintains that none has equalled its place in history or importance. However, components of its character could be found in the laboratories of Buskirk, Holloszy, Horvath, and Mitchell. If international productivity and recognition were the sole factors, then the laboratory directed by B. Saltin in Scandinavia would have to receive serious consideration.

It is unknown what will happen in the next 25 to 50 years. My prediction is that the research emphases will contain both integrative and molecular components, with departments of exercise science or kinesiology conducting the former and departments of molecular physiology and/or biochemistry performing the latter. Unlike the past, departments of physical education will have a limited role in conducting exercise physiology investigations and in the preparation of future researchers. A knowledge of genetics and immunology will be essential for new PhD graduates, and all will be expected to complete postdoctoral experiences before assuming academic or clinical responsibilities with institutions, clinics, or medical centers. Electronic publishing will prevail, and the assimilation of available information will become a major problem confronting scholars and investigators. Health care and delivery will be a national priority and, to receive federal funding, the majority of exercise physiology proposals will have to contain a disease or health focus. Although the general public will continue to be interested in the effects of exercise, they will be more critical of its benefits.

References—Part I

Anonymous. (1960). Russell Henry Chittenden. *The Physiologist*, **3**, 5-6.

Anonymous. (1961). William Henry Howell. *The Physiologist*, **4**, 5-11.

Anonymous. (1961). William Townsend Porter. *The Physiologist*, **4**, 28-31.

Bainbridge, F.A. (1923). *The physiology of muscular exercise* (3rd ed. 1931). New York: Longmans, Green. (Revised A.V. Bock and D.B. Dill)

Benedict, F.G., & Cathcart, E.P. (1913). *Publication No. 187: Muscular work: A metabolic study with special reference to the efficiency of the human body as a machine*. Washington, DC: Carnegie Institution of Washington.

Benedict, F.G., & Murschhauser, H. (1915). *Publication No. 231: Energy transformation during horizontal walking*. Washington, DC: Carnegie Institute of Washington.

Berryman, J.W. (1989). The tradition of the "six things non-natural": Exercise and medicine from Hippocrates through ante-bellum America. In K.B. Pandolf (Ed.), *Exercise and sport sciences reviews* (Vol. 17, pp. 515-559). Baltimore: Williams and Wilkins.

Berryman, J.W., & Park, R.J. (Eds.). (1992). *Sports and exercise: Essays in the history of sports medicine*. Urbana, IL: University of Illinois Press.

Billings, J.A. (1870). *Circular No. 4: A report on barracks and hospitals*. Washington, DC: Government Printing Office.

Bingham, N.W. (Ed.) (1895). *The book of athletics and out-of-door sports*. Boston: Lothrop.

Bock, A.V., van Caulaert, C., Dill, D.B., Fölling, A., & Hurxthal, L.M. (1928a). Studies in muscular activities: III. Dynamical changes occurring in man at work. *Journal of Physiology (London)*, **66**, 136-161.

Bock, A.V., van Caulaert, C., Dill, D.B., Fölling, A., & Hurxthal, L.M. (1928b). Studies in muscular activity: IV. The 'steady state' and the respiratory quotient during work. *Journal of Physiology (London)*, **66**, 162-174.

Brody, S. (1945). *Bioenergetics and growth*. New York: Reinhold.

Brooks, G.A. (1981). Physiology of exercise. In G.A. Brooks (Ed.), *Perspectives on the academic discipline of physical education*, (pp. 48-54). Champaign, IL: Human Kinetics.

Bursztein, S., Elwyn, D.H., Askanazi, J., & Kinney, J.M. (1989). *Energy metabolism, indirect calorimetry and nutrition.* Baltimore: Williams and Wilkins.

Buskirk, E.R. (1981). The emergence of exercise physiology. In G.R. Brooks (Ed.), *Perspectives on the academic discipline of physical education* (pp. 55-74). Champaign, IL: Human Kinetics.

Byford, W.H. (1855). On the physiology of exercise. *American Journal of Medical Science, 30,* 32-42.

Carpenter, T.M. (1948). *Publication No. 303C: Tables, factors and formulas for computing respiratory exchange and biological transformation of energy* (4th ed.). Washington, DC: Carnegie Institution of Washington.

Chapman, C.B. (1990). The long reach of Harvard's Fatigue Laboratory, 1926-1947. *Perspectives in Biological Medicine, 34,* 17-33.

Cleghorn, A., & Stewart, C.C. (1901). The inhibition of a voluntary muscle contraction. *American Journal of Physiology, 5,* 281-286.

Combe, A. (1843). *The principles of physiology applied to the preservation of health and to the improvement of physical and mental education.* New York: Harper & Row.

Cunningham, R.H. (1898). The restoration of coordinated volitional movement after nerve-"crossing." *American Journal of Physiology, 1,* 239-254.

Darling, E. (1899). The effects of training: A study of the Harvard University crew. *Boston Medical and Surgical Journal, 141,* 229-233.

Darling, E. (1901). The effects of training. *Boston Medical and Surgical Journal, 144,* 550-559.

Dawson, P.M. (1935). *The physiology of physical education.* Baltimore: Williams and Wilkins.

Deutsch, F., Kauf, E., & Warfield, L.M. (1927). *Heart and athletics.* St. Louis: Mosby.

Dill, D.B. (1967). The Harvard Fatigue Laboratory: Its development, contributions and demise. *Circulation Research, 20 & 21*(Suppl 1), 161-170.

Dill, D.B. (1980). Historical review of exercise physiology science. In W.R. Johnson & E.R. Buskirk (Eds.), *Structural and physiological aspects of exercise and sport* (pp. 37-41). Princeton, NJ: Princeton Books.

Dill, D.B. (1985). Arlie V. Bock, pioneer in sports medicine December 30, 1888-August 11, 1984. *Medicine and Science in Sports and Exercise, 17,* 401-404.

Donnelly, R.J. (1960). Laboratory research in physical education. *Research Quarterly, 31,* 232-234.

Dreyer, G. (1920). *The assessment of physical fitness.* New York: Hoeber.

Fenn, W.O. (1930). Frictional and kinetic factors in the work of sprint running, and work against gravity and work due to velocity changes in running. *American Journal of Physiology, 92,* 583-611; *93,* 433-462.

Fenn, W.O. (Ed.) (1968). *History of the International Congresses of Physiological Sciences 1889-1968* (A short history of the International Congresses of Physiologists, 1889-1938, by K.J. Franklin. The Minnekahda voyage, by Y. Zotterman. Physiology congresses, 1938-1968). Washington, DC: American Physiological Society.

Fitz, G.W. (1908). *Principles of physiology and hygiene*. New York: Holt Rinehart & Winston.

Flint, A., Jr. (1871). *On the physiological effects of severe and protracted muscular exercise; with special reference to its influence upon the excretion of nitrogen*. New York: Appleton-Century-Crofts.

Flint, A., Jr. (1878). *On the source of muscular power*. New York: Appleton-Century-Crofts.

Gould, A.G., & Dye, J.A. (1935). *Exercise and its physiology*. New York: Barnes.

Franz, S.I. (1900). On the methods of estimating the force of voluntary muscular contractions and on fatigue. *American Journal of Physiology*, **4**, 348-372.

Gerber, E.W. (1971). *Innovators and institutions in physical education*. Philadelphia: Lea and Febiger.

Haggard, H.W., & Greenberg, L.A. (1933). *Diet and physical efficiency*. New Haven, CT: Yale University Press.

Hill, A.V. (1925). The present tendencies and methods of physiological teaching and research. *Science*, **61**, 294-305.

Hill, A.V. (1927a). *Muscular movement in man*. New York: McGraw-Hill.

Hill, A.V. (1927b). *Living machinery*. New York: Harcourt Brace Jovanovich.

Horvath, S.M., & Horvath, E.C. (1973). *The Harvard Fatigue Laboratory: Its history and contributions*. Englewood Cliffs, NJ: Prentice Hall.

Hough, T. (1901). Ergographic studies in neuromuscular fatigue. *American Journal of Physiology*, **5**, 240-266.

Huber, G.C. (1889-1890). Observations on the degeneration and regeneration of motor and sensory nerve endings in voluntary muscle. *American Journal of Physiology*, **3**, 339-344.

Kleiber, M. (1932). Body size and metabolism. *Hilgardia*, **6**, 315-353.

Kleiber, M. (1961). *Fire of life*. New York: Wiley.

Kroll, W.P. (1982). *Graduate study and research in physical education*. Champaign, IL: Human Kinetics.

Latimer, C.W. (1898-1899). On the modification of rigor mortis resulting from previous fatigue of the muscle in cold blooded animals. *American Journal of Physiology*, **2**, 29-46.

McCloy, C.H. (1932). *The measurement of athletic power*. New York: Barnes.

McCurdy, J.H. (1901). The effect of maximum muscular effort on blood pressure. *American Journal of Physiology*, **5**, 95-103.

McCurdy, J.H. (1924). *The physiology of exercise* (1st ed.). Philadelphia: Lea & Febiger.

McCurdy, J.H. (1928). *The physiology of exercise* (2nd ed.). Philadelphia: Lea & Febiger.

McKenzie, R.T. (1910). *Exercise in education and medicine*. Philadelphia: Saunders.

Morehouse, L.E., & Miller, A.T. (1948). *Physiology of exercise*. St. Louis: Mosby.

Murphy, M.C. (1914). *Athletic training* (Introduction by R. Tait McKenzie; Preface by E.R. Bushnell) (2nd ed. 1920). New York: Scribner's.

Park, R.J. (1987a). Physiologists, physicians and physical educators: Nineteenth-century biology and exercise, hygienic and educative. *Journal of Sport History*, **14**, 28-60.

Park, R.J. (1987b). Athletes and their training in Britain and America, 1800-1914. *Journal of Sport History*, **14**, 57-107.

Schneider, E.C. (1931). *Physiology of muscular activity* (1st ed.). Philadelphia: Saunders.

Schneider, E.C. (1939). *Physiology of muscular activity* (2nd ed.). Philadelphia: Saunders.

Steinhaus, A.H. (1933). Chronic effects of science. *Physiological Reviews*, **19**, 103-147.

Steinhaus, A.H. (1941). Exercise. *Annual Review of Physiology*, **3**, 695-716.

Steinhaus, A.H. (1963). *Toward an understanding of health and physical education*. Dubuque, IA: Brown.

Stewart, C.C. (1898). Variations in daily activity produced by alcohol and by changes in barometric pressure and diet with a description of recording methods. *American Journal of Physiology*, **1**, 40-56.

Welch, J.C. (1898). On the measurement of mental activity through muscular activity and the determination of a constant of attention. *American Journal of Physiology*, **1**, 283-306.

Whitteridge, D. (1989). *One hundred years of congresses of physiology*. Litto Oy Oulu, Finland: International Union of Physiological Sciences.

Withington, E.T. (1894). *Medical history from the earliest times, a popular history of the healing art*. London: Scientific Press.

Withington, P. (Ed.) (1914). *The book of athletics*. Boston: Lothrop, Lee and Shepard.

References—Part II

ACSM. (1975). American College of Sports Medicine Position Statement on prevention of heat injuries during distance running. *Med. Sci. Sports*, **7**, vii-vii.

ACSM. (1976). American College of Sports Medicine Position Statement on weight loss in wrestlers. *Med. Sci. Sports*, **8**, xi-xiii.

ACSM. (1977). American College of Sports Medicine Position Statement on the use and abuse of anabolic-androgenic steroids in sports. *Med. Sci. Sports*, **9**, xi-xiii.

ACSM. (1978). American College of Sports Medicine Position Statement on the recommended quantity and quality of exercise for developing and maintaining fitness in healthy adults. *Med. Sci. Sports*, **10**, vii-ix.

ACSM. (1994). *American College of Sports Medicine-40th Anniversary lectures* (p. v). Indianapolis: American College of Sports Medicine.

APS. (1963). Training for the Ph.D. degree. *The Physiologist*, **6**, 7.

APS. (1977). Membership status. *The Physiologist*, **20**, 17.

APS. (1994). Membership status. *The Physiologist*, **37**, 94-95.

American College of Sports Medicine. (1975). *Guidelines for graded exercise testing and exercise prescription*. Philadelphia: Lea & Febiger.

American Men and Women of Science (1972). New York: J. Cattel Press.

Anonymous (1948). Foreword. *J. Appl. Physiol.* **1**, 1.

Asmussen, E., & Nielsen, M. (1955). Cardiac output during muscular work and its regulation. *Physiol. Rev.*, **35**, 778-800.

Astrand, P.-O. (1956). Human physical fitness with special reference to sex and age. *Physiol. Rev.*, **36**, 307-355.

Astrand, P.-O., & Rodahl, K. (1970). *Textbook of work physiology: Physiological bases of exercise*. New York: McGraw-Hill.

Balke, B. (1969). Editorial. *Med. Sci. Sports*, **1**, viii.

Balke, B., & Ware, R. (1959). An experimental study of physical fitness of Air Force personnel. *U.S. Armed Forces Med. J.*, **10**, 675-681.

Barnard, J.A. (1994). Personal communication.

Bartley, S.H. (1957). Fatigue and inadequacy. *Physiol. Rev.* **37**, 301-324.

Berger, R.A. (1982). *Applied exercise physiology*. Philadelphia: Lea & Febiger.

Bernauer, E.M. (1994). Personal communication.

Bevegard, R.S., & Shepherd, J.T. (1967). Regulation of the circulation during exercise in man. *Physiol. Rev.*, **47**, 178-213.

Blair, S.N., Kohl, H.W., & Powell, K.E. (1987). Physical activity, physical fitness, exercise, and the public health. In M.J. Safrit & H.M. Eckert (Eds.), *American Academy of Physical Education Papers* (Vol. 20, pp. 53-69). Champaign, IL: Human Kinetics.

Blomqvist, G. & Saltin. Cardiovascular adaptations to physical training. *Ann. Rev. Physiol.*, **45**, 169-190.

Booth, F.W. (1984). The future of exercise physiology as an academic discipline. *Specialization in physical education: The Alley legacy* (pp. 101-110). In C.M. Tipton & J.G. Hay, (Eds.), Iowa City: Department of Physical Education.

Booth, F.W. (1988). Perspectives on molecular and cellular exercise physiology. *J. Appl. Physiol.*, **65**, 1461-1471.

Booth, F.W. (1989). Application of molecular biology in exercise physiology. *Exerc. Sport Sci. Revs.*, **17**, 1-27.

Booth, F.W. (1991). Molecular and cellular adaptations of muscle in response to exercise. *Physiol. Rev.*, **71**, 541-585.

Bouchard, C., Shephard, R.J., & Stephens, T. (Eds.) (1994). *Physical activity, fitness, and health*. Champaign, IL: Human Kinetics.

Bouchard, C., Shephard, R.J., Stephens, T., Sutton, J.R., & McPherson, B.D. (Eds.) (1990). *Exercise, fitness, and health*. Champaign, IL: Human Kinetics.

Bowers, R.W. (1994). Personal communication.

Brenglemann, G.L. (1983). Circulatory adjustments to exercise and heat stress. *Ann. Rev. Physiol.*, **45**, 191-212.

Brobeck, J.R., Reynolds, O.E., & Appel, T.A. (Eds.) (1987). *History of the American physiological society: The first century 1887-1987.* Washington, DC: American Physiological Society.

Brooks, G.A. (1994a). Basic exercise physiology. In *American College of Sports Medicine-40th Anniversary lectures* (pp. 15-42). Indianapolis: American College of Sports Medicine.

Brooks, G.A. (1994b). Personal communication.

Brooks, G.A., & Fahey, T.D. (1984). *Exercise physiology: Human bioenergetics and its applications.* New York: Macmillian.

Bruce, R.A. (1973). Principles of exercise testing. In J.P. Naughton, H.K. Hellerstein, & I.C. Mohler, (Eds.), *Exercise testing and exercise training in coronary heart disease* (pp. 45-61). Philadelphia: Lea & Febiger.

Buckler, L. (1994). Personal communication.

Buskirk, E.R. (1996). Exercise physiology: Part I. In *History of exercise and sport science*, eds. J.D. Massengale and R.A. Swanson, 369-398. Champaign, IL: Human Kinetics.

Buskirk, E.R. (1994). Personal communication.

Buskirk, E.R. (1992). From Harvard to Minnesota: Keys to our history. *Exerc. Sport Sci. Revs.*, **20**, 1-26.

Carmack, M.A. (1995). Personal communication concerning Eugene Evonuk on 1-3.

Christensen, N.J., and Galbo, H. (1983). Sympathetic nervous system during exercise. *Ann. Rev. Physiol.*, **45**, 139-154.

Clarke, D.H. (1994). Personal communication.

Clarke, D.H. (1975). *Exercise physiology.* Englewood Cliffs, NJ: Prentice Hall.

Clausen, J.P. (1977). Effect of physical training on cardiovascular adjustments to exercise in man. *Physiol. Rev.*, **57**, 779-815.

Conant, J.B. (1963). *The education of American teachers.* New York: McGraw-Hill.

Cooper, K.H. (1968). *Aerobics.* New York: Bantam Books.

Cooper, K.H. (1970). *The new aerobics.* New York: M. Evans.

Corbin, D.E. (1986). *Jogging.* Glenview, IL: Scott, Foresman.

Costill, D.L. (1994a). Applied exercise physiology. In *American College of Sports Medicine-40th Anniversary lectures* (pp. 69-80). Indianapolis: American College of Sports Medicine.

Costill, D.L. (1994b). Personal communication.

Cureton, T.K. (1963). *Review of studies to improve cardiovascular fitness at the physical fitness research laboratory: University of Illinois, 1941-1963.* Unpublished bound document.

Cureton, T.K. (1964). *Physiology of exercise, physical fitness.* Unpublished document, 1-11.

Dempsey, J.D. (1993). Personal communication.

Dempsey, J.A., & Forster, H.V. (1982). Mediation of ventilatory adaptations. *Physiol. Rev., 62*, 262-346.

de Vries, H.A. (1994). Personal communication.

de Vries, H.A. (1966). *Physiology of exercise for physical education and athletics.* Dubuque, IA: Brown.

Edgerton, V.R. (1994). Personal communication.

Edington, D.W., & Edgerton, V.R. (1976). *The biology of physical activity.* Boston: Houghton Mifflin.

Falls, H.B. (Ed.). (1968). *Exercise physiology.* New York: Academic Press.

Faulkner, J.A. (1994). Personal communication.

Fenn, W.O. (1963). *History of American Physiological Society: The Third Quarter Century, 1937-1962.* Bethesda, MD: American Physiological Society.

Fishman, A.P. (1977). The journals of the American Physiological Society. *J. Appl. Physiol.: Respirat. Environ. Exerc. Physiol., 42*, 1-2.

Fishman, A.P. (1985). A rose by any other name. . . . *J. Appl. Physiol., 58*, 1-3.

Fitts, R.H. (1994). Cellular mechanisms of muscle fatigue. *Physiol. Rev., 74*, 49-94.

Fitz, G. (1934). Micromanipulator for pure culture and microchemical work. *Science, 79*, 233-234.

Fitz, G. (1931). A new micromanipulator. *Science, 76*, 72-75.

Fitz, G. (1926). A clinical study of muscular cramp: A physiological care. *Boston Med. Surg. J., 195*, 854-857.

Fitz, G. (1914). The physiological cost of insufficient protective clothing. *Boston Med. Surg. J., 170*, 648-651.

Fitz, G. (1895). A location reaction apparatus. *Psychol. Rev., 2*, 37-42.

Fitz, G. (1894). A study of types of respiratory movements. *Proc. Am. Assn. for Advancement of Phy. Ed., 9*, 57-68.

Forker, B.E. (1984). The Alley contribution and legacy. In C.M. Tipton & H.G. Hay (Eds.), *Specialization in Physical Education: The Alley Legacy* (p. 7). Iowa City: Department of Physical Education.

Fox, E.L., Bowers, R.W., & Foss, M.L. (1988). *The physiological basis of physical education and athletics* (4th ed.). Dubuque, IA: Brown.

Gerber, E.W. (1971). *Innovators and Institutions in Physical Education.* Philadelphia: Lea and Febiger.

Giebisch, G.H., Granger, J.P., Greenleaf, J.E., Lydic, R.B., Mitchell, R.H., Nadel, E.R., et al. (1990). What's past is prologue. *The Physiologist, 33*, 161-164.

Gisolfi, C.V. (1994). Personal communication.

Grodins, F.S. (1950). Analysis of factors concerned in the regulation of breathing during exercise. *Physiol. Rev., 30*, 220-239.

Hagberg, J., Blair, S., Ehsani, A., Gordon, N., Kapan, N., Tipton, C., & Zambraski, E. (1993). Position stand: Physical activity, physical fitness, and hypertension. *Med. Sci. Sports Exerc.*, i-x.

Hellerstein, H.K., Hirsch, E.Z., Ader, R., Greenblott, N., & Siegel, M. (1973). Principles of exercise prescription for normals and cardiac subjects. In J.P. Naughton, H.K. Hellerstein, & I.C. Mohler (Eds.), *Exercise testing and exercise training in coronary heart disease* (pp. 129-169). New York: Academic Press.

Henry, F.M. (1964). Physical education: An academic discipline. *Journal of Health, Physical Education and Recreation, 35*, 32-33, 69.

Henry, F.M., & Berg, W.E. (1950). Physiological and performance changes in athletic conditioning. *J. Appl. Physiol., 1*, 103-112.

Horvath, S.M. (1994). Personal communication.

Horvath, S.M., & Horvath, E.C. (1973). *The Harvard Fatigue Laboratory: Its History and Contributions*. Engelwood Cliffs, NJ: Prentice Hall.

Jackson, M.J., & Saunders, J.F. (1987). Spring and fall scientific meetings. In J.R. Brobeck, O.E. Reynolds, & Appel (Eds.), *History of the American Physiological Society: The first century 1887-1987* (pp. 315-332). Washington, DC: American Physiological Society.

Johnson, R.E. (1946). Applied Physiology. *Ann. Rev. Physiol., 8*, 535-558.

Johnson, W.R. (Ed.) (1960). *Science and medicine of exercise and sports*. New York: Harper & Row.

Jokl, E., Cluver, E.H., Goedvolk, G., & De Jongh, T.W. (1941). *Training and efficiency*. Johannesburg, South Africa: South African Institute for Medical Research.

Jones, J.H., & Lindstedt, S.L. (1993). Limits to maximal performance. *Ann. Rev. Physiol., 55*, 547-570.

Karpovich, P.V. (1959). *Physiology of Muscular Activity*, 5th ed. Philadelphia: Saunders.

Karpovich, P.V. (1947). Exercise. *Ann. Rev. Physiol., 9*, 149-162.

Karpovich, P.V., & Sinning, W.E. (1971). *Physiology of Muscular Activity*, 8th ed. Philadelphia: Saunders.

Katch, F.I. (1994). Personal communication.

Katz, A. (1954). Symposium of the regulation of the performance of the heart. *Physiol. Rev., 35*, 130-136, 143-155.

Kroll, W.P. (1982). *Graduate study and research in physical education*. Champaign, IL: Human Kinetics, 1-342.

Lamb, D.R. (1978). *Physiology of exercise responses and adaptations*. New York: Macmillian.

Lessler, M.A., & Hitchcock, F.A. (1985). History of physiology at the Ohio State University. *The Physiologist, 28,* 499.

Ludbrook, J. (1983). Reflex control of blood pressure during exercise. *Ann. Rev. Physiol., 45*, 155-168.

Mandel, R. (1994). NIH Anniversary History Project of the Division of Research Grants correspondence to C.M. Tipton.

Matthews, D.K., & Fox, E.L. (1971). *The physiological basis of physical education and athletics*. Philadelphia: Saunders.

McArdle, W.D., Katch, F.I., & Katch, V.L. (1981). *Exercise physiology, energy, nutrition and human performance.* Philadelphia: Lea & Febiger.

McCurdy, J.H., & Larson, L.A. (1939). *Physiology of exercise.* Philadelphia: Lea & Febiger.

Mitchell, J.H. (1994). Personal communication.

Mole, P.A. (1994). Personal communication.

Montoye, H.J., & Washburn, R. (1980). Genealogy of scholarship among Academy members. In M.G. Scott (Ed.), *The Academy papers,* (Vol. 13, pp. 94-101). Washington, DC: The American Academy of Physical Education.

Morehouse, L.E. (1972). *American men and women of science.* New York: R.R. Boroker Co.

Morehouse, L.E., & Miller, A.T., Jr. (1948). *Physiology of exercise.* St. Louis: Mosby.

Nadel, E.R. (1994). Personal communication.

Nagle, F.J. (1994). Personal communication.

Nagle, F.J., Clarke, K.S., Faulkner, J.A., Knuttgen, H.G., Thomas, C., & Tipton, C.M. (1968). Report of the ad hoc committee on the new quarterly journal. *ACSM Newsletter, 3*(2), 3.

Neufeldt, V., & Guralnik, D.B. (Eds.) (1988). *Webster's new world dictionary* (3rd ed.). Cleveland: Webster's New World Dictionaries.

Nieman, D.C. (1986). *The sports medicine fitness course.* Palo Alto, CA: Bull.

NIH advisory committees. (1991). U.S. Department of Health and Human Services, Public Health Service, Washington, DC: 408, 506.

NIH almanac. (1989). U.S. Department and Human Services. NIH Publication N. 89-3.

NIH extramural trends fiscal years 1984-1993. (1994). NIH Publication No. 94-3506. National Institutes of Health, Division of Research Grants.

Noble, B.J. (1986). *Physiology of exercise and sport.* St. Louis: Times Mirror/Mosby.

Oscai, L.B. (1994). Personal communication.

Otis, A.B. (1954). The work of breathing. *Physiol. Rev., 34,* 202-220.

Park, R.J. (1988). *Measurement of physical fitness: A historical perspective.* ODPHP Monograph Series. U.S. Department of Health and Human Services.

Passmore, R., & Durnin, J.V.G.A. (1955). Human energy expenditure. *Physiol. Rev., 35,* 301-324.

Pate, R.R. (1994). Personal communication.

Rabb, W. (1966). *Prevention of ischemic heart disease.* Springfield, IL: Thomas.

Raven, P.R. (1994). Personal communication.

Reddan, W.G. (1993). Personal communication.

Reynolds, O.E. (1976). Annual membership in APS. *The Physiologist, 19,* 32.

Robertson, C.M. (1995). Personal communication.

Rowell, L.B. (1974). Human cardiovascular adjustment to exercise and thermal stress. *Physiol. Rev., 54,* 75-159.

Rowell, L.B. (1993). *Human cardiovascular control*. New York: Oxford University Press.

Saltin, B., & Gollnick, P.D. (1983). Skeletal muscle adaptability: Significance for metabolism and performance. In L.D. Peachy, R.H. Adrian, & S.R. Geiger (Eds.), *Handbook of physiology: skeletal muscle* (pp. 555-631). New York: Oxford University Press.

Scheuer, J., & Tipton, C.M. (1977). Cardiovascular adaptations to physical training. *Ann. Rev. Physiol., 39*, 221-251.

Schneider, E.C., & Karpovich, P.V. (1948). *Physiology of muscular activity* (3rd ed.). Philadelphia: Saunders.

Serfass, R.C. (1994). Personal communication.

Shephard, R.H. (1982). *Physiology and biochemistry of exercise*. New York: Praeger.

Simonson, E. (Ed.). (1971). *Physiology of work capacity and fatigue*. Springfield, IL: Thomas.

Skinner, J.S. (1994). Personal communication.

Smith, A.H., Bernauer, E.M., Black, A.L., Burger, R.E., Crowe, J.H., Horowitz, J.M., et al. (1986). History of physiology at University of California, Davis. *The Physiologist, 29*, 46-57.

Stewart, I. (1994). Applied Physiology Study Section correspondence on 8-16, personal communication.

Taylor, C.R. (1987). Structural and functional limits to oxidative metabolism: Insights from scaling. *Ann. Rev. Physiol., 49*, 135-146.

Taylor, H.L., Buskirk, E.R., & Henschel, A. (1955). Maximum oxygen intake as an objective measure of cardiorespiratory performance. *J. Appl. Physiol., 8*, 73-80.

Tipton, C.M. (1994a). Guest editorial. *Med. Sci. Sports Exerc., 25*, 537.

Tipton, C.M. (1994b). Unpublished records of Exercise Science Programs at the University of Iowa, Big 10 universities, and Pacific coast universities between 1963 and 1984.

Tipton, C.M. (1994c, December 16). Inspection of Applied Physiology Study Section "Pink Sheets."

Tipton, C.M. (1993, June 3). Introduction to ACSM Gollnick Tutorial Lecture.

Tuttle, W.W., & Schottelius, B.A. (1969). Textbook of physiology. (16th ed.). Dubuque, IA: Brown.

Van Huss, W.D. (1994). Personal communication.

Wasserman, K., Hansen, J.E., Sue, D.Y., & Whipp, B.J. (1987). *Principles of exercise testing and interpretation*. Philadelphia: Lea & Febiger.

Wegner, N.K. (1994). Physical activity in primary and secondary prevention of heart disease. In *American College of Sports Medicine-40th Anniversary lectures* (pp. 43-54). Indianapolis: American College of Sports Medicine.

Welch, H.G. (1994). Personal communication.

Wilmore, J.H. (1976). *Athletic training and physical fitness*. Boston: Allyn & Bacon.

Wilmore, J.H. (1979). The challenge of change for physical education in the 1980's; physiological view. In M.G. Scott (Ed.), *The Academy Papers* (Vol. 13, pp. 27-32). Washington, DC: The American Academy of Physical Education.

Wilmore, J.H., and Costill, D.L. (1994). *Physiology of sport and exercise*. Champaign, IL: Human Kinetics.

Yoder, S.E. (1994). Personal communication.

Zeigler, E.F. (1979). Past, present and future developments of physical education and sport. In M.G. Scott (Ed.), *The Academy Papers* (Vol. 13, pp. 9-19). Washington, DC: The American Academy of Physical Education.

Current and Future Directions in Exercise and Sport Science

Richard A. Swanson
University of North Carolina at Greensboro
John D. Massengale
University of Nevada, Las Vegas

The present structure of the field of exercise and sport science within higher education is largely not the result of futures forecasting or trends extrapolation, but rather reactions to the challenges thrown out by visionary leaders some three decades or more ago. Of particular significance, of course, was Franklin Henry's call to identify a body of knowledge sufficient to qualify the field as an academic discipline. The result has been a burgeoning and maturing of research in a variety of areas and the consequent development of "subdisciplines." Of perhaps greater importance is the fact that this explosion of research and scholarship has provided the field with a substantive grounding that it formerly lacked. In fact, without this maturation into a discipline over the past three decades it might be safely postulated that by now physical education or exercise and sport science would have completely disappeared from the degree offerings of most major research universities.

The preceding chapters of this work have, in great detail, traced the twentieth-century evolution of the discipline of exercise and sport science in the United States. Each writer has described and analyzed the growth and maturation of the academic specialties that comprise the discipline today. But where, now, is the field as a whole and what is its future? In recent years there have been a number of efforts to ascertain that future and, of course, they all begin with a particular perception of the present. Is the field falling prey to fragmentation and are we in danger, at least within higher education, of being absorbed segmentally by more established "home" disciplines as Hoffman (1985a, 1985b) suggested in the mid-1980s? Or, is it merely in a transitional stage, undergoing normal growing pains? Has the move to develop a unique body of knowledge in exercise and sport science created an irreversible separation between scholars in higher education and physical education practitioners? Will this split result in an increasing number of departments of professional physical education separate from departments of exercise and sport science? In other words, who are we, and where are we headed?

Who Are We?

Undoubtedly, the efforts of scholars over the past several decades to develop a research-based body of knowledge have been spectacularly successful. (It could be argued that the term should be *bodies* of knowledge in recognition of the multiple highly developed subdisciplines.) The preceding chapters detail separate yet intertwined stories of the evolution of the field. They tell of scholars from the tradition of physical education, as well as those from other parent disciplines in the liberal arts and sciences, coming together to explore issues of mutual interest within the exercise and sport sciences. While acknowledging these joint efforts, it is also clear that in most cases it was members of the former group who initiated the organization of the subdiscipline by sponsoring conferences, founding societies, and conducting much of the early research.

Acknowledging the fact that scholars from more than one field contributed to the formation of the constituent subdisciplines, however, only partially answers the question, "Who are we?" Focusing exclusively on those who identify with the broader field of exercise and sport science by virtue of training and/or department affiliation in a college or university, we still have a rather fragmented picture. As many graduate professors will attest, over the past decade an increasing number of master's and doctoral degree candidates in exercise and sport science have come from undergraduate experiences in other fields. Unlike past generations, when virtually all graduate students came into programs with a rather common undergraduate base focused upon the preparation of physical education teachers and coaches, today's candidates are just as likely to have majored in psychology, biology, physics, history, sociology, nutrition, or gerontology, to name just a few. Today, many faculty members under the age of 40 have already been prepared with such a background.

Until the early 1980s, persons from outside the field wishing to pursue graduate study in exercise and sport science would have found most programs requiring them to fulfill literally all the undergraduate major requirements, often including student teaching, as a prerequisite to enrolling in the master's degree program. Generally, this was at least a two-year commitment. As the move toward specialization increased within the field, more and more programs began to either waive or substantially reduce the undergraduate major prerequisite. The rationale was that these individuals often brought excellent preparation for the area of specialization; often better than their peers who had majored in physical education. This preparation offered the graduate faculty specialist the opportunity to work with better-prepared students in that subdiscipline, and therefore to concentrate on more advanced course work and research. Undoubtedly, it has also contributed much to the advancement of knowledge and scholarship in the specialty. At the same time, others began to worry about the infusion of large numbers of specialists lacking at least a rudimentary understanding of the field as a whole (Hoffman, 1985a).

As noted in the first chapter, the 1970s and 1980s also brought major curriculum reform within exercise and sport science undergraduate programs. New career opportunities in the burgeoning fitness industry, as well as student interest in studying exercise and sport as a disciplinary major, spurred this rapid curriculum change. Increasingly, non-teacher education tracks were developed for those students wishing to focus their attention on the *study* of exercise and sport science, with no designs on teaching or coaching careers in K-through-12 settings. With heavy doses of course work in several areas, and perhaps a specific concentration in one, accompanied by supportive work in other disciplines, the individual was more appropriately prepared for a beginning career as well as graduate work in the new era of specialization, but with the added advantage of background in the discipline at large.

The answer to the question "Who are we?," then, is that we are both a discipline *and* a profession peopled with an increasing number of highly trained specialists in several areas, as well as thousands of what might be termed "generalists," each of whom forms a part of the whole of exercise and sport science. The specialists in the field come from different educational backgrounds, with varying degrees of understanding of the discipline as a whole. Moreover, some specialists and generalists see themselves solely as scientists, objectively examining evidence and asking new questions. Others see themselves primarily as practitioners, teaching others the skills and methods of sport and exercise. While it is probably safe to say that all share a common interest as human beings trained to work in the area of exercise and sport, the commonality may end there. And therein lies the current dilemma that, while not uncommon in contemporary disciplinary scholarship, is nevertheless perhaps the major professional concern in exercise and sport science today.

Where Are We?

The increased emphasis on specialization at the graduate level has hastened the rate at which research is enriching the body of knowledge and bringing exercise and sport science into the mainstream of American higher education, especially in the large research institutions. However, as more sophisticated research has generated new knowledge exponentially, it has become apparent that intellectual chasms have been developing within the discipline, frequently being played out at the department level in colleges and universities across the nation. The concerns expressed by Hoffman, Thomas, and others beginning in the mid-1980s are increasingly voiced by administrators and senior faculty in departments of exercise and sport science. Especially vocal are those in the hundreds of comprehensive and regional universities as well as the liberal arts colleges. Department heads in these institutions, the producers of the vast majority of undergraduate and master's degree majors annually, lacking the resources to appoint specialists unable to teach in more than one area, began to voice their complaints by the beginning of the 1990s.

At the 1991 summer workshop of the College and University Administrators' Council (CUAC) of the American Alliance for Health, Physical Education, Recreation and Dance (AAHPERD), their frustration broke into the open. Faced with growing difficulty in filling faculty positions they called upon the Council to address the issue. An ad hoc task force was charged with gathering facts regarding the preparation of doctoral candidates to assume new faculty positions.

That same year, Thomas (1991), an exercise and sport science scholar and administrator at one of the leading research institutions, asked the question, "Who is preparing PhDs, and for whom?" Noting that more than half of the PhDs produced annually come from large research universities where specialization is the rule, he concludes that "a greater number of PhDs are being produced than research universities and laboratories can absorb" (p. 4). At the same time, he observed, there are often not enough doctoral graduates from less specialized programs to meet the needs of the hundreds of comprehensive universities and liberal arts colleges of the nation.

As a result, many of the highly trained specialists are accepting positions in settings with missions that emphasize teaching over research and where a person usually must expect to teach in more than one area. Hence, we have in effect a clash of cultures, where the training and objectives of the specialist do not fit the mission of their institution. Unless the specialist then willingly accepts the situation and even redefines her or his career goals, frustration ensues on both sides, as neither the needs of the institution or the individual are satisfactorily met (Boyer, 1990; Massengale, 1994).

While the "quick and dirty" response to the problem described above is that both the candidate and the hiring institution must be clear in their career and institutional objectives in order to avoid inappropriate placements, longer-term solutions must be developed and put in place. In an earlier paper, Thomas (1987) suggested that while specialization itself is not wrong and is, in fact, healthy for the discipline, it has been pursued incorrectly. He concludes that, "we have become so narrow in our graduate preparation that doctoral students are not developing an adequate concept of the total field of inquiry and how the specialization fits within the sport science framework" (p. 120). He advocates each student being required "to obtain an adequate knowledge base in the physical, social, cultural, pedagogical, and statistical foundations of sport."

At the local level, faculty committees and administrators making personnel decisions need to clarify and verbalize the mission of the department when interviewing potential candidates for faculty positions, thus ensuring the best possible "fit." Doctoral granting units are well advised to follow the prescription of Thomas (1987) to require all graduate students to be at least minimally grounded in the broad foundations of the discipline. If the increasing number of conversations through journals and conferences, often led by faculty and administrators in the leading graduate programs, is any indication, there is hope that this is happening. If so, at least one of the most vexing outcomes of specialization in exercise and sport science can perhaps be at least minimized.

Placement of PhD specialists is, of course, not the only problem brought about by the creation of subdisciplines within exercise and sport science. The fragmentation that Hoffman (1985a) feared has indeed appeared in various guises. It is manifested in those young scholars who choose to identify themselves to others as exercise physiologists, biomechanists, sport psychologists, sociologists, or historians, with no reference to their home discipline or department. These same individuals frequently choose not to affiliate with umbrella professional organizations such as AAHPERD or the National Association for Physical Education in Higher Education (NAPEHE), opting instead for memberships exclusively in their subdiscipline or even within other "home" disciplines. Unfortunately, this specialization frequently translates into fragmentation within the person's academic department when little or no interest or commitment is given to its broader mission. Or, as has happened in more than one unit, a hierarchy of specialties develops, pitting the science people against the educationalists, or the pure versus the applied researchers, and so on. Overall is the fact that we even find it difficult to carry on meaningful conversations about one another's work because it has become so specialized that the languages and even the cultures appear foreign.

Where are we then, as a discipline/profession of Exercise and Sport Science? Are we fast becoming a collection of independent subgroups with little interest in talking with one another? Are we isolated pockets of self-absorbed specialists who are only interested in our own small corner of the exercise and sport science world, with little or no interest in the success of the practitioner working with lay people and trying to make sense of the whole? And so what if we are? As long as we are doing good science, what difference does it make? The answer is that it only makes a difference to those who believe in the overall mission of exercise and sport science, to those who believe that someone or some group has to make sense of the whole and put the fragmented pieces of data together for the benefit of society. Without that synthesis as the mission, the separate pieces of the disciplinary "pie" can be siphoned off to other appropriate disciplinary homes where they might or might not find hospitable surroundings as, again, one of many subspecialties. This particular picture of the future can, in fact, be seen in the isolated instances where universities have chosen to eliminate departments of exercise and sport science, and to distribute the tenured faculty to those departments that seem to be the closest fit. While the individuals are generally able to continue their research and teaching, they may also find themselves working at the local level in a vacuum outside sport studies.

Where Are We Going?

The perhaps bleak scenario painted above is not, of course, the total picture of exercise and sport science in the mid-1990s. In most colleges, comprehensive universities, and even doctoral-granting institutions, specialization has not as yet resulted in these extremes. In these departments, territorial battles between areas are rare, people talk to one another about their interests, and faculty focus not only upon their research but also upon curricula that serve the students well. Nevertheless, the potential for further erosion of the whole is certainly present. The erosion is partially illustrated by steady declines in membership in AAHPERD and NAPEHE over the past two decades as the subdisciplinary associations were formed.

Nevertheless, the preceding chapters are filled with positive signs that in the long run the building of a discipline, through the creation of subdisciplines, is resulting in a healthy whole rather than disintegration through fragmentation. First of all, the mere fact is hopeful that people prepared through and employed in exercise and sport science degree programs are leading participants within all of the subdisciplinary movements. It can be reasonably assumed that most such individuals have a loyalty to the whole and a commitment to advocacy for the delivery of programs and services that promote fitness and educationally sound sport experiences to all populations.

Equally positive is the recognition by several of the subdisciplines that future advancements in research will require interdisciplinary and cross-disciplinary collaboration within the broader field. In her perceptive analysis of the current status and future of pedagogy in chapter 2 of this work, Bain points repeatedly to the value of collaboration with both physical education practitioners and scholars from other subdisciplines. The action research projects done by Martinek and Schempp (1988) and

Anderson (1987, 1988) with K-through-12 teachers are singled out as prime examples of work that has captured great respect and is certain to be emulated. Of particular significance to the present discussion is Bain's conclusion "that pedagogy research in physical education must move beyond education as the sole source of theories and research questions. Knowledge and issues from health and from leisure and sport have implications for research on teaching, teachers, teacher education, and curriculum." One such implication might be that "A model that draws on health, leisure and sport research may . . . enable pedagogy researchers to reformat questions about the quality of school physical education programs." Since there is concern about "continuing tension around the relationship of pedagogy to the discipline of kinesiology or exercise and sport science," as well as concern about the "apparent failure of pedagogical research to influence school physical education programs," the search for a broader base of knowledge and expertise appears well founded. The prospect of physical education disappearing from the public school curriculum is perhaps reason enough for scholars from all appropriate subdisciplines to join together in collaborative work.

In the area of adapted physical activity and education (chapter 3), Sherrill and DePauw predict the future will bring more joint research and theorizing, more joint application, and more collaboration, as leaders create new paradigms and explore alternative strategies for facilitating equal access, integration, inclusion and infusion (p. 45). Contributing to and drawing from such areas as sport sociology, exercise and sport psychology, pedagogy, sport philosophy, and sport history, "adapted physical activity may act as a catalyst and a conscience in promoting scholarly inquiry into marginality of all kinds" (p. 45).

Sport history is in the interesting position of seeing increased scholarship in the field coming from researchers in other disciplines within the humanities and social sciences, while at the same time dwindling opportunities for employment of sport historians in departments of exercise and sport science has become commonplace. In fact, Professor Struna (chapter 5) comments, as sport history becomes increasingly incorporated into the fabric of other areas of social history, anthropology, and even literature, exercise and sport science administrators appear to be turning their backs on the subdiscipline. She worries that if sport history is lost from exercise and sport science, the loss of this "set of perspectives and research directions diminishes the vitality and viability" of the entire discipline. "This, in turn," she concludes, "raises the possibility that the remaining subdisciplines would no longer constitute a distinctive field of study, since they too could then become arms of other so-called home disciplines. In addition, who will then be the chronicler who researches, writes, teaches, and otherwise brings together the past and present, a key element in fostering both the sense and the reality of the discipline?"

Kretchmar, in his account of the development of sport philosophy (chapter 6), predicts that the area is growing increasingly disenchanted with the skeptical spirit that typifies much scientific inquiry, particularly within the field of philosophy itself. Suggesting that good sport philosophy is not just good philosophy, he theorizes that sport philosophers will demonstrate increasing willingness to chart new directions away from traditional philosophy. That new direction, because it focuses upon the world of sport, games, play, dance, and exercise, will create, in and of itself, greater interaction with the other subdisciplines of exercise and sport science.

Exercise and sport psychology, on the other hand, is being pulled in two directions. Some are definitely interested in applied psychology and counseling, while others are interested primarily in the development of a knowledge base, with both groups likely to remain solidly within exercise and sport science. Gill (chapter 8) predicts that sport and exercise psychology as a whole is very likely to not only remain within exercise and sport science, but, based upon present signs, will develop even closer ties with the other subdisciplines. Thomas (chapter 7) strengthens the notion of closer interdisciplinary ties by demonstrating that motor behavior has a solid and valuable place within exercise and sport science and progressively contributes to other disciplines such as physical therapy, leisure studies, medicine, neuroscience, psychology, and physiology.

Kretchmar, again in his chapter on the evolution of sport philosophy, while speaking specifically to an array of philosophy specialists, could also have been speaking for all of those in exercise and sport science who wish for greater unity and collaboration among the subdisciplines when he wrote:

> Today some indicators suggest that philosophy is returning to Aristotle's marketplace, where educated people with inquiring minds, common sense, a thirst for truth, and normal language abilities can communicate fruitfully with one another and make philosophic progress on practical human problems.

The fact that the current subdisciplinary movement in exercise and sport science allows for togetherness, interdisciplinary study, academic productivity, and improved collegiality, as well as the dreaded opportunity for ill will and fragmentation, has been mentioned by all of the contributors of this book. Sometimes contributors were subtle with their descriptions, and in other instances they were direct.

Sage (chapter 4) was very complimentary and thorough in his description of Gerald Kenyon as the spokesman, forerunner, and acknowledged leader of the sociology of sport movement in North America. What is additionally interesting about the Kenyon situation is that his graduate education is probably best described as exercise physiology.

Early exercise physiology as described by Buskirk (chapter 10, part 1) features a detailed history of how professors, physicians, and scientists representing many different areas created a completely new subdiscipline from the parent discipline of physiology. Tipton (chapter 10, part 2), taking a contemporary perspective, described how exercise physiology and exercise physiologists integrated and aided in the development of many of the subdisciplines found in modern exercise and sport science, while also fostering the concept that eventually became the American College of Sports Medicine.

Wilkerson (chapter 9) offers the most direct history of the development and purpose of a subdiscipline, and its cooperative relationship to exercise and sport science, while describing biomechanics. She clearly describes "borrowing" from physics, biology, physiology, and engineering, for the express purpose of establishing the subdiscipline that became known as biomechanics. She then describes how the main function of the subdiscipline is to bring its knowledge back to the core of exercise and sport science, in a rather "holistic" approach.

Working together to advance knowledge and promote healthy, active lifestyles has always been a stated purpose of exercise and sport science and physical education. Today more than ever, the knowledge base is growing and has, in fact, surpassed our ability to translate it all into successful programs. Whereas in past generations much promotion and curriculum work was done on the basis of untested theory, the present generation of scholars and practitioners has the opportunity to utilize a broad knowledge base gleaned from several subdisciplinary perspectives. The challenge is to work together productively.

What Will the Future Be?

Predicting the future of any human endeavor with any degree of precision is risky business. A good case in point is the increasing skepticism of the American public for the economic forecasts regularly bandied about by economists in both the public and private sectors. This skepticism is based upon too many predictions gone awry or the suspicions that political or corporate biases play too great a role in such forecasts.

On the other hand, while specificity is often risky, many predictions of trends or possibilities frequently materialize in smaller or altered form. For example, mid-twentieth-century predictions of climate-controlled cities under giant glass domes have yet to be realized, and yet the Houston Astrodome, opened in 1965, and its progeny, the giant shopping malls introduced in the early 1970s, are miniature versions of the science-fiction-like enclosed city. Similarly, predictions of self-propelled robots with electronic eyes and voices in every home to assist with the mundane chores of living have not yet come true. Nevertheless, like enclosed acres of retail space, the home computer has become a reality, as has the presence of computer-controlled home heating and cooling systems, appliances, and automobiles, as well as robotized manufacturing facilities in the industrial sector. There is, therefore, enough accuracy in our past predictions to keep us enthralled with the idea of planning for our futures based upon what we believe to be the most accurate data available. It is the examination of trends, which futurists often describe as trend extrapolation, that has received increasing attention over the past decade within the field of exercise and sport science.

Trend extrapolation is a method of predicting, forecasting, or projecting the future by assuming that events that shaped recent history caused a trend that will most likely extend into the future. It requires the assumption that items that shaped the past will continue and eventually shape the future. The use of trend extrapolation binds the researcher or futurist to the proposition that past history, current history, and future history are all points on a continuum (Massengale, 1987).

It is by far the simplest form of futures research. Trend extrapolation holds that things will be exactly like they have been in the past, or that things will change in the same way that they have in the past, or that what has been observed in the past will continue into the future. Assuming that the future will be like the past, or that past change will continue in the same direction, or that the rate of change will stay the same, are reasonable ways to attempt an understanding of the future.

Another important consideration is that trends extrapolation must be done with extreme care. Experimenting with trends can be misleading, and sometimes results in fluctuations or fads being mistaken for real trends. It is highly important to recognize appropriate issues and variables that are likely to affect the future, and to reject items that will not affect the future, while ignoring those items that have already been predetermined. There will always be items that can be identified as important, unimportant, or predetermined. For example, the growing violence in sport *is* important, hula hoops were *not* important as elementary physical education teaching aids, and many trends in licensure and/or certification *have already* been predetermined.

There is a serious weakness in using trend extrapolation, and that weakness is the possibility of a forecaster using personal prejudice, opinion, or intuition instead of sound professional judgment. For example, a researcher might extrapolate until a comfortable model is developed, which can easily be a model that meets predetermined views. An application of this inherent weakness can be seen by examining typical HPER textbooks and journals published in the 1960s that made forecasts such as, (1) "in the future coaches will be appointed on the basis of their educational qualifications and not their win/loss records," or (2) "in the future the certification of high school coaches will become standard practice in American education." Forecasts like these express collective wishful thinking, since there is very little evidence to support such extrapolations, and today it is clearly evident that forecasts like these may never come about.

Needless to say, none of the contributors to this book knows exactly what the future will be. However, professionals in the field of exercise and sport science can forecast almost all of the possible alternative futures that might come about (Massengale, 1987, 1988). That very notion rejects the idea that any single future is inevitable. Alternative futures can be identified, created, analyzed, planned, and even implemented as a process. Almost any future can be created, and then greatly influenced.

The process of creating alternative futures, studying them, and then selectively choosing the most appropriate future is not currently being done in the field of exercise and sport science. The leadership of the field needs to focus attention upon the creation of alternative futures, the selection of one, and then take the necessary steps to make that future come true.

A complicating factor is that the future will not be like the past, regardless of accurate trend extrapolation; it will be far more complex. New data that are yet to be established may not be like current data. Frames of reference will probably change. Demographics will change, as will science and technology. Social norms, cultural norms, and political institutions will vary independently of one another, as well as independently of science and technology.

When applied to exercise and sport science, the root of this problem appears to be that people are constantly predicting well into the twenty-first century by using 1980s methods and technology. The problem is further confounded when decision makers insist on using concepts and technology that they are comfortable with but which they may have acquired as graduate students in the late 1960s and early 1970s. Among the professional leaders caught in this dilemma are some of AAHPERD's board of governors, college deans, journal editors, Honor Academy members, Honor Society members, and Honor Fellows, who are mostly between the ages of 45 and 65.

Despite the professional risks involved, including lack of acceptance and outright error, scholars and practitioners in exercise and sport science, especially those in higher education, will continue to attempt to predict the future, and may often fail. Why might this failure persist? One reason may certainly lie in the fact that often the forecaster knows too much about the subject. That is, she or he becomes hamstrung because of past practice and is unable to break outside the boundaries of the past to create new possibilities for action in the future. The more one knows about past history, the more careful one should be when using trends extrapolation as a method of predicting the future. Experts in exercise and sport science seldom appear to lack self-confidence, and, like their peers in other disciplines and professions, are sometimes guilty of ignoring certain variables due to their highly specialized focus.

With this caveat in mind, the contributors to this book have attempted to accurately describe and analyze the history of exercise and sport science. It is anticipated that the knowledge base provided by these narratives, along with creative, imaginative leadership, can be the springboard required to create a bigger, better, and brighter future for exercise and sport science in the twenty-first century.

References

Anderson, W.G. (1987). Five years of program development: A retrospective. In G.T. Barrette, R.W. Reingold, C.R. Reese, & M. Peiron (Eds.), *Myths, models, & methods in sport pedagogy* (pp. 123-134). Champaign, IL: Human Kinetics.

Anderson, W.G. (1988). A school-centered collaborative model for program development. *Journal of Teaching in Physical Education,* **7**(3), 176-183.

Boyer, E.L. (1990). *Scholarship reconsidered.* Princeton, NJ: Carnegie.

Henry, F.M. (1964). Physical Education—An academic discipline. *67th Proceedings*: Annual Meeting of the National College Physical Education Association for Men (pp. 6-9).

Hoffman, S.J. (1985a). Specialization = Fragmentation = Examination: A formula for the demise of graduate education. *Journal of Physical Education, Recreation and Dance,* **56**(6), 19-22.

Hoffman, S.J. (1985b). Hoffman replies. . . . *Journal of Physical Education, Recreation and Dance,* **56**(9), 23.

Martinek, T.J., & Schempp, P.G. (Eds.) (1988). Collaboration for instructional improvement: Models for school-university partnerships. *Journal of Teaching in Physical Education,* **7**(3).

Massengale, J.D. (1987). *Trends towards the future in physical education.* Champaign, IL: Human Kinetics.

Massengale, J.D. (1988). The unprepared discipline: Selection of alternative futures. *Quest,* **40**(2), 107-114.

Massengale, J.D. (1994). Role conflict and administrative careers in AAHPERD. *The Physical Educator,* **51**(3), 157-161.

Thomas, J.R. (1987). Are we already in pieces or just falling apart? *Quest,* **39**(2), 114-121.

Thomas, J.R. (1991). Who is preparing Ph.D.'s and for whom? *Chronicle of Physical Education in Higher Education,* **3**(1), 4, 11.

Credits

Chapter 3

The photos of Josephine Rathbone, H. Harrison Clarke, William Hillman, Evelyn Davies, Louis Bowers, Geoffrey Broadhead, John Dunn, and Joseph Winnick are reprinted, by permission, from C. Sherrill, 1988, *Leadership Training in Adapted Physical Education* (Champaign, IL: Human Kinetics), 32-35, 74-76, and 121.

The photo of Arthur Daniels is reprinted, by permission, from the Archives of the American Alliance for Health, Physical Education, and Dance, 1900 Association Drive, Reston, VA 22091.

The photo of Julian Stein is reprinted, by permission, from J.P. Winnick, 1995, *Adapted Physical Education and Sport* (Champaign, IL: Human Kinetics), 7.

Chapter 5

The image of the NASSH seal is reprinted, by permission, of the North American Society for Sport History.

The photos of Allen Guttmann, David Voigt, Roberta Park, and the first NASSH Council are courtesy of Hal Ray, NASSH photographer.

Chapter 6

The cover of the 1973 Annual Meeting program is reprinted, by permission, from the Philosophical Society for the Study of Sport.

Chapter 8

The photo of Coleman Griffith is courtesy of University of Illinois Archives (record series 39/2/26).

The photos of Bruce Ogilvie, Dan Landers, and Tara Scanlan are reprinted, by permission, from R.S. Weinberg and D. Gould, 1995, *Foundations of Sport and Exercise Psychology* (Champaign, IL: Human Kinetics), 12, 18-19.

Chapter 10

The photo of Gerard, Bard, and Fenn is reprinted, by permission, from W.O. Fenn, 1963, *History of the American Physiological Society* (Bethesda, MD: The American Physiological Society), 11.

The photos of Glenn Cunningham, the Harvard Fatigue Lab Group, and David Bruce Dill are reprinted, by permission, from S.M. Horvath and E.C. Horvath, 1973, *The Harvard Fatigue Laboratory: Its History and Contributions* (Englewood Cliffs, NJ: Prentice Hall), 106.

The photo of F. Miescher is reprinted, by permission, from W.O. Fenn, 1968, *History of the International Congress of Physiological Sciences, 1889-1968* (Bethesda, MD: The American Physiological Society).

The photos of Archibald V. Hill, Thomas K. Cureton, and Erik Hohwu-Christensen are reprinted, by permission, from J.H. Wilmore and D.L. Costill, 1994, *Physiology of Sport and Exercise* (Champaign, IL: Human Kinetics), 6-9.

The photos of C.H. McCloy, William G. Anderson, and Clark W. Hetherington are reprinted, by permission, from E.W. Gerber, 1971, *Innovators and Institutions in Physical Education* (Philadelphia: Lea & Febiger), 404, 333, 390.

The photo of the Harvard Fatigue Laboratory reunion is courtesy of Steven M. Horvath.

The photo of Peter V. Karpovich is reprinted, by permission, of the American College of Sports Medicine.

The photo of Elsworth Buskirk is courtesy of Elsworth R. Buskirk.

The photo of Leonard A. Larson is courtesy of Leonard Larson.

The photo of Bruno Balke is courtesy of Bruno Balke.

The photo of Henry J. Montoye is courtesy of Henry Montoye.

The photo of the Bethesda Meeting participants is reprinted, by permission, from the American Physiological Society.

Author Index

Subject Index

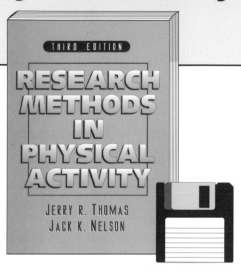